MW01631316

Greuze the Draftsman

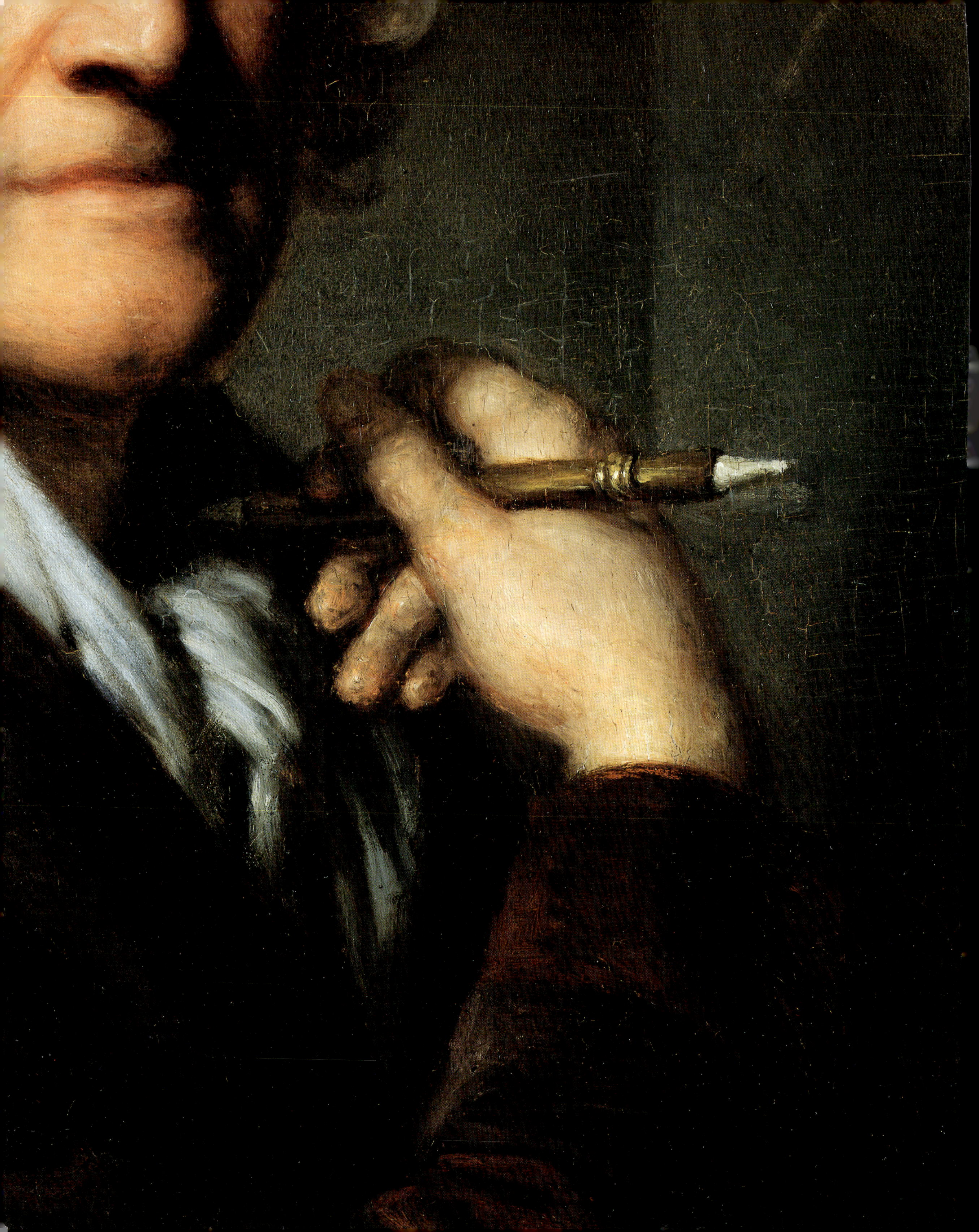

Greuze the Draftsman

Edgar Munhall

With an essay by Irina Novosselskaya

MERRELL in association with
The Frick Collection, New York

First published 2002 by
Merrell Publishers Limited
42 Southwark Street
London SE1 1UN

in association with
The Frick Collection
1 East 70th Street
New York, NY 10021

Published on the occasion
of the exhibition *Greuze the Draftsman*,
organized by Edgar Munhall

Exhibition itinerary:

The Frick Collection
New York
14 May – 4 August 2002

The J. Paul Getty Museum
Los Angeles
10 September – 1 December 2002

Front cover:
Greuze, *The Ungrateful Son*,
c. 1777 (no. 84)

Back cover:
Greuze, *Head of a Woman*,
c. 1765 (no. 47)

Frontispiece:
Greuze, *Portrait of the Artist* (detail),
1804 (no. 96)

Distributed in the USA by Rizzoli International
Publications, Inc. through St. Martin's Press,
175 Fifth Avenue, New York, NY 10010

A catalog record for this book is available from
the Library of Congress

British Library Cataloging-in-Publication Data:
Munhall, Edgar
Greuze the draftsman
1. Greuze, Jean-Baptiste, 1725–1805 – Criticism
and interpretation 2. Drawing – France
I. Title II. Frick Collection
741 ′.092

ISBN 1 85894 158 X (hardback)
ISBN 1 85894 159 8 (paperback)

Produced by Merrell Publishers Limited
Printed and bound in Italy

Designed by Nathan Garland
Edited by Fronia W. Simpson

Contents

Foreword

We are pleased to present at our respective institutions *Greuze the Draftsman,* the first exhibition devoted to the drawings of Jean-Baptiste Greuze. The selection of drawings comprises the finest and most representative sheets from international institutions and presents his graphic achievement in its fullest and most compelling scope.

While early photographs of Clayton, Henry Clay Frick's residence in Pittsburgh, show a Greuze-like *Head of a Girl* hanging in the Parlor, records indicate that the young collector returned it to Arthur Tooth & Sons less than a year after purchasing it in 1899 ("a wise decision," according to Edgar Munhall). Mr Frick never acquired another work by the artist, but in 1943 the Trustees of The Frick Collection purchased *The Wool Winder,* a major early painting that had formerly belonged to J. Pierpont Morgan. This picture will travel to Los Angeles to be part of an ancillary exhibition that The J. Paul Getty Museum is organizing to complement *Greuze the Draftsman.* In 1991, with funds recently bequeathed in memory of Suzanne and Denise Falk, The Frick Collection had the chance to acquire the extraordinary pair of pastel portraits by Greuze depicting the actor Baptiste *aîné* and his wife, which demonstrate in the present exhibition what the artist was capable of producing at the age of seventy-five (nos. 91, 92).

In 1983 The J. Paul Getty Museum had acquired Greuze's *The Laundress,* a work nearly contemporary with the Frick's *The Wool Winder.* By happy coincidence, the monograph devoted to it that the museum published in 2000 was written by Colin B. Bailey, who subsequently succeeded Edgar Munhall as the Chief Curator of The Frick Collection. In the same year *The Laundress* joined its collection, the Getty acquired its first Greuze drawing, *The Father's Curse: The Ungrateful Son* (no. 82)—a rare example of the sort of model Greuze prepared for engravers contracted to execute reproductive prints after his paintings—and a year later, in 1984, acquired the *Head of an Old Man* (no. 51). In 1999 the Getty made the daring acquisition of Greuze's painting *Cimon and Pero: Roman Charity* (fig. 154), which is based on a famous drawing in the collection of the Musée du Louvre (no. 65).

Greuze the Draftsman would have been inconceivable without the participation of its Guest Curator, Edgar Munhall. From the completion in 1959 of his PhD dissertation, "Jean-Baptiste Greuze: An Artist and His Critics," at Yale University, through his 1996 exhibition at The Frick Collection, *Greuze, a Portraitist for the 90s,* Mr Munhall has been the indefatigable keeper of the Greuze flame, which more than once has threatened to flicker out. Most notably, in 1976 he organized the first exhibition ever devoted to Greuze, *Jean-Baptiste Greuze/1725–1805,* which was seen at the Wadsworth Atheneum, the California Palace of the Legion of Honor, and the Musée des Beaux-Arts, Dijon.

For the present exhibition, which he conceived, Mr Munhall supervised all aspects of its organization, wrote the catalogue, and even participated in the fundraising required for the exhibition's presentation at The Frick Collection. All translations from the French are his.

Our thanks also go to Lee Hendrix, Curator of Drawings at The J. Paul Getty Museum, who coordinated the installation in Los Angeles.

We are immensely grateful to the institutional and private lenders who agreed so generously to part for a while with their Greuze treasures, in some cases, ones that were acquired only very recently. Special thanks are due to The State Hermitage Museum in St Petersburg, which has long held the finest group of Greuze drawings in the world; celebrated sheets, but rarely exhibited in the United States, twenty-two of them constitute nearly a quarter of the exhibition. Dr Mikhail Piotrovsky, Director; Mr Vladimir Matveyev, Deputy Director in charge of Exhibitions and Development; and Dr Irina Novosselskaya, Chief of the Western European Art Department, facilitated Mr Munhall's efforts to study this great ensemble and have helped him with unfailing generosity in the preparation of this catalogue and with all the details of their extraordinary loan. Dr Novosselskaya even managed to find the time amidst her many obligations to write the essay "The Collection of Drawings by Jean-Baptiste Greuze in St Petersburg," which recounts in detail and for the first time in English the story of how those drawings were acquired from the artist at the peak of his career.

The staff and Trustees of The Frick Collection are deeply appreciative of the support accorded this exhibition by The Florence Gould Foundation and The Isaacson-Draper Foundation, as well as by a group of friends of Mr Munhall—Mrs Russell Aitken, Monsieur Jean Bonna, Monsieur Michel David-Weill, Mr James Fairfax, Professor Joseph Koerner, Miss Diane Nixon, Mr Stephen K. Scher, and Mr Melvin R. Seiden. In addition, the presentation in New York of *Greuze the Draftsman* has benefited from the support of the Fellows of The Frick Collection.

To all those who have contributed to the success of this exhibition and its catalogue, we offer our deepest thanks.

Samuel Sachs II Director The Frick Collection	Deborah Gribbon Director The J. Paul Getty Museum

Preface

This publication and the exhibition that accompanies it are the fruits of over four decades I have devoted, in part, to Jean-Baptiste Greuze. In 1957 George Heard Hamilton, my mentor in graduate studies at Yale University, encouraged me to write my doctoral dissertation on the subject of Greuze and his critics, which I completed two years later. The research material for that project, assembled primarily in the Cabinet des Estampes at the Bibliothèque nationale de France—with the encouragement of its legendary curator Jean Adhémar—has constituted the basis of all my subsequent work on the artist. Much of it reappeared in the catalogue of the exhibition *Jean-Baptiste Greuze/1725–1805*, the first ever devoted to the artist, which I organized for the Wadsworth Atheneum in Hartford in 1976 on the invitation of its enlightened curator Peter Marlow.

Then, following some twenty years of articles, exhibition catalogue entries (most notably the important section on Greuze in *Diderot et l'art de Boucher à David* in 1984), and countless "opinions" supplied to colleagues, dealers, collectors, and auction houses, the idea of another Greuze exhibition, this one to be devoted to the artist's drawings, was proposed by Jeffrey E. Horvitz, a patron of the Fogg Art Museum. But eager to reach a larger audience than that beloved institution could attract—and specifically hoping for one in France—I first sought and obtained in New York the support of The Frick Collection, for which I am profoundly grateful. When no French museum seemed inclined to honor one of its greatest artistic sons, friends at The J. Paul Getty Museum—John Walsh, Director; Scott Schaefer, Curator of Paintings; and Lee Hendrix, Curator of Drawings—welcomed the project of *Greuze the Draftsman* enthusiastically. Deborah Gribbon, Mr Walsh's successor, has maintained the Getty's support of this undertaking, even extending it with an ancillary exhibition *Greuze the Painter*.

During the time it took to organize *Greuze the Draftsman* and write the exhibition catalogue, I have met with nothing but the warmest and most generous support from the collectors, colleagues, and historians whose help I sought so frequently. Special thanks are due to the following: Hervé Aaron, vicomte Jacques d'Arjuzon, Katharine Baetjer, Joseph Baillio, Julianna Bark, Charles Beye, Delphine Boeuf-Bernard, Jacqueline Chambord, Alvin L. Clark, Jr, James Crowley, Cara Dufour Denison, Emmanuel Ducamp, Vincent Ducourau, Philippe Durey, Carter Foster, Micheline Fried, Vivian Gill, Christine Giviskos, Margaret Morgan Grasselli, Nicholas Hall, Carlos van Hasselt, Michel Hilaire, Barbara Hinde, Sveteslao Hlopoff, John Ittmann, Shalaka Karbhari, Cynthia Katz, Mary Ann Kelly, Chantal Kensey, H.H. Prince Amyn Aga Khan, Bryan Knowles, Albert Kostenevich, Sylvain Laveissière, Fred Licht, Juan Luna, Suzanne Folds McCullagh, James Mitchell, Christina Peter, Mark Restellini, Gui Rochat, Marianne Roland Michel, Margaret Rose, Pierre Rosenberg, baron and baronne Elie de Rothschild, John Rowe, Alan Salz, Marjorie Shelley, Perrin Stein, Drew Stevens, Spencer Sutton, Don Swanson, David Tunick, comte de la Viñaza, marquis de Laborde, and Ragland Watkins. To this list should be added the name of Jacques Petithory, a great friend and one of the first of our generation to fully understand the genius of Greuze.

At The Frick Collection, it was Charles Ryskamp, then the director, who, with the enthusiasm of a connoisseur, welcomed the idea of this exhibition and won the crucial endorsement of the Board of Trustees. His successor, Samuel Sachs II, has generously continued to support our endeavor, as have the expanded Board of Trustees and the Council of The Frick Collection. Colleagues at the museum with whom I had been working on various exhibition projects for many years once again took up their battle stations and enabled *Greuze the Draftsman* to become a reality: Robert Goldsmith, Deputy Director for Administration; Susan Grace Galassi, Curator, and her Curatorial Assistant, Christine Minas; Richard di Liberto, Photographer, and William Stout, Registrar, to whom I am particularly grateful for his loyal support. Special thanks are due: Adrian Anderson, Martin Duus, Yuri Ito, Michael Paccione, Heidi Rosenau, Dennis Sweeney, and William Traylor. My successor as Chief Curator, Colin B. Bailey, has contributed the support of a distinguished fellow *dix-huitièmiste.*

On my retirement from The Frick Collection at the end of the last century, I was invited by Patricia Barnett, the Andrew W. Mellon Director of the Frick Art Reference Library, to become a resident scholar at that great institution. Gratefully ensconced in my elegant carrel there, I was able to write this catalogue under ideal circumstances, with practically every publication I needed at hand or readily available electronically. At the Frick Art Reference Library, I discovered I had become part of a large, diversified family of specialists, all eager to help me. My gratitude to these siblings is boundless.

I was honored that Merrell Publishers chose to publish this work, and I am grateful to my new friends at that firm for their thoughtful care in producing it: Hugh Merrell, Publisher; Julian Honer, Editorial Director; Anthea Snow, Managing Editor; and Matt Hervey, Art Director.

For the first time in my career, I had the pleasure of working with an editor—Fronia W. Simpson—who was not only meticulous in supervising the myriad details of such a book and apt in her suggestions, but actually encouraging to her author.

To work again with Nathan Garland, one of the finest graphic designers of our age, was not only a source of great professional satisfaction but a personal one, too, for it was he who designed the catalogue *Jean-Baptiste Greuze/1725–1805* just over a quarter of a century ago.

During this same period, I have been fortunate to benefit from the companionship, enriched with intellectual and moral support, of Richard Barsam, to whom I dedicate *Greuze the Draftsman* with deep affection and gratitude.

Edgar Munhall
Curator Emeritus
The Frick Collection

Introduction

Edgar Munhall

Facing page:
Fig. 1 Greuze, *Head of an Old Man, Study for "A Marriage Contract"* (no. 18), detail

"...this man draws like an angel."—Diderot, 1763[1]

In the pantheon of French masters of the eighteenth century—Watteau, Boucher, Fragonard, Chardin, Greuze, and David—Greuze holds his own as a draftsman, arguably right up with Watteau and nearby Chardin as a pastelist. In comparison with his achievement, Boucher appears monotonous; Fragonard, sublime but lacking a tragic, visceral quality; Chardin, practically nonexistent save for the pastels; and David, apart from his portraits, woefully dry. Yet, this is the first exhibition devoted to Greuze's drawings, and this, the first comprehensive publication of them.

In his own day, critics and collectors appreciated Greuze's graphic productions every bit as much as his paintings, the latter willing to pay—as Pierre-Jean Mariette noted—"prodigiously high prices for them."[2] As the artist's reputation waxed and waned during the nineteenth and twentieth centuries, the appreciation of his drawings seemed more constant than that of his paintings. This has been very much the case in the last thirty years, by which time all but a few of his great paintings had found their way into museums and were thus unavailable to the art market. But the drawings, resurfacing from an apparently endless stock, continue to appear again and again on the covers of catalogues issued by dealers and auction houses.

It can be said that Greuze began and ended his career with a drawing tool in his hand—as attested to by a self-portrait of 1750 (fig. 230) and another exhibited in 1804 (no. 96). Madame de Valori, Greuze's goddaughter and hagiographic biographer, recalled in 1813 that "without benefit of any teacher," Greuze "from the age of eight... was already drawing very well indeed... stealing time from his sleep to conceal work that the paternal authority forbade him."[3] Convinced finally of his talents, the budding artist decided to carry out the first of the many *tours de force* that would mark his career:

He made a pen drawing depicting St James, his father's patron saint, and he offered it to him on his feast day [25 July]. The imitation [of the engraving he had copied] was so perfect that his father was deceived, and thought that his son had given him a print. Greuze took pleasure for an instant in his father's mistake and... was given permission to be sent to Lyon, to work with Charles Grandon.[4]

Approximately sixty years later, the artist would die in his studio in the Louvre, having produced well over a thousand drawings of all sorts, and leaving his daughter Caroline about 150 of them, which she kept until her own death on 5 November 1842. They formed the nucleus of her posthumous sale held in Paris on 25–26 January 1843.[5] A number of drawings in the present exhibition have come down from that source (nos. 20, 61, 64, 66, 83, 88).

Nothing is known of Greuze's sojourn with Charles Grandon (1691–1762), beyond Madame de Valori's account: "Grandon... maintained what Greuze laughingly described as a picture factory. Grandon was enchanted with Greuze's aptitude and talent, and had him *make* a picture a day; which gave him the habit of using a brush and the facility that one day would give him the means to multiply his masterpieces."[6] Not the hack that Greuze described, Grandon was named *peintre ordinaire de la ville de Lyon* in 1749 and served as *maître du métier des peintres* between 1749 and 1751, probably about the time Greuze left his employ. He was also a dealer. Judging from two of his many portraits—a *Self-Portrait* and *M. Perrichon, Prévôt des marchands de Lyon,* both in the Musée des Beaux-Arts at Lyon[7]—he worked in a meticulous style reminiscent of Dutch masters of the seventeenth century such as Frans van Mieris (1635–1681) and Gerard Terborch (1584–1662), painting on a small scale, usually on panel.[8]

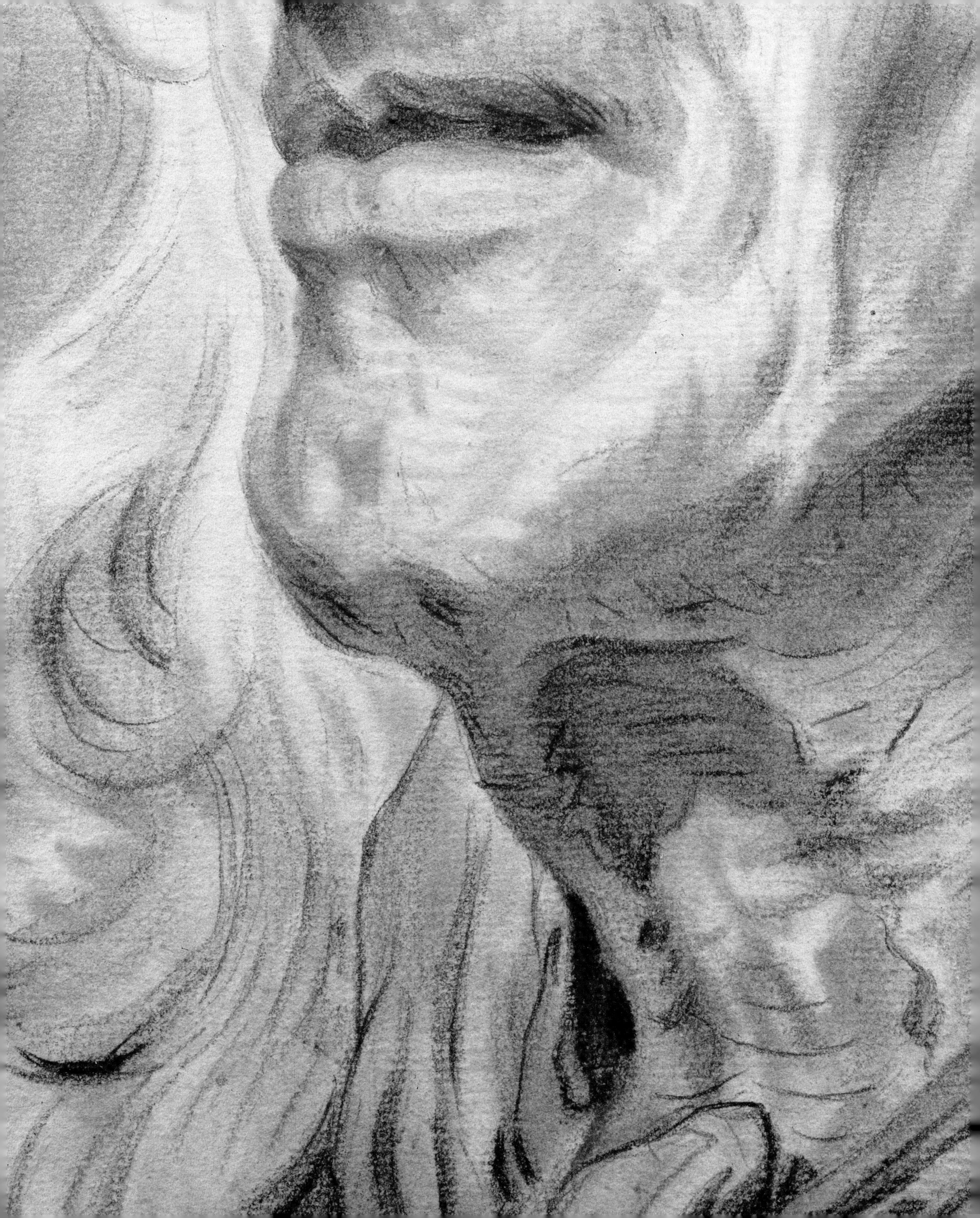

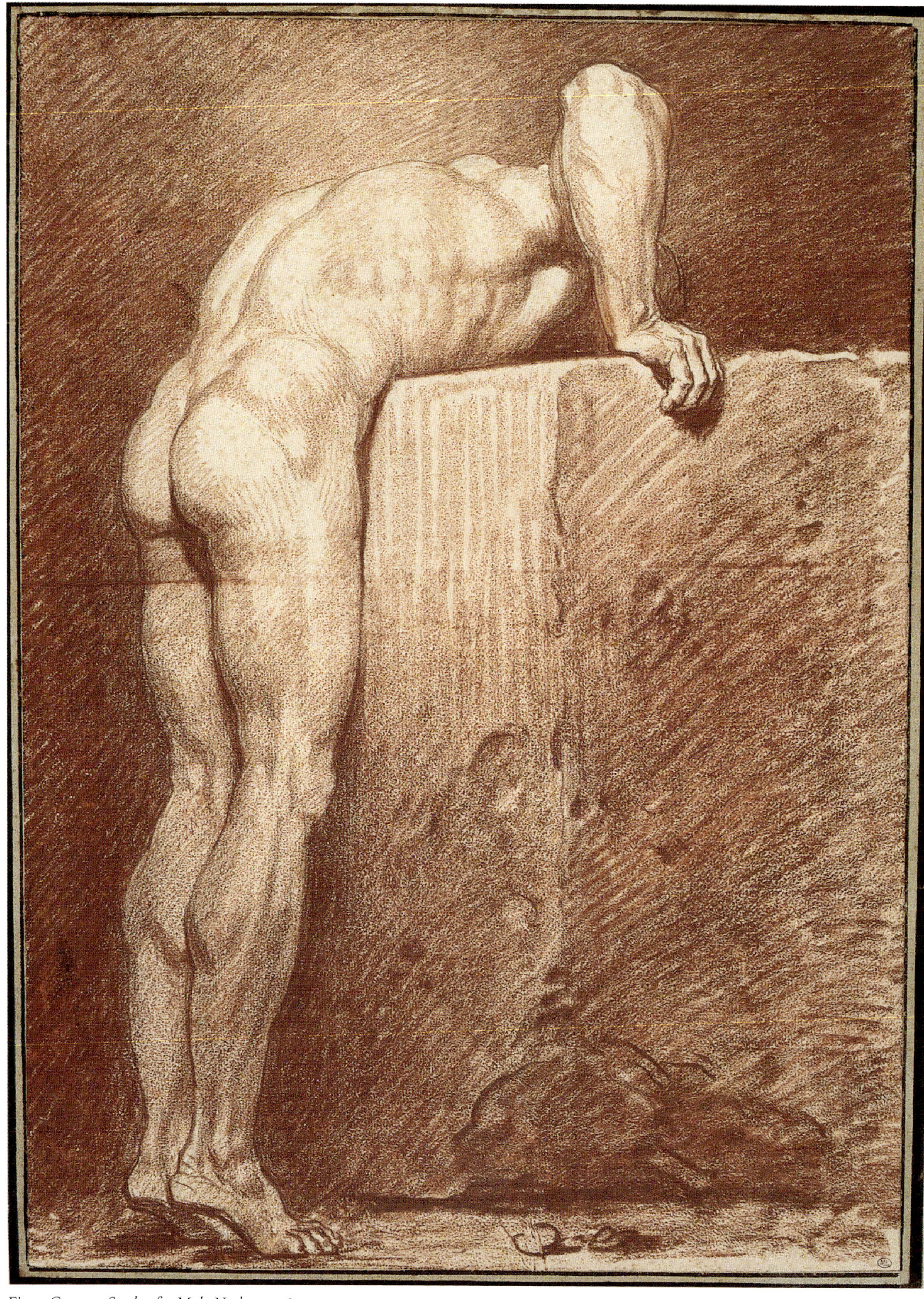

Fig. 3 Greuze, *Study of a Male Nude, c.* 1767, red chalk on cream paper, Bayonne, Musée Bonnat, Donation Petithory

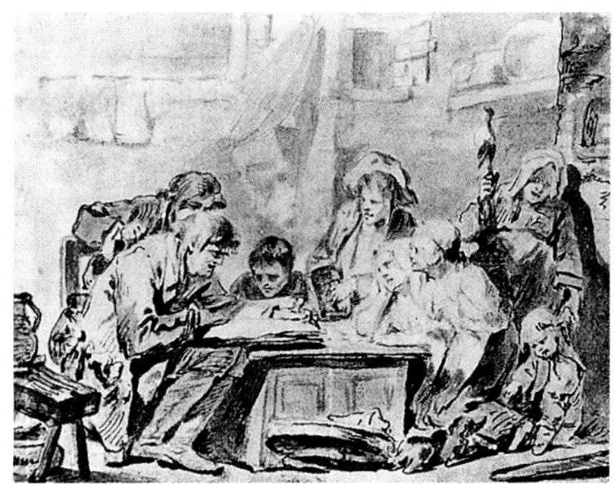

Fig. 2 Greuze, *Compositional Study for "The Family Bible Reading," c.* 1750–55, pen and brush with gray and brown ink wash on white paper, Paris, private collection

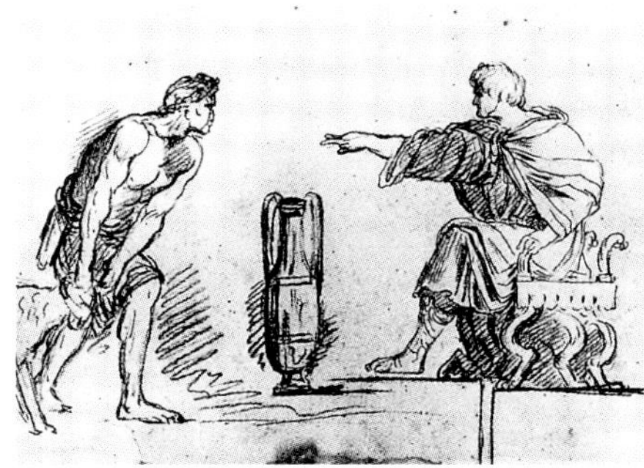

Fig. 4 Greuze, *Study after Domenichino's "Trial of Saint Cecilia,"* 1755–56, red chalk on cream paper, Tournus, Musée Greuze

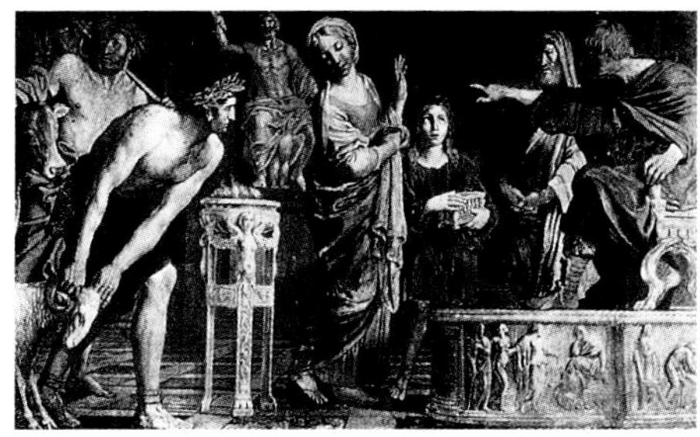

Fig. 5 Domenichino, *Trial of Saint Cecilia,* 1616–17, fresco, Rome, San Luigi dei Francesi

The two figural studies that this author earlier assigned to Greuze's period in Lyon exhibit a similar concentration on minute, even macabre details.[9] But this Grandonesque concern for precision was offset in them by a Rembrandtesque freedom with ink washes that characterizes even more Greuze's highly important compositional study for his first major work, *The Family Bible Reading* (figs. 2, 9). Apart from its stylistic significance, this drawing provides the first evidence of Greuze's unique ability to create a scene of many figures interacting with emotional intensity. Some perceptive amateur acquired this drawing early on, for Greuze's friend Johann Georg Wille (1715–1808) recalled purchasing it at a Paris auction in December 1759: "I bought at the sale that was held in M. Rémy's rooms... the first sketch that M. Greuze made for his picture *The Father of the Family Reading the Bible,* thirty-six livres.... The drawing has since passed into a German collection."[10] Perhaps it was the drawing's arresting drama that provoked Wille to describe its creator as "profound and solid."[11]

The next crucial phase in Greuze's development as a draftsman took place in Paris, where he must have arrived about 1750. Both Madame de Valori[12] and Louis Gougenot, abbé de Chezal-Benoît (see no. 4), recount the difficulties that Greuze, bereft of a protector, had in attending drawing classes at the Académie Royale de Peinture et de Sculpture. But the evidence of the large number of *académies*—studies of posed nude models—that Greuze would later sell General Ivan Ivanovitch Betskoy[13] and others (no. 2) suggest that the young artist spent many hours, presumably under the direction of Charles-Joseph Natoire (1700–1770) and Louis de Sylvestre (1675–1760), mastering his depiction of the human figure. Greuze's knowledge of anatomy, which he later claimed to disdain, is revealed in his lifelong ability to depict an ear, an eye, a finger—seen from any perspective—with perfect precision, something that connoisseurs keep in mind when faced with a copy or an imitation of an original drawing by Greuze. Also, his familiarity, perhaps even his boredom, with the genre of the *académie* led him to indulge in such highly original variations on it as number 66 and figure 3.

Greuze's year and a half in Italy (see no. 4) was highly productive, as reflected in what he brought back to exhibit at the Salon of 1757. In addition to the complex *Four Pictures in Italian Costume, The Neapolitan Sailor,* and the portrait of his patron the abbé Gougenot (fig. 34), the artist for the first time included a drawing in that exhibition: *A Sketch in Black Ink, Representing Some Italians Playing Morra* (Moscow, The Pushkin State Museum of Fine Arts). With Pierre Parrocel (1670–1739), Greuze was the only artist to exhibit a drawing in 1757—aside from the pastels of Maurice-Quentin de La Tour (1704–1788) and Jean-Baptiste Perronneau (1715?–1783).

By this time, according to Madame de Valori, Greuze felt he had developed his talents "so to say, to perfection."[14] Certainly the drawings that survive from the Italian sojourn (nos. 4–7) demonstrate a mastery of a broad range of types, as well as of media. The major change from this point on would be the artist's abandonment of the delicate, slightly Rococo style apparent in these Italian costume studies in pen and ink, the so-called *petite manière* that had been his speciality before leaving for Rome. While there, in addition to creating his own major works, he dutifully drew after ancient sculptures, Raphael (1483–1520), Michelangelo (1475–1564), Guido Reni (1575–1642), and Domenichino (1581–1641), but in a desultory manner, judging from a previously unidentified study after Domenichino's fresco *Trial of Saint Cecilia* in San Luigi dei Francesi (figs. 4, 5).[15]

Facing page:
Fig. 6 Greuze, *Head of a Girl* (no. 52), detail

From 1759 until his crisis-fraught Salon of 1769, Greuze regularly included drawings among his showings at the biennial exhibitions of the Académie: two in 1759, three in 1761 (see nos. 14, 23), none in 1763, four major works in 1765 (see nos. 41, 48, 49), none in 1767, when he was denied admission, and six in 1769 (see nos. 56, 69, Hartford *et al.* 1976–77, no. 51). On an average, only five or six other artists, including pastelists, would include drawings among their Salon entries—Jean-Baptiste Henri Deshays (1729–1765), Jean-Honoré Fragonard (1732–1806), Pierre-Antoine de Machy (1723–1807), André Portail (1695–1759), and Hubert Robert (1733–1808) among them. Greuze's decision to exhibit drawings at the Salon may reflect the influence of his patron Gougenot, who, as early as 1748, was urging artists to show their drawings this way: "One wishes that artists, instead of burying them [drawings] in the darkness of their portfolios, would make an effort to display them at the Salon more often than they have done to date.... By sharing their thoughts among themselves by such an exhibition, the masters could present at a glance the most serious aspect of their art."[16] In 1800, when Greuze reappeared at the Salon for the first time in thirty-one years, a drawing headed his list of entries: *The Departure for the Hunt* (no. 94).

From his Salon debut in 1755, when one critic characterized *The Family Bible Reading* (fig. 9) as "well drawn,"[17] to his surprise return appearance there in 1800, when his style of drawing was judged "too mannered,"[18] the ever-more-numerous critics focused on Greuze's drawings with considerable care. Concerning the three major drawings the artist showed in 1761, for instance, the abbé Philippe Bridard de la Garde wrote: "The several drawings by M. Greuze shown in the Salon do him as much honor by their execution as by the choice and genius of their invention. The subjects this young painter dreams up and renders so well could one day constitute a complete treatise on domestic morality."[19] They did, in fact, range from images of thieving children, to a family caring for a paralyzed father, to another family pathetically begging in unison.

That same year, 1761, Denis Diderot (1713–1784), the philosopher turned art critic, first spoke of Greuze's drawings in some detail, describing their subjects minutely and concluding with a vivid description of Greuze the draftsman that suggests he knew him well: "Greuze possesses a lot of spirit and taste. When he's working, he is completely wrapped up in what he's doing; he is profoundly moved: he expresses in the street the character of the subject he's dealing with in his studio, sad or gay, sprightly or serious, flirtatious or reserved, according to whatever engaged his brush and imagination in the morning."[20]

Two years later, when Diderot reached the apogee of his admiration for Greuze—exclaiming "That's really my man, that Greuze"[21]—he continued his description of him, specifically as a draftsman, in a highly personal and vivid way:

It's not surprising that this artist excels.... He is enthusiastic about his art; he makes endless studies; he spares neither care nor expenses in order to have the models that suit him. If he meets a head that strikes him, he would willingly fall on his knees before the bearer of that head to attract him to his studio. He is constantly on the lookout in the streets, in churches, in markets, at the theater, on promenades, in public gatherings. When he's thinking about a subject, he is obsessed with it, constantly preoccupied. Even his character is marked by it; he assumes that of his picture: he is brusque, sweet, insinuating, caustic, flirtatious, sad, gay, warm, serious, or mad, according to whatever he's working on.[22]

Diderot's final word on Greuze the draftsman was included in his lengthy review of the Salon of 1769, when he referred to the six drawings the artist was exhibiting:

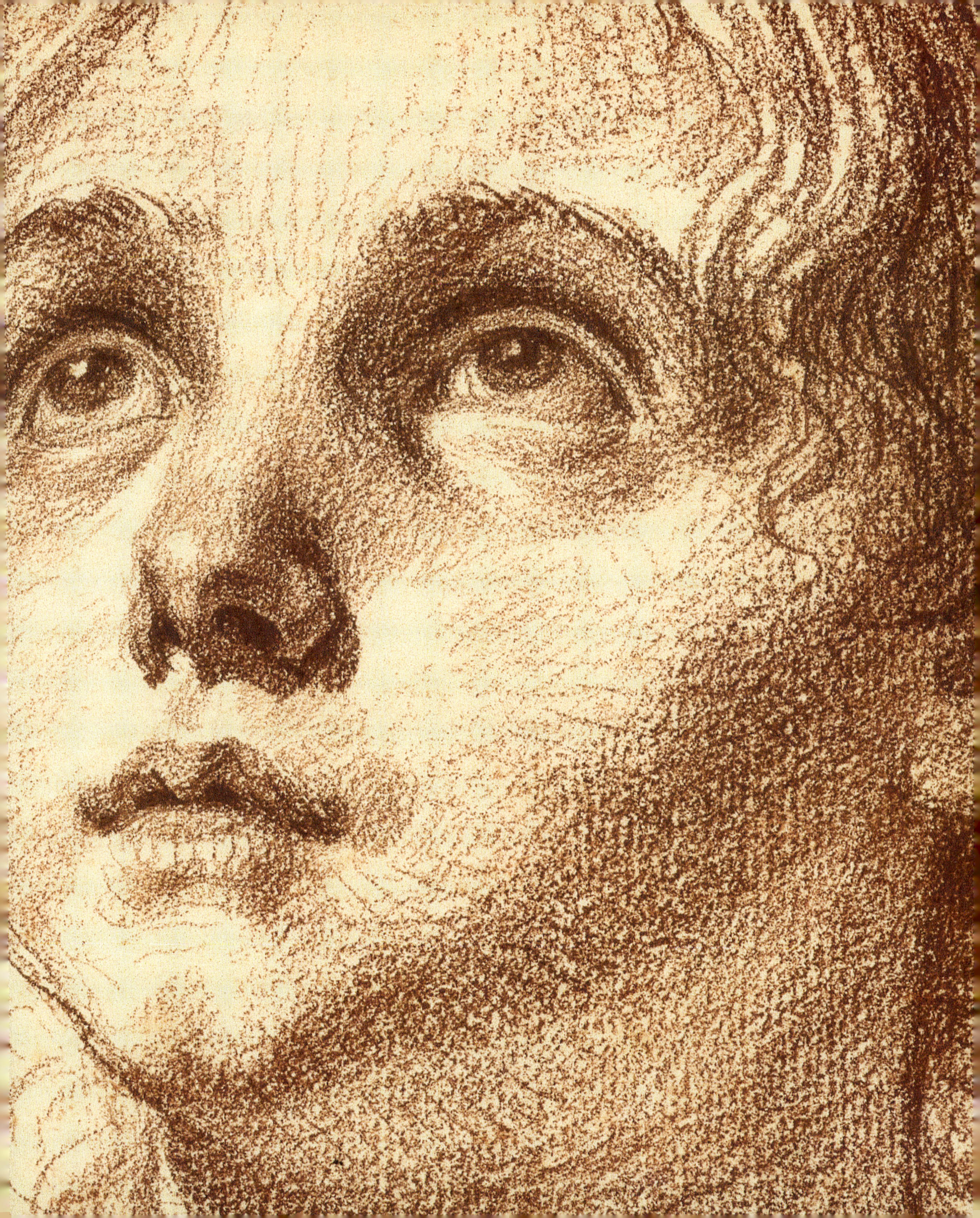

Facing page:
Fig. 7 Greuze, *Domestic Scene* (no. 88), detail

"And what about those *drawings*? Because that's where Greuze truly shows himself to be a man of genius. The one of *The Death of a Father Mourned by His Children* [fig. 168] is especially beautiful in composition, expression, and effect. He who understands art can imagine it painted."[23]

In 1767, when relations between Greuze and Diderot were souring, the latter sought to prevent the artist's being invited by Catherine II to Russia by writing in a letter to Étienne-Maurice Falconet (1716–1791) (that he knew the empress would probably see): "Say, my friend, all things considered, I think we shall never be sending Greuze to Russia. He's an excellent artist, but a very disagreeable character. One should have his drawings and his paintings, and leave the man at that."[24] Catherine II took the hint, as Dr Novosselskaya's essay here recounts in detail, writing to Falconet: "I renounce, not the works of Greuze, but indeed the man himself. . . ."[25]

With the eighteenth-century vogue not only for collecting contemporary drawings but for displaying them in frames,[26] Greuze had an enthusiastic and rich market for his work. Fellow artists and dealers possessed his drawings—Pierre-François Basan (1723–1797), Aignan-Thomas Desfriches (1715–1800), Claude Hoin (1750–1817), Jean-Baptiste-Pierre Le Brun (1748–1813), Joseph-Marie Vien (1716–1809), Johann Georg Wille—as well as collectors, such as Jean-Baptiste-Laurent Boyer de Fonscolombe, the chevalier de Damery, Louis-Antoine Vassal de Saint-Hubert, Vialart de Saint-Morys; aristocrats, such as the baron de Besenval, the marquis Jean-Joseph de Laborde, the comte de Vaudreuil; writers, such as Diderot, T.C. Bruun-Neergard; and distinguished foreigners, such as General Betskoy (with Catherine II behind him), count Karl Cobenzl, the baron d'Holbach, Duke Albert von Sachsen und Teschen, and Johann Friedrich Städel. Down to the present day, the greatest connoisseurs have savored their Greuze drawings—from Pierre-Jean Mariette in the eighteenth century (no. 57), to Edmond and Jules de Goncourt in the nineteenth (nos. 66, 94), to Frits Lugt in the twentieth (no. 80), and Pierre Rosenberg in the twenty-first.

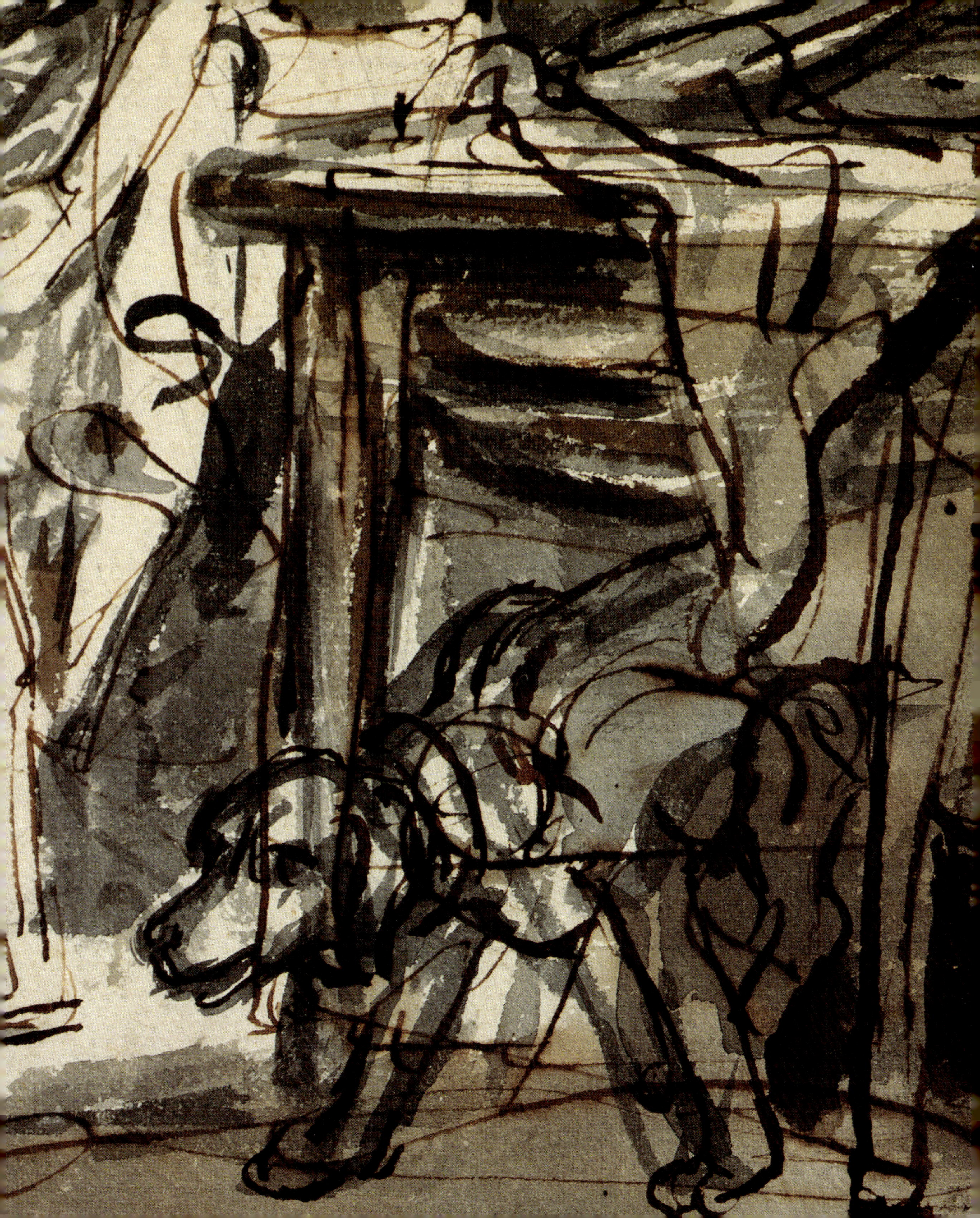

1. *"... cet homme dessine comme un ange."* Diderot *Salons,* I, p. 236.

2. *"Il a fait aussi nombre de desseins, qui dans le commencement lui ont été payés prodigieusement par quelques curieux."* Mariette 1851–60, II, p. 331.

3. *"Dès l'âge de huit ans, Greuze, sans avoir eu de maître, dessinait déjà fort bien, et prenait sur son sommeil pour cacher un travail que l'autorité paternelle lui interdisait."* Valori 1860, p. 249.

4. *"il dessina donc à la plume un saint Jacques, patron de son père, et le lui offrit pour le jour de sa fête; l'imitation était si parfaite avec l'original que son père s'y méprit, et crut que son fils lui présentait une gravure; Greuze jouit un instant de son erreur, et... obtint d'être envoyé à Lyon, chez Gromdon* [*sic*]." Valori 1860, p. 249.

5. The text of that sale catalogue was published in Valori 1860, pp. 377–86.

6. *"Grandon... tenait, comme le disait en riant Greuze, une fabrique de tableaux. Grandon fut enchanté des dispositions et du talent de son jeune élève, auquel il faisait* fabriquer *un tableau par jour; ce qui lui donna l'habitude du pinceau et la facilité qui devait un jour lui fournir les moyens de multiplier ses chefs-d'oeuvre."* Valori 1860, p. 249.

7. See P. Dissard, *Le Musée de Lyon, Les Peintures,* Paris 1912, p. 28, pl. 195.

8. See H. Blémont, "Charles Grandon," *Dictionnaire de biographie française,* Paris 1985, p. 988.

9. Hartford *et al.* 1976–77, nos. 2, 3.

10. *"J'ay acheté à la vente qui s'est faite chez M. Rémy... la première pensée que M. Greuze a fait pour son tableau* le Père de famille qui lit dans la Bible, *trente-six livres.... Ce dessein a passé depuis en Allemagne."* Wille 1857, I, p. 125. This is interesting evidence of Greuze's drawings appearing at auction during his earliest years in Paris. The drawing was eventually acquired by the family of its present owners at the Paris sale of 15 June 1938, lot 12.

11. *"profond et solide."* Wille 1857, I, p. 124.

12. Valori 1860, p. 250.

13. See Monod and Hautecoeur 1922, nos. 161–93; Leningrad 1977, nos. 6, 18, 19, 22, 23.

14. "[*Greuze*] *revint en France avec un talent qui s'était développé, pour ainsi dire, jusqu'à la perfection."* Valori 1860, p. 250.

15. See Martin and Masson 1906, no. 34; J. Martin, *Catalogue du Musée de Tournus,* Tournus 1910, no. 8; Rochette 2000, pp. 68–69, no. 13.

16. *"On voudroit que les Artistes, au lieu de les ensevelir dans l'obscurité de leurs porte-feuilles, s'empressent d'en exposer au Sallon plus souvent qu'ils n'ont encore fait.... Les Maîtres en se communiquant les uns aux autres leurs pensées par une pareille exposition, pourroient présenter sous un seul coup d'oeil la plus sçavante partie de leur Art."* Anonymous [L. Gougenot], *Lettre sur la peinture, la sculpture et l'architecture à M.***,* Amsterdam 1748, pp. 77–78. See B. Schreiber-Jacoby, "Watteau and Gabburri," in *Antoine Watteau (1684–1721): Le Peintre, son temps et sa légende,* exhib. cat., Paris, Musée du Louvre; Geneva, 1987, p. 270; and New York and Ottawa 2000, p. 81.

17. *"bien dessiné."* De la Porte, *Sentimens sur plusieurs des tableaux exposés cette année dans le grand sallon du Louvre,* Paris 1755, p. 17.

18. *"trop maniéré."* Anonymous, *Coup d'oeil sur le Salon de l'an VIII,* Paris 1800, p. 43.

19. *"Plusieurs desseins de M. Greuze, exposés au Salon, lui font autant d'honneur par l'exécution, que par le choix et le génie de l'invention. Les sujets qu'imagine et que rend si bien ce jeune peintre, pourront former un jour un traité complet de morale domestique."* Abbé Philippe Bridard de la Garde, *Observations d'une Société d'amateurs sur les tableaux exposés au Salon cette année 1761,* Paris 1761, p. 53.

20. *"Greuze a beaucoup d'esprit et de goût. Lorsqu'il travaille, il est tout à son ouvrage; il s'affecte profondément: il porte dans le monde le caractère du sujet qu'il traite dans son atelier, triste ou gai, folâtre ou sérieux, galant ou réservé, selon la chose qui a occupé le matin son pinceau et son imagination."* Diderot *Salons,* I, p. 135.

21. *"C'est vraiment là mon homme que ce Greuze."* Diderot *Salons,* I, p. 233.

22. *"Il serait surprenant que cet artiste n'excellât pas.... Il est enthousiaste de son art; il fait des études sans fin; il n'épargne ni soins ni dépenses pour avoir les modèles qui lui conviennent. Rencontre-t-il une tète qui le frappe, il se mettrait volontiers aux genoux du porteur de cette tête pour l'attirer dans son atelier. Il est sans cesse observateur dans les rues, dans les églises, dans les marchés, dans les spectacles, dans les promenades, dans les assemblées publiques. Médite-t-il un sujet: il en est obsédé, suivi partout. Son caractère même s'en ressent; il prend celui de son tableau: il est brusque, doux, insinuant, caustique, galant, triste, gai, froid, chaud, sérieux ou fou, selon la chose qu'il projette."* Diderot *Salons,* I, p. 236.

23. *"Et de ces* Dessins*? Que c'est là vraiment que Greuze s'est montré un homme de génie. Celui surtout de la Mort d'un père de famille regretté de ses enfans est beau de composition, d'expression et d'effet. Celui qui entend l'art le voit peint."* Diderot *Salons,* IV, p. 108.

24. *"Tenez, mon ami, tout bien considéré, je crois que nous n'enverrons point Greuze en Russie. C'est un excellent artiste, mais une bien mauvaise tête. Il faut avoir ses dessins et ses tableaux, et laisser là l'homme."* Diderot *Correspondance,* VIII, p. 104.

25. *"Je renonce non aux ouvrages de Greuze, mais bien au personnage...."* Quoted in Réau 1920, p. 277.

26. For a detailed discussion of this market, see Bailey 2000.

Facing page:
Fig. 8 Greuze, *Madame Baptiste* aîné (no. 92), detail

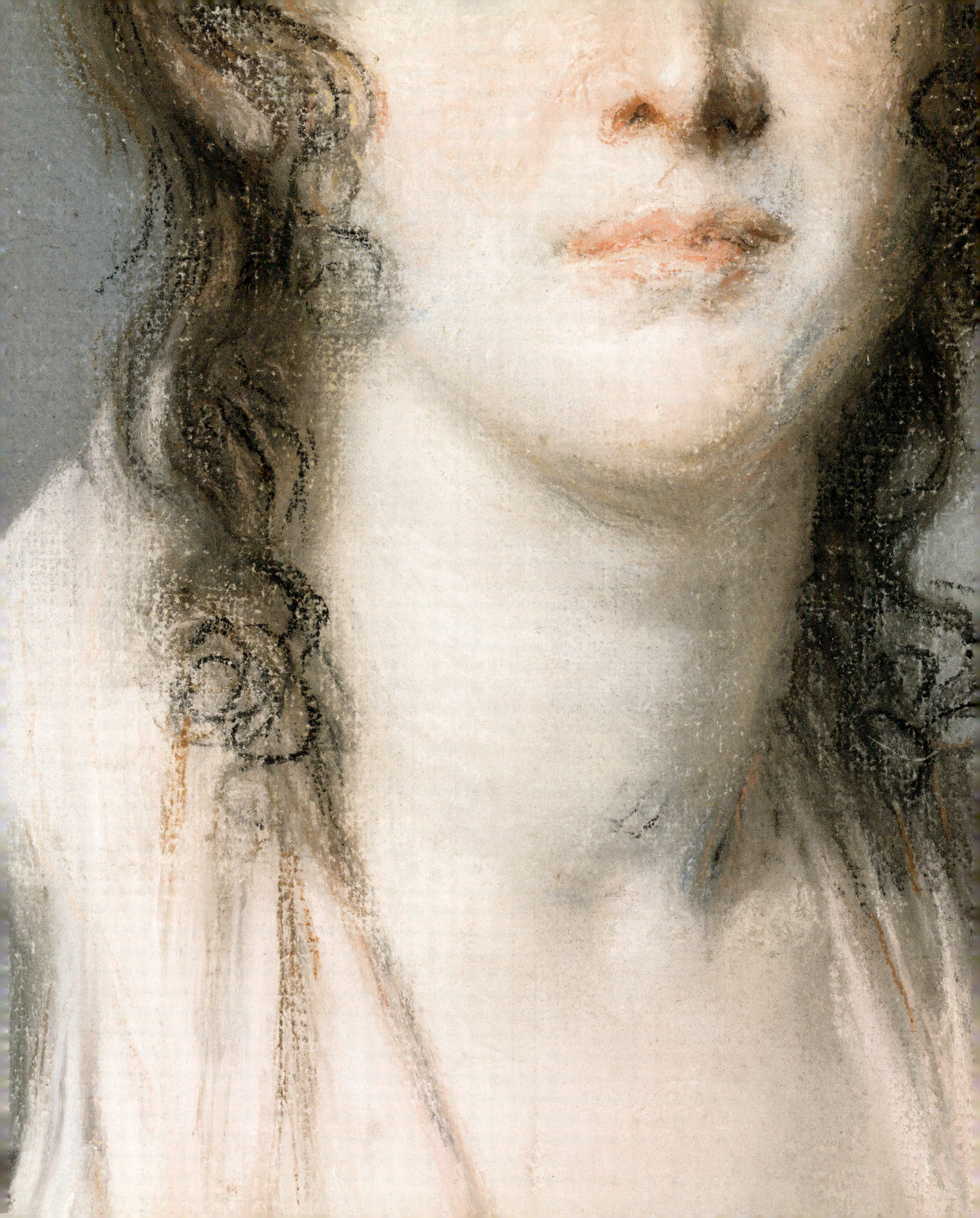

Summary Biography

Edgar Munhall

This chronology of the life of Jean-Baptiste Greuze is based on the more detailed one included in the exhibition catalogue *Jean-Baptiste Greuze/1725–1805* (Hartford *et al.* 1976–77, pp. 18–27), to which have been added some details discovered subsequently. For further information, the reader is referred to the studies of Arquié-Bruley 1983, Brookner 1972, Goncourt 1880, Guicharnaud 1999, Hautecoeur 1913, Laveissière 1980, Mauclair 1906, and Munhall (various) listed in the Selected Bibliography.

1697: Birth of Jean-Louis Greuze, father of the artist. Described as a "master roofer" *(maître couvreur)* in 1725, Greuze would later identify him as a "contractor-architect" *(entrepreneur-architecte).*

21 August 1725: Birth of the future artist, Jean Greuze, sixth of nine children born to Jean-Louis Greuze and his wife, née Claudine Roch, in the town of Tournus in Burgundy, roughly midway between Dijon and Lyon. The baptismal certificate specifies that the child was named simply "Jean Greuze" and that he had been baptized in the church of St-André the day he was born.

25 December 1732: Birth in Paris of Anne-Gabrielle Babuti, the artist's future wife.

25 July 1733: On the feast of St James, the eight-year-old Greuze presents his father with a copy he drew of an engraving depicting the saint. His father mistakes it for a print.

1740–50: At an unknown date, Greuze leaves Tournus to study painting in Lyon with Charles Grandon.

c. *1750:* Greuze arrives in Paris, where, eventually, he studies drawing at the Académie Royale de Peinture et de Sculpture with Charles-Joseph Natoire and Louis de Sylvestre (see nos. 1, 2). He seems to earn a living painting small pictures, perhaps copies.

28 June 1755: Through the influence of Sylvestre, named *directeur* of the Académie in 1752, and through that of the sculptor Jean-Baptiste Pigalle (1714–1785), Greuze is invited to show his work to members of the Académie. They vote to receive him as an associate member *(agréé)* of the institution on this date —classifying him specifically as a genre painter *(peintre de genre particulier).* At the time, he is instructed to consult Sylvestre concerning the customary reception picture expected from all artists named associate members of the Académie. Greuze, however, did not present it for another fourteen years.

Summer 1755: Greuze exhibits for the first time at the biennial exhibition of the Académie, called the "Salon" in reference to where it is traditionally held: in the Salon Carré of the Louvre. His entries included:

145 *The Blind Man Duped* (Moscow, The Pushkin State Museum of Fine Arts; fig. 125)
146 *The Family Bible Reading* (Paris, private collection; fig. 9)
147 *A Boy Asleep over His Book* (Montpellier, Musée Fabre)
148 *A Head, Done from Nature*
149 *Portrait of M. de Sylvestre, Director of the Academy* (Munich, Alte Pinakothek, Collection of the Bayerischen Hypotheken-und-Wechsel-Bank)

The first three entries are purchased by Ange-Laurent de Lalive de Jully, prominent collector of contemporary French art.

September 1755–April 1757: Greuze travels in Italy as the guest of Louis Gougenot, abbé de Chezal-Benoît (fig. 34), whom he had met probably through Pigalle. He spends a year in Rome (see nos. 4–7).

May 1756: Gougenot leaves the Eternal City for Paris, but Greuze declines to accompany his benefactor on his return to France. From Paris, the marquis de Marigny, *surintendant des bâtiments du roi,* instructs Natoire to give Greuze lodgings at the Palazzo Mancini, home of the French Academy in Rome, and commissions two paintings from Greuze for his sister, Madame de Pompadour. Greuze fails to execute this flattering commission until long after his return to Paris.

20 April 1757: Natoire informs Marigny that Greuze has left for Paris.

September 1757: Greuze shows at the Salon the products of his Italian journey and other works, including a drawing:

Four Pictures in Italian Costume
112 *The Broken Eggs* (New York, The Metropolitan Museum of Art; fig. 39)
113 *The Neapolitan Gesture* (Worcester Art Museum; fig. 40)
114 *The Lazy Italian Kitchen Maid* (Hartford CT, Wadsworth Atheneum)
115 *The Fowler* (Warsaw, Museum Narodowe)
116 *Portrait of M. Pigalle, Sculptor to the King*
117 *Portrait of M.**** (Dijon, Musée des Beaux-Arts; fig. 34)
118 *The Neapolitan Sailor* (perhaps London, The Wallace Collection)
119 *Boy with Lesson Book* (Edinburgh, National Galleries of Scotland)
120 *Two Heads; One of a Boy, One of a Girl*
121 *Sketch in India Ink, Depicting Some Italians Playing Morra* (Moscow, The Pushkin State Museum of Fine Arts; see no. 7)
122 *Other Works by the Same Artist*

Fig. 9 Greuze, *The Family Bible Reading,* before 1755, oil on canvas, Paris, private collection

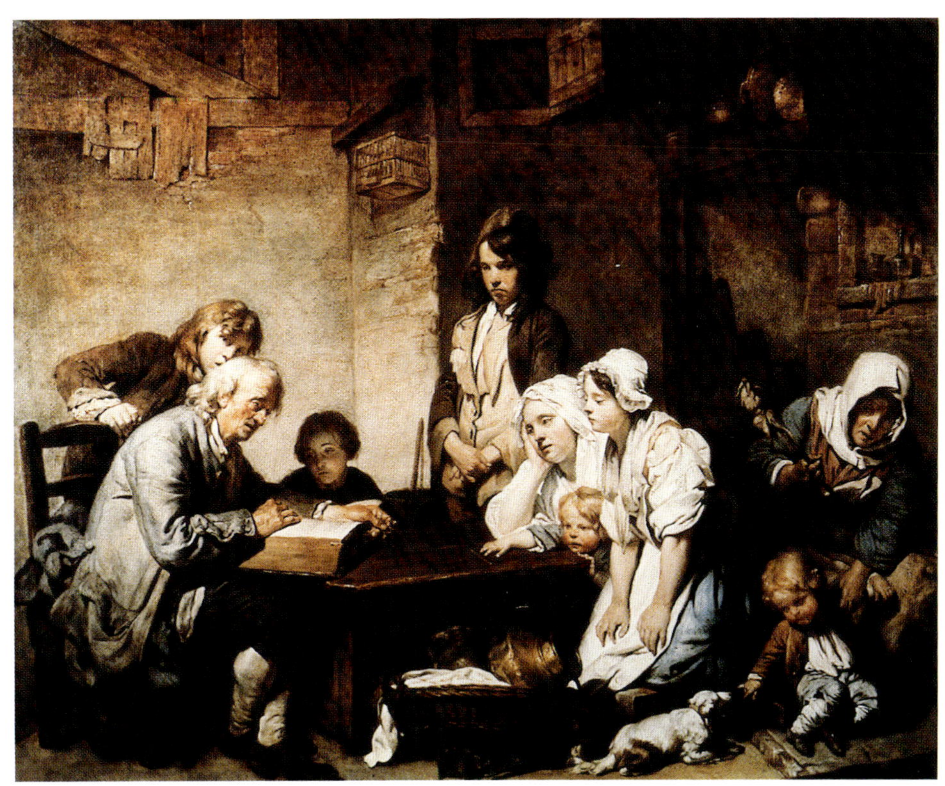

Fig. 10 Greuze, *A Marriage Contract,* 1760–61, oil on canvas, Paris, Musée du Louvre

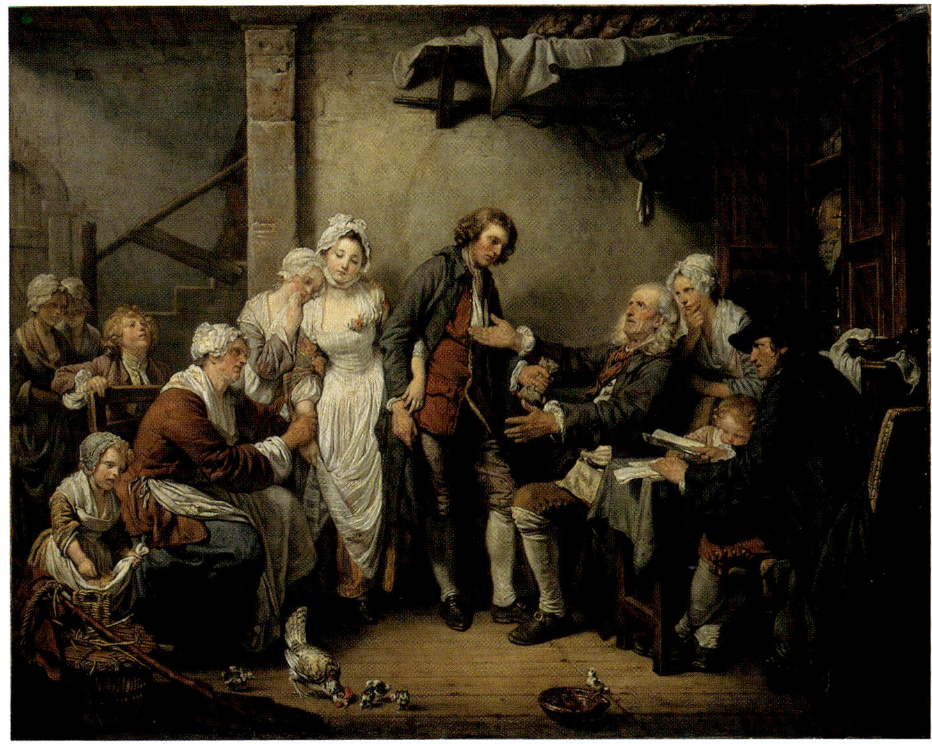

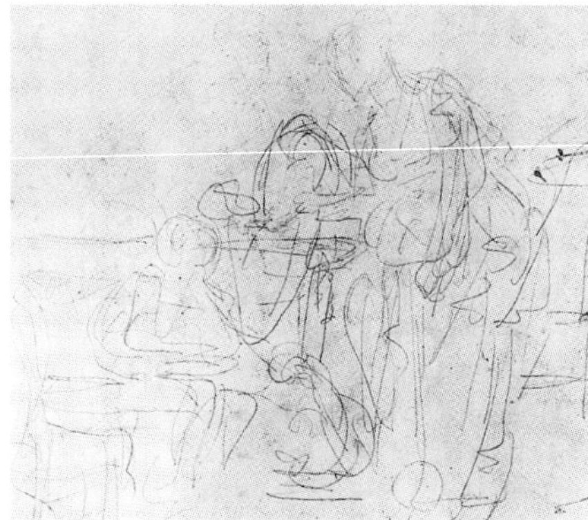

Fig. 11 Greuze, *Compositional Study for "The Motherly Reprimand"* (verso), *c.* 1760, black chalk on white paper, London, P. & D. Colnaghi & Co., Ltd

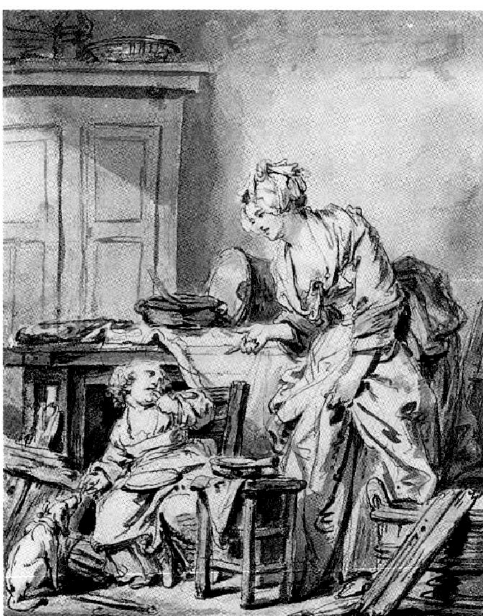

Fig. 12 Greuze, *The Motherly Reprimand* (recto), *c.* 1760, pen and brush with gray ink wash over graphite on white paper, London, P. & D. Colnaghi & Co., Ltd

31 January 1759: Greuze signs a marriage contract with Anne-Gabrielle Babuti, whom he marries on 3 February in St-Médard, Paris. She is the daughter of a successful bookseller. After an impassioned beginning—that coincided with the most successful phase of the artist's career—the marriage would soon disintegrate into a private nightmare and a public scandal, due largely to Madame Greuze's fiery character, her loose life, and meddling with her husband's affairs.

September 1759: Greuze exhibits twenty works at the Salon:

103 *Silence!* (London, Buckingham Palace, Royal Collection; fig. 44)
104 *Simplicity* (Fort Worth TX, Kimbell Art Museum; fig. 113)
105 *The Sleeping Knitter* (San Marino CA, Huntington Library, Art Collections and Botanical Gardens)
106 *The Wool Winder* (New York, The Frick Collection)
107 *Girl Weeping over Her Dead Bird* (Edinburgh, National Galleries of Scotland; fig. 53)
108 *Portrait of M. ***, Playing the Harp* (Washington D.C., National Gallery of Art)
109 *Portrait of Madame la marquise de ***, Tuning Her Guitar* (Baltimore Museum of Art)
110 *Portrait of M. ***, Doctor of the Sorbonne*
111 *Portrait of Mademoiselle de ***, Smelling a Rose* (Braunschweig, Herzog Anton Ulrich-Museum)
112 *Portrait of Mademoiselle de Amici, in Stage Costume* (West Lothian, Scotland, Dalmeny House, Rosebery Collection)
113 *Portrait of M. Babuti, Bookseller*
114 *Three Heads*
115 *Two Heads*
116 *A Head*
117 *Another Head*
118 *Two Sketches in India Ink*

November 1759: Birth of Greuze's first child, Marie-Anne Claudine, whose presumably early death is not recorded.

30 September 1760: The *philosophe* Denis Diderot (no. 55) refers to Greuze in a letter. He seems to have known him for some time. Diderot's enthusiastic writings about Greuze contribute greatly to the artist's reputation over the next decade, and for posterity. His reviews of the Salon exhibitions are first published in Baron Friedrich Melchior Grimm's privately circulated *Correspondance littéraire.*

August–September 1761: As usual, Greuze enjoys great success with his Salon entries, especially *A Marriage Contract,* which does not appear in the exhibition until 20 September:

96 *Portrait of the Dauphin* (New York, private collection)
97 *Portrait of M. Babuti* (Paris, private collection; fig. 65)
98 *Self-Portrait*
99 *Portrait of Madame Greuze as a Vestal Virgin*
100 *A Marriage Contract* (Paris, Musée du Louvre; fig. 10)
101 *Young Shepherd Holding a Flower* (Paris, Musée du Petit Palais)
102 *The Laundress* (Los Angeles, The J. Paul Getty Museum; fig. 85)
103 *Head of a Nymph*
104 *Several Heads (Paintings), under the Same Number*
105 *A Drawing Representing Children Stealing Chestnuts* (see no. 14)
106 *Another Drawing, of a Paralytic Cared for by His Family, or the Fruit of a Good Education* (Paris, Musée du Louvre; no. 23)
107 *Another* [Drawing]. *A Burnt-Out Farmer, Begging with His Family* (Chantilly, Musée Condé)

16 April 1762: Birth of Anne-Geneviève Greuze, called Caroline

August–September 1763: Greuze exhibits fourteen works in the Salon:

128 *Portraits of Monseigneur le duc de Chartres and of Mademoiselle*
129 *Portrait of the comte d'Angiviller* (New York, The Metropolitan Museum of Art; fig. 70)
130 *Portrait of the comte de Lupé*
131 *Portrait of M. Watelet* (Paris, Musée du Louvre; fig. 208)
132 *Portrait of Mademoiselle de Pange*
133 *Portrait of Madame Greuze*
134 *A Girl, Reading the "Croix de Jésus"*
135 *Head of a Boy*
136 *Head of a Girl*
137 *Another Head of a Girl*
138 *The Inconsolable Widow* (London, The Wallace Collection)
139 *The Broken Mirror* (London, The Wallace Collection; fig. 78)
140 *The Paralytic* (St Petersburg, The State Hermitage Museum; fig. 24)

11 November 1763: The German-born print maker and dealer Johann Georg Wille, a close friend of Greuze, notes in his journal that a Russian businessman had paid Greuze for a portrait, his second Russian commission.

19 November–10 December 1763: Wille records the seven sittings required for his portrait by Greuze. When completed, Wille's son Frédéric exclaims before it, *"Ah, c'est mon papa! C'est mon papa!"*

15 May 1764: Greuze's third child, Louise-Gabrielle, is baptized in St-Benoît, her godparents being Wille and his wife, whose name Louise she bears.

Fig. 13 Greuze, *Septimius Severus and Caracalla*, 1769, oil on canvas, Paris, Musée du Louvre

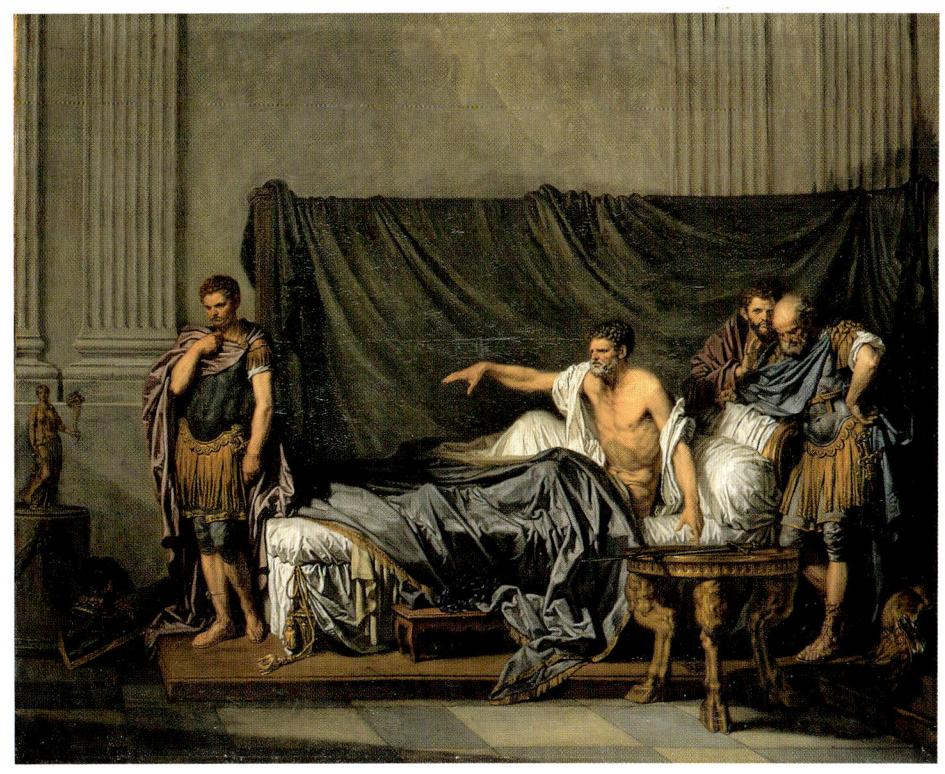

Fig. 14 Greuze, *The Beloved Mother*, 1769, oil on canvas, Madrid, collection comte de la Viñaza, marquis de Laborde

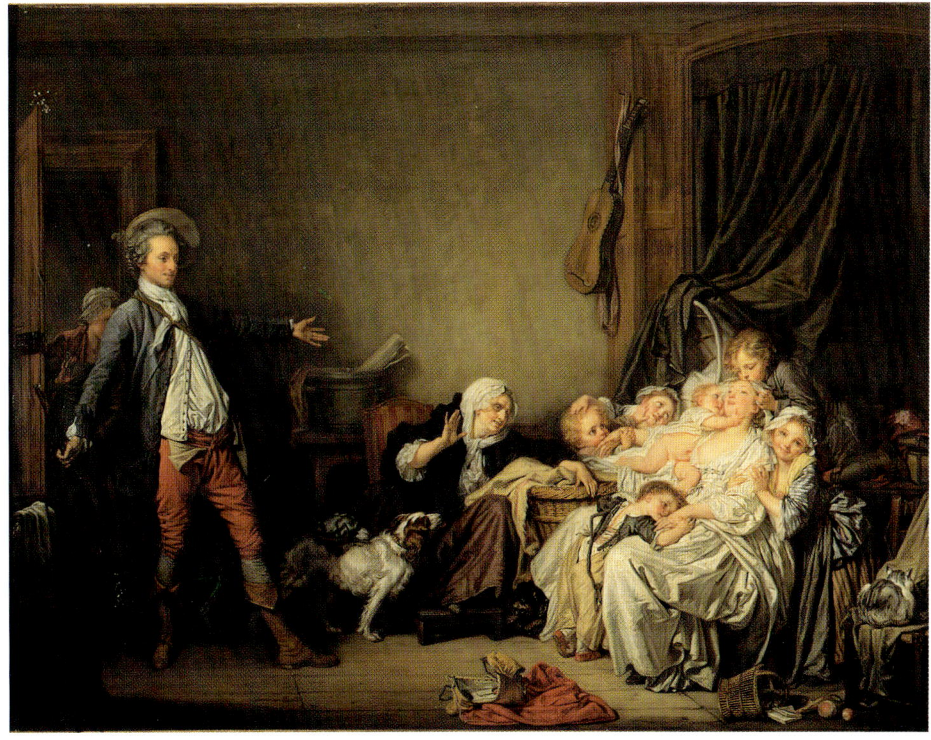

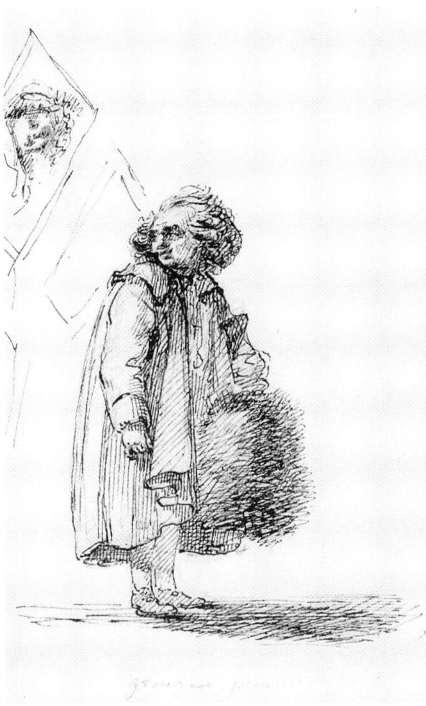

Fig. 15 Baron D. Vivant-Denon, *Greuze the Painter,* 1787, pen and black ink on white paper, whereabouts unknown

August–September 1765: Greuze exhibits sixteen works in the Salon:

110 *Girl Weeping over Her Dead Bird* (Edinburgh, National Galleries of Scotland; fig. 53)
111 *The Spoiled Child* (St Petersburg, The State Hermitage Museum; fig. 86)
112 *Head of a Girl*
113 *Another Girl, Holding a Doll Dressed as a Capuchin Monk* (St Petersburg, The State Hermitage Museum)
114 *Another Head of a Girl*
115 *A Head in Pastel*
116 *Portrait of M. Watelet* (Paris, Musée du Louvre; fig. 208)
117 *Portrait of M. Wille* (Paris, Musée Jacquemart-André)
118 *Portrait de M. Caffiéri* (New York, The Metropolitan Museum of Art)
119 *Portrait of M. Guibert*
120 *Portrait of Madame Tassart*
121 *Portrait of Madame Greuze*
122 *Portrait in Pastel of M. de la Live de July*
123 *The Beloved Mother* (see nos. 43, 70)
124 *The Ungrateful Son* (Lille, Musée des Beaux-Arts; no. 48)
125 *The Punished Son* (Lille, Musée des Beaux-Arts; no. 49)

18 April 1766: Greuze is named a nonresident member of the Académie des Sciences, Arts et Belles-Lettres of Dijon.

1766: Pierre-Charles Ingouf's (1746–1800) *Têtes de différents caractères,* a set of engravings after expressive heads in paintings by Greuze, is published with a dedication to Wille. Catherine II purchases *The Paralytic* (fig. 24), a picture the connoisseur Pierre-Jean Mariette had predicted would never sell because of its depressing subject.

1767: Charles-Nicolas Cochin (1688–1754), secretary of the Académie, writes Greuze to inform him that, because of his failure after twelve years to present his reception picture, he is barred from exhibiting at the Salon this year.

15 August 1767: Diderot writes to the sculptor Falconet in St Petersburg, telling him that he is awaiting two medals from General Ivan Betskoy, along with the diploma confirming the *philosophe*'s election to the Imperial Academy of Fine Arts as an associate member. This anticipated meeting with Betskoy may coincide with the latter's purchase of Greuze's drawings as recounted here by Irina Novosselskaya (pp. 29–30).

1768: Greuze's first book illustration is published: the frontispiece of Louis-Edme Billardon de Sauvigny's *Rose, ou la fête de Salency.*

23 July 1769: Greuze finally presents to the Académie his reception painting, *Septimius Severus and Caracalla* (fig. 13; see no. 67). Though received as a full academician, he is humiliated by being classed as a genre painter rather than as a history painter. This institutional row explodes in the press.

25 August–30 September 1769: Having been left at the Académie, Greuze's controversial *Septimius Severus* is shown at the Salon, along with a large number of other works by the artist:

151 *Septimius Severus and Caracalla* (Paris, Musée du Louvre; fig. 13)
152 *The Beloved Mother* (Madrid, collection comte de la Viñaza, marquis de Laborde; fig. 14)
153 *The Votive Offering to Cupid* (London, The Wallace Collection)
154 *The Kiss* (Pregny, Rothschild collection; fig. 122)
155 *Child Playing with a Dog* (London, private collection)
156 *Portrait of the Prince de Saxe*
157 *Portrait of M. Jeurat* (Paris, Musée du Louvre)
158 *Portrait of M. de ****
159 *Three Heads of Children, under the Same Number*
Drawings
160 *The Death of a Father Mourned by His Children* (Paris, Musée du Louvre, on deposit at the Musée des Beaux-Arts, Strasbourg; fig. 168)
161 *The Death of a Cruel Father Abandoned by His Children* (Tournus, Musée Greuze; no. 69)
162 *The Avaricious Man and His Children*
163 *The Paternal Benediction* (perhaps The Art Institute of Chicago)
164 *The Departure from Barcelonnette* (see nos. 56, 57)
165 *The Consolation of Old Age*

25 September 1769: Greuze publishes a letter in the *Avant-Coureur* defending his *Septimius Severus* against the avalanche of negative criticism directed at it. Infuriated over his treatment by the Académie, Greuze ceases to exhibit at the Salon until 1800 (see no. 94).

1769: Greuze's second book illustration is published in London, the frontispiece for Madame Benoist's novel *Sophronie* (fig. 165).

10 October 1769: Greuze's father dies in Tournus.

In St Petersburg, General Betskoy turns over his large collection of drawings by Greuze to the Imperial Academy of Fine Arts, of which he is the president.

Fig. 16 Greuze, *The Father's Curse: The Ungrateful Son,* 1777, oil on canvas, Paris, Musée du Louvre

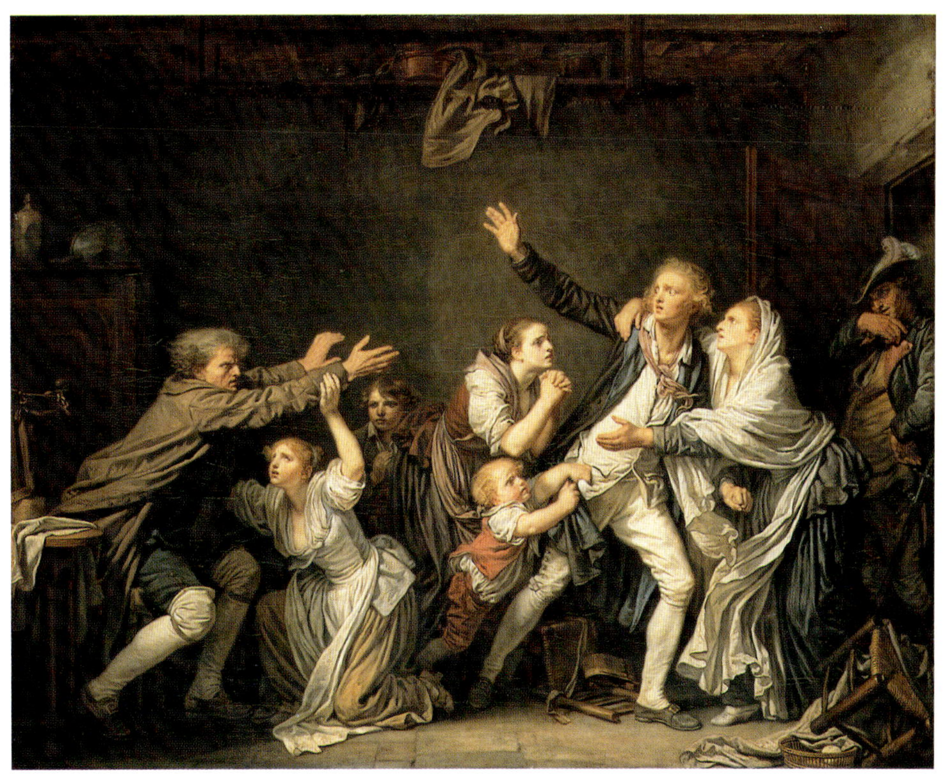

Fig. 17 Greuze, *The Father's Curse: The Punished Son,* 1778, oil on canvas, Paris, Musée du Louvre

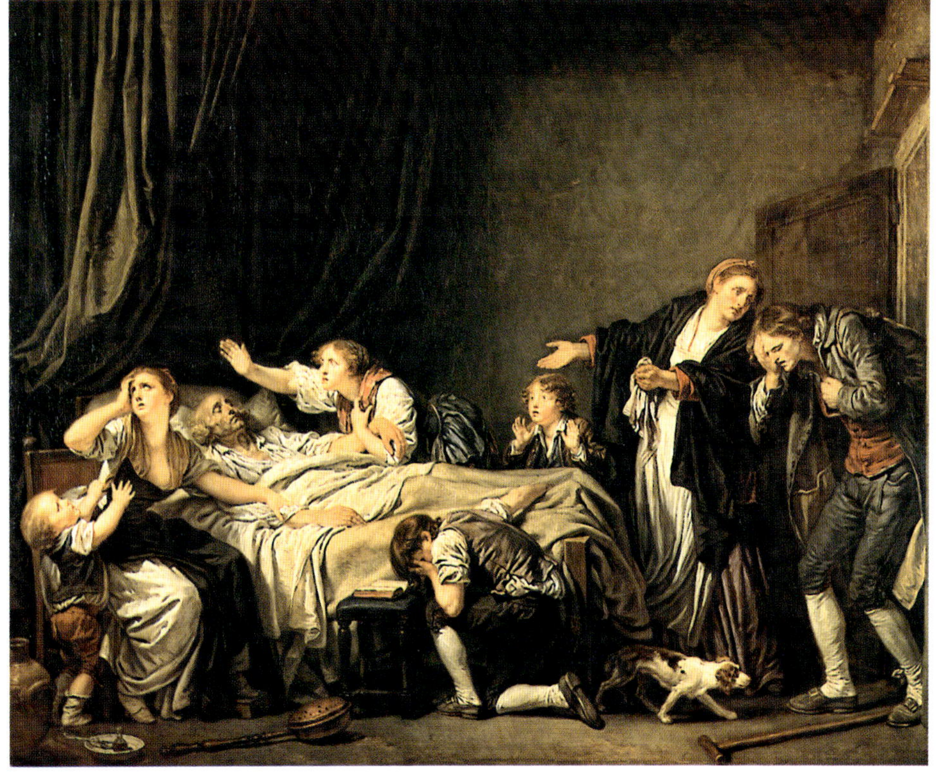

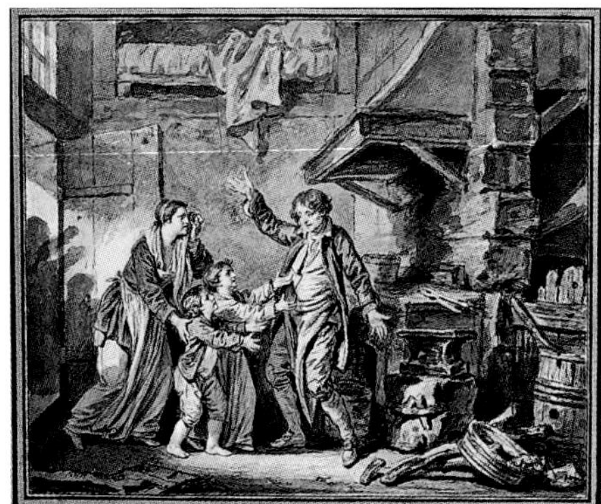

Fig. 18 Greuze, *Compositional Study for "The Drunken Cobbler,"* 1782, brush and gray ink wash over graphite on white paper, Frankfurt am Main, Städelsches Kunstinstitut

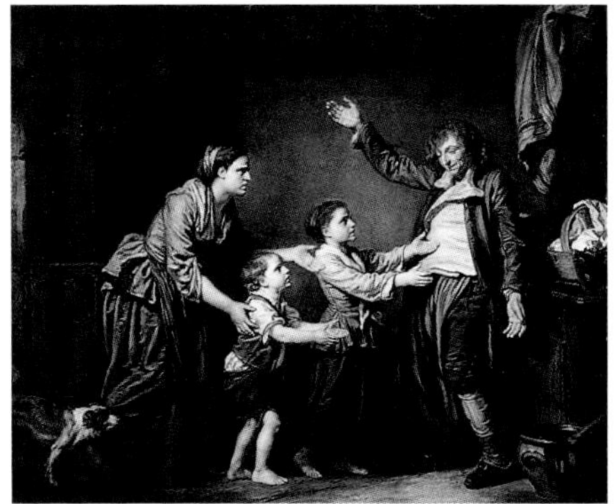

Fig. 19 Greuze, *The Drunken Cobbler,* 1782, oil on canvas, Portland Art Museum OR

28 September 1770: Though Greuze generally shuns meetings of the Académie, he occasionally appears when his vote could matter, as at this one concerning the admission of female members (a cause he supported).

1771: At the time of the Académie's Salon, Greuze begins to exhibit concurrently with it, but independently, in his studio in the Louvre. Among his many visitors is Gustav III of Sweden.

c. *1775:* Publication of the Baskerville edition of Ariosto's *Orlando furioso* with Greuze's illustration for canto XXIX (fig. 174).

6 July 1776: Balthazar Mollard recognizes before a notary that he owes Greuze and his wife the sum of 1428 livres for items belonging to them that his son had carried off. The boy, Greuze's pupil and a favorite of his wife, is seventeen years old; she is then forty-four.

June 1777: Greuze visits Benjamin Franklin at Passy and executes his portrait (pastel: Washington D.C., United States Department of State; oil: Philadelphia, American Philosophical Society). The artist receives the visit of Joseph II of Austria, brother of Marie-Antoinette, traveling as the comte de Falkenstein.

28 November 1778: Greuze is initiated into the Masonic Lodge Les Neuf Soeurs (see no. 13).

August 1779: Greuze exhibits with Jean-Antoine Houdon (1741–1828) at Les Neuf Soeurs, as well as in the Salon de la Correspondance, and at the Société des Beaux-Arts, Montpellier.

7 January 1780: Jean-Baptiste-Marie Pierre (1713–1789), *directeur* of the Académie, informs Charles-Claude de Flahaut de la Billarderie, comte d'Angiviller, *surintendant des bâtiments du roi* (fig. 70), that Greuze is offering to give up his apartment-studio in the Louvre in exchange for an annual pension of 1000 livres. D'Angiviller conveys the king's approval four days later.

2 February 1780: Pierre reports that Greuze has handed over all the documents concerning his apartment in the Louvre, and that the artist was pleased with the settlement from the state.

14 May 1782: Catherine II's son, Grand Duke Paul Petrovitch, traveling with his wife as the comte and comtesse du Nord, visits Greuze in his studio and commissions the painting *The Widow and Her Priest* (St Petersburg, The State Hermitage Museum).

June–September 1782: The idea of weaving tapestries at the Manufacture des Gobelins after paintings by Greuze (as a possible royal gift to the comte and comtesse du Nord) is considered, but dropped.

1785: In 1791 Madame Greuze would make a legal request to recover from her husband thirty-six livres she claims to have lost during her moving "about six years ago." This suggests that by 1785 the disputatious couple (see no. 89) were already separated.

11 December 1785: Following a particularly humiliating encounter with one of his wife's visitors, Greuze lodges a complaint over her behavior with the police. The text implies that the artist and his wife are living apart and that Greuze intends to make a more complete report on his marital problems.

1785–89: Greuze has dealings with Prince Nikolai Borisovitch Yusopov, selling him his own pictures as well as works by other French artists including François-André Vincent (1746–1816), Fragonard, and Élisabeth-Louise Vigée-Lebrun (1755–1842).

1786: Greuze exhibits three drawings in the Salon des Arts at Lyon.

5 December 1789: Anne-Gabrielle Babuti, calling herself "formally separated wife of J.-B. Greuze," obtains from the police the right to go to court to reply to a suit brought against her by her estranged husband.

1790: Greuze exhibits in the Salon de l'Encouragement des Arts. George Romney (1734–1802) visits Paris and dines with Greuze and Jacques-Louis David (1748–1825).

1791–92: Possibly with divorce in mind, Greuze dictates a lengthy and detailed account of his marital woes.

16 July 1792: Louis XVI awards Greuze a pension of 1537 livres 10 sols, retroactive to 1 January 1790.

4 August 1793: Greuze's divorce is granted, with Madame Greuze receiving a large settlement. The artist's two daughters, aged twenty-nine and thirty-one, remain with him.

27 August 1793: Anne-Gabrielle Babuti requests an inventory and appraisal of Greuze's possessions, which he and she are to divide. The inventory is begun on 2 September, the pictures are evaluated on 13 September, and on 18 September Greuze takes possession of his lodgings again, 14, rue Basse-Porte-St-Denis.

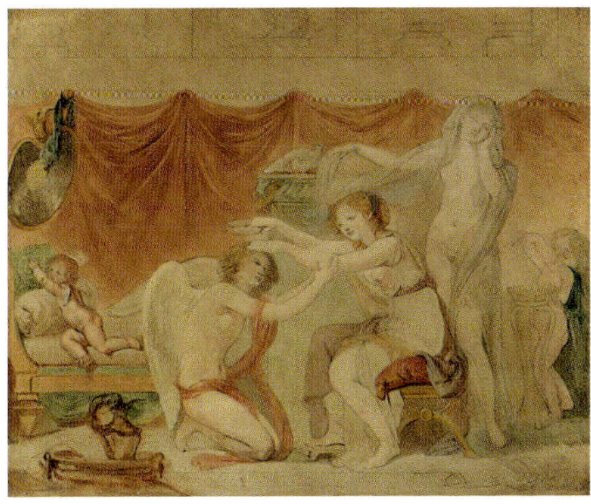

Fig. 20 Greuze, *Study for "Psyche Crowning Cupid," c.* 1790, graphite and oil on canvas, Marseille, Musée Borély, on deposit at the Musée des Beaux-Arts, Marseille

October 1792: Greuze joins the powerful Commune Générale des Arts, led by Jean-Bernard Restout (1732–1797) and David. The latter seems to encourage certain Revolutionary figures to commission their portraits from Greuze—Jacques-Nicolas Billaud-Varenne, Jean-Jacques Régis de Cambacérès, Jean-Antoine-Nicolas de Caritat, marquis de Condorcet, Philippe-François-Nazaire Fabre d'Églantine, Armand Gensonné.

18 September 1794: Greuze is spotted watching the execution of his notary and avid collector of his work, Charles-Nicolas Duclos-Dufresnoy.

29 April–21 November 1796: Desain de Saint-Gobert records nineteen sittings for his portrait by Greuze.

1797: Greuze settles a lengthy lawsuit over the will of his elder brother Jacques (a priest, who bequeathed him thirty livres) and rewards his lawyer, Jean Tupinier, by painting his portrait, completed on 19 March.

Summer 1800: For the first time since 1769, Greuze exhibits in the Salon. His eleven works, beginning with a drawing, include:

173 *The Departure for the Hunt, Portrait of the comte *** and His Wife, in a Landscape* (see no. 94)
174 *Two Pictures Forming Pendants (Same Number)*
A Child Hesitating to Touch a Bird in Fear that It Might Be Dead (Paris, Musée du Louvre)
A Young Woman Preparing to Write a Love Letter
175 *Portrait. A Young Woman at the Piano*
176 *Two Portraits of Men (Same Number)*
177 *Three Heads of Different Characters (Same Number)*
Fear of the Storm
Apprehension Mingled with Desire
Sleep
178 *Two Pendants (Same Number)*
Innocence Holding Two Doves (London, The Wallace Collection)
A Young Woman Covering Her Ears (formerly Paris, baronne Édouard de Rothschild)

Summer 1801: Greuze exhibits five works at the Salon:

158 *The Repentance of St Mary of Egypt in the Desert* (Norfolk VA, The Chrysler Museum of Art; fig. 228)
159 *A Farmer Handing over His Plow to His Son, in the Presence of the Family* (Moscow, The Pushkin State Museum of Fine Art)
160 *A Child*
161 *Portrait of a Man*
162 *Portrait of an Old Man*

Summer 1804: At the age of seventy-nine, Greuze exhibits for the last time in the Salon:

219 *The Repentance of St Mary of Egypt* (possibly the same exhibited in 1801 and again, posthumously, in 1808 [no. 271])
220 *Ariadne on Naxos* (London, The Wallace Collection)
221 *Portrait of the Artist* (no. 96)
222 *Portrait of a Woman*
223 *Two Heads of Girls: Timidity, Gaiety*

21 March 1805: Greuze dies in his studio in the Louvre, cared for in his last illness by Dr Guillotin. His funeral is sparsely attended, though the artist Jean-Simon Berthélémy (1743–1811) was there as Greuze had predicted, "like the poor man's dog." Marie-Françoise-Constance Mayer-Lamartinière (1775–1821) places on the artist's coffin a bouquet of immortelles. Greuze is buried in the cemetery of Montmartre.

March 1805: A few days after the artist's death, a letter addressed to him by Bidau, *commissaire* of the town of Tournus, announces that a street in which the artist's family had lived has been renamed "rue Greuze."

25 March 1805: Greuze's two daughters, equal heirs of their father, request an inventory of his possessions remaining in his studio in the Louvre.

1811: It is often stated that Anne-Gabrielle Babuti dies in 1811, but in fact, she inherits part of her daughter's estate the following year. There is no record of her death.

10 February 1812: Death of Louise-Gabrielle Greuze, buried with her father.

5 November 1842: Death of Anne-Geneviève (Caroline) Greuze, buried with her father.

25–26 January 1843: Caroline Greuze sale, Paris. Théophile Thoré prepares the important catalogue, listing what remains of the contents of Greuze's studio as preserved by his daughter.

The Collection of Drawings by Jean-Baptiste Greuze in St Petersburg

Irina Novosselskaya

In 1920 Louis Réau, a specialist in the field of French–Russian relations, published an article entitled "Greuze and Russia" in a Parisian magazine.[1] Toward the end of his article, the author noted that, in terms of the relative quantity and importance of works produced by the draftsman from Tournus held in various collections, St Petersburg trailed Paris by only a narrow margin. Since this article was published, new evidence has emerged that links Greuze to Russia. But the fundamental idea expressed by Réau holds true to this day—St Petersburg remains second only to Paris in the significance of its art collections. Furthermore, the St Petersburg collection of drawings by far outweighs other collections around the world, including those elsewhere in France.

In the late eighteenth and early nineteenth century, Jean-Baptiste Greuze, Hubert Robert, and Joseph Vernet (1714–1789) were among the most popular artists in Russia. The empress Catherine II, an avid collector of fine arts, whose acquisitions largely formed the foundation of the Hermitage, held the works of these masters in high esteem. In 1766, on the advice of Denis Diderot, and with the help of Prince Dmitry Alexeyevitch Golitsyn, who was at that time the Russian envoy in Paris, she acquired Greuze's painting *The Paralytic* (fig. 24), one of the artist's most significant works. It should be noted, however, that *The Paralytic,* praised by Diderot and met with great enthusiasm by the French public, was purchased in France, but not by a French collector. Nothing else is known about the empress's other purchases of works by Greuze. An anticipated trip of the draftsman to Russia never took place. Diderot, who opposed the trip, wrote to the sculptor Étienne-Maurice Falconet in 1767 expressing his views:

He's an excellent artist, but a very disagreeable character. One should have his drawings and his paintings, and leave the man at that. Furthermore, his wife is, by unanimous consent (and when I say unanimous, I leave out neither hers nor that of her husband), one of the most dangerous creatures on earth. I should not give up hope that one fine day, her Imperial Majesty might not send her on tour to Siberia. I tell you clearly here what I have given you to understand orally.[2]

Paul, Catherine's son, inherited his mother's love for Greuze's masterpieces. In 1782, the future Emperor Paul I of Russia was traveling in Europe together with his wife under the assumed names of the comte and comtesse du Nord. During this trip they commissioned a painting from Greuze entitled *The Widow and Her Priest* (St Petersburg, The State Hermitage Museum). It is widely known that the couple, while in Paris, expressed considerable interest in the theater, architecture, and the fine arts. Friedrich Melchior Grimm wrote to Diderot in July 1782 reporting on the Russians' activities: "When visiting the studios, he [the comte du Nord] displayed such profound knowledge of the arts that his compliments were considered a great honor by all our artists." Grimm continued: "He showed particular interest in the studios of Mr Greuze and Mr [Jean-Antoine] Houdon."[3]

Until recently Grimm's letter was the only evidence of contact between the successor to the Russian throne and Greuze. Subsequently I found a document in the state archives that not only corroborates the fact that Paul I visited Greuze's studio but also specifies the exact date this visit took place. A report compiled by Prince Baratinski, who accompanied the future czar during his trip, states: "Yesterday morning His Royal Highness expressed a desire to visit the Hôtel Dieu au Palais du Luxembourg and also to stop at the neighboring convent of the Carmelites, which possesses several paintings by well-known French artists. After that he wished to visit Greuze. After dinner his desire was to attend a French comedy."[4] With the report dated 26 May 1782, the visit must have taken place on the previous day. Solely on the basis of Grimm's letter, many scholars assumed that it was the comte du Nord who purchased the ensemble of Greuze's drawings in 1782.

There are other possible avenues by which Greuze's drawings could have entered the imperial collections. Prominent statesmen and public figures, patrons, and collectors of art—counts Nikita Akintitch Demidov, Alexander Sergeyevitch Stroganov, Andrey Petrovitch Shuvalov, and Prince Nikolai Borisovitch Yusopov—also collected Greuze's art. Some of them even developed personal relationships with the artist. Demidov, who purchased artwork from Greuze and commissioned over twenty-five paintings, lived in the same house in Paris with the draftsman. Greuze had extensive contacts with Prince Yusopov, an association known to many. The artist and Yusopov regularly corresponded regarding art the prince commissioned. While in Paris, Russians commissioned from the artist portraits of themselves and their loved ones. Thus the Hermitage collection was complemented by such works as *Portrait of Count Pavel Stroganov as a Child, Portrait of Countess Shuvalova,* and portrait heads from the Shuvalov and Yusopov collections. Mention of a second version of how the drawings got to Russia in the literature stems from the assumption that the collection of Greuze's drawings in the Hermitage was purchased by the Shuvalov family. In an article commemorating the 150th anniversary of the Imperial Academy of Fine Arts in St Petersburg, A. Rostislavov, an art critic and constant contributor to the magazine *Starie Godi,* wrote tantalizingly about the drawings by Greuze: "Less is known about its library [Imperial Academy of Fine Arts], which has existed since its inception: 17,000 volumes and as many original drawings, including an outstanding collection of Greuze's drawings (200), bought by Shuvalov [without specifying the first name] from the artist, were part of the library during the reign of Catherine the Great."[5] In reality, in 1758, Ivan Ivanovitch Shuvalov, the first president of the Imperial Academy of Fine Arts, presented the academy with one hundred paintings, among them Greuze's *Girl with a Doll:* "He offered the Academy as gifts a great number of wonderful paintings ... and rare drawings."[6] But Greuze's drawings were not among them.

In 1934, Tatiana Davidovna Kamenskaya,[7] who for a number of years headed the Department of Drawings in the Hermitage, first correctly identified the source of the acquisition of the drawings. Using unpublished information from the archives, she surmised that Ivan Ivanovitch Betskoy (1704–1795), president of the Imperial Academy of Fine Arts, had purchased the collection of drawings in 1769. Subsequently, I found supporting documents that show that until 1769 Greuze's drawings did indeed belong to Betskoy. Kiril Ivanovitch Golovachevski, the academy's treasurer and advisor, and from 1765 to 1772 the academy's librarian, submitted an inventory dated 23 June 1773[8] to the Imperial Academy of Fine Arts' Council when the new librarian, S.F. Belyaev, took over. Section 14 of the inventory, devoted to drawings, shows that on 31 January 1767 Betskoy transferred to the academy a large collection of "6979 original drawings by different artists in 31 folders."[9] Section 15, also devoted to drawings, has the following entry: in 1769 "received from His Highness Ivan Ivanovitch Betskoy, the President of the Academy, three hundred and sixty-three original drawings." Among them, under numbers 16–240, were drawings by Greuze.

A few words should be said about Ivan Ivanovitch Betskoy, a prominent dignitary at the court of Catherine the Great and a favorite of the empress. Beginning in 1762 all educational establishments in Russia were under his supervision, including the Imperial Academy of Fine Arts, which he headed for over thirty years. During that time he spared no effort to expand its collection. Furthermore, Betskoy contributed significantly to the development of the institution's library and the museum of casts and, as noted, gave a large number of drawings to the academy. Betskoy's background prepared him well for his position. He received an outstanding European education, worked for a number of years at the Department of Foreign Affairs, and resided for many years in European capitals, where he came into contact with figures in the international art world.

The academy received from Betskoy about seven thousand sheets, among which were numerous studies and paintings that most probably had been purchased as study materials for the academy's students. But there were also well-known masterpieces by artists of the French school—Jacques Bellange (act. 1600–1617), Daniel Dumoustier (1574–1646), Nicolas Poussin (1594–1665); the Italian school—Ercole de' Roberti (*c.* 1450–1496); the German school—Albrecht Dürer (1471–1528); and the Flemish school—Jacob Jordaens (1593–1678), among others.

The drawings given to the academy in 1767 were labeled individually by number, but Greuze's drawings, given in 1769, were grouped by category. And this we think might be of interest:

Number 16 Greuze	
1. Forty-five male heads done in red chalk	102
2. Fifty-seven female heads done in red chalk	
3. Seven heads done in black chalk	7
4. Twelve heads done in three chalks	12
5. Seven studies drawn in India ink	7
6. Twenty-two compositional studies done in red chalk	22
7. Ten compositional studies done in three chalks	10
8. Three compositional studies done in three chalks	3
9. Five portrait heads	5
10. Seventeen drawings of hands	17
11. Four drawings of dogs	4
12. Thirty-four clothed figures done in red chalk	34
13. Ten clothed figures done in black and white chalks	10
14. Five clothed figures done in three chalks	5
15. Two drawings from François [illegible]	2

It is not clear what prompted the successful artist to part with such a large number of his drawings, most of which, as indicated in this list, were study materials. Perhaps the extravagant tastes of the artist's wife had caused him financial difficulties. At the same time, it is important to remember that Betskoy, while living in Paris from 1756 to 1761, participated in French literary and art circles, was a guest at Madame Geoffrin's salon, and was close to Grimm and Diderot. Most probably, Betskoy purchased his collection of Greuze's drawings several years later on the recommendation of Diderot.

All the drawings that Betskoy gave to the academy in 1767 were marked by his stamp in the form of a star, which was placed in the lower corner of the sheet.[10] But Betskoy's stamp is missing from Greuze's drawings, and they are marked instead with the Imperial Academy of Fine Arts' two-headed eagle.[11] Most likely, the drawings were given to the library of the academy soon after they arrived from Paris. The rest of the collection transferred to the academy in 1769 was most probably kept by Betskoy for some time and therefore marked with his stamp.

The history of Greuze's drawings while in the academy's possession is also not without interest. In June 1818, Andrey Uhtomski, the academy's librarian, prepared a catalogue, *All Items of the Royal Academy of Arts under the Supervision of the Librarian.*[12] In it, Greuze's drawings, which at that time were kept in three crates, were mentioned. The list of works was rather general. Later, drawings either were under the supervision of the museum's curator or were transferred back to the custody of the librarian. On 12 July 1868 the supervisors of the Imperial Academy of Fine Arts issued a decree, signed by Isseev, conference secretary: Academician Klagus, the academy's librarian, was ordered to take custody from the museum of "books, prints, engravings, and other study materials."[13] Unfortunately, no lists concerning this transfer were preserved. But by the beginning of the twentieth century, the collection of Greuze's drawings, totaling 193, was kept in four folders and one box.[14] The smaller number of drawings can be explained by the fact that model and head studies had been used to teach students and were ruined over time by use. Proof of this use are oil stains and paint smears on several compositional studies.

For many years, Greuze's drawings were kept at the Imperial Academy of Fine Arts and were virtually unknown outside its walls. We have already mentioned the fact that the artist's studies were used to teach students. And only a few times, and only in the twentieth century, were some drawings included in exhibitions organized by the academy. The exhibition *Blanc et noir* was held in October 1903, and in 1908 the publication *Starie Godi* mentioned an exhibition of Greuze's drawings recently organized in the library of the academy.[15] But these exhibitions were private, not public, events.

In 1883 the magazine *Vestnick Izachnih Iskustv (Magazine of Fine Arts)* widely advertised its supplement, which it sent free of charge to all its subscribers, consisting of ten reproductions of Greuze's drawings from the academy's collection; the album was published by Stein and Laptev. Because the necessity of some such publication was raised on numerous occasions, Isseev, secretary of the academy, explained the institution's action in "Publishing Greuze's Drawings in Custody of the Academy of Arts."

The collection of drawings by Jean-Baptiste Greuze is such a unique treasure that no other museum in Europe can boast of such a possession. Even in the Louvre the number of drawings attributed to the now famous and highly esteemed artist is considerably fewer than in the Academy. And as to the importance of the works, the Louvre trails the Academy by far. But at the same time this collection remains unknown to the art world, which could not even imagine that such precious drawings by Greuze could have been kept under lock and key for a whole century in one of St Petersburg's establishments away from art lovers' eyes. And at the same time in foreign lands practically all works and even sketches done by this artist have been found and published in precise reproductions. Thus the Academy would have acted honorably and acquired the respect of all people interested in fine arts not only in Russia but in other countries if it attempted to publish Greuze's artwork in its possession using a reliable and relatively inexpensive method of reproduction—phototype.[16]

In 1910 F. Bernshtam, the academy's librarian, attempted to convince the academy to carry out another such project. He filed the state documents necessary to publish a second album of twelve reproductions of the artist's drawings. But the request was not granted because of the high cost of producing such an album.

Thus it comes as no surprise that the first complete edition of Greuze's drawings kept at the academy was published, not by the academy's staff, but by foreigners, and not in St Petersburg, but in Paris. In 1913 the French art historians François Monod and Louis Hautecoeur, who at that time were living in St Petersburg, published an article announcing their intention of publishing the academy's collection, praising it highly for its significance.[17] Monod and Hautecoeur, among the first researchers to investigate the academy's collection of Greuze's drawings thoroughly, in 1922 published their catalogue of the drawings.[18] Sixty-three of the 193 drawings included in the catalogue were reproduced. The catalogue's authors assumed that some of the sheets dated as late as the 1780s because they believed the collection most probably had been acquired by the heir to the Russian throne, Pavel Petrovitch, in 1782.

It would be unwise to underappreciate the research done by the two Frenchmen. For a considerable time this catalogue remained the only complete publication of the academy's collection. Because the catalogue was published in a limited, numbered edition, it now is a bibliographic rarity.

Of the four folders and one box of Greuze's drawings held at the academy, three folders and the box were transferred in 1924 from the Imperial Academy of Fine Arts to the Hermitage, together with other drawings by Western European artists. The drawings to be transferred were selected by prominent art specialists of the time, Professors Mikhail Vasilievitch Dobroklonski and Vladimir Fransovitch Levinson-Lessing, who were employed by the Hermitage. From Betskoy's collection they selected the most interesting objects (about 2000 drawings). It is difficult to understand how one folder of Greuze's drawings, including thirty head studies and busts, was left in the academy's custody. It is still kept by the Research and Development Museum of the Academy of Fine Arts in St Petersburg.

One hundred sixty-two drawings by Greuze were among the two thousand transferred to the Hermitage in 1924. Unfortunately, only 123 of them remain there; in the 1930s, following the redistribution of museums' collections, several drawings were transferred to the Museum of Fine Arts in Moscow and to the museums of fine arts in Krasnodar, Erevan, and other cities. Some of the drawings were sold at auctions.

Currently the Hermitage has 125 drawings by Greuze: 123 of these drawings come from the Betskoy collection, one from the collection of Pavel Vicktorovitch Delarov (1852–1913), which was transferred to the Imperial Academy of Fine Arts after 1913, and one drawing, *The School Mistress,* was acquired in 1768 in Brussels as part of the collection of Count Karl Cobenzl (1712–1770). This collection, which included over four thousand works of various schools, laid the foundation for the Hermitage's collection of drawings.

After 1924, when the collection of Greuze's work was transferred from the academy to the Hermitage, Tatiana Davidovna Kamenskaya, a specialist in the field of French drawings, mentioned above, took up research of his work. Her contribution to promoting the legacy of Greuze in Russia was most significant.[19] She also deciphered the meaning behind Greuze's drawing *The School Mistress* (no. 46).[20]

Before the 1960s it was a rarity to see Greuze's drawings exhibited domestically or abroad. But starting in the 1960s, a decade that witnessed an upsurge in exhibitions, selective drawings were shown in temporary exhibitions at the Hermitage and the Museum of Fine Arts in Moscow. And by the late 1960s these drawings were included on a regular basis in exhibitions devoted to Western European drawings organized in museums abroad: Australia, Austria, Czechoslovakia, Denmark, England, France, Germany, Hungary, Japan, the United States, and other countries.

The year 1975 marked the 250th anniversary of Greuze's birth. Unfortunately, the Hermitage did not take part in the outstanding exhibition of Greuze's work that was seen in Hartford, San Francisco, and Dijon the following year. But the catalogue of works included in the exhibition, by Edgar Munhall, the leading scholar of Greuze, gave rise to a fresh interest in the artist.[21]

In 1977 the author of the present essay organized an exhibition that displayed all of Greuze's drawings that are kept at the Hermitage. The catalogue of the exhibition included for the first time references to archival documents attesting to the collection's origins and its tenure at the Imperial Academy of Fine Arts.[22] Brief statements included in Monod and Hautecoeur's catalogue were supplemented by new data. And later several publications were issued in Russia devoted to Greuze's art and particularly to his drawings, which were considered a significant aspect of his work.[23]

The importance of Betskoy's collection can be compared only with that of the collection preserved by the daughter of the artist, Caroline Greuze. This included an

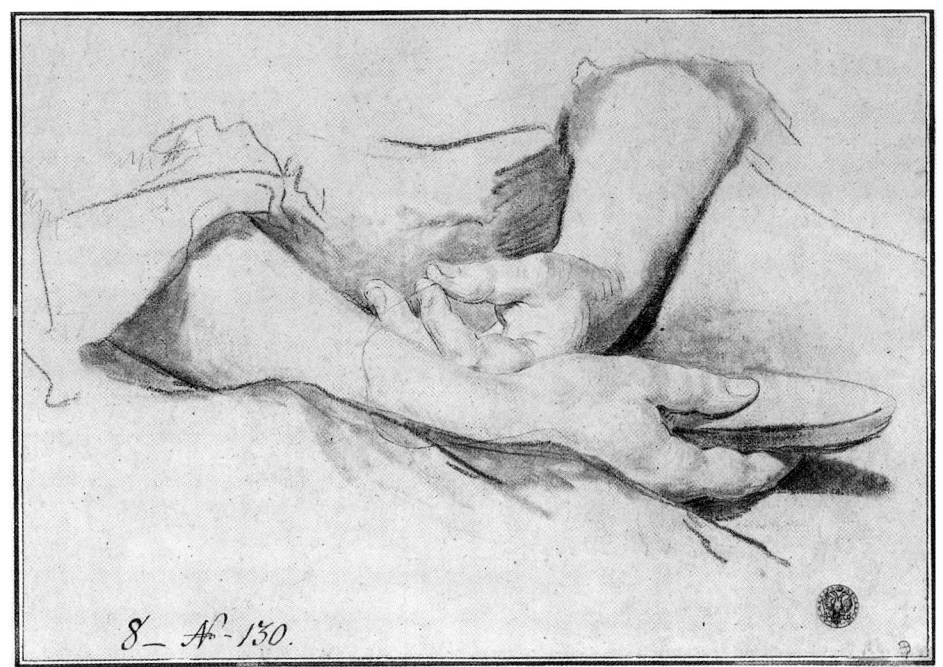

Fig. 21 Greuze, *Study of a Lady's Hands, One Holding a Thread, the Other, a Navette,* 1757, black chalk, stumped, on cream paper, St Petersburg, The State Hermitage Museum

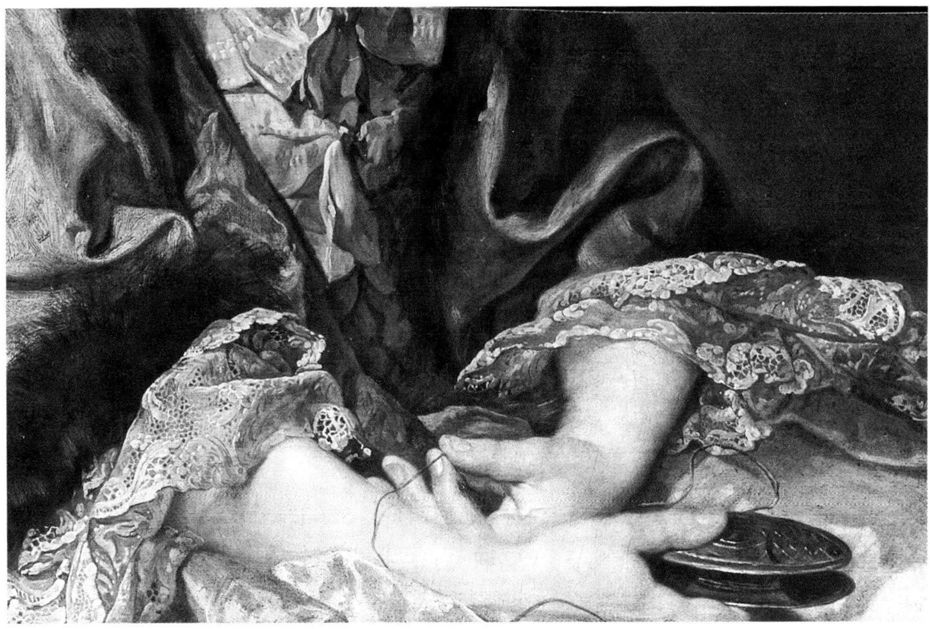

Fig. 22 Greuze, *Portrait of Marie-Angélique de Varenne, Madame George Gougenot de Croissy* (detail), 1757, oil on canvas, New Orleans Museum of Art

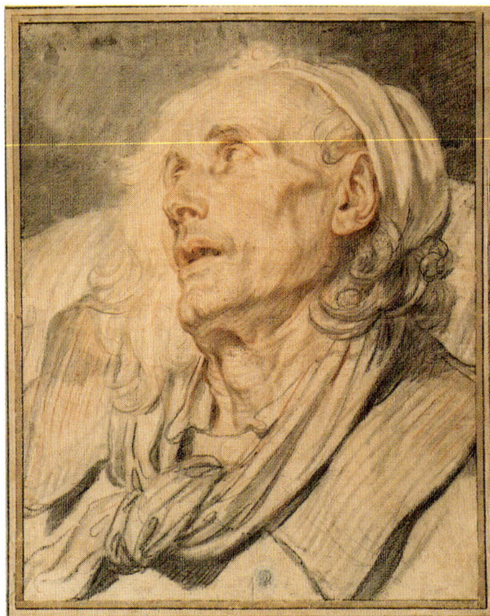

Fig. 23 Greuze, *Bust of an Old Man, Study for "The Paralytic,"* 1763, red and black chalks, stumped, on cream paper, St Petersburg, The State Hermitage Museum

album of sketches and over one hundred drawings on separate sheets, covering a broader period of time and a wider variety of subjects and compositions than Betskoy's. But the collection was sold in parts in 1843, when the artist's drawings, no longer in vogue, brought only a fraction of their worth.[24]

The Hermitage collection of Greuze's artwork includes over thirty studies made from life—the *académies*. Such studies are rarely found in other collections. But even though this group of drawings is unique, it serves only as a preamble to the main collection, the most valuable part of which are the preparatory studies of figures, heads, and hands, which Greuze used in later compositions dating from the mid-1750s to the late 1760s. Among the studies are two or three for *The Neapolitan Gesture* (Worcester Art Museum), *Silence!* (London, Buckingham Palace, Royal Collection; no. 8), *The Spoiled Child* (St Petersburg, The State Hermitage Museum; no. 30), five studies for *The Beloved Mother* (Madrid, collection comte de la Viñaza, marquis de Laborde; nos. 40, 44, 45), six studies for *The Dry Nurses* (Kansas City MO, The Nelson-Atkins Museum of Art; nos. 34, 35), and nine studies for *The Paralytic* (St Petersburg, The State Hermitage Museum; nos. 24, 25). The list does not end with these examples, as the collection includes studies for twenty significant works of the artist.

Drawings constituted a special place in Greuze's work. Without exaggeration it can be said that no other eighteenth-century French artist made so many careful studies for his paintings. It suffices to look at only one example, *The Paralytic,* for which numerous preparatory drawings have been preserved. Among them are a composition done in India ink (Le Havre, Musée des Beaux-Arts; fig. 71), several sketches of the head of the ailing man, including two uncontested masterpieces—drawings in black chalk, red chalk, and gray washes in the collections of the National Museum in Copenhagen and the Hermitage—a sketch of the figure of the paralyzed man done in red chalk (Wijhe, The Netherlands, Stichting Hannema-de Stuers Fundatie), several sketches done in red chalk in the Hermitage collection: *The Wife of the Paralytic,* two sketches of the figure of the son-in-law (and a sketch of his head retained by the Museum of the Academy of Arts in St Petersburg), two sketches of a boy carrying a cup, a sketch of a figure of another boy covering the sick man's legs, a sketch of a dog (done in red and black chalk; no. 25), and a sketch of the hand of an elderly person, probably one of the sketches of the paralyzed man's hand (no. 24). Though minor differences are apparent between the drawings and the final painting, each study was clearly intended for a specific use in that complex work.

Greuze's sketches, often done in different tones of red chalk, are almost always done on large sheets (40 to 50 centimeters high), and they almost always depict figures, heads, and hands in large scale. Strong, bold strokes produce forms and portray movement. The artist usually did not draw the smallest details. Although general in character, the sketches nonetheless precisely depict the essential elements of the painting. In *Standing Man, Study for "Italians Playing le Jeu de la main chaude"* (see no. 7), the figure swinging his arm conveys abrupt movement. The artist was constantly searching for the correct placement or movement of hands (fig. 21), utilizing such studies in portraits (fig. 22). The drawing of the head (fig. 23) for *The Paralytic* (fig. 24) is both expressive and noble. Though executed in half-tones and in a palette limited to grays and browns, it remains extremely expressive. Even the sketches of young women so popular with the artist's contemporaries (nos. 17, 53) are more direct and expressive in drawings than in paintings.

In concluding the history of the Hermitage collection of Jean-Baptiste Greuze's drawings, their origin, and research, it would be useful to expand the reader's knowledge of Greuze's contacts with Russia. These contacts were not limited to

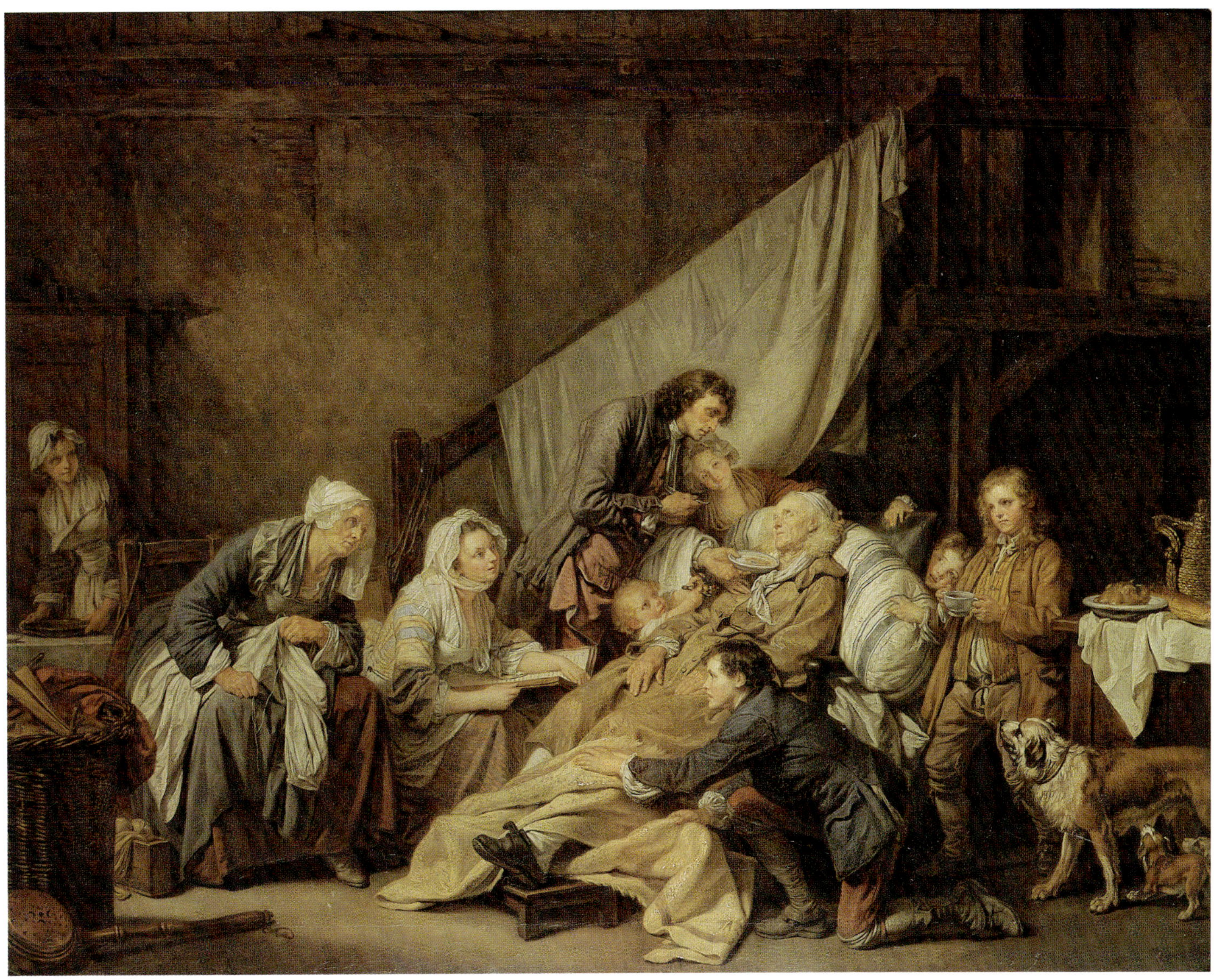

Fig. 24 Greuze, *The Paralytic,* 1763, oil on canvas, St Petersburg, The State Hermitage Museum

fulfilling important commissions and selling paintings to the Russian court and to Russian art patrons. Greuze literally flooded St Petersburg with heads, sometimes producing original paintings, but more often, especially in his later years, repeating or adapting existing works. In addition, Russian copyists relentlessly multiplied his designs. Almost every respectable and well-to-do family had its own "Greuze," which was most likely a head. Large collections mostly consisted of heads: girls with letters, dogs, or birds. Although these heads were of varying quality, there were, of course, true masterpieces, but sometimes Greuze produced his works, according to Alexander Benua, simply in the manner of a "fashionable pastry chef."[25] The Yusopov collection had approximately twenty heads, and they held a prominent position in collections such as those of the Demidov and Naryshkin. These heads also appeared in smaller collections and in homes of many of the Russian intelligentsia. It is well known that the famous Russian writer Ivan Sergeyevitch Turgenev, who despised Greuze, "with all the forces of his soul,"[26] nevertheless purchased one of Greuze's heads in Paris and took special care in its preservation and placement in his home. In the home of Modest Il'yich Tchaikovsky, brother of the famous composer, there were two heads by Greuze: one of a blond, curly-haired boy and the other of a frowning girl who personified Anger.

It was these heads, rather than portraits, drawings, or even genre scenes, that established the image of Greuze as an artist in Russia. The dominance of these *têtes d'expression* was responsible for the negative attitude of late-nineteenth-century progressive Russian art critics toward Greuze's art. In the late eighteenth and early nineteenth century Greuze was not simply famous; he was one of the most popular French artists in Russia. In the Age of Sentimentalism this interest can be justified. The Russian public at that time enjoyed "tear-jerking comedy," and Diderot's, Jean-Jacques Rousseau's, and Pierre-Augustin Caron Beaumarchais's works were translated into Russian.
It is worth mentioning in this respect that the well-known Russian writer of fables I.I. Hemnitser used scenes from Greuze's drawings as the basis for his stories.[27]

When Hemnitser visited Greuze's studio in Paris in 1777, two drawings left a lasting impression on the writer: *The Boat of Happiness* (Rotterdam, Boijmans-van Beuningen Museum) and *The Boat of Misfortune* (Boston, Jeffrey E. Horvitz Collection). Hemnister, an advocate of family virtues, not only described in detail both drawings—allegories of family happiness and family misfortune—but also dedicated a parable in verse to the drawings, which reads in part:

It has been known throughout the ages, not only now,
That agreement makes things grow,
And disagreement destroys.
I will prove this truth with examples,
And Greuze's drawings will tell the story.

Multiple ties linked Greuze and his art to Russian culture and its people. From documents obtained through the archives,[28] it has been established that in 1767 Greuze had a Russian student, Ivan Grinev (who died in Paris), training him free of charge and teaching him to work mostly with images from life. Teachers for such students were chosen with the advice of the Russian envoy in Paris, D.A. Golitsyn. Greuze's artwork was used to teach students, a fact attested by the multiple copies of Greuze's work kept at the St Petersburg Imperial Academy of Fine Arts and the Moscow School of Fine Arts and Sculpture.[29] Greuze's popularity in Russia can be supported by the inclusion of his paintings in numerous exhibitions that were held on a regular basis by different establishments in the second half of the nineteenth century. And now audiences in the United States, on the East and West Coasts, can enjoy some of the treasures by this eighteenth-century artist held in the State Hermitage Museum in St Petersburg.

1. Réau 1920, pp. 273–86.

2. Diderot, *Oeuvres complètes,* ed. J. d'Assézat, Paris 1876, XVIII, p. 247.

3. *Correspondance littéraire, philosophique et critique de Grimm et de Diderot,* Paris 1830, XI: *1782–1783,* p. 351.

4. The State Archive of the Russian Federation, f. 653, p. 2, c. 459: report of Prince Baratinsky, visit of Paul I abroad, L. 58; message of Prince Baratinsky, no. 10 from Paris, 26 May 1782. The author thanks Rifat Gaffifulin, who kindly pointed out this document.

5. A. Rostislavov, "Notes from the 150th Anniversary of the Academy of Arts," *Starie Godi,* nos. 10–12, 1914, p. 132.

6. *Compilation of Materials on the History of the St Petersburg Royal Academy of Arts and Its One Hundred Years of Existence,* St Petersburg 1864, s. 1, pp. 4, 5.

7. Kamenskaya 1934, p. 79.

8. The Russian State Historical Archive: list of possessions in the custody of Kiril Golovachevski, f. 789, p. 1, s. 1, c. 570.

9. The Russian State Historical Archive: list of possessions in the custody of Kiril Golovachevski, f. 789, p. 1, s. 1, c. 570.

10. Lugt S. 2878a. Lugt stated that Catherine bought the drawings from Betskoy (p. 409): *"Ce mécène avait réuni un ensemble de dessins qui fut acheté en 1767 par la reine [sic] et offert par elle à L'Académie des Beaux-Arts."* No information corroborates the fact that a considerable collection of drawings was purchased by Catherine the Great from Betskoy in 1767 or that she later gave these drawings to the academy.

11. Lugt S. 2699a.

12. The Russian State Historical Archive: f. 789, p. 1, no. 2866, c. 139.

13. The Russian State Historical Archive: f. 789, p. 34, no. 1172, c. 1.

14. This number was included in Monod and Hautecoeur 1922. The catalogue was completed in 1914, but publication was delayed by World War I.

15. *Starie Godi,* February 1908, p. 98.

16. The Russian State Historical Archive: f. 789, p. 2, c. 45.

17. F. Monod and L. Hautecoeur, "Les Dessins de Greuze conservés à l'Académie des Beaux-Arts de Saint-Pétersbourg," *BSHAF,* 1913, pp. 228–30.

18. Monod and Hautecoeur 1922.

19. Kamenskaya 1934, pp. 79–93; *eadem,* 1947.

20. T. Kamenskaya, "Greuze et Madame Geoffrin," *GBA,* November 1934, pp. 221–23.

21. Hartford *et al.* 1976–77.

22. Leningrad 1977.

23. U. Tarasov, "Drawings of Jean-Baptiste Greuze from the Collection of the Academy of Fine Arts," *Mir Iskusstvo,* no. 8, 1981; I. Novosselskaya, "Artists of the Wille Family and Jean-Baptiste Greuze," *Announcements of the State Hermitage,* issue XLVII, 1982; *eadem* 1985; *eadem, Paintings of Jean-Baptiste Greuze in Museums of the Soviet Union* (The works of the State Hermitage XXV), Leningrad 1985; *eadem* 1987; *eadem, Greuze and Russia: Russia–France. Age of the Enlightenment,* St Petersburg 1992.

24. *Catalogue de tableaux et dessins de Greuze, provenant de la succession de sa fille mademoiselle Caroline Greuze,* Paris 1843.

25. A. Benua, "Yusopov's Gallery," *Mir Iskusstvo,* nos. 13–24, 1900, p. 135.

26. I.S. Turgenev, *Complete Works and Letters,* Moscow and Leningrad 1961, XII, bk. 1, pp. 48, 111, 120, 126. See also P.R. Zaborov, "Turgenev and Western European Fine Art," in *Russkaya literatura i zarubejnoe iskustvo,* Leningrad 1986, pp. 138, 139.

27. See P.U. Danilevski, "Notes on Themes of West European Fine Art in Russian Literature," *Russkaya literatura i zarubejnoye iskustvo,* Leningrad 1986, pp. 268–81.

28. R. Golovenskaya, "Pensioner-Artists of the Academy of Arts in the Eighteenth Century," *Voprosi hydojestbenogo obrazovanija,* issue VIII, Leningrad 1974, pp. 73–83.

29. N. Kovalevskaya, "Russian Genre on the Eve of the Peredvizhnik Movement (Artistic and Social Features of Moscow)," *Russkaya jivonis XIX veka,* Moscow 1929, p. 80, appendix 91.

1 *Young Artist at a Drawing Board*

Pen and brush, brown ink over graphite on beige paper, 232 × 165 mm (9 1/8 × 6 1/2 in.)
Signed at lower left *Greuze;* inscribed on mat at lower left *Greuse*
Madison WI, Elvehjem Museum of Art, University of Wisconsin–Madison,
Class of 1943 Gift Fund purchase

Provenance: P. van der Dussen van Beeftingh, Rotterdam (d. 1876); his sale, Rotterdam, 29–30 May 1876, lot 614; private collection, Paris; Wildenstein & Co., Inc., New York, by 1968; acquired by the Elvehjem Art Center in 1973
Exhibitions: French Graphics from the Elvehjem Art Center Collection, Elvehjem Museum of Art, Madison WI, April–May 1975, no. 16; *The Hand of the Master,* Elvehjem Museum of Art, Madison WI, May–July 1985, no cat.; *Old Master Prints from Area Collections,* Milwaukee Art Museum, April–June 1997, no. 20
Bibliography: Elvehjem Art Center, University of Wisconsin–Madison Bulletin, 1973–74, ill. 5; M.F. Rogers (ed.), *Handbook of the Collection of the Elvehjem Art Center, University of Wisconsin–Madison,* Madison WI 1974, p. 97; R. Panczenko (ed.), *Handbook of the Collection, Elvehjem Art Center, University of Wisconsin–Madison,* Madison WI 1990, no. 62

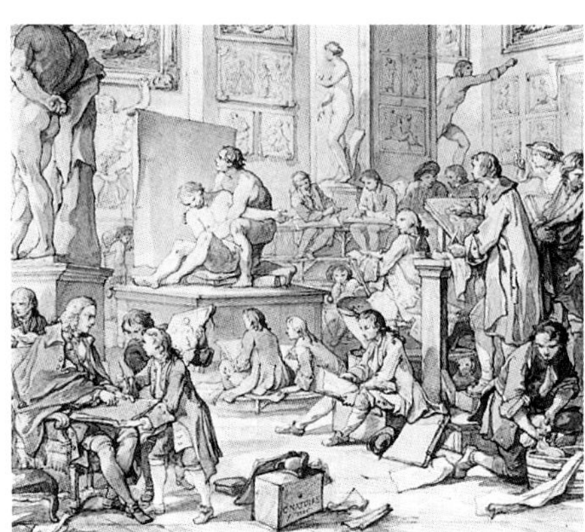

Fig. 25 C.-J. Natoire, *The Interior of a School of Art* (detail), 1746, watercolor over black chalk, London, Courtauld Institute of Art (Witt Collection)

This study of a young artist stepping back from his drawing board is so evocative of descriptions of Greuze's student days at the Académie in Paris that it is tempting to regard it as a self-portrait. The abbé Gougenot, for example, in his "Voyage en Italie" recalled that

he [Greuze] came to Paris and attended school without competing for any prizes, deprived thereby of the prerogative held by those who have won them of being placed more advantageously in the life drawing classes; he contented himself with the most distant spot, which the students derisively call the Bucket because, being directly under the lamp, whoever occupies it catches the drippings.[1]

Executed in the feathery *petite manière* style of Greuze's early work (see figs. 30–33), and with the pen that he largely abandoned after his Italian sojourn, this drawing nevertheless conveys vividly a sense of exhaustion or anxiety—characteristic of the emotional states that the artist would focus on and exploit pictorially for life. The drawing from which the young artist has turned away appears to be a depiction of two models, one upright, one crouched, as a pair are shown in Natoire's depiction of a contemporary life-class (fig. 25).

The large bucket in the foreground must have been one of those vessels in which the Académie students washed the chalk from their hands after a drawing session, as shown in the same Natoire drawing. It might also be a reference to the "Bucket" referred to above by the abbé Gougenot.

1. *"Il vint à Paris et suivit l'école sans s'assujetter à mettre à aucun prix, privé par là de la prérogative qu'ont ceux qui les ont remportés d'être placés plus avantageusement dans l'école pour dessiner d'après le modèle, il se contentait de la dernière place, que les élèves appellent par dérision le Baquet par ce qu'en étant directement dessous la lampe, celui qui l'occupe en reçoit les égoutures."* Gougenot, p. 139.

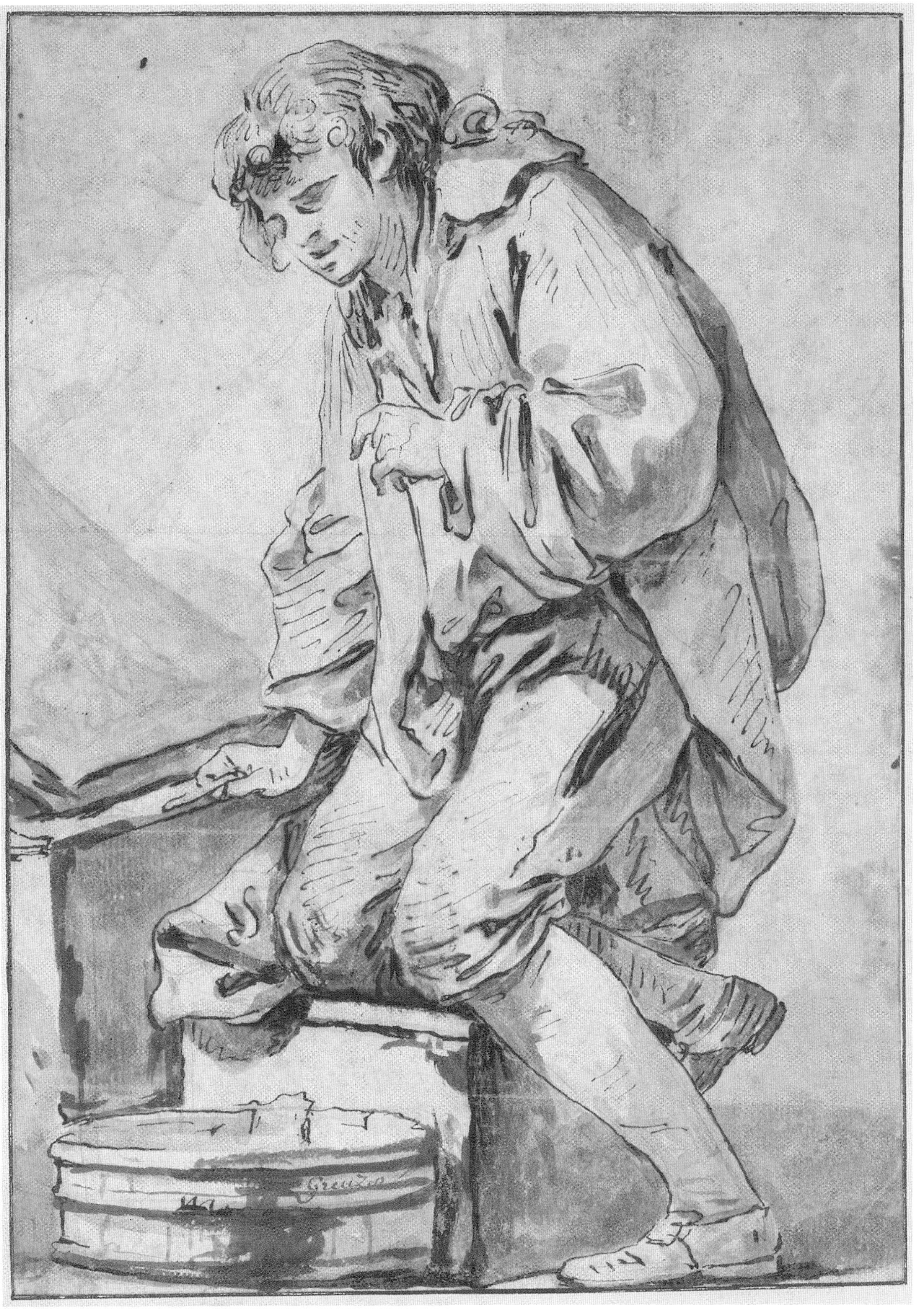

2 *Seated Male Nude with Left Leg Outstretched*

Black and red chalks, stumped, on cream paper, 380 × 490 mm ($14\frac{15}{16} \times 19\frac{5}{16}$ in.)
Signed and dated at lower right *Greuze 1758;* inscribed on mount (see n. 1 below)
Paris, Bibliothèque nationale de France, Cabinet des Estampes

Provenance: Nicolas de Livry, bishop of Callinique, Sens, eighteenth century; Paris, Bibliothèque de l'Arsenal, 1858; transferred to the Bibliothèque nationale between 1861 and 1864 (Lugt 248)
Exhibition: Hartford *et al.* 1976–77, no. 4
Bibliography: Martin and Masson 1906, no. 1303; A. de Montaiglon (ed.), "Pièces communiquées par M. Leperlier, et annotées par M. de Montaiglon," *Archives de l'art français,* VI, 1858–60, p. 236; Munhall 1966, pp. 88–89, fig. 10

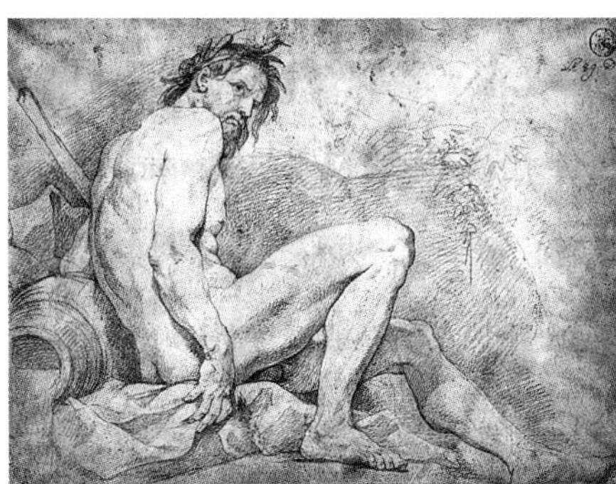

Fig. 26 C.-J. Natoire, *River God,* 1744, red chalk, Düsseldorf, Kunstmuseum

Of the many drawings from the model that Greuze must have executed at the Académie during his early years there, few have survived, aside from the important group now in the State Hermitage Museum, St Petersburg (see no. 3). The present one bears on its eighteenth-century mount an inscription vividly suggestive of the young artist's budding personality: "This figure is by Mr Greuze; when he did it, Mr Natoire was professor; the latter, after having praised it, nevertheless called to his attention that the figure looked crippled. Sieur Greuze, displeased, answered him: Monsieur, you would be happy if you could do one equal to it."[1] If this anecdote is accurate, the date on the drawing (1758) must have been added later, for Greuze could have been working in Natoire's studio only until 1751, when the latter was appointed *directeur* of the Académie in Rome. A similar confrontation of professor and student, of a more respectful character, is evoked in Natoire's own drawing *The Interior of a School of Art* (fig. 25), dated 1746.[2]

Greuze's precise rendering of such anatomical details as the feet and ears in this drawing may well reflect the instruction of Natoire, whose drawing of a river god (fig. 26), dated 1744, exhibits similar characteristics. Though he became an instinctive master of anatomy, Greuze would subsequently denigrate such skill, telling the engraver Michel Nitot, called Charles Dufresne (b. 1759): "this science was pushed too far, [it] was more suited to a surgeon than a painter."[3]

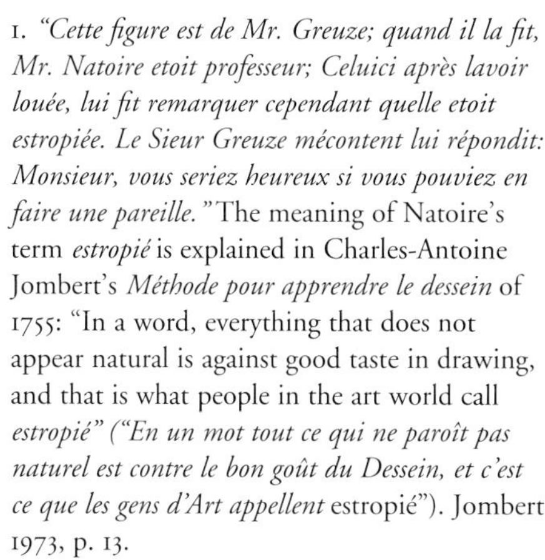

1. *"Cette figure est de Mr. Greuze; quand il la fit, Mr. Natoire etoit professeur; Celuici après lavoir louée, lui fit remarquer cependant quelle etoit estropiée. Le Sieur Greuze mécontent lui répondit: Monsieur, vous seriez heureux si vous pouviez en faire une pareille."* The meaning of Natoire's term *estropié* is explained in Charles-Antoine Jombert's *Méthode pour apprendre le dessein* of 1755: "In a word, everything that does not appear natural is against good taste in drawing, and that is what people in the art world call *estropié" ("En un mot tout ce qui ne paroît pas naturel est contre le bon goût du Dessein, et c'est ce que les gens d'Art appellent* estropié"). Jombert 1973, p. 13.

2. See *Charles-Joseph Natoire,* exhib. cat., Troyes, Musée des Beaux-Arts; Nîmes, Musée des Beaux-Arts; Rome, Villa Medicis, 1977, no. 42.

3. Quoted in P. Ratouis de Limay, "Un Chanteur de l'Opéra, graveur et collectionneur du début du dix-neuvième siècle," *BSHAF,* 1949, p. 70.

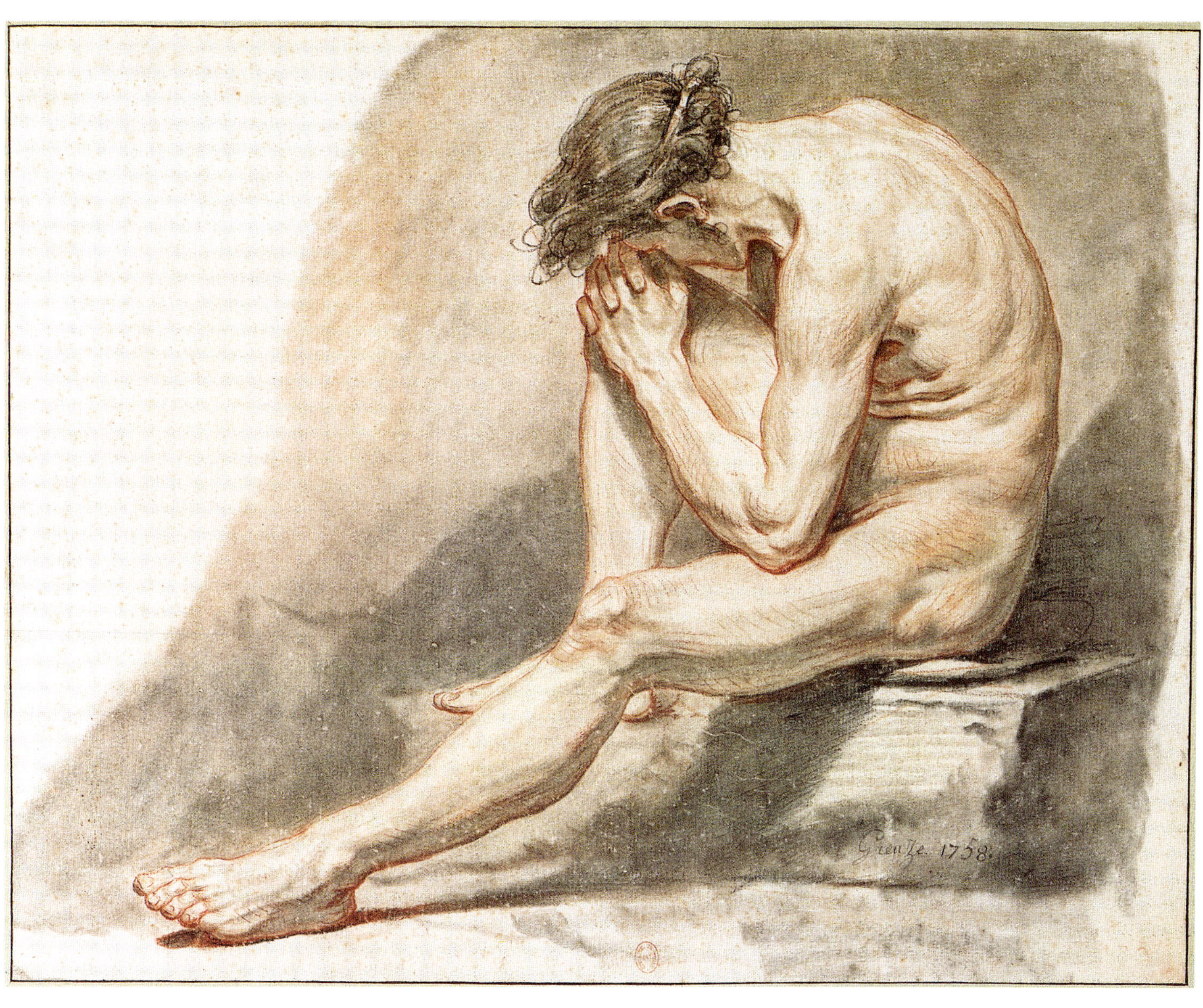
Greuze 1758

3 *Seated Satyr*

Red and black chalks, stumped, 413 × 334 mm (16 ¼ × 13 3/16 in.)
Inscribed in pen and black ink at lower left *9-31*
St Petersburg, The State Hermitage Museum

Provenance: Ivan Ivanovitch Betskoy, St Petersburg; Imperial Academy of Fine Arts, St Petersburg, 1769 (Lugt S. 2699a); transferred to the Hermitage in 1924
Exhibition: Leningrad 1977, no. 25
Bibliography: Monod and Hautecoeur 1922, no. 189; Novosselskaya 1985, p. 75

Essentially a simple study of a male nude like number 2, and perhaps drawn after the same model, this sheet was transformed by Greuze into an image of a satyr through rapid reworking in red chalk. A repositioned left leg or paw, hooves, the base of a tail, and a pointed ear change the erstwhile studio model into a mythological being.

Irina Novosselskaya related this *Satyr* to the model and pose of another *académie* in the collection of the State Hermitage Museum (fig. 27).[1]

Although male sea-monsters appear in Greuze's *Triumph of Galatea* (fig. 28), a work dating from about 1750 like the present drawing,[2] no satyrs appear in his oeuvre.

1. Novosselskaya 1985, p. 75. See Monod and Hautecoeur 1922, no. 175.

2. See H. Gibert, *Catalogue du Musée d'Aix,* Aix-en-Provence 1867, p. 222, no. 478; E. Aude, *Le Musée d'Aix-en-Provence,* Paris 1921, pp. 17, 52; Brookner 1972, p. 92, pl. 4; B. Ély, *Cézanne, l'École de dessin et le musée d'Aix dans Cézanne au Musée d'Aix,* Aix-en-Provence 1984, pp. 184, 187, 188; *La Représentation de la femme dans la peinture française au Musée Granet,* exhib. cat. by Kochi *et al.,* Aix-en-Provence, Musée Granet, 1999–2000, no. 26.

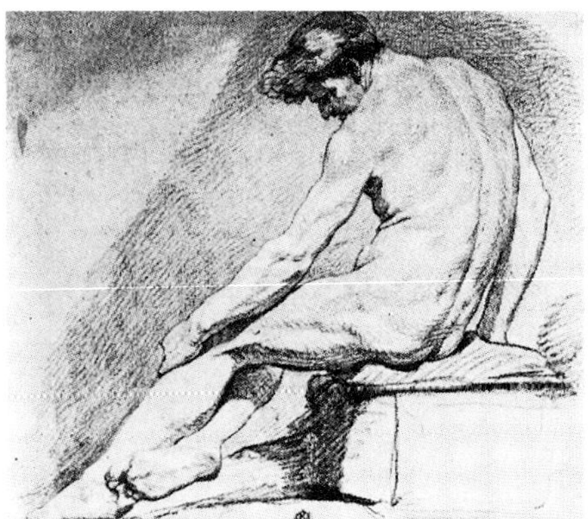

Fig. 27 Greuze, *Seated Male Nude, c.* 1750, red chalk on white paper, St Petersburg, The State Hermitage Museum

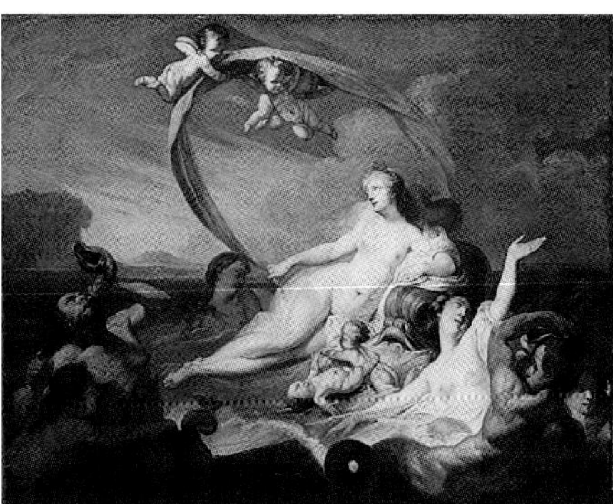

Fig. 28 Greuze, *Triumph of Galatea, c.* 1750, oil on canvas, Aix-en-Provence, Musée Granet

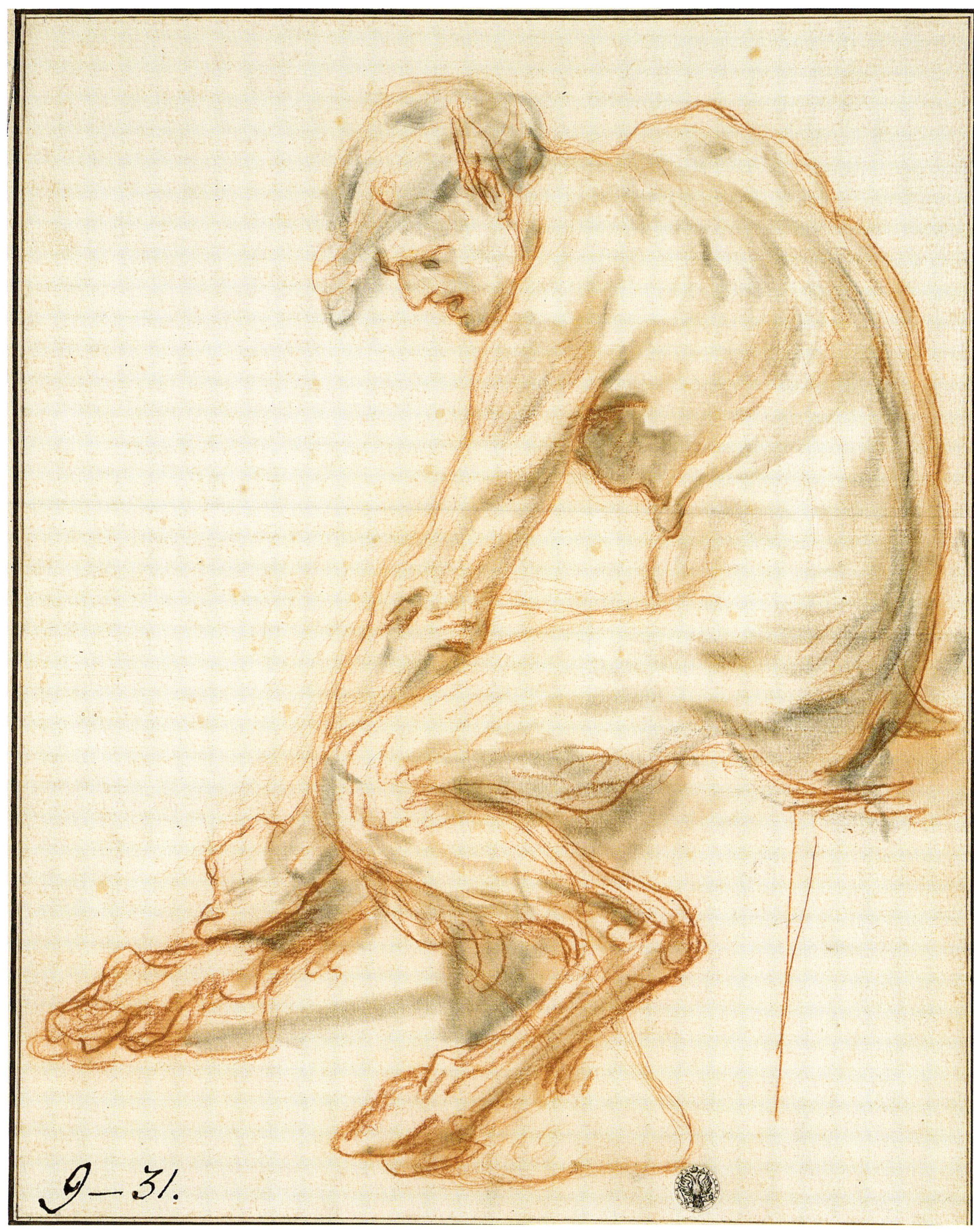
9—31.

4 *Louis Gougenot, "Voyage en Italie, Année 1755 et 1756," Manuscrit de M. l'Abbé Gougenot*

Volume I, bound in 4°, in gray-green calf, with stamped, gilded borders on front and back covers, the spine stamped *Voyage en Italie/ Année 1755 et 1756/ Manuscrit de M. L'Abbé/ GOUGENOT/ I* (bound in 1792), 320 × 230 × 75 mm (12 9/16 × 9 1/16 × 2 15/16 in.), containing the following eight drawings by Greuze, in watercolor over graphite, with inscriptions on the support sheet by Gougenot in pen and ink: *Marons du Mont Cenis portant un voyageur* (fig. 29), 194 × 130 mm (7 5/8 × 5 1/8 in.), facing p. 254; *Savoyarde* (fig. 33), 196 × 130 mm (7 3/4 × 5 1/8 in.), between pp. 254–55; *Païsanne Piémontaise,* 196 × 130 mm (7 3/4 × 5 1/8), between pp. 254–55; *Bourgeoise de Gênes avec le mezzo sur la tête* (fig. 32), 195 × 132 mm (7 11/16 × 5 1/4 in.), between pp. 301–02; *Bourgeoise de Gênes avec le mezzo rabattu sur les épaules* (fig. 31), 195 × 133 mm (7 11/16 × 5 1/4 in.), between pp. 301–02; *Bourgeoise de Bologne,* 192 x 134 mm (7 9/16 × 5 7/16 in.), facing p. 365; *Parmesane,* 195 × 131 mm (7 11/16 × 5 3/16 in.), between pp. 338–39; *Païsanne Bolonaise* (fig. 30), 195 × 131 mm (7 11/16 × 5 3/16 in.), facing p. 429
Paris, private collection

Provenance: Louis Gougenot, abbé de Chezal-Benoît (1719–1767), Paris, and by descent to the present owner
Exhibition: L'Italia vista dai pittori francesi del XVIII e XIX secolo, Rome, Palazzo delle esposizioni, 1961, no. 181
Bibliography: G. des Mousseaux, "Notice sur l'abbé Gougenot," *Revue universelle des arts,* I, 1855, pp. 443–44; F. Lacroix, "Nécrologie des artistes et des curieux de 1765 à 1782. (Suite) (1). X. L'Abbé Gougenot, amateur," *Revue universelle des arts,* XII, 1860, pp. 175–76; R. Michéa, "Quelques détails inédits sur le voyage en Italie de Greuze et de Gougenot," *Études italiennes,* April–June 1934, p. 138; Brookner 1956, p. 158; baron de Soucy, "Le Voyage en Italie de Greuze par l'abbé Gougenot de Croissy," *BSHAF,* 1958, p. 95; P. Quarré, "Acquisitions pour le musée: *Portrait de l'abbé Gougenot* par Greuze," *Bulletin de la Société des amis du Musée de Dijon,* 1970–72, p. 96; Brookner 1972, pp. 57–58; Hartford *et al.* 1976–77, pp. 18–20, 38–39, 52–53; McPherson 1985, pp. 94–95; Munhall 1994, p. 639; Guicharnaud 1999, pp. 15–41

The present volume is the first of three containing the abbé Louis de Gougenot's manuscript record of the tour of Italy he undertook in 1755–56, totaling over two thousand pages. Exhibited only once before, and little known until the author's summary description of it in 1976 and Hélène Guicharnaud's detailed study of 1999, the "Voyage en Italie" contains a wealth of information concerning Greuze's Italian sojourn, as well as eight watercolors by the artist.

Abbé Louis de Gougenot (1719–1767; fig. 34), Greuze's long-suffering host on that trip, was born into a family associated with the house of Condé, and indeed lived in its Parisian *hôtel.* Trained for the law, he became a member of the Grand Conseil de France, but he also held various ecclesiastical posts, eventually becoming—three years before his death—commendatory abbot of the abbey of St-Pierre de Chezal-Benoît. Gougenot was deeply interested in the arts from an early age, absorbed especially with theory and criticism, but also producing biographies of Louis Galloche (1670–1761), Jean-Baptiste Oudry (1686–1755), Louis-Joseph Le Lorrain (1715–1759), and Guillaume Coustou I (1677–1746), and advising Pigalle on the iconography of the Maréchal de Saxe monument. In 1748 he published anonymously a *Lettre sur la peinture, la sculpture et l'architecture à M***.*

After traveling widely in France and recording in journals what he had seen—and illustrating them with his own drawings—Gougenot finally decided in 1755 to undertake a grand tour of Italy, even though the state of his health made him fearful of the possible hazards involved. When his traveling companion, Pierre d'Alègre d'Ousteyres,

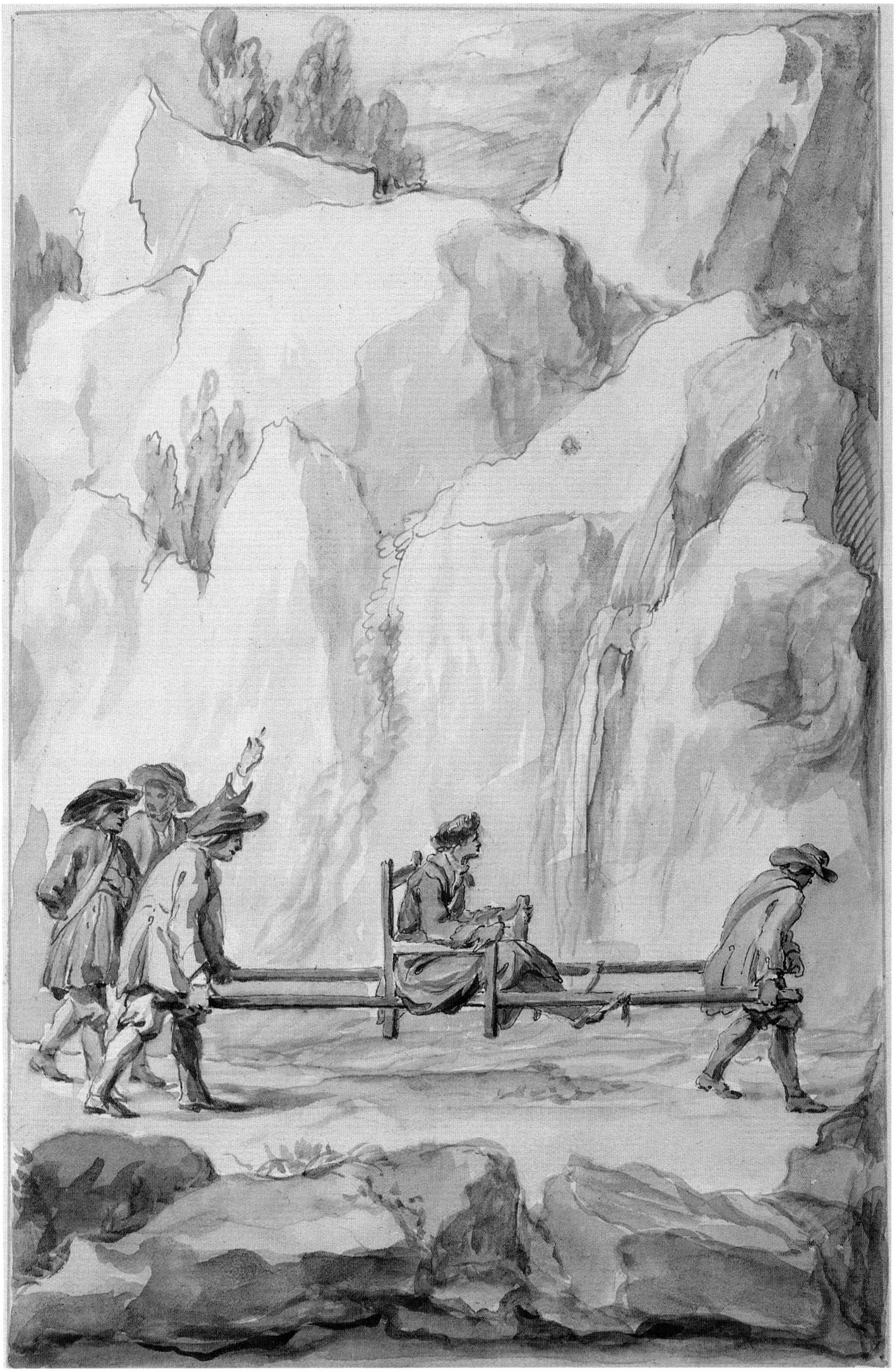

Fig. 29 Greuze, *Marons du Mont Cenis portant un voyageur,* 1755, watercolor over graphite, in Gougenot, facing p. 254

a partner at the Grand Conseil, bowed out at the last moment, Gougenot invited Greuze in his place. This extraordinary stroke of luck, probably orchestrated by Pigalle, meant that the young artist could profit from a tour of Italy without having to compete for it with his fellow artists, without being subject to the constraints of the Académie's supervision, and at no cost. Gougenot summed up the situation in the introduction to his "Voyage en Italie": "On the point therefore of breaking off all my plans because of this untoward event [d'Alègre's withdrawal], I proposed to M. Greuze, the young painter of genre scenes who had just been enthusiastically received into the Académie, to accompany me entirely at my expense during the trip. He welcomed this offer as a continuation of good fortune."[1]

For his troubles, the Académie rewarded Gougenot by electing him an honorary member on 10 January 1756. Greuze, however, was less generous. He stayed in Rome, obliging his benefactor to find another companion for his return to France; he had little to do with Gougenot after he went back to Paris, and later Greuze claimed that he had paid for the Italian trip himself. All this Gougenot's grandnephew recalled in his "Notice sur l'abbé Gougenot": "Cherished, loved, and admired by all who knew him, he knew neglect only on the part of Greuze, who, however, always found him as indulgent as eager to be of use to him."[2]

The manuscript "Journal" that constitutes the "Voyage en Italie" begins on page 144 of the first volume and occupies the totality of the other two. Gougenot intended to write a guidebook to Italy on the basis of these voluminous notes, but the astronomer J.-J. Le Français de Lalande obtained Gougenot's text shortly after the latter's early death in 1767 and published the material in his own *Voyage d'un françois en Italie* (1769), which remained the most popular French guide to Italy until the mid-nineteenth century.

Although engravings and drawings by Gougenot and others are integrated within the three volumes, only the first one includes drawings by Greuze, all executed in watercolor. With one exception, they record, in depictions of single figures with no background, the picturesque female garb typical of various cities and provinces through which the visitors passed. They include—in order of appearance and citing Gougenot's inscriptions—a *Savoyarde* (fig. 33), a *Païsanne Piémontaise,* a *Bourgeoise de Gênes avec le mezzo sur la tête* (fig. 32), a *Bourgeoise de Gênes avec le mezzo rabattu sur les épaules* (fig. 31), a *Bourgeoise de Bologne,* a *Parmesane,* and a *Païsanne Bolonaise* (fig. 30).[3] In each case, a passage in Gougenot's "Journal" describes the costume depicted in the drawing. In reference to the *Bourgeoise de Gênes avec le mezzo sur la tête* (figs. 32, 38), for instance, Gougenot noted: "The [Genoese] ladies do not differ at all [from the ladies of Novi] in their headdress. But they wear a Mezzo, which is a piece of silk or printed cotton which they use like a veil or mantilla, in covering their head and shoulders."[4] With the *Bourgeoise de Bologne,* Greuze, surprisingly, based his image on a well-known painting by Jean Barbault (1705–1766), an artist who had been living in Rome since 1747.[5]

Six of these images and eighteen others by Greuze reappear in a set of engravings published in 1768 by members of Pierre-Étienne Moitte's (1722–1780) family—the *Divers habillements suivant le costume d'Italie. Dessinés d'après nature par J.B. Greuze... ornés de fonds par J.B. Lallemand et gravés d'après des dessins tirés du cabinet de M. l'abbé Gougenot.*[6] Jean-Baptiste Lallemand (1716–1803) provided a frontispiece for these prints, as well as elaborate backgrounds for each of Greuze's simple, monumental figures (figs. 36, 38)—transforming them with interiors, landscapes, and architectural settings, replete with fountains, boats, clocks, birdcages, fragments of ancient sculpture, brooms, and dogs. Although the title page states that the drawings the Moitte family copied belonged to the abbé Gougenot, he had died the year before the *Divers habillements* appeared, and no such drawings are referred to specifically in his will or in the

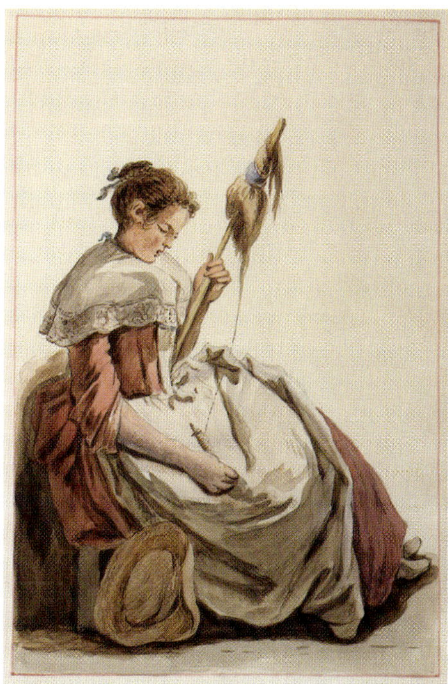

Fig. 30 Greuze, *Païsanne Bolonaise,* 1755, watercolor over graphite, in Gougenot, facing p. 429

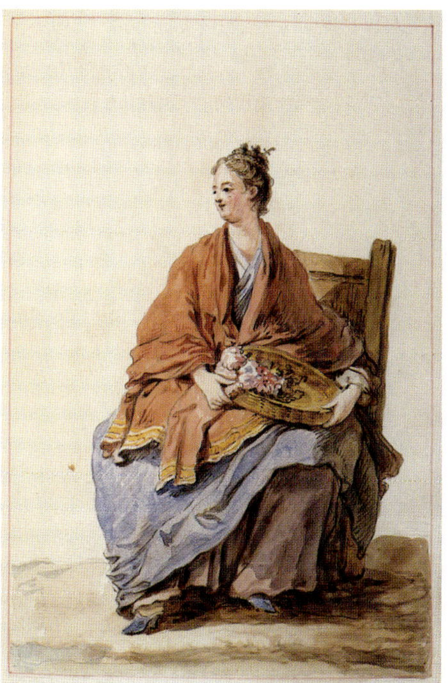

Fig. 31 Greuze, *Bourgeoise de Gênes avec le mezzo rabattu sur les épaules,* 1755, watercolor over graphite, in Gougenot, between pp. 301–02

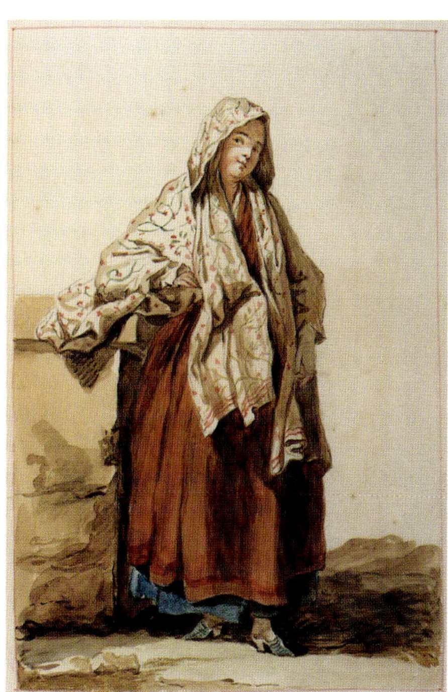

Fig. 32 Greuze, *Bourgeoise de Gênes avec le mezzo sur la tête,* 1755, watercolor over graphite, in Gougenot, between pp. 301–02

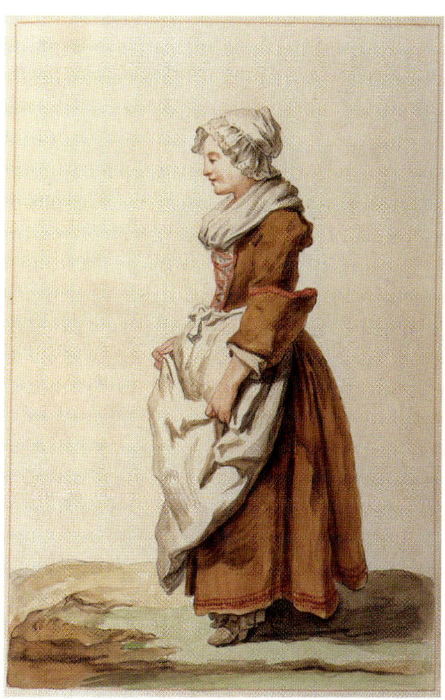

Fig. 33 Greuze, *Savoyarde,* 1755, watercolor over graphite, in Gougenot, between pp. 254–55

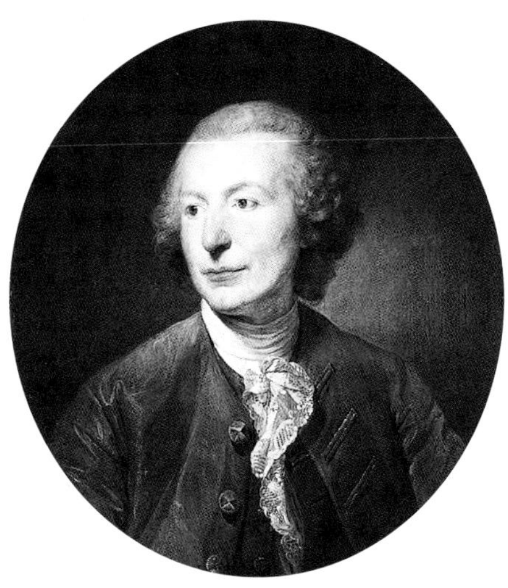

Fig. 34 Greuze, *Portrait of Louis Gougenot,* 1757, oil on canvas, Dijon, Musée des Beaux-Arts

inventory of his possessions that included, besides his portrait by Greuze (fig. 34), *The Broken Eggs* (fig. 39) and *The Neapolitan Gesture* (fig. 40).[7]

These engravings, however, were not based on the watercolor drawings that Greuze produced for Gougenot to have bound into his album, but rather on the original versions of them and additional drawings that Greuze executed in pen and brush with ink wash, while traveling with his benefactor. For instance, Moitte's engraving *Contadina di Bolognese/ Paysanne Bolonaise* (fig. 36) is based on Greuze's drawing (fig. 35), whose mat is inscribed *Greuze f. 1755*, and F.-A. Moitte's engraving *Cittadina Di Genovese Col Mezzo In Testa/ Bourgeoise de Gênes avec le mezzo sur la tête* (fig. 38) is based on Greuze's drawing (fig. 37), inscribed identically. From the group of twenty such drawings that once belonged to Paul Randon de Boisset and Louis-Antoine Vassal de Saint-Hubert,[8] two are preserved today in the Museum Boijmans-van Beuningen, Rotterdam,[9] and another pair, in the Metropolitan Museum of Art, New York.[10] Others have appeared at sales or on the art market at various times.

In contrast to these costume studies, Greuze recorded for Gougenot's album one of the most dramatic moments of their trip—the crossing of the Mont Cenis pass on 18 October 1755 (fig. 29). Beset with rain, wind, hail, and freezing temperatures, they crossed "the highest point of the Alps" carried in stretchers, as Gougenot recorded:

Mr Greuze and I were carried, each of us in a little wicker armchair in the form of a stretcher where they had us seated.... Though it takes only two men to carry each person, they generally bring along six and take turns alternately.... These porters are called marons *[growlers]. Ours took only five hours to cross the Mont Cenis, whose route is about twenty kilometers.... Nothing is comparable to the skill with which they carried us.*[11]

1. *"Sur le point donc de rompre tous mes projets pour ce contre temps, je proposai à M. Greuze jeune peintre de Bambochades qui venoit d'être reçu avec applaudissements à l'Académie de m'accompagner en le défrayant tout pendant le voyage. Il reçut cette offre comme une suite de bonne fortune."* Gougenot, pp. 138–39.

2. *"Chéri, aimé et estimé de tous ceux qui le connurent, il n'éprouva d'oubli que de la part de Greuze, qui, cependant, le trouva toujours aussi indulgent qu'empressé de lui être utile."* Mousseaux 1855, p. 442.

3. Guicharnaud 1999, p. 20, fig. 18; p. 21, fig. 20; p. 21, fig. 19; p. 22, fig. 21; p. 20, fig. 17; p. 23, fig. 23; p. 22, fig. 22.

4. *"Les bourgeoises [de Gênes] n'en diffèrent point par leurs coiffures. Mais elles portent un Mezzo qui est une pièce de soye ou d'indienne dont elles se servent comme de voile et de mantille, en se couvrant la tête et les épaules."* Gougenot, p. 266.

5. See Guicharnaud 1999, p. 19, fig. 16.

6. Portalis and Béraldi 1880–82, III, pt. I, pp. 112–13, 114; Martin and Masson 1906, no. 410; Guicharnaud 1999, p. 19.

7. Guicharnaud 1999, pp. 44, 46.

8. Randon de Boisset sale, Paris, 27 February–25 March 1777, lot 376; Vassal de Saint-Hubert sales, Paris, 29 March–13 April 1779, lot 164; 24 April–5 May 1783, lot 159.

9. See Hartford *et al.* 1976–77, nos. 7, 8; *From Pisanello to Cézanne: Master Drawings from the Museum Boymans-van Beuningen, Rotterdam,* exhib. cat., ed. Ger Luijten and A.W.F.M. Meij, New York, The Pierpont Morgan Library; Fort Worth TX, Kimbell Art Museum, 1990; The Cleveland Museum of Art, 1990–91, no. 89.

10. See Bean and Turčić 1986, p. 118, nos. 123, 124.

11. *"nous fûmes portés Mr Greuze et moi chacun dans un petit fauteuil d'ozier en forme de brancard où l'on nous fit asseoir.... Quoiqu'il ne faille que deux hommes pour porter chaque personne, on en prend ordinairement six et ils se relayent alternativement.... Ces sortes de porteurs s'appellent vulgairement les Marons.... Nos porteurs ne mirent que cinq heures à nous faire passer le Mt Cenis dont la traversée est de cinq lieux.... Rien n'est comparable à l'adresse avec laquelle ils nous portèrent."* Gougenot, pp. 193–94; Guicharnaud 1999, p. 24, fig. 25, and repr. cover of *GBA*, July–August 1999.

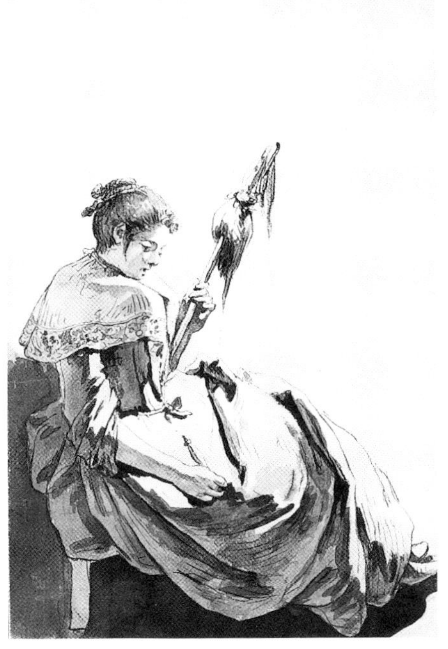

Fig. 35 Greuze, *Bolognese Peasant Girl with a Distaff,* 1755, pen and brush with gray ink wash, New York, The Metropolitan Museum of Art, Harry G. Sperling Fund, 1982

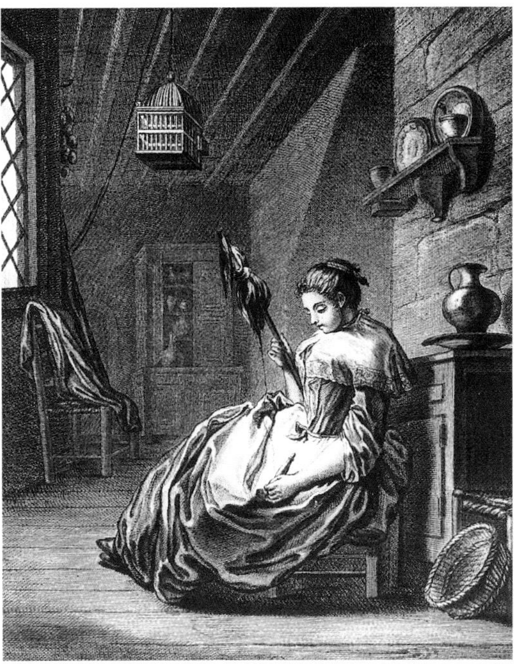

Fig. 36 Moitte, after Greuze, *Paysanne Bolonaise,* 1768, engraving, Paris, Bibliothèque nationale de France

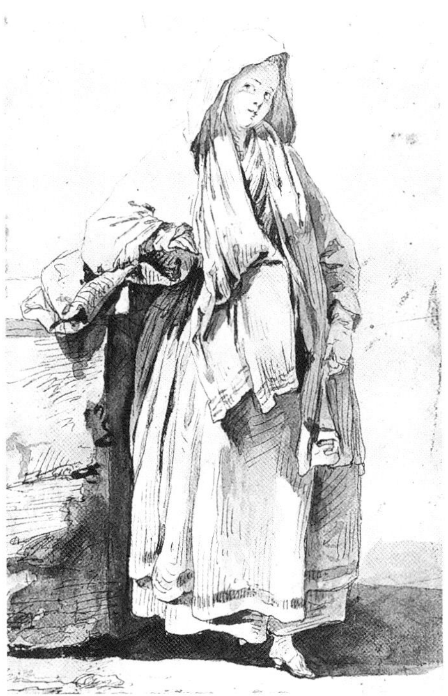

Fig. 37 Greuze, *Bourgeoise de Gênes avec le mezzo sur la tête,* 1755, pen and brush with gray ink wash, whereabouts unknown

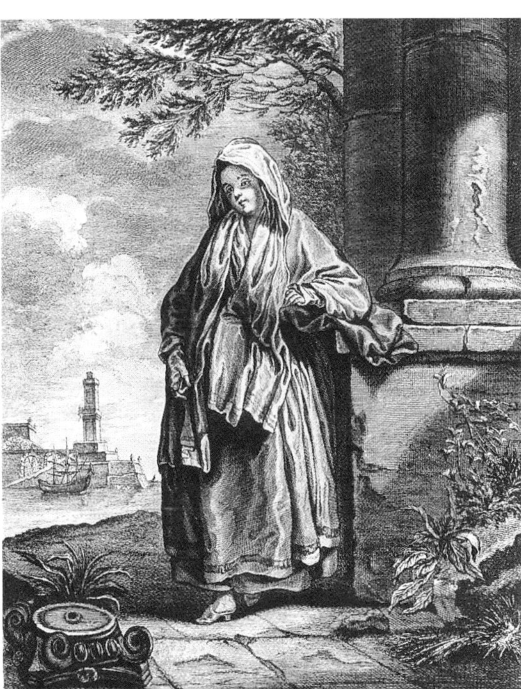

Fig. 38 F.-A. Moitte, after Greuze, *Bourgeoise de Gênes avec le mezzo sur la tête,* 1768, engraving, Paris, Bibliothèque nationale de France

5 *Boy with a Broken Egg, Study for "The Broken Eggs"*

Black, red, and white chalks on tan paper, 338 × 274 mm (13 15/16 × 10 3/4 in.)
Vienna, Graphische Sammlung Albertina

Provenance: Duke Albert von Sachsen und Teschen (1738–1822), Vienna (Lugt 174)
Exhibitions: None known
Bibliography: "Les Belles Sanguines," *Je Sais Tout,* 15 March 1911, p. 153 (as by François Boucher); J. Thompson, "A Study by Greuze for Broken Eggs," *The Metropolitan Museum Journal,* XVII, 1982, pp. 47–48

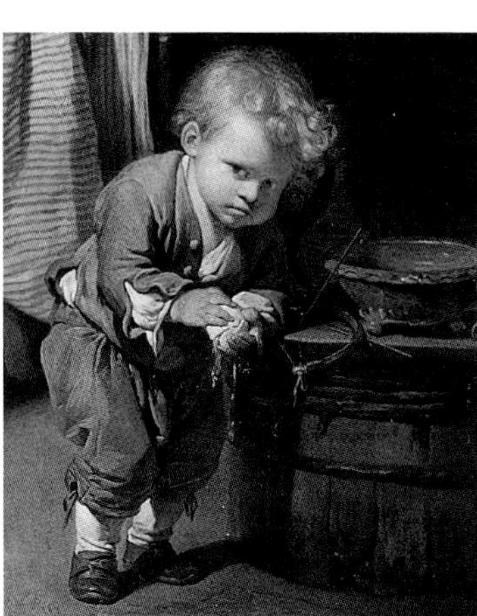

Fig. 39 Greuze, *The Broken Eggs* (detail), 1756, oil on canvas, New York, The Metropolitan Museum of Art

It was James Thompson who first spotted the relationship of this drawing, traditionally attributed to Boucher, to the foreground figure of Greuze's *The Broken Eggs* (fig. 39), which the artist executed in Rome during the spring of 1756.[1] Furthermore, Thompson was to analyze the significance of the boy's role in Greuze's pictorial drama with greater subtlety than anyone had before. In describing the recently completed picture to the comte de Caylus on 12 May 1756, for instance, the abbé Barthélémy made reference merely to "a child thrown into the corner of the picture [who] takes one of the eggs and tries to repair it."[2] The title Greuze provided for the Salon catalogue of 1757 referred simply to "a child [who] attempts to repair a broken egg."[3] Subsequently, historians have tended to consider the boy with his egg as an example of uncomprehending innocence faced with a spectacle of moral downfall. But stressing the importance of the small bow and arrow on which the child is shown leaning, Thompson rightly saw him as a "solemn, plainclothes Cupid, silently commenting on the irreparable consequences of erotic abandon."[4]

The use of black, red, and white chalks is unusual in Greuze's work done in Rome, evidence of his inclination to experiment with various combinations of media at this time: brush and ink or watercolor, pen and ink, pastel, black and white chalks, and gouache.

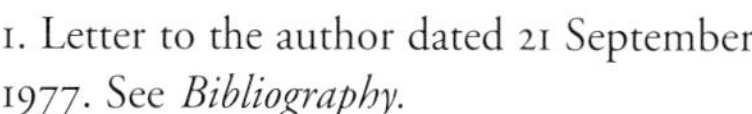

1. Letter to the author dated 21 September 1977. See *Bibliography.*

2. *"un petit enfant jeté sur le coin du tableau prend un de ces oeufs cassés et tâche de le rajuster."* Abbé J.-J. Barthélémy, *Voyage en Italie,* Paris 1801, p. 134.

3. *"Un enfant tente de raccomoder un oeuf."* See Hartford *et al.* 1976–77, no. 9.

4. Thompson 1989–90, p. 14.

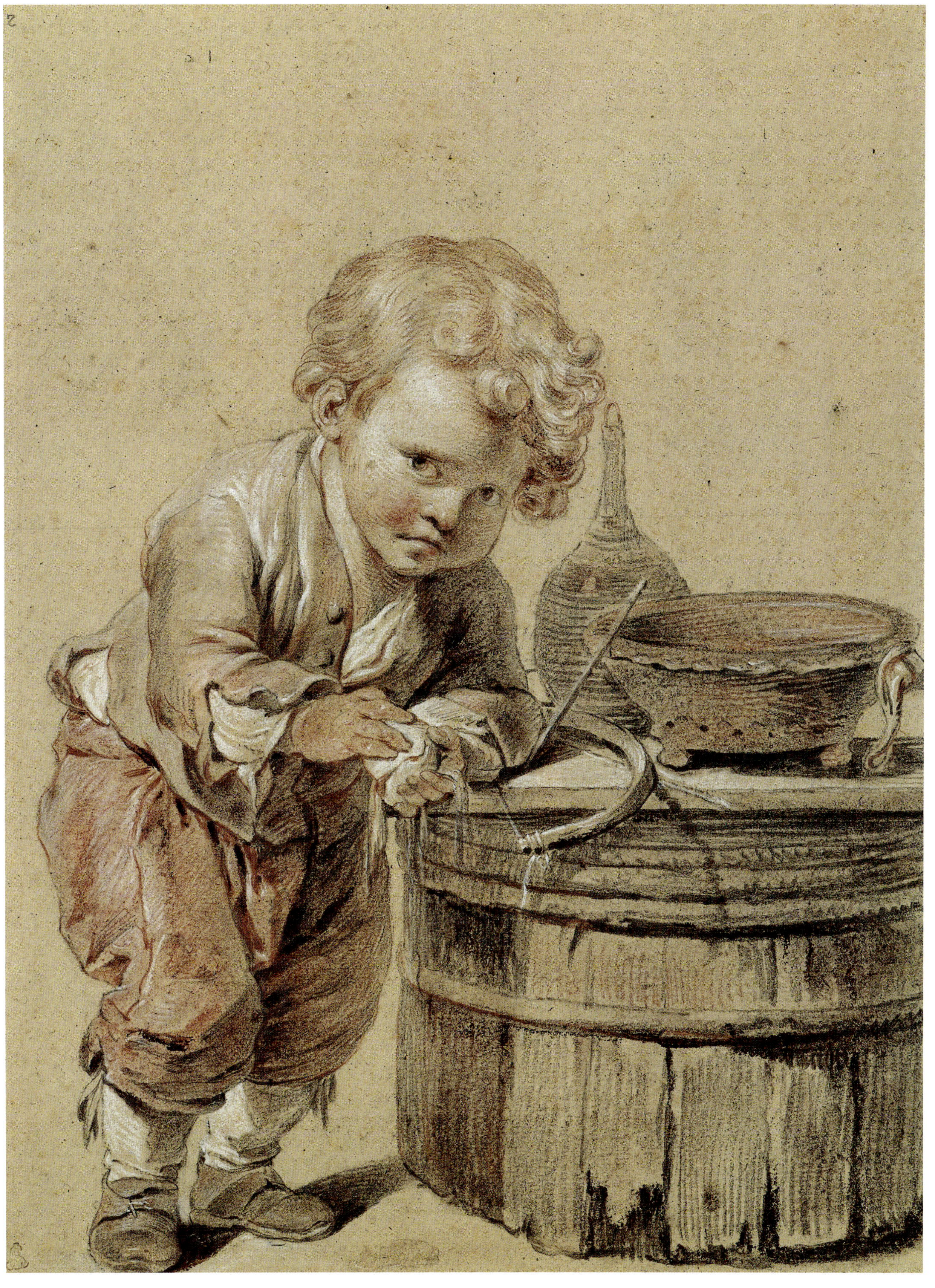

6 *Old Woman with Arms Outstretched, Study for "The Neapolitan Gesture"*

Black chalk, stumped, heightened with white chalk, on faded blue paper, 470 × 316 mm (18½ × 12½ in.)
Signed and dated lower left *Greuze. f. Romae an. 1756*
New York, Collection of Joseph F. McCrindle

Provenance: sale, London, 13 April 1965, lot 51; acquired from P. & D. Colnaghi & Co. Ltd, London, 1965
Exhibitions: Old Master Drawings, London, P. & D. Colnaghi & Co. Ltd, 1965, no. 34; Hartford *et al.* 1976–77, no. 13; *French Master Drawings,* New York, Didier Aaron, Inc., 1984, no. 18; *Old Master Drawings from the Collection of Joseph F. McCrindle,* The Art Museum, Princeton *et al.,* 1991, no. 88
Bibliography: McPherson 1985, p. 104

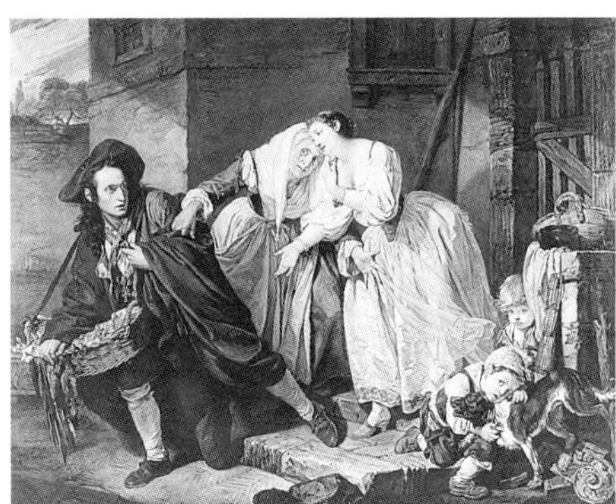

Fig. 40 Greuze, *The Neapolitan Gesture,* 1757, oil on canvas, Worcester Art Museum, Charlotte E.W. Buffington Fund

The drawing is a study for Greuze's painting *The Neapolitan Gesture* (fig. 40), which the abbé Barthélémy described to the comte de Caylus on 22 February 1757 as having been recently completed.[1] In that work, the old woman represented here is depicted as a servant who pulls back with her right hand the cloak of a Portuguese nobleman disguised as a peddler to reveal his double cross of the Order of Christ. The old woman appears here much as she does in the painting, though there her eyes are focused sharply on the intruder rather than looking out at the viewer, the knotted end of the *mezzo* over her head hangs more conspicuously in front of her waist, and her apron falls between her legs, giving her left knee a more protective character.

The model, whom Greuze utilized as well for *The Broken Eggs* of 1756, must have been one of those described by the abbé Gougenot's grandnephew as subject to the artist's capricious ways during his Roman sojourn: "In order to satisfy him [Greuze] it was necessary to assemble in the greatest haste the characters necessary for the composition of the picture he was working on at the moment. Then, once they were all brought together, his verve, he would say, had died out; he no longer felt in a creative state, and he would dismiss his models, who nevertheless received the payment agreed upon for the posing session [from the abbé Gougenot]. Such freakish whims occurred often with this bizarre man."[2]

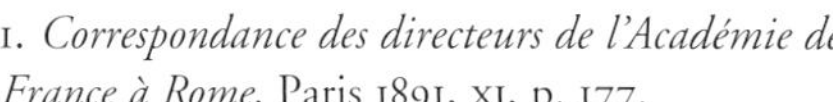

1. *Correspondance des directeurs de l'Académie de France à Rome,* Paris 1891, XI, p. 177.

2. *"Pour le satisfaire, il fallait réunir en toute hâte les personnages nécessaires à la composition du tableau dont il s'occupait dans le moment. Puis, une fois les personnages rassemblés, sa verve, disait-il, était éteinte; il ne se sentait plus en état de travailler, et il congédiait ses modèles, qui recevaient cependant le prix convenu pour la séance. De pareilles fantaisies étaient fréquentes chez cet homme bizarre."* Chevalier G. des Mousseaux, "Notice sur l'abbé Gougenot," *Revue universelle des arts,* I, 1855, p. 441.

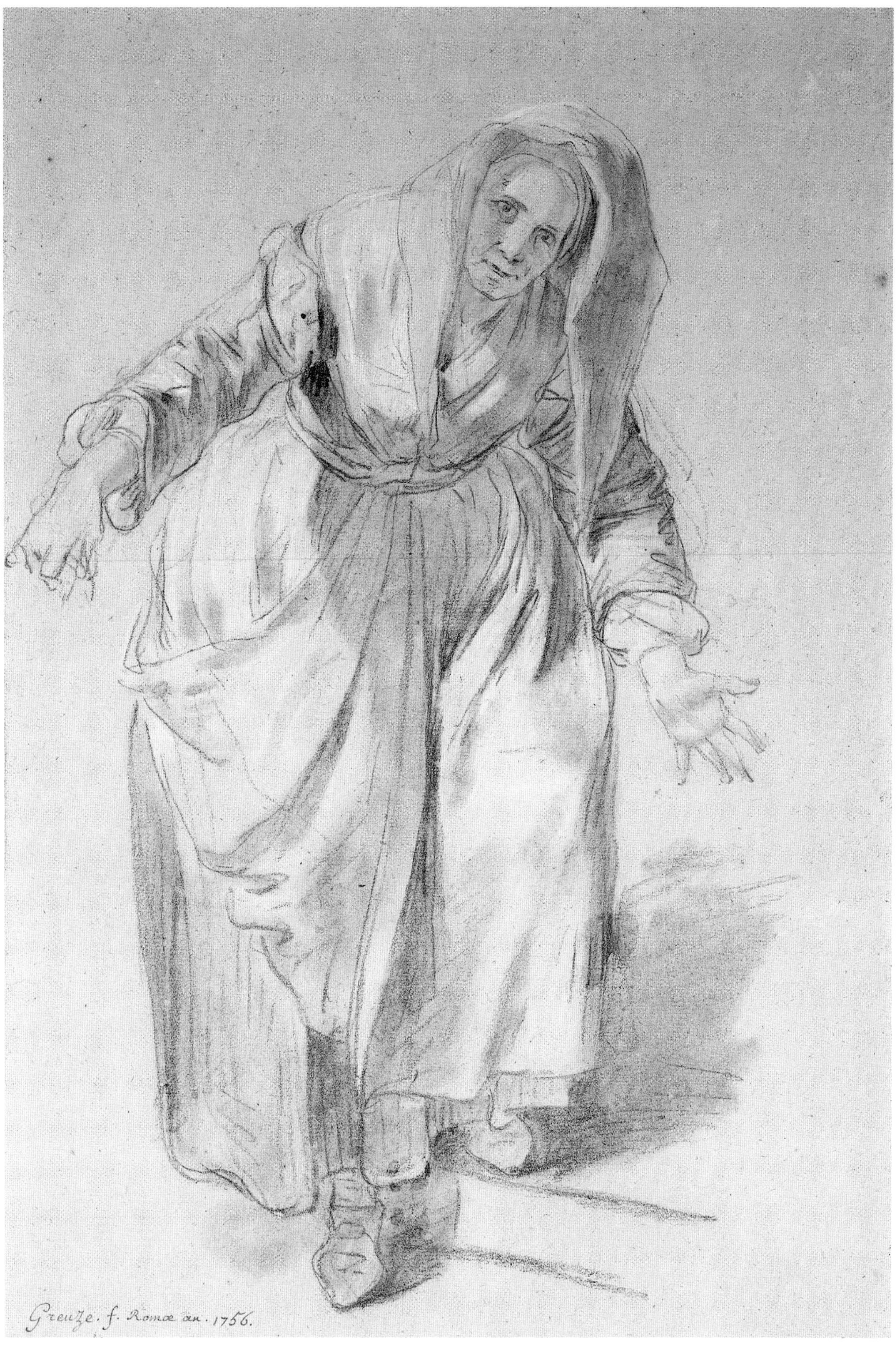
Greuze. f. Romæ an. 1756.

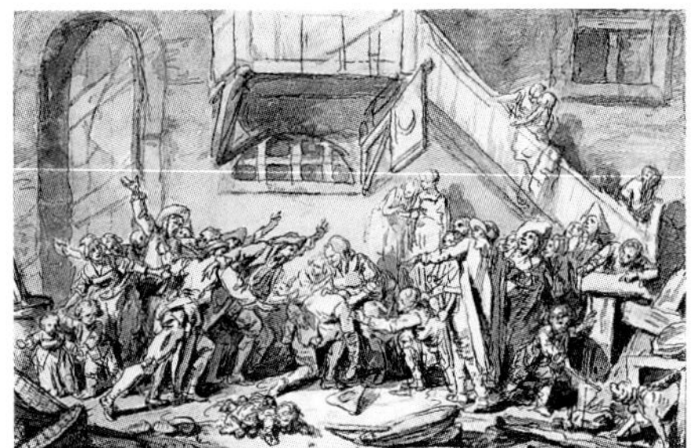

Fig. 41 Greuze, *Italians Playing le Jeu de la main chaude,* 1756, pen and brush with brown and gray ink wash, Berlin, © Kupferstichkabinett-Sammlung der Zeichnungen und Druckgraphik-Staatliche Museen zu Berlin–Preussischer Kulturbesitz

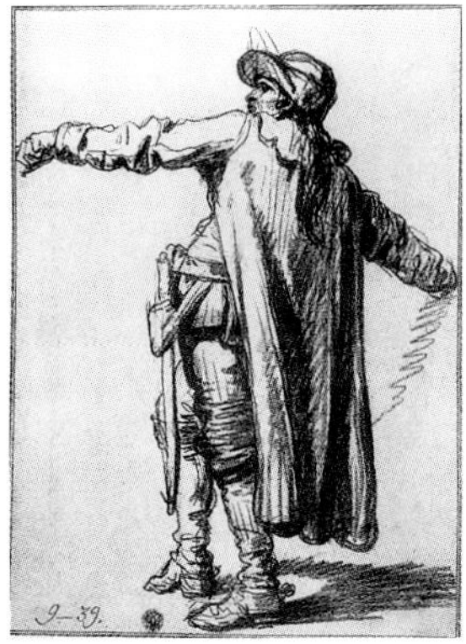

Fig. 42 Greuze, *Standing Man, Study for "Italians Playing le Jeu de la main chaude,"* 1756, red chalk on white paper, St Petersburg, The State Hermitage Museum

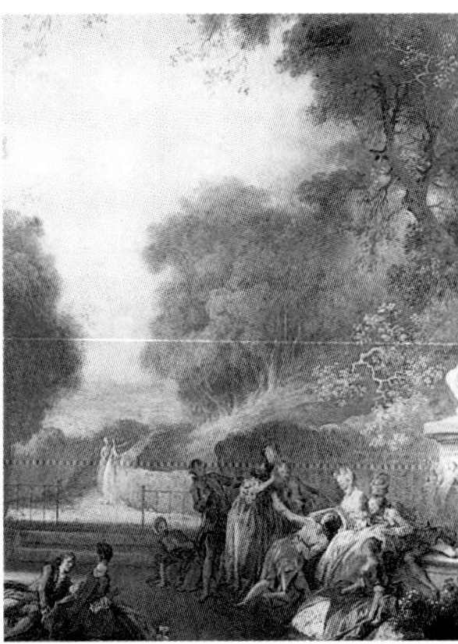

Fig. 43 J.-H. Fragonard, *The Game of Hot Cockles* (detail), 1778–80, oil on canvas, Washington D.C., National Gallery of Art, Samuel H. Kress Collection

7 *Standing Man, Study for "Italians Playing le Jeu de la main chaude"*

Red chalk on white paper, 550 × 450 mm (21 11/16 × 17 11/16 in.)
Inscribed in pen and black ink at lower left *9-53;* in pen and brown ink on verso of old mount *Étude de la main chaude*
St Petersburg, The State Hermitage Museum

Provenance: Ivan Ivanovitch Betskoy, St Petersburg; Imperial Academy of Fine Arts, St Petersburg, 1769 (Lugt S. 2699a); transferred to the Hermitage in 1924
Exhibitions: Leningrad 1977, no. 50; Leningrad 1983, no. 23; Karlsruhe 1996, no. 65
Bibliography: Monod and Hautecoeur 1922, no. 55, pl. XXI

As the inscription, *Étude de la main chaude*, on the reverse of this drawing's old mount indicates, this vigorous figural study is related to a major drawing by Greuze depicting the game *la main chaude* (fig. 41).[1] In it, a kneeling player whose head is buried in a woman's lap is shown having his open left hand slapped by a crowd of rowdy men. According to the rules of the game, this would continue until he succeeded in guessing the identity of the partner slapping him.[2] The present drawing and another in the State Hermitage Museum (fig. 42)[3] correspond respectively to figures to the left and right of the kneeling man, preparing to deliver him what were once aptly described as "formidable slaps."[4] Fragonard would paint a gentler and more aristocratic depiction of the game some years later (fig. 43).[5]

The flamboyant costumes suggest that all these drawings relate to a scene observed by Greuze during his Italian sojourn. At his first Salon after his return to Paris, that of 1757, the artist exhibited a drawing entitled *Des Italiens qui jouent à la more,* a scene as tumultuous as figure 41 but depicting the ancient Roman game of *morra.* In this work signed and dated 1756, the figures wear costumes identical to those in this drawing and figure 41.[6]

1. Martin and Masson 1906, no. 314; G. Arnolds, *Zeichnungen des Kupferstichkabinetts in Berlin. Französische Zeichnungen,* Berlin 1949, pp. 56–57, pl. 34. Huquier sale, Paris, 9 November 1772, lot 407; M. Bénard, *Cabinet de M. Paignon-Dijonval,* Paris 1810, p. 155, no. 3859; Émile Galichon sale, Paris, 10–14 May 1875, lot 60.

2. *"Main chaude: jeu dans lequel un des joueurs, la tête sur les genoux d'un autre et la main ouverte sur le dos, reçoit des coups sur cette main jusqu'à ce qu'il ait deviné qui l'a frappé." Larousse universel en 2 volumes,* Paris 1923, II, p. 129.

3. St Petersburg, The State Hermitage Museum, inv. no. 14789. Monod and Hautecoeur 1922, no. 49, pl. XVII.

4. *"formidables tapes."* Émile Galichon sale, Paris, 10–14 May 1875, lot 60 (Martin and Masson 1906, no. 314).

5. J.-P. Cuzin, *Jean-Honoré Fragonard. Vie et oeuvre,* Fribourg 1987, no. 341.

6. Moscow, The Pushkin State Museum of Fine Arts. Martin and Masson 1906, nos. 286, 310. Repr. in sale, Paris, 20 March 1899, no. 41.

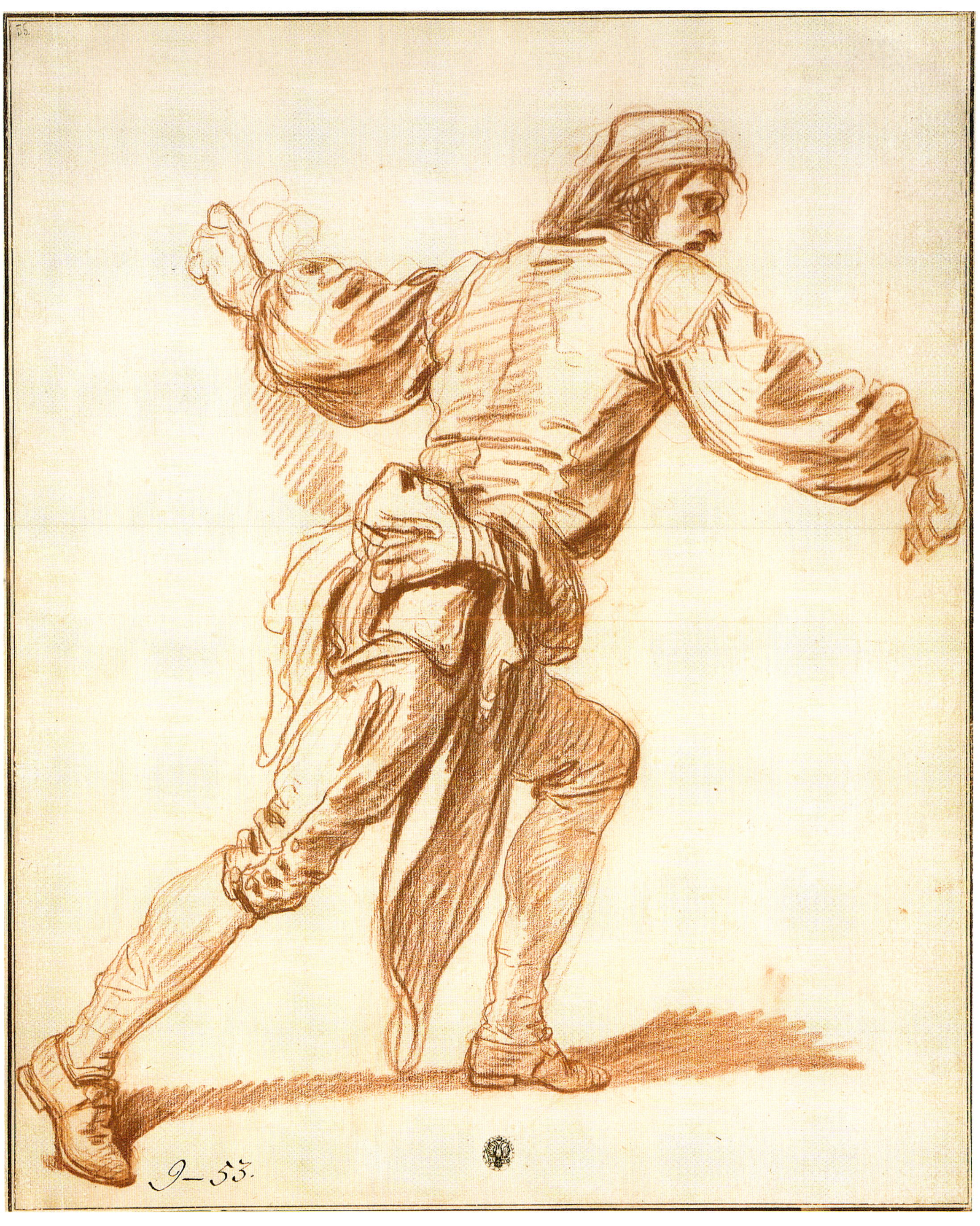
9–53.

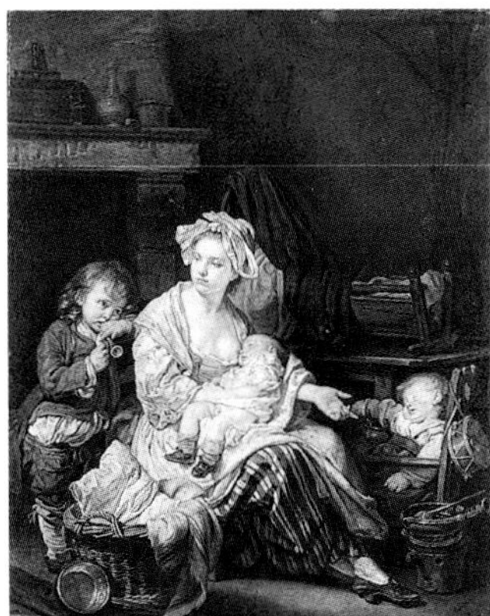

Fig. 44 Greuze, *Silence!* 1759, oil on canvas, London, Buckingham Palace, Royal Collection

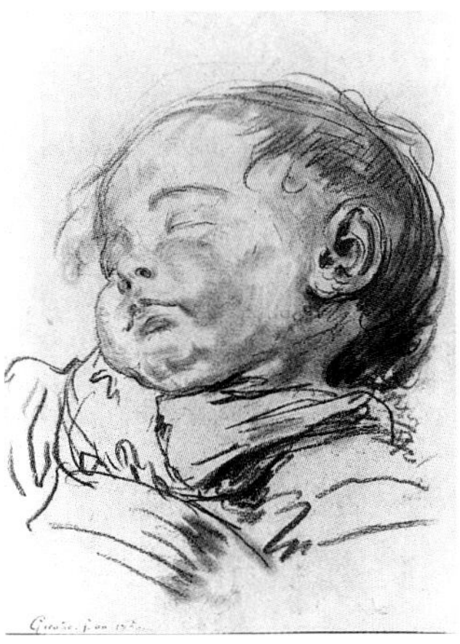

Fig. 45 Greuze, *Head of a Sleeping Child,* 1759, red, black, and white chalks, France, private collection

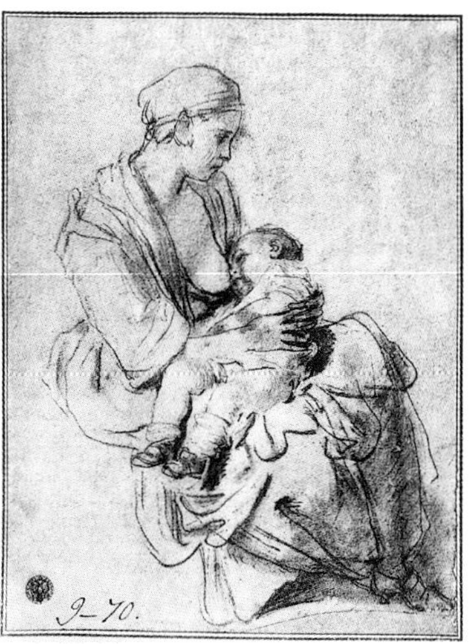

Fig. 46 Greuze, *Seated Woman Nursing a Child, Study for "Silence!"* red and black chalks, stumped, whereabouts unknown

8 *Child Sleeping in a Chair, Study for "Silence!"*

Red and black chalks, stumped, on white paper, 226 × 189 mm (8 15/16 × 7 15/16 in.)
Inscribed in pen and black ink at lower left *9-36*
St Petersburg, The State Hermitage Museum

Provenance: Ivan Ivanovitch Betskoy, St Petersburg; Imperial Academy of Fine Arts, St Petersburg, 1769 (Lugt S. 2699a); transferred to the Hermitage in 1924
Exhibitions: Leningrad 1977, no. 47; *Works of Western European Masters from the Hermitage* (in Japanese), Sapporo, The Hokkaido Museum of Modern Art; Fukuoka, The Fukuoka Prefectural Museum, 1985, no. 62, repr.; Karlsruhe 1996, no. 62, repr.
Bibliography: Monod and Hautecoeur 1922, no. 29, pl. v; Hartford *et al.* 1976–77, p. 66

This is one of four surviving studies for the painting *Silence!* that Greuze included among his Salon entries of 1759, listing it in the catalogue as *Un tableau représentant le Repos, caractérisé par une Femme qui impose silence à son fils, en lui montrant ses autres enfants qui dorment* (fig. 44).[1] As opposed to the lax, indulgent mother of *The Spoiled Child* (no. 33), the imposing young woman in this picture reprimands her disheveled son, eager to blow his small horn and indifferent to the slumber of his infant brothers. In its conception, *Silence!* owes much to the example of Nicolaes Maes's (1634–1693) *The Naughty Drummer* of 1655, in which a mother by a crib reprimands a boy about to beat a drum (the one in Greuze's picture is depicted as already broken).[2]

Although Diderot brusquely dismissed Greuze's Salon works in 1759, the anonymous author of the controversial *Lettre critique à un ami sur les ouvrages de M.M. de l'Académie exposés au Salon* remarked that, although Greuze worked in a "sterile genre," "he holds his own against several great men because he knows nature and he cherishes it."[3] That observation is borne out by the evidence of Greuze's various preparatory drawings for *Silence!* and by the advice he gave to Joseph Ducreux (1735–1802): "Make studies before painting, especially by drawing."[4]

Executed much in the powerful style of Maes or his master Rembrandt (1606–1669), the present drawing is a study for the center of the mother's attention: the child at the right, blissfully asleep in his small armchair. A study for the same child's head (fig. 45) is signed and dated *Greuze.f.an.1759.*[5] The child asleep on his mother's lap is taken from another drawing by Greuze (fig. 46) in which the mother is more preoccupied with nursing him.[6]

1. See O. Millar, *The Queen's Pictures,* London 1977, p. 156; *Carlton House, The Past Glories of George IV's Palace,* exhib. cat., London, The Queen's Gallery, Buckingham Palace, 1991–92, pp. 203–04, no. 182.

2. W. Valentiner, *Nicolaes Maes,* Berlin and Leipzig 1924, pp. 42, 45, pl. 16; I. Gaskell, *The Thyssen-Bornemisza Collection. Seventeenth-Century Dutch and Flemish Painting,* London 1989, pp. 244–47, no. 53.

3. *"Il se soutient dans un genre aussi stérile contre plusieurs grands hommes, parce qu'il connaît la Nature et qu'il la chérit." Lettre critique à un ami sur les ouvrages de M.M. de l'Académie exposés au Salon,* Paris 1759, p. 27.

4. *"Faites des études avant que de peindre en dessinant surtout."* Quoted in Goncourt 1880, p. 385 n. 1.

5. Hartford *et al.* 1976–77, p. 66.

6. Monod and Hautecoeur 1922, no. 71, pl. xxviii; sale, Leipzig, 29 April 1931, lot 106.

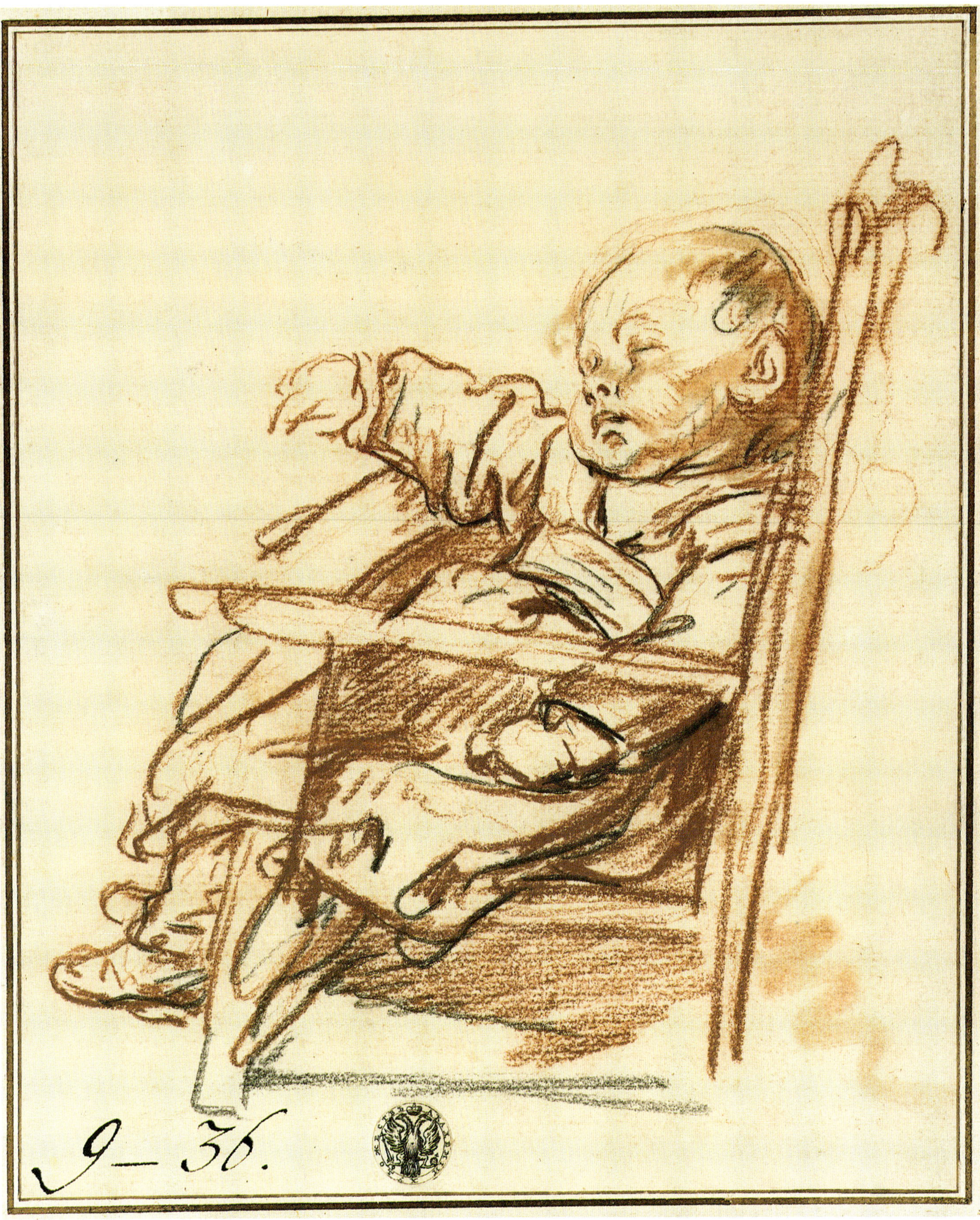
9– 36.

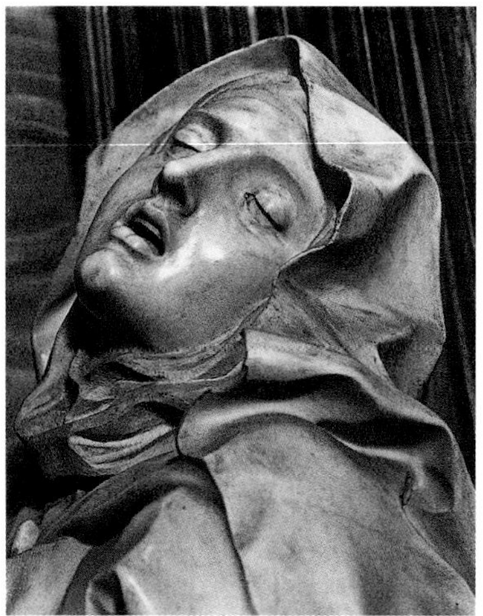

Fig. 47 G.L. Bernini, *The Ecstasy of St Teresa* (detail), 1647–51, marble, Rome, Santa Maria della Vittoria

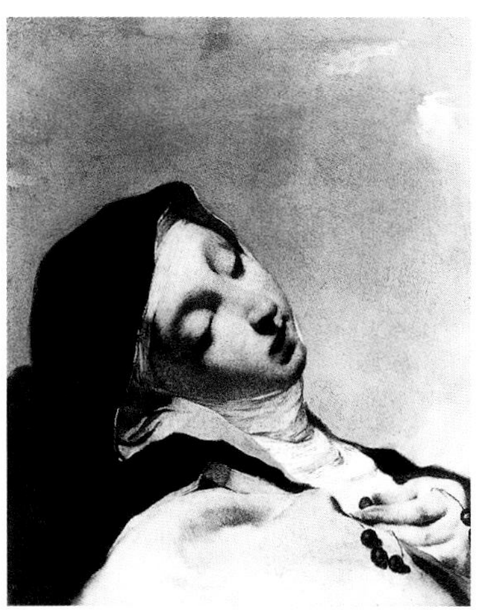

Fig. 48 G.B. Piazzetta, *St Teresa in Ecstasy*, 1737, oil on canvas, Stockholm, Nationalmuseum

9 *Head of a Woman Leaning Back to the Left*

Red chalk on white paper, 369 × 326 mm (14 9/16 × 12 13/16 in.)
Inscribed in pen and black ink at lower left *8-No 59*
St Petersburg, The State Hermitage Museum

Provenance: Ivan Ivanovitch Betskoy, St Petersburg; Imperial Academy of Fine Arts, St Petersburg, 1769 (Lugt S. 2699a); transferred to the Hermitage in 1924
Exhibition: Leningrad 1977, no. 122
Bibliography: Monod and Hautecoeur 1922, no. 126

The drawing is clearly based on Gian Lorenzo Bernini's (1598–1680) marble sculpture *The Ecstasy of St Teresa* in Santa Maria della Vittoria, Rome (fig. 47).[1] The fact that it is reversed may be the result of Greuze's experimenting with a counterproof of an earlier drawing, perhaps one executed in the Cornaro Chapel. Certainly the extreme distortion of the thrown-back head corresponds to how the figure appears from a viewer's low angle of vision in the church.[2]

Besides providing evidence of what Greuze was looking at during his Roman sojourn, this image also suggests an important source for the artist's later images of women in erotic ecstasy (nos. 41, 47). What Bernini was representing was the supreme moment of the saint's visions, the Transverberation (or Transfixion) of her heart by the arrow of Divine Love that occurred in 1559, as described in her *Vida:* "In his [the angel's] hands I saw a long golden spear, and at the end of the iron tip I seemed to see a point of fire. With this he seemed to pierce my heart several times so it penetrated to my entrails. When he drew it out, I thought he was drawing them out with it and he left me completely afire with a great love for God."[3]

The tendency to see sexual sublimation in Bernini's representation of such spiritual passion has been constant since *The Ecstasy of St Teresa* was first viewed in 1651 until the present day. Greuze's patron the abbé Gougenot was no exception, as this entry in his "Journal" (see no. 4) indicates:

If the figure of St Teresa were naked, she would not be more licentious. The sculptor has given her an expression which one would not dare translate into words. The angel (who seems to be a Cupid) has a brazen look; the saint's draperies are very rumpled, but hardly at all considering her frenzied attitude.... The expression of this work is most vivid, the head of the angel is of a singular delicacy, and that of St Teresa perfectly beautiful.[4]

About twenty years before Greuze's graphic variation on Bernini's *St Teresa,* Giovanni Battista Piazzetta (1683–1754) painted a *St Teresa in Ecstasy* (fig. 48) that curiously resembles it, though the figure's expression is more becalmed. Piazzetta would not have known Bernini's sculpture firsthand, but Greuze might have seen Marco Pitteri's (1702–1786) engraving after Piazzetta's painting.[5]

1. R. Wittkower, *Gian Lorenzo Bernini: The Sculptor of the Roman Baroque,* London 1966, pp. 216–18, no. 48.

2. See R.T. Petersson, *The Art of Ecstasy. Teresa, Bernini, and Crashaw,* New York 1970, pl. XXI.

3. Quoted in Petersson 1970, p. 40.

4. *"Quand la figure de Sainte Thérèse serait nüe, elle ne seroit pas plus licentieuse. Le sculpteur y a mis une expression que le Papier ne peut souffrir.... L'ange (qui semble être un amour) a l'air hardi; les Draperies de la Sainte sont très chifonnées, mais peu eu égard à son attitude d'égarement.... L'expression de ce morceau est des plus vives, la Tête de l'Ange est d'une finesse singulière et celle de Sainte Thérèse parfaitement belle."* Quoted in Guicharnaud 1999, p. 34.

5. R. Pallucchini, *L'Opera completa del Piazzetta,* Milan 1982, nos. 76, 78a.

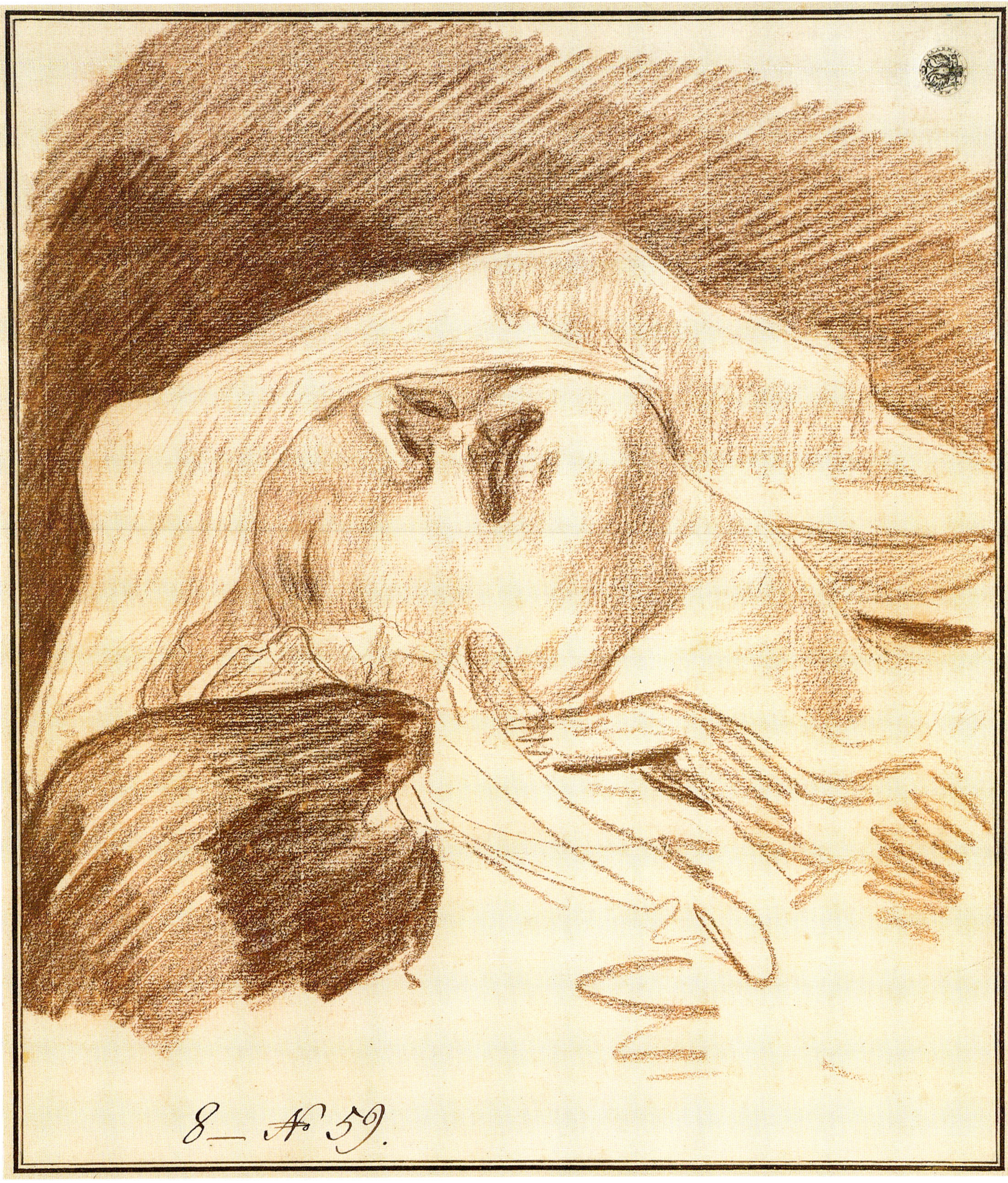

10 *Head of a Woman Seen from Above*

Red chalk on white paper, 389 × 311 mm (15 3/8 × 12 1/4 in.)
Inscribed in pen and black ink at lower left *8-No 45*
St Petersburg, The State Hermitage Museum

Provenance: Ivan Ivanovitch Betskoy, St. Petersburg; Imperial Academy of Fine Arts, St Petersburg, 1769 (Lugt S. 2699a); transferred to the Hermitage in 1924
Exhibition: Leningrad 1977, no. 123
Bibliography: Monod and Hautecoeur 1922, no. 128

This deceptively simple study of a hooded woman might have been selected by Greuze to include in the group of drawings he was selling General Betskoy as a demonstration of the proper rendering of draperies, one of the basic preoccupations of academic draftsmanship. But more specifically, this study demonstrates how, with deft shading, to suggest the volume of a head contained within a cloth cone, looking rather like the hood of a hair drier. The resulting sculptural effect invites comparison to the head of Houdon's *Winter* (fig. 49), a work dating from the early 1780s.[1] The costume specialist Michele Majer describes the headgear in Greuze's drawing as a hooded mantle, probably attached to a cloak, but light enough to be worn over a cap or an elaborate coiffure. C. Willett and Phillis Cunnington point out that such hoods, "always soft... and large enough to cover any day cap worn under it, completely covering the head, ...were sometimes worn indoors."[2]

The pensive attitude of the subject and her majestic cowl suggest that this drawing may be related to Greuze's lost painting entitled *Reflections,* for which a full figural study has survived (fig. 50).[3] It seems to relate as well to number 11.

1. H.H. Arnason, *The Sculptures of Houdon,* New York 1975, pp. 67–68.

2. C. Willett and P. Cunnington, *Handbook of English Costume in the Eighteenth Century,* London 1957, p. 160. I am grateful to Michele Majer for pointing out this source.

3. See Hartford *et al.* 1976–77, p. 135, no. 61.

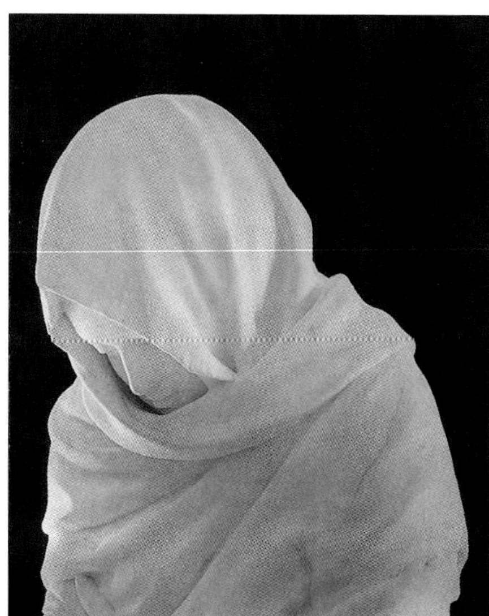

Fig. 49 J.-A. Houdon, *Winter* (detail), 1783, marble, Montpellier, Musée Fabre

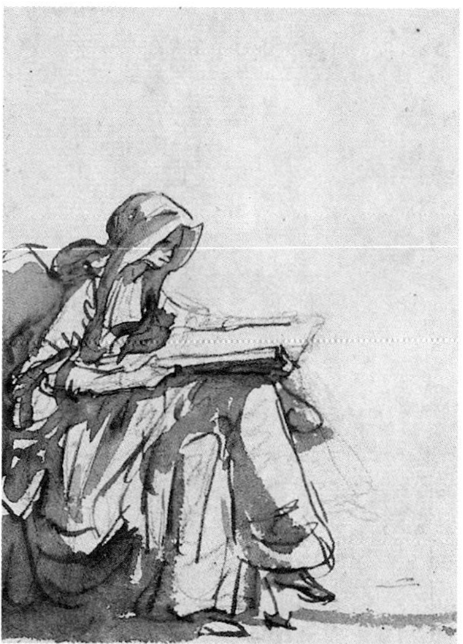

Fig. 50 Greuze, *Seated Woman Holding a Book, Study for "Reflections", c.* 1768, brush with black and brown ink over graphite, Tournus, Musée Greuze

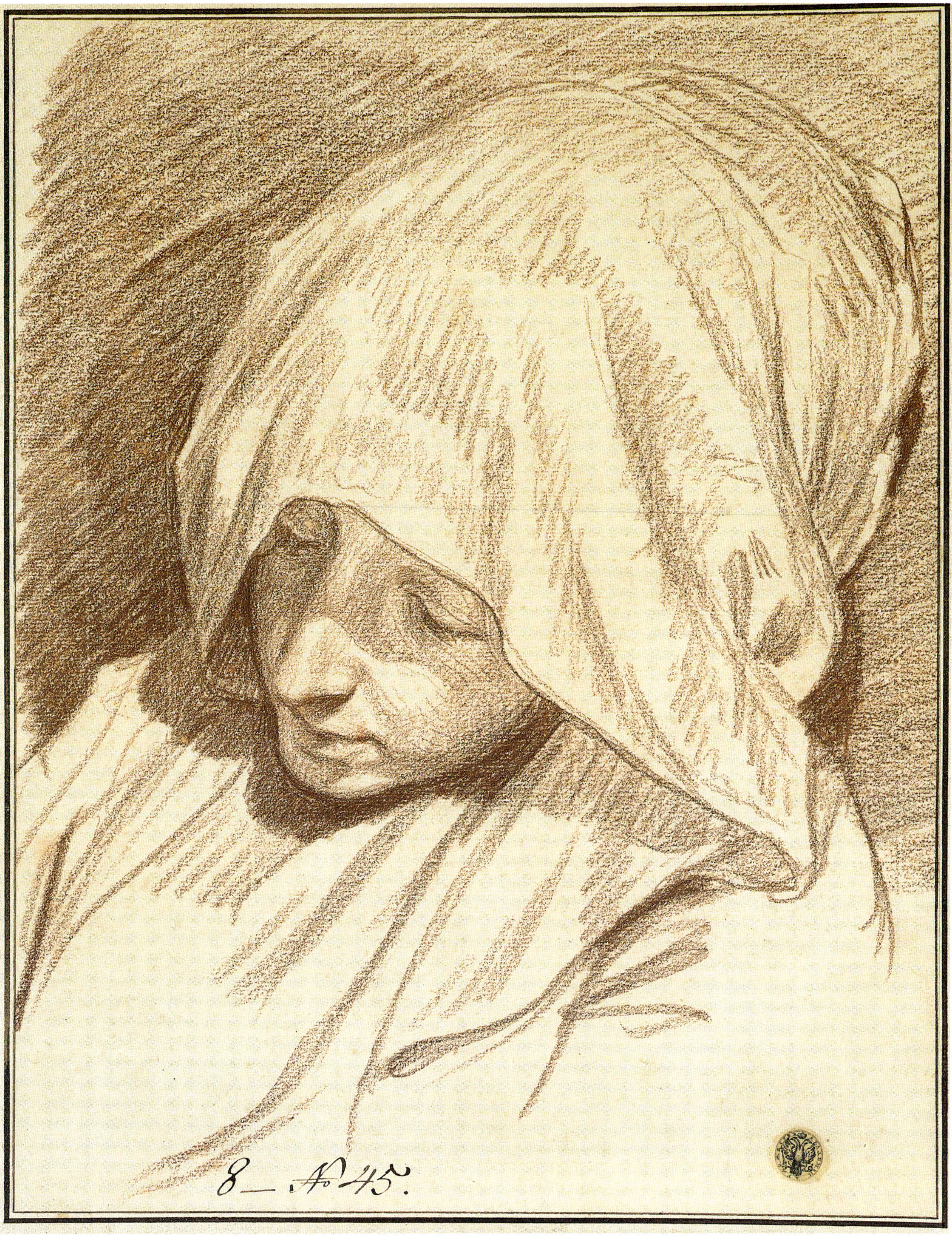
8_ .No.45.

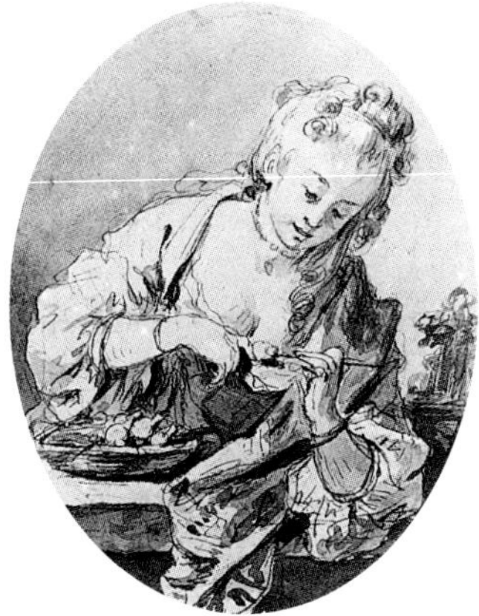

Fig. 51 Greuze, *The Young Nurse,* 1757, brush with gray ink wash over graphite, Rouen, Musée des Beaux-Arts

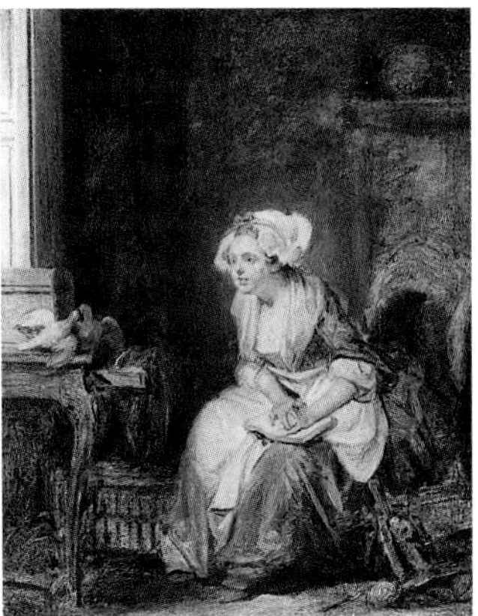

Fig. 52 Greuze, *The First Lessons in Love,* *c.* 1760, oil on canvas, Manchester NH, The Currier Gallery of Art

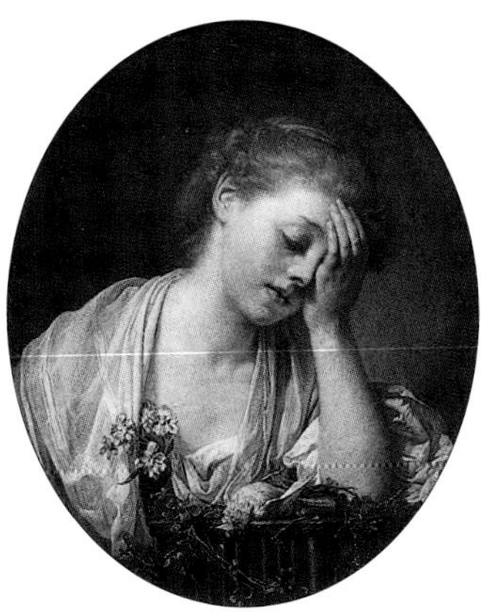

Fig. 53 Greuze, *Girl Weeping over Her Dead Bird,* 1765, oil on canvas, Edinburgh, National Galleries of Scotland

11 *Study of a Seated Woman*

Red chalk on white paper, 388 × 309 mm (15 5/16 × 12 9/16 in.)
Signed in red chalk on the footstool *Greuze;* inscribed in pen and black ink at lower left *9-50*
St Petersburg, The State Hermitage Museum

Provenance: Ivan Ivanovitch Betskoy, St Petersburg; Imperial Academy of Fine Arts, St Petersburg, 1769 (Lugt S. 2699a); transferred to the Hermitage in 1924
Exhibition: Leningrad 1977, no. 108
Bibliography: Monod and Hautecoeur 1922, no. 69, pl. XXVI; E. Munhall, *"The First Lessons in Love* by Jean-Baptiste Greuze," *The Currier Gallery of Art Bulletin,* 1977, p. 6

The subject here of a young woman watching a dove pecking at its dead partner belongs to an iconographic theme that preoccupied Greuze over many years: young women interacting with birds.

The earliest example, signed and dated *Greuze anno 1757* (fig. 51), was executed in Rome and belonged to the abbé Gougenot.[1] It depicts a woman feeding some young birds. This was followed a year later by a study (signed and dated *Greuze.f.an.1758*) of a young women leaning forward to watch a pair of billing doves,[2] a subject Greuze treated in a painting of about 1760, *The First Lessons in Love* (fig. 52).[3]

At the Salon of 1765, Greuze achieved a great success with his *Girl Weeping over Her Dead Bird* (fig. 53). By introducing death into his program of women-with-birds, Greuze provoked the famous response of Diderot, who, muttering "That child is weeping over something else, I tell you,"[4] equated the death of the girl's sparrow with her own loss of virginity. While Greuze was capable of playing on such a *double entendre,* this author and certain critics of 1765 were more inclined to consider the subject to be the shock a young person experiences in his or her first confrontation with the mystery of death. Such seems to be the tenor of the present drawing, too, in which the young woman appears withdrawn, saddened by the spectacle at her feet.

So strong was Greuze's preoccupation with this theme that among his entries at the Salon of 1800, his first since 1769, was a painting entitled *A Child Hesitating to Touch a Bird for Fear that It Might be Dead* (Paris, Musée du Louvre).[5]

The bold and complex rendering of the woman's voluminous skirt here, so similar to that of number 42, is counterbalanced by such precious touches as the effect of reflected light on the woman's chin. A study of a woman's hands holding a bird, like this sheet, dates probably from about 1765 (fig. 54).

1. Martin and Masson 1906, no. 797; Musée des Beaux-Arts, Rouen, *Catalogue des dessins, sculptures, et architecture,* Rouen 1911, p. 125, no. 1005.

2. Montpellier, Musée Fabre, inv. no. 837-1-306. Martin and Masson 1906, no. 1804; A. Joubin, *Le Musée de Montpellier, Musée Fabre, Dessins,* Paris 1929, p. 37, repr.

3. Munhall 1977, pp. 3–6.

4. *"Cet enfant pleure autre chose, vous dis-je."* Diderot *Salons,* II, p. 147.

5. Rosenberg, Reynaud, and Compin 1974, I, p. 157, no. 330, repr.

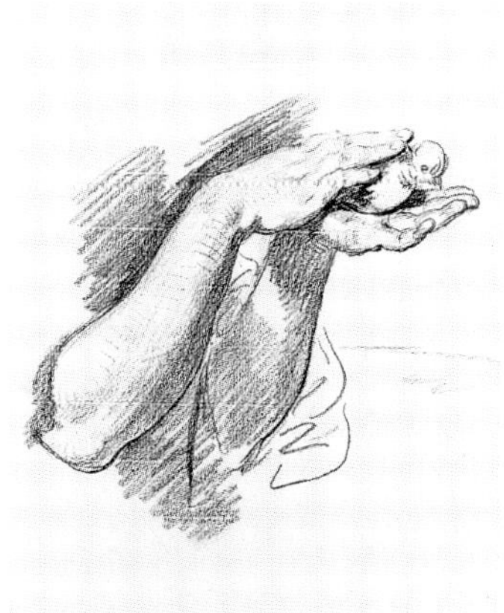

Fig. 54 Greuze, *A Woman's Hands Holding a Bird, c.* 1765, red chalk on white paper, Austin, Jack S. Blanton Museum of Art at the University of Texas in Austin

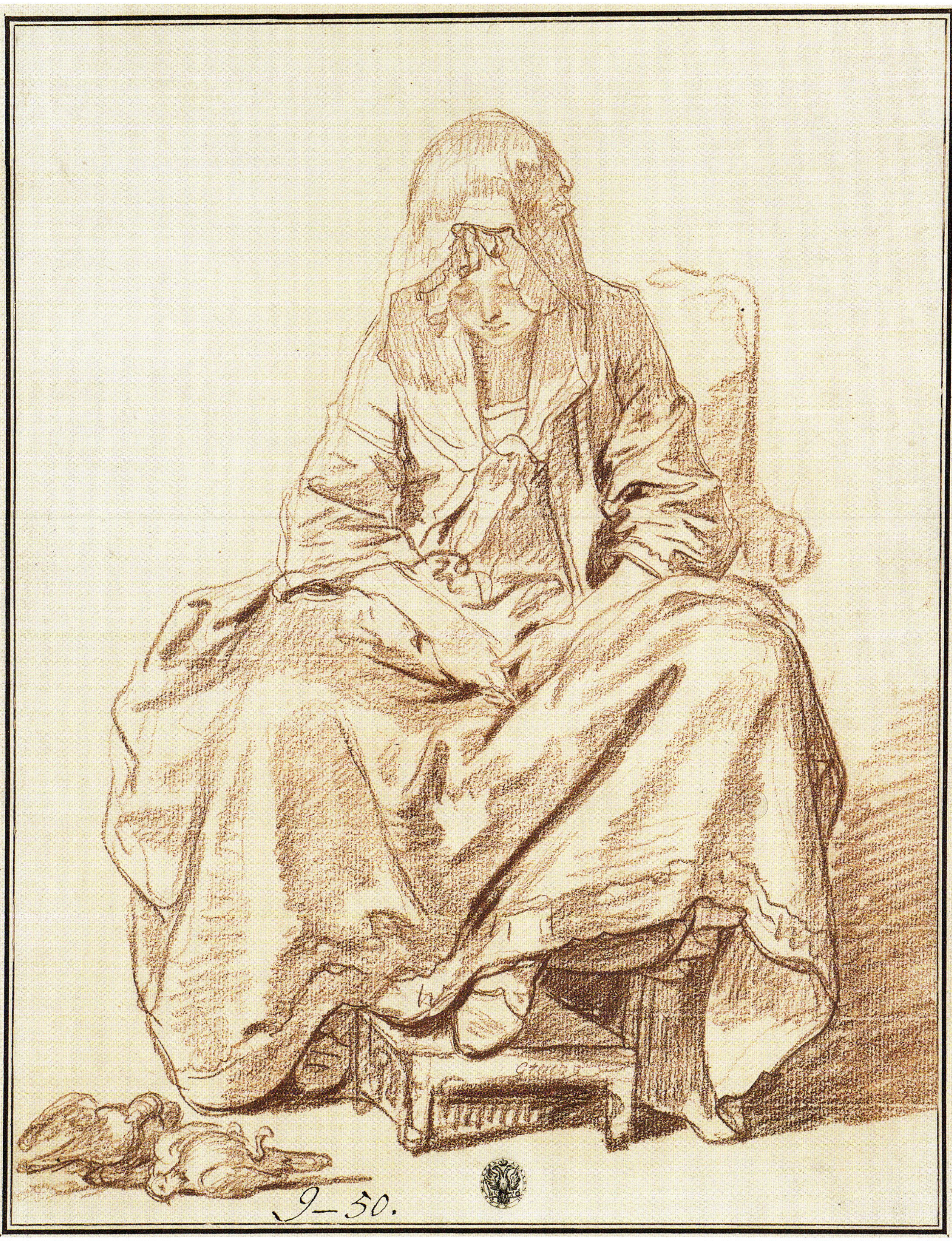
9–50.

12 *Melancholy*

Brush with black ink and gray ink wash over graphite on white paper, 370 × 284 mm (14 9/16 × 11 3/16 in.)
Inscribed in pen and black ink at lower left *9-85*.
St Petersburg, The State Hermitage Museum

Provenance: Ivan Ivanovitch Betskoy, St Petersburg; Imperial Academy of Fine Arts, St Petersburg, 1769 (Lugt S. 2699a); transferred to the Hermitage in 1924; sale, Leipzig, 29 April 1931, lot 100 (bought in); St Petersburg, Hermitage
Exhibition: Leningrad 1977, no. 102
Bibliography: Smith, no. 59; Martin and Masson 1906, no. 334; Monod and Hautecoeur 1922, no. 63, pl. XXIII

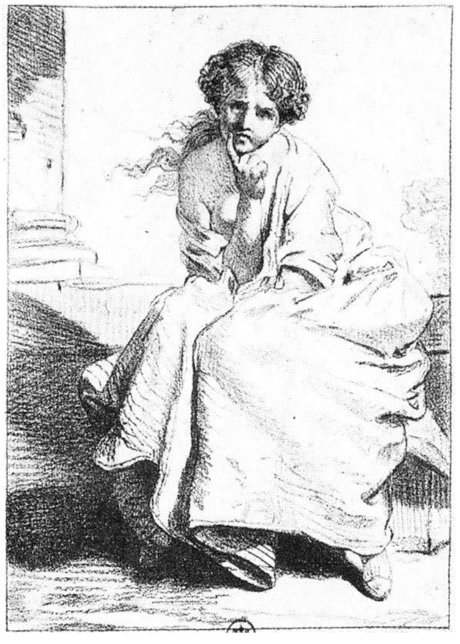

Fig. 55 Massard, after Greuze, *La Mélancolie*, c. 1768, engraving, Paris, Bibliothèque nationale de France

If this drawing was used as a model for the Massard engraving entitled *La Mélancolie* (fig. 55), the engraver took great liberties with it, reproducing it like a chalk drawing, varying the pose, partially denuding the subject, and placing her in an outdoor setting.[1] Whatever the intent of the engraver and, presumably, Greuze himself, the reproduction lessened rather than heightened the dramatic effect of the drawing. There, the woman appears trapped in her voluminous draperies, clutching her throat or chin as though shocked or frightened. Her confused state and pose approximate those of the mother in Greuze's early compositional study for *Sophronie* (no. 68), and the bold brushwork here is similar too.

A painting by Greuze entitled *La Mélancolie* appeared in the Choiseul-Praslin sale, Paris, 18 February 1793, lot 176, but it was a bust-length composition depicting a woman veiled in black.

1. Portalis and Béraldi 1880–82 (III, pt. 1, p. 54, no. 9) attributed the print to Jean Massard, whereas Martin and Masson (p. 110) attributed it alternately to M.P. Massard (no. 334) and Jean-Baptiste-Félix Massard (p. 110).

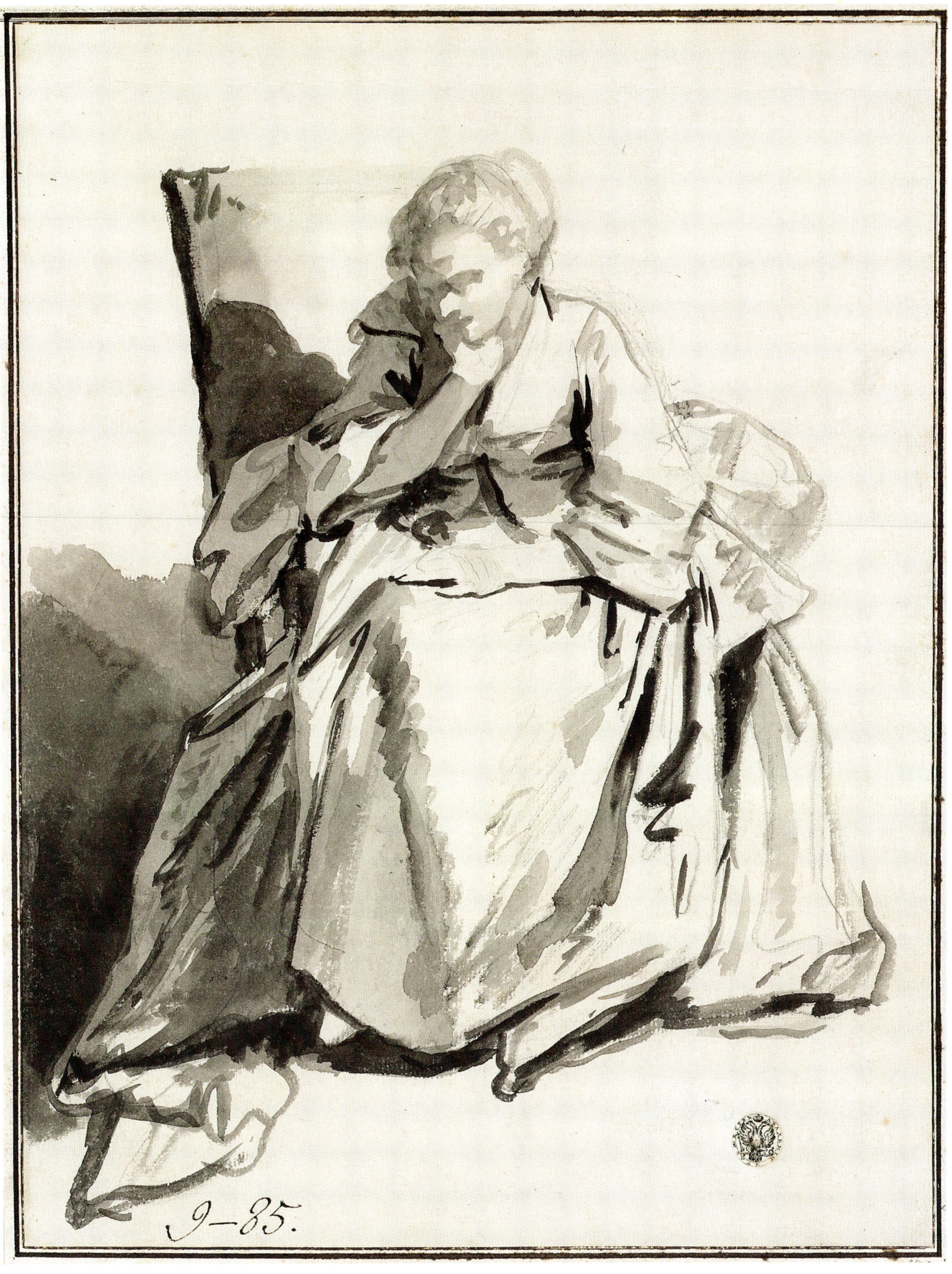
9–85.

13 *The Philosopher*

Brush with black ink and gray ink wash over graphite on white paper, 378 × 284 mm ($14\frac{7}{8} \times 11\frac{3}{16}$ in.)
Inscribed in pen and black ink at lower left *9-86.;* in pen and brown ink on reverse of old mount *Le Philosophe*
St Petersburg, The State Hermitage Museum

Provenance: Ivan Ivanovitch Betskoy, St Petersburg; Imperial Academy of Fine Arts, St Petersburg, 1769 (Lugt S. 2699a); transferred to the Hermitage in 1924
Exhibition: Leningrad 1977, no. 103
Bibliography: Monod and Hautecoeur 1922, no. 24, pl. 11

The inscription on the old mount of this drawing, probably in Greuze's hand, *Le Philosophe,* contributes little to our understanding of it. Far removed from the spoofing attitude of Greuze's *Philosophy Asleep* (fig. 99), it seems rather a meditative image, probably with Masonic overtones, considering the presence of the skull, the crossed bones, the sword, and the sputtering candle. All these relate to the third degree of Masonry, in which a candidate would enact his own funeral, his fellow members pointing their swords at his prone body.[1] The philosopher Greuze depicted here seems lost in thought, indifferent to the two adults and children sketchily indicated on the other side of his table.

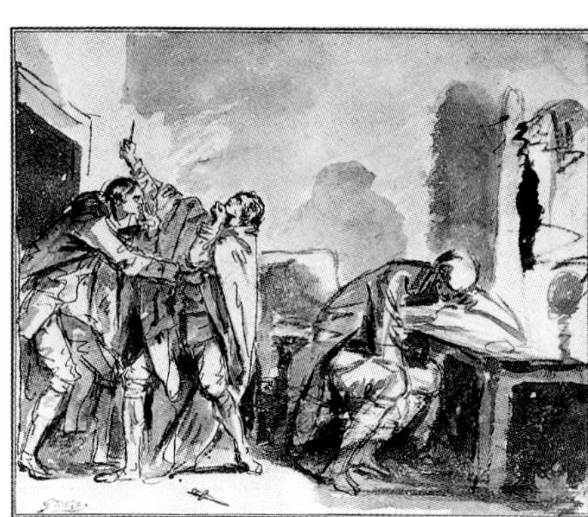

Fig. 56 Greuze, *Scene of a Murder, c.* 1768, pen and brush with black ink and gray and brown ink wash, London, British Museum

The drawing relates to another one, equally enigmatic, in which the philosopher is depicted collapsed at his table, perhaps murdered by the young cloak-and-dagger man at the left (fig. 56). The artist apparently attached such importance to this work that he signed it twice: *Greuze* at lower left and *JBG* at mid-right.[2]

Greuze was a member of the influential Paris Masonic lodge known as Les Neuf Soeurs, but he was elected to it only in 1778, at least ten years after executing *The Philosopher.*[3]

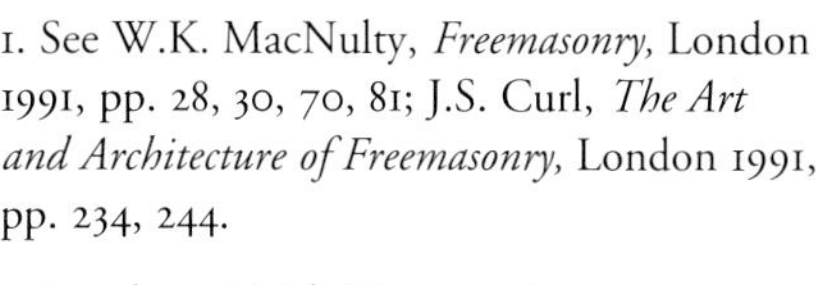

1. See W.K. MacNulty, *Freemasonry,* London 1991, pp. 28, 30, 70, 81; J.S. Curl, *The Art and Architecture of Freemasonry,* London 1991, pp. 234, 244.

2. London, British Museum, inv. no. 1919.6.16.187.

3. See Hartford *et al.* 1976–77, p. 168.

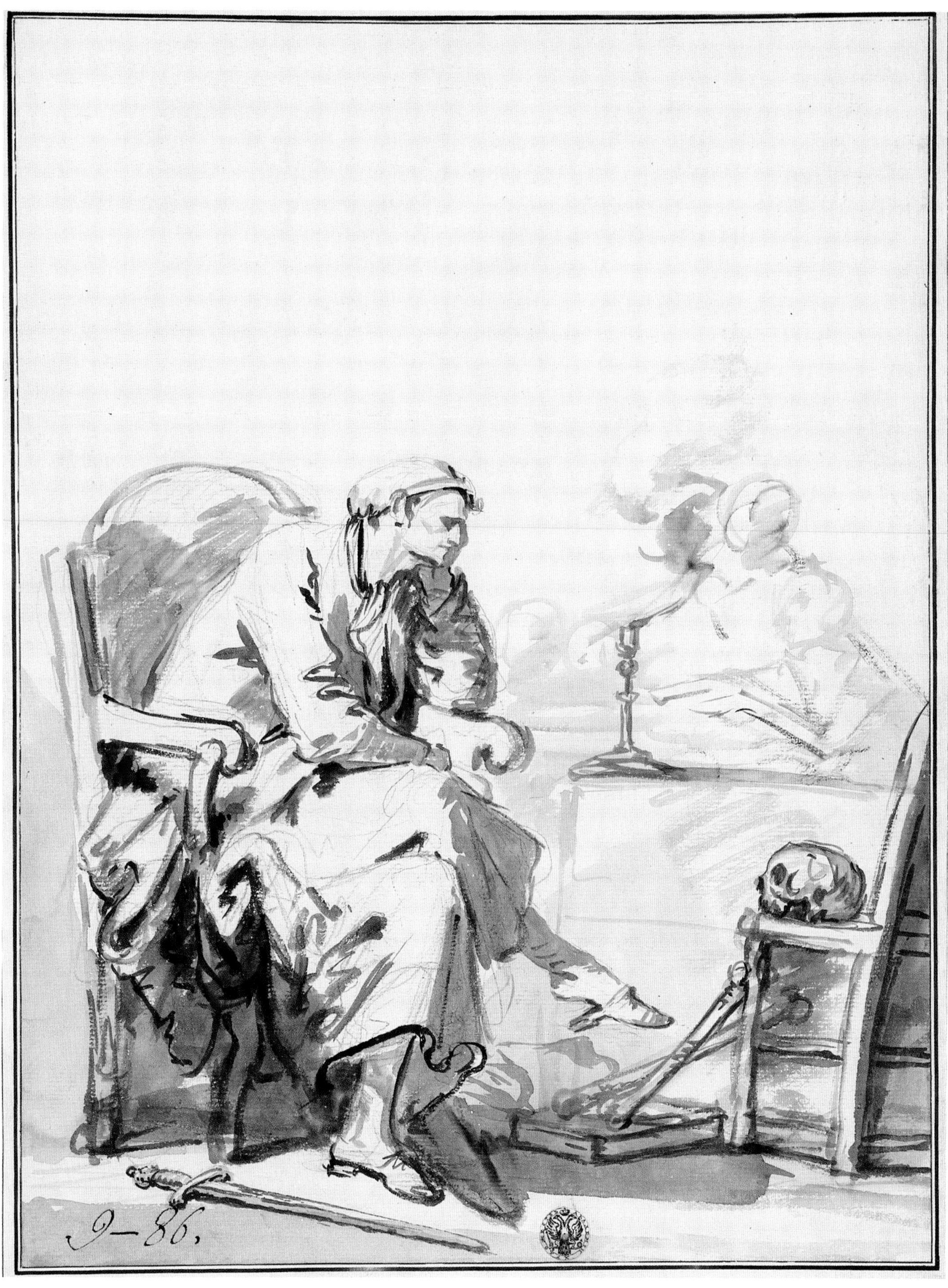
9–86,

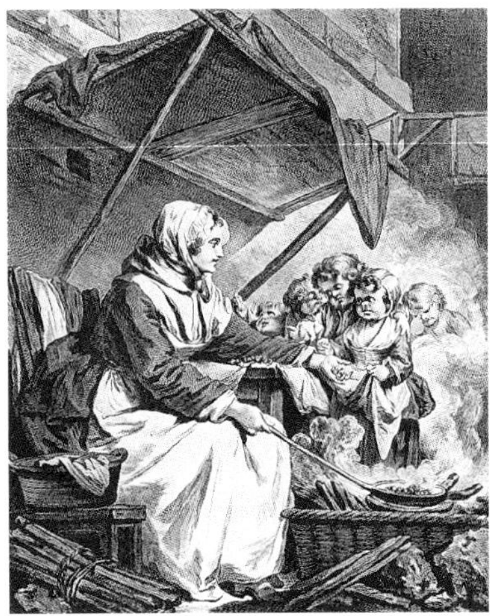

Fig. 57 J.-F. Beauvarlet, after Greuze, *La Marchande de marrons,* 1761, engraving, New York, The Metropolitan Museum of Art, Dick Fund

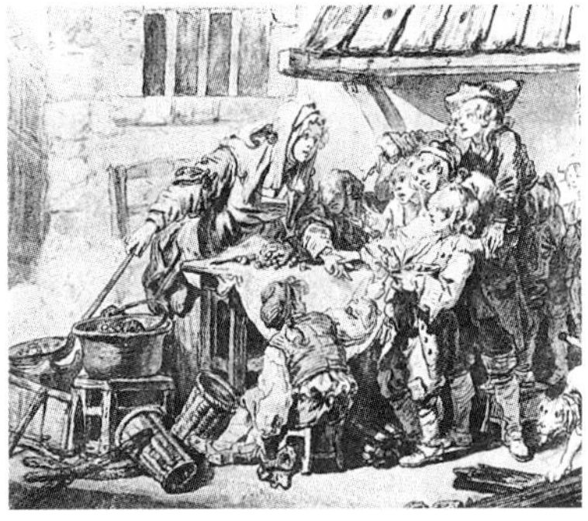

Fig. 58 Greuze, *The Chestnut Vendor,* *c.* 1760, brush with black and brown ink, whereabouts unknown

14 *The Chestnut Vendor*

Brush with black and brown ink over graphite on white paper, 420 × 315 mm (16 1/2 × 12 3/8 in.)
Paris, private collection

Provenance: chevalier de Damery, Paris, 1783;[1] Pierre-François Basan *père,* Paris; his sale, Paris, 1–19 December 1798, lot 98; Paillet, Paris; comte Jacques de Bryas, Paris; his sale, Paris, 4–6 April 1898, lot 73; Pierre Decourcelle, Paris; his sale, Paris, 29–30 May 1911, lot 97; private collection, France, until 1996; Didier Aaron & Co., New York
Exhibition: perhaps Salon de la Correspondance, 1783[2]
Bibliography: Smith, no. 161; Martin and Masson 1906, no. 327; M. Roux, *Inventaire du fonds français, Graveurs du dix-huitième siècle. Bibliothèque Nationale, département des estampes,* Paris 1933, II, p. 227, no. 51; *Didier Aaron, Catalogue,* London, New York, and Paris [1998], no. 10

Chestnut vendors seemed to fascinate Greuze in the early 1760s, with their picturesque equipment and the largely young and rambunctious clients they attracted. The sweet variety of the chestnuts that were sold hot in the streets were called *marrons (Castaneau sativa).* With their shells slashed, they were roasted over hot embers in special long-handled pans, precisely as shown in this drawing. The bundles of faggots in the foreground supplied the fuel for the brazier.

At about the same time, Greuze executed another drawing depicting a chestnut vendor whose history has often been confused with that of the present one (fig. 58). Exhibited at the Salon of 1761 (no. 105) as *Un Dessein représentant des enfans qui dérobent des Marrons,* it was briefly described then by Diderot: "There is a great variety of action, of physiognomies and of characters in all those little rascals, some of whom attract the attention of that poor *Chestnut Vendor,* while the others steal from her."[3]

What the abbé de la Garde wrote in reference to the drawings Greuze exhibited at the Salon of 1761—"Several drawings of Monsieur *Greuze*... do him as much honor by their execution as by the choice and genius of their dramatic invention"[4]—applies just as well to the present sheet, where the range of emotions so deftly indicated among the crowded children—confident, pleading, frightened, assertive—is set off by the imposing yet gracious figure of the vendor, the whole scene composed and rendered with force and elegance.

Jacques-Firmin Beauvarlet's (1731–1797) engraving of the drawing in reverse (fig. 57) proved to be a popular motif in the domain of the decorative arts. Its low-life subject was reproduced on a gold and enameled snuffbox dated 1763–64 as well as on a Sèvres porcelain jardinière dated 1765 (see *Didier Aaron, Catalogue* in *Bibliography*).

1. This provenance is cited on Jacques-Firmin Beauvarlet's engraving after the drawing (fig. 57): *"Ce dessin est au cabinet de Monsieur Damery, Chevalier de l'Ordre Royal Militaire de St. Louis."* For information on this important collector of Greuze's drawings and the presumed subject of a portrait by the artist, see Hartford *et al.* 1976–77, no. 40.

2. So indicated by Martin and Masson 1906 (see *Bibliography*), but only paintings by Greuze are listed in the manuscript catalogue of the exhibition preserved in the Frick Art Reference Library ("Essai d'un tableau historique des peintres de l'école française... avec le catalogue des ouvrages des mêmes maîtres qui sont offerts à présent... dans le Salon de la Correspondance," Paris 1783, p. 85).

3. *"Il y a une grande variété d'actions, de physionomies et de caractères dans tous ces petits fripons dont les uns occupent cette pauvre Marchande de marrons, tandis que les autres la volent."* Diderot *Salons,* I, p. 134. This is the drawing Martin and Masson catalogued as no. 328 and probably the drawing Wille described buying from Greuze on 18 December 1759 (Wille 1857, I, p. 125) and the one that appeared at the Jacob de Vos sale, Amsterdam, 22–24 May 1883, lot 735.

4. *"Plusieurs desseins de M.* Greuze... *lui font autant d'honneur par l'exécution, que par le choix et le génie de l'invention."* Abbé Philippe Bridard de la Garde, "Observations d'une Société d'amateurs sur les tableaux exposés au Salon cette année 1761," *Observateur littéraire,* Paris, October 1761, p. 53.

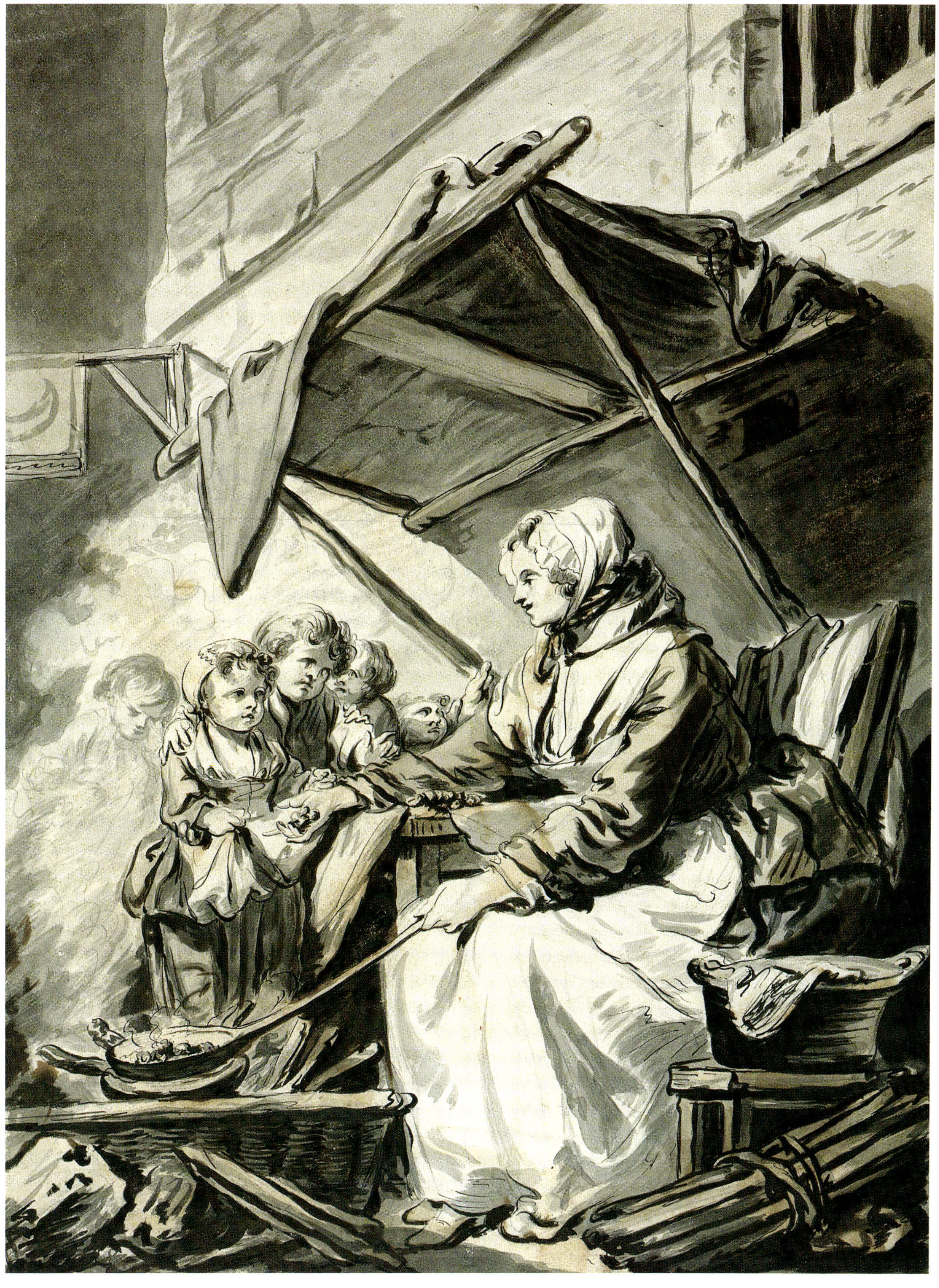

15 *Compositional Study for "A Marriage Contract"*

Brush, black and brown ink wash over graphite on white paper, 350 × 495 mm (13 ¾ × 19 ½ in.)
Paris, Musée du Petit Palais

Provenance: possibly marquis Jean-Joseph de Laborde, Paris; possibly his sale, Paris, 16 May 1783, lot 38; Jean-Baptiste-Laurent Boyer de Fonscolombe, Aix-en-Provence; his sale, Paris, 18 January 1790, lot 189; baron Roger, Paris; his sale, Paris, 23–24 December 1842, lot 131; Auguste Simon, Paris; his sale, Paris, 10–15 March 1862, lot 30; Clément, Paris; Eugène Dutuit, Rouen (Lugt 709a); bequeathed by him to the city of Paris in 1902
Exhibitions: Dessins des maîtres anciens, Paris, École des Beaux-Arts, 1879, no. 569; *Chefs-d'oeuvre du Petit Palais,* Zurich, Kunsthaus, 1947, no. 75; *French Art,* Washington D.C., *et al.* 1952 (not in cat.); Hartford *et al.* 1976–77, no. 30; *Chefs-d'oeuvre du musée du Petit Palais,* Tokyo, Idemitsu Museum, 1982–83, no. 70; *Fragonard et le dessin français au XVIIIe siècle,* Paris, Musée du Petit Palais, 1992–93, no. 36
Bibliography: P. de Chennevières, "Les Dessins des maîtres anciens exposés à l'École des beaux-arts," *GBA,* II, 1879, p. 203; Martin and Masson 1906, no. 114; H. Lapauze, *Catalogue sommaire des collections Dutuit,* Paris 1907, no. 968; *idem, Le Palais des Beaux-Arts de la Ville de Paris (Petit Palais),* Paris 1910, pp. 255–56; H. Lapauze, C. Gronkowski, and A. Fauchier-Magnan, *Catalogue sommaire des collections Dutuit,* Paris 1925, no. 1014; Paris 1984, p. 227; J. Chouillet, "Le Regard jaloux de la soeur dans *L'Accordée de village,* Réflexions sur le thème de la jalousie dans l'oeuvre de Diderot," *Diderot et Greuze, Actes du Colloque de Clermont-Ferrand (16 novembre 1984),* Clermont-Ferrand 1986, pp. 69–70, pl. XXIV

In this final compositional study for the painting Greuze exhibited to great acclaim at the Salon of 1761 as *Un Mariage, et l'instant où le père de l'Accordée délivre la dot à son gendre* (fig. 10), a picture more familiarly known as *L'Accordée de village,* the artist included all the essential details of the painting with these minor differences: the full figure shown mounting the staircase, a different cupboard door, the absence of a cloth hanging from the cupboard's middle shelf, and certain nuances of expression among the figures. Patterns of light and shade are precisely established, and the variety of gray and brown washes even suggests the coloring of the final work. It is conceivable that the present drawing was presented as a *modello* to the marquis de Marigny, who commissioned *L'Accordée de village.*[1]

The scene depicted represents the ceremony of *promesses de mariage,* the registration of a civil marriage contract before a notary. As Emma Barker has observed, "The drawing up of a marriage contract prior to the religious ceremony was standard practice in France among all but the very poor."[2] The cast of characters so minutely described by Diderot in his *Récapitulation* of the Salon of 1761 includes, from right to left,

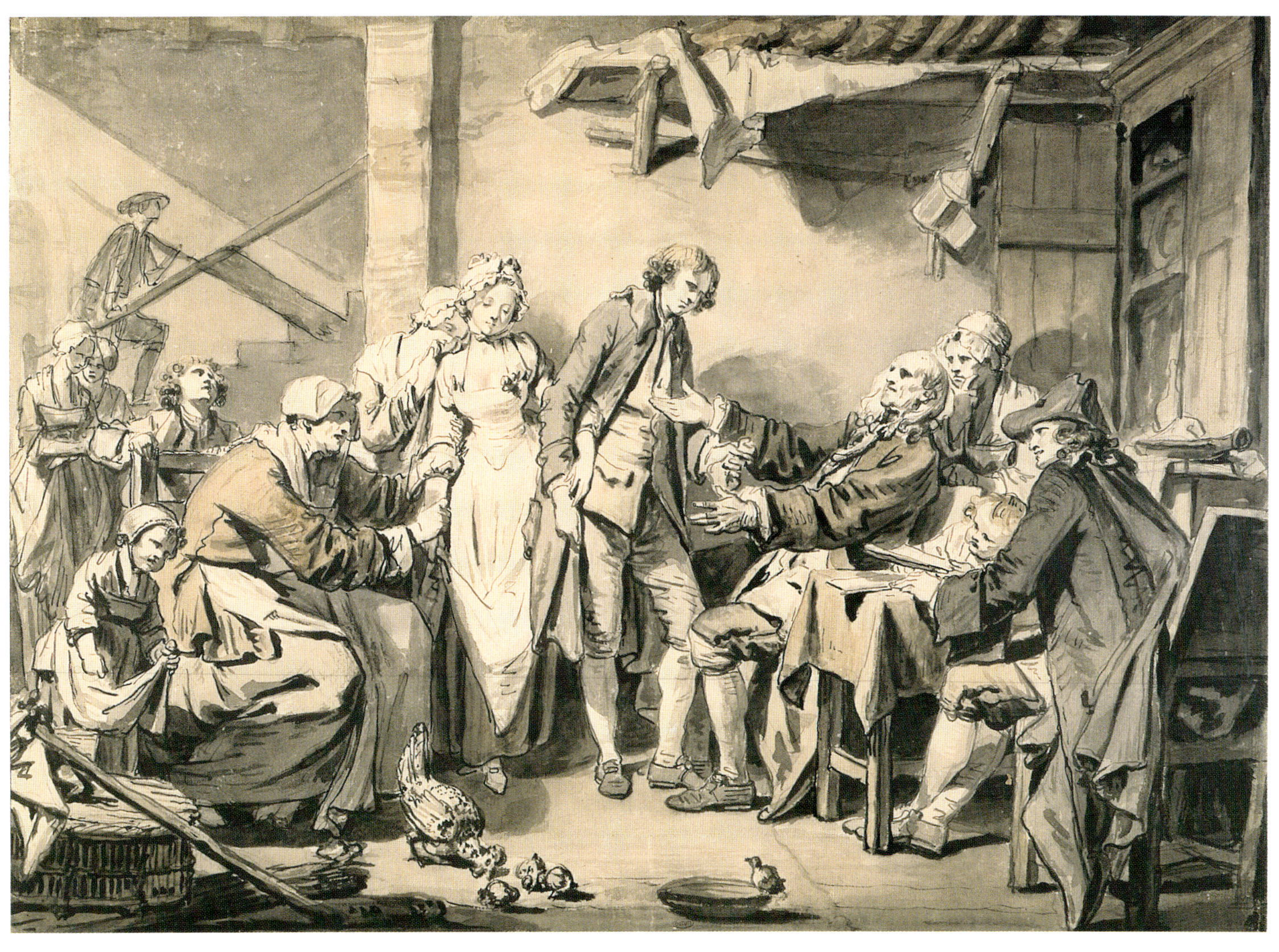

the notary, a heedless child, the jealous older sister, the father, the fiancé, the future bride, her saddened younger sister, the mother, a child feeding a hen and her brood, a younger brother straining to see the action, two servants, and a worker mounting the stairs.

The large number of studies Greuze produced for *L'Accordée de village* was the means by which he achieved the remarkable fluidity of his final composition, so justly praised by Diderot: "Its composition seemed to me very beautiful.... There are twelve figures; each is in its proper place, and does what it should do. How they are all linked together! how they move along rippling and rising in a pyramid!"[3] More recently, José-Luis de Los Llanos rightly claimed that Greuze's genius as a draftsman "exploded" in this work that, in comparison with the painting, possesses something "more incisive and more natural, in a word, stronger."[4]

To appreciate the finesse of this drawing, and to understand the artist's working methods, compare his earliest surviving compositional study for the same subject (fig. 59). Here, working like a filmmaker, Greuze established his *dramatis personae* in precisely the roles they would play in the final painting, but with no concern for aesthetic niceties in executing the drawing.

1. Other compositional studies for the painting are recorded, but none has survived except fig. 59. Françoise Arquié-Bruley pointed out that the present drawing could not have been the model for Jean-Jacques Flipart's (1719–1782) engraving that was lot 162 in the Vaudreuil sale, 26 November 1787, of different dimensions, and described, with its pendant, as "the most highly finished by the master" *("les plus rendus du maître").* Arquié-Bruley 1983, pp. 127, 132 n. 43.

2. Barker 1997, p. 44.

3. *"La composition m'en a paru très-belle.... Il y a douze figures; chacune est à sa place, et fait ce qu'elle doit. Comme elles s'en enchaînent toutes! comme elles vont en ondoyant et en pryamidant!"* Diderot *Salons,* 1, p. 141.

4. *"quelque chose de plus incisif et de plus naturel, en un mot de plus fort."* In *Fragonard et le dessin français au XVIIIe siècle* (see *Exhibitions*), p. 78.

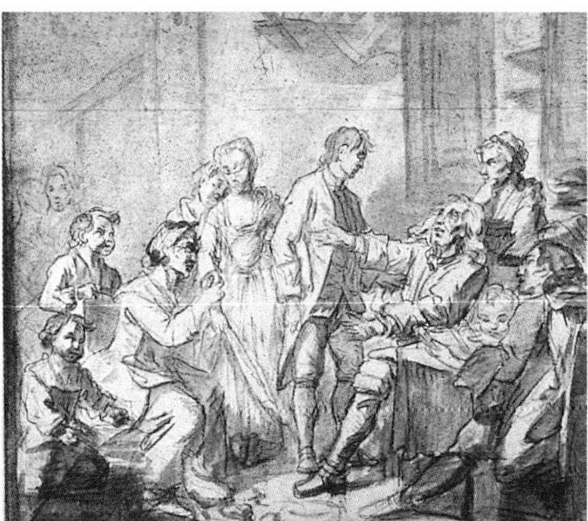

Fig. 59 Greuze, *Compositional Study for "L'Accordée de village,"* 1761, brush and brown ink on white paper, Paris, private collection

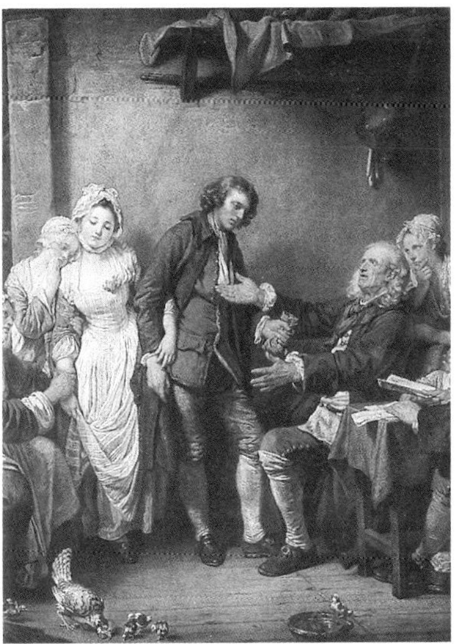

Fig. 60 Greuze, *A Marriage Contract* (detail), 1761, oil on canvas, Paris, Musée du Louvre

16 *Young Woman Standing, Study for "A Marriage Contract"*

Black and white chalks over graphite on tan paper, 515 × 325 mm (20 ⁵⁄₁₆ × 12 ¹³⁄₁₆ in.)
Inscribed in pen and brown ink on the mount at lower right *Greuze fec.*
Chalon-sur-Saône, Musée Denon

Provenance: chevalier de Damery (d. 1803); acquired by the museum in 1902
Exhibitions: Musées de Bourgogne, Dijon, Musée des Beaux-Arts, 1952, no. 109; *De Watteau à David: Peintures et dessins des musées de province français,* Brussels, Palais des Beaux-Arts, 1975, no. 104; *Balzac et la peinture,* Tours, Musée des Beaux-Arts, 1999, no. 8
Bibliography: Smith, no. 164; Martin and Masson 1906, no. 388; L. Armand-Calliat, *Musée Vivant-Denon: Catalogue de la Section des Beaux-Arts,* Chalon-sur-Saône 1963, no. 256, pl. XXIII; Brookner 1972, p. 102, pl. 30; Hartford *et al.* 1976–77, pp. 82, 85; Wakefield 1984, pp. 129–30, fig. 156; Paris 1984, p. 227; Rand 1996, p. 233 n. 47

The bride in *A Marriage Contract* (fig. 60) differs from this full-scale study for that figure in that she inclines her head slightly to her left to accommodate the head of her weeping younger sister; she lifts her apron in her right hand; and she has a nosegay tucked into her bodice. However, Greuze anticipated here—down to the positioning of each finger—the important gesture of her left arm passing around her future husband's (even though it is not included) so that her fingers barely touch his hand. As in the study for her head (no. 17), the bride appears here more reflective than coquettish.

When *A Marriage Contract* finally appeared at the Salon of 1761 and provoked general enthusiasm, the author of the *Observations d'une Société d'amateurs sur les tableaux exposés au Salon cette année 1761*—whom Jean Seznec identified as the abbé Philippe Bridard de la Garde (Madame de Pompadour's librarian)[1]—particularly appreciated Greuze's device of the interlocking arms and its significance:

The young bride has one arm linked around that of the young man. One can see that modesty and the presence of her parents hold back the hand, all ready to place itself on that of her future husband, whom she desires but dares not touch.... Nothing is more piquant than the figure of this bride.... One can recognize just a bit of hypocrisy, sweet and honest, that covers up what is really preoccupying her at this moment.[2]

Diderot's comments after finally viewing *A Marriage Contract* indicate that the care Greuze lavished on his preliminary studies for the bride were not in vain:

She is dressed marvelously. That white linen apron could not be better; there is a bit of richness in its finishing; but this is the day of the betrothal. You have to see how true are all the folds of everything this figure wears, as well as the others.... She is really pretty, even very pretty. A bosom turned on a lathe, which you don't see at all; but I bet there's nothing there that holds it up, and that it stands on its own. Were she closer to her fiancé, she would not have been sufficiently decent; were she closer to her mother or her father, she would have been false. One of her arms passes under that of her future husband, and the tips of her fingers fall and rest softly on his hand; it is the only mark of tenderness that she gives him, and perhaps without even knowing it herself; it is a delicate idea on the painter's part.[3]

Later, Diderot cites the observation of a "very bright" woman *("une femme de beaucoup d'esprit")* that while the principal male figures in *A Marriage Contract* look like peasants, the mother and the bride look like women from the Paris markets, the latter having the air of "a pretty flower-seller" *("une jolie bouquetière").*[4]

The way in which Greuze exploited here the potential of the tinted tan paper was consistent with the instructions of contemporary drawing masters, such as Charles-Antoine Jombert:

Tinted papers were invented to spare the work of the chalk in those passages which should have the tone of the tinted paper, and then one uses white chalk or pastel to bring out the highlights. In this fashion, the color of the paper serves as a mid-tone; then one needs only to indicate shadows with colored chalk in those areas where they are deepest and to highlight, as we just said, the lightest points with white.[5]

The present drawing, when in the possession of the chevalier de Damery, was engraved by Catherine-Jeanne-Françoise Deschamps (1740–1769), first of the engraver Jacques-Firmin Beauvarlet's three wives (fig. 61).

1. Seznec in Diderot *Salons,* 1, p. 76.

2. *"La jeune accordée a un bras entrelacé dans celui du jeune homme. On s'apperçoit que la pudeur et la présence des parens retiennent la main, prête à se poser sur celle du futur, qu'elle désire, mais qu'elle n'ose toucher.... Rien n'est si piquant que la figure de cette accordée.... On y distingue jusqu'à une petite hypocrisie, douce et honnête, qui couvre le véritable intérêt dont elle est occupée dans ce moment."* Abbé Philippe Bridard de la Garde, *Observations d'une Société d'amateurs sur les tableaux exposés au Salon cette année 1761,* Paris 1761, pp. 48–49.

3. *"Elle est vêtue à merveille. Ce tablier de toile blanc fait on ne peut pas mieux; il y a un peu de luxe dans sa garniture; mais c'est un jour de fiançailles. Il faut voir comme tous les plis de tous les vêtements de cette figure et des autres sont vrais.... Elle est jolie vraiment, et très-jolie. Une gorge faite au tour qu'on ne voit point du tout; mais je gage qu'il n'y a rien là qui la relève, et que cela se soutient tout seul. Plus à son fiancé, et elle n'eût pas été assez décente; plus à sa mère ou à son père, et elle eût été fausse. Elle a le bras à demi passé sous celui de son futur époux, et le bout de ses doigts tombe et appuie doucement sur sa main; c'est la seule marque de tendresse qu'elle lui donne, et peut-être sans le savoir elle-même; c'est une idée délicate du peintre."* Diderot *Salons,* 1, pp. 142–43.

4. Diderot *Salons,* 1, p. 144.

5. *"On a inventé les papiers de demie teinte, pour épargner le travail du crayon, dans les endroits qui doivent être de la même force que la teinte du papier, et l'on se sert de craye, de crayon, ou de pastel blanc pour rehausser, c'est-à-dire, pour faire paroître les endroits éclairés. De cette façon, la couleur même du papier sert de demie teinte: il ne s'agit plus que d'ombrer avec un crayon de couleur, les endroits où sont les plus fortes ombres, et de rehausser, comme nous venons de dire, les jours avec du blanc."* Jombert 1973, pp. 54–55.

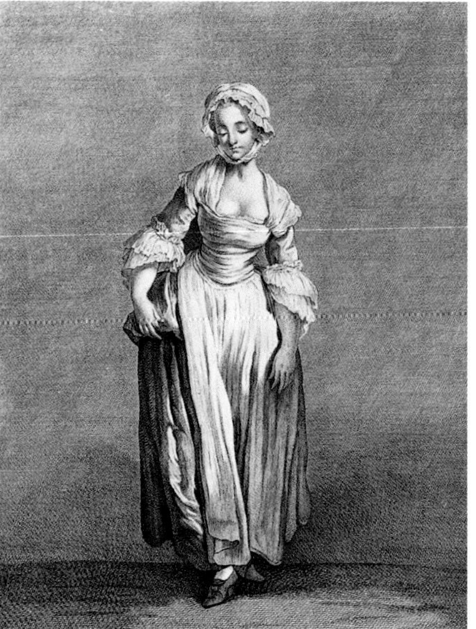

Fig. 61 C.-J.-F. Deschamps, after Greuze, *Standing Young Woman, c.* 1761, engraving, Paris, Bibliothèque nationale de France

Facing page:
16 *Young Woman Standing, Study for "A Marriage Contract"*

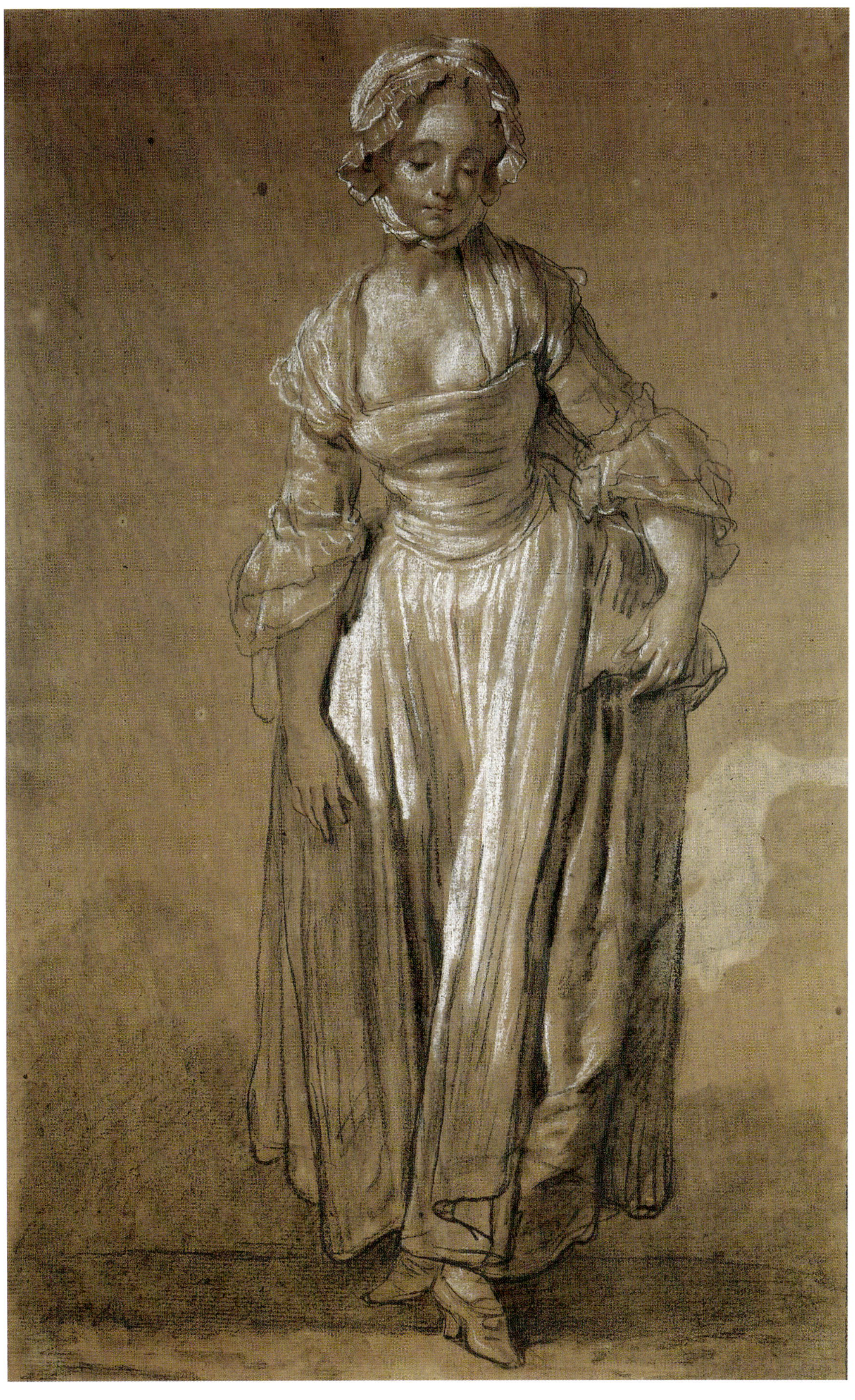

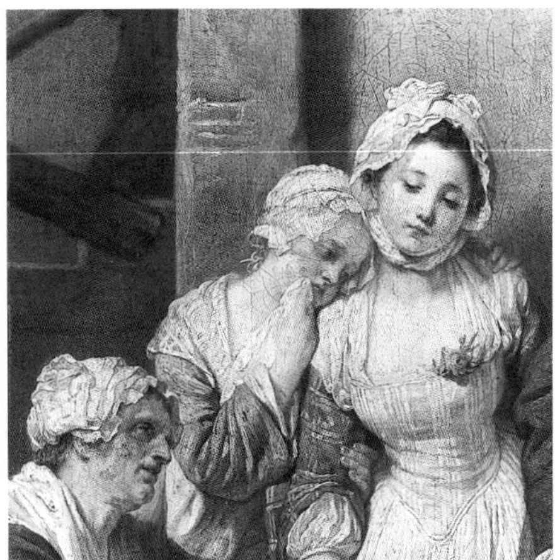

Fig. 62 Greuze, *A Marriage Contract* (detail), 1761, oil on canvas, Paris, Musée du Louvre

17 *Head of a Girl with Eyes Downcast, Study for "A Marriage Contract"*

Red and black chalks, stumped, over graphite on white paper, 395 × 301 mm (15 9/16 × 11 13/16 in.)
Inscribed in pen and black ink at lower left *8-No 110.*
Private collection

Provenance: Ivan Ivanovitch Betskoy, St Petersburg; Imperial Academy of Fine Arts, St Petersburg, 1769 (Lugt S. 2699a); transferred to the Hermitage in 1924; sale, Leipzig, 29 April 1931, lot 105; sale, Geneva, 15 June 1960, lot 204; Slatkin Gallery, New York; Louis Silver, Chicago
Exhibitions: Hartford *et al.* 1976–77, no. 32; *Eighteenth-Century Drawings in New York Collections,* New York, The Metropolitan Museum of Art, 1999, no. 49
Bibliography: Martin and Masson 1906, no. 114; Monod and Hautecoeur 1922, no. 103, pl. XL; Paris 1984, p. 227; Rand 1996, p. 225

In Greuze's painting *A Marriage Contract* (fig. 62), in the compositional study for it (no. 15), and in the study for her full figure (no. 16), the bride, for whom this drawing is another study, tips her head slightly to her left to accommodate a younger sister weeping on her shoulder. In his *Récapitulation* of the Salon of 1761, Diderot described this movement as "a light and gentle bending . . . that fills her with grace and truth."[1] But here, she maintains a more upright, withdrawn, and contemplative air, described again by Diderot as "charming, decent, and reserved."[2]

It was Baron Grimm rather than Diderot who described with the greatest subtlety the complex emotions Greuze succeeded in capturing in this haunting image:

How to describe to you all that is going on in her soul, at the moment of this revolution so longed for and so feared that is going to occur in her life? . . . The tender feelings for her fiancé, the sorrow at leaving her parents' home, the inclinations toward love opposed by her modesty and the decency of a well-brought-up young lady; a thousand feelings of tenderness, voluptuousness, of fear that rise up in an innocent soul at the moment of this change in her condition, you read all that in the face and attitude of this charming creature. . . . How was the artist able to render so many divers sentiments, and so delicate, with a few strokes of his brush?[3]

In addition to number 16 and a painted study for the bride Baron Grimm mentions as being in the Salon of 1761,[4] a pastel study of the bride's head appeared in the sales of three great eighteenth-century collectors in the 1770s—those of Lalive de Jully, Pierre-Jean Mariette, and Randon de Boisset.[5]

1. *"une légère et molle inflexion . . . qui la remplit de grâce et de vérité."* Diderot *Salons,* I, p. 142.

2. *"charmante, décente et réservée."* Diderot *Salons,* I, p. 142.

3. *"mais comment vous peindre tout ce qui se passe dans son âme, au moment de cette révolution si désirable et si redoutée qui va se faire dans toute sa vie? . . . La tendresse pour son fiancé, le regret de quitter la maison paternelle, les mouvements de l'amour combattus par la modestie et par la pudeur dans une fille bien née; mille sentiments confus de tendresse, de volupté, de crainte qui s'élèvent dans une âme innocente au moment de ce changement d'état, vous lisez tout cela dans le visage et dans l'attitude de cette charmante créature. . . . Comment le peintre a-t-il pu rendre tant de sentiments divers, et délicats, en quelques coups de pinceau?"* Baron Grimm in Diderot *Salons,* I, p. 145.

4. Perhaps one of the *Plusieurs Têtes peintes, sous le même numéro,* listed among Greuze's entries in the Salon catalogue under no. 104. See Diderot *Salons,* I, p. 145. Grimm wrote of it "One would, I think, be quite happy already with this sketch, if one weren't familiar with the sublime execution [of this head] in the final painting" *("On serait, je crois, déjà fort aise d'avoir cette esquisse, si l'on n'en connoissait pas la sublime exécution dans le tableau").* In Diderot *Salons,* I, p. 145.

5. La Live de Jully sale, Paris, 5 March 1770, lot 137; Pierre-Jean Mariette sale, Paris, 15 November 1775, lot 1263; Randon de Boisset sale, Paris, 25 February–25 March 1777, lot 15. See C.B. Bailey, *Ange-Laurent de La Live de Jully, a Facsimile Reprint of the Catalogue Historique (1764) and the Catalogue Raisonné des Tableaux (March 5, 1770),* New York 1988, pp. 47, 62.

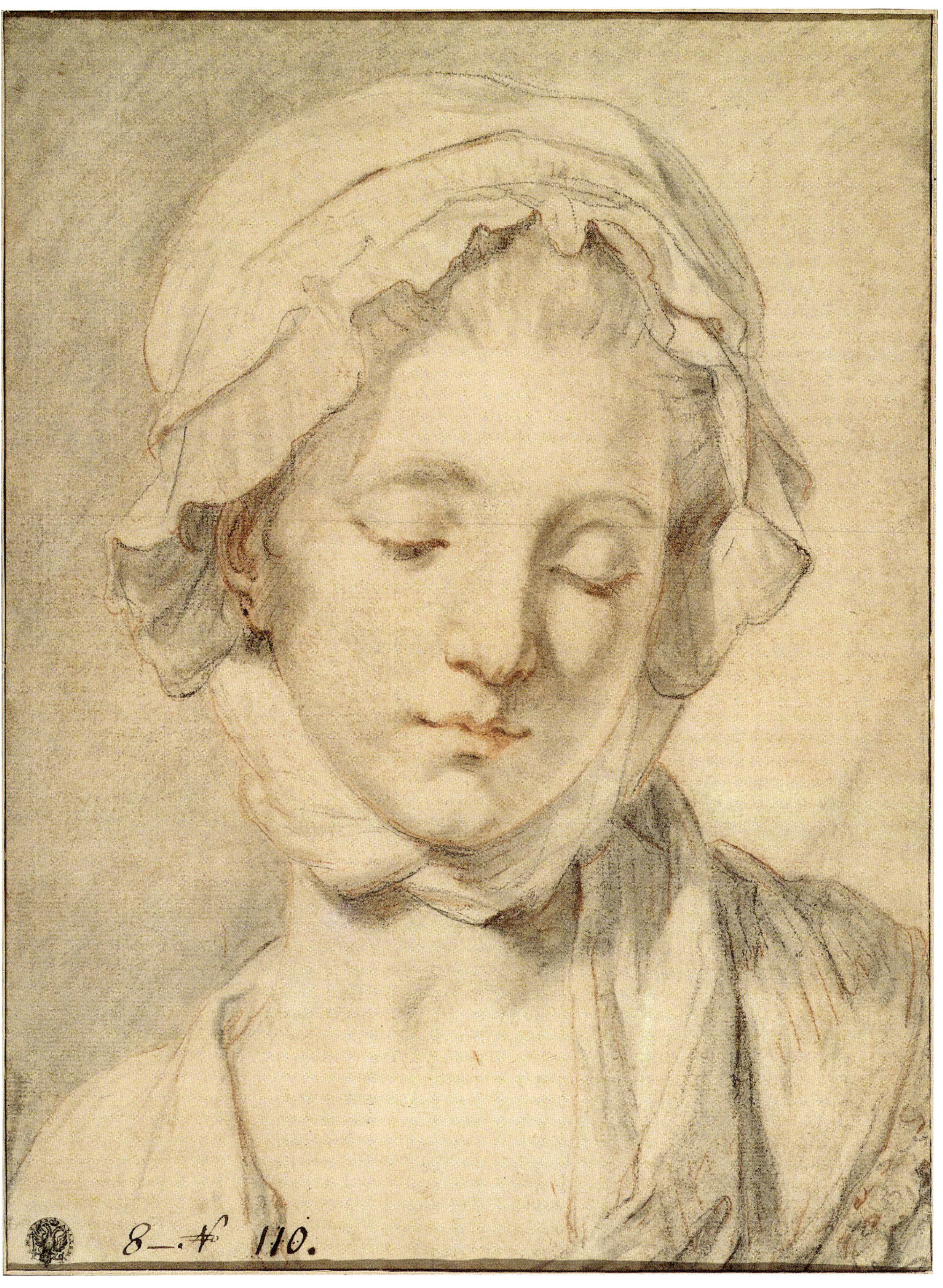
8—N° 110.

18 *Head of an Old Man, Study for "A Marriage Contract"*

Red and black chalks, stumped, over graphite on white paper, 476 × 330 mm (18 ¾ × 12 ¹⁵⁄₁₆ in.)
Inscribed on mat *Ce même monogramme est fait au crayon rouge derrière ce dessin par Greuze, donné par lui à Vien* [Joseph-Marie Vien, 1716–1809], *peintre, maître de David et depuis à Monsieur Chevin* [?] *de Troyes*[1]
New York, private collection

Provenance: according to the inscription cited above, given by Greuze to Joseph-Marie Vien; then to Monsieur Chevin (?), Troyes; or purchased from Greuze on 17 July 1761 by Johann Georg Wille; French private collection; Fabrice Faré, Paris, 1984; Alain Moatti, Paris
Exhibitions: None known
Bibliography: Paris 1984, p. 227

Before the present drawing was known, another one nearly identical to it (fig. 63) was included in the exhibition *Jean-Baptiste Greuze/1725–1805* (no. 31). Though described in the exhibition catalogue as being on white paper, it is in fact on tan paper. This crucial detail suggests that the present study for the father of the bride in *A Marriage Contract* (fig. 10) and not the version belonging to the Yale University Art Gallery was the drawing Wille purchased from Greuze on 17 July 1761 and described that day in his diary: "I have bought from M. Greuze a large head of an old man drawn in black and red chalk on white paper. It is the head of the father in *The Marriage Agreement,* a picture he is now working on. It cost me three gold louis."[2] Though the inscription on the mount of the present drawing contradicts the Wille provenance, there can be no question of its superiority over the variant, albeit an autograph, copy. Its boldness and fluidity of handling contrast with the more precise handling of the other (fig. 1).

The model appears to be the same old man who posed for *The Paralytic* (fig. 24), a painting Greuze exhibited in 1765 but for which he was already making preliminary

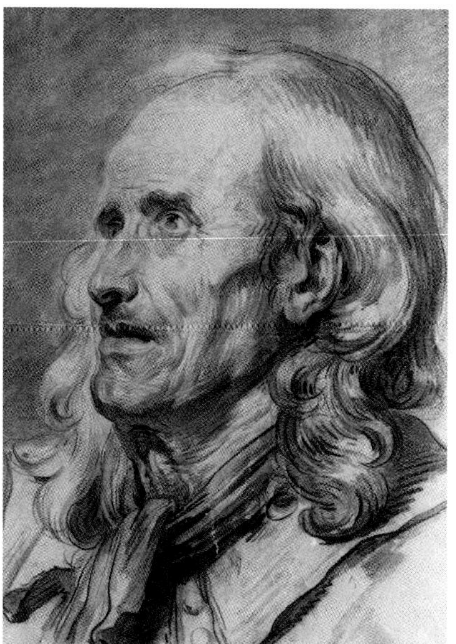

Fig. 63 Greuze, *Head of an Old Man,* 1761, red and black chalks on tan paper, New Haven, Yale University Art Gallery

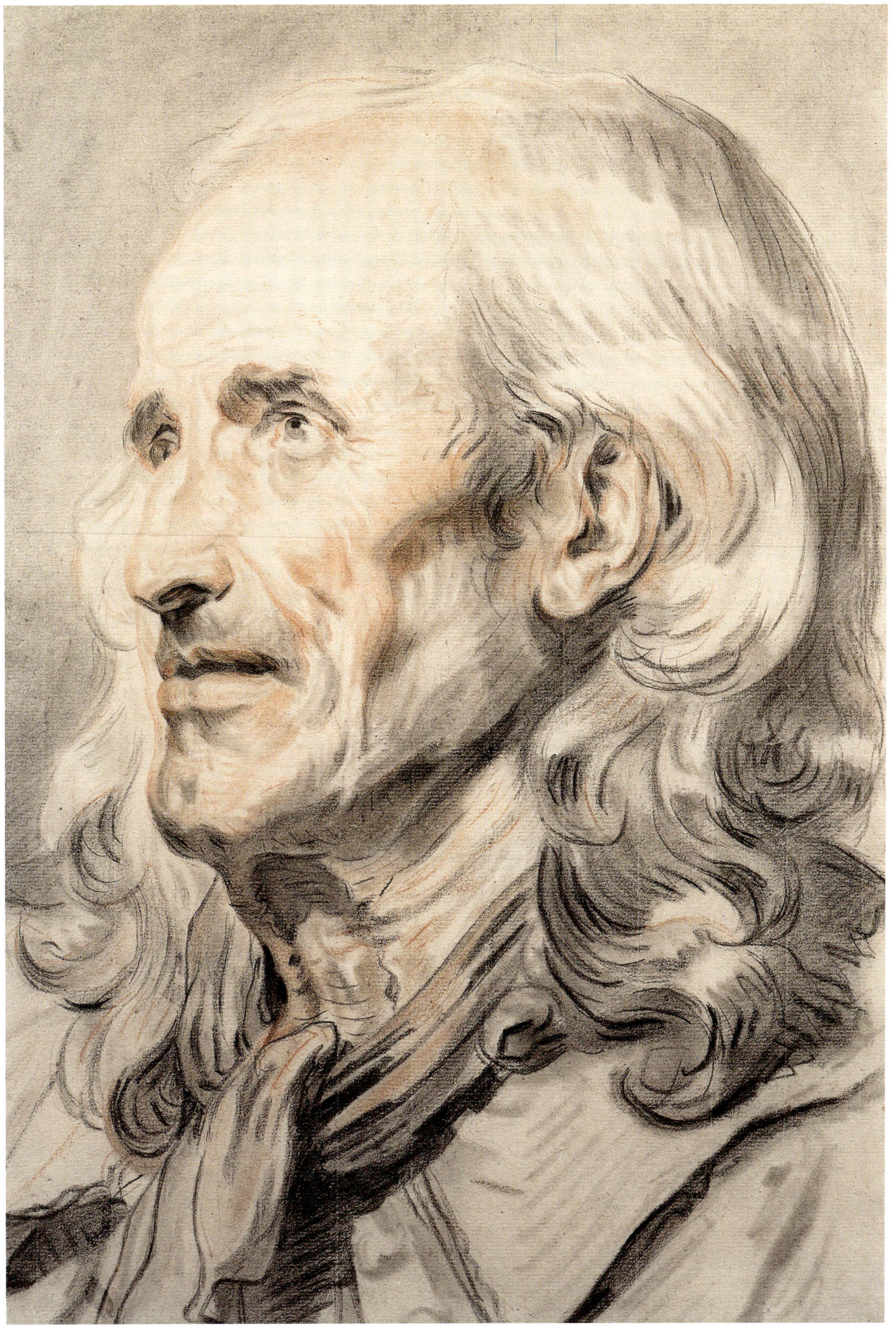

studies in 1761. In contrast to the upright posture in this drawing, in *A Marriage Contract* (fig. 64), Greuze positioned the old man's head tilted back, as though he were speaking more forcefully.

The resemblance between this figure and Greuze's own father-in-law, whose portrait (fig. 65) the artist exhibited at the same Salon as *A Marriage Contract,* is surely no coincidence. After all, this was the man who in 1759 provided his daughter with a dowry of 10,000 livres, when her future husband could offer only 4000 on his side, and who, on his death in 1769, left his life annuity to his daughter and son-in-law.[3]

In his description of *A Marriage Contract* in his *Récapitulation* of the Salon of 1761, Diderot referred to the father as "an old man of sixty years, with gray hair, a kerchief twisted around his neck; he has an air of simple good-heartedness that pleases."[4] Baron Grimm, always a bit more effusive, wrote of the same figure:

One cannot look at this old man of Greuze's without feeling tears coming to the eyes. What a good father! How surely deserving he is of the mellowness that he feels at this moment!... Certainly he must be saying to his son-in-law: My son, do not thank me for the money; it is for my daughter that you must thank me; she is more precious to me than all that I possess.[5]

1. "This same monogram was inscribed in red chalk on the back of this drawing by Greuze, given by him to Vien, painter, master of David and later to Monsieur Chevin [?] of Troyes."

2. *"J'ay acheté de M. Greuze une grande tête de vieillard dessiné sur papier blanc aux crayons noir et rouge. C'est la tête du père de l'Accord du marriage, tableau qu'il fait actuellement. Elle m'a coûté trois louis d'or."* Wille 1857, I, p. 173.

3. Wildenstein 1960, p. 231.

4. *"un vieillard de soixante ans, en cheveux gris, un mouchoir tortillé autour de son cou; il a un air de bonhomie qui plaît."* Diderot *Salons,* I, p. 142.

5. *"On ne peut regarder ce vieillard de Greuze dans se sentir venir les larmes aux yeux. Quel bon père! Qu'il est bien digne de la douceur qu'il éprouve en ce moment!... Le père lui dit certainement: Mon fils, ne me remercie pas de l'argent; c'est de ma fille qu'il faut me remercier; elle m'est bien plus chère que tout ce que je possède."* In Diderot *Salons,* I, pp. 144–45.

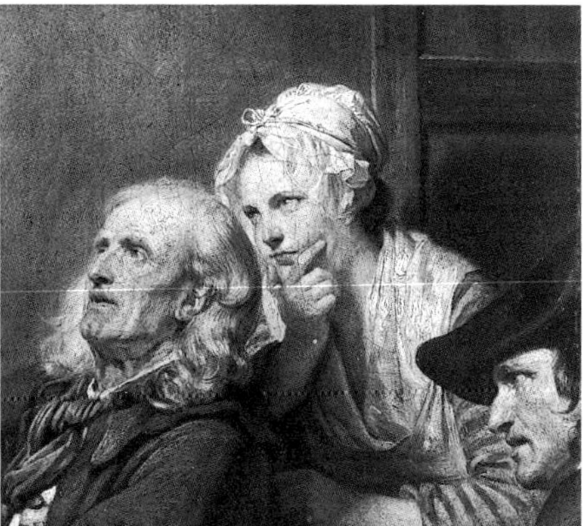

Fig. 64 Greuze, *A Marriage Contract* (detail), 1761, oil on canvas, Paris, Musée du Louvre

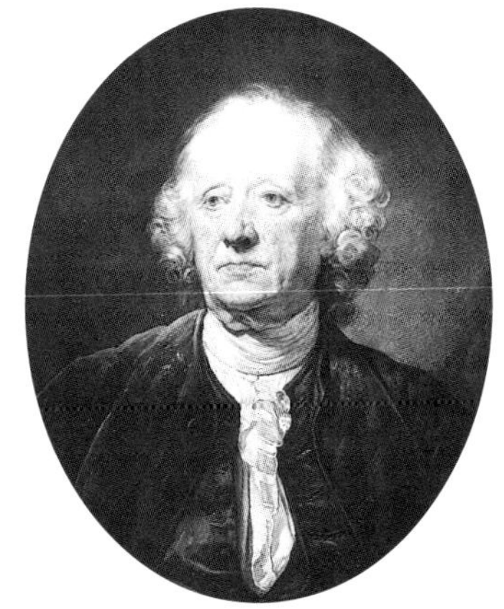

Fig. 65 Greuze, *Portrait of François Babuti,* 1761, oil on canvas, private collection

19 *The Notary*

Black chalk, with stumping, and red chalk, heightened with white chalk, on buff paper, 435 × 426 mm (17 1/8 × 16 13/16 in.)
Signed in graphite at lower right *J.B. Greuze*
The Art Institute of Chicago, Wirt D. Walker Endowment

Provenance: baronne Domitille-Louis-Mélanie de Lagny (mid-nineteenth century), and by descent until 1986; sale, Monaco, 22 February 1986, lot 47; Thos. Agnew & Sons Ltd, London; Jaime Ortiz-Patiño, Geneva; Agnew's, London, 1993; Spink-Leger Pictures, London, through 1998
Exhibitions: From Claude to Géricault, The Arts in France 1630–1830, London, Thos. Agnew & Sons Ltd, 3 June–25 July 1986, no. 28; *Agnew's 1993 Catalogue,* London, Agnew's, 2 June–30 July 1993, no. 16; *Master Drawings: 17th to 20th Century,* London, Spink-Leger Gallery, 1998, no. 6
Bibliography: Munhall 1964, pp. 8–9; Hartford *et al.* 1976–77, p. 86; Paris 1984, p. 227; Rand 1996, p. 223; S.F. McCullagh, "Drawings in The Art Institute of Chicago," *Master Drawings,* fall 2000, pp. 247, fig. 5, 248

The man depicted here is clearly the same individual who occupies the lower right corner of Greuze's *A Marriage Contract* (fig. 66), exhibited at the Salon of 1761. As all the critics noted, he represents the notary who would have prepared the documents of the civil marriage contract that in the painting he holds in his right hand and covers with his left. As the artist made clear in his title for the Salon catalogue of 1761, his picture was intended to represent "A Marriage, and the moment when the father of the betrothed hands over the dowry to his son-in-law" *("Un Mariage, et l'instant où le père de l'Accordée délivre la dot à son gendre").* Besides preparing the necessary paperwork, the notary's role was that of a witness to this civil marriage ceremony. Presumably, that is why, of all the men depicted, he alone wears a hat.

The civil marriage document so prominently depicted here and in Greuze's painting would have corresponded to the one prepared for the artist's own marriage to Anne-Gabrielle Babuti, signed and witnessed "in the home of Monsieur and Madame Babuti on the afternoon of Wednesday 31 January 1759."[1] Among other details, that document specified that Greuze, aged thirty-four, held documents proving he had obtained his parents' permission to marry, as had his future wife; that, in anticipation

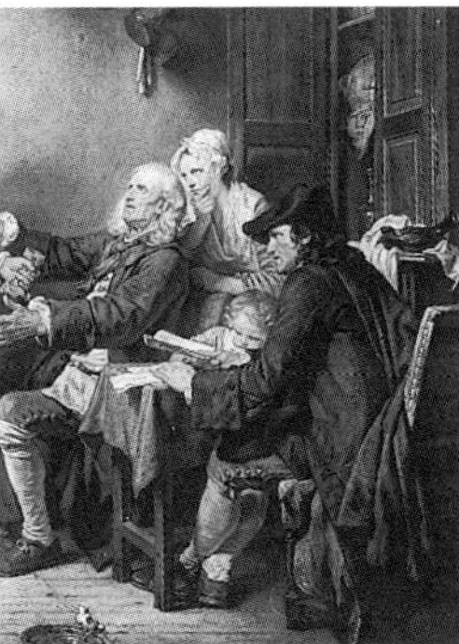

Fig. 66 Greuze, *A Marriage Contract* (detail), 1761, oil on canvas, Paris, Musée du Louvre

of the religious marriage ceremony to be celebrated "forthwith" *("incessamment")*—as it was, three days later in the Paris church of St-Médard—the two had prepared together the "treaty, agreement, and articles of marriage that follow" *("les traittés, accords et conventions de mariage").* These stipulated that the artist engaged himself to share his possessions up to a value of 4000 livres, and that the bride's parents would provide a dowry of 10,000 livres.

Most of the critics who commented on Greuze's *A Marriage Contract* at the Salon of 1761 mentioned the notary, from Diderot—"The notary is dressed in black, colored breeches and stockings, wearing a coat and judicial collar, a hat on his head. He looks like a bit of a crafty haggler, as suits a peasant of his profession; it's a beautiful figure. He listens to what the father is saying to his son-in-law"[2]—to the abbé Aubert, who composed a *conte moral* in verse inspired by the picture—"A peasant, coiffed with a flat hat/ In black coat, white stockings, rather crimson [breeches],/ In a corner holds the contract."[3]

Although the present drawing has traditionally been regarded as a preparatory study for the figure of the notary in *A Marriage Contract,* the dramatic differences in the man's posture between drawing and final painting, as well as his expression, suggest that the drawing was executed after the painting, as an independent creation. By turning the figure around to a frontal position and making both his arms expressive, as well as by depicting his mouth open as though speaking, Greuze created an image that stands by itself. Moreover, the care and bravura of the technique raise this drawing above the lowly genre of a preparatory study. It possesses the beauty and importance of those presentation drawings by Greuze that Mariette described as fetching "prodigious prices from some collectors."[4]

A red chalk study for the notary's head appeared in the Marcille sale, Paris, 4–7 March 1857, and in the Defer-Dumesnil sale, Paris, 10–12 May 1900, lot 153.

1. These details and others that follow are quoted from Greuze's marriage contract as published in Wildenstein 1960, pp. 231–32. For the interpretation of *A Marriage Contract* as depicting a civil marriage ceremony, see Munhall 1964, pp. 8–10; Paris 1984, p. 225; Rand 1996, pp. 222–23; and Barker 1997, p. 44.

2. *"Le tabellion est vêtu de noir, culotte et bas de couleur, en manteau et en rabat, le chapeau sur la tête. Il a bien l'air un peu matois et chicanier, comme il convient à un paysan de sa profession; c'est une belle figure. Il écoute ce que le père dit à son gendre."* Diderot *Salons,* I, p. 142.

3. *"Un paisan, coëffé d'un chapeau plat,/ En manteau noir, bas blancs cramoisie,/ Dans un coin dressoit le contrat."* Abbé Aubert, *L'Accordée de village,* quoted in M. Fréron, *Année littéraire,* VI, Paris 1761, p. 214.

4. *"payés prodigieusement par quelques curieux."* Mariette 1851–60, p. 331.

Facing page:
19 *The Notary*

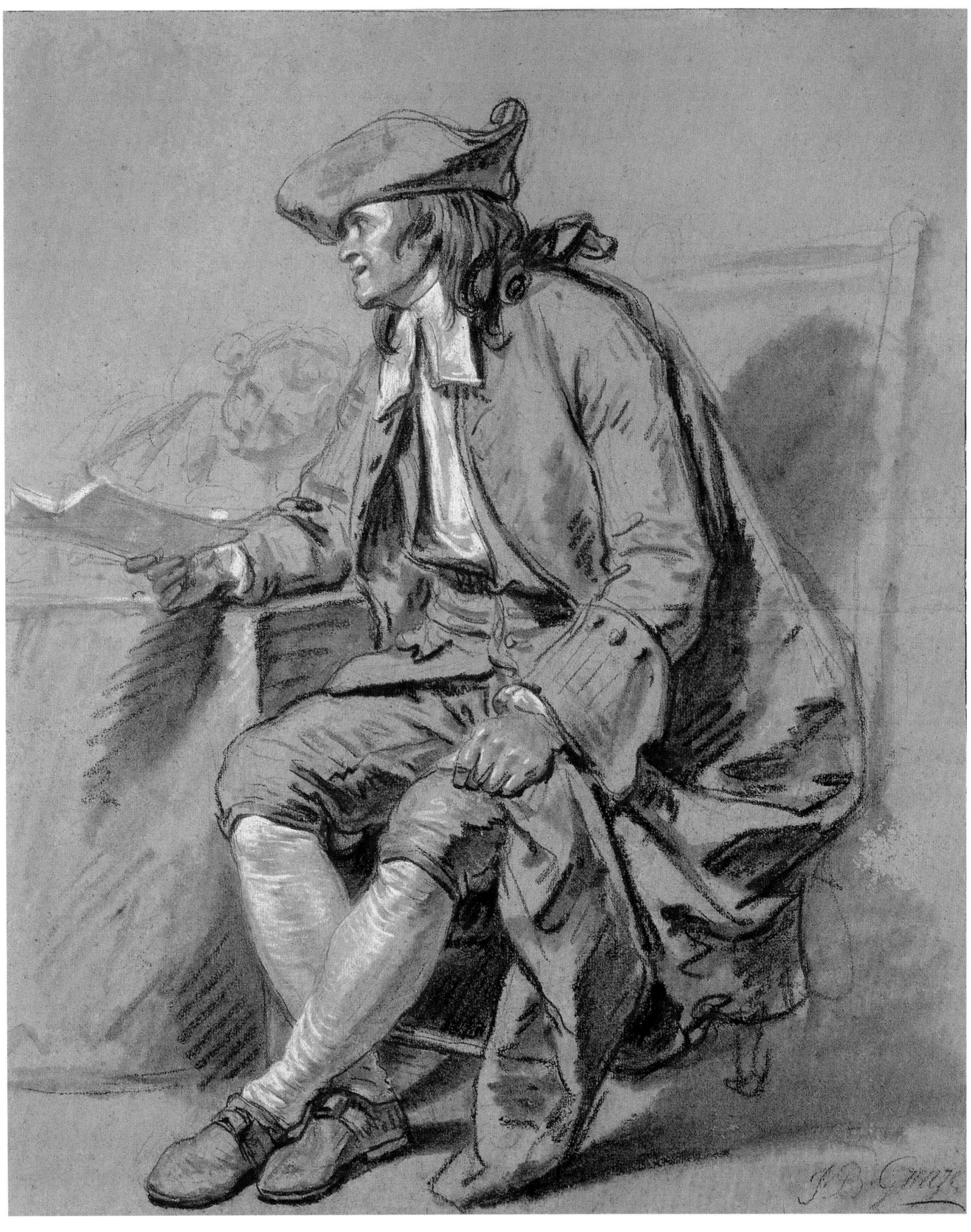

20 *The Departure of the Married Couple*

Brush and gray ink over graphite, 539 × 650 mm (21 3/16 × 25 5/8 in.)
Paris, Musée du Louvre, Département des arts graphiques

Provenance: Anne-Geneviève (Caroline) Greuze (d. 1842), Paris; her sale, Paris, 25–26 January 1843, lot 10; according to Martin and Masson (see *Bibliography*), bought in and then sold to Laperlier; his sale, Paris, 11–13 April 1867, lot 62; purchased by the Musée du Louvre in 1984
Exhibitions: None known
Bibliography: Martin and Masson 1906, no. 278; "Récentes Acquisitions des musées nationaux," *La Revue du Louvre et des Musées de France,* IV, 1984, p. 285; Rand 1996, pp. 228, 233; Barker 1997, p. 48, fig. 2

When the present drawing appeared in the sale of Caroline Greuze's collections in 1843, it was described in the sale catalogue by Théophile Thoré as "executed as an intended pendant to *L'Accordée de village.*"[1] Similarly, in the catalogue of the Laperlier sale in 1867, it was described as "The tearful village bride leaving her family."[2] These statements, of which the earlier may depend from a verbal tradition going back to Greuze himself, echoed critical notions expressed in 1763 with the exhibition of *The Paralytic* (fig. 24), to the effect that Greuze was conceiving a series of pictures that would depict the changing lives of the same *dramatis personae* who made their debut in *A Marriage Contract* (fig. 10), or even in the much earlier *Family Bible Reading* of 1755 (fig. 9). Diderot, for instance, wrote of *The Paralytic* in 1763: "all the heads in this scene are the same as those in his picture *A Marriage Contract,* and those of *A Marriage Contract* the same as those in his *Family Bible Reading.*... Agreed; but what if the painter wanted it that way? [but what if] he were following the history of the same family?"[3]

If it was indeed Greuze's intention to create a Hogarth-like sequence of family scenes, it is easy to recognize in the present composition the major players from *A Marriage Contract:* the bride, the groom, the mother of the bride, and her father, as well as assorted minor figures, minus the notary and the disappointed elder sister. Their apparent ages and physical types remain similar, though the bride has lost her youthful delicacy—quickly it would seem, if the departure is supposed to be occurring soon after the marriage. Even the ratio of proportions of this enormous sheet are in scale with those of the canvas of 1761, which measures 92 by 117 centimeters (36 1/4 × 46 1/8 in.).

Barker recognized that the present drawing corresponds in almost every detail to the "Marriage of Bazile" episode in Greuze's scenario *Bazile et Thibault:*

Bazile marries Manon Bastier. The tender farewells of Manon to her mother. The scene takes place in the presence of several village girls, her friends. Some weep, the others laugh, and each in her own manner expresses her pain or pleasure. The mother, standing near the horse on which her daughter is mounted, dressed in riding garb, holds out her hand to her and turns away her head to hide the tears that overcome her, the father seems to wish her every sort of happiness. The daughter, at this moment, grasps the hand of her father to kiss it. Bazile, on horseback near his wife, awaits impatiently the conclusion of all these good wishes.[4]

1. *"exécuté pour faire pendant à l'Accordée de village."*

2. *"L'Accordée de village quittant sa famille en larmes."*

3. *"toutes les têtes de cette scène sont les mêmes que celles de son tableau des* Fiançailles, *et celles de son* Paysan qui fait la lecture à ses enfants.... *D'accord; mais si le peintre l'a voulu ainsi? s'il a suivi l'histoire de la même famille?"* Diderot *Salons,* I, p. 236.

4. Barker 1997, p. 48: *"Bazile épouse Manon Bastier. Tendres adieux de Manon à sa mère. La scène se passe en présence de plusieurs filles du village, de ses amies. Les unes pleurent, les autres rient et chacune à sa manière exprime la peine ou le plaisir. La mère, debout près du cheval sur lequel sa fille est montée, vêtue en habit d'amazone, lui tient la main et détourne la tête pour cacher les larmes qui la suffoquent, son père lui semble souhaiter toute sorte de bonheur. La fille, dans ce moment, saisit la main de son père pour la baiser. Bazile, à cheval près de son épouse, attend avec impatience la fin de tous ces compliments."* Quoted in Brookner 1972, p. 161.

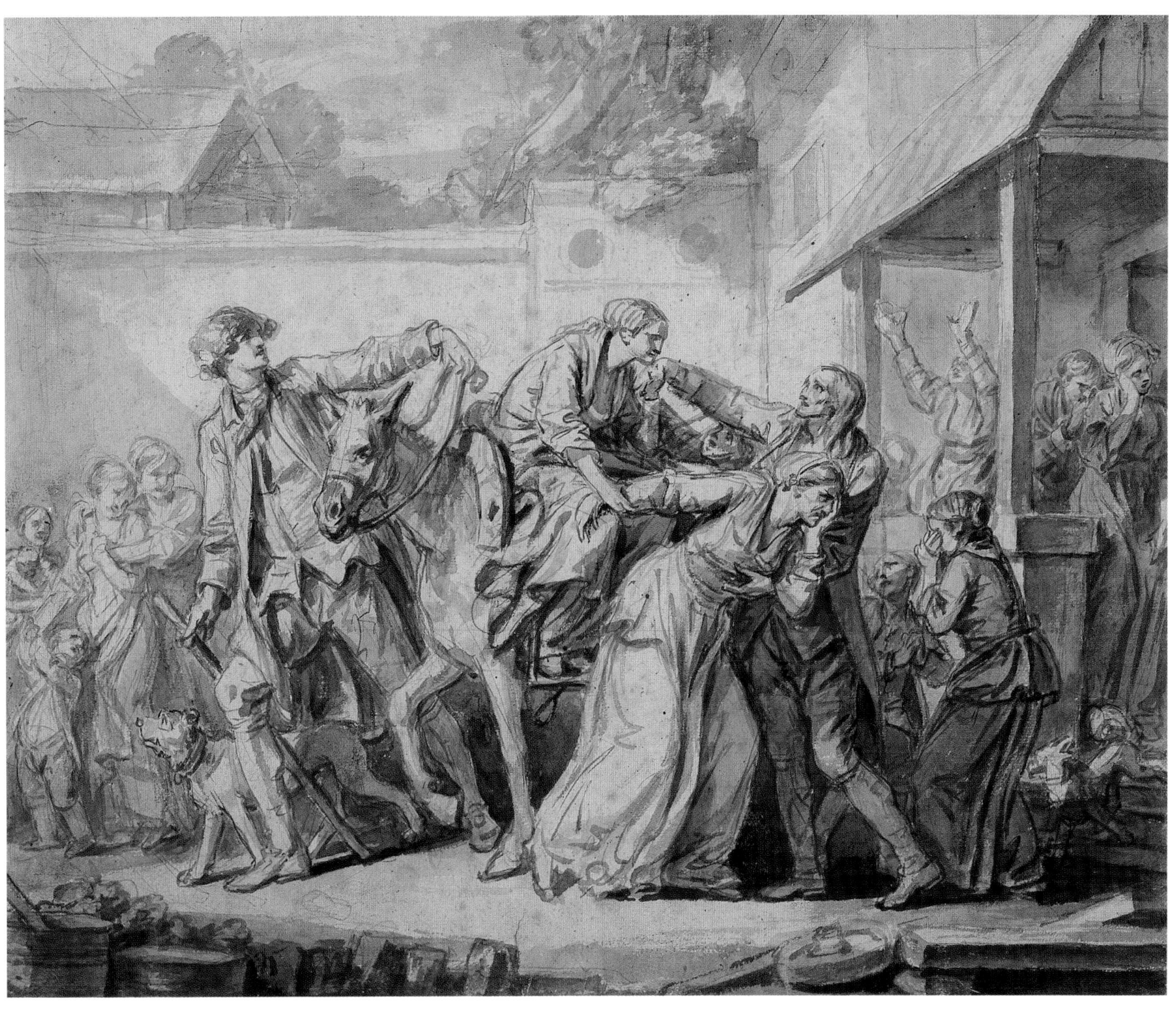

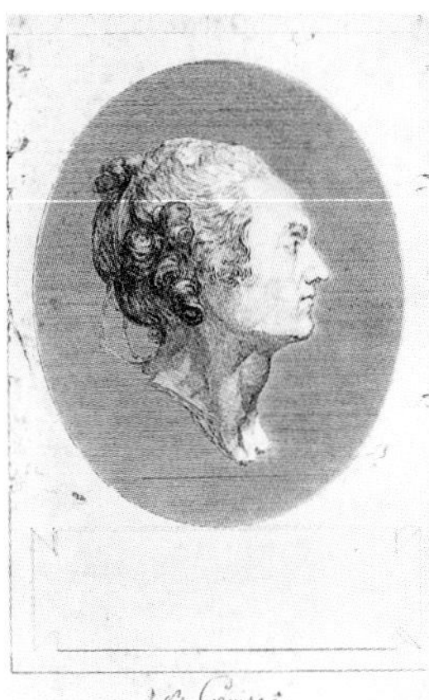

Fig. 67 J.-J. Flipart, after Greuze, *Jean-Bte. Greuze,* 1763, engraving, Paris, private collection

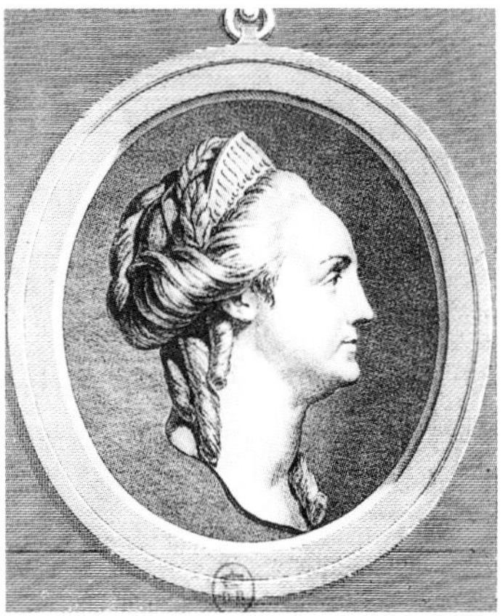

Fig. 68 C.-E. Gaucher, after Greuze, *Catherine II, Impératrice des Russies,* 1782, engraving, Paris, Bibliothèque nationale de France, Cabinet des Estampes

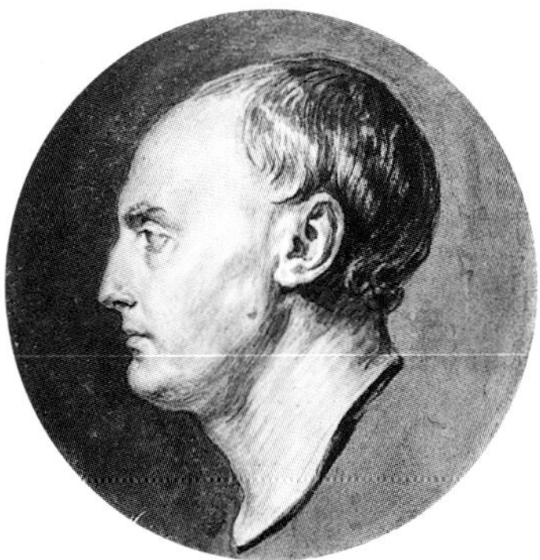

Fig. 69 Greuze, *Portrait of Sir Robert Strange,* 1760 (?), brush and gray ink wash, Edinburgh, Scottish National Portrait Gallery, on loan from the National Museum of Antiquities of Scotland

21 *Self-Portrait in Profile*

Brush and gray ink on white paper cut to oval format, 157 × 134 mm (6 3/16 × 5 3/8 in.)
Inscribed in three hands on an old label from the backing of a former frame *J. B. Greuze Peint/ Par lui-même a l'âge/ de 35 ans/ donné par Mme Trognon/ le 30 décembre 1854/ Donné par M. Henriquel-Dupont./ le 18 octobre 1887* [1]
Oxford, The Ashmolean Museum, Lent by the Visitors of the Ashmolean Museum

Provenance: Trilha, Paris; G. Duplessis, Paris; Madame Trognon, Paris, 1854; Henriquel-Dupont, Paris, 1887; A. Fauchier-Magnan, Paris; his sale, London, 4 December 1935, lot 22; P. & D. Colnaghi Ltd, London; T.H. Cobb, London; K.T. Parker, Oxford; presented by him to the museum in 1947
Exhibitions: London 1968, no. 332; Hartford *et al.* 1976–77, no. 36
Bibliography: Smith, no. 1; Martin and Masson 1906, no. 1150; Ashmolean Museum, *Annual Report,* Oxford 1947, p. 44; Bailey 2000, frontispiece

With this small drawing, Greuze recorded his appearance at the height of his career in the early 1760s. It would be the model for the best-known image of the artist: J.-J. Flipart's engraving, dated 1763, illustrated here in a rare proof stage (fig. 67).[2]

The severe classical quality of the drawing, startling for its time, links it to a number of other profile portraits by Greuze, including that of Diderot (no. 55), engraved by C.-E. Gaucher (1741–1804) in 1766; one of Catherine II (fig. 68), based on a portrait bust Houdon exhibited at the Salon of 1773, and one of the Scottish engraver Sir Robert Strange (1721–1792), engraved by the subject just before his death in 1792. Greuze's drawing of Strange (fig. 69) could well have been executed about the time of Greuze's self-portrait, for Wille mentioned in his diary receiving a visit from Strange on 22 August 1760, just as the Scotsman was setting out for Italy.[3]

In contrast to the "antique" male coiffures Greuze featured in his portraits of Diderot and Strange, his own elaborately dressed and powdered curls strike an old-fashioned note. The engraver Charles Dufresne recounted in his memoirs that Greuze's mode of dressing his hair "in the form of a pigeon wing and with spirals" had been created for him by a lover during his Roman sojourn of 1755–57; it remained his model for life.[4]

An anonymous miniature on copper reproducing this drawing belongs to the Ashmolean Museum (inv. no. 1979.48), and a copy in oil after Flipart's engraving by Jean-Daniel Heimlich (1740–1796) is in the collection of the Musée des Beaux-Arts, Strasbourg (inv. no. 1286).[5]

1. "J.B. Greuze Painted/ By himself at the age/ of 35 years/ given by Mme Trognon/ 30 December 1854/ Given by M. Henriquel-Dupont./ 18 October 1887." I am grateful to Mr J.J.L. Whiteley for photocopying and transcribing this inscription.

2. Portalis and Béraldi 1880–82, II, pt. 1, p. 201; C. Le Blanc, *Manuel de l'amateur d'estampes,* Paris [1854–89], II, p. 240, no. 17; Arsène Bonafous-Murat, *Estampes, 1490–1989,* cat., Paris, December 1989, no. 33a. I am grateful to Colin Harrison for drawing my attention to this proof of Flipart's engraving and for supplying a photograph of it.

3. Wille 1857, I, p. 142. See also Valori 1860, p. 367 n. 1; J. Denniston, *Memoirs of Sir Robert Strange,* London 1855, II, pp. 223–24; C. Ffoulk, "Sir Robert Strange, Engraver," *The Connoisseur,* XI, 1905, p. 153; D. Sutton, "Paris-Londres," *Apollo,* May 1984, p. 334.

4. Dufresne's full account is cited in Hartford *et al.* 1976–77, pp. 89, 90.

5. See *A qui ressemblons-nous? Le Portrait dans les musées de Strasbourg,* exhib. cat., Strasbourg, Musée des Beaux-Arts, 1988, no. 153.

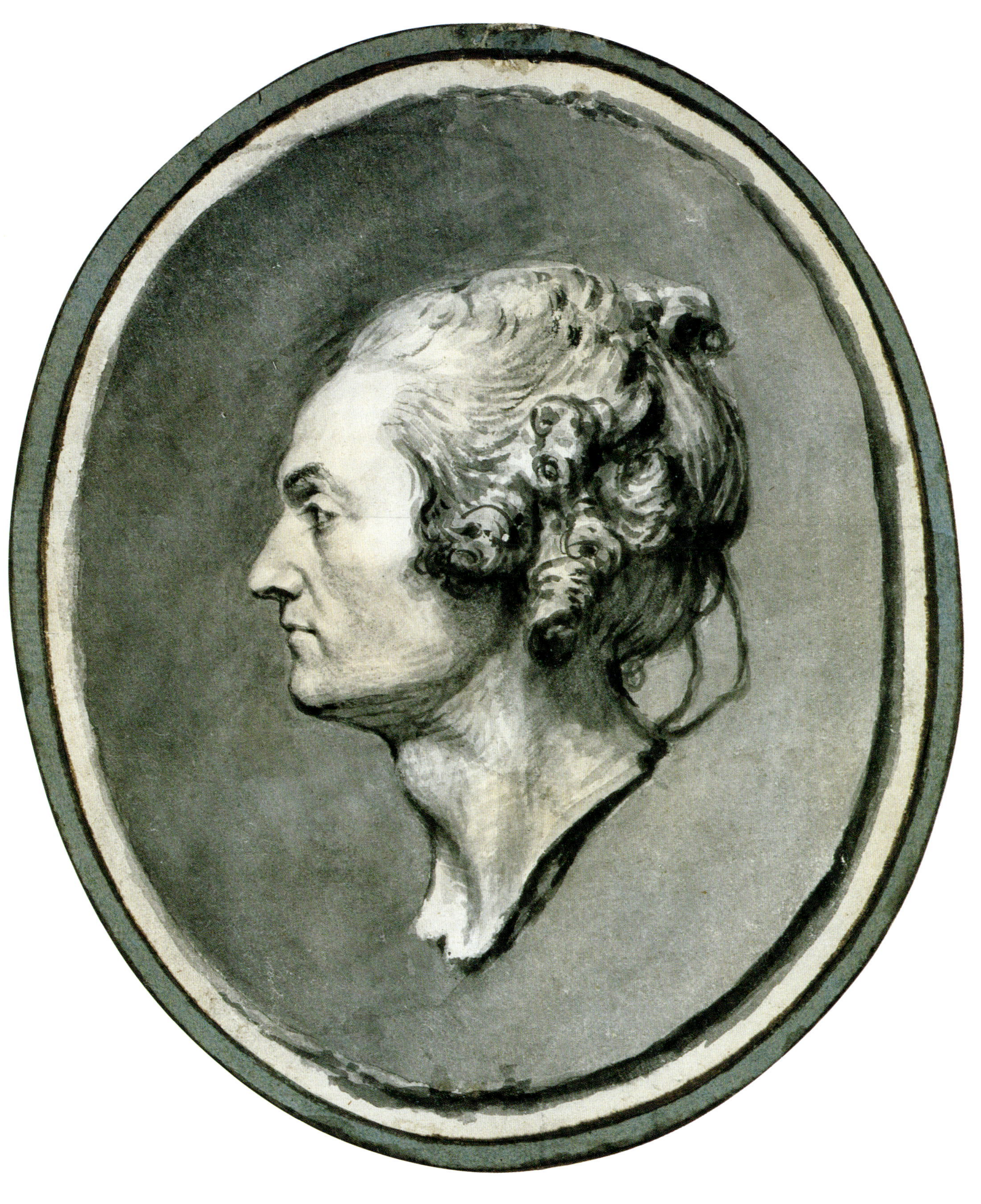

22 *Presumed Portrait of Louis-Philippe, duc d'Orléans*

Red and black chalks, stumped, over graphite on white paper, 519 × 326 mm (20 7/16 × 12 7/8 in.)
Paris, Musée du Louvre, Département des arts graphiques

Provenance: Paignon-Dijonval, Paris (d. 1792); his grandson, vicomte Charles-Gilbert Morel de Vindé, Paris; Samuel Woodburn, London, 1816; Pierre Defer, Paris; purchased from him by the museum in 1842

Exhibitions: London 1932, no. 828; *Le Dessin français dans les collections du XVIIIe siècle,* Paris, Gazette des Beaux-Arts, 1935, no. 312; *Exposition du costume,* Paris, Palais Galliéra, 1937; *La Révolution française,* Paris, Musée Carnavalet, 1939; *Les Goncourt et leur temps,* Paris, Musée des Arts Décoratifs, 1946, no. 385; *French Drawings: Masterpieces from Seven Centuries,* The Art Institute of Chicago *et al.*, 1955, no. 70; *Pastels et miniatures des XVIIe et XVIIIe siècles,* Paris, Musée du Louvre, Cabinet des Dessins, 1963; Hartford *et al.* 1976–77, no. 38

Bibliography: M. Bénard, *Cabinet de M. Paignon-Dijonval,* Paris 1810, no. 3691; Reiset 1866–69, no. 769; Goncourt 1880, pp. 346–47; Martin and Masson 1906, no. 1268; Guiffrey and Marcel 1911, no. 4568; Bouchot-Saupique 1939, no. 13, pl. VII; D. Sutton, *French Drawings of the XVIII Century,* London 1949, p. 42; M. Levey, review of *Jean-Baptiste Greuze/1725–1805, Master Drawings,* XV, no. 3, autumn 1977, p. 281; E. Launay, *Les Frères Goncourt, collectionneurs de dessins,* Paris 1991, p. 167 n. 514

The traditional identification of this superb sheet, one of Greuze's rare full-length portrait drawings, as representing Louis-Philippe, duc d'Orléans (1725–1785), father of Louis-Philippe-Joseph, known as Philippe Égalité, goes back to Théodore Reiset's catalogue of 1866. But he titled the drawing simply *Portrait of a Standing Man* and suggested an identification of the subject only hesitantly: "it is thought to represent the duc d'Orléans."[1] Earlier, M. Bénard's 1810 catalogue of the Paignon-Dijonval collection provided no name for the subject, describing it merely as a "portrait of a man."[2] While the Goncourt brothers admired the drawing sufficiently for Jules to reproduce it as an etching,[3] Edmond expressed a strong disbelief in the traditional identification, writing in *L'Art du dix-huitième siècle:* "Among the drawn portraits [by Greuze] there is in the Louvre a very important drawing in red and black chalks, stumped, of a standing man leaning on a cane and which passes as representing the duc d'Orléans, father of Philippe Égalité!"[4]

The present author proposed in 1976 that this drawing might depict instead Charles-Claude de Flahaut de la Billarderie, comte d'Angiviller, on the basis of its

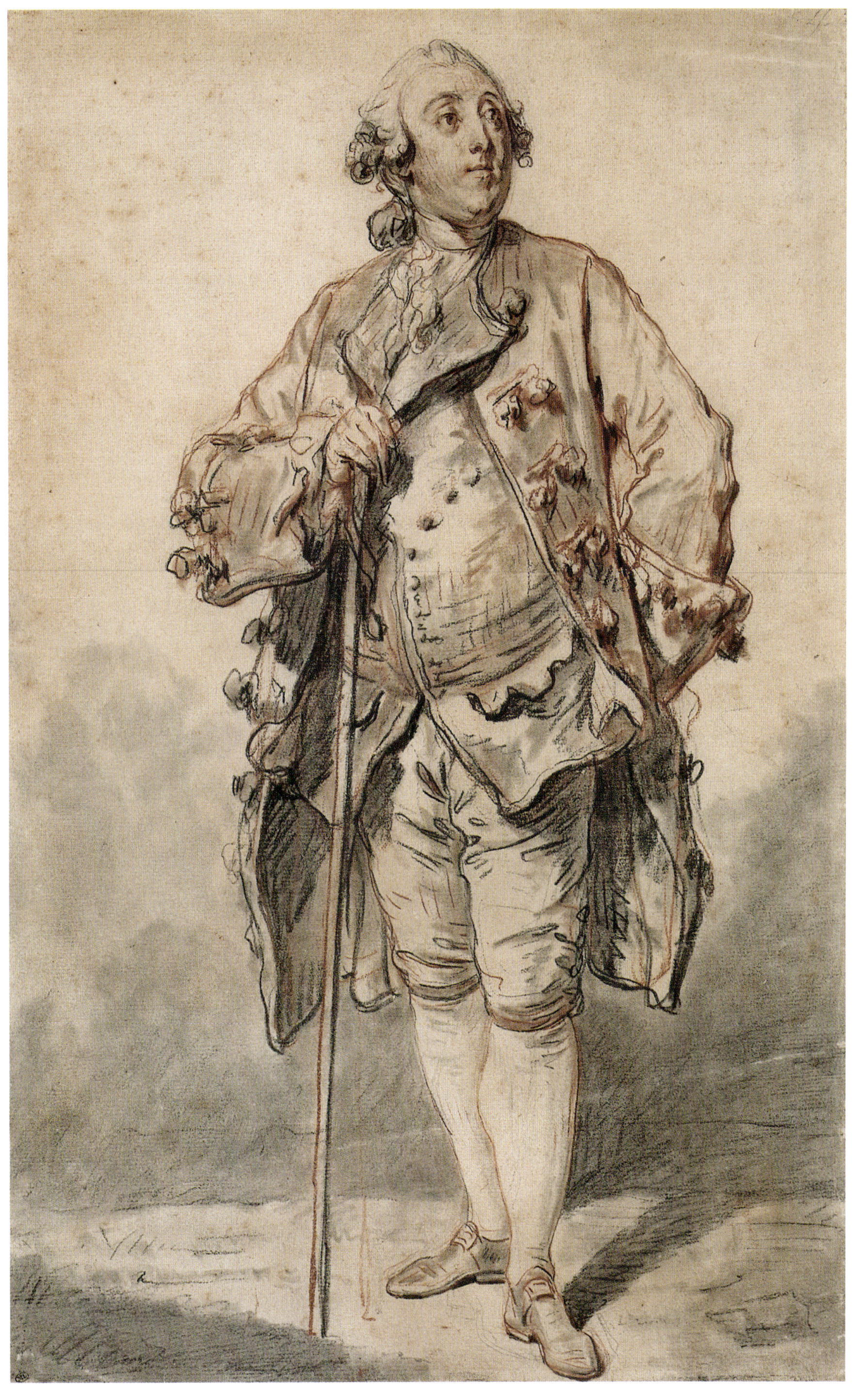

resemblance to the portrait of the latter in the Metropolitan Museum of Art (fig. 70), both physically and in terms of dress.[5] Furthermore, although no evidence exists of any contact Greuze might have had with the duc d'Orléans, there are many indications of d'Angiviller's supportive interest in the artist's career once the former assumed the role of *surintendant des bâtiments du roi* in 1774, culminating in his purchase of *A Marriage Contract* for the king in 1782.

At the time Greuze might have executed this portrait drawing—about 1763—d'Angiviller held the post of *gentilhomme de la maison des enfants de France,* supervising the education of the children of the Dauphin Louis, whose portrait Greuze painted in 1761.[6]

In addition, d'Angiviller's wife, Élisabeth-Josèphe, was the daughter of Jean-François de Laborde, for whose brother Greuze was painting *The Beloved Mother* (fig. 14) and numerous family portraits (see no. 70) at the same time as he was executing the portrait on canvas of d'Angiviller, exhibited at the Salon of 1763. Although d'Angiviller did not marry Élisabeth-Josèphe until 1781, the two had commenced a liaison twenty years earlier.[7]

1. *"Portrait en pied d'homme debout. On croit y reconnaître le duc d'Orléans."* Reiset 1866–69.

2. *"portrait d'homme."* Bénard 1810.

3. Goncourt 1880, p. 347 n. 1.

4. *"Parmi les portraits dessinés figure au Louvre un très important dessin aux crayons noir et rouge et à l'estompe, d'un homme debout appuyé sur une canne, et qui passe pour le duc d'Orléans, père de Philippe Égalité!"* Goncourt 1880, pp. 346–47.

5. Hartford *et al.* 1976–77, no. 38. The suggestion was accepted by at least one critic—Sir Michael Levey, writing in *Master Drawings,* xv, no. 3, autumn 1977, p. 281.

6. This portrait strongly resembles the one Greuze painted of d'Angiviller. See Bailey 2000, fig. 13.

7. See H. Stein, "Angiviller (Charles-Claude de La Billarderie, comte d')," and R. d'Amat, "Angiviller (Élisabeth-Josèphe de La Borde, baronne de Marchais, puis comtesse d')," *Dictionnaire de Biographie française,* Paris 1936, II, pp. 1130–34.

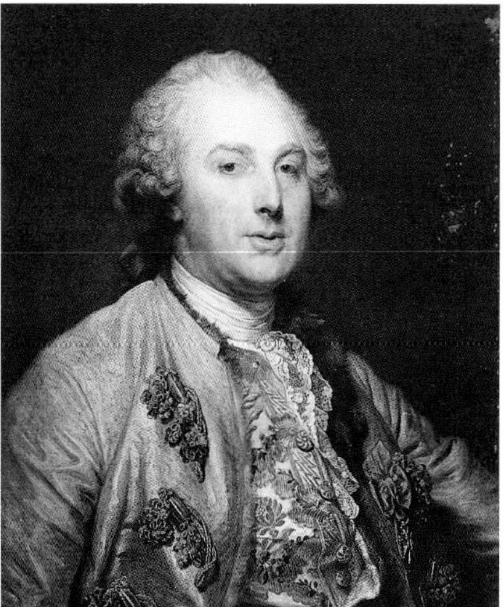

Fig. 70 Greuze, *Portrait of Charles-Claude de Flahaut de la Billarderie, comte d'Angiviller,* 1763, oil on canvas, New York, The Metropolitan Museum of Art, Gift of Edith C. Blum *(et al.),* Executors, in memory of Mr. and Mrs. Albert Blum

23 *Compositional Study for "The Paralytic"*

Brush with gray and brown ink wash, heightened with white, on tan paper, 522 × 640 mm (20 5/16 × 25 3/16 in.)
Paris, Musée du Louvre, Département des arts graphiques

Provenance: sale, Paris, 16 March 1977, purchased by the Musée du Louvre
Exhibitions: None known
Bibliography: Acquisitions du Cabinet des Dessins 1973–1983, exhib. cat., Paris, Musée du Louvre, 1984, p. 124; Paris 1984, p. 236; Paris 1986–87, p. 203

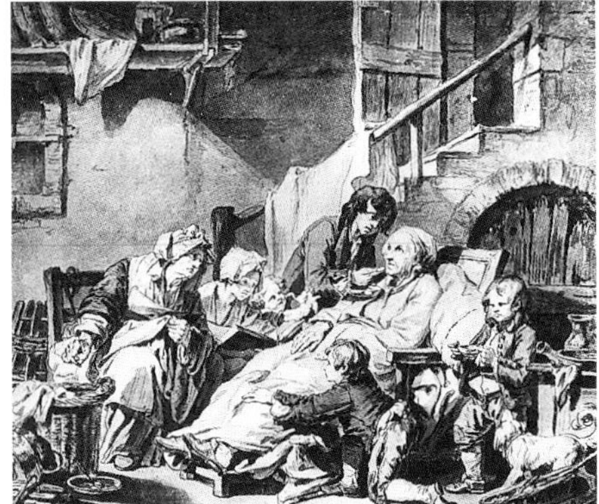

Fig. 71 Greuze, *Compositional Study for "The Paralytic,"* 1760 (?), brush with gray and brown ink on white paper, Le Havre, Musée des Beaux-Arts

Though the early history of this drawing is not documented, it is possible that it was the work Greuze exhibited at the Salon of 1761 as "Another Drawing of a Paralytic cared for by his family, or the fruit of a good education."[1] The only other surviving compositional study for the painting to be called *Filial Piety,* which Greuze exhibited in 1763 (fig. 24), appears to be earlier than this one, sketchier in style, and lacking the crucial dramatic distinction of including three generations of the same family (fig. 71).[2] Diderot praised the drawing shown in 1761 mostly for its moralizing subject: "a picture with moral principles in which one can see that this genre will produce compositions capable of bringing honor to the talents and feelings of the artist,"[3] but he also singled out the expressive heads with enthusiasm: "His head [that of the old man], his son's, and that of his wife are of a rare beauty."[4] Writing of the finished painting in 1763, he could as well have been speaking of this apparently final preparatory composition: "The number of characters assembled in a rather small space is quite large; however, they are there without confusion, because this master excels especially at coordinating his scenes."[5]

In contrast to the painting shown in 1763, the most striking differences in this drawing are the servant at the far right and the different breed of dog.

Greuze's choice of subject was a daring one, in terms of possible sales: the paralyzed victim of a stroke being cared for by his family. Viewing the drawing shown in 1761, Baron Grimm opined that a man suffering from the gout would have been less painful to look at, arguing that at least he would have been capable of smiling.[6] Two years later, commenting on the trouble Greuze was having selling his painting, Mariette wrote that not only was the asking price excessively high, but that the subject was frankly "depressing" and unlikely to appeal to rich collectors.[7] It took a patron of the grandeur of Catherine II to settle the matter; she purchased the picture in 1766.

The abbé de la Garde, one of many critics prone to see Greuze conceiving dramatic suites of subjects, wrote that *The Paralytic* might one day be part of a "complete treatise of family morals."[8] In defense of those who saw a reappearance in *The Paralytic* of the family who composed *A Marriage Contract* (fig. 10), it must be noted that the placement of the major figures is remarkably similar in both pictures, as are such details as the form of the staircase and banister.

When Diderot wrote in 1767 that Greuze "broods for whole months over the composition of a single painting and sometime takes a year to execute it,"[9] he was probably thinking of *The Paralytic* and of the great number of preparatory studies of all kinds that Greuze produced during its evolution (see nos. 24–26, fig. 23).

1. *"Autre Dessein d'un Paralytique soigné par sa famille, ou le fruit de la bonne éducation."* Diderot *Salons,* I, p. 98, no. 105. For the fullest discussion of the history and meaning of the work later entitled *Filial Piety,* see Paris 1984, pp. 230–37.

2. In addition to these compositional studies, one appeared in the Vaudreuil sale, Paris, 26 November 1787, described as signed, and on white paper, and another in the Revil sale, Paris, 24–29 February 1845, lot 30, described as heightened in gouache, signed and dated 1760, and including eight figures.

3. *"un tableau de moeurs où l'on voit que ce genre fournira des compositions capables de faire honneur aux talents et aux sentiments de l'artiste."* Diderot *Salons,* I, p. 135.

4. *"Sa tête, celle de son fils, et celle de sa femme sont d'une beauté rare."* Diderot *Salons,* I, p. 135.

5. *"Le nombre des personnages rassemblés dans un assez petit espace est fort grand; cependant ils y sont sans confusion, car ce maître excelle surtout à ordonner sa scène."* Diderot *Salons,* I, p. 234.

6. In Diderot *Salons,* I, p. 146.

7. *"triste."* Mariette 1851–60, II, p. 330.

8. *"un Traité complet de la morale domestique."* Abbé Philippe Bridard de la Garde, *Observations d'une Société d'amateurs sur les tableaux exposés au Salon cette année 1761,* Paris 1761, p. 53.

9. *"couve pendant des mois entiers la composition d'un seul* [*tableau*], *et met quelque fois un an à l'exécuter!"* Diderot *Salons,* III, p. 113.

Facing page:
23 *Compositional Study for "The Paralytic"*

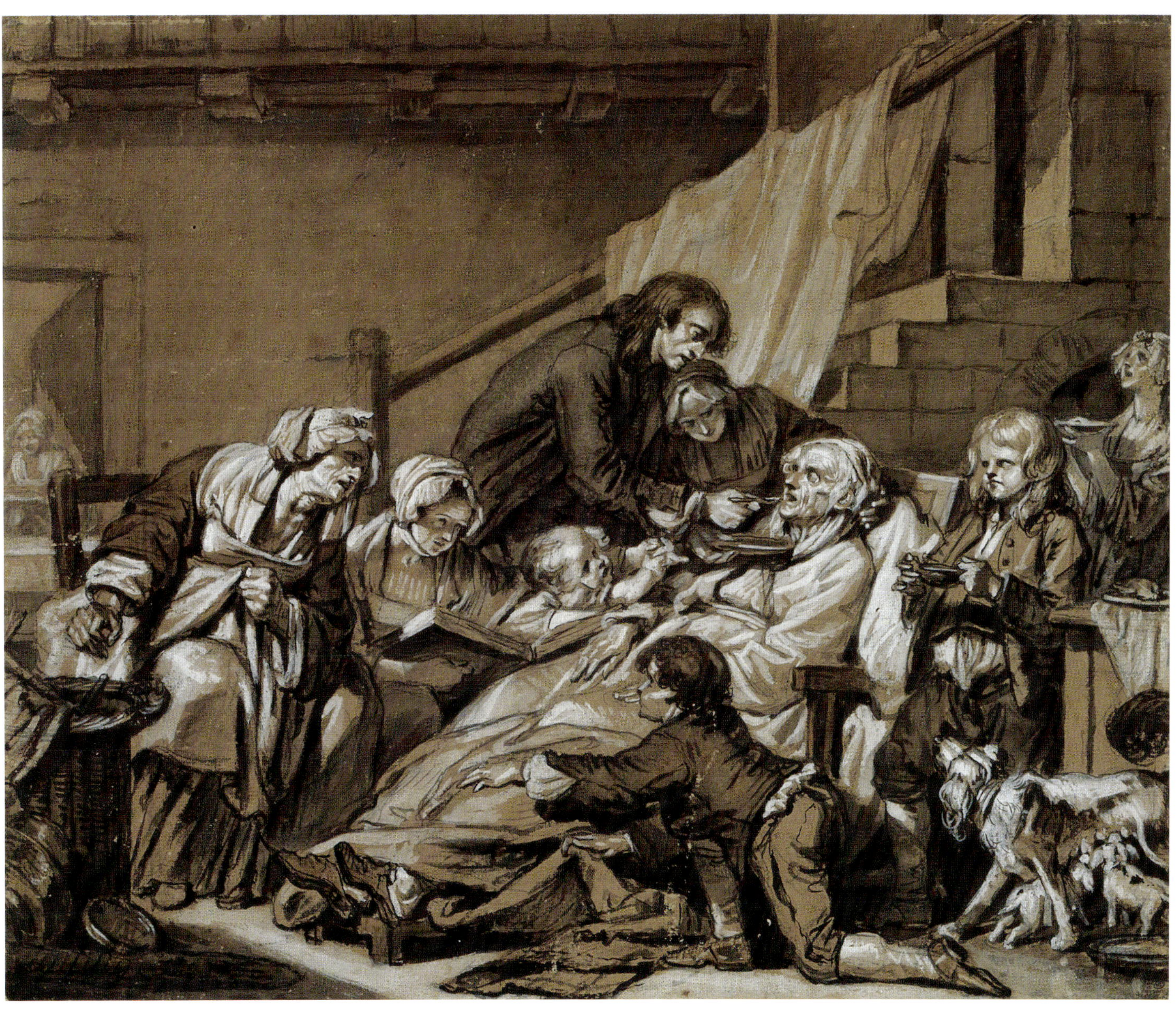

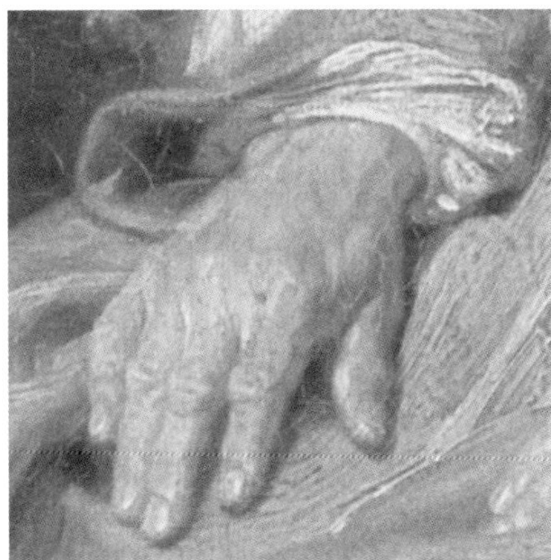

Fig. 72 Greuze, *The Paralytic* (detail), 1763, oil on canvas, St Petersburg, The State Hermitage Museum

24 *A Man's Right Hand, Study for "The Paralytic"*

Red chalk on white paper, 305 × 440 mm (12 × 17 3/8 in.)
Inscribed in pen and black ink at lower left *8-No 119.;* inscribed in pen and brown ink on verso of old mount *Etude du Paralytique*
St Petersburg, The State Hermitage Museum

Provenance: Ivan Ivanovitch Betskoy, St Petersburg; Imperial Academy of Fine Arts, St Petersburg, 1769 (Lugt S. 2699a); transferred to the Hermitage in 1924
Exhibitions: Leningrad 1977, no. 65; Copenhagen 2000, no. 9, fig. 14
Bibliography: Monod and Hautecoeur 1922, no. 5; Paris 1984, p. 237; Novosselskaya 1987, p. 7; Fischer *et al.* 2000, pp. 48–49, fig. 16

Just below the center of Greuze's intricately composed *Paralytic* lies the extended right hand of the subject, isolated and still amid the action taking place around it (figs. 24, 72). Its stasis is almost more effective dramatically than the calculated expressiveness of the old man's face looking up at his caregiver, and possibly contributed to Diderot's reaction to the subject when he viewed the painting at the Salon of 1763: "When I see that eloquent and pathetic old man, I feel . . . my soul affected and tears about to flow from my eyes."[1]

Particularly for a draftsman like Greuze (see frontispiece), a hand was more than just a useful appendage of the body, particularly this weathered, old example, hanging limply from the arm of the stroke victim who is the subject of *The Paralytic.* Greuze focused attention on it to remind his viewers that this was a hand that had labored, had prayed, had caressed loved ones, had held children, had petted dogs. The attention Greuze devoted to hands in general (see no. 50, figs. 21, 22) and the skill with which he drew them suggest the importance he attached to them as expressive elements secondary only to faces and gestures in conveying the meaning of his dramatic scenes.

Because of its reversed viewpoint, the present sheet cannot be considered a precise model for the right hand of the subject of *The Paralytic,* but it was in all likelihood drawn by Greuze during one of the many posing sessions that preceded the execution of that painting.

Farther along in his discussion of it mentioned above, Diderot said: "And then this man draws like an angel. . . . He has spirit and sensibility . . . he makes endless studies."[2] The latter remark is particularly apt in the case of *The Paralytic,* which Catherine II purchased in 1766, for Greuze selected no fewer than sixteen studies for that work to follow it to St Petersburg with the drawings he sold to Ivan Betskoy shortly thereafter. These included two further depictions of an old man's hand.[3]
In 1765 Baron Grimm had noted that such studies for *The Paralytic* had cost the artist 200 louis, presumably for models and materials.[4]

1. *"Lorsque je vis ce vieillard éloquent et pathétique, je sentis . . . mon âme s'attendrir et des pleurs prêts à tomber de mes yeux."* Diderot *Salons,* I, p. 233.

2. *"Et puis cet homme dessine comme un ange. . . . Il a de l'esprit et de la sensibilité. . . . il fait des études sans fin."* Diderot *Salons,* I, p. 236.

3. Monod and Hautecoeur 1922, nos. 3, 4. Another pair of drawings of hands by Greuze, in red chalk, one described as being a study for *The Paralytic,* appeared at the Paul Defer sale, Paris, 28–29 January 1861, lot 367.

4. *"ce tableau . . . lui a coûté 200 louis en études."* Grimm in Diderot *Salons,* II, p. 149.

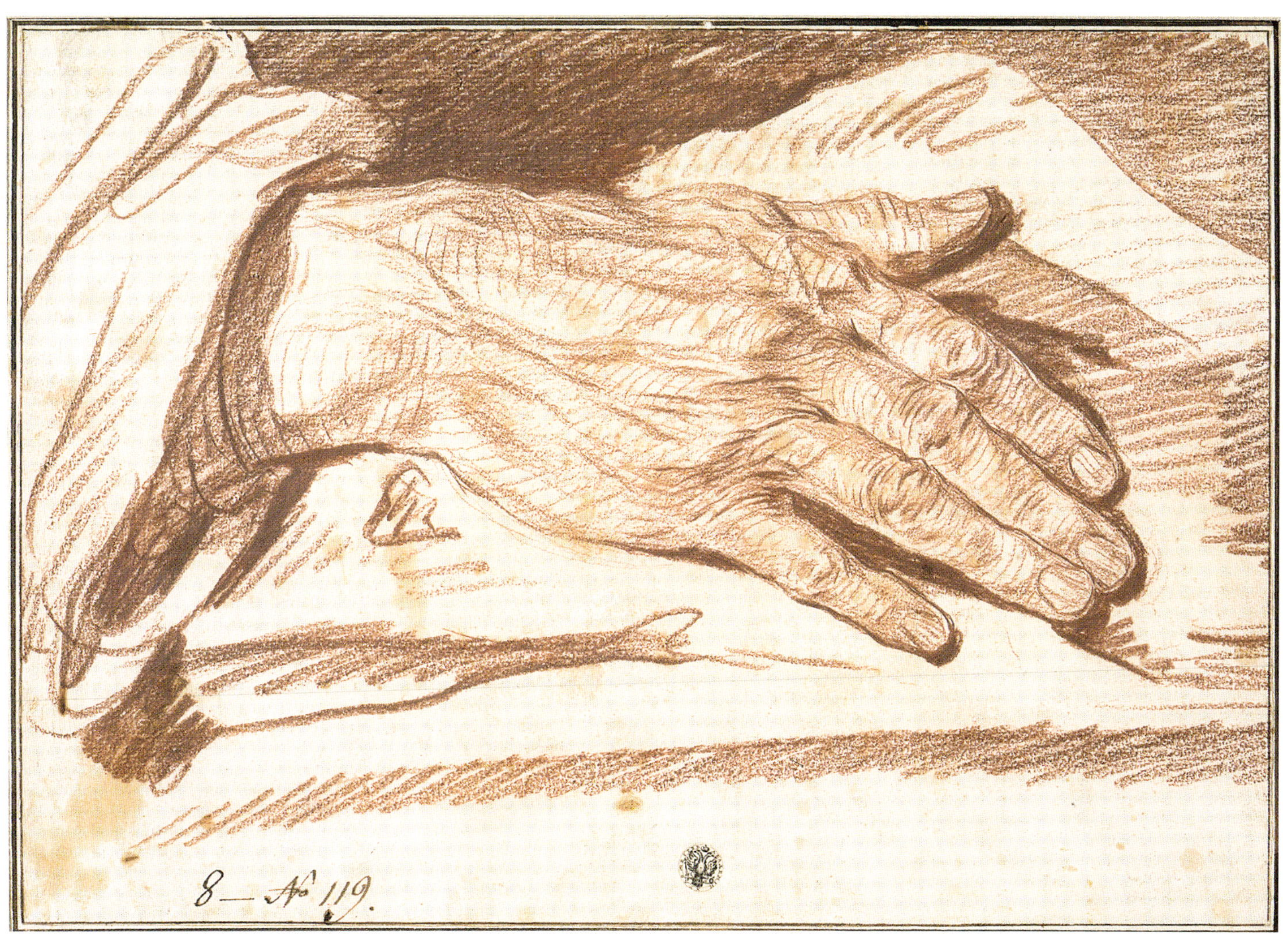
8— № 119.

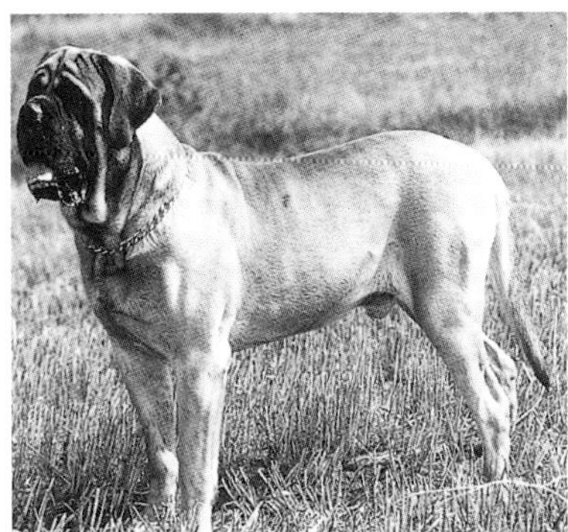

Fig. 73 A Mastiff

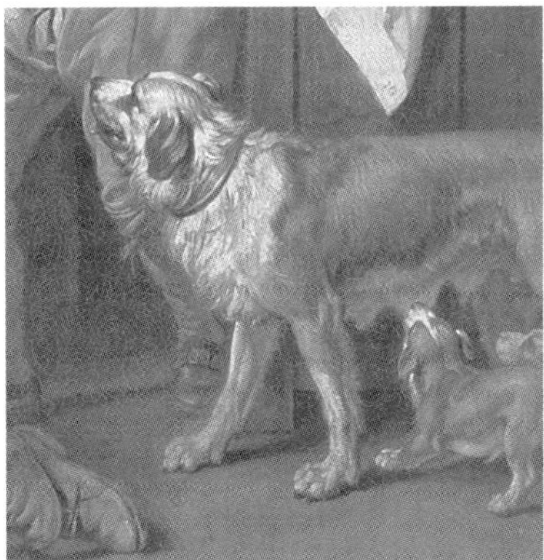

Fig. 74 Greuze, *The Paralytic* (detail), 1763, oil on canvas, St Petersburg, The State Hermitage Museum

25 *A Dog Facing Left, Study for "The Paralytic"*

Red and black chalks on cream paper, 328 × 453 mm (12 15/16 × 17 3/16 in.)
Inscribed in pen and black ink at lower left *9 81.;* in pen and brown ink on verso of old mount *Etude du Paralytique*
St Petersburg, The State Hermitage Museum

Provenance: Ivan Ivanovitch Betskoy, St Petersburg; Imperial Academy of Fine Arts, St Petersburg, 1769 (Lugt S. 2699a); transferred to the Hermitage in 1924
Exhibitions: St Petersburg 1903, no. 18; Prague 1972, no. 45; Manchester 1974, no. 37; *Tegninger fra det Statslige Eremitage-Museum og det Statslige Russiske Museum i Leningrad,* Aarhus, Aarhus Kunstmuseum; Copenhagen, Thorvaldsens Museum, 1975, no. 31; Leningrad 1977, no. 64; *Hermitage and Tretiakov. Master Drawings and Watercolors,* Melbourne, National Gallery of Victoria; Sydney, Art Gallery of New South Wales, 1978–79, no. 22; Paris 1986–87, no. 324; Leningrad and Moscow 1987, no. 388; Karlsruhe 1996, no. 71; Copenhagen 2000, no. 10
Bibliography: Monod and Hautecoeur 1922, no. 18; Kamenskaya 1934, p. 93; Novosselskaya 1987, p. 6

Dogs often appear in Greuze's pictures (see figs. 9, 13, 17, 19, 24, 40), but this study of a mastiff bitch—the lioness of the canine world (fig. 73)—is probably his most memorable creation in that field. In Diderot's discussion of *The Paralytic,* for which this is a study for the dog at lower right (fig. 74), the critic singled out the inclusion of that animal as an inspired "accessory" *("accessoire")* to the composition: "In this one *[The Paralytic],* he has placed next to the boy bringing his infirm father something to drink a large bitch standing up with her nose in the air and suckling the puppies at her feet."[1] A little farther along, he returned to this detail: "I'm in raptures over that bitch suckling its pups."[2] It seemed to Diderot an inspired detail because it underlined the meaning of this picture that he would have preferred to entitle *The Rewards of a Good Upbringing (De la récompense de la bonne éducation donnée)*—as opposed to Greuze's *Filial Piety (La Piété filiale).* In other words, just as a dog instinctively nurtures her pups, so parents feed and train their children (and, if fortunate, are later rewarded by receiving their care in return).

The obscure Latin poem that the critic of the *Affiches de Paris* cited in 1763 as Greuze's inspiration for *The Paralytic*—Marco Girolamo Vida's *Parentum manibus*—stressed this idea of reciprocal care exchanged by two generations of a family, as a son addressed these regrets to his deceased parents: "your old age would not have caused me any trouble, and the inconveniences inseparable from that stage of life would not have diminished my affection, nor inspired any distaste . . . by my affectionate cares, you would have enjoyed only pleasures."[3]

Thus, Greuze employed his sharp-eyed, realistic study of an animal toward a symbolic end, just as he did in the case of the old man's hand discussed with number 24.

1. *"Dans celui-ci, il a placé à côté du garçon qui apporte à boire à son père infirme une grosse chienne debout qui a le nez en l'air, et que ses petits tettent toute droite."* Diderot *Salons,* 1, p. 236.

2. *"Cette chienne qui ses petits tettent me transporte."* Diderot *Salons,* 1, p. 238.

3. *"votre vieillesse ne m'aurait point causé d'ennuis, et les incommodités inséparables de cet âge ne pouvaient porter atteinte à mon affection, ni m'inspirer de dégoût . . . par mes soins affectueux, vous n'auriez goûté que des douceurs."* M.G. Vida, *Les Vers à soie, poème de Jérôme Vida de Crémone,* trans. J.B. Levée, Paris 1809, p. 194. See Paris 1984, p. 235.

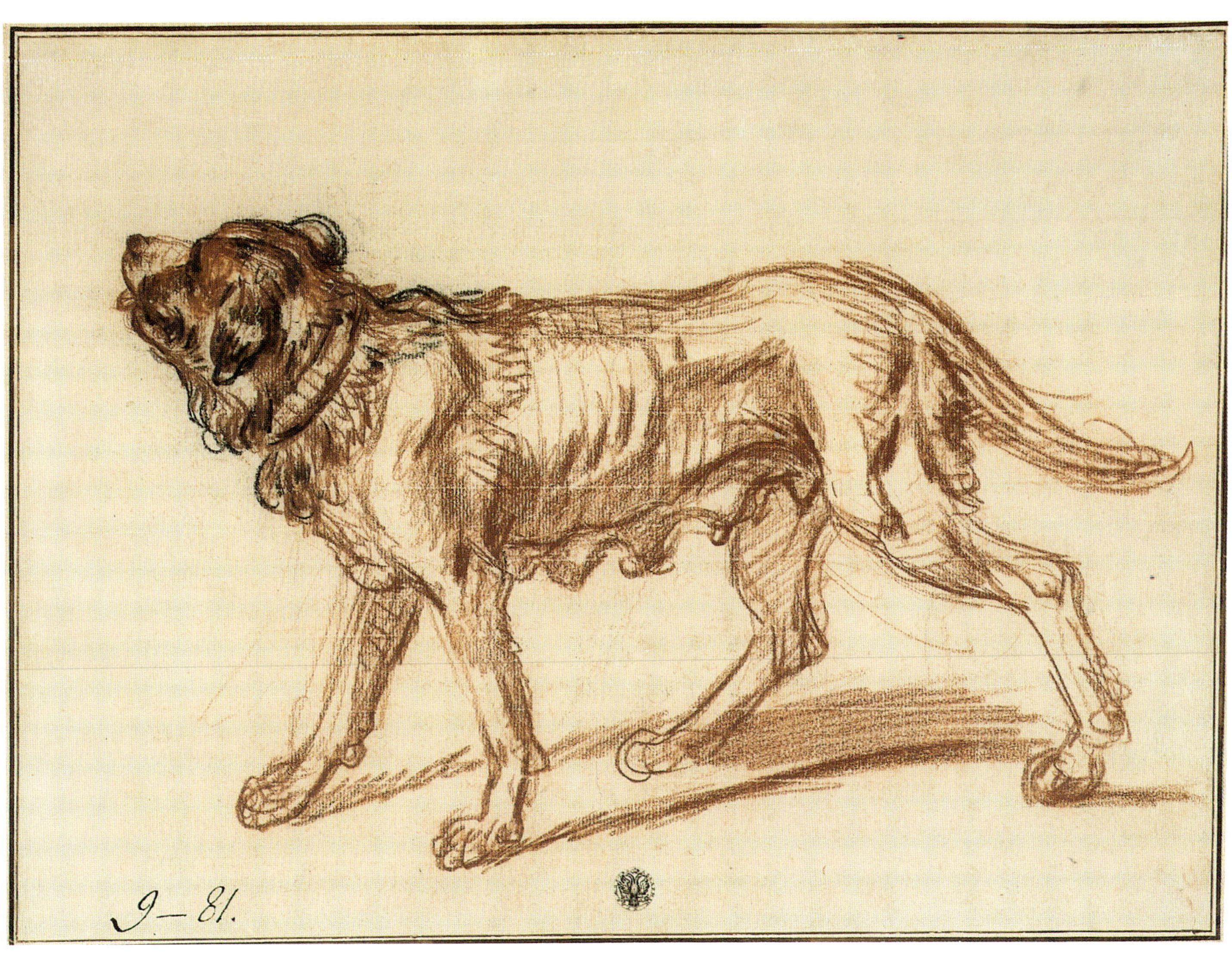
9– 81.

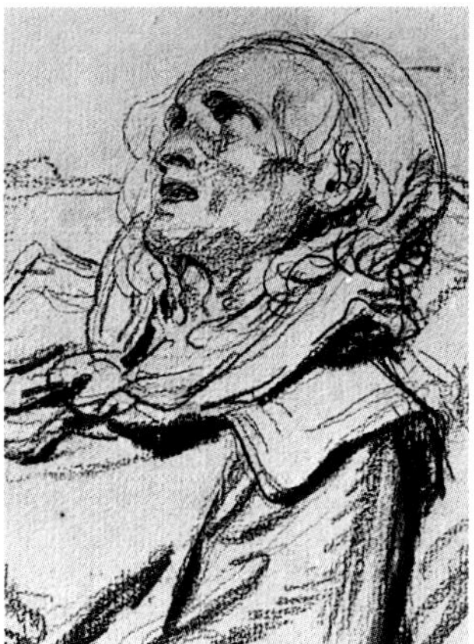

Fig. 75 Greuze, *The Paralytic* (detail), 1761 (?), red chalk on white paper, Wijhe, The Netherlands, Stichting Hannema-de Stuers Fundatie

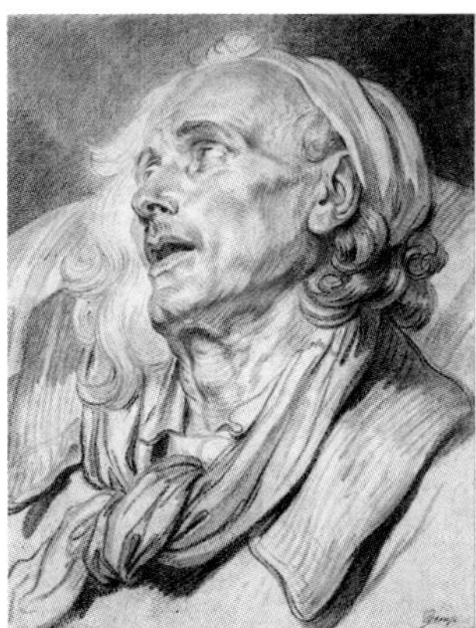

Fig. 76 Greuze, *Bust of an Old Man*, 1763, red and black chalks on white paper, Copenhagen, Den Kongelige Kobberstiksamling, Statens Museum for Kunst

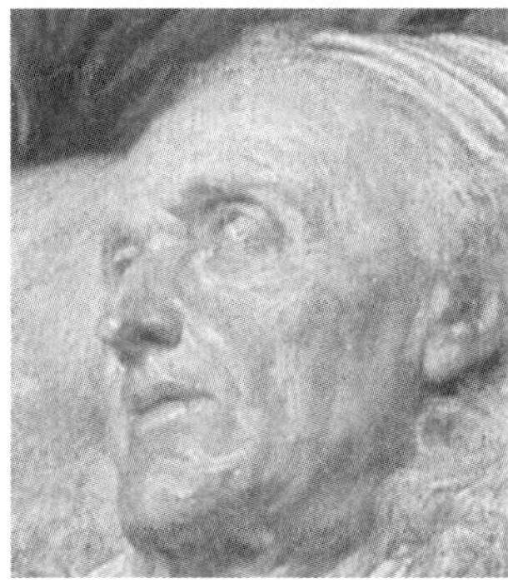

Fig. 77 Greuze, *The Paralytic* (detail), 1763, oil on canvas, St Petersburg, The State Hermitage Museum

26 *Bust of an Old Man*

Red, black, and white chalks with stumping, wetting, and erasure on light brown paper, 466 × 376 mm (18 3/8 × 14 13/16 in.)
The Woodner Family Collection

Provenance: Destouches, Paris; his sale, Paris, 5 March 1847, lot 48; Mahérault, Paris; his sale, Paris, 27–29 May 1880, lot 102; Charles Brück; his sale, Paris, 2 February 1917, lot 59; David David-Weill, Neuilly, 1952; Wildenstein and Co., Inc., New York; Cranbrook Academy of Art, Bloomfield Hills MI; sale, London, 13 July 1972, lot 13; Woodner Collections (Shipley Corporation)
Exhibitions: French Pastels and Drawings from Clouet to Matisse, New York, Wildenstein and Co., Inc., 1944, no. 45; *Old Master Drawings from the 15th to the 18th Century,* New York, William H. Schab Gallery *et al.*, 1973–74, no. 110; *Master Drawings from American Collections,* Los Angeles County Museum of Art, 1976, no. 158; *Master Drawings from the Woodner Collection,* Malibu CA, J. Paul Getty Museum *et al.*, 1983–85, no. 58; *Die Sammlung Ian Woodner,* Vienna, Graphische Sammlung Albertina *et al.*, 1986, no. 98; *Master Drawings: The Woodner Collection,* London, The Royal Academy of Arts, 1987, no. 81; *Woodner Collection: Master Drawings,* New York, The Metropolitan Museum of Art, 1990, no. 102; *The Touch of the Artist: Master Drawings from the Woodner Collections,* Washington D.C., National Gallery of Art, 1995–96, no. 89
Bibliography: G. Henriot, *Collection David-Weill,* Paris 1928, III, pp. 213–14; Hartford *et al.* 1976–77, p. 80; Fischer *et al.* 2000, p. 20, fig. 5

Like numbers 19, 32, and 84, this life-size bust of an old man was conceived probably as an independent presentation drawing after a major painting—in this case, *The Paralytic* (fig. 24)—rather than as a study for it. Indeed, the appearance of the old man in the actual preparatory drawings (figs. 23, 75, 76) and in the final painting (fig. 77) is harrowing, as Greuze depicted a stroke victim with unsparing realism: paralyzed, with a sagging, open mouth; speechless with fear, his hair matted with sweat. Greuze's intent to move his viewers with this spectacle of human suffering evidently worked, as Diderot wrote of the paralyzed man in the painting shown in 1763: "His beautiful head is of a character so touching; he appears so responsive to the care being offered him; it is so hard for him to speak, his voice is so weak, his expression so tender, his complexion so pale, that you would have no bowels of mercy not to feel them moved."[1]

The subject of the present drawing instead radiates a sense of beatific resignation and is positively *soigné* in his appearance. As Greuze removed himself here from the grim reality of his preparatory studies, he could allow himself to indulge in a bravura demonstration of his drawing capabilities, achieving effortlessly those qualities a knowing connoisseur would appreciate.

1. *"Sa belle tête est d'un caractère si touchant; il paraît si sensible aux services qu'on lui rend; il a tant de peine à parler, sa voix est si faible, ses regards si tendres, son teint si pâle, qu'il faut être sans entrailles pour ne les pas sentir remuer."* Diderot *Salons,* I, p. 234.

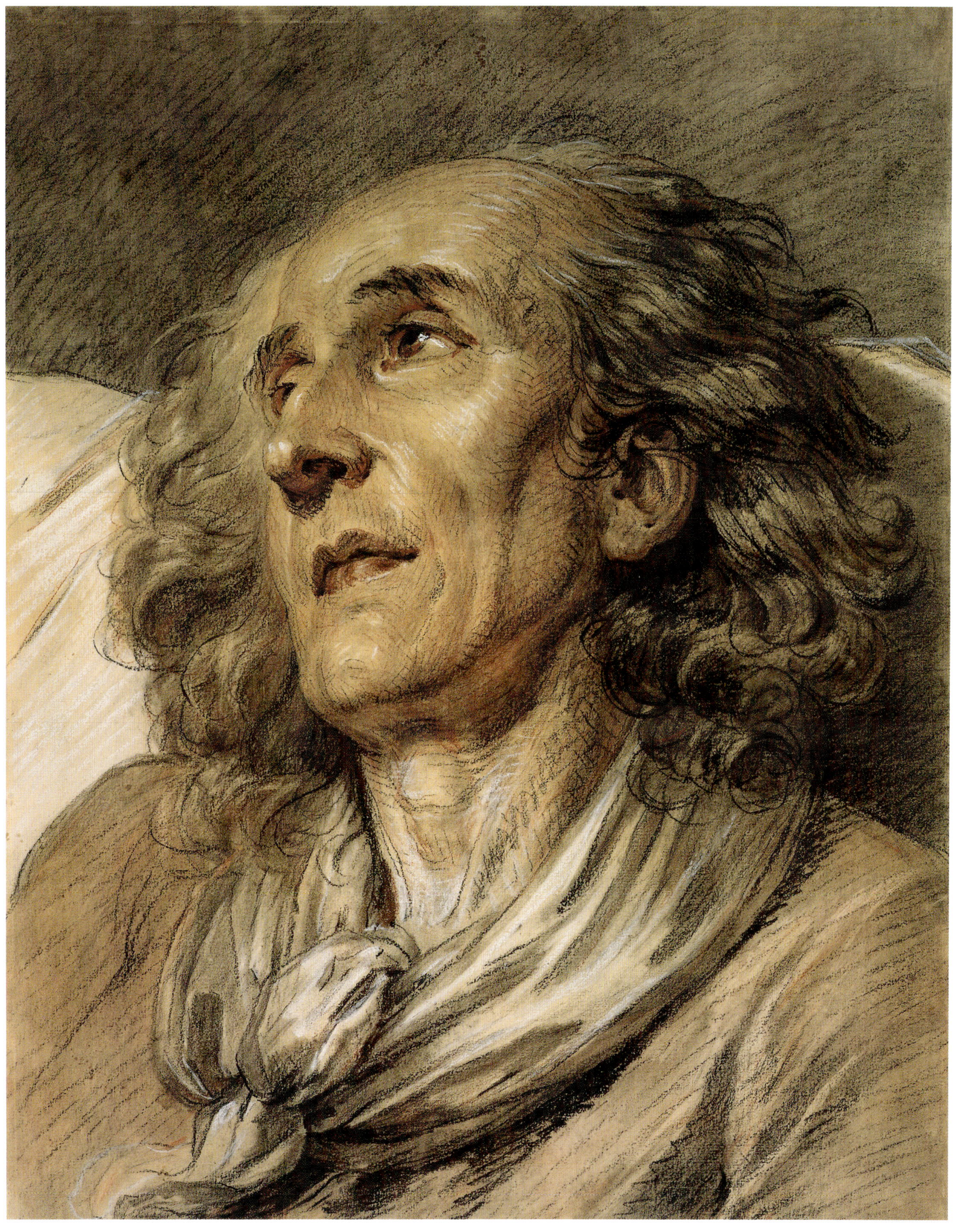

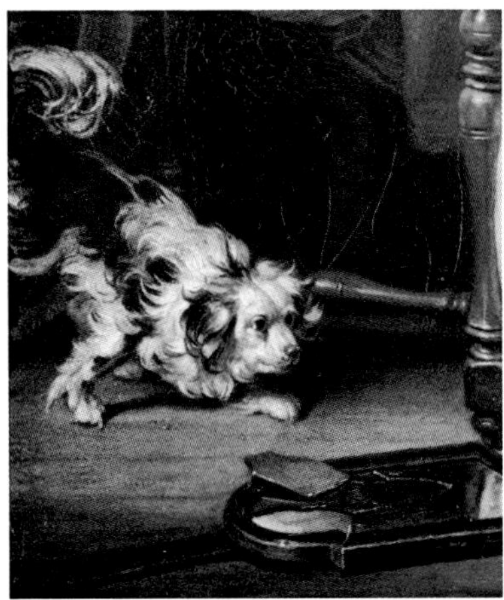

Fig. 78 Greuze, *The Broken Mirror* (detail), 1763, oil on canvas, London, The Wallace Collection

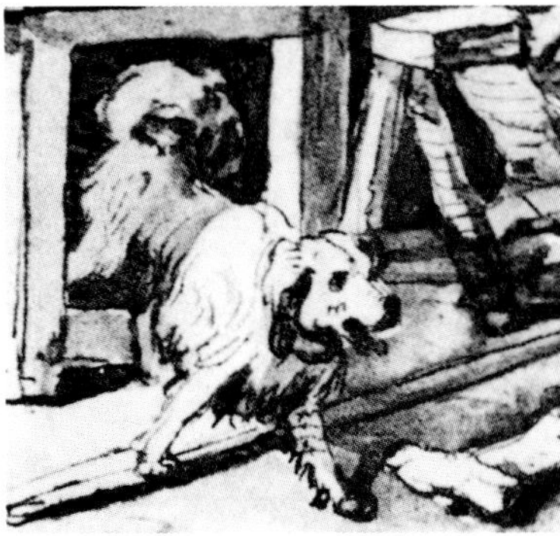

Fig. 79 Greuze, *Italians Playing Morra* (detail), 1756, pen and brush with gray and brown ink wash on white paper, Moscow, The Pushkin State Museum of Fine Arts

27 *A Dog Running to the Right, Study for "The Broken Mirror"*

Red, black, and white chalks, stumped, on blue paper, 211 × 269 mm (8 5/16 × 10 9/16 in.)
Inscribed in pen and black ink at lower left *9-82*.
St Petersburg, The State Hermitage Museum

Provenance: Ivan Ivanovitch Betskoy, St Petersburg; Imperial Academy of Fine Arts, St Petersburg, 1769 (Lugt S. 2699a); transferred to the Hermitage in 1924
Exhibition: Leningrad 1977, no. 56
Bibliography: Monod and Hautecoeur 1922, no. 19

In Greuze's *The Broken Mirror* (fig. 83), a brilliant pastiche of Terborch, a cavalier King Charles spaniel is depicted rushing in to inspect the mirror his mistress has just broken (fig. 78). Employing the *trois crayons* medium on blue paper, a relative rarity for him, the artist captured the speed and weightlessness of the dog through short, curling strokes of the chalks and soft stumping—in contrast to his sculpturesque rendering in red chalk of the muscular mastiff in number 25.

According to superstition, breaking a mirror is a serious matter, portending death or bad luck, traditionally, for seven years.[1] The young woman's grief would therefore seem justified (mirrors were also expensive), but crafty Diderot suspected Greuze here of playing with a *double entendre,* similar to the one he noted in the case of the *Girl Weeping over Her Dead Bird* of 1765 (see no. 11):

Greuze already painted the same subject once before; he set by a cracked mirror a large young lady in white satin, overcome with a profound melancholy. Don't you think there would be as much absurdity in attributing the tears of the girl in this Salon to the loss of her bird, as the melancholy of the girl from the preceding Salon to her broken mirror? That child is weeping over something else, I tell you.[2]

As John Ingamells pointed out, this encoded message in Greuze's *The Broken Mirror* may owe something to William Hogarth's (1697–1764) print of 1736 entitled *After,* in which a broken mirror lying on the floor is part of the general disorder that accompanied that young lady's fall from grace.[3]

Greuze had introduced a dog in a similar pose, but of a less elegant breed, into a drawing signed and dated *J.B. Greuze à Rome 1756: Italians Playing Morra,* exhibited at the Salon of 1757 (fig. 79).

1. See I. Opie and M. Tatem (eds.), *A Dictionary of Superstitions,* Oxford and New York 1989, pp. 249–50.

2. *"Greuze a dejà peint une fois le même sujet; il a placé devant une glace fêlée une grande fille en satin blanc, pénétrée d'une profonde mélancolie. Ne pensez-vous pas qu'il y auroit autant de bêtise à attribuer les pleurs de la jeune fille de ce Salon à la perte d'un oiseau, que la mélancolie de la jeune fille du Salon précédent à son miroir cassé? Cet enfant pleure autre chose, vous dis-je."* Diderot *Salons,* II, p. 147.

3. J. Ingamells, *The Wallace Collection Catalogue of Pictures,* III, *French before 1815,* London 1989, p. 206. See R. Paulson, *Hogarth's Graphic Works,* London 1989, pl. 142.

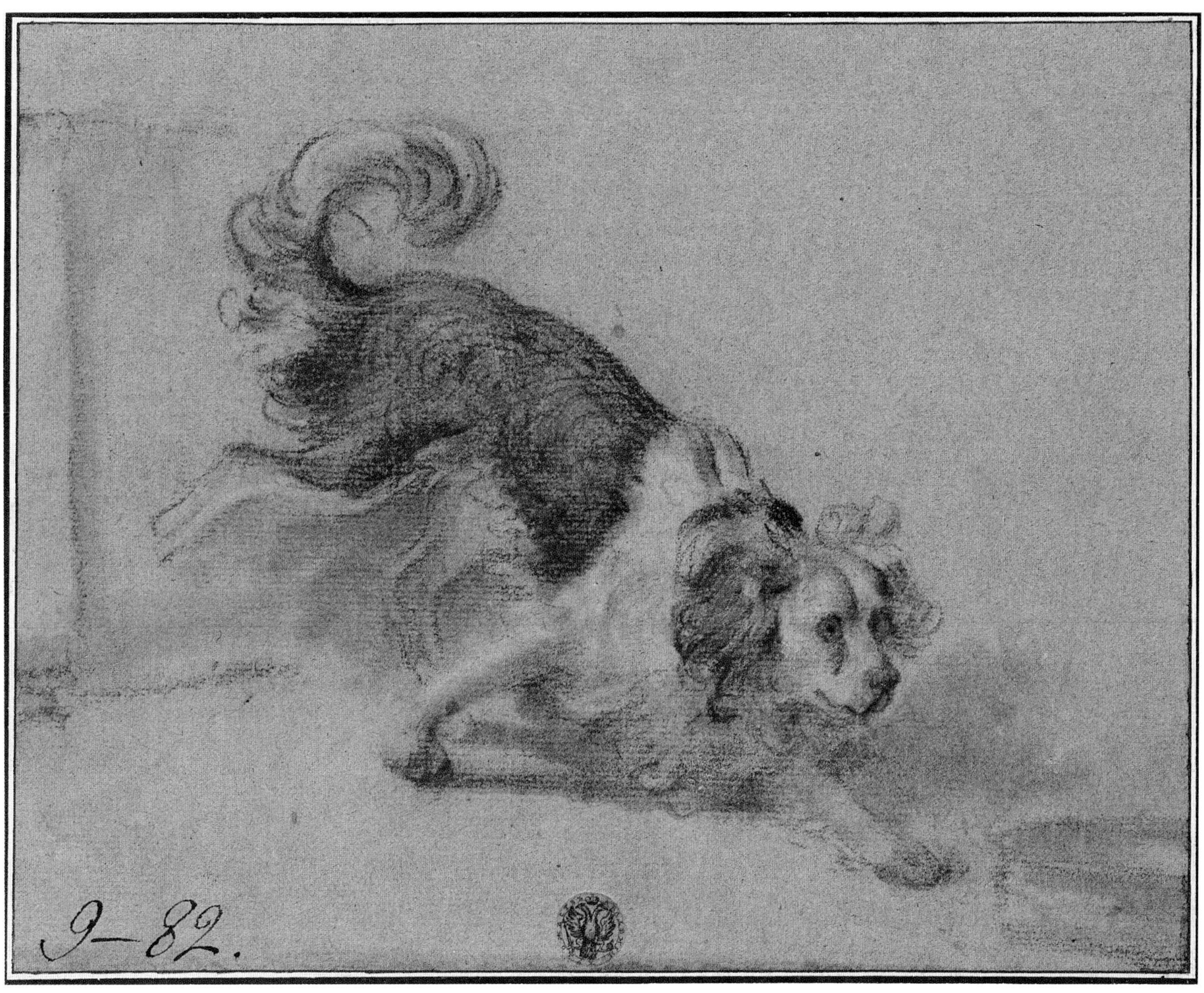
9–82.

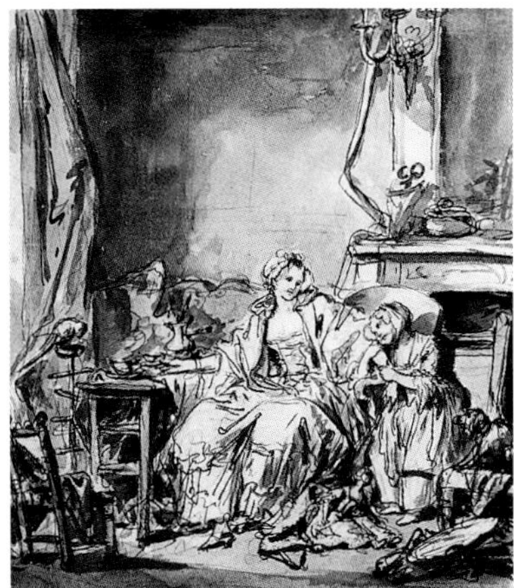

Fig. 80 Greuze, *Interior Scene, c.* 1765, pen and brush with black and brown ink on white paper, Vienna, Graphische Sammlung Albertina

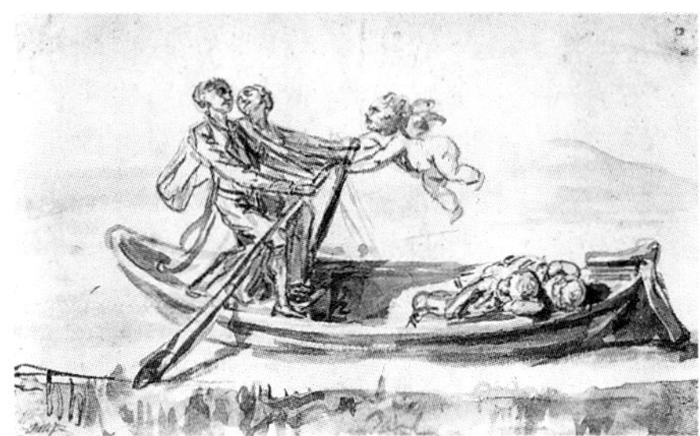

Fig. 81 Greuze, *The Boat of Happiness, c.* 1778, brush with black ink on white paper, Rotterdam, Museum Boijmans-van Beuningen

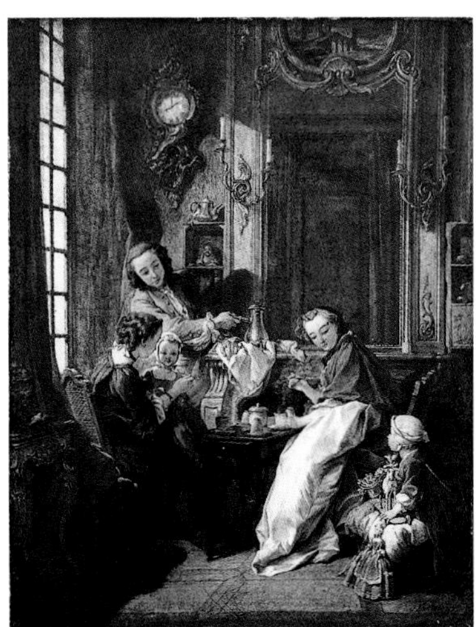

Fig. 82 F. Boucher, *Morning Coffee, c.* 1739, oil on canvas, Paris, Musée du Louvre

28 *A Family Scene*

Brush with black and brown ink wash over graphite on white paper, 457 × 400 mm (18 × 15 ¾ in.), including an addition of 127 mm (5 in.) at top and another of 1.27 mm (½ in.) at bottom
St Petersburg, The State Hermitage Museum

Provenance: Ivan Ivanovitch Betskoy, St Petersburg; Imperial Academy of Fine Arts, St Petersburg, 1769 (Lugt S. 2699a), 1769; transferred to the Hermitage in 1924
Exhibitions: St Petersburg 1903, no. 431; Leningrad 1926, no. 206; Moscow 1955, no. 73; Leningrad 1977, no. 86; Tokyo 1994, no. 69; Karlsruhe 1996, no. 76
Bibliography: "Dessins de J.-B. Greuze de la Bibliothèque de l'Académie des Beaux-Arts," *Mir Iskusstvo,* XII, 1903, p. 231; Martin and Masson 1906, no. 377; Monod and Hautecoeur 1922, no. 25, pl. III; Barker 1994, p. 119

This image of domestic bliss appears to be a major reworking of a nearly identical composition in the Graphische Sammlung Albertina (fig. 80), but of slightly different proportions. Here, Greuze has shifted the group of mother and daughter, with all their paraphernalia, to the left to introduce the figure of the father. Essentially the image is autobiographical, in the sense that it evokes the early, happy years of Greuze's own marriage, or at least how he had wanted them to be. Since the surviving texts dictated by him concerning his union with Anne-Gabrielle Babuti date from the time of their separation in 1785, there are no references in them to such peaceful idylls as illustrated here. In his "Mémoire contre sa femme," the artist recalled only that "The first seven years of our marriage [1759–66] were not accompanied by extraordinary events; we had had three children; there remained two to look after."[1] In his remarks concerning the well-known allegorical drawing *The Boat of Happiness* (fig. 81), Greuze made specific reference to this early stage of his marriage, when "the harmony that reigns between these happy spouses enables them to face and overcome danger, and Love... encourages them and smiles on their happiness."[2]

As Irina Novosselskaya has pointed out,[3] the present drawing recalls Boucher's *Morning Coffee* (fig. 82), which Greuze could have known through Bernard-François Lépicié's (1698–1755) engraving of 1744.[4] The resemblance is less for its familial character than for the similar accoutrements of a successful artist's dwelling: the fine furniture, the pier glass over the chimneypiece, the candelabra, the cascading curtains, the doll, the coffee service. Although Greuze's interior lacks Boucher's oriental porcelains, it does boast a reduction of the Venus de' Medici on the chimneypiece, a sculpture that reappears elsewhere in his work (see no. 87). The tassel swinging wildly alongside the chimneypiece must be a bell pull for servants.

1. *"Les sept premières années de notre mariage ne furent point accompagnées d'événements extraordinaires; nous avions eu trois enfants; il nous en restait deux à qui il fallait veiller."* J.-B. Greuze, "Mémoire de Greuze contre sa femme," ed. P. de Chennevières, *Archives de l'art français,* II, 1852–53, p. 160.

2. *"l'accord qui règne entre ces heureux époux, les fait braver et vaincre le danger, et l'Amour... les anime et sourit à leur bonheur."* Valori 1860, p. 373. See Cambridge *et al.* 1998–2000, no. 79.

3. Leningrad 1977, p. 38.

4. See A. Ananoff, *François Boucher,* Lausanne and Paris 1976, I, pp. 284–86.

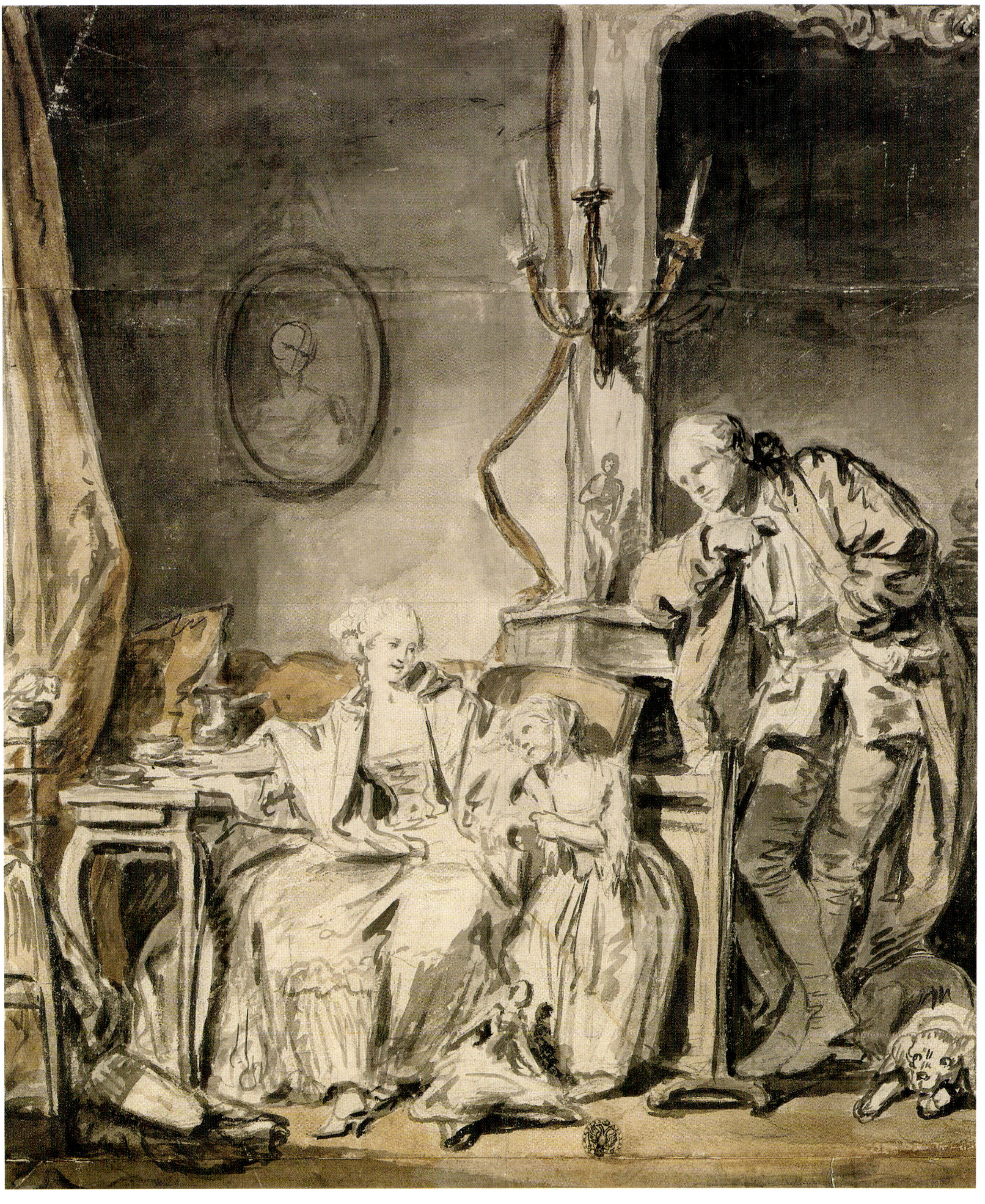

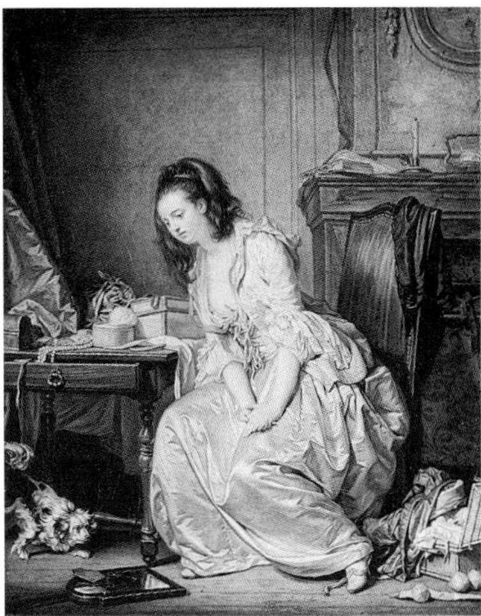

Fig. 83 Greuze, *The Broken Mirror,* 1763, oil on canvas, London, The Wallace Collection

29 *The Angry Mother*

Brush with black and gray ink wash over graphite on cream paper, 357 × 305 mm (14 1/16 × 12 in.)
Washington D.C., National Gallery of Art

Provenance: chevalier de Damery, Paris;[1] Coutan, Paris; his sale, Paris, 19 April 1830, lot 239; sale, Paris, 26 March 1958, lot 54; Galerie Cailleux, Paris; Rosenberg & Stiebel, Inc., New York; Arthur Liebman, Lake Forest IL; given by him to the National Gallery of Art in 1992
Exhibitions: None known
Bibliography: Smith, no. 100; Martin and Masson 1906, no. 336; Brookner 1972, pp. 99, 127; "Cour des tableaux anciens et modernes," *Connaissance des arts,* December 1958, p. 122, repr.

One of Greuze's earliest depictions of a domestic quarrel, this scene of a mother confronting her daughter over an incriminating letter possesses a Mozartean lightness in comparison with the thundering drama of later scenes of family strife such as *The Father's Curse: The Ungrateful Son* (nos. 48, 82) or *The Angry Wife* (no. 89). Indeed, the luxurious setting and voluminous gowns relate it to such contemporary cabinet pictures as *The Broken Mirror* (fig. 83) and *The Inconsolable Widow,* both listed in the Salon catalogue of 1763, but not exhibited.[2]

The Angry Mother shares with the former, as well as with number 28, the presence of an important chimneypiece, surmounted, as in the case of the other works, by a large mirror. The architectural setting and furnishings in the present drawing are slightly more Rococo in character than the contemporary paintings, with the serpentine curves of the large armchair, the frames of the mirror and the painting above it, and the indentations of the wall panel—all typical of the style of a Parisian interior of a slightly earlier period.[3]

The open chest in the lower left corner provides a hint of interrupted activity, much as the door shown ajar in the mirror conveys a sense of time.

Pierre-Étienne Moitte, one of the first artists to reproduce Greuze's works in engravings, executed a nearly full-scale print after *The Angry Mother* (fig. 84).

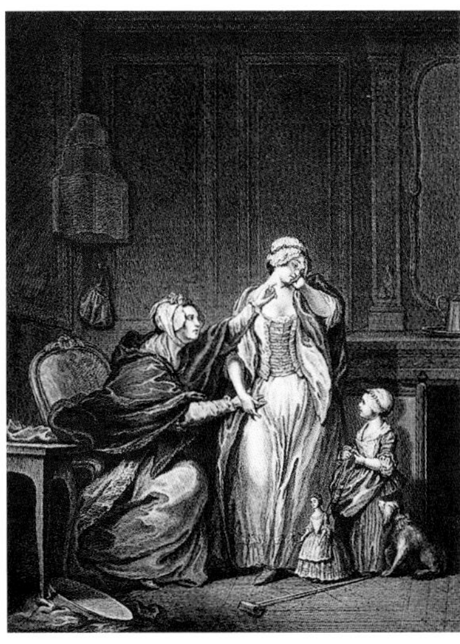

Fig. 84 P.-É. Moitte, after Greuze, *The Angry Mother,* 1763, engraving, New York, The Metropolitan Museum of Art

1. His ownership indicated by the dedication on Moitte's engraving of the drawing (fig. 84). See Portalis and Béraldi 1880–82, III, pt. 1, p. 114, no. 5.

2. See J. Ingamells, *The Wallace Collection Catalogue of Pictures,* III, *French before 1815,* London 1989, pp. 205–09.

3. Three large pier glasses of the sort depicted here are listed in the inventory established after Greuze's divorce in 1793. See Arquié-Bruley 1983, pp. 141–42, nos. 6, 23, 31.

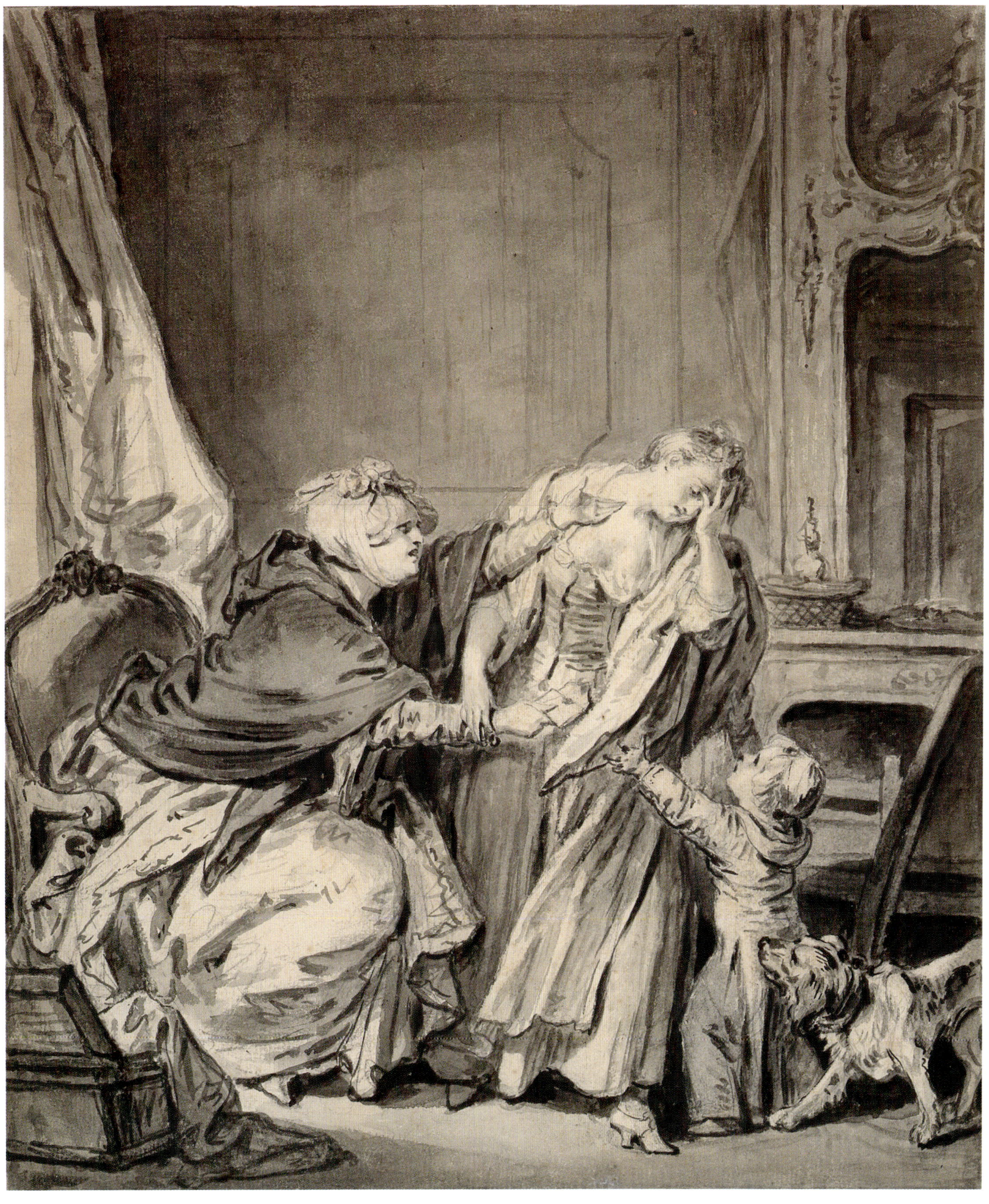

30 *A Seated, Smiling Woman, Looking Up*

Black, red, and white chalks on tan paper, 389 × 281 mm (15 5/16 × 11 1/16 in.)
Inscribed in pen and black ink at lower left *9-71.*
St Petersburg, The State Hermitage Museum

Provenance: Ivan Ivanovitch Betskoy, St Petersburg; Imperial Academy of Fine Arts, St Petersburg, 1769 (Lugt S. 2699a); transferred to the Hermitage in 1924
Exhibitions: Leningrad 1926, no. 210; Leningrad 1956, no. 86; Stockholm 1963, no. 45; Prague 1972, no. 44; Leningrad 1977, no. 76; Tokyo 1994, no. 68; Karlsruhe 1996, no. 73
Bibliography: Monod and Hautecoeur 1922, no. 45, pl. xv; *Eremitaget i Leningrad. 100 Malingar och teckningar fran Eremitaget: Vasteuropeisk konst fran 1500–1700 talen,* Göteborg, Göteborgs Konstmuseum, 1970, p. 18

With the present drawing and numbers 31–33, one can follow Greuze imagining a subject (no. 30), characterizing the head of the principal figure (no. 31), pausing to execute a dazzling variation on it (no. 32), and finally, dutifully reproducing for an engraver the painting that was the final result (no. 33, fig. 86).

When the term *trois crayons* is mentioned, most people immediately envisage a page of ethereal head and hand studies by Watteau, executed in red, black, and white chalks. Greuze reminds us here that the mixed-chalk medium can produce images of robust earthiness as well, complete with luscious, globelike breasts that attract the viewers' eyes as much as does the subject's beguiling smile.

This study is the earliest known preparation for *The Spoiled Child,* a work shown at the Salon of 1765 and popularized through Pierre Maloeuvre's engraving of 1772 (fig. 87). Although its primary subject is the rather sober one of child training, from the beginning Greuze must have intended to lighten its message by presenting a mother with abundant physical charms, a decision immediately noted by the critics of 1765 (see pp. 112, 114). In contrast to her somewhat doll-like appearance in the final work, the mother in the present drawing appears monumental: broad-shouldered, full in the hips, and encased in a skirt double the size of the one in the painting. Her cap is less of a confection and her gown less *haute couture.*

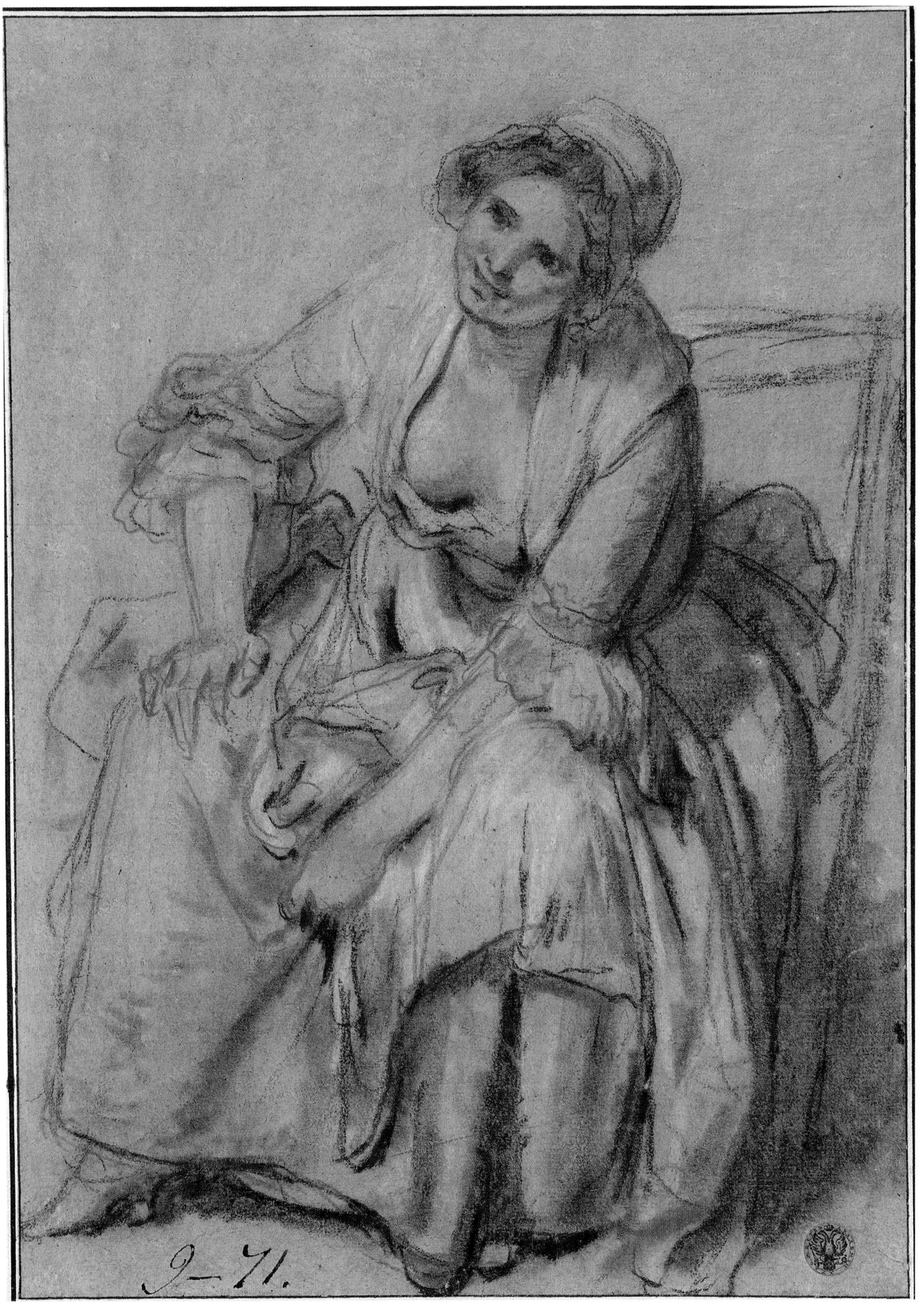
9–71.

31 *Head of a Smiling Woman Inclined to the Left, Study for "The Spoiled Child"*

Red chalk on white paper, 397 × 309 mm (15 5/8 × 12 1/8 in.)
Private collection

Provenance: Villenave, Paris; his sale, Paris, Alliance des Arts (Lugt 61), 1 December 1842, no. 646; sale, New York, 28 January 1999, lot 65; Agnew's, London
Exhibitions: None known
Bibliography: None known

If number 30 was Greuze's first study for the mother in *The Spoiled Child* (fig. 86), this would seem to be his initial study of her head. From the simplified form of the bonnet in the former, the artist has conceived a more convoluted and flattering headdress, complete with bows and floating lappets. The model too appears generally less stolid and on her way to becoming the seductive personage of the final painting.

Besides its intrinsic quality, in which the carefully manipulated hatching and cross-hatching that define the planes of the head are played off against the exploding curling lines of the bonnet, the drawing demonstrates Greuze's innate comprehension of the anatomy of the human head—the relationship of brow to nose, the strength of the chin, the setting of the eyes—so like his contemporary Houdon's. Also, as Théophile Thoré noted in the catalogue of the Villenave sale of 1842, this study is life-size *("grandeur naturelle").* This anatomical skill of Greuze is equaled by his ability to capture the personality of this young woman—humorous, intelligent, frank.

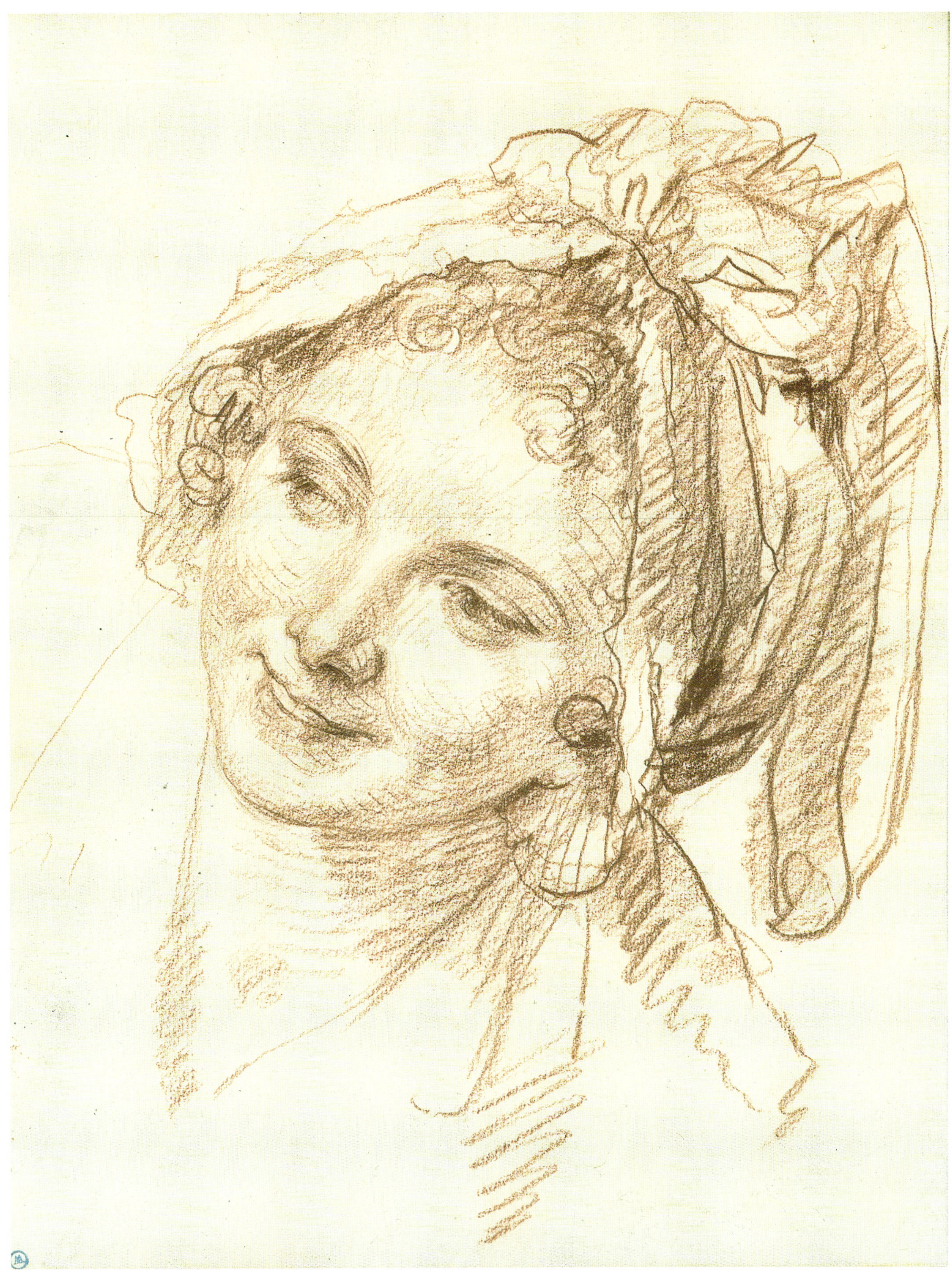

32 *Head of a Smiling Woman*

Black and white pastel chalks, charcoal, red chalk, with stumping, on white paper rubbed with red chalk, 342 × 260 mm (13 7/16 × 10 1/4 in.)
Vienna, Graphische Sammlung Albertina

Provenance: Duke Albert von Sachsen und Teschen, Vienna
Exhibitions: London 1932, no. 1016; *Le Dessin français dans les collections du XVIIIe siècle,* Paris, Wildenstein & Cie, 1935, no. 209; *Chefs d'oeuvre de l'art français,* Paris, Palais national des arts, 1937, no. 549; *Meisterwerke aus Oesterreich/Zeichnungen, Gemälde, Plastik,* Zurich, Kunsthaus, 1946–47, no. 158; *Cent-cinquante Chefs d'oeuvre de l'Albertina de Vienne,* Paris, Bibliothèque nationale, 1950, no. 147; *Meisterwerke aus Frankreichs Museen,* Vienna, Albertina, 1950, no. 110; *Das Dresdner Kupferstichkabinett und die Albertina, Meisterzeichnungen aus zwei alten Sammlungen,* Vienna, Albertina, 1978, no. 112; *Zeichnungen alter Meister aus der Albertina,* Washington D.C., National Gallery of Art; New York, The J. Pierpont Morgan Library; Vienna, Albertina, 1984–86, no. 75
Bibliography: J. Schönbrunner and J. Meder, *Handzeichnungen alter Meister aus der Albertina und anderen Sammlungen,* Vienna 1896–1908, no. 289; Martin and Masson 1906, no. 622; Royal Academy of Arts, *French Art, 1200–1900,* commemorative cat., London 1933, no. 695; O. Benesch, *Meisterzeichnungen der Albertina,* Vienna 1964, no. 220; Bailey 2000, p. 250

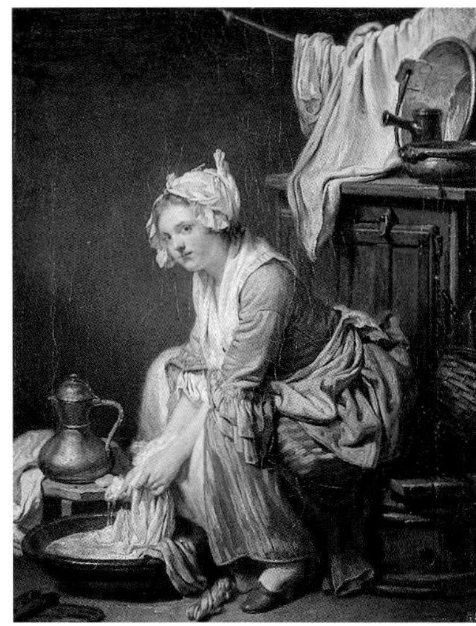

Fig. 85 Greuze, *The Laundress,* 1761, oil on canvas, Los Angeles, The J. Paul Getty Museum

One of Greuze's best-loved drawings, this dazzling exercise in *trois crayons* would seem to be the final study for the head of the mother in *The Spoiled Child* (fig. 86). In contrast to the rough study of the full figure of the same model (no. 30) and her rather daft appearance in the highly finished rendition of the composition (no. 33), this close-up is vividly realistic. One could imagine that, pleased with his resolution of the pose and the appearance of this figure in number 33, Greuze decided to execute this drawing as an independent variation on it, simply to show off his technical prowess.

Of the mother's appearance in *The Spoiled Child* when exhibited at the Salon of 1765, Diderot wrote: "The head of the mother is charming in its coloring; but her headdress does not sit on her head, and prevents it from appearing three-dimensional"[1] —a justifiable point, but not appropriate to this study. Diderot went on to link the mother in *The Spoiled Child* to the personage of *The Laundress* (fig. 85) exhibited four years before: "it's his little laundress of four years ago who's gotten married, and whose life story he is proposing to follow."[2] This supposition would seem based mostly on the similarity of the cap with ribbons and lappets worn by the two figures.

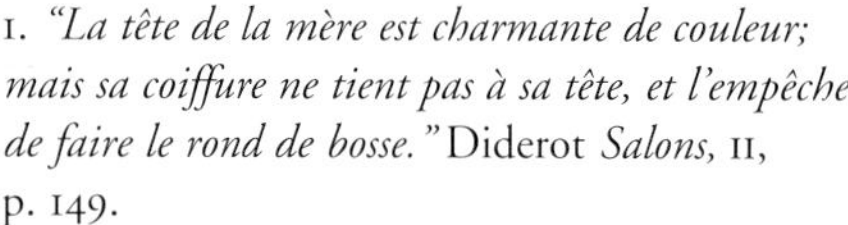

1. *"La tête de la mère est charmante de couleur; mais sa coiffure ne tient pas à sa tête, et l'empêche de faire le rond de bosse."* Diderot *Salons,* II, p. 149.

2. *"c'est sa petite blanchisseuse d'il y a quatre ans qui est mariée, et dont il se propose de suivre l'histoire."* Diderot *Salons,* II, p. 149.

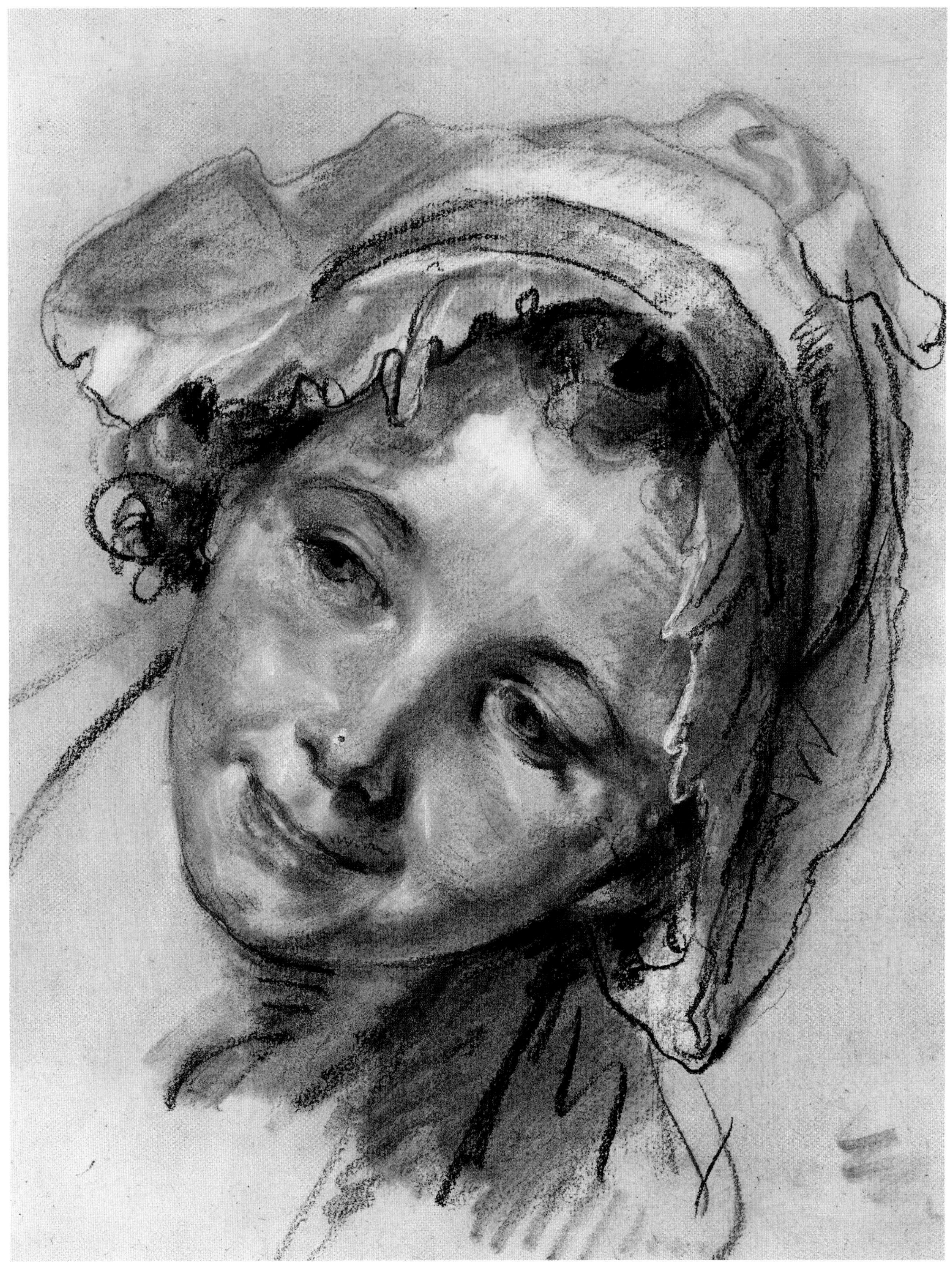

33 *The Spoiled Child*

Brush with gray wash over graphite on cream paper, 450 × 340 mm (17 ¾ × 13 7/16 in.)
Inscribed on the mount *ce dessin a été gravé par/ Maloeuvre sous la direction de/ Le Bas*
Vienna, Graphische Sammlung Albertina

Provenance: Vassal de Saint-Hubert, Paris; his sales, Paris, 29 March–13 April 1779, lot 165, and 29 April 1783, lot 161; Villeminot, Paris; his sale, Paris, 25 May 1807, lot 159; Duke Albert von Sachsen und Teschen (Lugt 174), Vienna
Exhibitions: None known
Bibliography: Martin and Masson 1906, no. 136; Novosselskaya 1987, p. 7

This highly finished drawing is an early example of the model Greuze would have provided an engraver commissioned to reproduce one of his paintings, in this case, *The Spoiled Child* (fig. 86). That work, exhibited at the Salon of 1765 (no. 111), was acquired immediately by the duc de Choiseul-Praslin who, presumably, was unwilling to part with it for the months required to execute an engraved reproduction.

When the present drawing appeared in the Villeminot sale in 1807, it was described in the catalogue thus: "The very finished drawing, by J.-B. Greuze, which appears to have been executed as a model for the engraving of the subject known by the title of *The Spoiled Child*."[1] Yet Pierre Maloeuvre, the engraver in question, appended to his print (fig. 87) a notice that it had been "engraved . . . after the original painting of Jean-Baptiste Greuze removed from the cabinet of Monseigneur the duc de Praslin."

When that canvas had appeared at the Salon of 1765, its provocative subject was much commented on, especially by Charles-Joseph Mathon de La Cour, who described it succinctly:

M. Greuze produced another picture that he has called The Spoiled Child. *To convey this subject, he has painted one of those lazy and complaisant women who let their children do anything they want. . . . This woman is, naturally, chubby; she rests her elbow on her knee, and exposes her breasts in a nonchalant way. Her little boy is quite fresh, quite well nourished, and quite stupid. You can see in his face the traces of that boredom to which children*

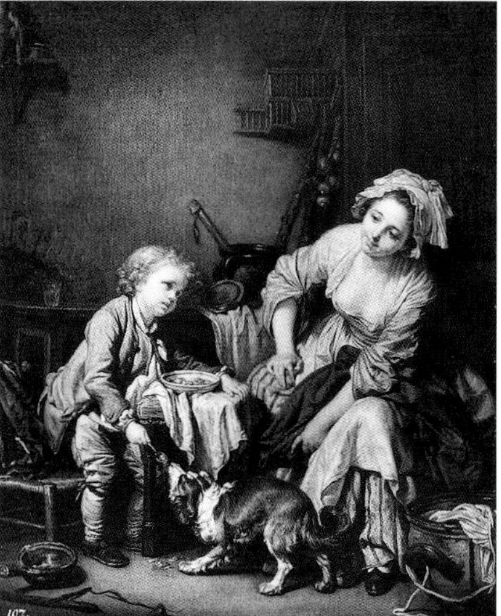

Fig. 86 Greuze, *The Spoiled Child*, 1765, oil on canvas, St Petersburg, The State Hermitage Museum

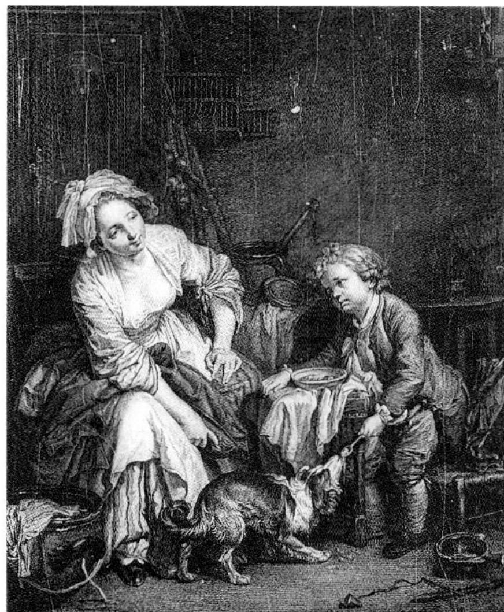

Fig. 87 P. Maloeuvre and P. Le Bas, after Greuze, *The Spoiled Child*, 1772, engraving, Paris, Bibliothèque nationale de France

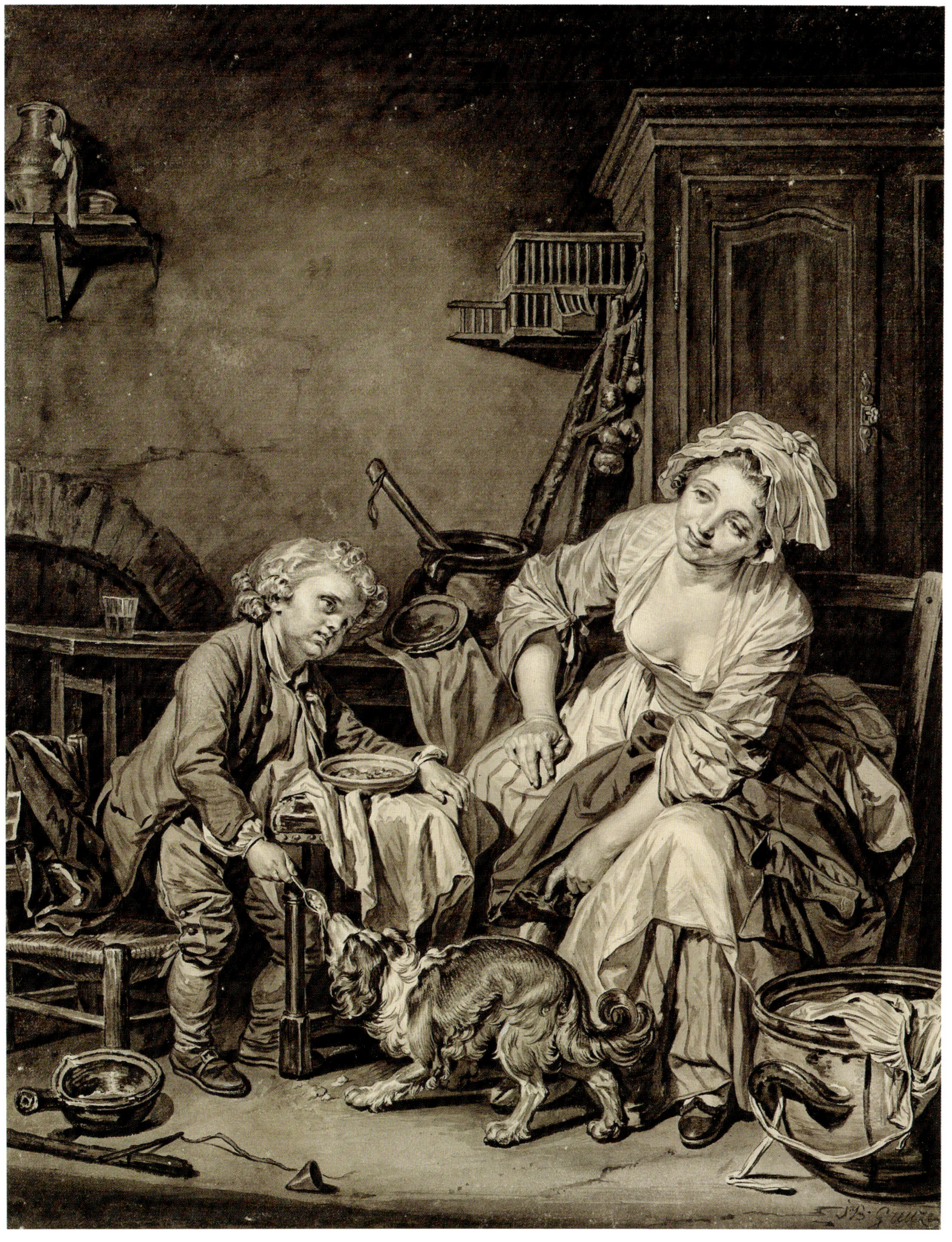

are inclined when they are given nothing to do, for fear of exhausting them. He has just been given soup; instead of eating it, he gives some gently, spoonful by spoonful, to a dog. The mother laughs and observes that act of kindness with extreme complaisance.[2] Greuze's belief that such minor examples of childhood misbehavior are the prelude to more heinous crimes to follow was a constant one throughout his career and forms the basis for his *Bazile et Thibault, ou les deux éducations,* a dramatic scenario he conceived in the manner of Hogarth.[3]

In *The Motherly Reprimand* (figs. 11, 12), a subject closely related to the present one, the mother is depicted scolding her child for giving his food to the dog, rather than looking on indulgently.[4]

The present drawing demonstrates with what fanatical precision Greuze rendered each telling detail of his picture: the highlight on the wineglass (is the mother a tippler?), the key in the lock of the cabinet, and its hinges; the glint on the edge of the boy's spoon, the gleaming coat of the cringing dog—an English toy spaniel—described in the catalogue of the Choiseul-Praslin sale, Paris, 18 February 1793, as "a large, pure-bred dog."[5]

1. *"Le Dessin très terminé, par J.-B. Greuze, qui paroît avoir été fait pour diriger la Gravure du sujet connu sous le tire de 'Enfant gâté.' "* Catalogue of the Villeminot sale, 25 May 1807, lot 159.

2. *"M. Greuze a donné un autre tableau qu'il a appellé* l'Enfant gâté. *Pour bien rendre ce sujet, il a peint une de ces femmes paresseuses et faciles, qui laissent faire à leurs enfants tout ce qu'ils veulent.... Cette femme a, comme de raison, beaucoup d'embonpoint; elle s'accoude sur ses genoux, et laisse voir sa gorge par nonchalence. Son petit garçon est bien frais, bien nourri, bien stupide. On voit sur sa physionomie les traces de cet ennui, où sont sujets les enfans, quand on ne les occupe à rien, de peur de les fatiguer. On vient de lui donner une soupe; au lieu de la manger, il en donne tout doucement les cuillierées à un chien. La mère rit et regarde cette gentillesse avec une complaisance extrême."* Mathon de La Cour 1765, pp. 6–7.

3. See Brookner 1972, pp. 156–64.

4. See *An Exhibition of Master Drawings,* exhib. cat., P. & D. Colnaghi, London, 2001, no. 29.

5. *"un grand chien de belle race."*

34 *Seated Woman Holding a Child, Study for "The Dry Nurses"*

Red chalk on cream paper, 380 × 270 mm (14 15/16 × 10 5/8 in.)
Inscribed in pen and black ink at lower left *9-60.*
St Petersburg, The State Hermitage Museum

Provenance: Ivan Ivanovitch Betskoy, St Petersburg; Imperial Academy of Fine Arts, St Petersburg, 1769 (Lugt S. 2699a); transferred to the Hermitage in 1924
Exhibition: Leningrad 1977, no. 68
Bibliography: Monod and Hautecoeur 1922, no. 64, pl. XXIV; Novosselskaya 1985, p. 78, fig. 9

This roughly executed drawing is a study for the central pair of figures in Greuze's lost painting *The Dry Nurses (Les Sevreuses),* known today only from a version in the Nelson-Atkins Museum of Art, Kansas City, which the author does not consider autograph (fig. 88). Because the figure in this drawing faces right, as in Jean-Baptiste Tilliard's (1740–1813) and Pierre-Charles Ingouf's engraving of the composition (fig. 89), Greuze may have positioned his model in that way to see what she would look like in the future print. Certainly the drawing demonstrates that he was already anticipating the patterns of light and shade caused by light emanating from the window at upper left in the engraving—such as the shadows along the woman's back, over her skirt beneath the child, and across the floor to the right.

Greuze's celebrated drawings *The Departure for the Wet Nurse* and *The Return from the Wet Nurse* (fig. 90) showed his interest in the subject of nursing, one much debated by his contemporaries.[1] They suggest that the artist shared the point of view of Diderot, as presented in the *Encyclopédie,* that mothers should nurse their own children rather than turning them over to professional wet nurses. However, a recollection of Greuze's friend Wille indicates that Anne-Geneviève Greuze, born in April 1762, was still with her wet nurse in September 1763 and that she was visited only occasionally by her parents.[2]

The title of the composition to which this study is related—*The Dry Nurses*—refers to that stage of nursing in which a child is gradually weaned from breast-feeding.

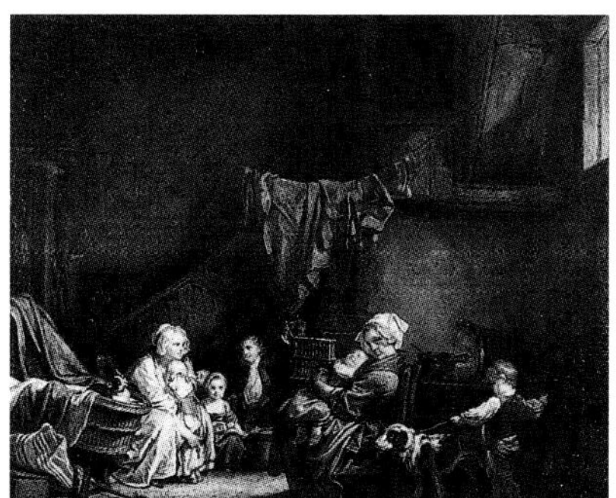

Fig. 88 After Greuze, *The Dry Nurses,* 1765, oil on canvas, Kansas City MO, The Nelson-Atkins Museum of Art

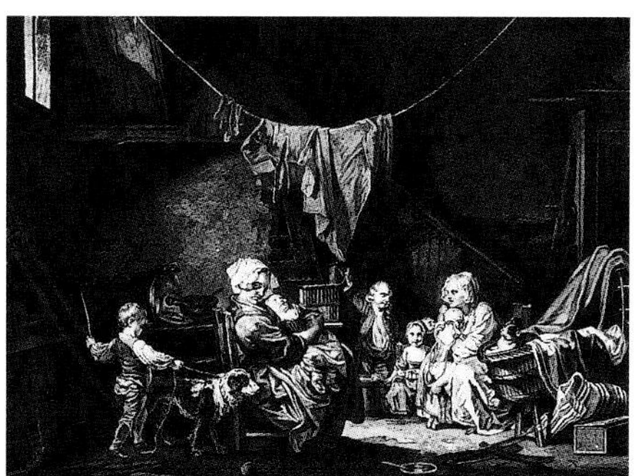

Fig. 89 J.-B. Tilliard and C. Ingouf, *The Dry Nurses,* 1769, engraving, Paris, Bibliothèque nationale de France

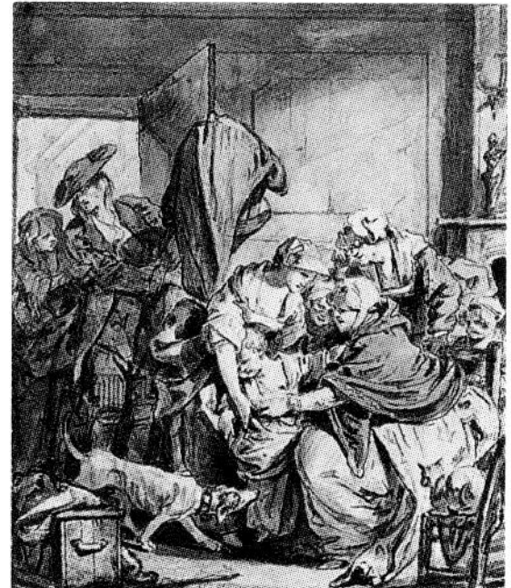

Fig. 90 Greuze, *The Return from the Wet Nurse, c.* 1763, brush with gray ink wash over graphite on white paper, private collection

This was to be accomplished by substituting one breast-feeding per day by a serving of light broth, then a second one replaced a week later by some milk soup. After several months, all breast-feeding would be gradually replaced by servings of milk or eggs beaten in milk.[3]

Greuze exhibited *The Dry Nurses* at the Salon of 1765, but it was not listed in the catalogue. Diderot noted that Chardin, who hung the exhibition, had placed it beneath Alexander Roslin's (1718–1793) *Father Arriving at His Estate, Where He Is Received by His Children Who Love Him Tenderly* to suggest that the latter was "a model of discord" and Greuze's painting, "a model of harmony."[4] Describing the subject of the present drawing as "a peasant woman on whose lap a little girl is sleeping,"[5] Diderot said that Adriaen van Ostade (1610–1685) would not have disclaimed the authorship of this painting, which he proceeded to describe enthusiastically: "No one paints with more vigor. The effect is real. One does not look for the source of light. The groups are charming. It is a little composition the least fussed-over and the best resolved. You believe you are in a cottage. Nothing disappoints, neither the subject itself, nor the art.... for me, it's the picture that I want."[6]

1. See Hartford *et al.* 1976–77, pp. 98–101, nos. 41, 42.

2. Wille 1857, I, p. 230.

3. See *sevrage* in *Larousse universel en 2 volumes,* Paris 1923, II, p. 939.

4. *"Modèle de discordance"; "modèle d'harmonie."* Diderot *Salons,* II, p. 160.

5. *"une paysanne, sur le giron de laquelle une petite fille est endormie."* Diderot *Salons,* II, p. 160.

6. *"On ne peint pas avec plus de vigueur. L'effet en est vrai. On ne cherche pas d'où vient la lumière. Les grouppes sont charmans. C'est la petite ordonnance la moins recherchée et la mieux entendue. Vous croyez être dans une chaumière. Rien ne détrompe, ni la chose, ni l'art.... pour moi, c'est le tableau que je demande."* Diderot *Salons,* II, p. 160.

Facing page:
34 *Seated Woman Holding a Child, Study for "The Dry Nurses"*

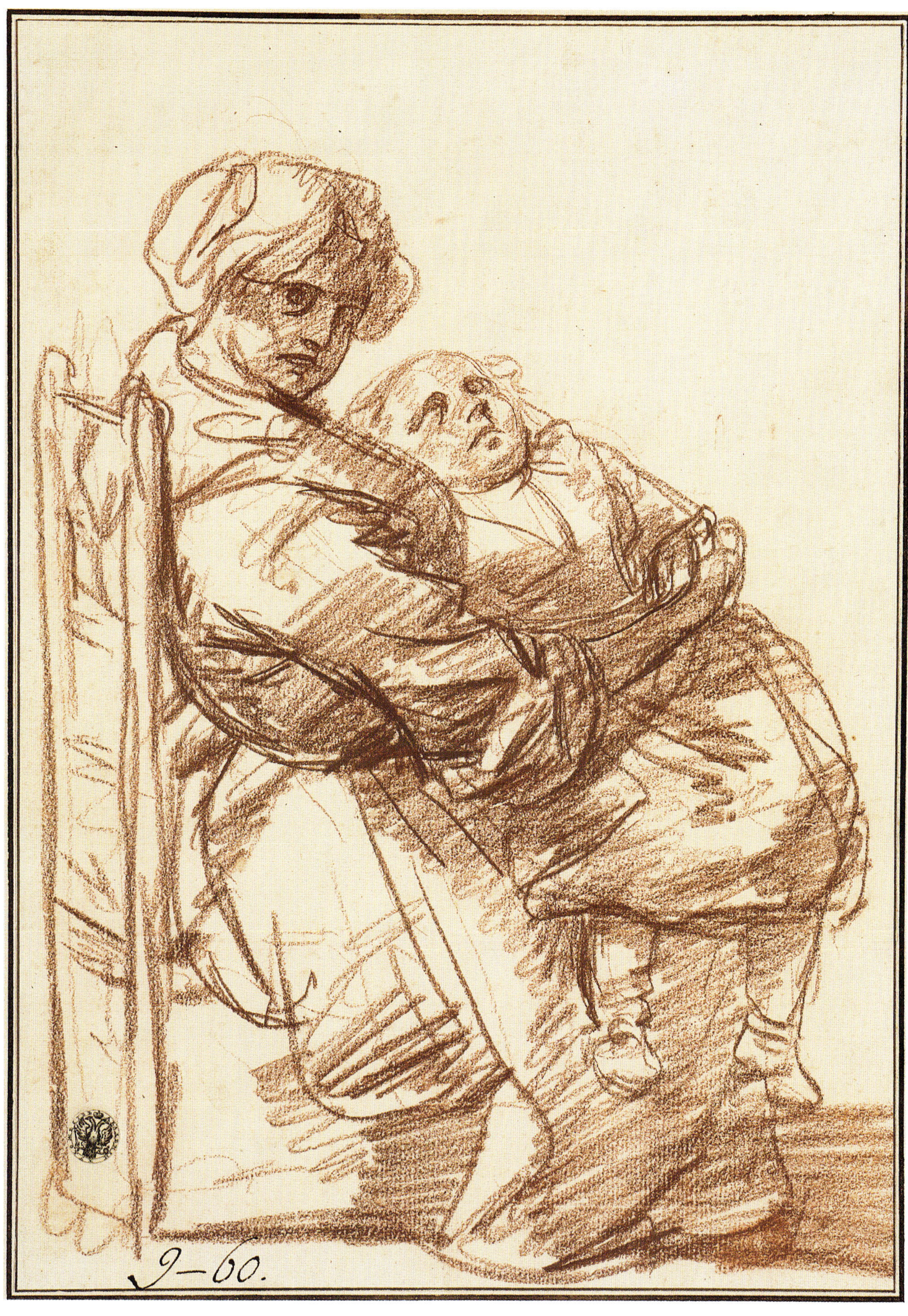
9-60.

35 *Standing Boy Seen from Behind, Study for "The Dry Nurses"*

Red chalk on cream paper, 291 × 190 mm ($11\frac{7}{16} \times 7\frac{7}{16}$ in.)
Inscribed in pen and black ink at lower left *9-42.*
St Petersburg, The State Hermitage Museum

Provenance: Ivan Ivanovitch Betskoy, St Petersburg; Imperial Academy of Fine Arts, St Petersburg, 1769 (Lugt S. 2699a); transferred to the Hermitage in 1924
Exhibition: Leningrad 1977, no. 72
Bibliography: Monod and Hautecoeur 1922, no. 36; Novosselskaya 1985, p. 78, fig. 14

This is a study for the boy parading a dog in *The Dry Nurses* (fig. 88), described by the critic Mathon de la Cour in 1765: "in the corner of the picture, a little boy leads a large dog with a cord around his neck, and holds a whip in his other hand. The look of boredom with which the dog puts up with this game is totally amusing."[1] Diderot mentioned him simply as: "In the foreground, a child who leads a dog around with a cord."[2] For a full discussion of the painting, see number 34.

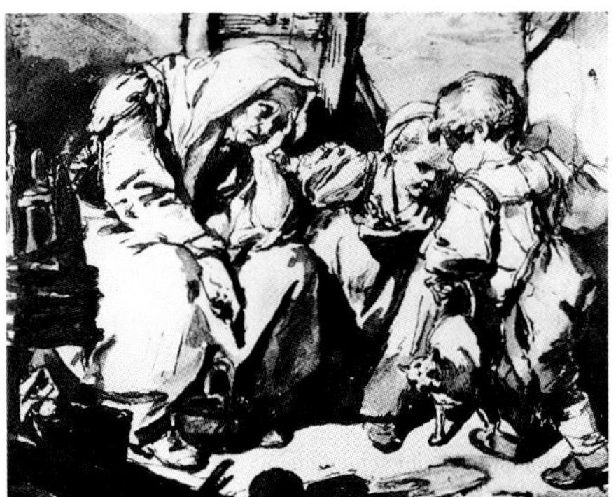

Fig. 91 Greuze, *The Sleeping Grandmother*, *c.* 1765, pen and brush with gray and brown ink on white paper, Épinal, Musée départemental des Vosges, Fonds Oulmont

Greuze's memorable invention of this droopy-drawered child mimicking a heroic figure restraining a wild animal such as Guillaume Coustou I's (1677–1746) *Chevaux de Marly,* at the entrance to the Champs-Élysées, may be what Mathon de La Cour had in mind when he referred to *The Dry Nurses* as demonstrating "the ingenious simplicity of its creator . . . [who] sees nature as an artist ought to see it, that is to say, as a lover, with eyes that miss nothing and embellish everything."[3]

Greuze re-employed the same image, minus the dog, in a drawing entitled *The Sleeping Grandmother* (fig. 91).

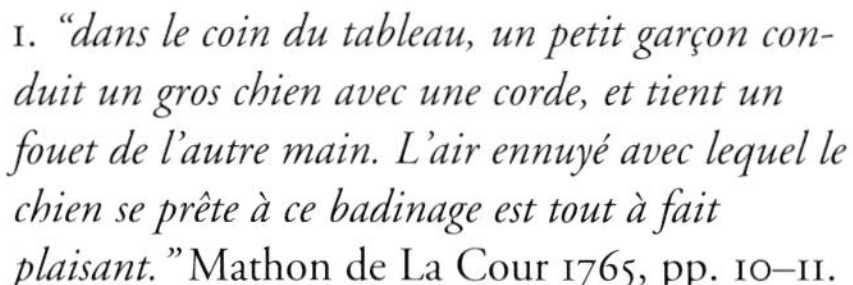

1. *"dans le coin du tableau, un petit garçon conduit un gros chien avec une corde, et tient un fouet de l'autre main. L'air ennuyé avec lequel le chien se prête à ce badinage est tout à fait plaisant."* Mathon de La Cour 1765, pp. 10–11.

2. *"Sur le plan antérieur, un enfant qui conduit un chien avec une corde."* Diderot *Salons,* II, p. 160.

3. *"on y reconnoît la naïveté ingénieuse de l'Auteur . . .* [qui] *voit la nature comme un Artiste doit la voir, c'est-à-dire, en Amant, avec des yeux à qui rien n'échappe, et qui embellissent tout."* Mathon de La Cour 1765, p. 11.

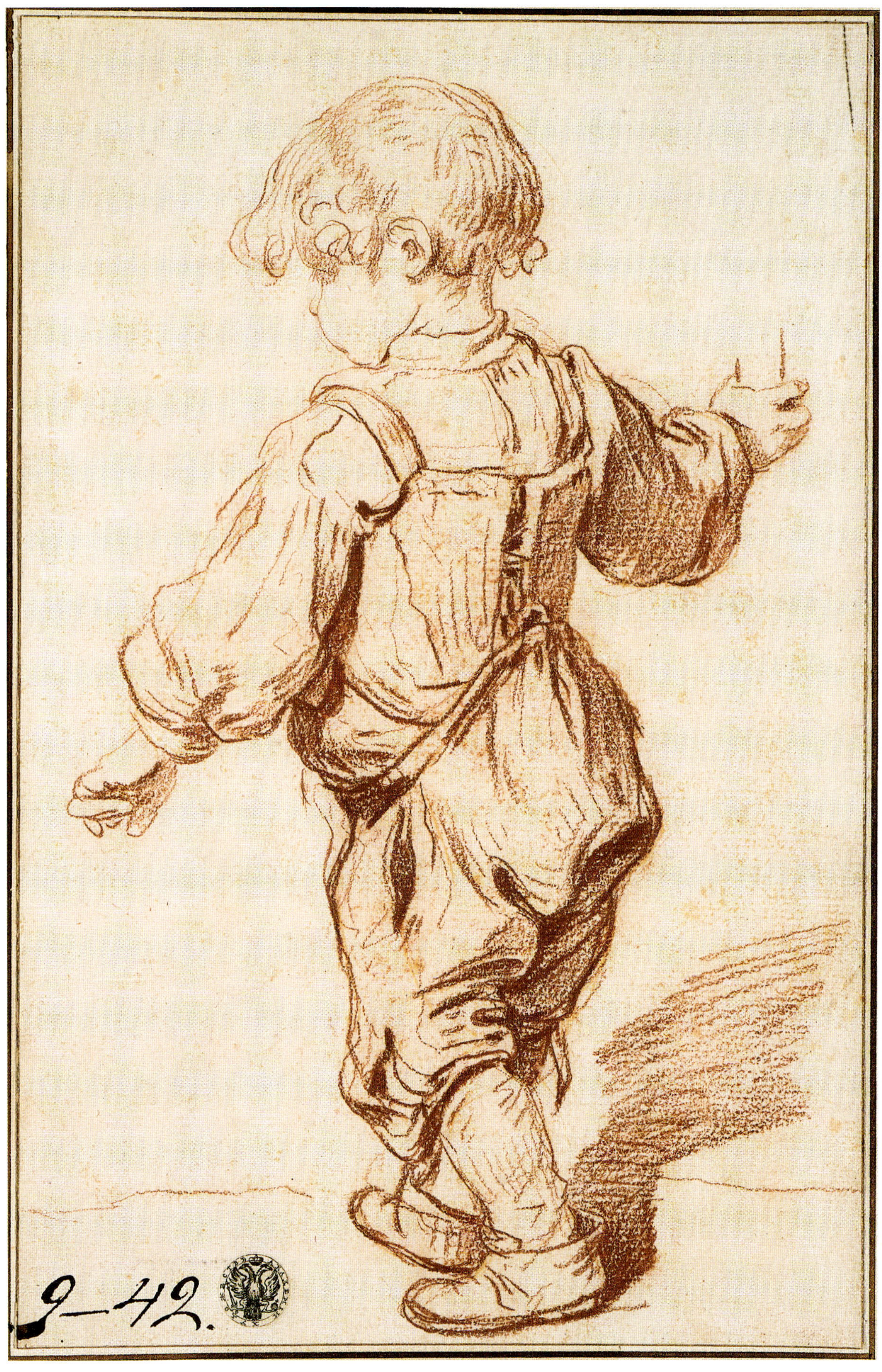
9–42.

36 *Head of an Old Woman Looking Up, Study for "The Stepmother"*

Red chalk on white paper, 410 × 325 mm (16 1/8 × 12 13/16 in.)
New York, The Metropolitan Museum of Art, Rogers Fund

Provenance: Jules Porgès, Paris; comtesse de Fitz-James, Paris; Baron Rudolf, Ritter von Gutmann, Vienna; William H. Schab Gallery, New York; acquired by the museum in 1949
Exhibitions: Hartford *et al.* 1976–77, no. 27; New York 1990
Bibliography: Portalis and Béraldi 1880–82, II, pt. 2, p. 691; Martin and Masson 1906, no. 121; *The Metropolitan Museum of Art. Annual Report of the Trustees,* New York 1949, p. 28; Bean and Turčić 1986, pp. 120–21; C. Michell, "La Diffusion des gravures d'après Greuze," in *Diderot et Greuze, Actes du colloque de Clermont-Ferrand (16 novembre 1984),* Clermont-Ferrand 1986, pp. 46–47; Thompson 1989–90, p. 22; V. Ducourau, "Le Legs Petithory au Musée Bonnat de Bayonne," *Revue du Louvre, La Revue des musées de France,* no. 4, 1994, pp. 13–14; *La Donation Jacques Petithory au Musée Bonnat, Bayonne; objets d'art, sculptures, peintures, dessins,* exhib. cat., Paris, Musée du Luxembourg, 1997, p. 206

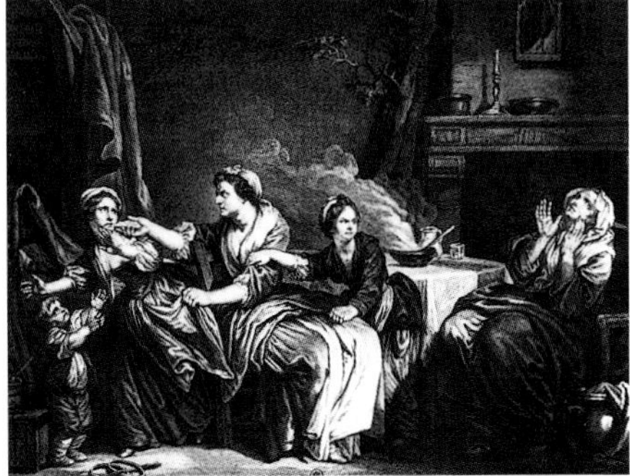

Fig. 92 J.-C. Le Vasseur, after Greuze, *The Stepmother,* 1781, engraving, Paris, Bibliothèque nationale de France

The drawing is a study for the head of the sorrowing grandmother in Greuze's composition *The Stepmother.*

Though the word *pinxit* appears after Greuze's name on Jean-Charles Le Vasseur's (1734–1816) second engraving of that subject (fig. 92), in fact, Greuze seems never to have executed a painting on the theme. Instead, as indicated in the contract Le Vasseur and Greuze signed before a notary on 18 October 1779,[1] the engraver most likely followed as his model the large and highly finished drawing by Greuze that reappeared in 1983 (fig. 93).

Greuze's fascination with this painful subject of a stepmother abusing her stepchild goes back to the early 1760s, when the same Jean-Charles Le Vasseur produced a sketchy rendering of *The Stepmother* in a caricature dedicated to the "most high, most amusing and most ridiculous lady, the wife of J.-B. Greuze," that included as well a rendering of Flipart's engraving of Greuze's *Self-Portrait* of about 1763 (fig. 67).[2]

When the second and larger print appeared on the market, Greuze drew attention to it in a letter published in the *Journal de Paris* on 13 April 1781. In it, he claimed to have been inspired by some gossips on the Pont Neuf talking about a stepmother who thrust a piece of stale bread in her stepdaughter's face. Greuze described the child's grandmother, depicted in the present drawing, as follows: "grieved to the very heart, she raises toward heaven her eyes and her trembling hands, and seems to say: 'Ah, my daughter, where are you? What misery, what bitterness!' "[3]

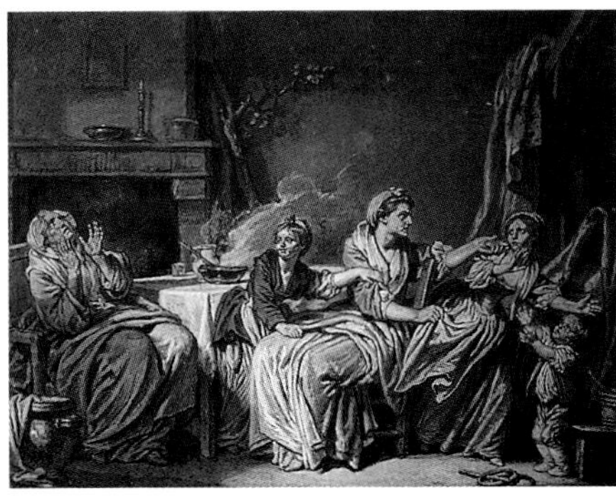

Fig. 93 Greuze, *The Stepmother,* 1779, brush with gray ink wash, heightened with white gouache, over graphite on tan paper, Bayonne, Musée Bonnat, Donation Petithory

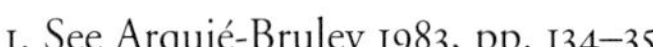

1. See Arquié-Bruley 1983, pp. 134–35.

2. *"très-haute, très-plaisante et très-ridicule dame, femme de J.-B. Greuze."* Impression in the Bibliothèque nationale de France, Cabinet des Estampes. See *Diderot,* exhib. cat., Paris, Bibliothèque nationale, 1963–64, no. 297; J. Renouvier, *Histoire de l'art pendant la Révolution,* Paris 1863, p. 519.

3. *"pénétrée de la plus vive douleur, elle élève vers le ciel ses yeux et ses mains tremblantes, et semble dire: 'Ah, ma fille, où es-tu? Que de malheurs, que d'amertume!' "* The full text is cited in Goncourt 1880, p. 302 and, with translation, in Hartford *et al.* 1976–77, p. 74.

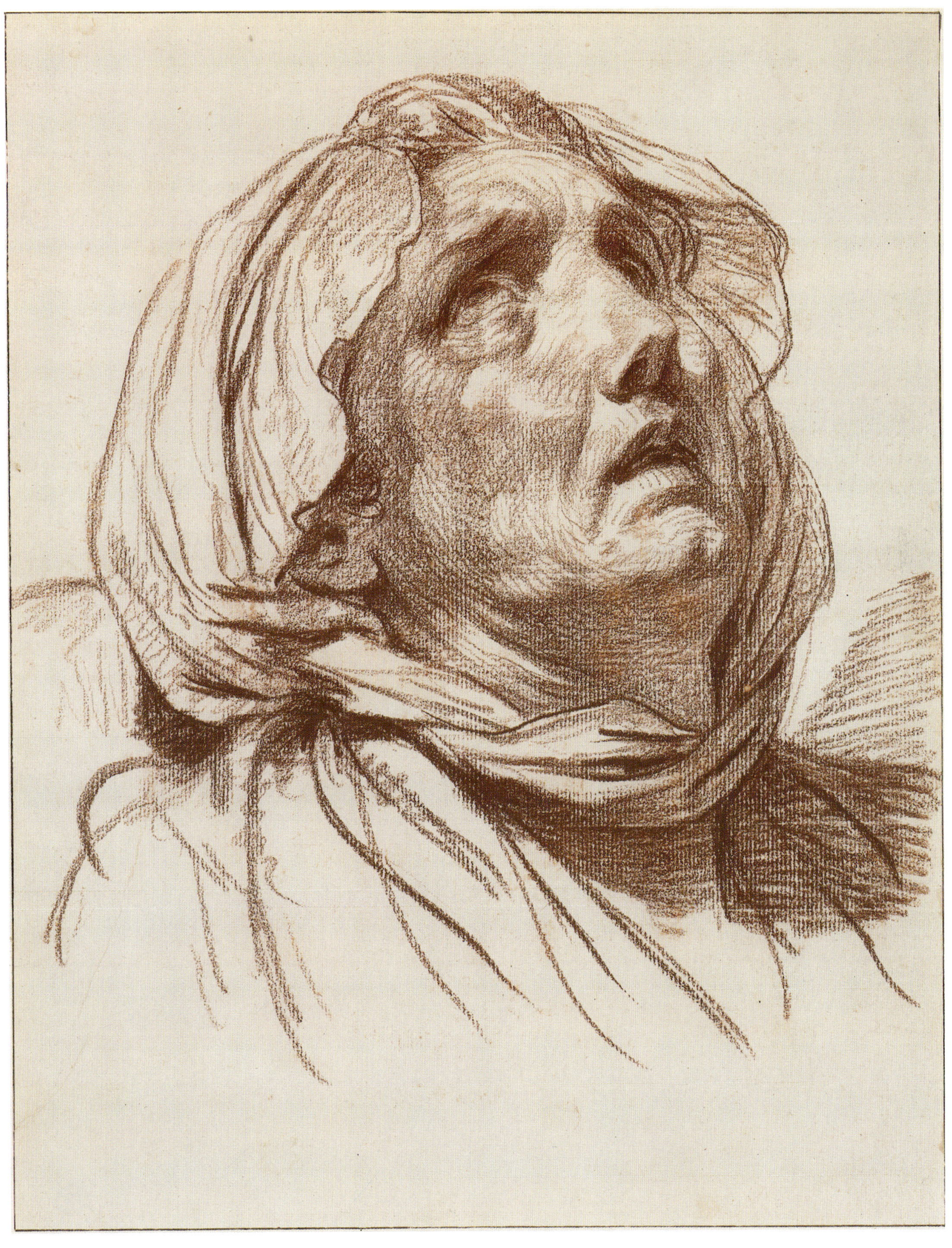

37 *Head of a Woman Turned to the Right*

Red chalk on cream paper, 437 × 328 mm (17 3/16 × 12 15/16 in.)
Inscribed in pen and black ink at lower left *8-No. 67.*
St Petersburg, The State Hermitage Museum

Provenance: Ivan Ivanovitch Betskoy, St Petersburg; Imperial Academy of Fine Arts, St Petersburg, 1769 (Lugt S. 2699a); transferred to the Hermitage in 1924
Exhibition: Leningrad 1977, no. 103
Bibliography: Monod and Hautecoeur 1922, no. 132, pl. LIV

Whereas Monod and Hautecoeur related this powerful *tête d'expression* to the figure of the daughter in *The Angry Mother* (no. 29), Novosselskaya (in Leningrad 1977) more logically cited its resemblance to the mother in that composition—because of the similar turn of the head and the bonnet tied under the chin—but as she observed, the model's expression here is quite different: less angry than alarmed or fearful. Perhaps inspired by that detail of *The Angry Mother,* Greuze transformed it later into this independent study of expression. With its sculpturesque density and bravado execution, the present drawing compares closely with number 36.

Two copies executed after this *Head of a Woman* have survived, providing vivid evidence of just how Greuze's drawings, and specifically those acquired for the Imperial Academy of Fine Arts, St Petersburg, were utilized as models for students. One version formerly in the Bryas collection and later with the Galerie Cailleux, Paris (fig. 94), is nearly identical in size (435 × 323 mm) and of high quality. But examined closely, it is apparent that the copyist lacked Greuze's instinctive grasp of anatomy, as the brow, cheeks, nose, and chin in the copy disperse rather than coalesce harmoniously. And whereas Greuze was able to convey the rolling curves of the bonnet's edge with subtly varied strokes, the copyist's comparable lines lie flat on the surface. In the second copy (fig. 95), measuring 457 × 340 mm, these faults are even more exaggerated, along with a total inability to render the complex structure of the woman's bonnet.

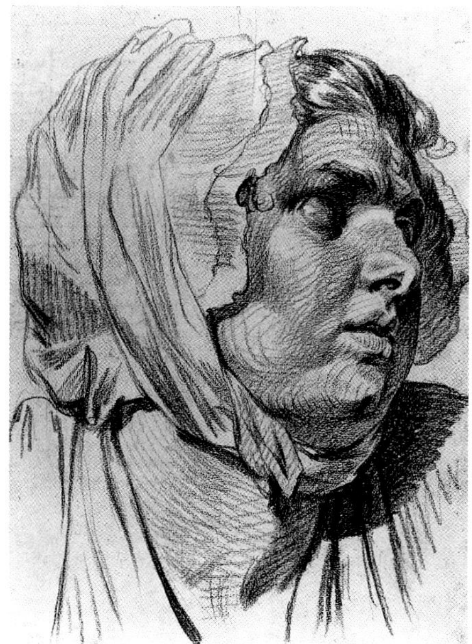

Fig. 94 Unknown artist, after Greuze, *Head of a Woman Turned to the Right, c.* 1775, red chalk on white paper, whereabouts unknown

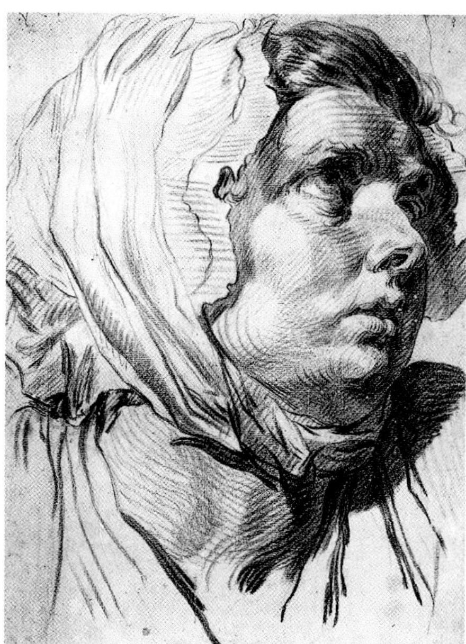

Fig. 95 Unknown artist, after Greuze, *Head of a Woman Turned to the Right, c.* 1775, red chalk on white paper, Kansas City MO, The Nelson-Atkins Museum of Art

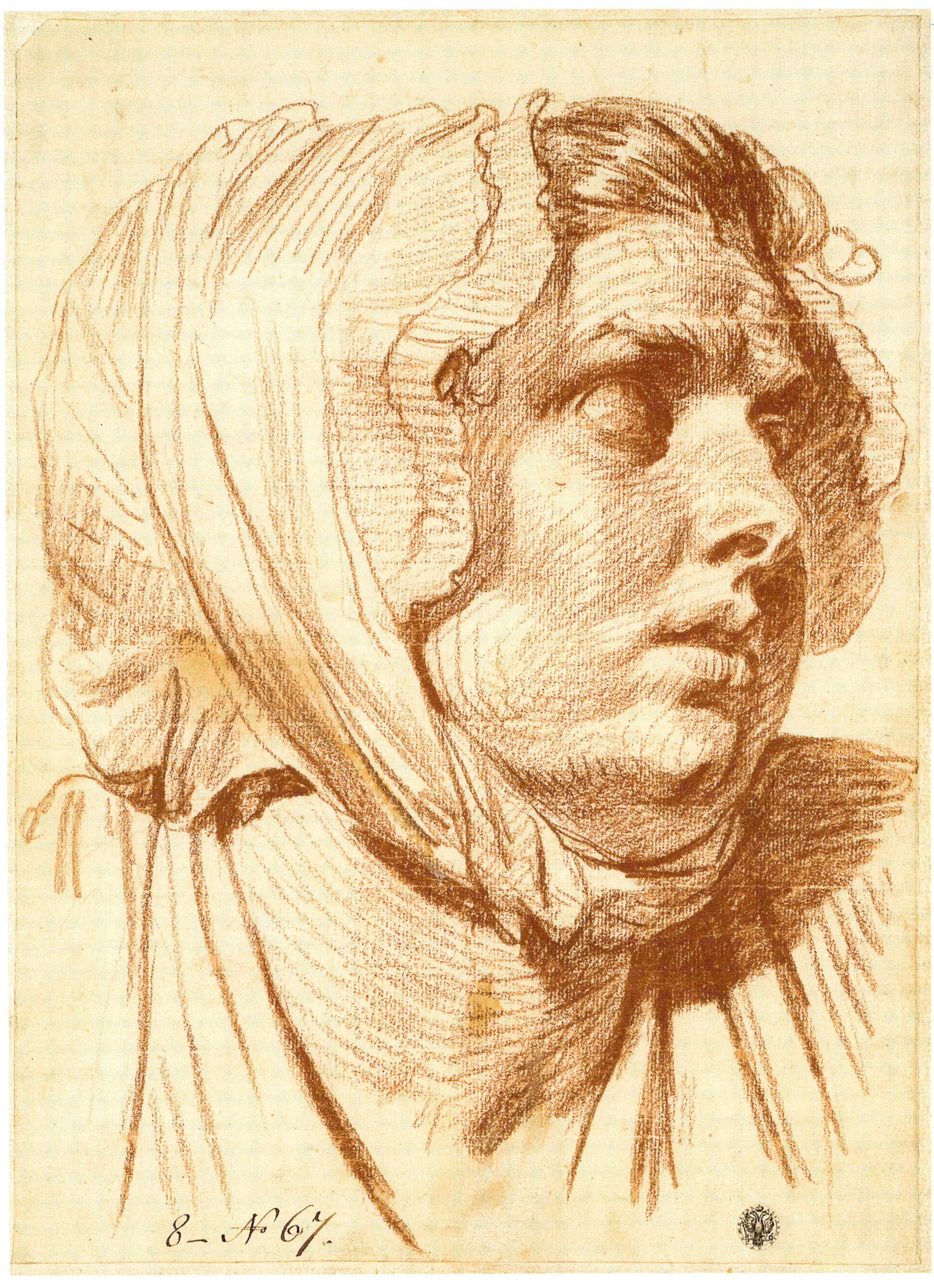
8_ N° 67.

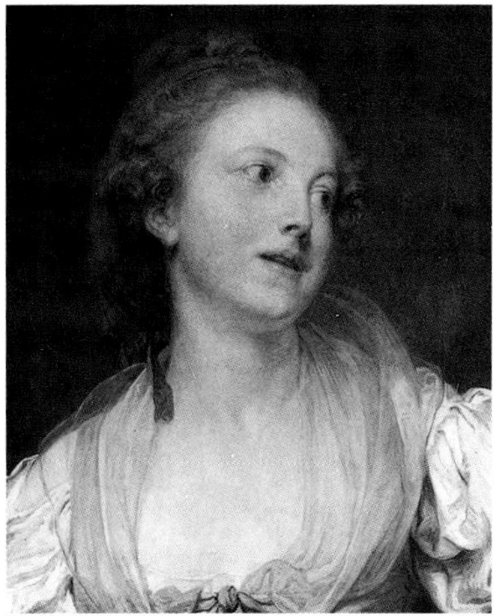

Fig. 96 Greuze, *Portrait of a Young Woman,* 1760, oil on canvas, Zurich, Collection Rau

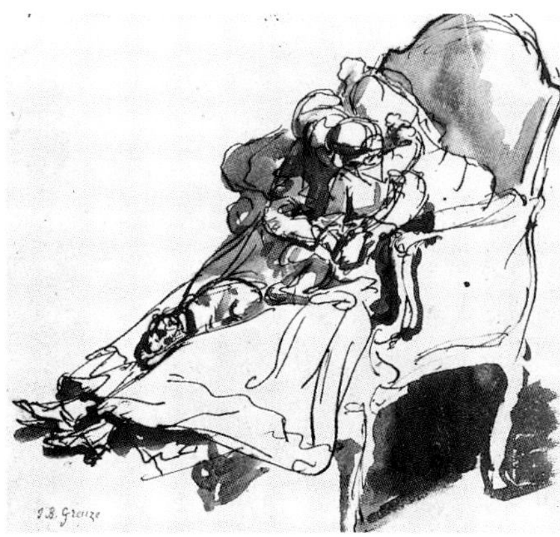

Fig. 97 Greuze, *Woman on a Chaise Longue, Holding a Dog, c.* 1763, pen and brush with black ink, Stockholm, Nationalmuseum

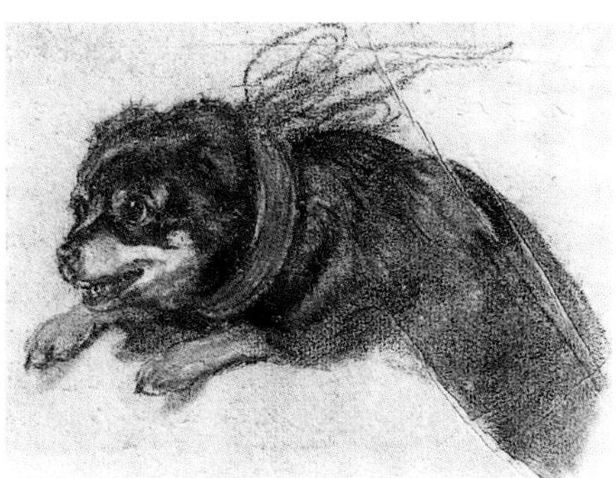

Fig. 98 Greuze, *Study of a Dog,* 1764, pastel, Dijon, Musée Magnin

38 *Madame Greuze on a Chaise Longue with a Dog*

Brush with gray ink wash over black and red chalk, 343 × 470 mm (13 ½ × 18 ½ in.)
Inscribed at lower left in brown ink, reinforced in black ink *Madame/ Greuze dessinée par/ J.B. Greuze son mari*
Amsterdam, Rijksmuseum

Provenance: Albert Meyer, Paris, 1932; Dr. F. Mannheimer; acquired by the museum in 1960 from the Dienst voor's Rijks Verspreide Kunstvoorwerpen
Exhibitions: London 1932, no. 773; *Le Dessin français dans les collections hollandaises,* Paris, Institut Néerlandais; Amsterdam, Rijksmuseum, 1964, no. 94; London 1968, no. 316
Bibliography: The Royal Academy of Arts, *French Art, 1200–1900,* commemorative cat., London 1933, no. 697; S. de Ricci, *Dessins du XVIIIe siècle, Collection Albert Meyer,* Paris 1935, no. 31; *Verslag van de Hoofd Directeur over het jaar 1953,* The Hague 1953, pp. 59–60; L.C.J. Frerichs, *Keuze van tekeningen bewaard in het Rijksprentenkabinet te Amsterdam,* Amsterdam 1963, no. 84 (English ed., 1965); J. Bean, "French Drawings in Dutch Collections," *Master Drawings,* II, no. 3, 1964, p. 294; J. Hulton, "'France in the Eighteenth Century' at the Royal Academy," review, *Master Drawings,* autumn 1968, p. 167; Roland Michel 1987, p. 219, fig. 264

While this drawing has often been linked to Greuze's *Philosophy Asleep* (fig. 99), the actual resemblances are slight and the satirical tone of that composition is absent here. More likely, this celebrated sheet is but one of many images the artist recorded of his wife, Anne-Gabrielle Babuti, during the happy, early years of their marriage. Her face has been rendered with great care, as a portrait, and corresponds in its delicate features and the coiffure bound tightly with ribbons to an oil portrait of his wife Greuze dated 1760 (fig. 96).[1]

A much less finished variant of the present drawing is in the Nationalmuseum, Stockholm, depicting Madame Greuze again on the same chaise longue with a dog between her legs, but holding a very active baby (fig. 97).[2] That infant could be Anne-Geneviève Greuze, later called Caroline, born in April 1762.

The little spaniel on Madame Greuze's lap reappears in a number of works by the artist and was the subject of an independent study in pastel (fig. 98).[3] Commenting on its appearance in the portrait of Madame Greuze the artist exhibited in 1765, Diderot wrote: "His eyes are full of life. If you look at him for a while, you will hear him bark."[4]

1. See *De Fra Angelico à Bonnard, Chefs-d'oeuvre de la Collection Rau,* exhib. cat., Paris, Musée du Luxembourg, 2000–2001, no. 40.

2. See *Fem Sekler Fransk Konst,* exhib. cat., Stockholm, Nationalmuseum, 1958, no. 244.

3. See Hartford *et al.* 1976–77, no. 45.

4. *"Il a les yeux pleins de vie. Si vous le regardez quelque temps, vous l'entendrez aboyer."* Diderot *Salons,* II, p. 152.

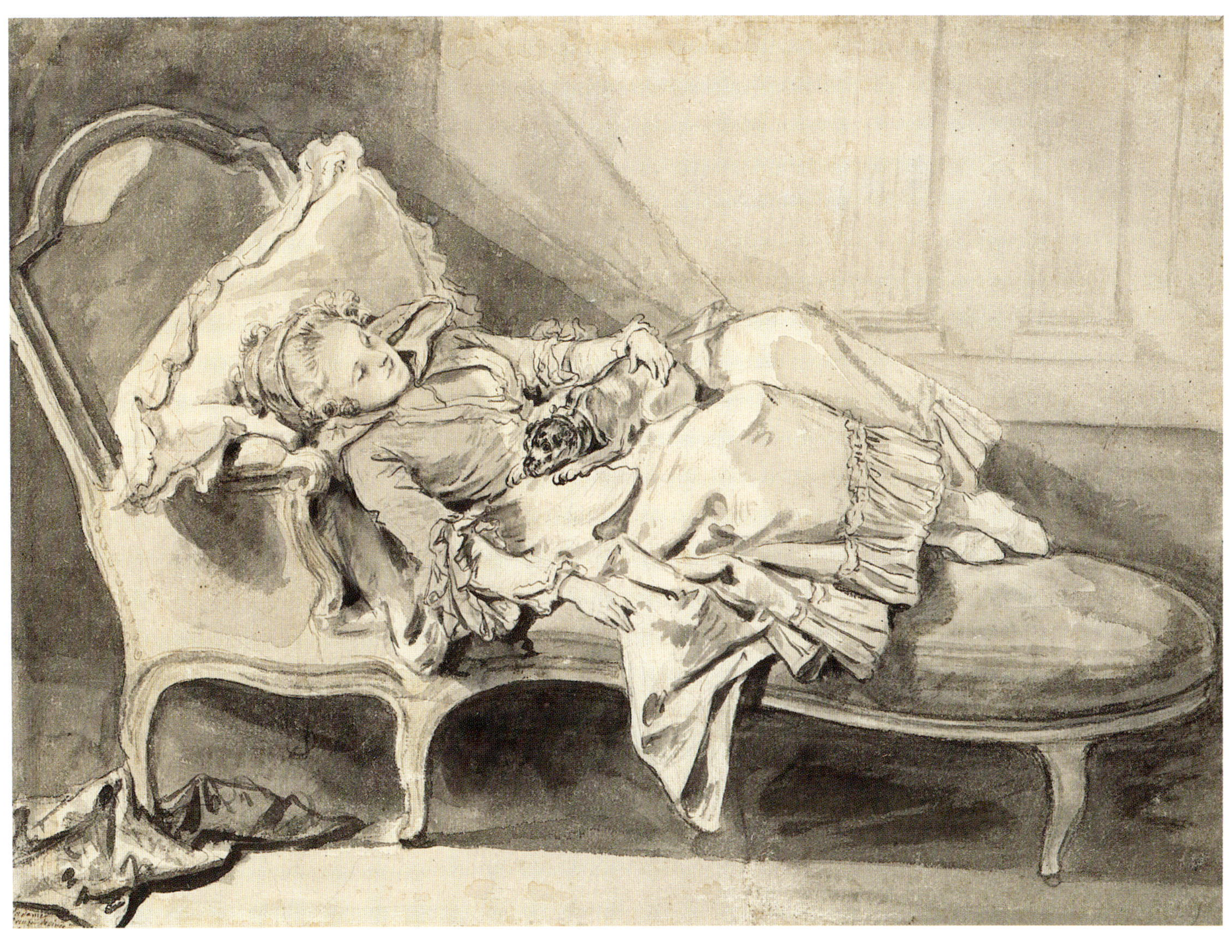

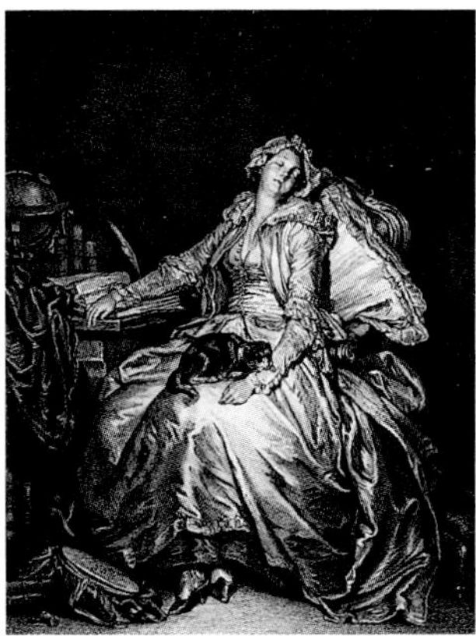

Fig. 99 J.-M. Moreau and J.-J. Aliamet, after Greuze, *Philosophy Asleep,* 1777, etching and engraving, New York, The Metropolitan Museum of Art, Gift of the Estate of Mrs Robert B. Noyes

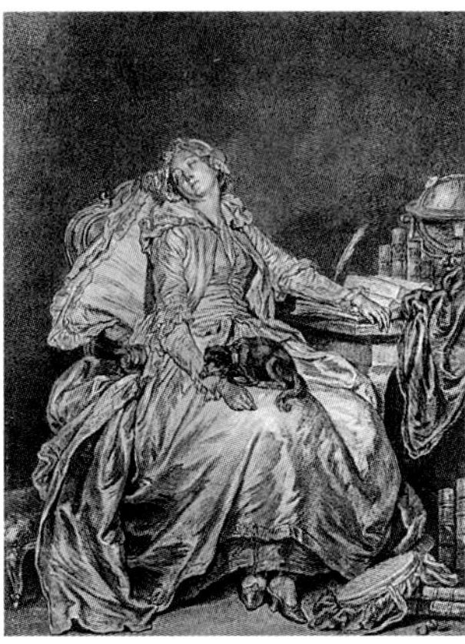

Fig. 100 J.-M. Moreau, *Philosophy Asleep,* *c.* 1776, pen and black ink, gray wash, heightened in white, whereabouts unknown

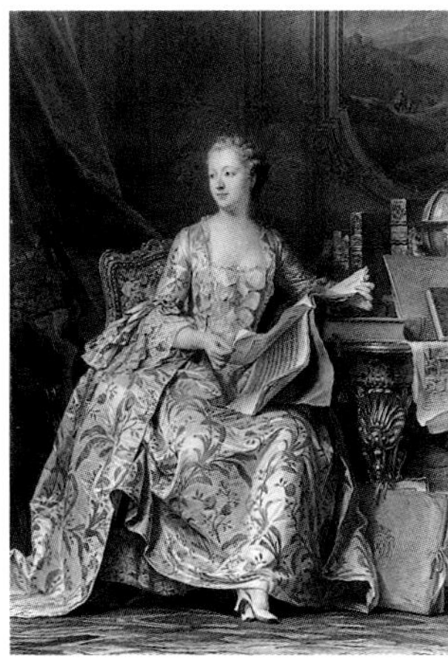

Fig. 101 M.-Q. de La Tour, *Madame de Pompadour,* 1752–55, pastel on paper, Paris, Musée du Louvre, Département des arts graphiques

39 *Head of a Sleeping Woman (Anne-Gabrielle Babuti)*

Red chalk on white paper, 373 × 318 mm (14 11/16 × 12 1/2 in.)
Karlsruhe, Staatliche Kunsthalle

Provenance: Jacques Petithory, Paris; purchased by the museum from R.M. Light, Boston, in 1975
Exhibition: Die französischen Zeichnungen, 1570–1930, Karlsruhe, Staatliche Kunsthalle, Kupferstichkabinett, 1983, no. 31
Bibliography: Smith, nos. 125, 136; Goncourt 1880, p. 311; Martin and Masson 1906, nos. 353, 1154; Hartford *et al.* 1976–77, pp. 13, 21, fig. 11; "Principales Acquisitions des musées en 1975," *GBA* ("Chronique des arts"), March 1976, p. 22, no. 75; *Jahrbuch der Staatlichen Kunstsammlungen in Baden-Württemberg,* XIII, 1976, pp. 156–57; V. Carlson in *Regency to Empire: French Printmaking, 1715–1814,* exhib. cat., The Baltimore Museum of Art; The Minneapolis Institute of Arts, 1984–85, p. 218, no. 72

Greuze must have executed this extraordinary drawing about the time of number 38, but its utilization as a partial model for the print *Philosophy Asleep* (fig. 99) did not occur until 1777.[1] In the interval, Greuze exhibited at the Salon of 1765 two portraits of his wife, of which one was a study for the mother in *The Beloved Mother* (no. 41), and the other, a lost portrait whose composition, judging from Diderot's comments,[2] must have resembled *Philosophy Asleep*—a woman depicted dozing in a chair with a dog on her lap.

The actual model for the print of 1777, however, was a drawing long attributed to Greuze but that was executed most likely by the engraver Jean-Michel Moreau (1741–1814) (fig. 100).[3] Anticipating the reversal of the printing process, Moreau drew the figure inclining to the left and took special care to reverse the titles on the spines of the books so that they would read properly as *Newton, Epicure, Platon, Descartes,* and *Copernic.* Each detail of the ruffles and folds of fabric, and the various textures of flesh, leather, and wood are rendered with an engraver's precision, not with the loose bravado of Greuze's original drawing.

Developed from the casual study of Madame Greuze asleep, the resulting print is a masterful spoof of the intellectual pretensions of the artist's contemporaries, especially Diderot and such bluestockings as Madame Geoffrin (see no. 46). Indeed, *Philosophy Asleep,* particularly in Moreau's drawing, seems to mock specifically the aspirations and person of Madame de Pompadour, as she was portrayed by Maurice-Quentin de La Tour in his monumental pastel exhibited at the Salon of 1755 (fig. 101), down to the pose, the form of the armchair, the placement of the table, the globe, the books (that in Madame de Pompadour's portrait include the *Encyclopédie*), and Madame Greuze's humble sewing frame that replaces the portfolio of Madame de Pompadour's comparable handiwork—her own engravings.

1. M.J.-F. Mahérault, *L'Oeuvre de Moreau le jeune,* Paris 1880, p. 109, no. 145; Portalis and Béraldi 1880–82, III, pt. 1, pp. 123, 157, no. 8, p. 173, no. 15; E. Bocher, *Jean-Michel Moreau le jeune,* Paris 1882, p. 95, no. 251; A. Moureau, *Les Moreau,* Paris 1893, p. 19; Martin and Masson 1906, pp. 105, 111.

2. Diderot *Salons,* II, p. 152. A gouache by Pierre-Antoine Baudouin (d. 1769), *La Lecture interrompue,* may recall Greuze's lost pastel of 1765 (Jacques Doucet sale, Paris, 6 June 1912, lot 1, repr.).

3. Laborde sale, Paris, 16 April 1783, lot 45; Demidov, Paris; Edmond and Jules de Goncourt, Paris; Laughlin sale, London, 10 June 1959, lot 29; baron Hatvany, London; sale, London, 6 July 1965, lot 111.

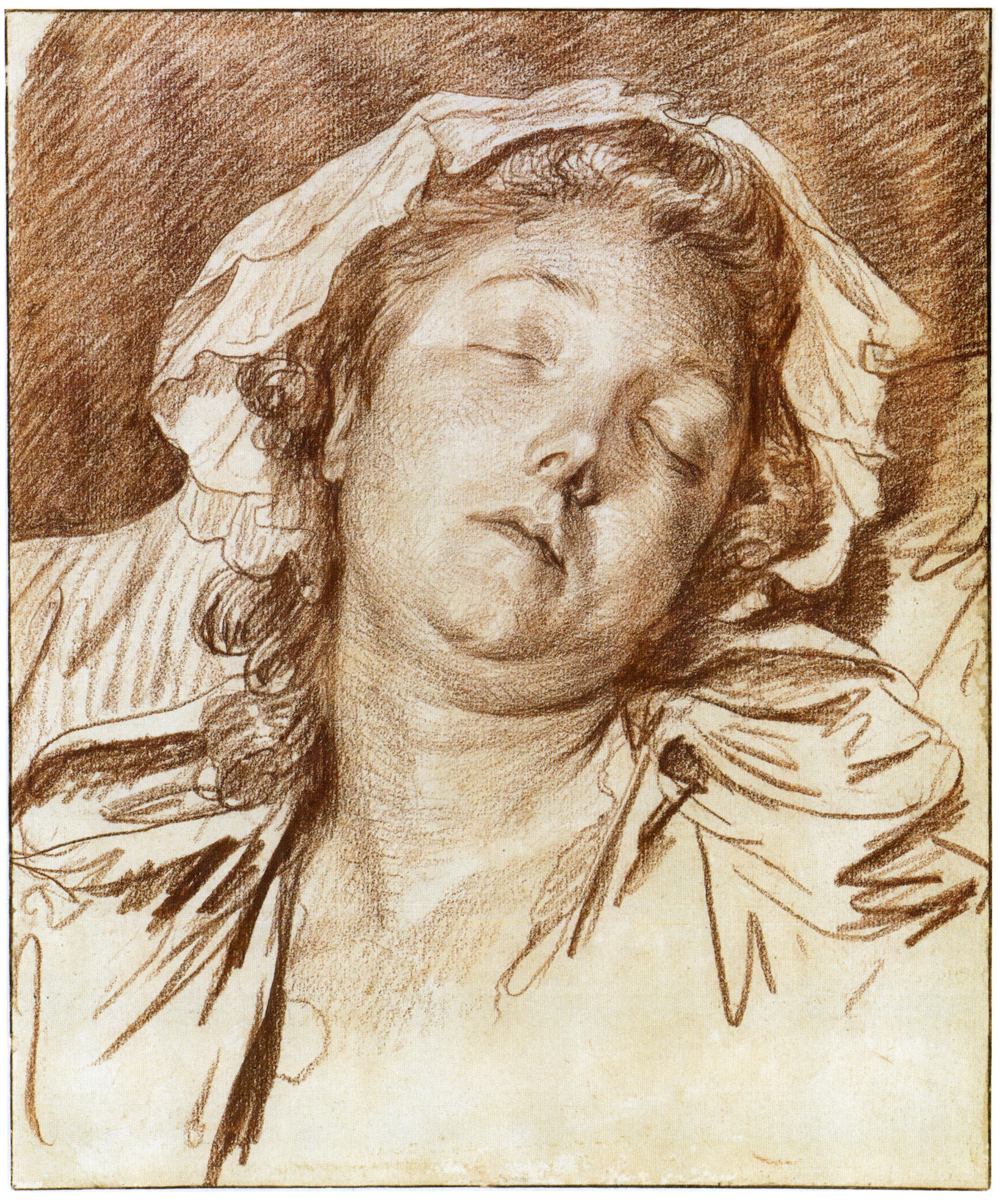

40 *A Seated Woman, Study for "The Beloved Mother"*

Black chalk on cream paper, 405 × 325 mm (16 × 12¾ in.)
Inscribed in pen and black ink at lower left *9-76.;* in pen and brown ink on reverse of old mount *Etude de la mère bien aimée*
St Petersburg, The State Hermitage Museum

Provenance: Ivan Ivanovitch Betskoy, St Petersburg; Imperial Academy of Fine Arts, St Petersburg, 1769 (Lugt S. 2699a); transferred to the Hermitage in 1924
Exhibitions: Leningrad 1926, no. 208; Moscow 1955, p. 73; Leningrad 1956, p. 86; Leningrad and Moscow 1969, no. 11; Budapest 1970, no. 46; Prague 1972, no. 46; Leningrad 1977, no. 80; Florence 1982, no. 90; Leningrad 1983, no. 24; *Masterpieces of Western European Art from the Hermitage,* New Delhi, National Museum of India, 1987, no. 105; *Masterpieces from the Hermitage, Leningrad: Western European Art of the Fifteenth–Twentieth Centuries,* Sydney, Art Gallery of New South Wales; Melbourne, National Gallery of Victoria, 1988, no. 58; Karlsruhe 1996, no. 74; New York 1998–99, no. 97
Bibliography: Monod and Hautecoeur 1922, no. 44, pl. XIV; Kamenskaya 1934, pp. 879–80; Novosselskaya 1975, pp. 473, fig. 8, 474; *eadem* 1985, pp. 78, 83; *eadem* 1987, p. 9; *eadem* in *The State Hermitage: Masterpieces from the Museum's Collections,* London 1994, II, pp. 426–27, no. 351

Probably the earliest surviving study for *The Beloved Mother* (fig. 14), this drawing established the pose and character of the principal subject of that picture, down to her dazed expression, exposed breast, and the vast skirt that anchors her among the bevy of her juvenile admirers. In the only known compositional study for *The Beloved Mother* (no. 43), Greuze repeated the figure as she appears here, with certain adjustments to the skirt that would be followed in the final painting.

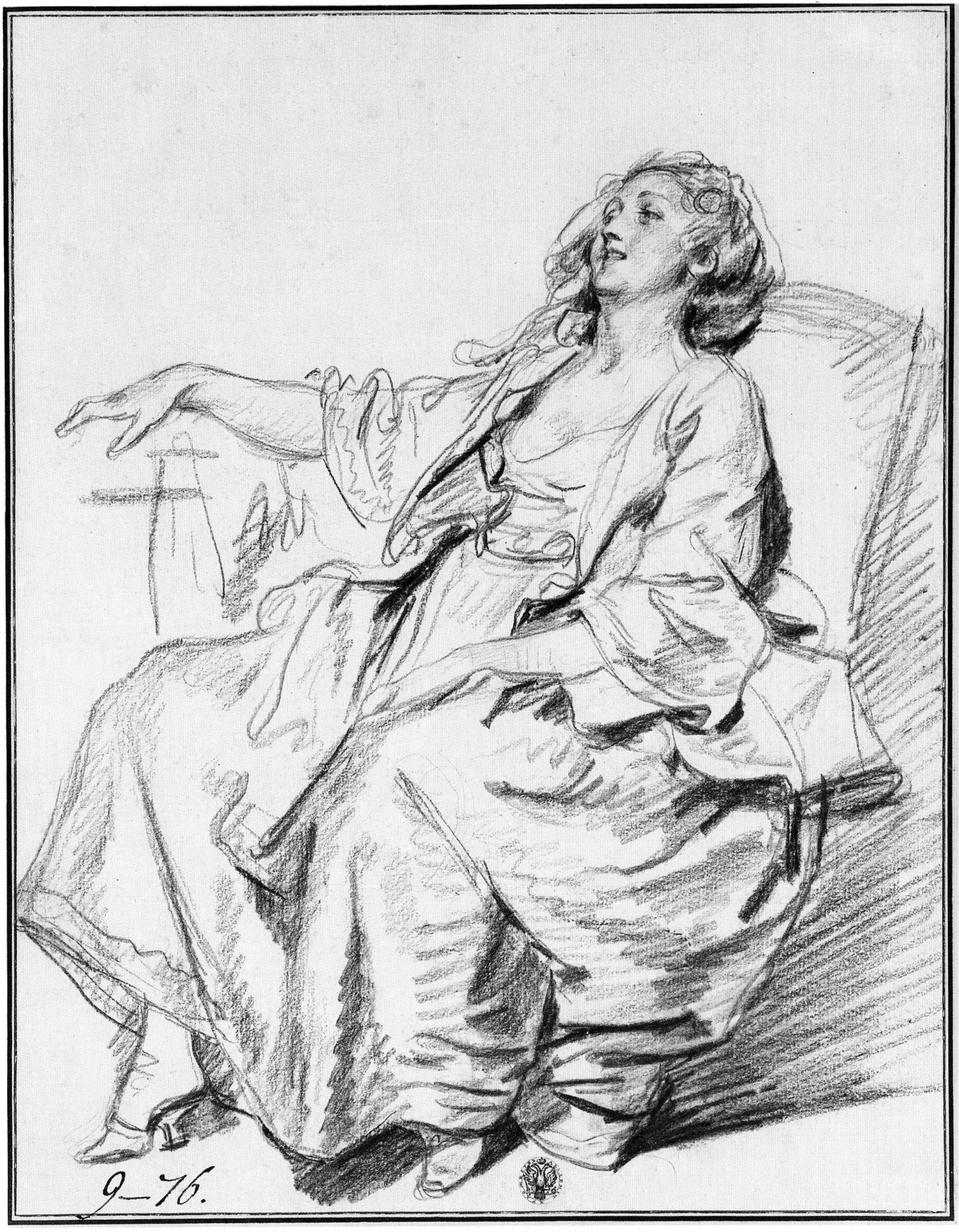
9–76.

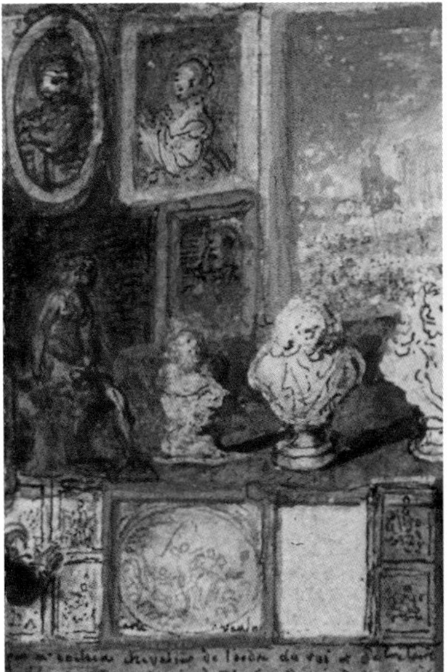

Fig. 102 G. de Saint-Aubin, *The Salon of 1765* (detail), 1765, pen and ink, brush with watercolor, Paris, Musée du Louvre, Département des arts graphiques

41 *The Beloved Mother*

Pastel with red, black, and white chalks on light brown paper, 440 × 322 mm (17 5/16 × 12 11/16 in.)
Washington D.C., National Gallery of Art, New Century Gift Committee

Provenance: Pierre-Joseph-Victor de Besenval, Paris, 1765 (d. 1791); perhaps his sale, Paris, 10 August 1795, lot 86;[1] Jacques Doucet, Paris, by 1899; his sale, Paris, 5 June 1912, no. 73; Édouard de Rothschild, Paris;[2] François Coty, Paris (d. 1934); his sale, Paris, 30 November 1936, lot 21; private collection, France; sale, Paris, 15 November 1999, lot 59; Thomas Agnew & Sons, London
Exhibitions: Exposition de cent pastels du XVIIIe siècle, Paris, Galerie Georges Petit, 1908, no. 20; *Art for the Nation: Collecting for a New Century,* Washington D.C., National Gallery of Art, 2000–2001, pp. 192–93
Bibliography: "Mémorial des Laborde," nos. 7, 11; Lady Dilke, *French Painters of the XVIIIth Century,* London 1899, pp. 132 n. 5, 137; M. Tourneux, "La Collection Jacques Doucet. Pastels et dessins," *Les Arts,* December 1904, pp. 24, 26, repr. p. 27; Martin and Masson 1906, nos. 169, 1181; A. Joubin, "Jacques Doucet, 1853–1929," *GBA,* February 1930, repr. p. 75, fig. 3; Florence 1982, p. 81; F. Chapon, *Mystère et splendeurs de Jacques Doucet, 1853–1929,* Paris 1984, p. 88; Barker 1994, pp. 119, 127

At the Salon of 1765, Greuze exhibited as number 115 *A Head in Pastel (Une Tête en pastel)* that must correspond to the present work. While Jean Seznec stated that the critic Mathon de La Cour wrote that number 115 was not exhibited, what the latter said was in fact not that specific: "We had been promised another head and a portrait that were not exhibited," possibly referring to numbers 114 and 120.[3] Other critics described the *Head in Pastel* in sufficient detail to attest to its presence there at least at some point. Moreover, Margaret Morgan Grasselli was sharp enough to spot its presence in Gabriel de Saint-Aubin's (1724–1780) celebrated view of the Salon of 1765 (fig. 102).[4]

The *Critique des peintures et sculptures* that year specified that number 115 was "the study for the sketch of the good mother," certainly meaning "the beloved mother."[5] Diderot, in the text quoted and discussed below, made the same observation: "it's the sketch, the study for the beloved mother."[6] It was Mathon de La Cour who specified that in the pastel sketch for *The Beloved Mother* (no. 123 in the Salon) the model was Greuze's wife: "Greuze took pleasure in inserting as this beloved mother the portrait of Madame Greuze."[7] Visitors to the Salon were thus able to compare this now-lost compositional sketch for *The Beloved Mother* to the present sheet. In a similar fashion, visitors to the present exhibition can compare the partial compositional sketch for *The Beloved Mother* (no. 43) to the black chalk study for the figure of the mother (no. 40) and this bust. The three were executed probably in that order, the pastel being the ultimate preparation for the mother's head in the painting (fig. 103).

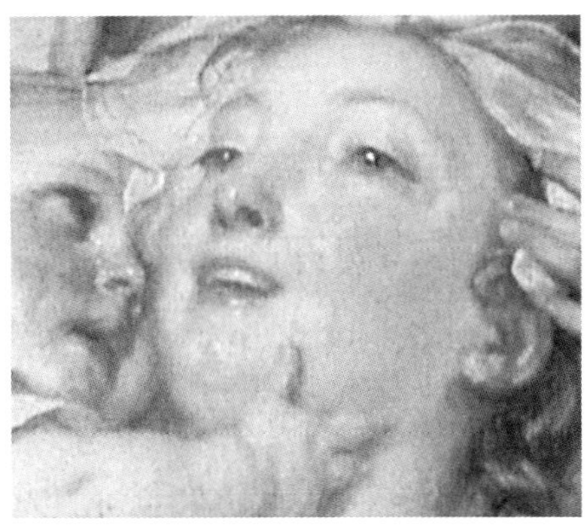

Fig. 103 Greuze, *The Beloved Mother* (detail), 1769, oil on canvas, Madrid, collection comte de la Viñaza, marquis de Laborde

It was the art historian Marcel Nicolle, cataloguing Jacques Doucet's paintings and drawings for the 1912 sale, who first connected Diderot's familiar text of 1765 with the present drawing, not quoting it, but providing the precise bibliographical reference and stating: "the sketch inspired Diderot [to write] one of his most celebrated passages."[8]

Obviously composing from his notes, Diderot began to write, in reference to "114. *Tête en pastel*" (in fact, no. 115): "This is another rather beautiful thing. It is full of truth about flesh, of an infinite freshness and delicacy.... The corners of the mouth, which go down, give her an air of suffering mixed with pleasure." Then he worried that he was confusing the present work with the portrait of Madame Greuze shown at the same Salon—"I'm not sure, my friend, if I'm not mixing up two pictures. I rub my brow in vain, paint and repaint in the air, drag my imagination back to the Salon;

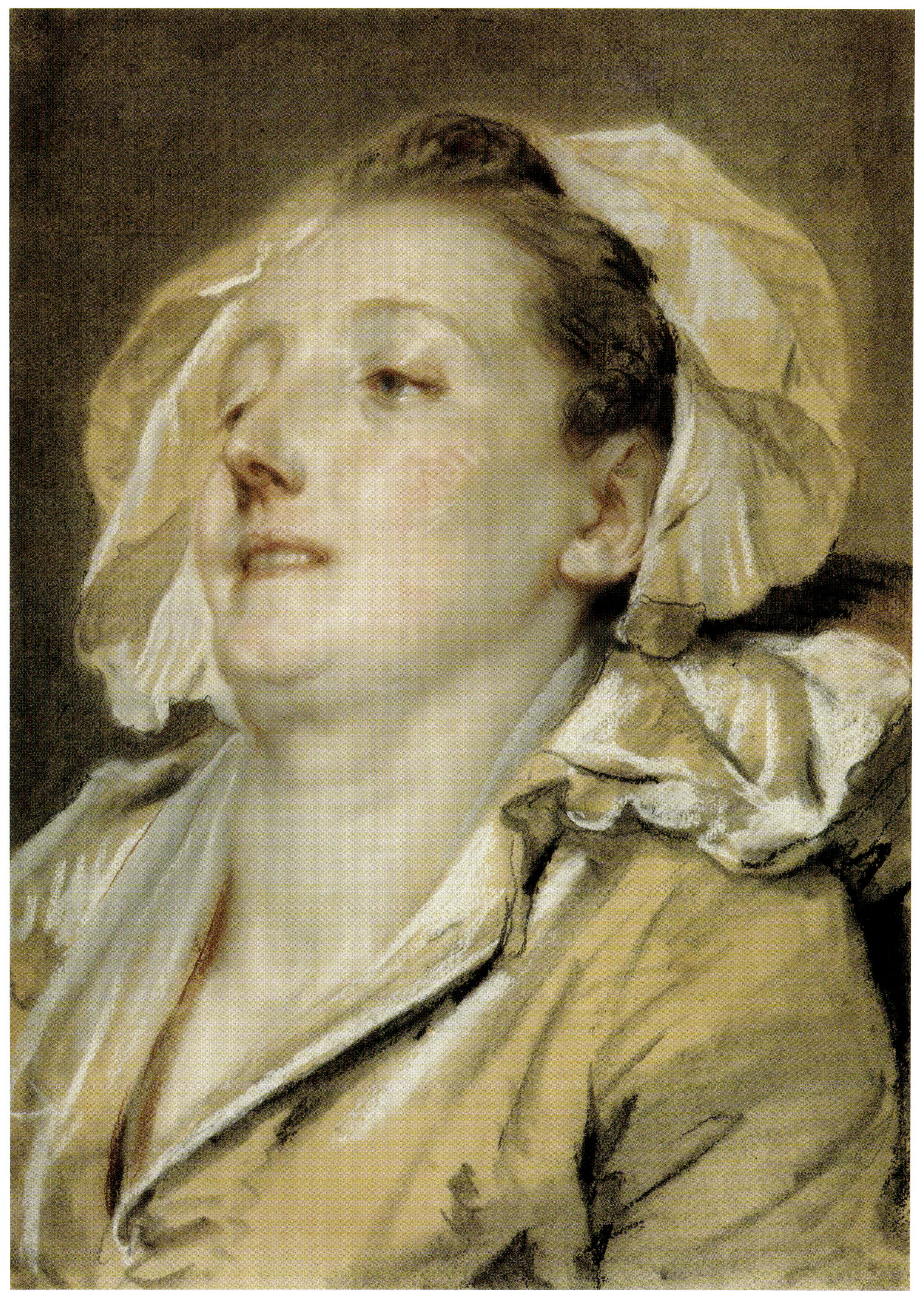

all in vain. There it must stand, just like that."[9] Then, still using the heading "114. *Portrait de madame Greuze,*" he recommenced:

Here, my friend, is evidence of how much ambiguity there may be in the best picture. You see this lovely fish wife, rather plump, who has her head thrown back, her coloring pale, her elaborate bonnet in disarray, with her expression a mixture of pain and pleasure, revealing a moment of ecstasy sweeter to experience than suitable to paint? Now then, this is the sketch, the study of the beloved mother. How is it that here a figure is decent and there it ceases to be?... This half-open mouth, these watery eyes, this thrown-back pose, this swollen throat, this voluptuous mixture of pleasure and pain cause eyes to be averted and all decent women to blush.... Besides, if women quickly pass by this work, men stop in front of it for a long time; that is, those men who are connoisseurs and those who, pretending to be connoisseurs, come to enjoy a spectacle of powerful voluptuousness, and those who, like myself, combine both motivations. There are, on her forehead, and between the forehead and the cheeks, and from the cheeks to the bosom, incredible tonal passages; this teaches you to see nature and reminds you that there is such a thing. You must see the details of that swollen throat, which words cannot describe. This is absolutely beautiful, true to life, and scientifically observed.[10]

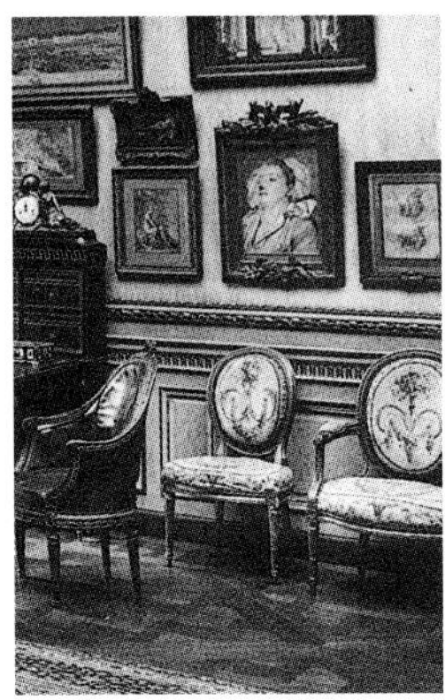

Fig. 104 Unknown photographer, *Salon des pastels of Jacques Doucet's Hôtel,* prior to 1912, Paris, Bibliothèque d'Art et d'Archéologie

If Diderot's sexually charged interpretation of this drawing seems excessive, it must be admitted that the image—with Greuze's uncanny ability to imitate living flesh—is vividly frank in its depiction of swooning ecstasy. Nor was Diderot alone in his reaction, for the above-cited *Critique* noted: "Several people appeared troubled in understanding in what state she is represented. One sees her with her head thrown back, her eyes half-closed and languishing, her mouth open, and her teeth clenched.... The expression captures rather well the tearful joy of a mother responding to the caresses of her babies."[11] Even Lady Dilke, that bluestocking historian, responded intensely to this drawing, when she viewed it in Doucet's *hôtel* in the rue Spontini (fig. 104): "The study in pastel which he made from his wife for the head of 'La Mère bien-aimée' excites our warmest admiration, not only for the marvelous mother-o'-pearl tones of the flesh, but by the masterly drawing, especially noticeable in the rendering of the mouth."[12]

Commenting on Greuze's audacious mixture of expressions in this bust, Diderot said: "Never have you seen the presence of two contrary expressions so precisely characterized. This *tour de force* Rubens did not exceed in the Galerie of the Luxembourg Palace, where the painter depicted in the visage of the queen both the pleasure of having given birth to a son, and the marks of the painful state that preceded it."[13] He was referring, of course, to Peter Paul Rubens's (1577–1640) *Birth of Louis XIII* from the Medici series (fig. 105), which Greuze had studied, mounted on a ladder, in the summer of 1760.[14] From Moreau de Mautour in 1704 to Falconet in 1781, many had commented on this ingenious depiction by Rubens of wildly divergent emotions.[15]

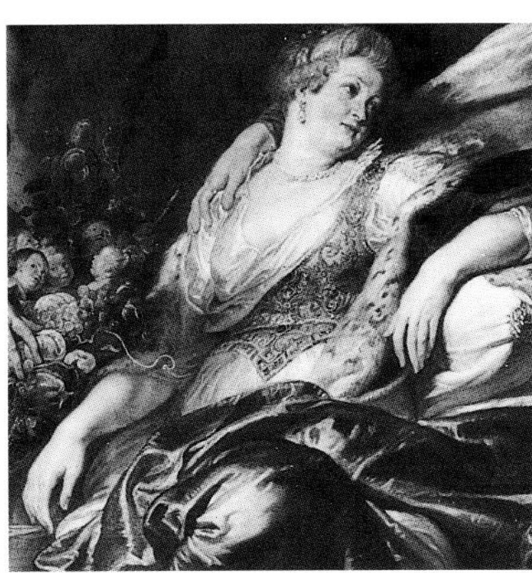

Fig. 105 P.P. Rubens, *The Birth of Louis XIII* (detail), 1622–25, oil on canvas, Paris, Musée du Louvre

The extraordinary, original frame, which barely contains this explosive image (fig. 106), was described in the Doucet sale catalogue as being of the period of 1765 (though, ironically, characterized as *Louis XVI*), with its decorative components partially detailed: "phoenix, foliage... horse's head, urn disgorging its water."[16] The "phoenix" or pelican at the top of the frame, depicted feeding its young with its own blood—a traditional Christian symbol of Christ caring for his Church—is perfectly appropriate to the subject of *The Beloved Mother,* as is the cornucopia, emblem of abundance, at the left, while the imagery below of the straining horse would apply equally well to the subject of the father in this picture, shown returning from the hunt (fig. 14). Such an elaborate frame corresponds generally to those cartouche-adorned ones depicted in Henri-Pierre Danloux's (1753–1809) portrait of the original owner of the present drawing, as specified in the catalogue of the Salon of 1765, the baron de Besenval (fig. 107), commander-in-chief of the ill-fated Swiss Guards, who were slaughtered by a Parisian mob while defending the royal family.[17]

Fig. 106 Unknown sculptor, frame, 1765, gilded wood, Washington D.C., National Gallery of Art

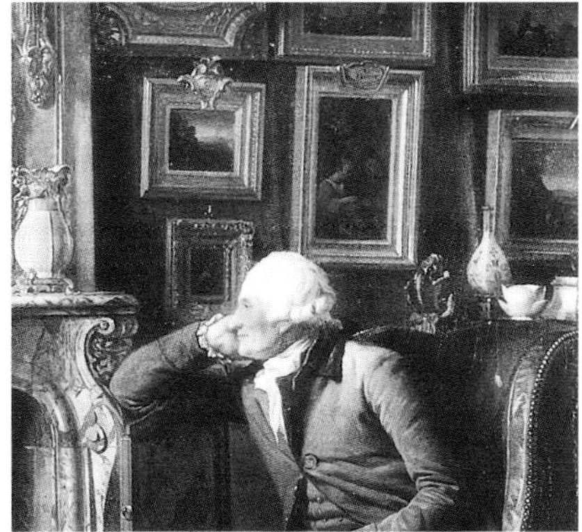

Fig. 107 H.-P. Danloux, *The Baron de Besenval in His "Salon de Compagnie"* (detail), 1791, oil on canvas, private collection

1. Under no. 86 in the catalogue of the de Besenval sale, it is noted: *"Différentes belles gouaches, dessins et estampes faisant suite du cabinet mais que le temps ne nous a pas permis de détailler comme plusieurs morceaux l'auroient mérités, seront détaillées sous ce numéro."* This was the only listing for drawings in the sale.

2. A note in the annotated copy of the Doucet sale catalogue in the Frick Art Reference Library states: *"35,000/ Danlos pour Ed. de Rothschild."*

3. Seznec in Diderot *Salons,* II, p. 36: *"On avait promis une autre tête et un portrait qui n'ont pas été exposés."* Mathon de La Cour 1765, p. 8.

4. See *Art for the Nation. Collecting for a New Century* 2000–2001, p. 311 n. 1.

5. *"l'étude pour l'esquisse de la bonne mère." Critiques des peintures et sculptures de Messieurs de l'Académie royale l'an 1765,* Paris 1765, p. 27.

6. *"c'est l'esquisse, l'étude de la mère bien-aimée."* Diderot *Salons,* II, p. 151.

7. Mathon de La Cour 1765, pp. 26–27.

8. *"L'esquisse a inspiré à Diderot un de ses passages les plus célèbres."* M. Nicolle in Doucet sale catalogue, 5 June 1912, p. 77.

9. *"C'est encore une assez belle chose. Il y a tout plein de vérité de chair, et un moelleux infini.... Les coins de la bouche qui baissent, lui donnent un air de douleur mêlé de plaisir. Je ne sais, mon ami, si je ne brouille pas ici deux tableaux. J'ai beau me frotter le front, peindre et repeindre dans l'espace, ramener l'imagination au Salon; peine inutile. Il faut que cela reste, comme le voilà."* Diderot *Salons,* II, pp. 150–51.

10. *"Voici, mon ami, de quoi montrer combien il reste d'équivoque dans le meilleur tableau. Vous voyez bien cette belle poissarde, avec son gros embonpoint, qui a la tête renversée en arrière, dont la couleur blême, le linge de tête étalé en désordre, l'expression mêlée de peine et de plaisir, montrent un paroxisme plus doux à éprouver qu'honnête à peindre? Eh bien! c'est l'esquisse, l'étude de la mère bien-aimée. Comment se fait-il qu'ici un caractère soit décent, et que là il cesse de l'être?... Cette bouche entr'ouverte, ces yeux nageans, cette attitude renversée, ce cou gonflé, ce mélange voluptueux de peine et de plaisir, font baisser les yeux et rougir toutes les honnêtes femmes dans cet endroit. Tout à côté, c'est la même attitude, les mêmes yeux, le même cou, le même mélange de passions, et aucune d'elles ne s'en aperçoit... Au reste, si les femmes passent vîte devant ce morceau, les hommes s'y arrêtent longtemps; j'entends ceux qui s'y connoissent, et ceux qui, sous prétexte de s'y connoître, viennent jouir d'un spectacle de volupté forte, et ceux qui, comme moi, réunissent les deux motifs. Il y a au front, et du front sur les joues, et des joues vers la gorge, des passages de tons incroyables; cela vous apprend à voir la nature, et vous la rappelle. Il faut voir les détails de ce cou gonflé, et n'en pas parler. Cela est tout-à-fait beau, vrai et savant."* Diderot *Salons,* II, p. 151.

11. *"Plusieurs personnes ont parues inquiets de savoir dans quel état elle est représentée. On la voit la tête panchée, les yeux à demi-fermés et languissants, la bouche ouverte et les dents serrés.... L'expression désigne assez un état d'attendrissement d'une mère qui jouit des caresses de sa famille." Critiques* 1765, p. 27.

12. Dilke 1899, p. 137.

13. *"Jamais vous n'avez vu la présence de deux expressions contraires aussi nettement caractérisés. Ce tour de force, Rubens ne l'a pas mieux fait à la galerie du Luxembourg, où le peintre a montré sur le visage de la reine et le plaisir d'avoir mis au monde un fils, et les traces du douloureux état qui a précédé."* Diderot *Salons,* II, p. 155.

14. See Wille 1857, I, p. 139.

15. See J. Thuillier and J. Foucart, *Rubens' Life of Marie de Medici,* New York 1967, pp. 80–81; Seznec in Diderot *Salons,* II, pp. 36–37.

16. *"cadre d'époque Louis XVI, orné de motifs: phénix, feuillages.... tête de cheval, urne épanchant son onde."* Doucet sale catalogue, 5 June 1912, p. 77.

17. See C.B. Bailey in *An Aspect of Collecting Taste,* exhib. cat., New York, Stair Sainty Matthiesen, 1986, pp. 48–53, no. 17, repr. p. 49.

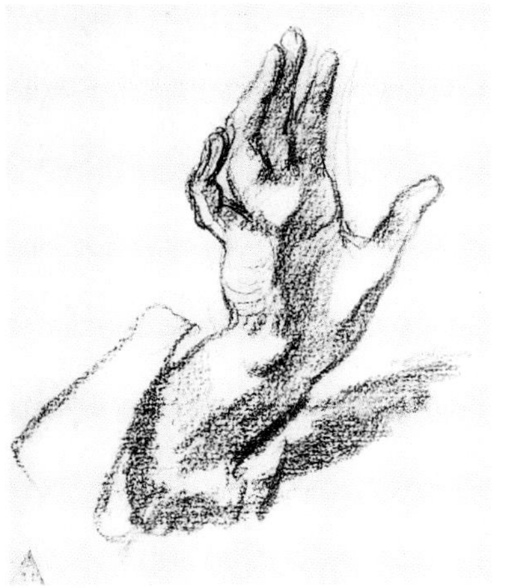

Fig. 108 Greuze, *A Woman's Right Hand, Study for "The Beloved Mother,"* red chalk on white paper, 1765, whereabouts unknown

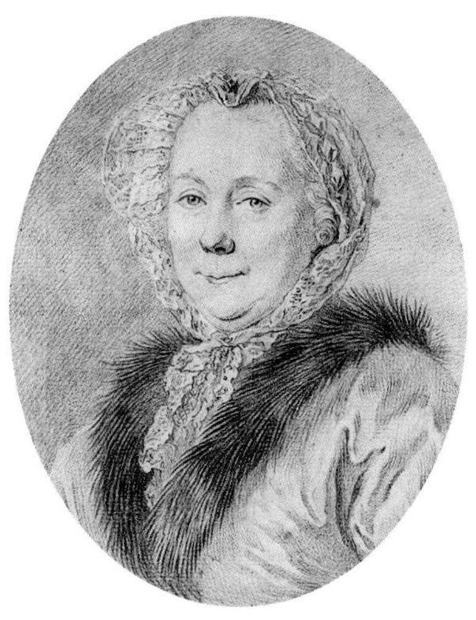

Fig. 109 A. de Saint-Aubin (?), after J. Bernard, *Portrait of Barbe-Louise, vicomtesse de Nettine,* graphite on white paper, 1763, New Haven, Yale University Art Gallery, gift of Edward B. Greene, B.A. 1900

42 *Seated Elderly Woman, Study for "The Beloved Mother"*

Red chalk on cream paper, 378 × 289 mm (14⅞ × 11⅜ in.)
Paris, Musée du Louvre, Département des arts graphiques

Provenance: original collection of the Cabinet des Dessins du Louvre (Saint Morys collection) (Lugt 1886, 2207)
Exhibitions: Rococo: Masterpieces of XVIII Century French Art from the Museums of France, San Francisco, California Palace of the Legion of Honor, 1949, no. 22; *Art français,* Tokyo, Kyoto, and Fukuoka, 1954–55, no. 54; *Le XVIIIe siècle français,* Venice, Vienna, and Zurich, 1955, no. 120; *Kunst und Geist Frankreichs im 18. Jahrhundert,* Vienna, Oberes Belvedere, 1966, no. 84; Hartford *et al.* 1976–77, no. 46
Bibliography: Morel d'Arleux, no. 12645/12; "Mémorial des Laborde," p. 100; Normand 1892, repr. facing p. 19; Martin and Masson 1906, nos. 169, 1520; Guiffrey and Marcel 1911, p. 58, no. 4559; Hautecoeur 1913, pl. xxiv; Bouchot-Saupique 1939, no. 5; Brookner 1972, p. 111, pl. 44; Arquié-Bruley *et al.* 1987, ii, p. 499; Roland Michel 1987, p. 214, fig. 255

This study for the central figure of the grandmother in *The Beloved Mother* (fig. 14) depicts the mother-in-law of the man who commissioned that painting, the marquis Jean-Joseph de Laborde, Barbe-Louise, vicomtesse de Nettine (1706–1775). Born Mademoiselle Stoupy, she married the Belgian banker Matthias de Nettine. Following his death, Empress Maria-Theresa conferred on her the title of vicomtesse, for the services Madame de Nettine was rendering her as banker in The Netherlands, as her father's successor. Madame de Nettine's daughter Rosalie-Claire-Josèphe Nettine (1737–1811) married Laborde in 1760.[1]

In addition to this majestic depiction of the grandmother-banker, Greuze executed a study of her right hand, open in a gesture of excitement (fig. 108). Though difficult to spot in the painting, the servant girl only partially indicated at the doorway repeats this movement. A contemporary portrait drawing of Madame de Nettine, considered to be a copy, perhaps by Augustin de Saint-Aubin (1736–1807), after a lost drawing by Joseph Bernard, presents the woman's features in a more conventional way (fig. 109).[2]

In his description of the sketch of *The Beloved Mother* exhibited at the Salon of 1765, Mathon de La Cour referred to the figure of the grandmother thus: "The grandmother is moved to the point of tears by this tender scene."[3] The same year, Diderot chided an imaginary person who might have said, "Oh, I could have painted that," by asking, "And that grandmother, you would have thought of putting her there; you are quite sure of it!"[4] He went on to describe her appearance, in a setting different from both the final composition and the early compositional study exhibited here (no. 43): "At the rear of the room, her back turned to a fireplace surmounted by a mirror, the grandmother seated in an armchair, and very grandmotherly in expression and attire, bursting into laughter at the scene taking place."[5] What Diderot wrote that year on Greuze's draftsmanship in general could have been written about this drawing in particular: "The pen of the poet, the chalk of the skillful draftsman, seem to run along and frolic together."[6]

1. For biographical details, see F. Courboin, *Histoire illustrée de la gravure en France,* Paris 1924, ii, p. 141; T. de Morembert, "Laborde (Jean-Joseph de)," *Dictionnaire de biographie française,* Paris 1989, xviii, p. 1371; J.-P. Poisson, "Le Notariat parisien à la fin du 18e siècle," *Dix-huitième siècle,* no. 7, 1975, p. 109.

2. A. Wolf, *The Edward B. Greene Collection of Engraved Portraits and Portrait Drawings at Yale University,* New Haven and London 1952, no. 13, pl. xxxv, fig. 3; E. Haverkamp-Begemann and A.-M.S. Logan, *European Drawings and Watercolors in the Yale University Art Gallery,* New Haven 1970, i, no. 38.

3. *"La grand'mère est touchée jusqu'aux larmes de cette scène tendre."* Mathon de La Cour 1765, pp. 11–12.

4. *"Et cette grand'mère, vous auriez songé à l'amener là; vous en êtes sûr!"* Diderot *Salons,* ii, p. 154.

5. *"Sur le fond du salon, le dos tourné à une cheminée couverte d'une glace, la grand'mère assise dans un fauteuil, et bien grand'mèrisée de tête et d'ajustemens, éclatant de rire de la scène qui se passe."* Diderot *Salons,* ii, p. 155.

6. *"La plume du poète, le crayon du dessinateur habile, ont l'air de courir et de se jouer."* Diderot *Salons,* ii, p. 154.

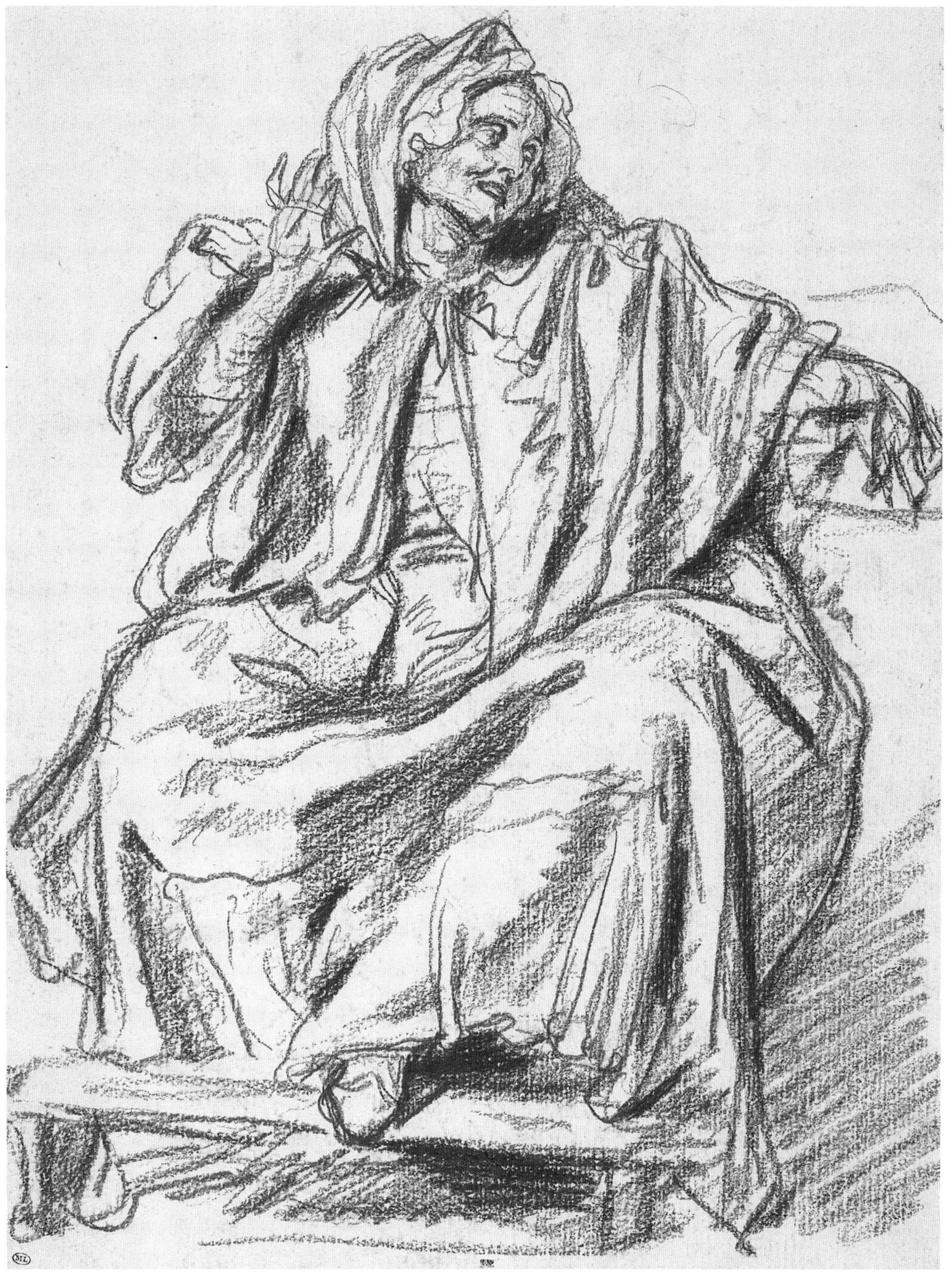

43 *Compositional Study for "The Beloved Mother"*

Pen and brush with black and brown ink over graphite on white paper, 332 × 378 mm (13 1/16 × 4 7/8 in.)
Signed in ink at lower right *Greuze*
Vienna, Graphische Sammlung Albertina

Provenance: Duke Albert of Sachsen und Teschen (Lugt 174), Vienna
Exhibitions: None known
Bibliography: "Mémorial des Laborde," p. 101; J. Seznec in Diderot *Salons,* II, p. 37; Wildenstein 1960, pp. 229, fig. 2, 230

This must be a preliminary compositional study for the right half of *The Beloved Mother* (fig. 14), a painting listed in the catalogue of the Salon of 1769 but not exhibited (see no. 70).

An *esquisse* of this subject appeared in the Salon of 1765 (no. 123). While it is clear from Diderot's detailed description of the latter that he was not speaking of the present drawing, his opening words certainly seem appropriate to it: "Sketches have in common a flame that the finished painting does not. It is the moment of heat for the artist, pure zest, with no admixture of the stiffening that reflection adds to everything; it is the soul of the painter that spreads itself freely across the canvas."[1] The unknown compiler of the "Mémorial des Laborde" was also right in characterizing the present drawing as "rather bold in its coloring,"[2] for this is a powerful work and signed with a vigor equal to its draftsmanship.

With a few discrepancies, Diderot's remarks about the group around the mother as represented in the sketch exhibited in 1765 apply equally well to the present drawing: *then the beloved mother falling back onto her chaise longue, and with all the children strewn over her. There must be six at least: the smallest one is between her arms; a second one hangs from one side; a third one hangs from the other; a fourth one, who has climbed over the back of the chair, kisses her forehead; a fifth one is chewing her cheeks; a sixth one, standing, his head resting on her [the mother's] lap, and not happy with his role. The mother of these children has joy and tenderness painted on her face, with a bit of that malaise inseparable from the movement and weight of so many children who overwhelm her, and whose violent caresses will sooner or later wear her out if they go on. It is this feeling close to pain, mingling with tenderness and joy, with that thrown-back position and sense of exhaustion, plus that half-open mouth, that give this head, considered apart from the rest of the composition, such a singular character.*[3]

The genesis and meaning of *The Beloved Mother* are discussed with number 70.

1. *"Les esquisses ont communément un feu que le tableau n'a pas. C'est le moment de chaleur de l'artiste, la verve pure, sans aucun mélange de l'apprêt que la réflexion met à tout; c'est l'âme du peintre qui se répand librement sur la toile."* Diderot *Salons,* II, pp. 153–54.

2. *"assez accusé de couleurs."* "Mémorial des Laborde," p. 101.

3. *"puis la mère bien-aimée renversée sur sa chaise longue, et tous ses enfans répandus sur elle. Il y en a six au moins: le plus petit est entre ses bras; un second est pendu d'un côté; un troisième est pendu de l'autre; un quatrième, grimpé au dossier de la chaise, lui baise le front; un cinquième lui mange les joues; un sixième, debout, a la tête penchée sur son giron, et n'est pas content de son rôle. La mère de ces enfans a la joie et la tendresse peintes sur son visage, avec un peu de ce mal-aise inséparable du mouvement et du poids de tant d'enfans qui l'accablent, et dont les caresses violentes ne tarderoient pas à l'excéder si elles duroient. C'est cette sensation qui touche à la peine, fondue avec la tendresse et la joie, avec cette position renversée et de lassitude, et cette bouche entr'ouverte, qui donnent à cette tête, séparée du reste de la composition, un caractère si singulier."* Diderot *Salons,* II, pp. 154–55.

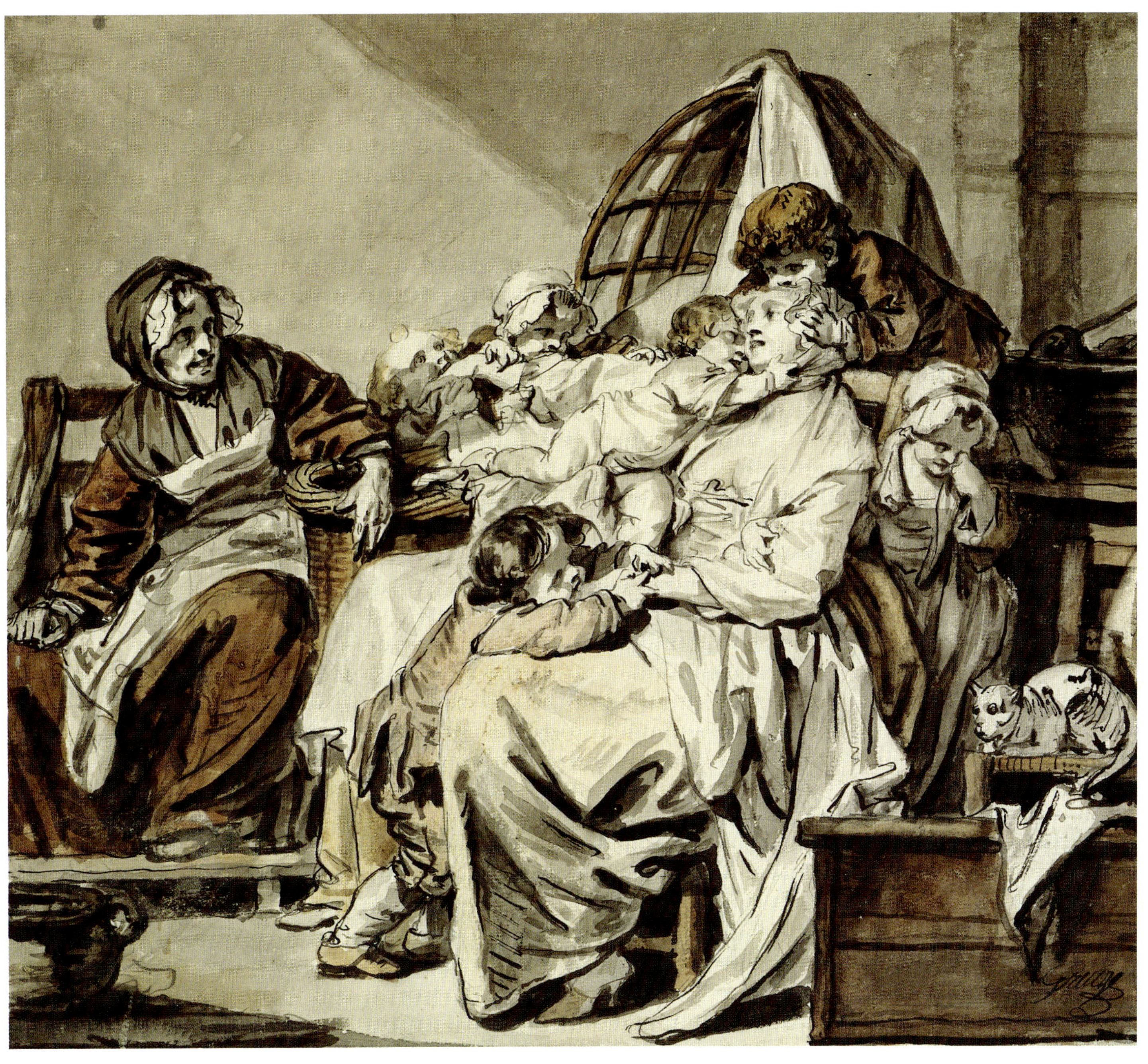

44 *A Child Seen from Behind, Study for "The Beloved Mother"*

Black chalk on white paper, 301 × 248 mm (11 $^{13}/_{16}$ × 9 $^{3}/_{4}$ in.)
Inscribed in pen and black ink at lower left *9-77.;* in pen and brown ink on reverse of old mount *Etude de la mère bien aimée*
St Petersburg, The State Hermitage Museum

Provenance: Ivan Ivanovitch Betskoy, St Petersburg; Imperial Academy of Fine Arts, St Petersburg, 1769 (Lugt S. 2699a); transferred to the Hermitage in 1924
Exhibitions: Budapest 1970, no. 47; *Meisterzeichnungen aus der Eremitage in Leningrad, des Puschkin-Museum und der Tretjakow-Galerie in Moskau,* Vienna, Graphische Sammlung Albertina; Graz, Neue Galerie, 1972, no. 27; Leningrad 1977, no. 82
Bibliography: Monod and Hautecoeur 1922, no. 32, pl. VIII; Kamenskaya 1934, pp. 79–80

In this study for the child nestled between its mother's legs in *The Beloved Mother,* he appears much as he does in the final painting (fig. 14), though his expression here is more frightened than dreamy. But details such as the opened bodice and the raised left foot are established in this preparatory study. While the sex of the child in the present drawing is uncertain (very young children were usually dressed as girls), in the earlier, general compositional study, the comparable figure is definitely a boy, eagerly trying to distract his mother (no. 43). Describing the lost sketch of *The Beloved Mother* shown at the Salon of 1765, Diderot described this child as "standing, his head resting on her [the mother's] lap, and not happy with his role."[1]

A separate study for the head of the child in the present drawing also figured among the drawings acquired by Betskoy (fig. 110). Though presumably drawn at the same time, it was executed in red chalk.[2]

1. *"debout, a la tête penchée sur son giron, et n'est pas content de son rôle."* Diderot *Salons,* II, p. 154.

2. The State Hermitage Museum, inv. no. 14474. See Martin and Masson 1906, no. 1766; Monod and Hautecoeur 1922, no. 144, pl. LVII. What appears to be a copy of it was sold in Paris, 26 March 1973, lot 15, repr.

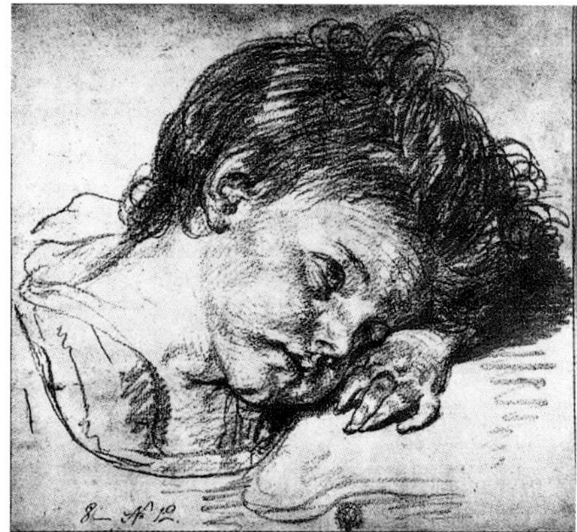

Fig. 110 Greuze, *Head of a Child, c.* 1765, red chalk on white paper, St Petersburg, The State Hermitage Museum

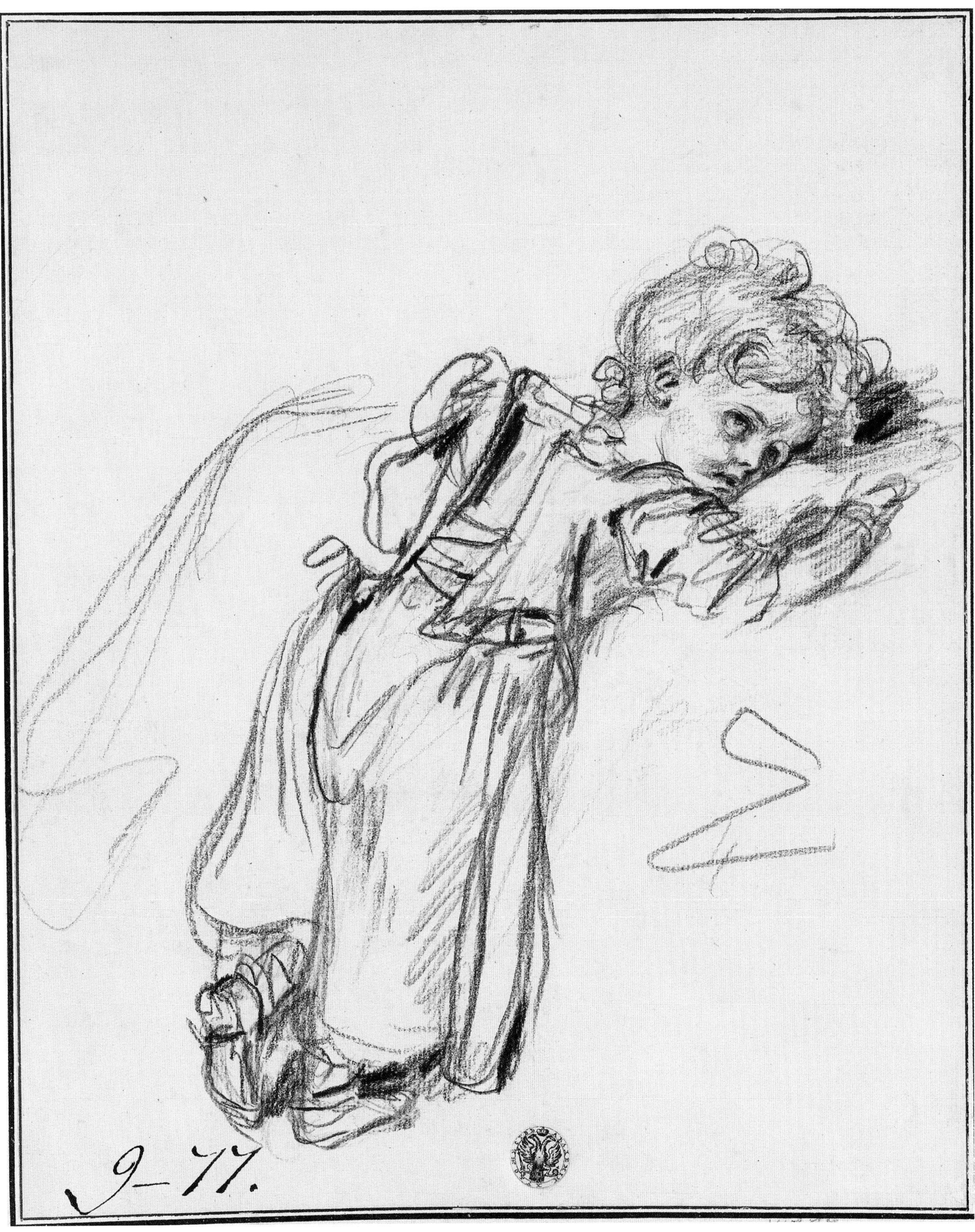
9-77.

45 *A Girl Leaning Forward, Study for "The Beloved Mother"*

Red chalk on cream paper, 320 × 214 mm (12 9/16 × 8 7/16 in.)
Inscribed in pen and black ink at lower left *9-54.;* in pen and brown ink on reverse of old mount *Etude de la mère bien aimée*
St Petersburg, The State Hermitage Museum

Provenance: Ivan Ivanovitch Betskoy, St Petersburg; Imperial Academy of Fine Arts, St Petersburg, 1769 (Lugt S. 2699a); transferred to the Hermitage in 1924
Exhibition: Leningrad 1977, no. 81
Bibliography: "Mémorial des Laborde," no. 8; Monod and Hautecoeur 1922, no. 34, pl. x; Kamenskaya 1934, pp. 79–80; Barker 1994, pp. 118–19, 128

This is a study for the girl at the far right of *The Beloved Mother* (fig. 14), where she appears to be the eldest of the six children clambering around and over their mother. The sole figure in the picture to address her gaze to the viewer, she does so with flirtatious directness. The comparable figure in the compositional sketch (no. 43) appears slightly younger and weeps with disappointment for failing to hold her mother's attention, even though her right arm remains clasped around the mother's. In the final painting, as Emma Barker observed, she seems eager to aspire to her mother's fecund role.

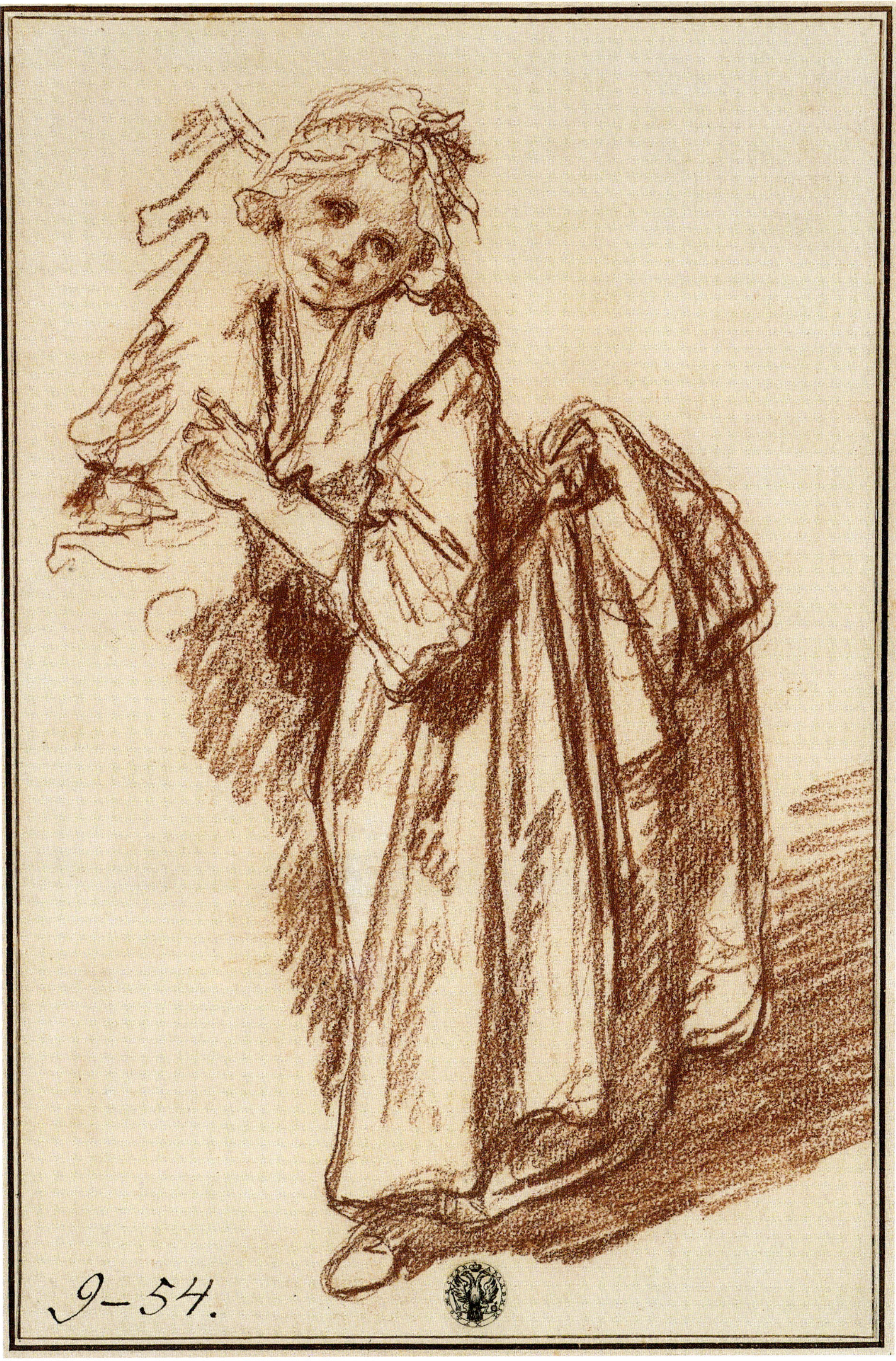

46 *The School Mistress*

Black chalk, pen and black ink, brush with black and brown ink wash on white paper, 330 × 444 mm (13 × 17 ½ in.)
Signed in pen and black ink both at lower left and on the back of the kneeling figure in the center of the drawing *J. B. Greuze*
St Petersburg, The State Hermitage Museum

Provenance: Count Karl Cobenzl, Brussels (Lugt S. 2858b);[1] acquired by the Hermitage in 1768 (Lugt 2061)
Exhibitions: Leningrad 1926, no. 205; Moscow 1955, p. 73; Leningrad 1956, p. 86; Stockholm 1963, no. 44; Leningrad and Moscow 1969, no. 17; Leningrad 1977, no. 85; Leningrad 1983, no. 25; Karlsruhe 1996, no. 75; New York 1998–99, no. 98
Bibliography: N. Makarenko, *Khudozhestvennye sokrovishcha Imperatorskogo Ermitazha* (The artistic treasures of the imperial Hermitage), Petrograd 1916, pp. 222, 224; I. Ioffe, *Frantsuzskoe iskusstvo epokhi razlozheniia feodaizma* (French art from the end of feudalism), Leningrad 1932, p. 80; "Mémorial des Laborde," p. 105; Kamenskaya 1934, pp. 221–22; *eadem* 1947, pp. 2–6; Brookner 1972, p. 100; Novosselskaya 1975, p. 474, fig. 9; Hartford *et al.* 1976–77, pp. 22–23, fig. 12; The State Hermitage Museum, *Western European Drawing,* Leningrad 1981, no. 92

As Kamenskaya demonstrated in her delicious article of 1934, this drawing is the one Greuze made on learning that Madame Geoffrin, noted Parisian hostess and art patron, had described his *Beloved Mother* of 1765 (see no. 43) as a "fricassee of babies."[2]

Already aware five years earlier of Madame Geoffrin's criticism of his work, the artist had then exclaimed, according to Diderot: "By God! if she annoys me, she had better watch out. I'll do a painting of her."[3] This time, Greuze was more specific in his threats, as recorded by Baron Grimm: "What right has she to speak of a work of art? Let her tremble that I might immortalize her! I'll paint her as a school mistress, a whip in her hand, and she will frighten every child alive and every one yet to be born!"[4]

Greuze, who had attended Madame Geoffrin's Monday gatherings of artists and was familiar with his hostess's prudish demands for proper behavior at them, ingeniously captured their ambiance in *The School Mistress,* where the tyrannical teacher

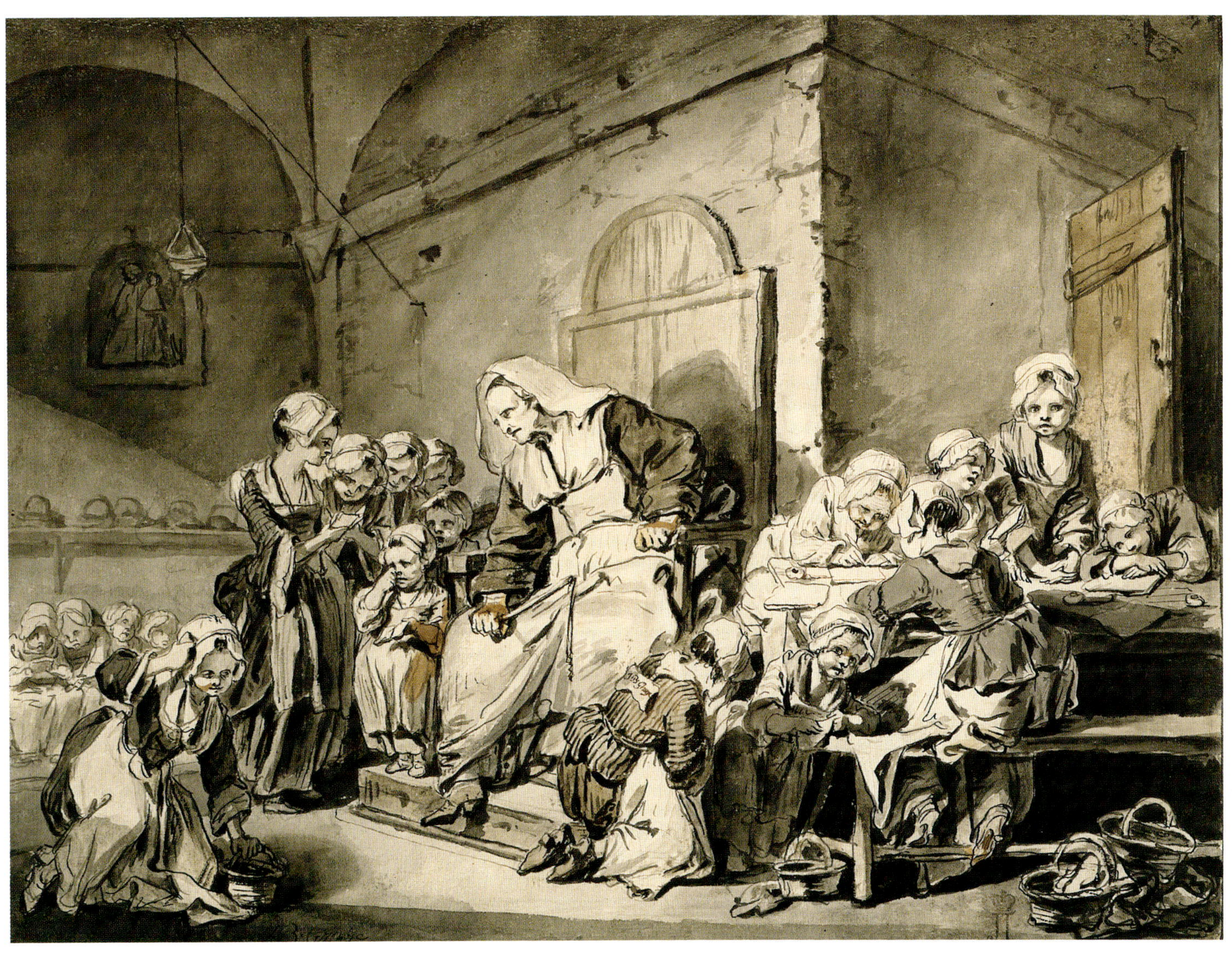

dominates her timorous crowd from her high-backed chair, just as François Boucher (1703–1770) had depicted *la Geoffriniska* doing in her own salon (fig. 111). For the principal figure, Greuze adapted the pose from a contemporary study for his composition *The Severe Mother* (fig. 112).[5]

Madame Geoffrin's negative reaction to Greuze's *The Beloved Mother* was no doubt provoked by the overt sexuality of that picture. Preferring idealized images of children—her collection included five by François-Hubert Drouais (1727–1775)—she owned a single work by Greuze: one of the two versions of his *Simplicity* (fig. 113), painted on commission for the marquis de Marigny, brother of Madame de Pompadour and a close friend of Madame Geoffrin.[6]

1. See catalogue of the Cobenzl collection: "Catal[ogue] de Cabin[et], Catalogue de Desseins, troisième Grandeur," ms., fol. 44 verso, *carton* no. 5: *"Greuze, no. 25,* La Maîtresse d'école."

2. *"fricassé d'enfants."* Quoted in Kamenskaya 1934, p. 222.

3. *"Mort Dieu! si elle me fâche, qu'elle y prenne garde, je la peindrai."* Diderot, *Oeuvres complètes,* ed. J. d'Assézat, Paris 1876, XVIII, p. 467.

4. *"De quoi s'avise-t-elle, de parler d'un ouvrage de l'art? Je la peindrai en maîtresse d'école, le fouet à la main, et elle fera peur à tous les enfants présents et à naître."* Diderot 1876, XI, p. 441. For Madame Geoffrin, see P. de Ségur, *Le Royaume de la rue Saint-Honoré,* Paris 1897; G. de Lastic Saint-Jal, "La Reine de la Rue Saint-Honoré," *L'Oeil,* September 1957, pp. 50–57; B. Scott, "Madame Geoffrin: A Patron and Friend of Artists," *Apollo,* February 1967, pp. 98–103; P.R. Radisich, *Hubert Robert, Painted Spaces of the Enlightenment,* Cambridge 1998, pp. 15–53.

5. See Hartford *et al.* 1976–77, p. 110, no. 47.

6. See Hartford *et al.* 1976–77, pp. 68–69, no. 24; Paris 1984, pp. 227–28, no. 60; *In Pursuit of Quality: The Kimbell Art Museum,* Fort Worth TX 1987, p. 228.

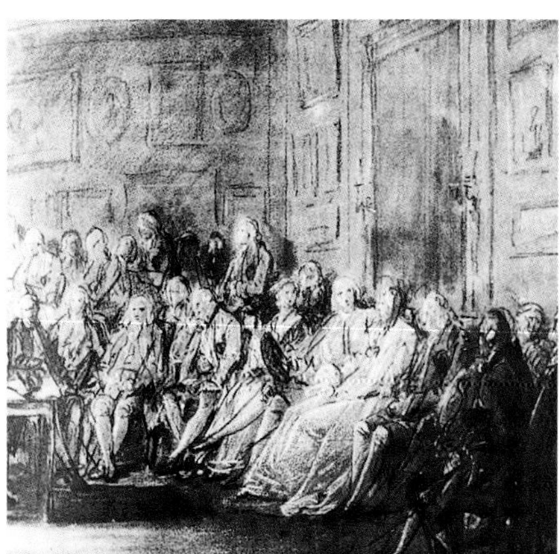

Fig. 111 F. Boucher, *A Reading by d'Alembert in the Salon of Madame Geoffrin* (detail), *c.* 1760, black and white chalks on blue paper, private collection

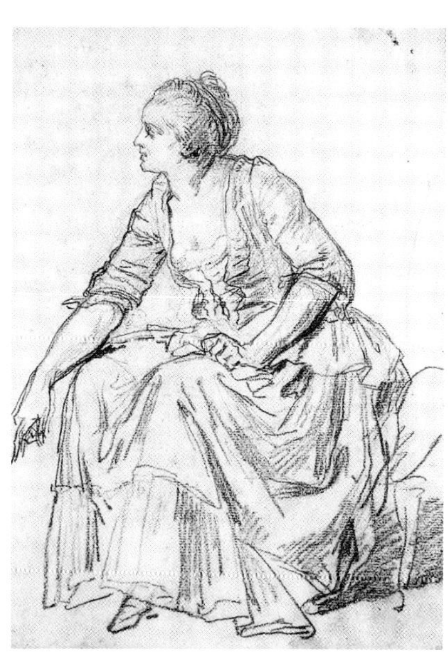

Fig. 112 Greuze, *Seated Female Figure, Study for "The Severe Mother," c.* 1765, red chalk on white paper, Hartford CT, Wadsworth Atheneum, Henry and Walter Keney Fund

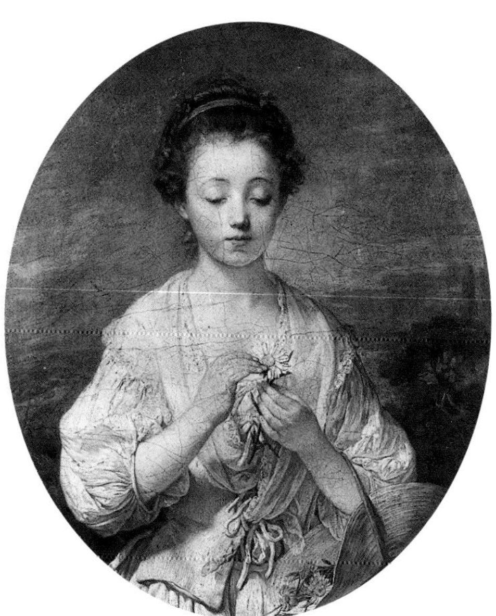

Fig. 113 Greuze, *Simplicity,* 1758, oil on canvas, Fort Worth TX, The Kimbell Art Museum

47 *Head of a Woman*

Red chalk on cream paper, 430 × 330 mm (16 15/16 × 13 in.)
Private collection

Provenance: London, Matthiesen Gallery, 1950; Paris, Galerie Cailleux, 1951; sale, New York, 8 January 1991, lot 7
Exhibitions: French Master Drawings of the 18th Century, London, Matthiesen Gallery, 1950, no. 37; *Le Dessin français de Watteau à Prud'hon,* Paris, Galerie Cailleux, 1951, no. 65
Bibliography: Martin and Masson 1906, no. 1367; E. Munhall, "The Dreamer," *Hall & Knight MMI,* London and New York 2001, p. 149, fig. 84

This depiction of postorgasmic ecstasy must be a preparatory study for the picture known as *La Volupté,* of which at least two versions exist today (figs. 114, 115).

The image derives from portraits of his wife that Greuze had begun exhibiting in 1761, two years after their marriage: *Portrait of Madame Greuze as a Vestal Virgin* (Diderot: "That one, a vestal virgin!");[1] another in 1763, *Portrait of Madame Greuze* (Diderot: "portrait of the pregnant Madame Greuze");[2] and the two presented at the Salon of 1765: number 41 and a portrait of Madame Greuze with a dog. Critics' remarks concerning the latter two (see pp. 130, 126) could apply almost as well to this drawing, which is probably contemporary with them, but it is doubtful that even Greuze would have exhibited at the Salon so frankly carnal an image as *La Volupté,* let alone identifying it as a portrait of his wife.

Diderot, who remarked in 1765 that "This painter is certainly in love with his wife, and he has reason to be so,"[3] had concluded his eulogy of number 41 by describing it as *"savant,"* or "scientifically observed." The adjective is apt in terms of modern studies of human sexual behavior. Alfred Kinsey, for instance, described the female "whole body" orgasm as resulting in such "rapture" as Greuze has depicted here. In particular, the swollen throat in number 41 and here was noted by Kinsey, who cited "neck muscles . . . nipples . . . and the whole breast" as being "liable to enlargement" in orgasm. Finally, the "unfocused stare," the "glistening eye," "the mouth open to

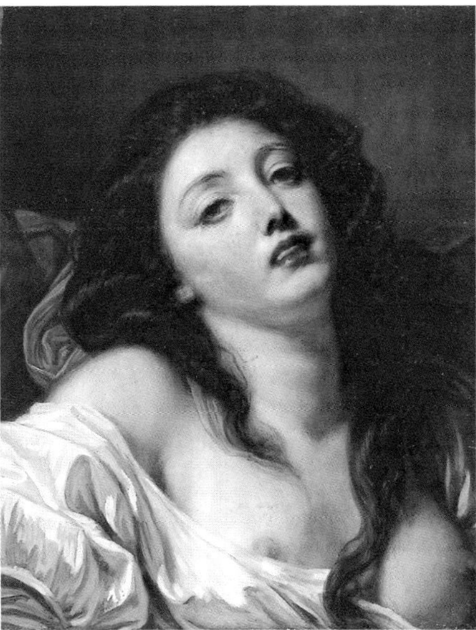

Fig. 114 Greuze, *La Volupté,* 1765, oil on panel, private collection

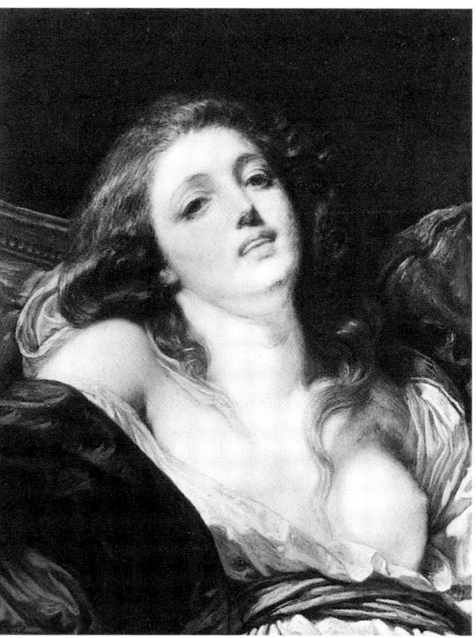

Fig. 115 Greuze, *La Volupté,* 1765, oil on panel, St Petersburg, The State Hermitage Museum

secure air," and the general impression of a "state of unconsciousness" that characterize Greuze's subjects were linked by Kinsey to the French term for orgasm: *la petite mort* ("the little death") or *la mort douce* ("the sweet death").[4]

The origins of this daring image are to be found, as Emmanuelle Brugerolles first pointed out,[5] in a rather more innocent depiction by Greuze of a young woman resting alongside two copulating doves (fig. 116), a drawing in which first appeared the pose, the supporting pillows, and even the style of armchair found in this drawing and its related paintings. Of the latter, one (fig. 114) appears to have been painted rapidly before the model or after the present drawing, while the other (fig. 115) appears more elaborately worked up, as a work intended for exhibition or sale.[6]

Charles-François Letellier (1743–1800) engraved the present drawing for his fourth *Cahier de têtes de différents caractères* (fig. 117).

1. *"Le* Portrait de madame Greuze en vestale. *Cela, une vestale!"* Diderot *Salons,* I, p. 134.

2. *"Il y avoit au Salon dernier* [1763], *un* portrait de madame Greuze enceinte." Diderot *Salons,* II, p. 152.

3. *"Ce peintre est certainement amoureux de sa femme, et il n'a pas tort."* Diderot *Salons,* II, p. 152.

4. A.C. Kinsey *et al., Sexual Behavior in the Human Female,* Philadelphia 1953, pp. 638, 604–05, 622–23, 615.

5. In *De Michel-Ange à Géricault, Dessins de la Donation Armand-Valton,* exhib. cat., Paris, École Nationale Supérieure des Beaux-Arts, 1981, p. 244.

6. See I.S. Nemilova, *The Hermitage, Catalogue of Western European Painting, French Painting, Eighteenth Century,* Moscow and Florence 1986, pp. 113–14, no. 61.

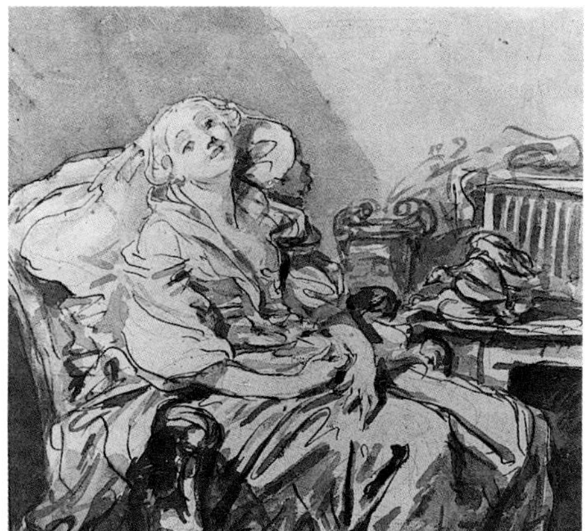

Fig. 116 Greuze, *The Girl with Doves,* 1763 (?), brush with brown and black inks, Paris, École Nationale Supérieure des Beaux-Arts

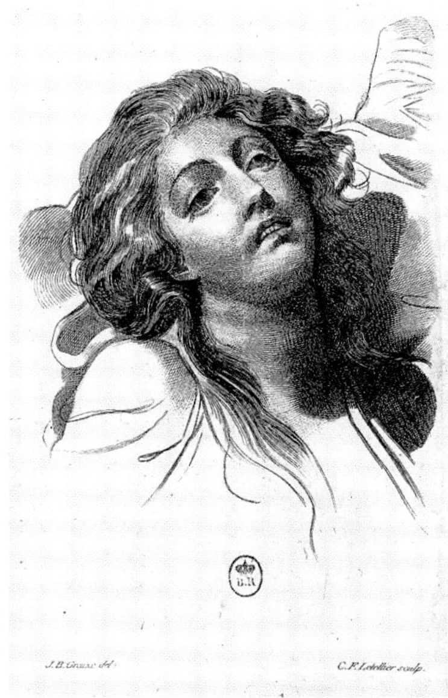

Fig. 117 C.-F. Letellier, after Greuze, *Head of a Woman, c.* 1770, engraving, Paris, Bibliothèque nationale de France

Facing page:
47 *Head of a Woman*

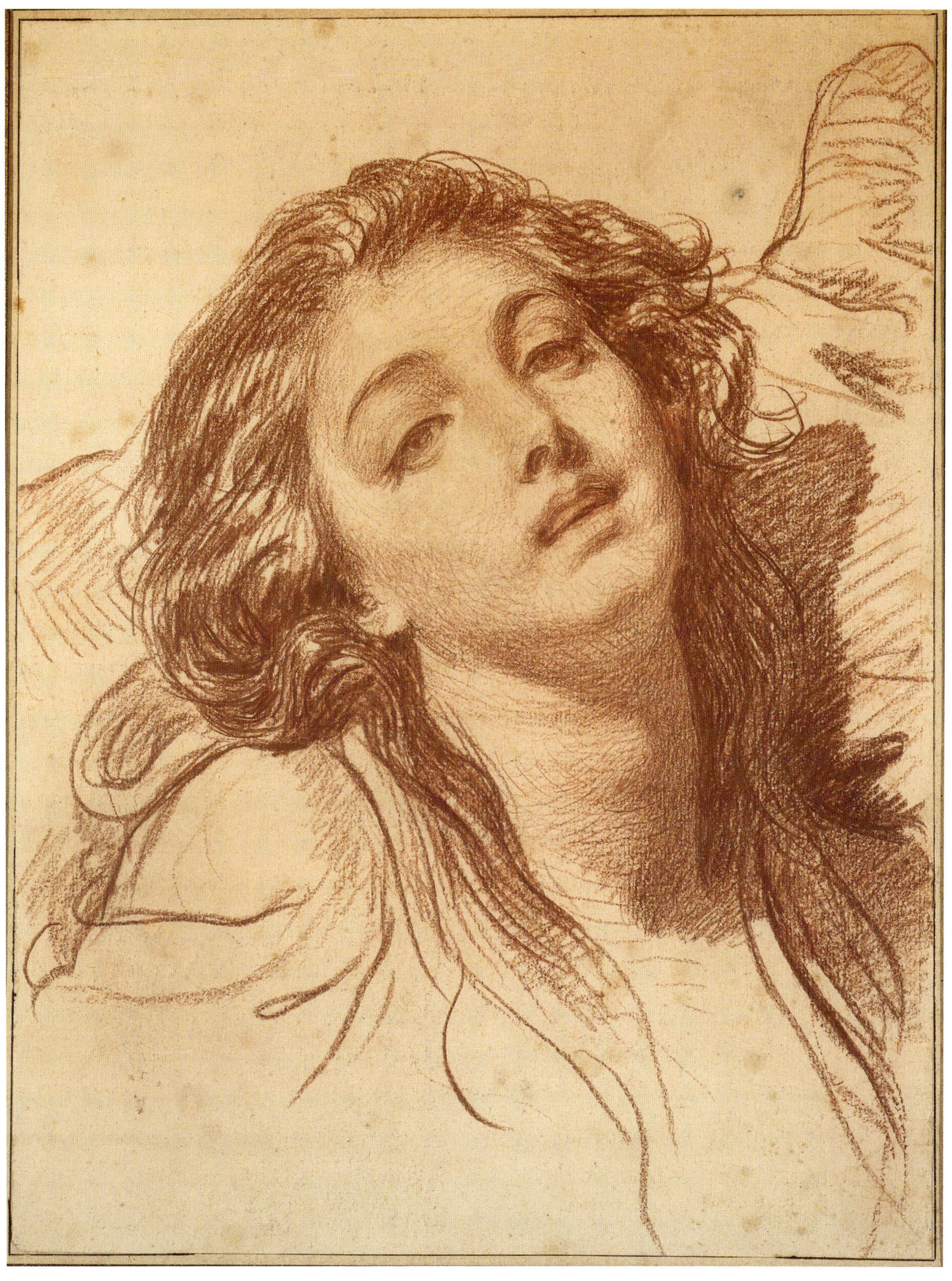

48 *The Father's Curse: The Ungrateful Son*

Brush with brown and gray ink over graphite on white paper, 320 × 420 mm (12 5/8 × 16 9/16 in.)
Lille, Musée des Beaux-Arts

Provenance: marquis Jean-Joseph de Laborde, Paris, with pendant; his sale, Paris, 16 May 1783, lot 40, sold to Dulac; Houtelart, Lille, with pendant;[1] given by him to the museum, with pendant, in 1864
Exhibitions: Salon of 1765, no. 124 (?); *From Poussin to Puvis de Chavannes: A Loan Exhibition of French Drawings from the Collection of the Musée des Beaux-Arts at Lille,* London *et al.* 1974–75, no. 53; Hartford *et al.* 1976–77, no. 48; Paris 1984, no. 66; *Tradition and Revolution in French Art, 1700–1880: Paintings and Drawings from Lille,* London, The National Gallery, 1993, no. 61
Bibliography: See the full listing in Raux 1995, pp. 102, 104; and P. Stein, "Sophie Raux, *Catalogue des dessins français . . . ,*" review, *Master Drawings,* xxxv, no. 1, 1997, pp. 74, 75; P. Déan, *Diderot devant l'image,* Paris and Montréal 2000, p. 100; M. Ledbury, *Sedaine, Greuze and the Boundaries of Genre,* Oxford 2000, pp. 252–57; Fischer *et al.* 2000, pp. 61, fig. 17, 62, fig. 18

This is Greuze's earliest surviving rendition of *The Father's Curse: The Ungrateful Son,* a subject he would treat in a major painting of 1777 (fig. 16). It was the most violent domestic scene he had yet taken up, and the first to be conceived with a pendant. In the scene, an aged man implores his son not to abandon his family to follow a recruiting officer and join the army. Other members of the family, down to the barking dog, react to the drama in various ways appropriate to their age and position in the household. The major differences between the drawing and the final painting, whose composition is reversed, are the change of the father's entreaties into a violent curse and the transformation of the son's insolent stance and menacing gesture into a pose of astonishment and fear. Though wielding his brush with great freedom, Greuze nevertheless defined the path of light flooding in from the open door with dramatic precision, a cinematic effect maintained in the painting of 1777.

Though the present author and others have long tended to associate this sheet with the sketch entitled *The Ungrateful Son* that Greuze exhibited at the Salon of 1765 (no. 122), the discrepancies in detail between the drawing and Diderot's description of what he saw in 1765 are simply too important to ignore. More likely, what the artist

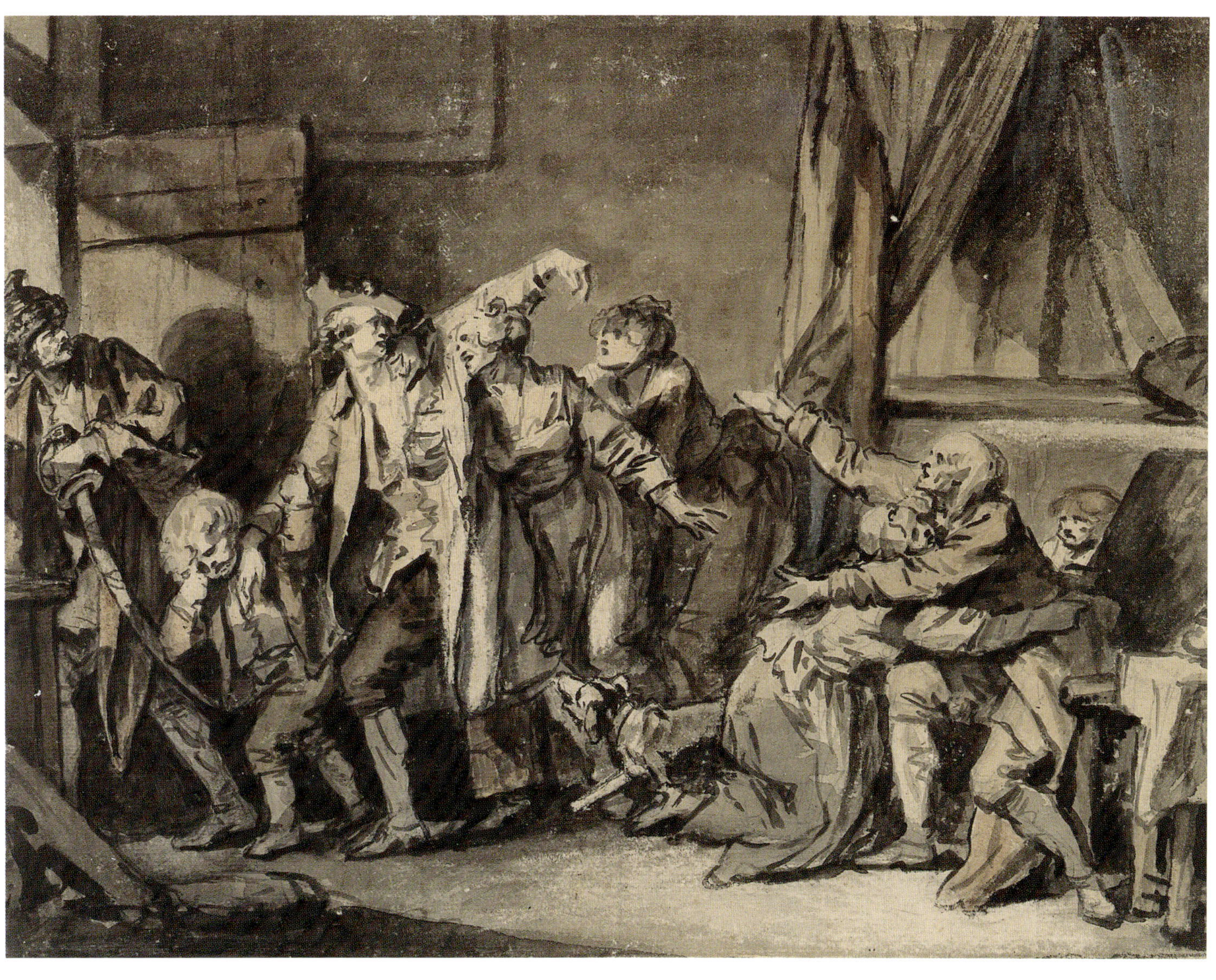

showed in 1765 was the pair of drawings that appeared in the Saint-Maurice sale, Paris, 6 February 1786, lot 382, and are now lost. These were considerably larger than the Lille drawings (580 x 720 mm), included nine figures, and were more elaborately worked up in gray wash with white highlights on blue paper.

For Diderot, the drawing he saw in 1765 was "very beautiful.... Everything in this sketch is understood, ordered, well characterized, clear."[2] But in his lengthy, detailed description, he stressed, among other elements shown differently here, the significance of the recruiting officer reacting to the turbulent scene by "leaving, his back turned to what is going on, his sword under his arm, his head lowered,"[3] very different from his appearance here. Another critic, Mathon de La Cour, also fascinated by the scene of family discord, suggested that the youngest children might be the sons, rather than the brothers, of the departing man: "all the children weep, on seeing that their father is going to leave the family home."[4]

A later rendering of *The Ungrateful Son* is number 81, and Greuze's drawing after the final painting, intended as the engraver's model, is number 82.

1. This drawing and no. 49 were photographed and published between 1851 and 1855 by Blanquart-Évrard and described as "belonging to M. Houtelart." See I. Jammes, *Blanquart-Évrard et les origines de l'édition photographique française, catalogue raisonné des albums photographiques édités, 1851–1855,* Geneva 1981, nos. 164, 165. I am grateful to Madame Brejon de Lavergnée for having drawn my attention to this publication.

2. *"très belle.... Tout est entendu, ordonné, caractérisé, clair dans cette esquisse."* Diderot *Salons,* II, p. 157.

3. "[*il*] *s'en va, le dos tourné à ce qui se passe, son sabre sous le bras, et la tête baissée."* Diderot *Salons,* II, p. 157.

4. *"tous les enfans pleurent, en voyant que leur père va quitter la maison paternelle."* Mathon de La Cour 1765, p. 11.

49 *The Father's Curse: The Punished Son*

Brush with brown and gray ink over graphite on white paper, 320 × 420 mm (12 5/8 × 16 9/16 in.)
Lille, Musée des Beaux-Arts

Provenance: marquis Jean-Joseph de Laborde, Paris, with pendant; his sale, Paris, 16 May 1783, lot 41, sold to Paillet; acquired by Houtelart in 1810, Lille; given by him to the museum, with pendant, in 1864
Bibliography: see no. 48
Exhibitions: Salon of 1765, no. 125 (?); *From Poussin to Puvis de Chavannes: A Loan Exhibition of French Drawings from the Collection of the Musée des Beaux-Arts at Lille,* London *et al.* 1974–75, no. 54; Hartford *et al.* 1976–77, no. 49; *Dessins néo-classiques du Musée des Beaux-Arts de Lille,* Lille, 1983, no. 102; Paris 1984, no. 67 (repr. flopped); *Triumph und Tod des Helden,* exhib. cat., Cologne *et al.* 1988, no. 145; *Tradition and Revolution in French Art, 1700–1880: Paintings and Drawings from Lille,* London, The National Gallery, 1993, no. 62

This pendant to *The Ungrateful Son* (no. 48) depicts the wayward son returning home, crippled and wasted, at the very moment of his father's death. As was the case with its pendant, Greuze executed a major painting on the same theme, in 1778 (fig. 17). With its composition simplified into Poussinesque grandeur, the latter includes an additional mourning figure in the foreground and omits such details as the window, the candle, and the holy-water vessel.

As with no. 48, there are too many differences between this drawing and Diderot's description of the *esquisse* he viewed at the Salon of 1765 for them to have been the same: "the eldest daughter... one hand raised to her brow, and the other... still holding the crucifix," "the poor mother... her back against the wall," "that flask alongside the book."[1] Again, one must suppose that it was one of the pair of drawings in the Saint-Maurice sale of 1786 that appeared in the Salon.

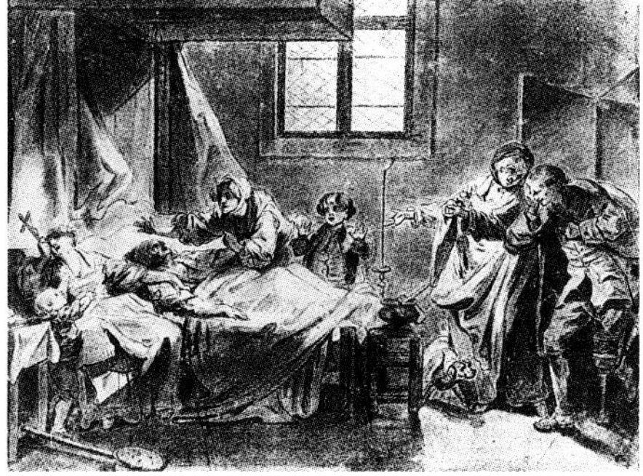

Fig. 118 Greuze, *The Father's Curse: The Punished Son,* 1765, black chalk, brush with gray and brown ink over graphite on white paper, Vienna, Graphische Sammlung Albertina

In his usual way, Diderot spoke only of the dramatic minutiae of Greuze's compositions rather than of their formal qualities, noting, for instance, that the son "has lost the leg with which he pushed away his mother, and is crippled in the arm with which he threatened his father."[2] His general reaction was ecstatic: "This is beautiful, very beautiful, sublime; everything, everything."[3]

But not everyone in 1765 could contemplate with ease such scenes of human suffering. After describing the drawing in detail, Mathon de La Cour, for instance, noted: "These two frightening scenes are conveyed in the strongest manner in the sketches. I would never advise M. Greuze to execute them. They poison the soul with a feeling so profound and terrible that one is forced to turn one's eyes away from them."[4] Even twenty years later, a historian of contemporary French art would write of these subjects: "perhaps it would be better not to admit the existence of such monsters."[5] Diderot too

Facing page:
49 *The Father's Curse: The Punished Son*

felt that Greuze might never execute paintings on the theme of the Father's Curse, but for different reasons: "With all that, taste is so wretched, so trifling, that perhaps these two sketches will never be painted, and if they are, Boucher will sooner have sold fifty of his indecent and insipid marionettes than Greuze these two sublime pictures."[6]

No fewer than four variations by Greuze on the theme of the Punished Son exist, demonstrating the evolution of his style away from the picturesque manner of the 1765 sketches to the noble simplicity of his final painting of 1778 (fig. 17), so reminiscent of seventeenth-century models of history painting: one in the Albertina that may actually predate the Lille drawing because of its uncertain treatment of light (fig. 118), a second in the École Nationale Supérieure des Beaux-Arts that dramatically resolves that same element by eliminating the window (fig. 119), a third in the Albertina that introduces a window at the left and substitutes ceiling beams for the canopy of the bed (fig. 120), and a fourth in the same collection that brings in the crucial foreground figure of the weeping boy (fig. 121). The latter sketch is also the first to particularize the features of the dead father so that he bears an uncanny resemblance to Greuze himself.

1. *"La fille aînée... une main portée à la tempe, et l'autre... tenant encore le crucifix," "la pauvre mère... le dos contre le mur," "cette fiole qui est a côté du livre."* Diderot *Salons,* II, pp. 157–58.

2. *"Il a perdu la jambe dont il a repoussé sa mère, et il est perclus du bras dont il a menacé son père."* Diderot *Salons,* I, p. 158.

3 *"Cela est beau, très-beau, sublime; tout, tout."* Diderot *Salons,* I, p. 158.

4. *"Ces deux scènes effrayantes sont rendues de la manière la plus forte dans les esquisses. Je ne conseillerois jamais à M. Greuze de les exécuter. On souffre trop à les voir. Elles empoissonnent l'âme d'un sentiment si profond et si terrible, qu'on est forcé d'en détourner les yeux."* Mathon de La Cour 1765, p. 13.

5. *"peut-être vaudroit-il mieux de ne pas supposer l'existence de pareils monstres." Discours sur l'origine, les progrès et l'état actuel de la peinture en France...,* Paris 1785, pp. 24–25.

6. *"Avec tout cela, le goût est si misérable, si petit, que peut-être ces deux esquisses ne seront jamais peintes, et que si elles sont peintes, Boucher aura plutôt vendu cinquante de ses indécentes et plates marionnettes que Greuze ces deux sublimes tableaux."* Diderot *Salons,* II, p. 159.

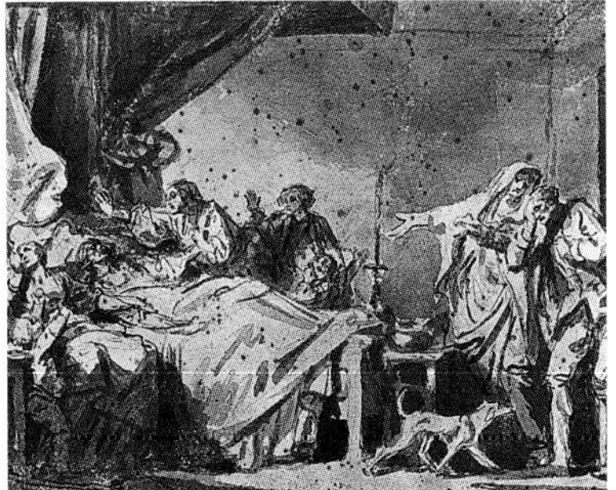

Fig. 119 Greuze, *The Father's Curse: The Punished Son,* 1777–78, black chalk, brush with gray ink, Paris, École Nationale Supérieure des Beaux-Arts

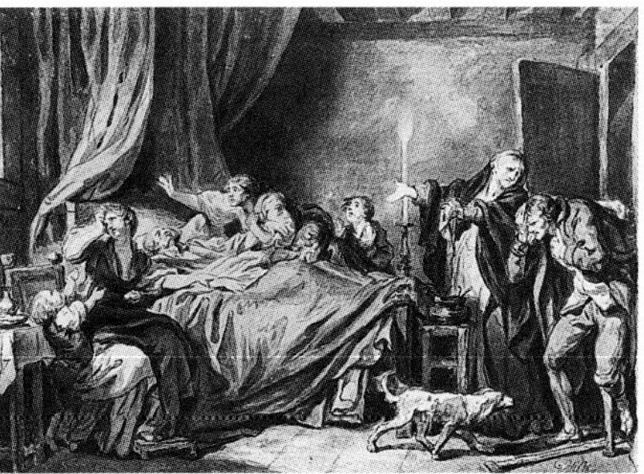

Fig. 120 Greuze, *The Father's Curse: The Punished Son,* 1777–78, brush with gray and brown ink, heightened in white, Vienna, Graphische Sammlung Albertina

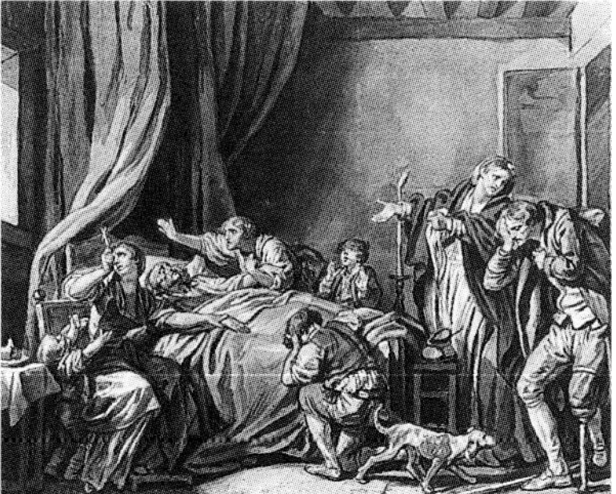

Fig. 121 Greuze, *The Father's Curse: The Punished Son,* 1777–78, brush with gray and brown ink, Vienna, Graphische Sammlung Albertina

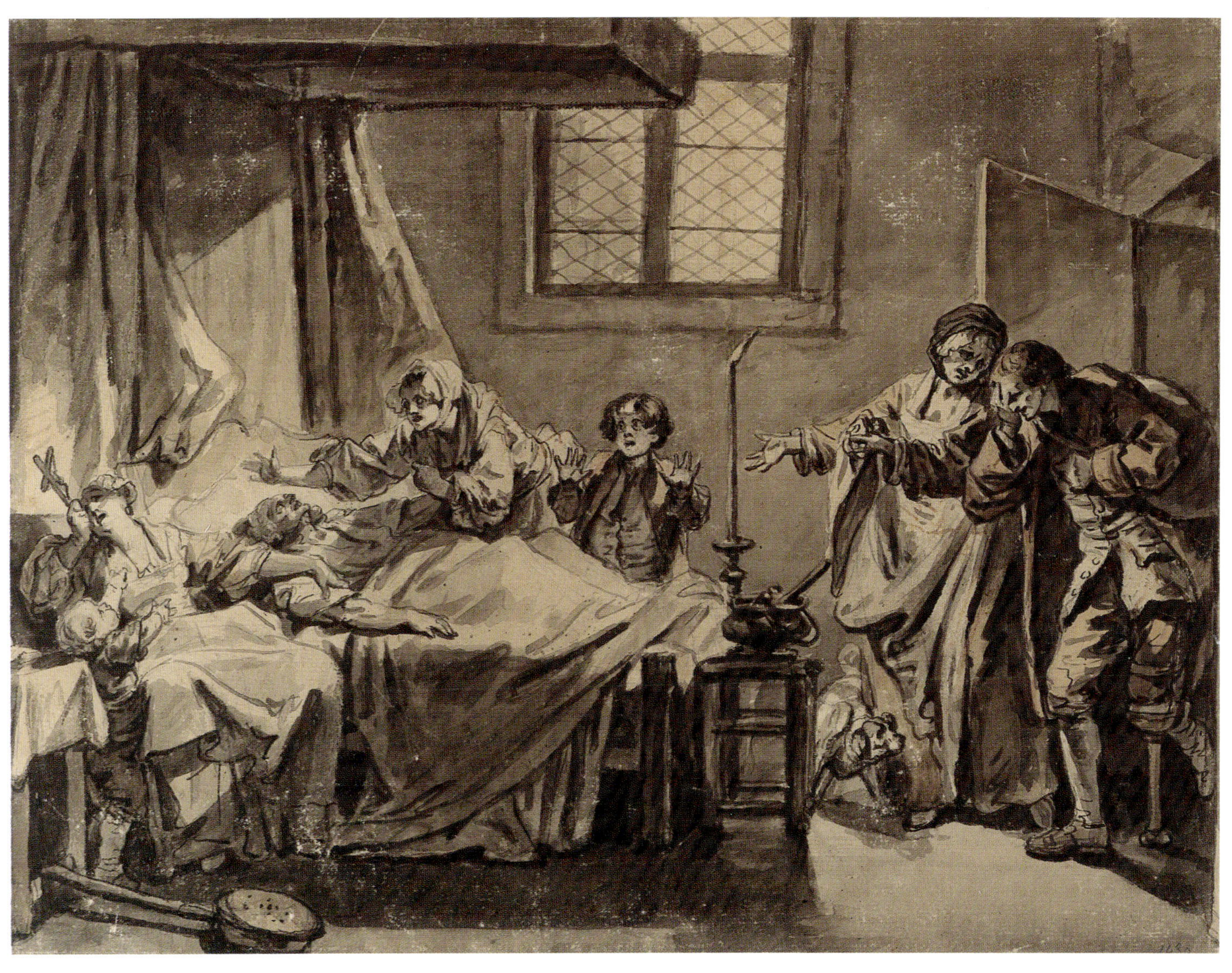

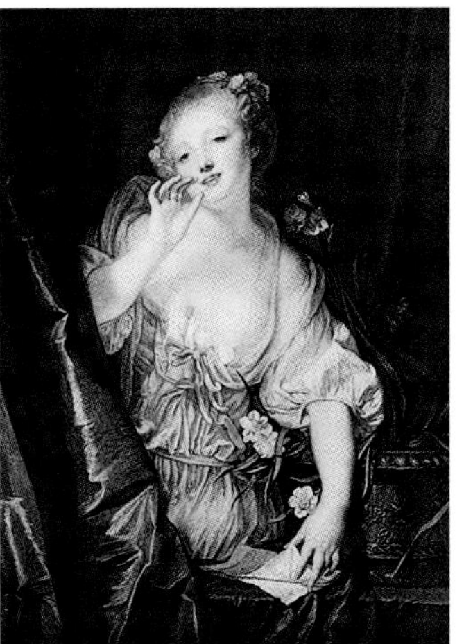

Fig. 122 Greuze, *The Kiss,* 1765, oil on canvas, Pregny, Rothschild collection

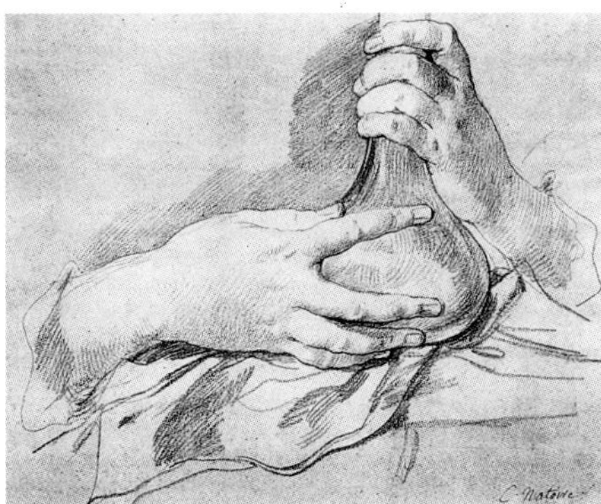

Fig. 123 C.-J. Natoire, *Study of a Hand, c.* 1750, red chalk on white paper, private collection

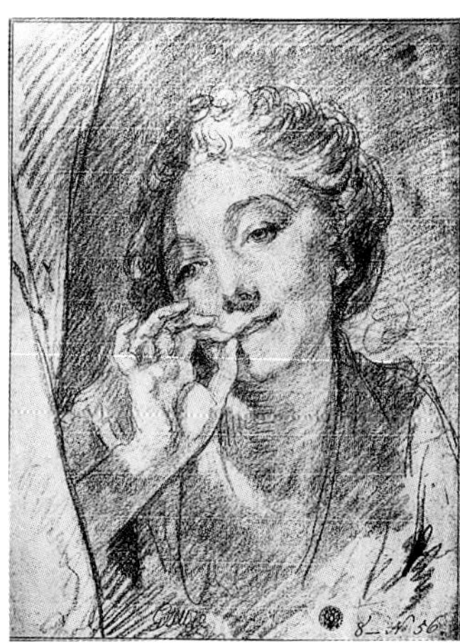

Fig. 124 Greuze, *Study for "The Kiss,"* 1765, red chalk on cream paper, whereabouts unknown

50 *A Woman's Left Hand, Study for "The Kiss"*

Red chalk on cream paper, 415 × 324 mm (16 3/8 × 12 3/4 in.)
Inscribed in pen and black ink at lower left *8-No 123.*
St Petersburg, The State Hermitage Museum

Provenance: Ivan Ivanovitch Betskoy, St Petersburg; Imperial Academy of Fine Arts, St Petersburg, 1769 (Lugt S. 2699a); transferred to the Hermitage in 1924
Exhibition: Leningrad 1977, no. 67
Bibliography: Monod and Hautecoeur 1922, no. 2

This drawing of a trembling hand was a study for one of Greuze's major works, *The Kiss (Le Baiser envoyé)* (fig. 122), completed in 1765 on commission from the duchesse de Grammont, who intended the picture to be a New Year's gift to her brother, the duc de Choiseul.[1] In the painting, the subject's left hand fingers an open letter. Though one of the artist's largest, most complex, and most beautiful works, *The Kiss* has not been publicly exhibited since 1831.[2]

Diderot, who saw it in Greuze's studio, discussed it enthusiastically at the end of his review of the Salon of 1765, giving particular emphasis to the importance of this left hand:

She has just received a note from her lover. This lover is passing below her window and she throws him a kiss as he goes by. It is impossible to represent for you all the voluptuousness of this figure.... This left arm that she no longer has the force to hold up, has come to rest upon a flowerpot... the note has fallen from her hand; the tips of her fingers have come to rest on the windowsill, which has set their position. You must see how they are slightly raised.... [You must see] the voluptuous softness of it all, from the tips of the fingers of that hand, which one follows up through the rest of the figure; and how that softness overcomes you and snakes through the veins of the viewer, who sees it snaking through the figure itself! It is a picture to make you lose your head, even yours, which is so good.[3]

Studies by Charles-Joseph Natoire, Greuze's early teacher at the Académie (see no. 2), suggest that it was from this master that Greuze learned how to exploit to expressive ends the intricate anatomy of hands (fig. 123). Greuze's study of the subject's head and right hand for *The Kiss,* for instance (fig. 124), succeeds in conveying not only an action different from the present sheet, but even a different emotional tone.[4]

1. Martin and Masson 1906, no. 422.

2. *Catalogue of Pictures by Italian, Spanish, Flemish, Dutch and English Masters,* London, British Institution for Promoting the Fine Arts in the United Kingdom, 1831, p. 19, no. 169, lent by Sir Richard Wigram, Bart.

3. *"Elle vient de recevoir un billet de son amant. Cet amant passe sous sa fenêtre, et elle lui jette un baiser en passant. Il est impossible de vous peindre toute la volupté de cette figure.... Ce bras gauche qu'elle n'a plus la force de soutenir, est allé tomber sur un pot de fleurs... le billet s'est échappé de sa main; l'extrémité de ses doigts s'est allée reposer sur le bord de la fenêtre qui a disposé de leur position. Il faut voir comme ils sont mollement repliés....* [*Il faut voir*] *la mollesse voluptueuse qui règne depuis l'extrémité des doigts de la main, et qu'on suit de-là dans tout le reste de la figure; et comme cette mollesse vous gagne et serpente dans les veines du spectateur, comme il la voir serpenter dans la figure! C'est un tableau à tourner la tête, la vôtre même qui est si bonne."* Diderot *Salons,* II, pp. 205–06.

4. Monod and Hautecoeur 1922, no. 113, pl. XLV.

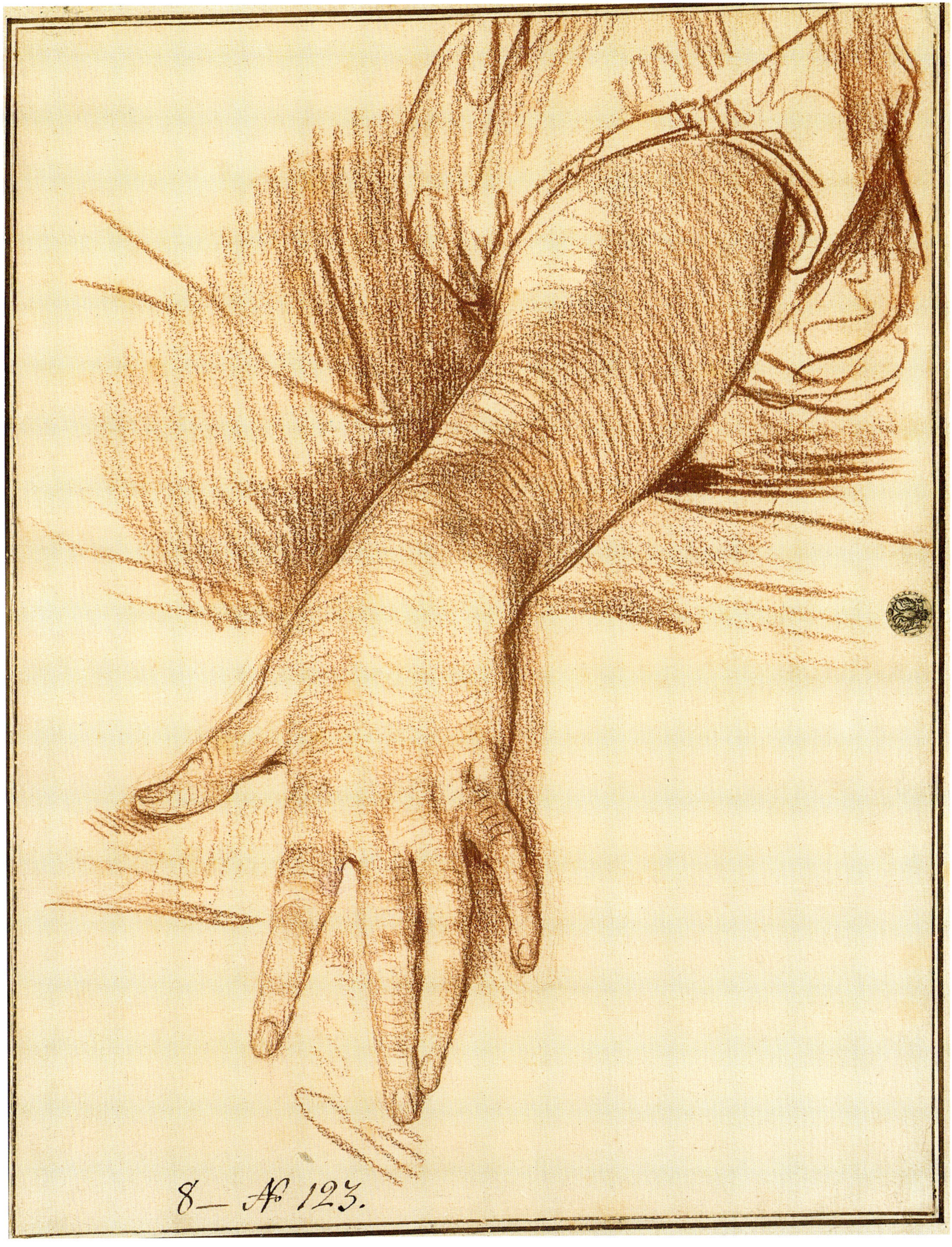
8— № 123.

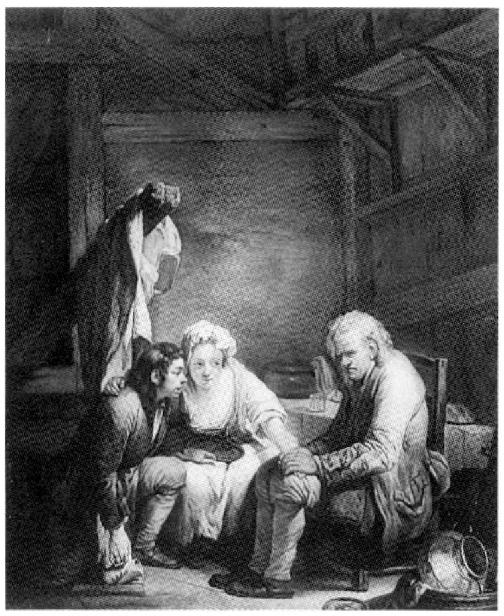

Fig. 125 Greuze, *The Blind Man Duped,* 1755, oil on canvas, Moscow, The Pushkin State Museum of Fine Arts

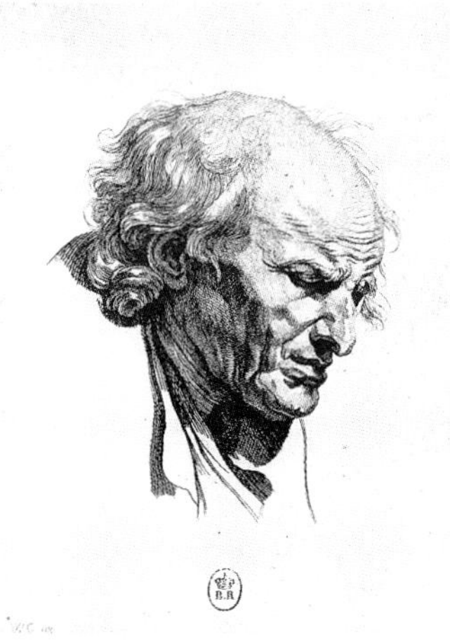

Fig. 126 P.-C. Ingouf, after Greuze, *Head of an Old Man,* 1766, engraving, Paris, Bibliothèque nationale de France

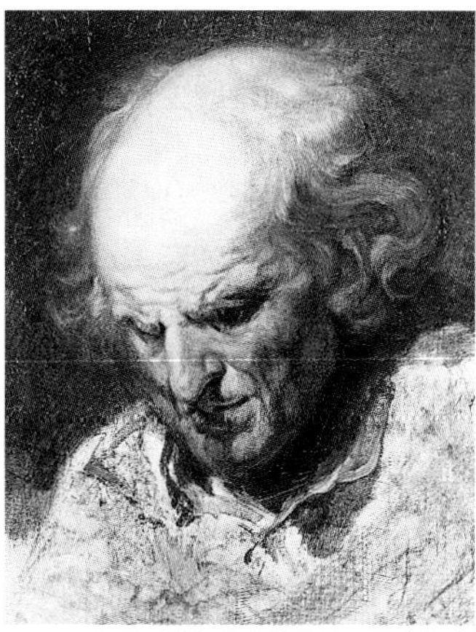

Fig. 127 Greuze, *Head of an Old Man,* 1755, oil on canvas, private collection

51 *Head of an Old Man*

Red chalk on white paper, 396 × 320 mm ($15\frac{5}{8} \times 12\frac{5}{8}$ in.)
Inscribed on verso in brown ink *No 31,* in blue chalk *0009/ 746;* with ink mark of a stamp in the form of an upright triangle (Austrian customs stamp) and a note in brown chalk *J.B. Greuze fecit*
Los Angeles, The J. Paul Getty Museum

Provenance: Friedrich van Amerling (1803–1887), Vienna; his widow, Marie, Gräfin Hoyos-Amerling, Vienna; their sale, Vienna, 3–6 May 1916, lot 96; private collection, Switzerland; private collection, London, 1968
Exhibition: Red Chalk Drawings, Los Angeles, The J. Paul Getty Museum, 1999
Bibliography: Martin and Masson 1906, no. 1350; "Acquisitions/ 1984," *The J. Paul Getty Museum Journal,* XIII, 1985, p. 189, no. 88; G. Goldner *et al., European Drawings, Catalogue of the Collections,* Malibu CA, 1988, I, pp. 164–65, no. 72

Although clearly related to the head of the old blind man Greuze depicted in his *The Blind Man Duped* (fig. 125), a painting he exhibited at his Salon debut in 1755 (no. 145), this drawing seems to have been executed by Greuze about ten years later as a model for the engraver Pierre-Charles Ingouf. In 1766 the latter published his *Têtes de différents caractères, dédiées à Mr. J.-G. Wille, Graveur ordinaire du Roy, Par son amy J.B. Greuze,* a set of six engravings of expressive heads based on various figures in paintings by Greuze. Though not the most talented engraver of his age, Ingouf managed to produce a faithful rendition of Greuze's pathetic image, rendering with particular care the forceful accents of dark shadows in the drawing as well as the wispy loose hairs on the bald man's head (fig. 126). Greuze's friend Wille, to whom the set of prints was dedicated, proudly recorded the event in his diary on 21 February 1766: "M. Greuze has dedicated to me a little book of six heads that he has had engraved for me after his own drawings. He dedicated them to me as an old friend."[1]

Such engravings, intended for use by student artists, naturally were widely copied and are the origin of the many mediocre versions of the present sheet, including the one in the Musée du Berry, Bourges, cited by George Goldner.[2]

An important related work is an oil sketch by Greuze of the same model, seen from a slightly higher position (fig. 127), that is probably a study for the painting exhibited in 1755.

1. *"M. Greuze m'a dédié un petit cahier de six têtes qu'il m'a fait graver d'après ses dessins. Il me les a dédiées en qualité d'ancien ami."* Wille 1857, I, p. 313.

2. Goldner *et al.* 1988, p. 164.

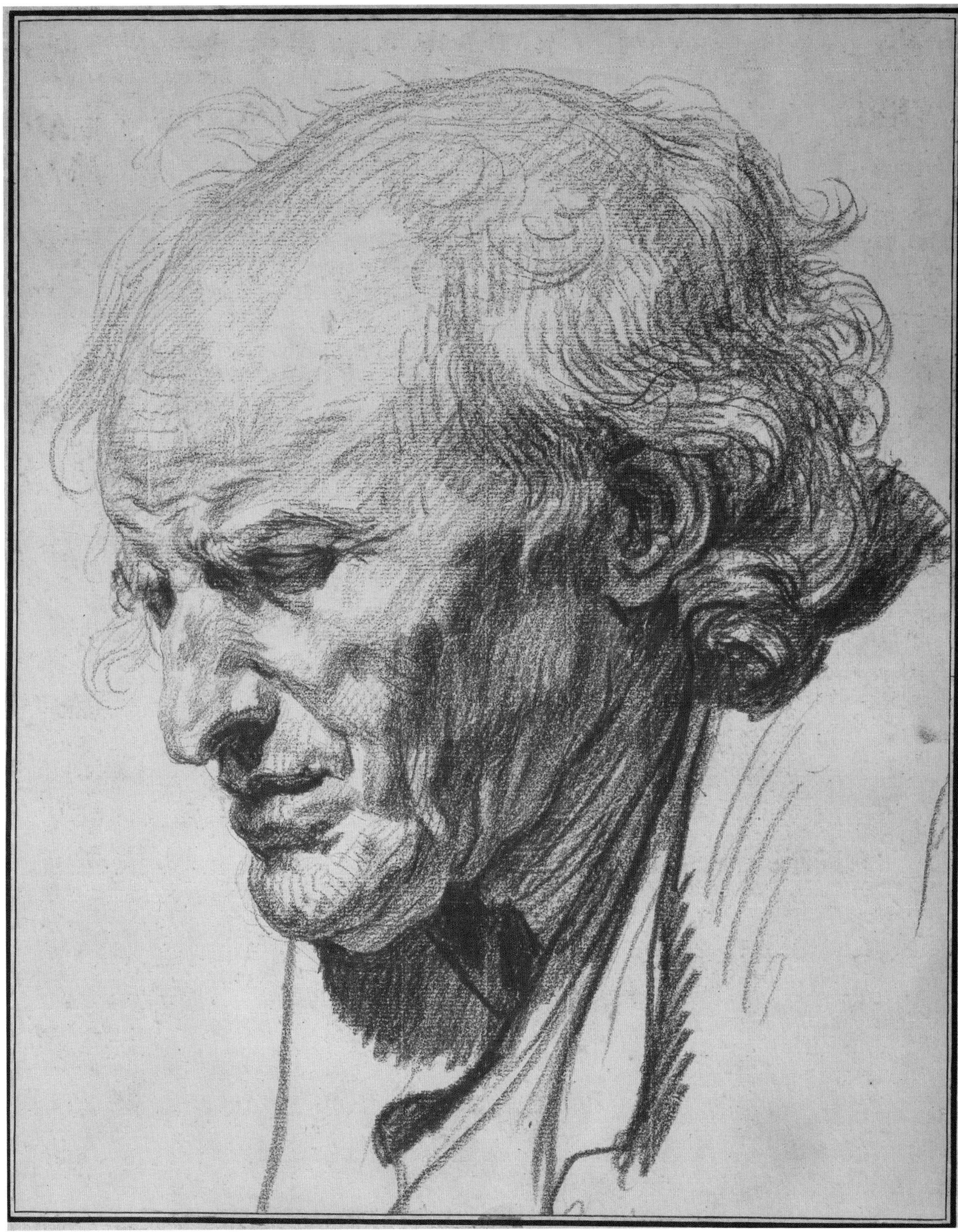

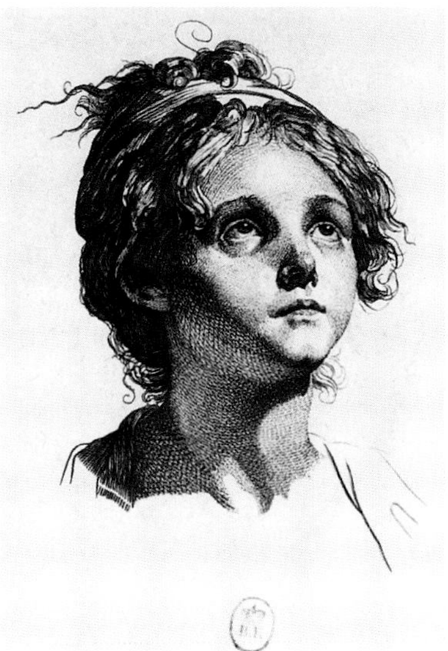

Fig. 128 P.-C. Ingouf, after Greuze, *Head of a Girl,* 1766, engraving, Paris, Bibliothèque nationale de France

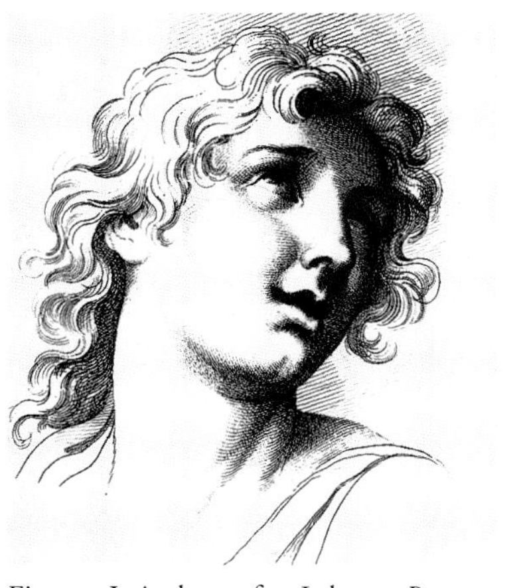

Fig. 129 J. Audran, after Lebrun, *Rapture,* 1727, engraving, photograph courtesy of the Frick Art Reference Library

52 *Head of a Girl*

Red chalk on cream paper, 356 × 284 mm (14 × 11 3/16 in.)
New York, The Metropolitan Museum of Art, Rogers Fund 1949

Provenance: Jules Porgès, Paris; comtesse de Fitz-James, Paris; baron Rudolf, Ritter von Gutmann, Vienna; William H. Schab Gallery, New York; acquired by the museum in 1949
Exhibition: New York 1990
Bibliography: Martin and Masson 1906, no. 1353; *The Metropolitan Museum of Art, Annual Report of the Trustees,* New York 1949, p. 28; *The Metropolitan Museum of Art Bulletin,* February 1959, p. 166; E. Munhall, "Jean-Baptiste Greuze: An Artist and His Critics," diss., Yale University 1959, p. 204 n. 13; Bean and Turčić 1986, p. 121; Thompson 1989–90, pp. 21, 23

As different from number 51 in its manner of execution as in its subject and the emotion depicted, this *Head of a Girl* was, like it, engraved by Ingouf for the same *Cahier de têtes de différents caractères* published in 1766. Unlike it, however, the subject is not to be found in any known painting by Greuze.

The artist's exquisite precision in delineating the head of his youthful subject reveals his instinctive sense of anatomy, and the execution demonstrates his control of the sharpened chalk in handling the varieties of cross-hatching, nowhere more subtle than in the light passage under the chin suggestive of a reflection. Throughout, Greuze played off the general indication of shadows achieved by rubbing his chalk against the grain of the paper and then spinning the delicate web of hatchings over it—the processes of *grainant* and *hachant,* as described by Jombert.[1] Then, the important highlight in the proper right eye was carefully scraped out of the red chalk with a knife (see fig. 6).

There is even a haunting sense of a rapport between the forty-year-old artist and his teenage model, whom he coached into assuming and maintaining such an evanescent expression. Ingouf the engraver did Greuze justice in rendering the varieties of shading in his drawing and every loose curl of hair (fig. 128).

As with other studies of expression, Greuze here seemed consciously to be producing a modern version of one created by Charles Lebrun (1619–1690) in the seventeenth century. Whereas Jean Audran's (1667–1756) engraving of 1727 after the latter's image of Rapture seems to depict an angel (fig. 129), Greuze's comparable subject clearly depicts a girl one might have passed on the rue de la Sorbonne, Greuze's address cited on the title page of the *Cahier.* Nevertheless, her features correspond to Lebrun's original description of that emotional state: "the head will incline to the side of the heart, and the eyebrows will be lifted, as will the eyes. The inclination of the head seems to suggest the abasement of the soul. It is for that reason too that the eyes and eyebrows... are raised to heaven, where they seem to be drawn to discover what the soul cannot know."[2]

Copies after Ingouf's engraving include a *Head of a Girl* in the Morin sale, Paris, 19 March 1925, lot 74.

1. Jombert 1973, pp. 62, 64–65.

2. *"la tête sera panchée du côté du coeur, et les sourcils élevés en haut, et la prunelle sera de même. La tête penchée comme je viens de dire, semble marquer l'abaissement de l'âme et son incapacité. C'est pour cela aussi que les yeux et les sourcils...* [*seront*] *élevés vers le ciel, où ils semblent être attachés pour découvrir ce que l'âme ne peut concevoir."* H. Jouin, *Charles Le Brun et les arts sous Louis XIV,* Paris 1889, II, p. 380; see also C. Lebrun, *L'Expression des passions et autres conférences, correspondance,* ed. J. Philipe, Paris 1994, p. 115, and Montagu 1994, pp. 117, 147, fig. 185, p. 181.

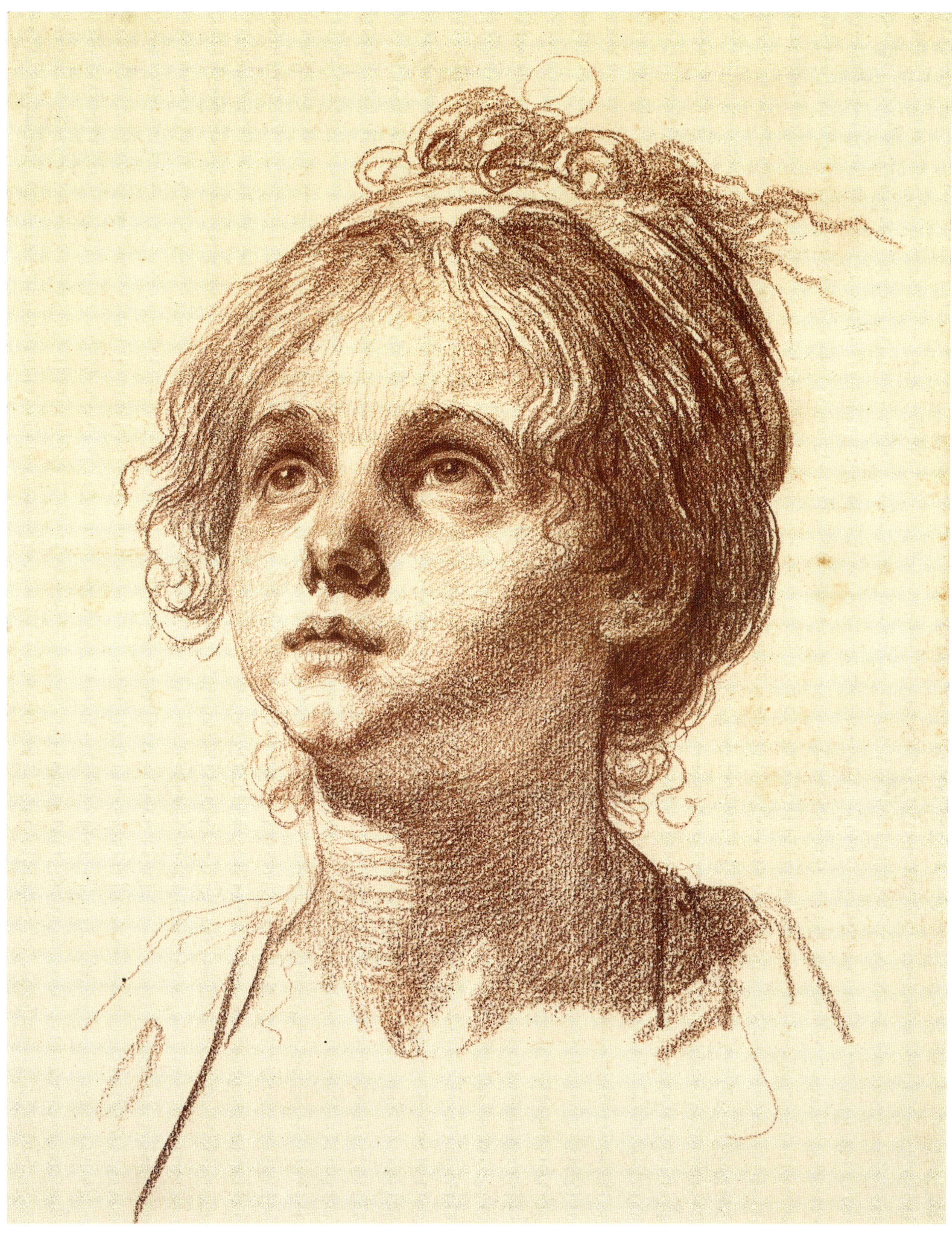

53 *A Woman Dressing Her Hair*

Red chalk on cream paper, 226 × 200 mm (8 15/16 × 7 7/8 in.)
Inscribed in pen and black ink on old mount, lower left *8-No 95.*
St Petersburg, The State Hermitage Museum

Provenance: Ivan Ivanovitch Betskoy, St Petersburg; Imperial Academy of Fine Arts, St Petersburg, 1769 (Lugt S. 2699a); transferred to the Hermitage in 1924
Exhibition: Leningrad 1977, no. 94
Bibliography: Monod and Hautecoeur 1922, no. 160, pl. LXI

The artist served as this young woman's mirror, creating an image of rare intimacy, suggestive even of neurotic introspection. Within the long tresses held out from the head, Greuze established an intricate, impressionistic pattern of light and shade, with shadows and reflections giving the head a sculpturesque density. In a slightly smaller format, Greuze drew a similarly disheveled subject face-on (fig. 130).

The model depicted in the present drawing reappears, still fingering her hair, in another study in the Hermitage collection (fig. 131).[1]

1. Monod and Hautecoeur 1922, no. 65, pl. XXV; Leningrad 1977, no. 66.

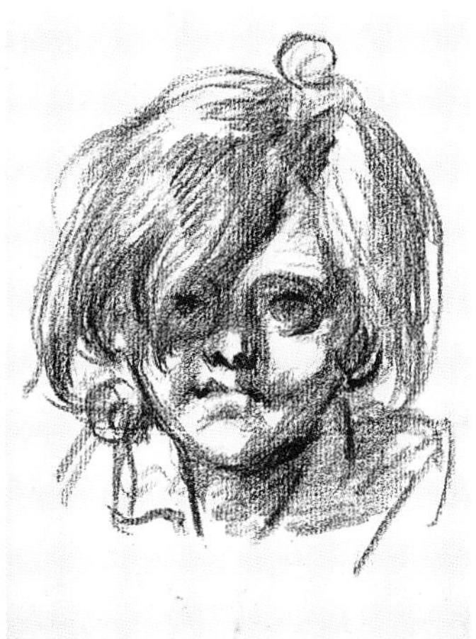

Fig. 130 Greuze, *Head of a Girl, c.* 1765, red chalk on white paper, whereabouts unknown

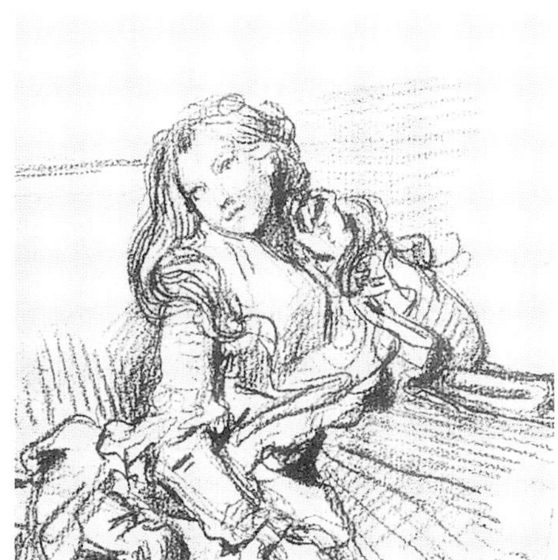

Fig. 131 Greuze, *A Woman Seated in an Armchair* (detail), *c.* 1765, red chalk on white paper, St Petersburg, The State Hermitage Museum

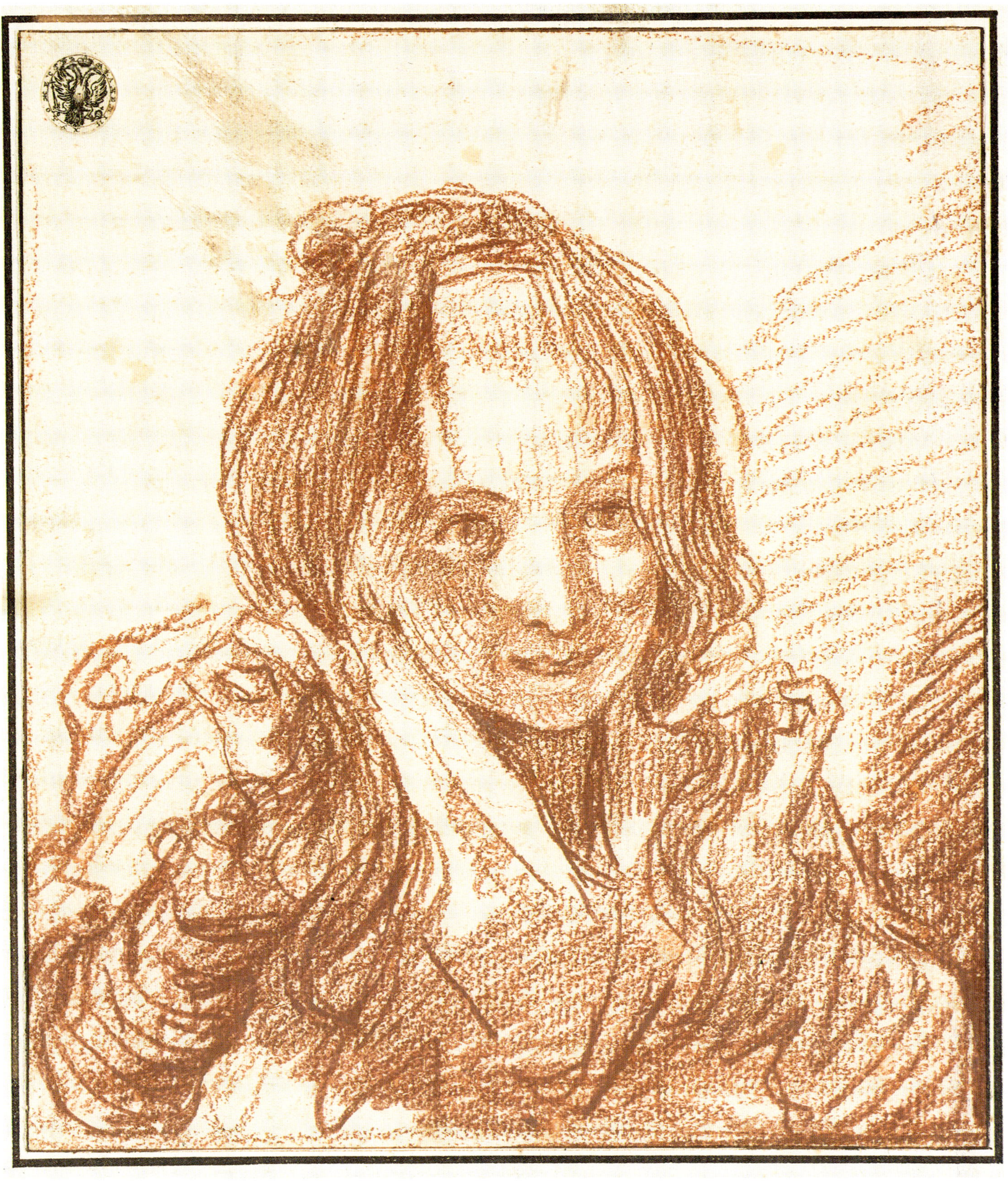

54 *Head of a Woman in Profile*

Red chalk on cream paper, 390 × 318 mm ($15^{5}/_{16}$ × $12^{1}/_{2}$ in.)
Jeffrey E. Horvitz Collection

Provenance: Galerie Cailleux, Paris; acquired in 1988
Exhibition: Cambridge *et al.* 1998–2000, no. 78
Bibliography: Cambridge *et al.* 1998–2000, cover and pp. 268–69, 377, 436, 448

Although Greuze must have drawn this *Head of a Woman in Profile* in the mid-1760s, at the same time as numbers 51 and 52, no engraving appears to have been after it. As in the case of number 52, Greuze seems here to have been "modernizing" one of Charles Lebrun's expressive heads, in this instance the one depicting Fear.[1] Yet the emotion captured in this sheet is more enigmatic—memorably characterized by Marianne Roland Michel as "attentive and almost incensed"[2]—which may explain why it was not utilized for one of the *Cahiers de têtes de différents caractères,* which tended to feature only archetypical examples of emotions.

The same robust model with her chipmunk cheeks posed, again in profile, for a more complete figural study Greuze chose to include in the group he sold Betskoy (fig. 132), and which in turn was included in the sale of some Hermitage drawings at Leipzig in 1931.[3]

Many years later, Greuze appears to have recalled the present sheet in establishing the appearance of the mother in *The Drunken Cobbler* (fig. 19), where her appalled expression is well suited to the situation of a destitute mother of two children confronting a feckless, drunken husband.

1. See Cambridge *et al.* 1998–2000, p. 268.

2. *"attentive et presque courroucée."* From the information sheet provided by the Galerie Cailleux at the time of sale in 1988.

3. Monod and Hautecoeur 1922, no. 134, pl. LV; sale, Leipzig, 29 April 1931, lot 114, sold to Halberstamm.

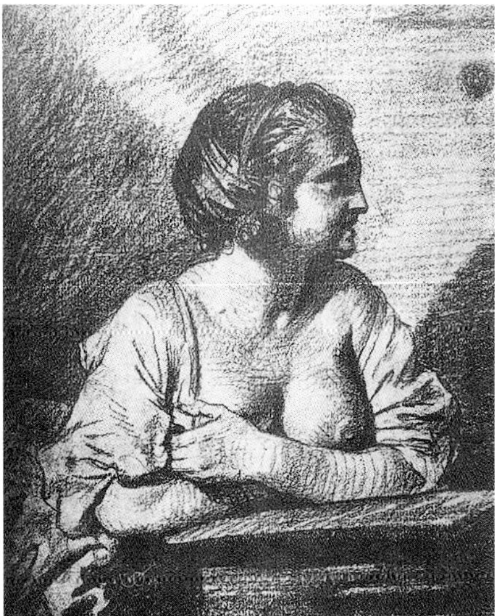

Fig. 132 Greuze, *Study of a Woman in Profile,* 1765, red chalk on cream paper, whereabouts unknown

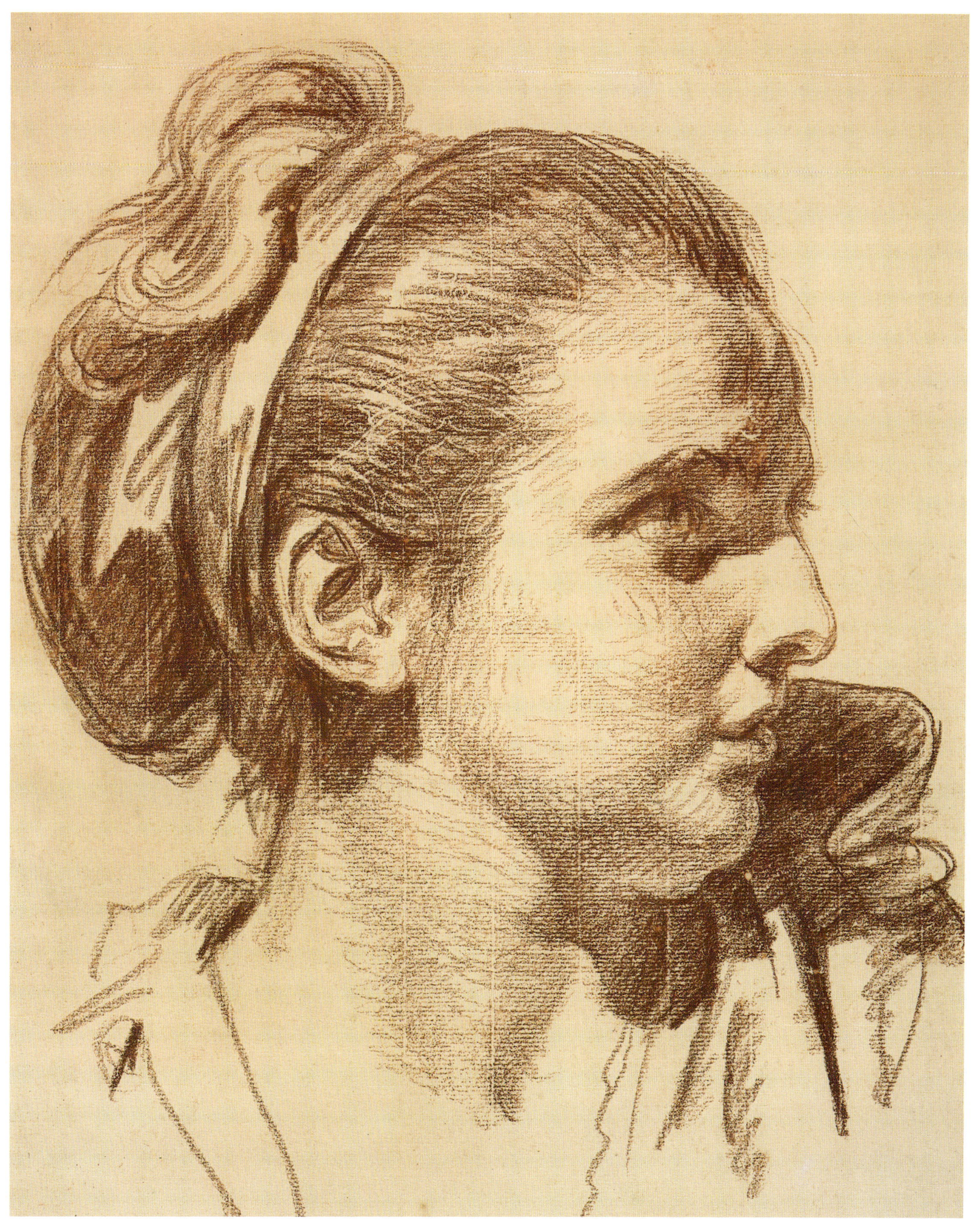

55 *Portrait of Denis Diderot*

Black and white chalks, with stumping, on warm brown paper, 361 × 283 mm (14¼ × 11 3/16 in.)
Signed in graphite at upper right *J.B. Greuze;* inscribed on label once pasted on back of frame *Portrait de Diderot/ Dessiné par Greuze pour le Baron d'Holbach/ donné par Mr d'Holbach fils à Made de Vandeul/ fille de Diderot./ Après la mort de Made de Vandeul, il m'a été donné par Monsr. de Vandeul son fils, le 21 décembre 1824./ E.S.*[1]
New York, The Pierpont Morgan Library

Provenance: Denis Diderot, Paris;[2] Paul-Henri Dietrich, baron d'Holbach, Paris (d. 1789); his son, M. d'Holbach; Madame de Vandeul, Diderot's daughter; her son, M. de Vandeul; E.S. (Eugène Salverte?); Martial François Marcille (1790–1856), Paris; his sale, 4–7 March 1857;[3] Hippolyte Walferdin, Paris; his sale, Paris, 3 April 1880, lot 76; David David-Weill, Neuilly; acquired in 1958 as the gift of John M. Crawford
Exhibitions: La Peinture française depuis la fin du dix-huitième siècle, Paris, Salon of 1846; *French Eighteenth-Century Pastels, Water Colors and Drawings from the David-Weill Collection,* New York, Wildenstein and Co., 1938, no. 97; *The French Revolution,* New York, Wildenstein and Co., 1943, no. 10; *French Pastels and Drawings from Clouet to Degas,* New York, Wildenstein and Co., 1944, no. 43; London 1968, no. 321; *The World of Voltaire,* Ann Arbor, University of Michigan Museum of Art, 1969, no. 47; Hartford *et al.* 1976–77, no. 50; *European Drawings, 1375–1825,* New York, The Pierpont Morgan Library, 1981, no. 104; *French Drawings, 1550–1825,* New York, The Pierpont Morgan Library, 1984, no. 67; Paris 1984, no. 68; *Diderot et son temps,* Brussels, Bibliothèque Royale Albert Ier, 1985, no. 1; *French Master Drawings from The Pierpont Morgan Library,* Paris, Musée du Louvre; New York, The Pierpont Morgan Library, 1993–94, no. 65
Bibliography: see C.D. Denison, *French Master Drawings from The Pierpont Morgan Library,* exhib. cat., New York 1993, p. 148; and J. Geffriaud Rosso, *Diderot et le portrait,* Pisa 1998, pp. 27–34

This portrait, executed in Greuze's studio in 1766, is a moving testimony to the friendship that for a while linked the artist and the *philosophe* and art critic Denis Diderot (1713–1784), Greuze's most enthusiastic and influential admirer.

Diderot's star was then at its zenith, as he saw the completion in 1766 of the monumental *Encyclopédie* that he had undertaken with Jean Le Rond d'Alembert in 1747 and received that same year from Catherine II a fifty-year advance on the pension she had offered him.

Diderot had first written of Greuze with some familiarity in his *Salon* of 1759. By 1761 he was calling him "our friend Greuze"[4] and writing his enthusiastic description of *A Marriage Contract* (fig. 10). In 1763 he addressed him as *tu,* and that same year began his account of *The Paralytic* with the exclamation: "That's really my man, that

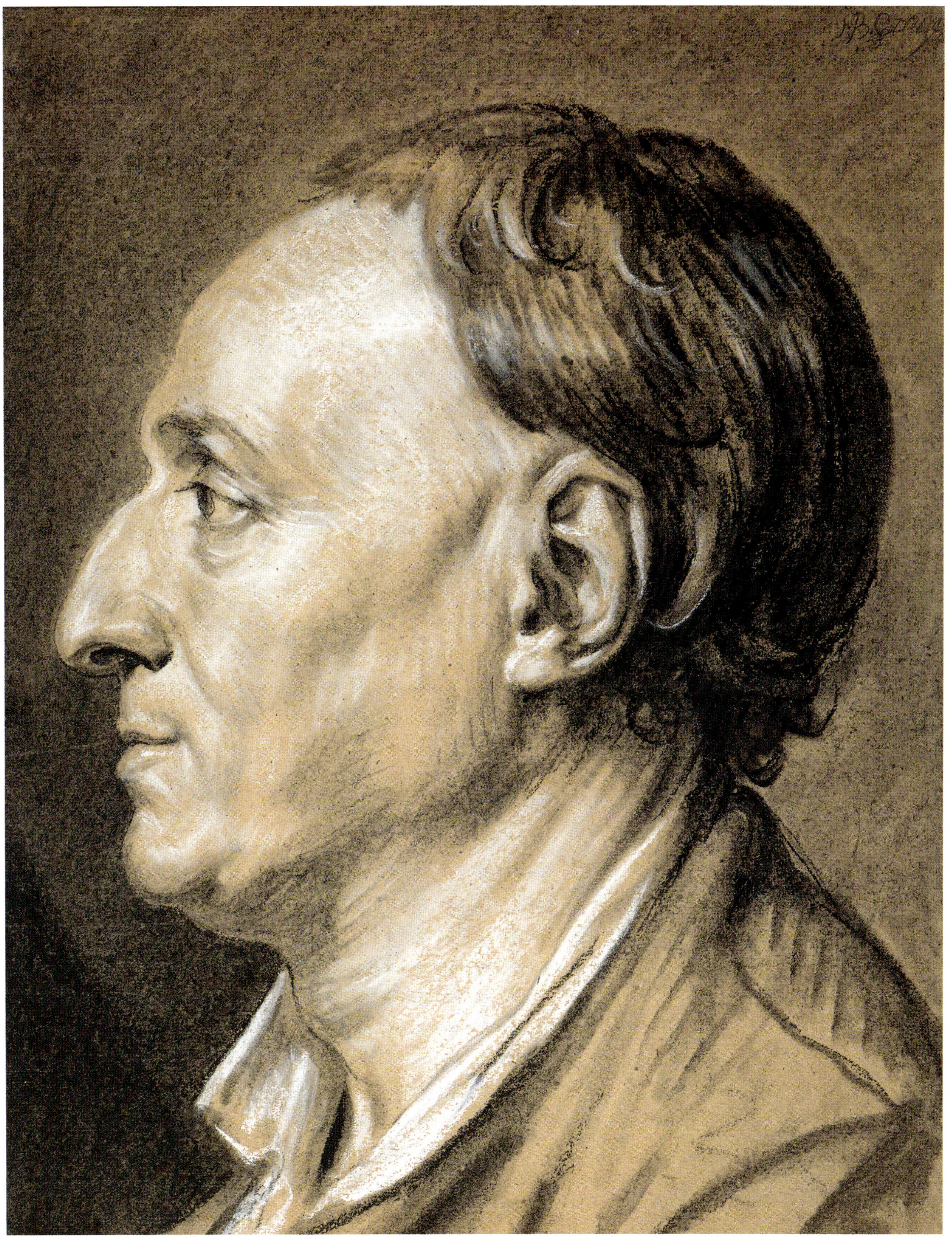

Greuze!"[5] By 1765 Diderot was saluting Greuze publicly as "your painter and mine, the first among us to take it upon himself to instill moral principles in art," and revealing as well something of the private side of Greuze: "He is a bit vain, our artist, but his vanity is that of a child; it is the drunkenness of talent: *Look at that, will you? That's really beautiful!*... I truly fear that, should he become modest, he will have reason to be so."[6] But by 1767, relations between the two men were disintegrating, probably for personal as well as professional reasons. The end came that year with Diderot's withering reference to the artist as "my late friend Greuze."[7]

With this portrait—life-size—Greuze followed the format he had employed a few years earlier for his own portrait (no. 21) and of a few others, a format launched by Charles-Nicolas Cochin in 1750 in emulation of antique medals. But the portrait of Diderot is drawn with greater freedom, power, and color, making us feel we are seeing the man as he saw himself: "I had a high forehead, very lively eyes, rather large features, a head totally in the character of an ancient orator, a guilelessness that nearly bordered on simplicity, on the rusticity of ancient times.... I have a face that fools artists."[8]

Stating that his portrait by Louis-Michel Van Loo (1707–1771) of 1767 (fig. 133) gave him the air of "an old coquette who still knows how to charm," Diderot acknowledged Greuze's superiority: "without the exaggeration of all the features in the engraving made after Greuze's drawing, I would be infinitely better."[9]

Diderot's fame and the relative scarcity of portraits of him led to the production of many engravings after the model of Greuze's drawing—by Augustin de Saint-Aubin, C.-E. Gaucher (fig. 134), Guillaume-Philippe Benoît (1675–1770?), Jean-Victor Dupin (b. 1718), A.-B. Duhamel (b. 1736), and Thomas Ryder (1746–1810). These were disseminated across Europe and as far as China, were reproduced on porcelain, and even as gilt-bronze furniture mounts, served as visual arguments for Johann Kasper Lavater,[10] and as models for Pablo Picasso (1881–1973) (fig. 135).[11]

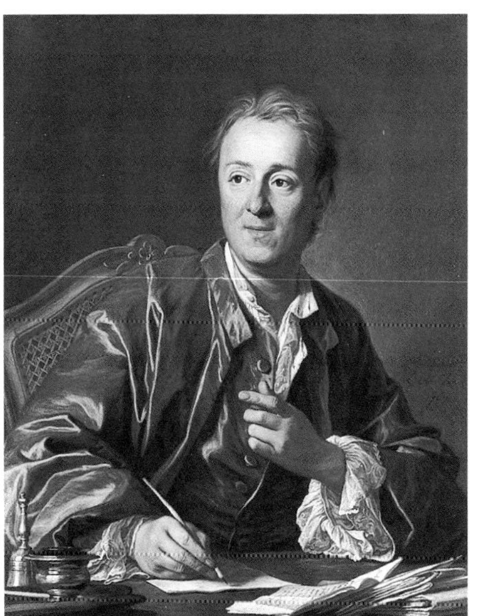
Fig. 133 L.-M. Van Loo, *Portrait of Diderot,* 1767, oil on canvas, Paris, Musée du Louvre

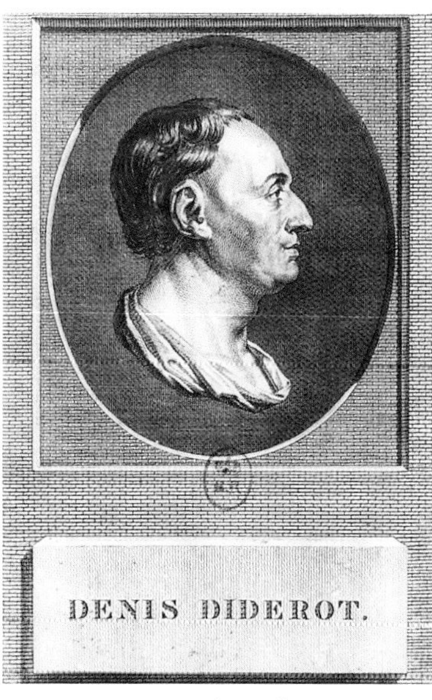

Fig. 134 C.-E. Gaucher, after Greuze, *Portrait of Diderot,* 1766, engraving, Paris, Bibliothèque nationale de France

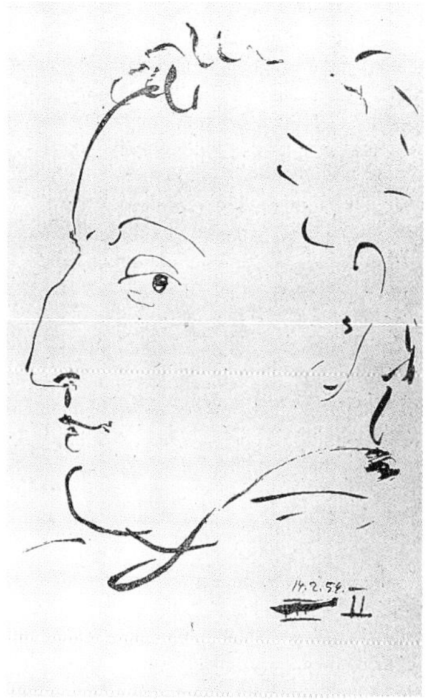

Fig. 135 P. Picasso, *Diderot,* 1954, brush and black ink, Succession Picasso

1. "Portrait of Diderot/ Drawn by Greuze for Baron d'Holbach/ given by Mr d'Holbach Junior to Madame de Vandeul/ Diderot's daughter./ After the death of Madame de Vandeul, it was given to me by Monsieur de Vandeul her son, 21 December 1824./ E.S."

2. Writing in January 1767, Baron Grimm described the circumstances in which the drawing was executed and stated that Greuze gave Diderot the drawing, along with the first one hundred proofs of Saint-Aubin's engraving after it. Baron F.M. von Grimm, *Correspondance littéraire, philosophique et critique,* ed. M. Tourneux, Paris 1879, VII, p. 202. Quoted in Hartford *et al.* 1976–77, pp. 116–17.

3. The Marcille provenance is given by Martin and Masson 1906 (no. 1108), but the drawing is not listed in his sale of 4–7 March 1857, nor in the earlier one of 16–17 January 1857.

4. *"notre ami Greuze."* Diderot *Salons,* I, p. 134.

5. Diderot *Salons,* I, p. 233.

6. *"votre peintre et le mien, le premier qui se soit avisé, parmi nous, de donner des moeurs à l'art." "Il est un peu vain, notre peintre; mais sa vanité est celle d'un enfant; c'est l'ivresse du talent....* Voyez-moi cela! C'est cela qui est beau!... *Je crains bien, lorsqu'il deviendra modeste, qu'il n'ait raison de l'être."* Diderot *Salons,* II, p. 144.

7. *"feu mon ami Greuze."* Diderot *Salons,* II, p. 197.

8. *"J'avois un grand front, des yeux très-vifs, d'assez grands traits, la tête tout-à-fait du caractère d'un ancien orateur, une bon-homie qui touchait de bien près à la bêtise, à la rusticité des anciens tems.... J'ai un masque qui trompe l'artiste."* Diderot *Salons,* I, p. 167.

9. *"une vieille coquette qui fait encore l'aimable.... Sans l'exagération de tous les traits dans la gravure qu'on a faite d'après le crayon de Greuze, je serais infiniment mieux."* Diderot *Salons,* II, p. 167.

10. See Rosso 1998, pp. 192–95.

11. Rosso 1998, pp. 181–85.

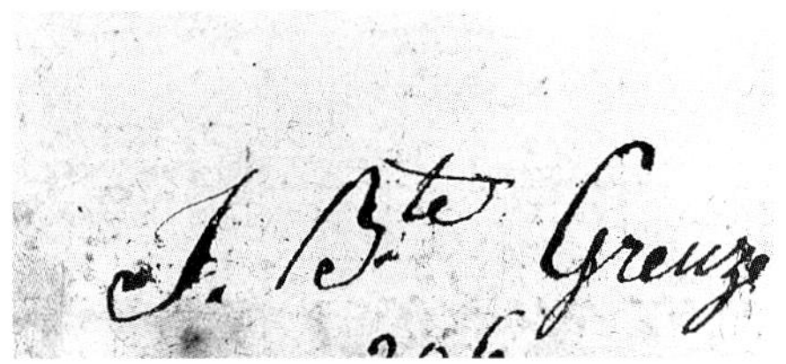

Fig. 136 Greuze, signature on no. 56

56 *The Departure of a Young Savoyard*

Brush with black, gray, and brown ink wash over graphite on white paper,
333 × 278 mm (13 1/8 × 10 15/16 in.)
Signed on verso *J. Bte Greuze* (fig. 136)
Amsterdams Historisch Museum

Provenance: perhaps Meynier Saint-Fal, Paris;[1] Carel Joseph Fodor (1801–1860), Amsterdam; Stedelijk Museum, Amsterdam, until 1975, when transferred to the Amsterdams Historisch Museum
Exhibitions: Exposition rétrospective d'art français, Amsterdam, Rijksmuseum, 1926, no. 168 *bis; Fodor 100 jaar,* Amsterdam, Fodor Museum, 1963, no. 75; Hartford *et al.* 1976–77, no. 54
Bibliography: Beschrikving der Schilderijen . . . in Het Museum Fodor, Amsterdam 1863, p. 77; Martin and Masson 1906, nos. 133, 135; R.A. Weigert, "Les Dessins français conservés dans les principales collections publiques de Hollande," *BSHAF,* 1933, p. 217; Munhall 1968, p. 94, fig. 11

Greuze here depicts a hesitant Savoyard child embarking on his itinerant career under his mother's forceful direction, a marmot box strapped over his shoulders, a walking stick in his left hand. His younger brother, oblivious to the drama occurring before him, continues to play at left. A large standing figure—perhaps the father—has been obliterated from the doorway.

From antiquity, it had been customary for male inhabitants —especially children— of Savoy, in present-day southeastern France and northern Italy to leave their mountainous homeland during the winter to earn their living abroad, providing amusements at street fairs and performing such menial tasks as sweeping chimneys and selling water. French artists from Watteau to Drouais had recorded their picturesque appearance, but only Greuze evoked the physical and psychological hardships endured by these child laborers.

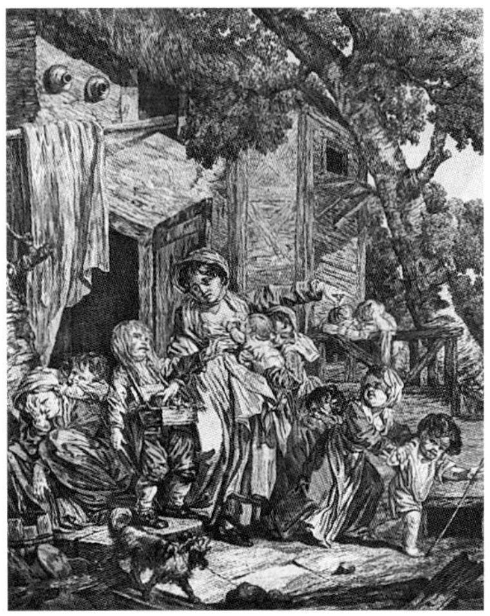

Fig. 137 Unknown artist, after Greuze, *The Departure from Barcelonnette,* after 1769, engraving, Paris, Bibliothèque nationale de France

Greuze actually knew the area from which he drew these subjects, for he and the abbé Gougenot had passed through Chambéry and rural Savoy on their way to Italy in 1755.[2] Reminiscences of this experience appear not only in the bizarre costumes and rough masonry houses he drew, but also in his evocations of the trauma of disrupted families. His depictions of Savoyards thus possess a realism lacking in his contemporaries' representations of these folk.

In addition to *The Education of a Young Savoyard* included here (no. 57), Greuze executed another drawing of a Savoyard subject that he showed at the Salon of 1769 (no. 164), *The Departure from Barcelonnette.* Now lost but recorded by an unknown engraver (fig. 137), this composition appears to have been an elaboration of the present one but lacking its visceral impact. Still, the critic of *L'Avant-Coureur* described it as "possessing a great deal of truth, of movement, and even of human interest."[3] Barcelonnette, by the way, is a village in Savoy.

1. Provenance cited by Martin and Masson 1906, no. 133.

2. See Guicharnaud 1999, pp. 23–24.

3. *"beaucoup de vérité, de mouvement et même d'intérêt."* "Arts. Exposition des peintures, sculptures, gravures de M.M. de l'Académie Royale," *L'Avant-Coureur,* 11 September 1769, p. 7. See Seznec in Diderot *Salons,* IV, p. 45.

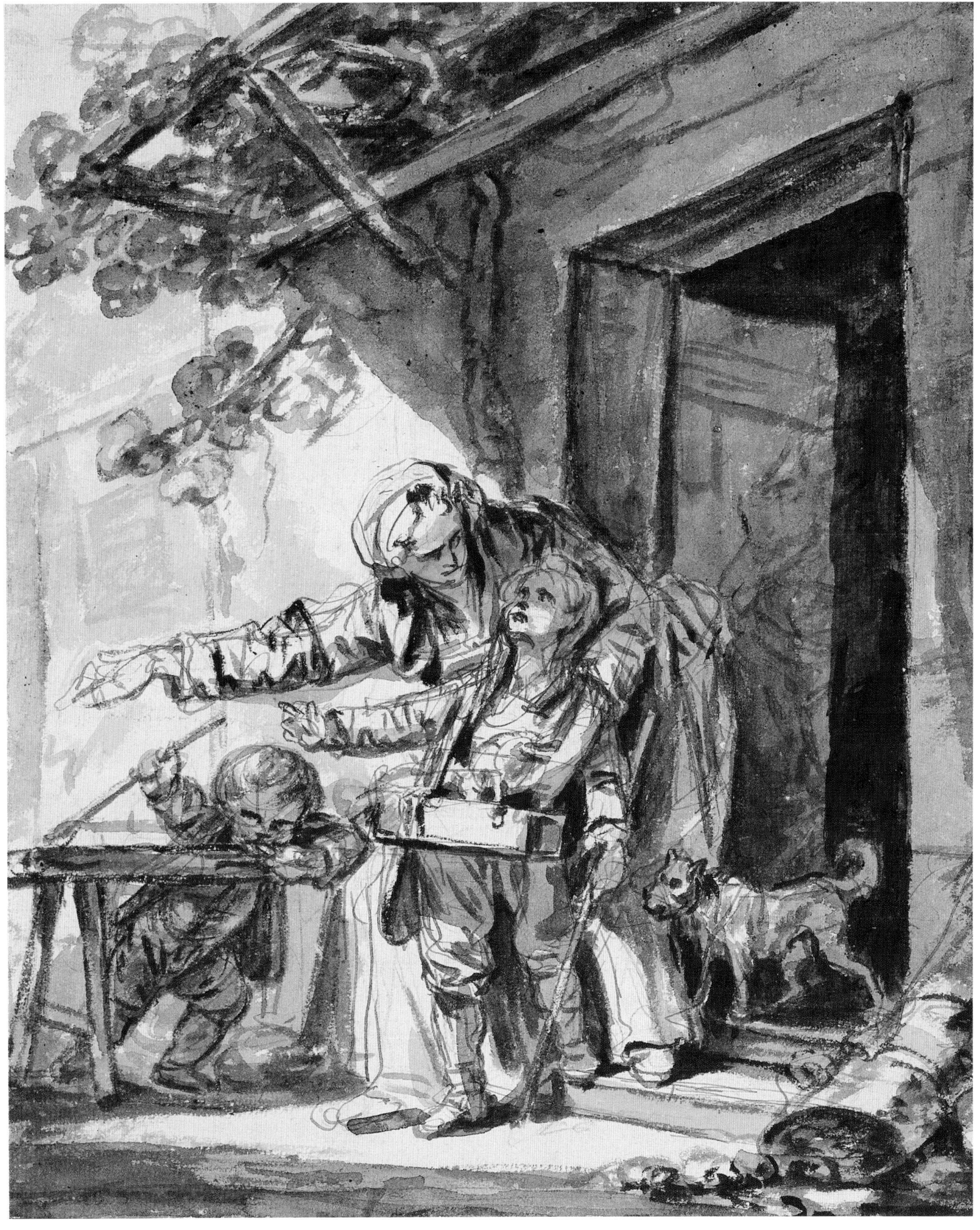

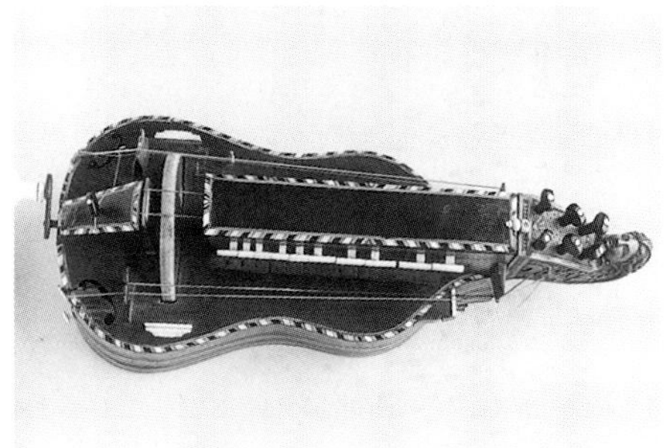

Fig. 138 F. Lejeune, Hurdy-Gurdy, *c.* 1750, various inlaid woods, New York, The Metropolitan Museum of Art

57 *The Education of a Young Savoyard*

Red, black, and white chalks, with stumping, on cream paper, 434 × 342 mm (17 1/16 × 13 3/8 in.)
Vienna, Graphische Sammlung Albertina

Provenance: Pierre-Jean Mariette (1694–1774), Paris; his sale, Paris, 15 November 1775–30 January 1776, lot 1262; Duke Albert von Sachsen und Teschen, Vienna (Lugt 174)
Exhibitions: None known
Bibliography: Normand 1892, repr. facing p. 28; Munhall 1968, pp. 93, fig. 10, 94

Even more than in *The Departure of a Young Savoyard* (no. 56), this drawing captures the emotional distress caused by the impending separation of the young mother and child. Her role is suggested by the *marmite* and spoon resting on the windowsill and by her enveloping arms; his obedient but apprehensive state, by his expression and posture, seemingly overwhelmed by the large, guitar-shaped hurdy-gurdy he balances on his tiny thighs. His departure seems imminent, as his *tricorne* is ready at lower right, his marmot box and staff at the left. The image is imbued with sadness, tenderness, and fear.

Greuze utilized his white chalk sparingly, to define the anatomy of the mother's face and to bring forward certain forms—her kerchief, the boy's cuffs and stockings. In a similar way, the few touches of red chalk—perhaps the final strokes—accent the mother's shoulder and the edge of the caned seat.

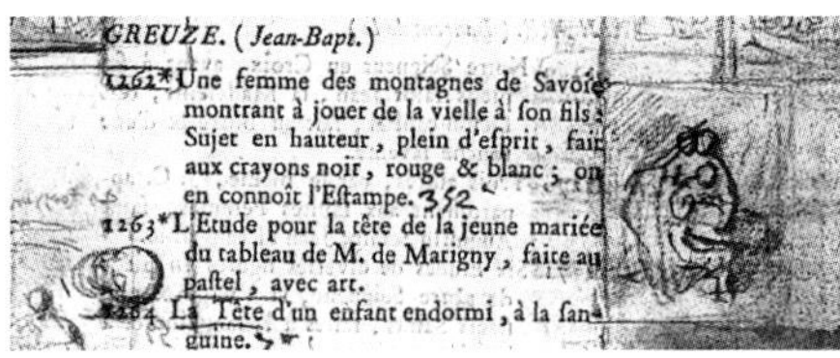

GREUZE. (*Jean-Bapt.*)
1262*Une femme des montagnes de Savoie montrant à jouer de la vielle à son fils: Sujet en hauteur, plein d'esprit, fait aux crayons noir, rouge & blanc; on en connoît l'Estampe. 352
1263*L'Etude pour la tête de la jeune mariée du tableau de M. de Marigny, faite au pastel, avec art.
1264 La Tête d'un enfant endormi, à la sanguine.

Fig. 139 G. de Saint-Aubin, sketch of no. 57 in the Mariette sale catalogue, 1775, graphite, Boston, Museum of Fine Arts, Bequest of William A. Sargent

The hurdy-gurdy, or *vielle à roue* (fig. 138), was an ancient musical instrument indelibly associated with the Savoyards. Louis-Sébastien Mercier's *Tableau de Paris* cites it as standard equipment: "Some of them carry a *vielle* in their arms and accompany its sound with a nasal voice."[1] Its sound was heard at street fairs and country gatherings across Europe in the eighteenth century, and occasionally in the Paris Métro today.

The drawing was acquired soon after its execution by the renowned collector Pierre-Jean Mariette, who knew Greuze and provided some important information about the artist in his *Abécédario.* When *The Education of a Young Savoyard* appeared in Mariette's posthumous sale, Gabriel de Saint-Aubin was sufficiently impressed to make a sketch of it in his copy of the sale catalogue (fig. 139),[2] in which it was described as "A woman of the mountains of Savoy showing her son how to play the *vielle.*" As that catalogue entry went on to state: "We know the engraving of it"[3]—*The Education of a Young Savoyard,* engraved by Jean-Michel Moreau and Jean-Jacques Aliamet (fig. 140). This was the only reproductive print after one of his works that Greuze actively helped execute.[4]

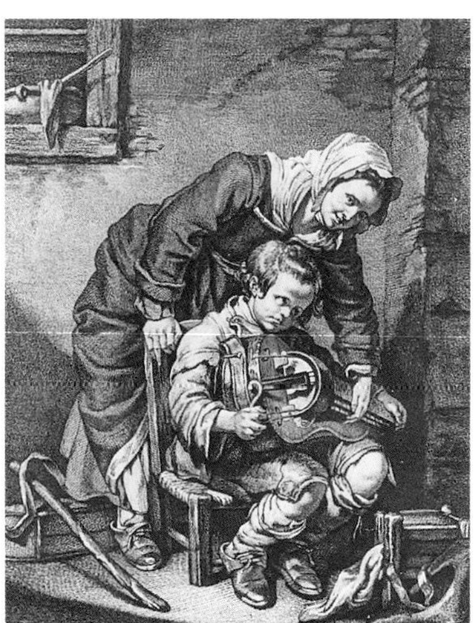

Fig. 140 J.-M. Moreau and J.-J. Aliamet, after Greuze, *The Education of a Young Savoyard, c.* 1770, etching and engraving, Paris, Bibliothèque nationale de France

1. *"Les uns portent une vielle entre leurs bras et l'accompagnent d'une voix nasale."* L.-S. Mercier, *Tableau de Paris,* Paris 1781, I, p. 250.

2. E. Dacier, *Gabriel de Saint-Aubin,* Paris and Brussels 1931, II, p. 193, no. 1042.

3. *"Une femme des montagnes de Savoie montrant à jouer de la vielle à son fils"; "on en connoît l'Estampe." Catalogue de différens objets de curiosité... Dépendant de la succession de M. Mariette,* Paris 1775, no. 1262.

4. F. Courboin, *Histoire illustrée de la gravure en France,* Paris 1924, II, p. 151.

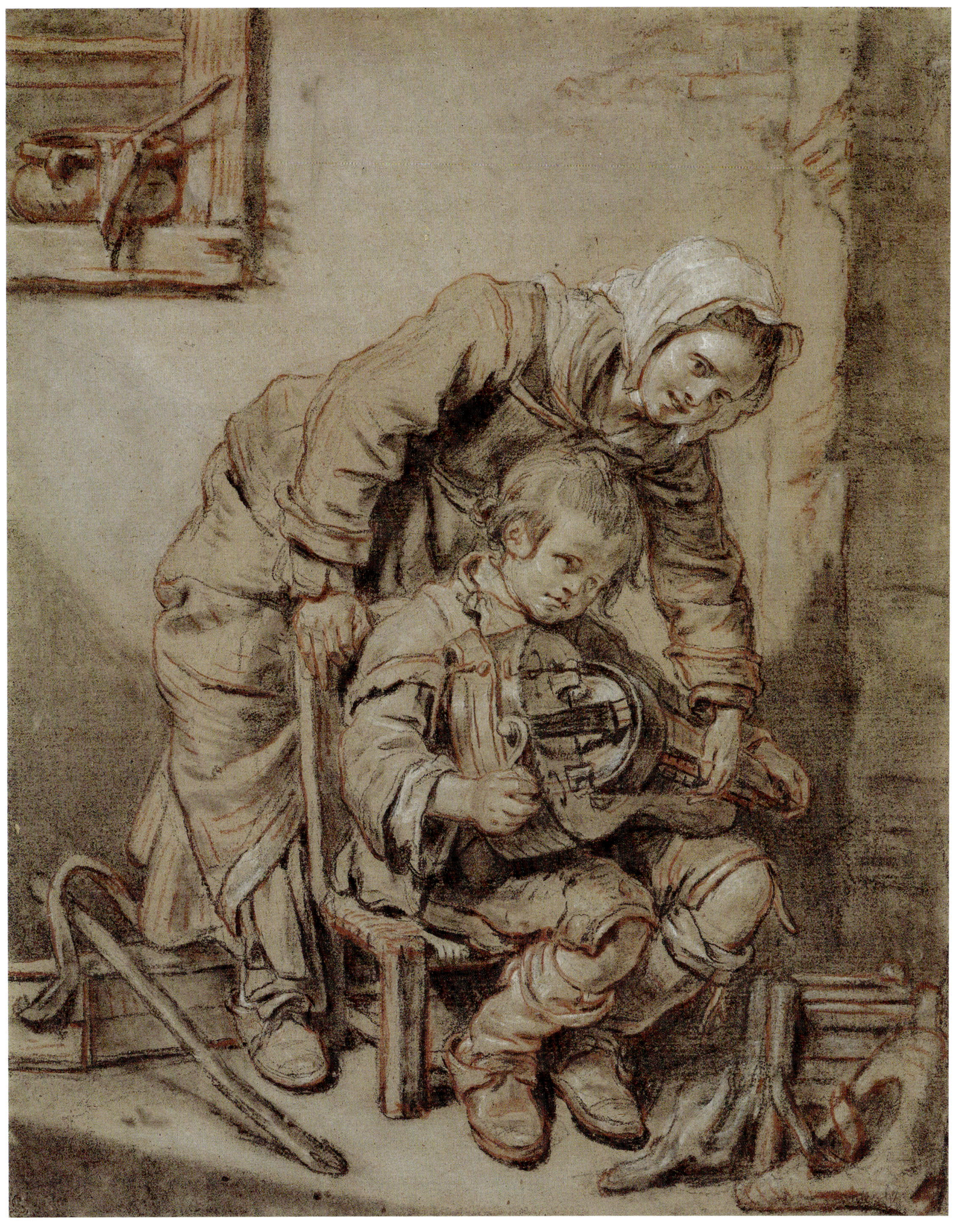

58 *The Dancing Doll*

Brush, black and brown ink, with watercolor over graphite on white paper, 324 × 275 mm (12 ¾ × 10 13/16 in.)
Vienna, Graphische Sammlung Albertina

Provenance: chevalier de Damery (Lugt 2862); Duke Albert von Sachsen und Teschen, Vienna (Lugt 174)
Exhibitions: Meisterwerke aus Oesterreich/Zeichnungen, Gemälde, Plastik, Zurich, Kunsthaus, 1946–47, no. 159; *Cent-cinquante Chefs d'oeuvre de l'Albertina de Vienne,* Paris, Bibliothèque nationale, 1950, no. 148
Bibliography: Goncourt 1880, p. 353; Martin and Masson 1906, no. 405; Brookner 1972, p. 114, pl. 48

With this unusual, outdoor subject, Greuze has captured a more joyous side of Savoyard life than in his depiction of their family woes (nos. 56, 57). Here, a group of twenty figures and a highly excited dog stare in wonderment as the Savoyard causes a doll to dance, probably by jiggling with his left hand a thread connected to it under the table. Such "dancing" figures, known as *marionettes à la planchette,* were seen performing on street corners across Europe throughout the eighteenth century, as well as in elegant homes (fig. 141).[1] They were one of the specialities of the wandering Savoyards. Greuze's protagonist and his assistants would have been recognized as such immediately, with their "long hair . . . cocked hat . . . and breeches."[2]

Greuze often dared to treat "verbal" subjects. Here, the open mouth of the Savoyard and his pointing finger convey the sense of his speaking, to which the audience responds by straining forward, pointing, embracing, or holding hands excitedly.

1. See A. Chapus and E. Droz, *Automata: A Historical and Technological Study,* London 1959, pp. 315–18. The author is grateful to Dr Manu von Miller for her help with this entry.

2. *"les cheveux longs . . . le chapeau bicorne . . . des guêtres ou des chausses."* C. Borlet and J. Poncer, "Le Type Savoyard," *Bibliothèque de la Science sociale,* Paris 1907, p. 58.

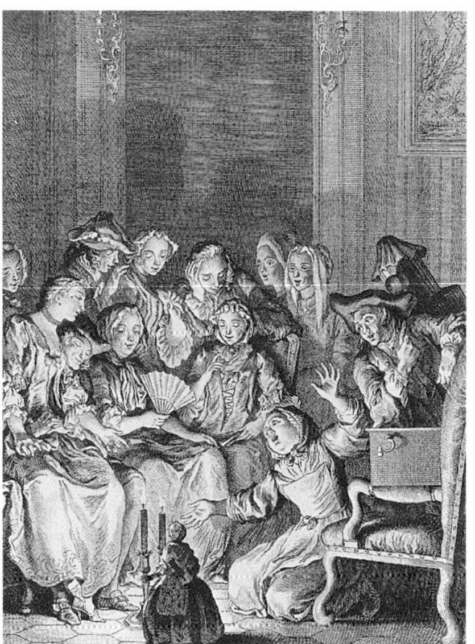

Fig. 141 M. Cochin, after C.-N. Cochin, *The Charming Doll,* 1780, engraving, New York, The Metropolitan Museum of Art, Harris Brisbane Dick Fund, 1953

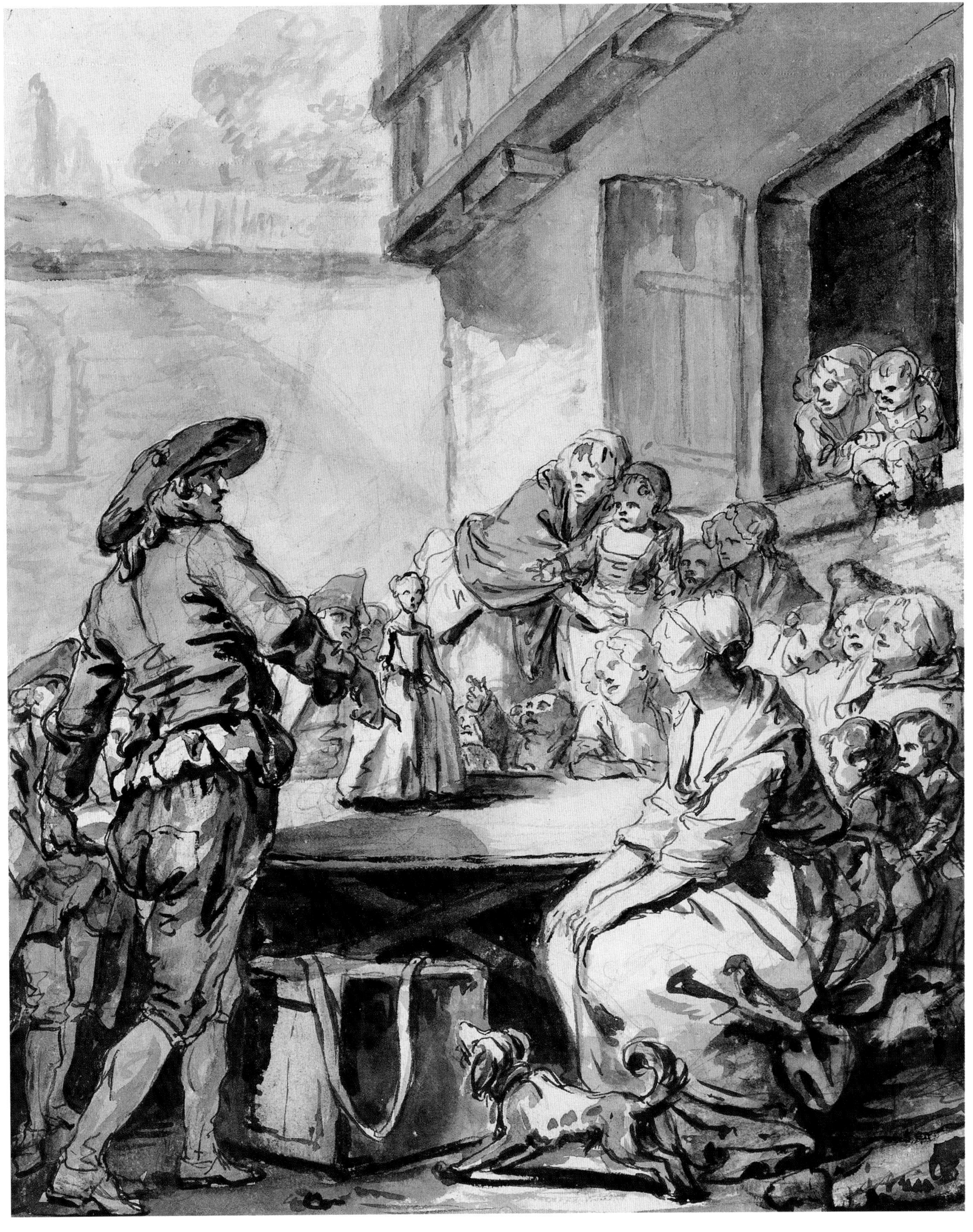

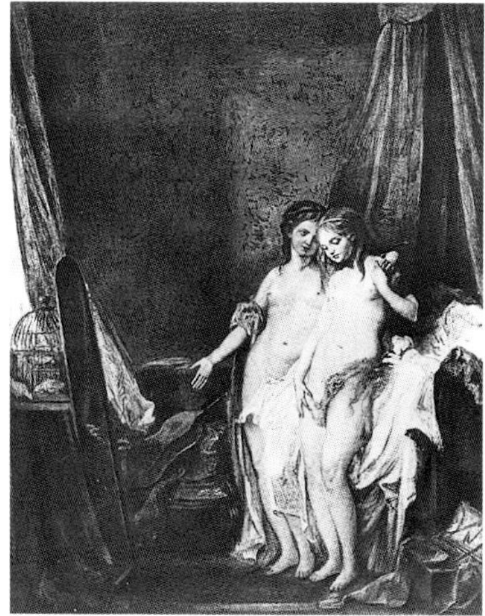

Fig. 142 Greuze, *The Two Sisters*, 1770 (?), oil on canvas, whereabouts unknown

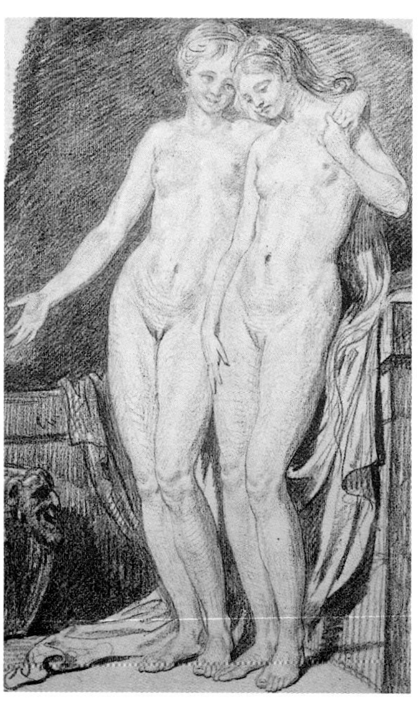

Fig. 143 Greuze, *The Two Sisters*, 1770 (?), red chalk on white paper, private collection

59 *The Two Sisters*

Brush with brown ink wash over graphite on white paper, 385 × 344 mm (15 3/16 × 13 5/16 in.)
Lyon, Musée des Beaux-Arts

Provenance: Coutan, Paris; his sale, Paris, 14–16 April 1812, lot 32; perhaps Prince Nicolas J. Soutzo;[1] bequeathed to the museum by Madame du Marest in 1913
Exhibitions: None known
Bibliography: Martin and Masson 1906, no. 1243; W.M. Brady & Co., Inc., and Thomas William Fine Art Ltd, *Old Master Drawings*, New York 2000, under no. 32

This spirited drawing is a study for *The Two Sisters* (fig. 142), a large picture that once hung in the bedroom of the twelfth Earl of Pembroke's apartment on the place Vendôme, and appeared in his sale of 30 June 1862 (lot 27). It was last recorded in the sale of the marquise Landolfo Carcano, Paris, 31 May 1912 (lot 156).

Between this first compositional study, steamy with its erotic overtones and sense of conspiracy, and the final painting, Greuze executed another study of the two figures alone (fig. 143), much as they would appear—though covered—in the painting *The Two Sisters.* There, the barking dog in the foreground of the Lyon sheet appears farther up, on a bed, and the table mirror is transformed into a full-length mirror, or *psyché.*

Given Greuze's tendency to exploit pictorially aspects of his private life, it is tempting to relate the figures in this composition to his two daughters, Anne-Geneviève (Caroline) and Louise-Gabrielle. In substantiation of this, it is worth noting that the inventory of the latter's effects executed on 22 February 1812 listed among four "unfinished" *("ébauchés")* canvases, one representing "two girls looking at themselves in a mirror" *("deux jeunes filles se regardant dans un miroir").*[2]

Though sexual undertones are common in Greuze's work, such echoes from the world of his friend Diderot's *romans licencieux* are rare. One thinks of the conversation between Soeur Suzanne and her perverse mother superior in *La Religieuse:* "Have you never been tempted to look, with pleasure, at how beautiful you are? No, dear mother. I don't know if I am so beautiful as you say.... You have never thought of letting your hands wander over those beautiful breasts, those thighs, that tummy, over that flesh so firm, so sweet, and so white?"[3]

1. Provenance cited by Martin and Masson 1906, but no such drawing is listed in either of his sales, 7 April 1876 or 17–19 December 1877.

2. Arquié-Bruley 1983, p. 151, no. 34t.

3. *"Jamais vous n'avez été tentée de regarder, avec complaisance, combien vous êtes belle? Non, chère mère. Je ne sais pas si je suis si belle que vous le dites.... Jamais vous n'avez pensé à promener vos mains sur cette belle gorge, sur ces cuisses, sur ce ventre, sur ces chairs si fermes, si douces et si blanches?"* D. Diderot, *La Religieuse,* in *Oeuvres,* ed. A. Billy, Paris 1959, p. 383.

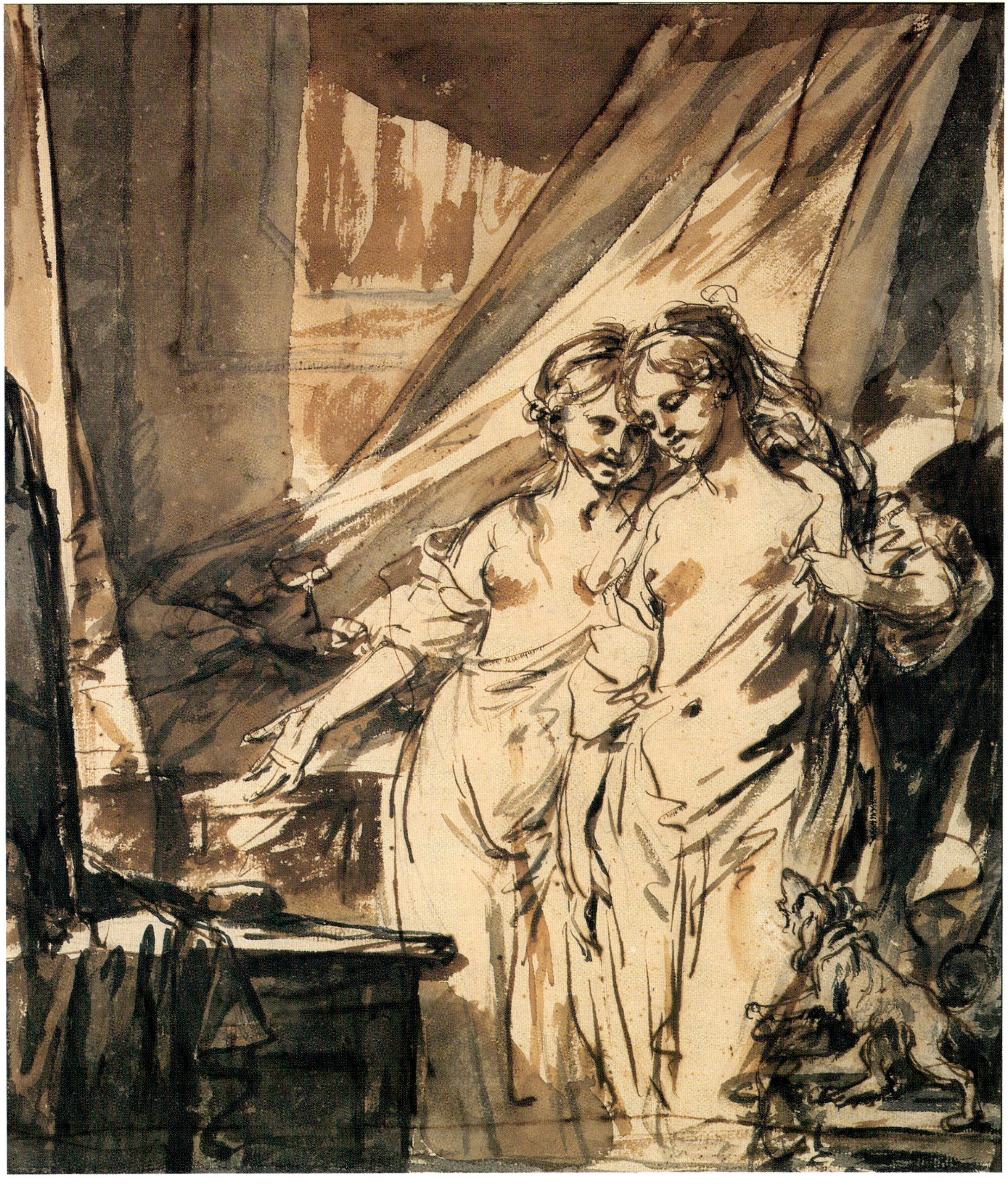

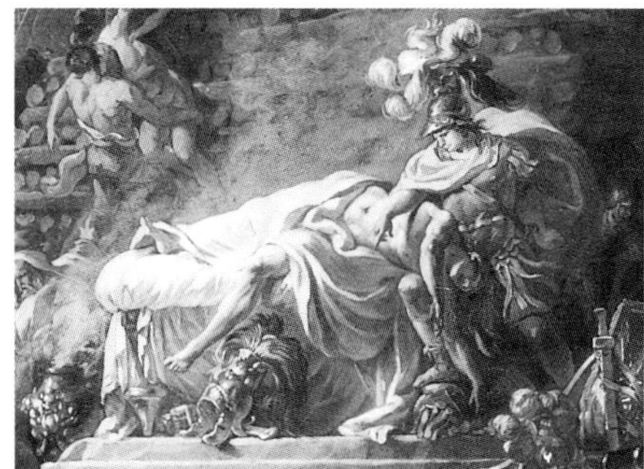

Fig. 144 J.-L. David, *The Funeral of Patroklos* (detail), 1779, oil on canvas, Dublin, National Gallery of Ireland

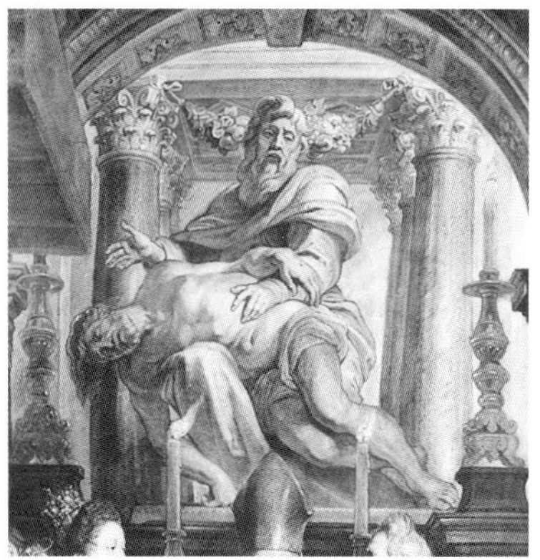

Fig. 145 P.P. Rubens, *Marriage by Proxy* (detail), 1622–25, oil on canvas, Paris, Musée du Louvre

60 *The Funeral of Patroklos*

Red chalk on white paper, 450 × 570 mm (17 ¾ × 22 7/16 in.)
Signed in red chalk at lower right *Greuze*
Private collection, lent in memory of Denise Cailleux, Madame Frédéric Mégret

Provenance: Madame de Conantré, Paris; her daughter, baronne de Ruble, Paris; her daughter, Madame de Witte, Paris; marquise de Bryas, née de Witte, Paris; Galerie Cailleux, Paris, until 1973
Exhibitions: Paris 1951, no. 186; *Autour du néoclassicisme,* Paris, Galerie Cailleux, 1973, no. 12; Hartford *et al.* 1976–77, no. 66
Bibliography: Schnapper 1978, p. 375; Munhall 1994, p. 642

Though the subject of this drawing was long described generically as representing "an entombment," it seems reasonable to identify the two heroic figures as representing Achilles preparing the body of his beloved Patroklos for his funeral pyre, suggested by the large stone structure at the left.

The funeral of Patroklos, as recounted by Homer, was a popular theme at the time Greuze executed this sheet. It was, for instance, the subject of the Académie's Prix de Rome competition in 1769, oil sketches for which survive from the hands of Jean-Simon Berthélémy (1743–1811), Pierre Lacour (1745–1814), Joseph-Barthélémy Le Bouteux (b. 1744), Joseph-Benoît Suvée (1743–1807), and Jean-Joseph Taillasson (1745–1809).[1] Ten years later David produced his enormous canvas *The Funeral of Patroklos* that focuses on a pair of figures not unlike those Greuze drew here (fig. 144).[2] But in contrast to David's panoramic depiction of Patroklos's funeral pyre, Greuze characteristically focused on the distraught Achilles struggling to cope with the reality of his companion's death. The artist's simple design seems intended to illustrate Homer's description of Achilles trying to embrace the ghost of Patroklos: "He opened his arms towards him as he spoke and would have clasped him in them, but there was nothing, and the spirit vanished as a vapor, gibbering and whining into the earth."[3]

Greuze's recumbent Patroklos recalls the sculpture representing the dead Christ in Rubens's *Marriage by Proxy* (fig. 145), a painting from which Greuze copied two heads in 1760.[4] The reversal of the pose may have resulted from one of Greuze's frequent uses of a counterproof to suit the composition at hand. According to Jakob Burckhardt, Rubens's model—featuring another pair of heroic male figures—was Baccio Bandinelli's (1493–1560) *Christ and God the Father,* once installed at the high altar of the Duomo in Florence and now in Santa Croce.[5]

1. See H. Siefert, *Themen aus Homers Ilias in der französischen Kunst (1750–1831),* Munich 1988, pp. 403–04.

2. See *French Painting, 1774–1830: The Age of Revolution,* exhib. cat., The Detroit Institute of Arts; New York, The Metropolitan Museum of Art, no. 27, repr. p. 54.

3. Homer, *The Iliad,* trans. Samuel Butler, bk. XXIII, stanza iv, ll. 73–75.

4. Hartford *et al.* 1976–77, no. 25.

5. J. Burckhardt, *Recollections of Rubens,* London 1950, pp. 118–19; M. Raymond, *La Sculpture florentine,* Florence 1900, IV, p. 126; J. Thuillier and J. Foucart, *Rubens' Life of Marie de' Medici,* New York 1972, p. 77.

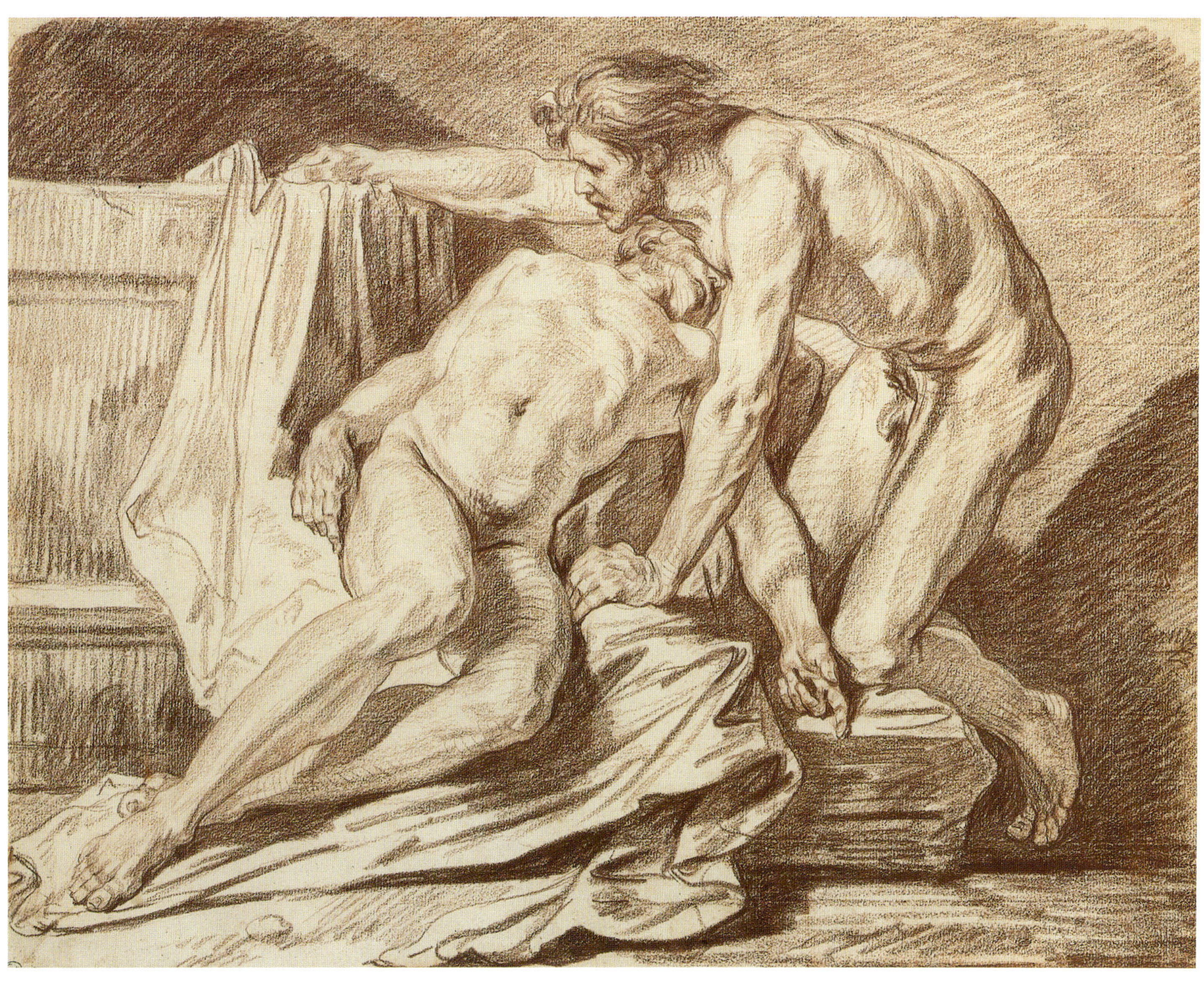

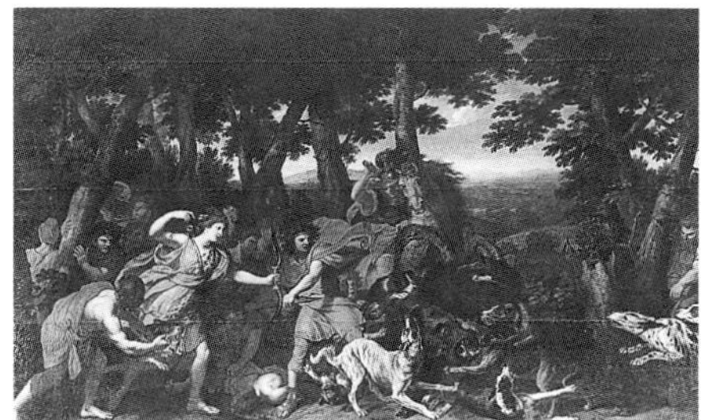

Fig. 146 C. Lebrun, *The Hunt of Meleager and Atalanta, c.* 1658, oil on canvas, Paris, Musée du Louvre

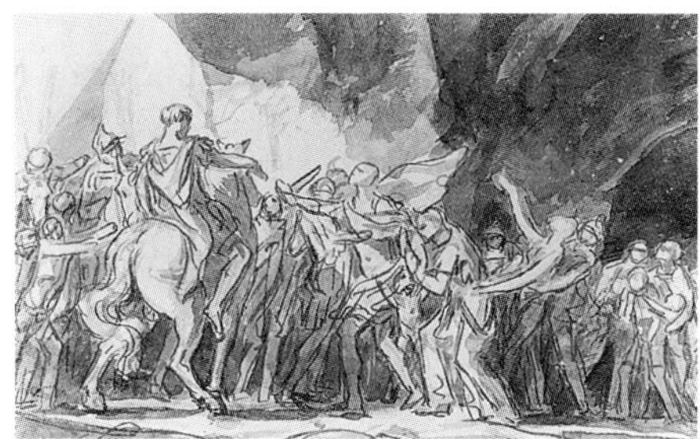

Fig. 147 Greuze, *Compositional Study for "The Arrest of Sabinus," c.* 1767, brush with brown and gray ink wash over graphite on white paper, Graphische Sammlung, Staatsgalerie Stuttgart

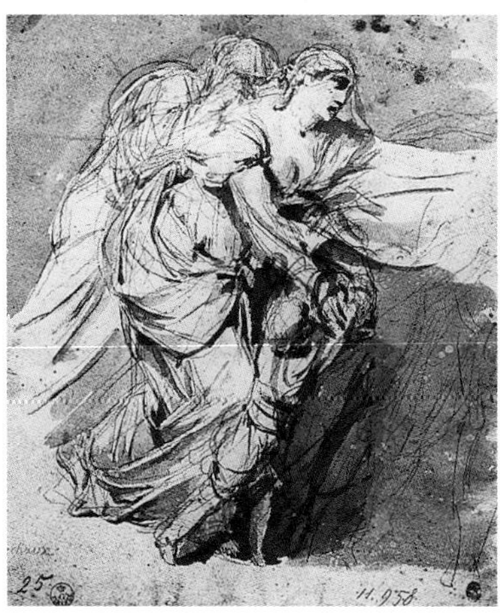

Fig. 148 Greuze, *Study for "The Arrest of Sabinus," c.* 1767, red chalk, brush and gray ink wash on white paper, Florence, Galleria degli Uffizi

61 *The Arrest of Sabinus*

Brush with black ink over graphite on white paper, 490 × 640 mm (19 1/8 × 25 3/16 in.)
Inscribed on mount *Dessin original de Greuze légué au Musée/ de Chaumont par Sylvain Mollot./ Paris le 9 décembre 1859./ H. Walferdin*
Chaumont, Musée Municipal

Provenance: perhaps Caroline Greuze (d. 1842), Paris; her sale, Paris, 25–26 January 1843, no. 22;[1] Sylvain Mollot, Paris; bequeathed by the latter to the museum and transferred there by H. Walferdin on 9 December 1859
Exhibitions: The Age of Neoclassicism, London, The Royal Academy of Arts, 1972, no. 631; Paris 1974–75, no. 74; Hartford *et al.* 1976–77 (Dijon only, no. 66 *bis*)
Bibliography: Martin and Masson 1906, nos. 25, 25 *bis; Catalogue du Musée de Chaumont,* Chaumont 1912, no. 8; Munhall 1965, pp. 23–27; J. Seznec, "Diderot et l'affaire Greuze," *GBA,* May 1966, p. 353; *Mostra di disegni francesi da Callot a Ingres,* exhib. cat., Florence, Galleria degli Uffizi, 1968, pp. 67–68; Brookner 1972, p. 109; Schnapper 1977, p. 89; Schnapper 1978, p. 375; H. Geissler in *Meisterwerke aus der graphischen Sammlung, Zeichnungen der 15. bis 18. Jahrhunderts,* exhib. cat., Stuttgart, Staatsgalerie, 1984, p. 264, no. 197, repr. p. 287; Munhall 1994, p. 642

This powerful drawing provides evidence of yet another experiment on Greuze's part with a historical subject during the period in the late 1760s when he was evolving his *morceau de réception.* Following Tacitus's account in his *Annals* (IV. 67), Greuze has represented the rebellious Gaul Julius Sabinus being arrested by the emperor Vespasian at the entrance to the cave where he had been hiding for nine years with his wife, their twin children, and two devoted servants. The latter group, including Sabinus's sorrowing wife, Epponina, react to the event with distress and fear. The subject is typically obscure and emotional, but it also reflects contemporary interest in themes drawn from French history. The same subject was employed by Taillasson in a painting exhibited at the Salon of 1789 and by Nicolas-André Monsiau (1754–1837) in a sketch shown in 1800.

The drawing recalls Charles Lebrun's *Hunt of Meleager and Atalanta* (fig. 146) in a number of ways: its horizontal format, its friezelike design, the clearly defined gestures and expressions, the billowing cloak of Sabinus, the rearing horse, and the gesture of Atalanta used here with Vespasian and repeated by Greuze with the figure of Septimius Severus in his *morceau de réception* (fig. 13). It is conceivable that in creating his own new, grand manner, Greuze studied this seventeenth-century master of dramatic expression, to whom critics would often compare him.

A preliminary compositional study for the present sheet (fig. 147) suggests the attention the artist was lavishing on this subject.[2] It demonstrates that Greuze subsequently chose to reverse his composition and reduce the number of figures to differentiate them for greater dramatic effect. An additional study for the figure of Epponina and her children (fig. 148) reveals Greuze's new interest in generalized draperies of a classical style, as he was moving away from the realism of contemporary dress that characterized his earlier work.

1. Described in the sale catalogue as *"Scene from Roman History.*—A man on horseback, surrounded by numerous figures.—Brush and wash" ("Scène de l'histoire romaine.—*Un homme à cheval, entouré de figures nombreuses.—A la plume et lavé*").

2. See Geissler 1984. The Stuttgart sheet was illustrated in the de Vries catalogue *Dessins de maîtres anciens et modernes,* Amsterdam, 1929, no. 115, and may have been lot 320 in the Hippolyte Walferdin sale, Paris, 12–16 April 1860. Martin and Masson 1906 assigned the latter provenance to the Chaumont drawing.

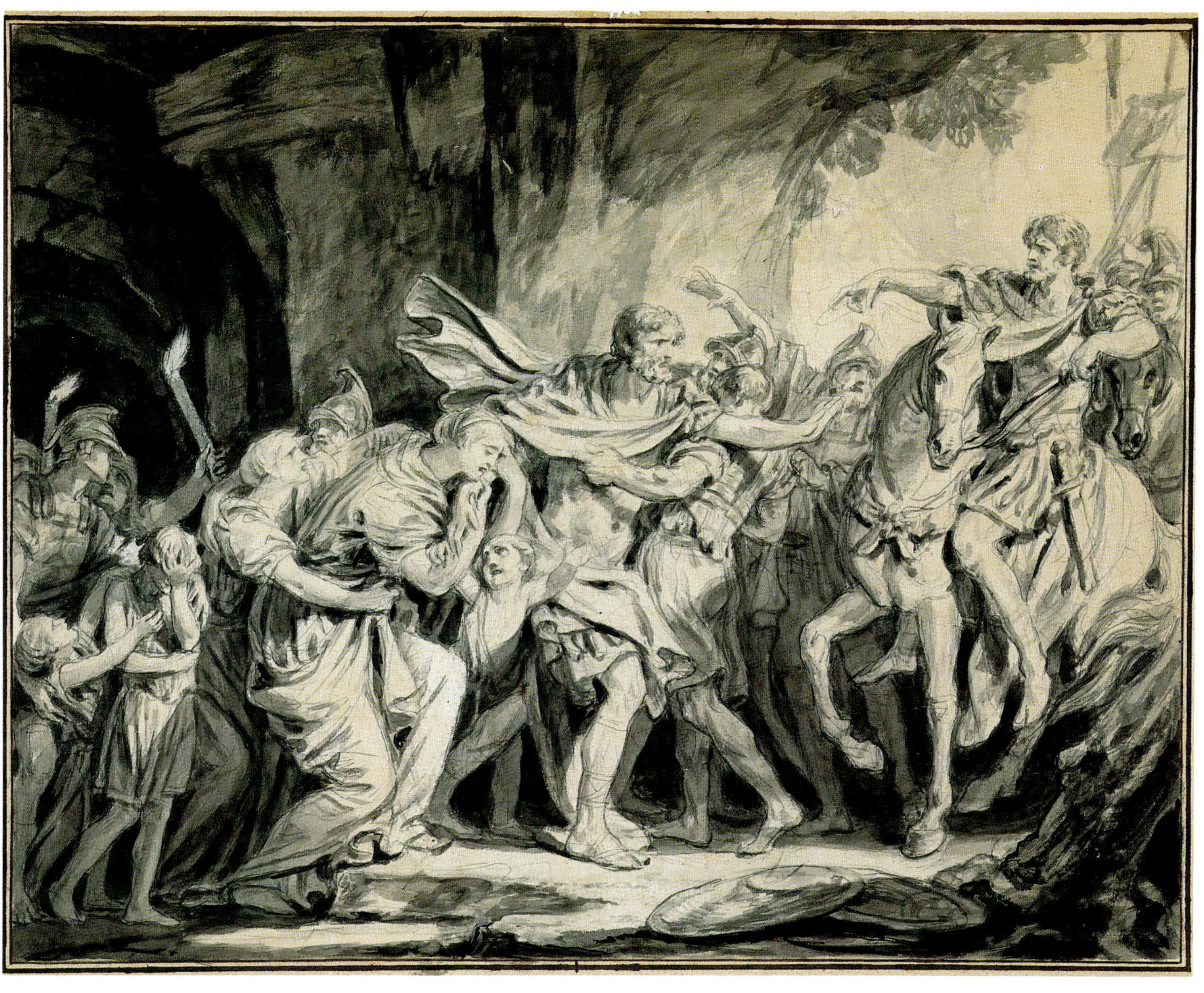

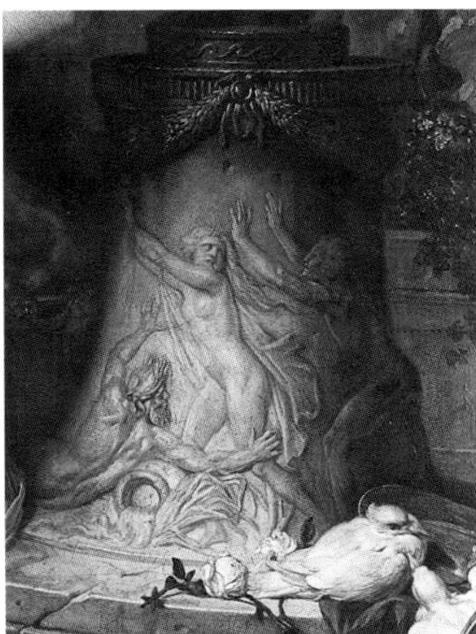

Fig. 149 Greuze, *The Votive Offering to Cupid* (detail), 1767, oil on canvas, London, The Wallace Collection

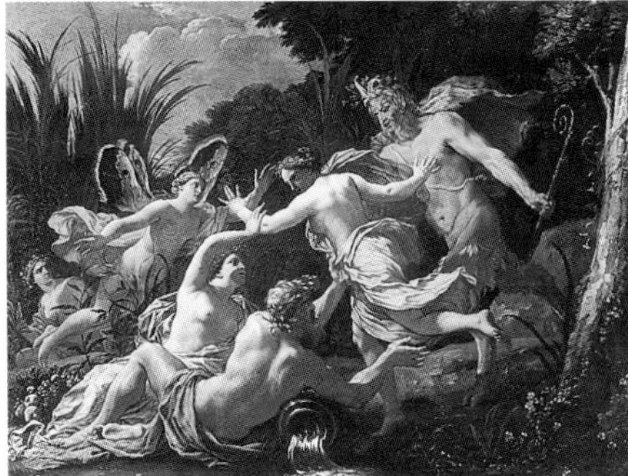

Fig. 150 M. Dorigny, *Pan and Syrinx,* 1657, oil on canvas, Paris, Musée du Louvre

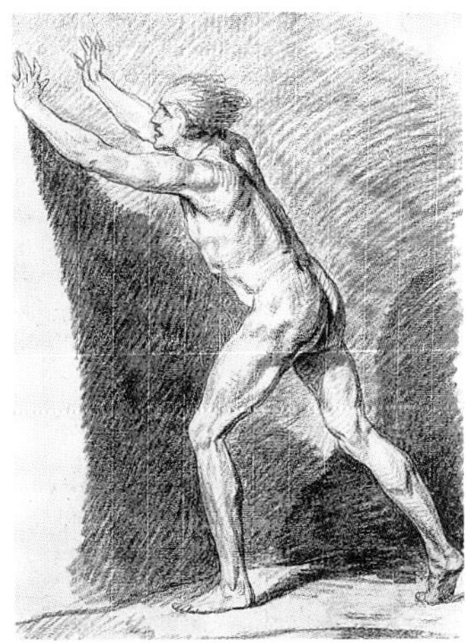

Fig. 151 Greuze, *Naked Man Rushing to the Left,* 1767, red chalk on white paper, private collection

62 *River God*

Red chalk on cream paper, 470 × 634 mm (18 ½ × 24 15/16 in.)
New York, The Metropolitan Museum of Art, Joseph Pulitzer Bequest

Provenance: Galerie Cailleux, Paris; acquired by the museum in 1961
Exhibitions: Paris 1951, no. 185; *Figures nues d'école française,* Paris, Galerie Charpentier, 1953, no. 9; London 1968, no. 319; *French Drawings and Prints of the Eighteenth Century,* New York, The Metropolitan Museum of Art, 1972–73, no. 26; Hartford *et al.* 1976–77, no. 56
Bibliography: Cailleux 1960, p. 292 n. 7; *The Metropolitan Museum of Art Bulletin,* October 1961, pp. 47, 63–64; J.H. Rubin in *Eighteenth-Century French Life Drawing. Selections from the Collection of Mathias Polakovits,* exhib. cat., Princeton University, The Art Museum, 1977, p. 33; Bean and Turčić 1986, p. 122, no. 130; J. Ingamells, *The Wallace Collection Catalogue of Pictures,* III, *French before 1815,* London 1989, pp. 204–05

Of the many drawings Greuze executed in preparing his *The Votive Offering to Cupid* (London, The Wallace Collection)—compositional schemes, studies of figures, heads, and sculptural reliefs[1]—Anita Brookner identified this one as a study for the base of the altar of Cupid in that painting (fig. 149).[2] Though exhibited in the Salon of 1769 (no. 153), Diderot referred to it as completed in 1767, both in his *Salons* and in a letter to Falconet dated July 1767.[3] The river god's presence in this pseudo-relief alludes to his role in protecting Syrinx when she was fleeing Pan by transforming her into the reeds that appear alongside the flowing urn in Greuze's painting.

Jacob Bean associated the present study with a drawing by Louis de Boullogne the Younger (1654–1733), also in the Metropolitan Museum of Art (inv. no. 61.28), representing a similar figure of a river god, and subsequently, Dean Walker suggested a common source for both drawings in Michel Dorigny's (1617–1685) *Pan and Syrinx* (fig. 150). To complicate the issue further, the figure of Syrinx on the altar base of *The Votive Offering to Cupid* has been recognized as based on a relief on an urn that is part of Louis-Claude Vassé's (1716–1772) *Nymph Drying Her Hair,* a marble signed and dated 1763 now in the Metropolitan Museum of Art, and the present author recently identified a red chalk drawing in a private collection (fig. 151) as a study for the all-too-human figure of Pan on the same altar base. Finally, among the drawings by Greuze acquired by Betskoy and today in the State Hermitage Museum is a red chalk drawing of a river nymph seen from behind, a female counterpart to the male god in the present sheet, with a similar flowing urn and crumpled foreground draperies.[4]

That Greuze lavished such attention on a single element of a picture, even indulging in uncharacteristic borrowings from other artists, suggests the importance he attached to *The Votive Offering to Cupid* at this crucial turning point in his career.

1. See Ingamells 1989, p. 204.

2. A. Brookner, "Cent Antiquaires parisiens," *Connaissance des arts,* May 1958, p. 55.

3. Diderot *Salons,* III, p. 225; Diderot *Correspondance,* VII, p. 103.

4. Inv. no. 14742; Monod and Hautecoeur 1922, no. 172.

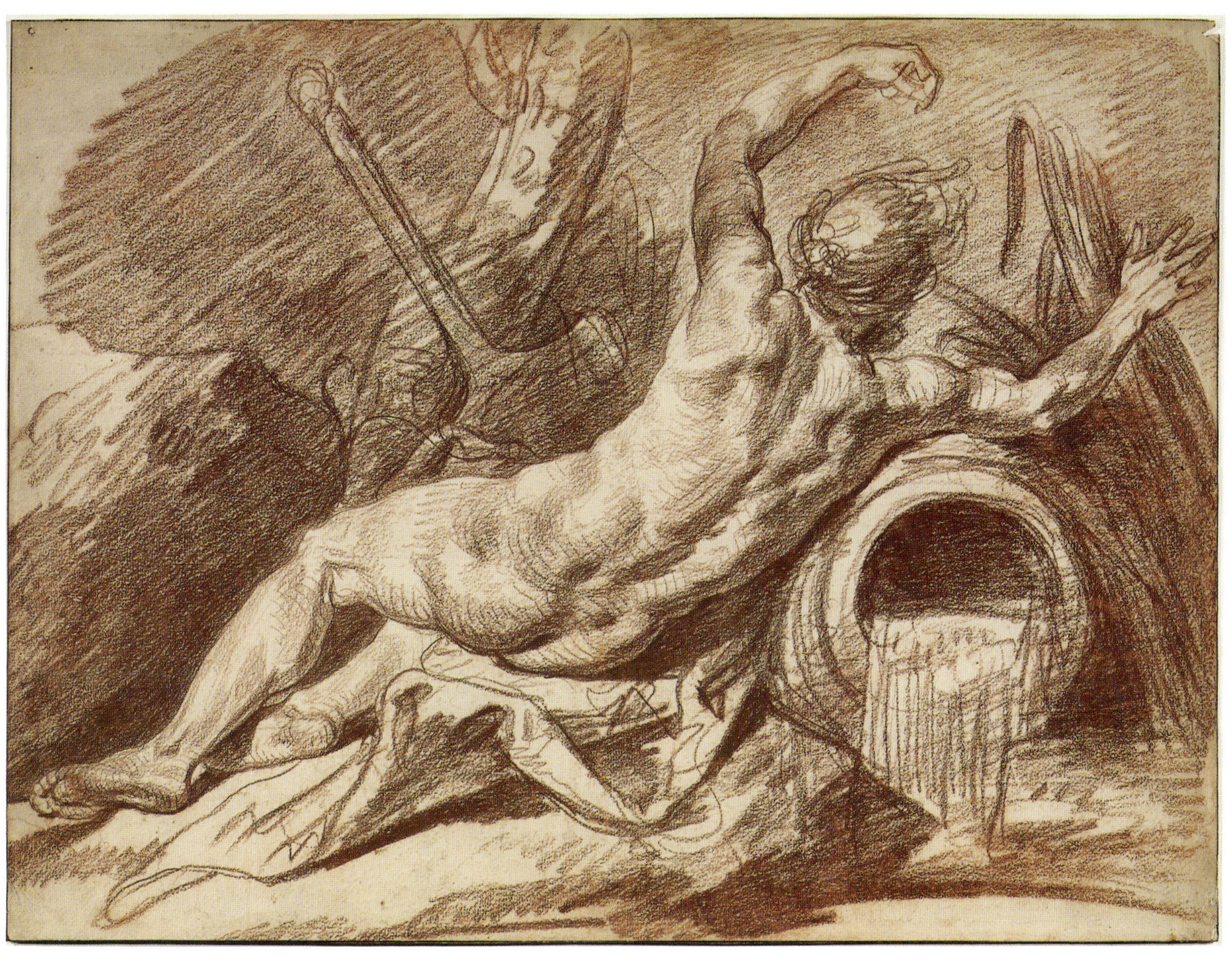

63 *Seated Female Nude Leaning Forward*

Red chalk on cream paper, 407 × 301 mm (16 1/16 × 11 13/16 in.)
Paris, Musée du Louvre, Département des arts graphiques

Provenance: acquired from Paul Prouté S.A., Paris, in 1979
Exhibition: Acquisitions du Cabinet des Dessins, 1973–1983, Paris, Musée du Louvre, 1984, no. 87
Bibliography: Paul Prouté S.A., *Catalogue "Centenaire,"* Paris 1978, no. 47; "Chronique des Arts," *GBA,* March 1980, p. 70

The figure's pose in strict profile and bending forward to the right would suggest that this drawing is yet another preparatory study by Greuze for his *Cimon and Pero: Roman Charity* (fig. 154). The full-breasted woman depicted here with an unapologetic realism worthy of Gustave Courbet (1819–1877) was obviously chosen with that nursing subject in mind. The artist's preference for such solid, muscular female models reflects not only personal tastes but also a familiarity with and emulation of the antique sculpture he was drawing at the same period (fig. 152).

Another drawing of the same model, partially clothed, is discussed in reference to number 54 (fig. 132).

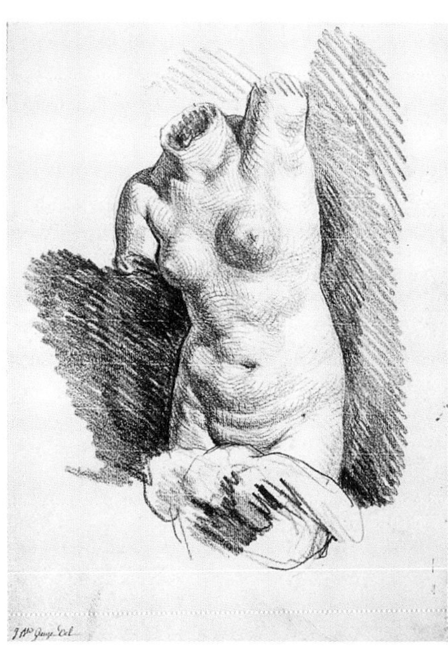

Fig. 152 Greuze, *Female Torso, Study after the Antique, c.* 1767, red chalk on white paper, Warsaw, University Library

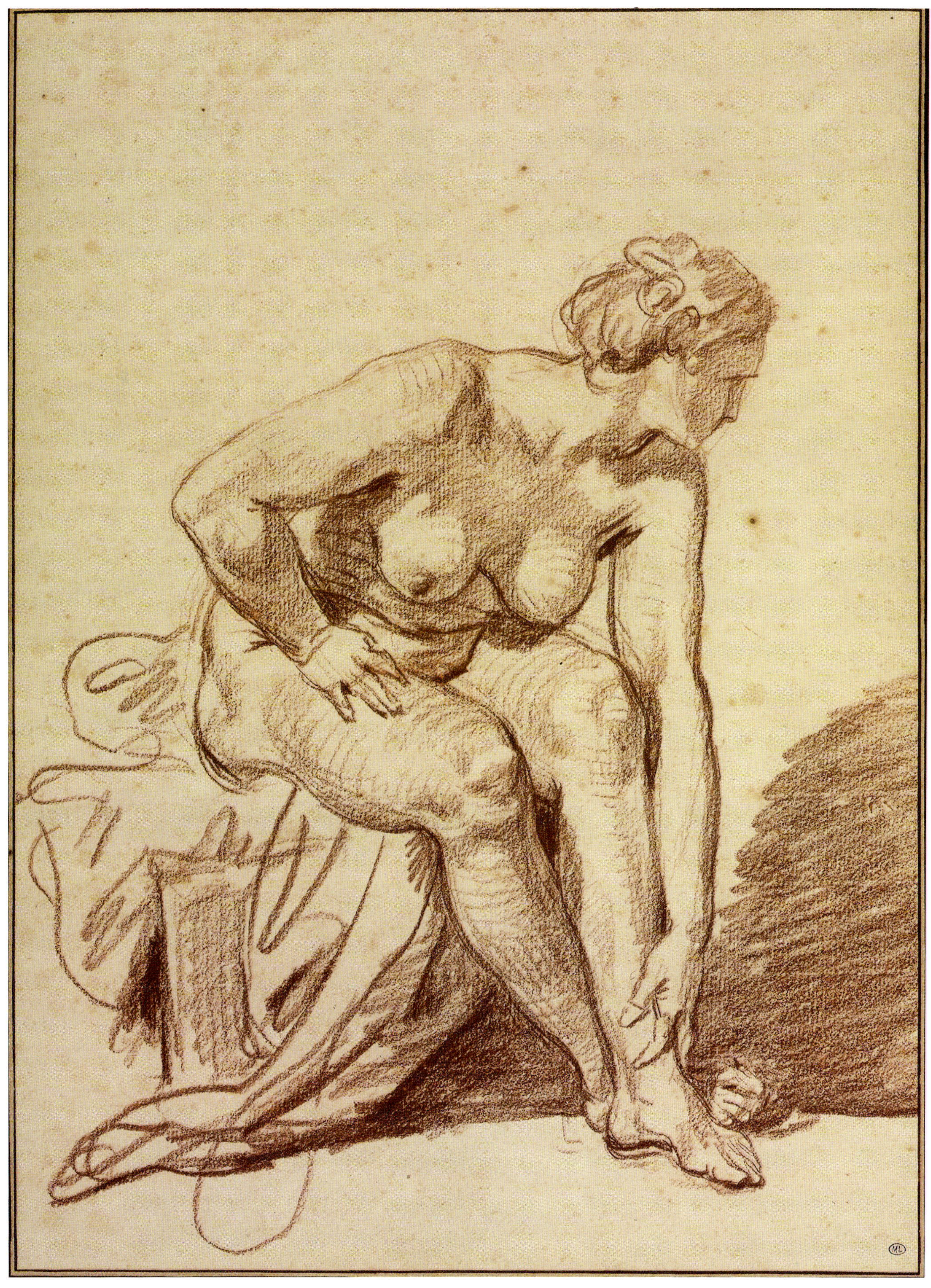

64 *Seated Female Nude*

Red chalk on cream paper, 445 × 370 mm (17 ½ × 14 ⅝ in.)
Signed in red chalk at lower right *J B G*
Cambridge MA, Fogg Art Museum, Harvard University, Bequest of Meta and Paul J. Sachs

Provenance: Caroline Greuze (d. 1842), Paris; her sale, Paris 25–26 January 1843, lot 29; Delbecq, Ghent; his sale, Paris, 20 January 1845, lot 104; Émile Straus, Paris, 1886; his sale, Paris, 3 June 1929, lot 72; sold by Birnbaum to Paul J. Sachs in 1929; entered the Fogg Art Museum in 1965
Exhibitions: up to 1959, see listing in Hartford *et al.* 1976–77, no. 59; *Drawing on Tradition: The Lost Legacy of Academic Figure Studies,* Cambridge MA, Fogg Art Museum, 1994–95, no. 10; *Behind the Line. The Materials and Techniques of Old Master Drawings,* Cambridge MA, Fogg Art Museum, 1998, no. 5
Bibliography: up to 1965, see listing in Hartford *et al.* 1976–77, no. 59, but not including Normand 1892, repr. facing p. 89; Cailleux 1960, pp. 292, 294 n. 7; R. Klessmann, review of *Jean-Baptiste Greuze/1725–1805, Pantheon,* XXXV, April–June 1977, repr. p. 175; N. Goldstein, *Guide to 100 American and European Drawings: A Portfolio,* Englewood Cliffs NJ 1982, pl. 19; A. Scottez in *Au temps de Watteau, Fragonard et Chardin. Les Pays-Bas et les peintres français du XVIIIe siècle,* exhib. cat., Lille, Musée des Beaux-Arts, 1985, p. 107; E. Saywell, "Behind the Line: The Materials and Techniques of Old Master Drawings," *Harvard University Art Museums Bulletin,* fall 1998, pp. 9–10, 36

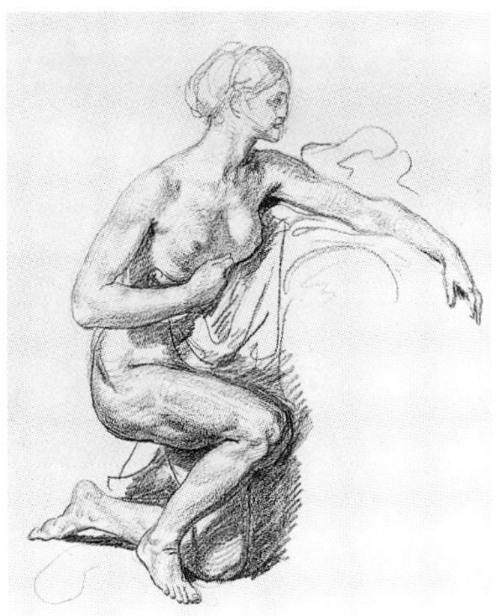

Fig. 153 Greuze, *Kneeling Female Nude, Study for "Cimon and Pero: Roman Charity,"* *c.* 1767, red chalk on cream paper, Boston, Jeffrey E. Horvitz Collection (inv. no. D-F-820)

Through its frequent appearance in exhibitions and publications, this sheet has contributed considerably to Greuze's renown as a draftsman.

The gesture of the woman pressing her breast suggests that this was a study for a depiction of the classical theme known as Roman Charity, the story taken from Valerius Maximus of Pero breast-feeding her imprisoned father Cimon after he had been sentenced to die of starvation.[1] Théophile Thoré was the first to make this association in cataloguing the present drawing for the Caroline Greuze sale in 1843.[2] With this subject, Greuze was able to transfer the theme of a nursing woman, which he had treated in numerous genre scenes, into the realm of history painting. It would also have appealed to him as a demonstration of filial piety, as Valerius Maximus himself wrote: "Such an action would appear unnatural, if the first commandment of nature were not to love our parents."[3]

Another study by Greuze for Roman Charity, but with the model turned to the right—as she would appear in his painting of that subject (fig. 154)—was recently acquired by an American collector (fig. 153).

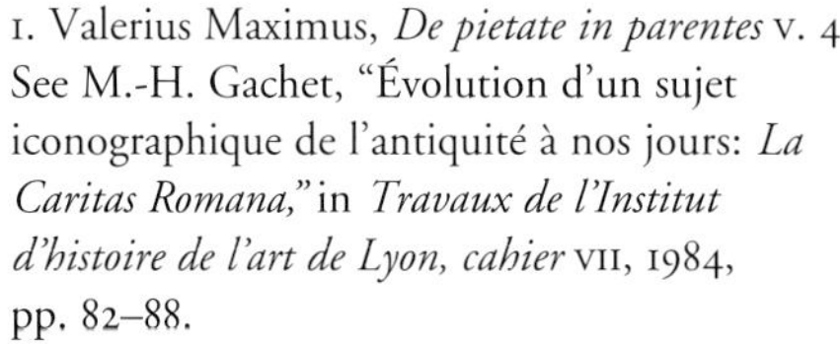

1. Valerius Maximus, *De pietate in parentes* V. 4. See M.-H. Gachet, "Évolution d'un sujet iconographique de l'antiquité à nos jours: *La Caritas Romana,"* in *Travaux de l'Institut d'histoire de l'art de Lyon, cahier* VII, 1984, pp. 82–88.

2. "Appears to be the study for the Roman Charity" *("Paraît être l'étude pour la Charité romaine").* T. Thoré, catalogue of the Caroline Greuze sale, lot 29.

3. Gachet 1984, p. 82.

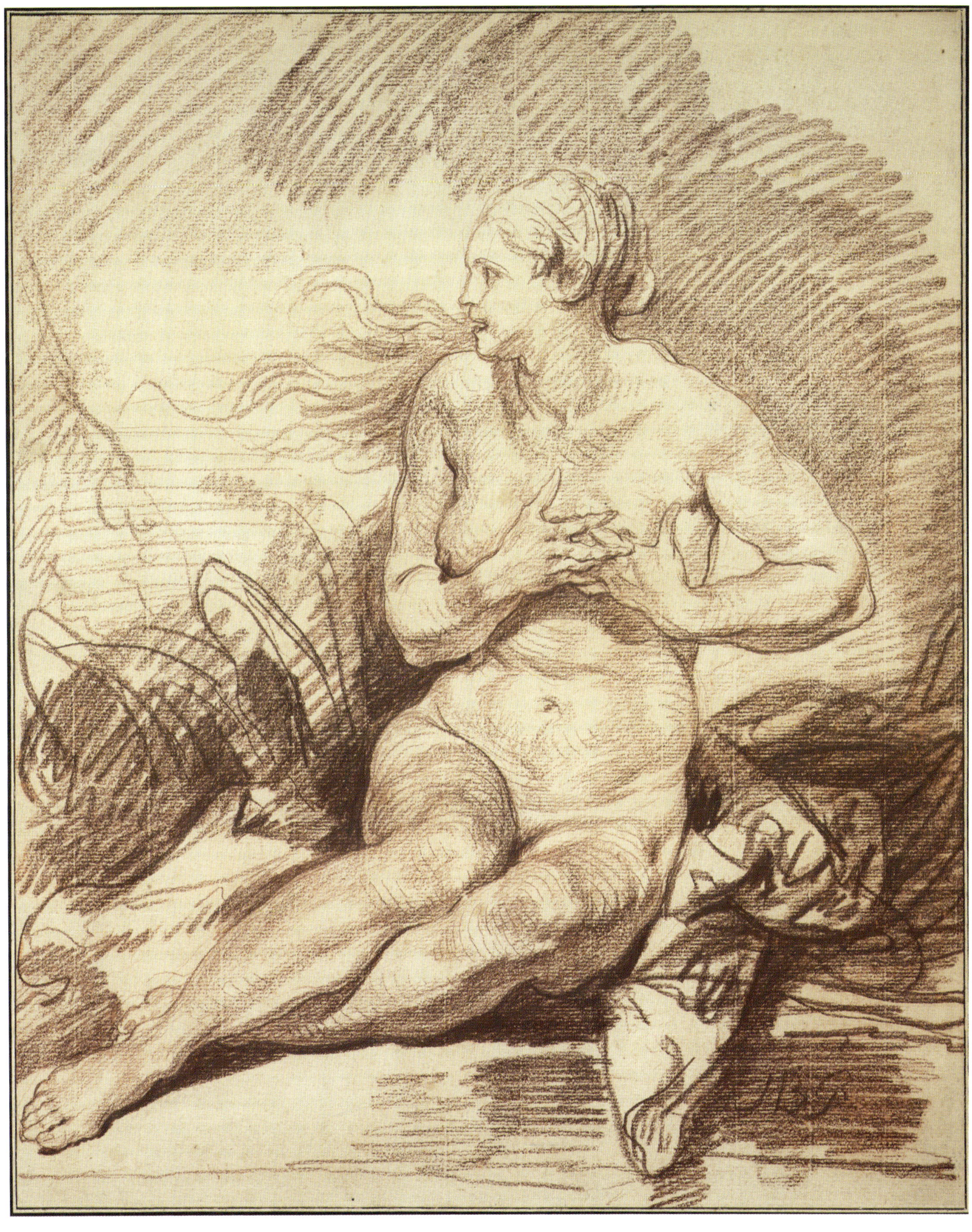

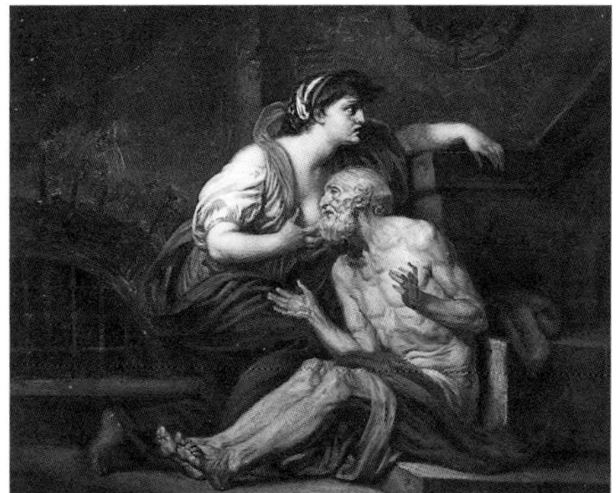

Fig. 154 Greuze, *Cimon and Pero: Roman Charity,* 1767, oil on canvas, Los Angeles, The J. Paul Getty Museum

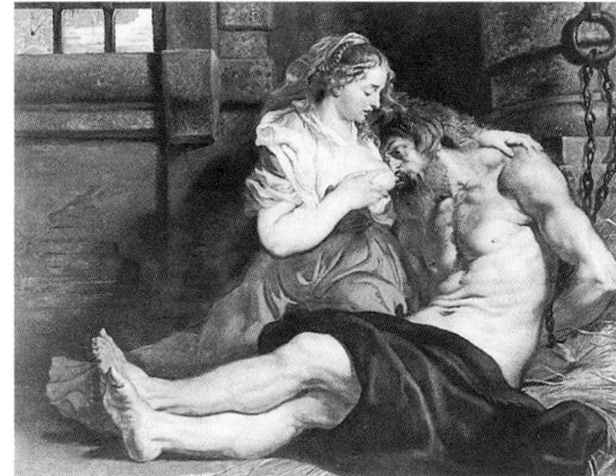

Fig 155 P.P. Rubens, *Roman Charity,* 1611–12, oil on canvas, St Petersburg, The State Hermitage Museum

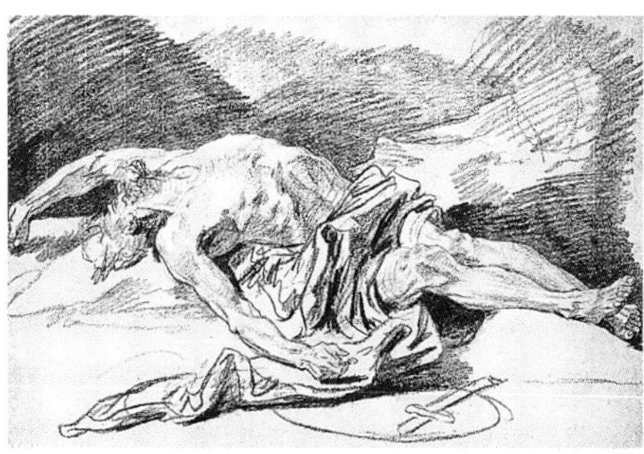

Fig. 156 Greuze, *The Death of Cato of Utica,* 1767–68, red chalk on white paper, Tournus, Musée Greuze

65 *Cimon and Pero: Roman Charity*

Brush, black ink, and gray ink wash over graphite on cream paper, 326 × 416 mm (12 15/16 × 16 3/8 in.)
Paris, Musée du Louvre, Département des arts graphiques

Provenance: original collection of the Cabinet des Dessins, Musée du Louvre (Saint-Morys collection)
Exhibitions: Dessins français de 1750 à 1825: Le Néo-classicisme, Paris, Musée du Louvre, Cabinet des Dessins, 1972, no. 10; Hartford *et al.* 1976–77, no. 60
Bibliography: Morel d'Arleux, no. 12645; Martin and Masson 1906, no. 226; Guiffrey and Marcel 1911, VI, p. 56, no. 4542; J. Mathey, "Greuze et Fragonard copistes de Rubens," *BSHAF,* no. 2, 1933, pp. 183–84; A. Pigler, *Barockthemen,* Budapest 1956, II, p. 284; Munhall 1965, pp. 24, 27; Brookner 1972, p. 108; Schnapper 1977, p. 89; Schnapper 1978, p. 375; Arquié-Bruley *et al.* 1987, II, p. 499; Munhall 1994, p. 642; H. Mouradian in *Jean-Jacques Bachelier (1724–1806), Peintre du Roi et de Madame de Pompadour,* exhib. cat., Versailles, Musée Lambinet, 1999–2000, p. 168; Fischer *et al.* 2000, p. 73, fig. 21

For information concerning the iconographic and historical background of this drawing and related works, see number 64.

Both the present *Cimon and Pero* and the recently rediscovered painting Greuze executed after it (fig. 154) so closely resemble Rubens's painting of the same subject (fig. 155) that it seems likely Greuze had seen Rubens's painting when it appeared as lot 97 in the de Jullienne sale, Paris, 30 March–22 May 1767. The disposition of the two figures is similar, both heads are in profile, Pero's arm encircles Cimon to draw him closer, and a barred window is indicated at the left. What is unique about Greuze's interpretation of the subject is the element of fear, hauntingly conveyed in Pero's face in the painting, in the present sheet, and even in the reversed study for her figure (no. 64).

In 1765 both Jean-Jacques Bachelier (1724–1806) and Louis Lagrenée (1725–1805) presented pictures of Roman Charity at the Salon, the former now in the collection of the École des Beaux-Arts, Paris, and the latter now lost.[1] Though neither resembles Greuze's composition, they attest to the contemporary popularity of the theme and, for that reason, may have influenced Greuze in abandoning it as a possible vehicle for his *morceau de réception.*

Greuze frequently had recourse at this time to the same bearded, thin old model who posed here for the figure of Cimon.[2] Most notably, Greuze drew him as the fallen figure in *The Death of Cato of Utica* (fig. 156), another historical subject the artist experimented with in the late 1760s.[3]

1. See Mouradian 1999–2000, pp. 168–170, no. 122; and M. Sandoz, *Les Lagrenée,* Paris 1983, I, p. 203, no. 151.

2. See Hartford *et al.* 1976–77, p. 134, no. 60.

3. See Rochette 2000, pp. 70–71, no. 14.

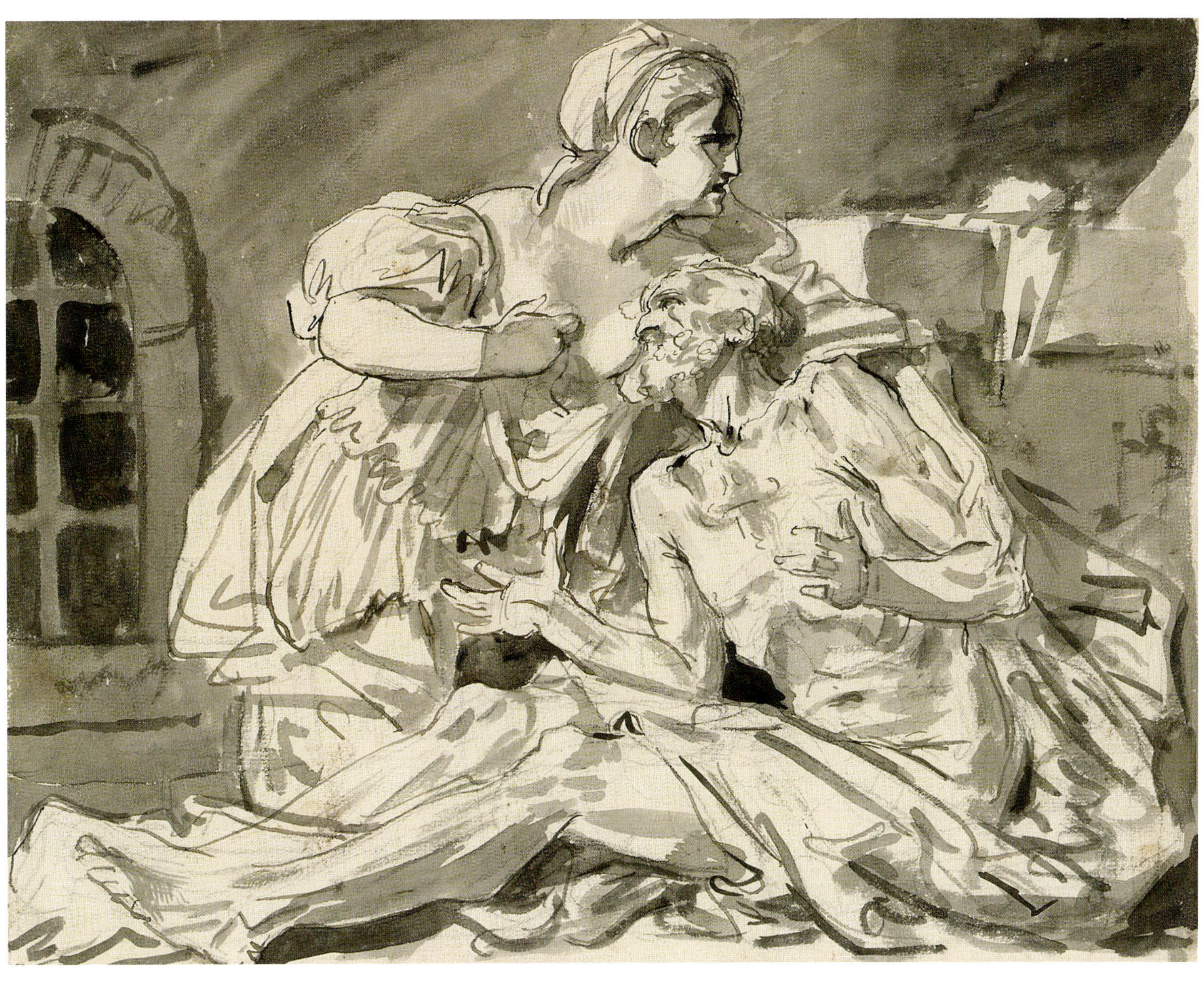

66 *A Woman Going to Bed*

Red and black chalks, stumped, on white paper, 580 × 370 mm (22 13/16 × 14 9/16 in.)
Signed in black chalk at lower right *J B G*
Lyon, Musée des Beaux-Arts

Provenance: Caroline Greuze (d. 1842), Paris; her sale, Paris, 25–26 January 1843, lot 35; Pierre Defer, Paris; his sale, Paris, 28 February–1 March 1859, lot 377; Edmond and Jules de Goncourt, Paris (Lugt 1089); their sale, Paris, 15–17 February 1897, lot 121; Brame *fils,* Paris; A. Marmontel, Paris; his sale, Paris, 28–29 March 1898, lot 30; anonymous sale, Paris, 9 March 1950, lot 17; Galerie Cailleux, Paris, 1951; sold to the museum in 1960

Exhibitions: Paris 1951, no. 63; *Figures nues d'école française,* Paris, Galerie Charpentier, 1953, no. 98; *Schönheit des 18. Jahrhunderts,* Zurich, Kunsthaus, 1955, no. 122; Hartford *et al.* 1976–77 (Dijon only, no. 57 *bis*); *Au temps de Watteau, Fragonard et Chardin. Les Pays-Bas et les peintres français du XVIIIe siècle,* Lille, Musée des Beaux-Arts, 1985, no. 63

Bibliography: E. de Goncourt, *La Maison d'un artiste,* Paris 1881, I, p. 89; Martin and Masson 1906, nos. 1033, 1318, 1324; R. Jullian, "Le 'Coucher à l'italienne' de Jacob van Loo," *Proporzioni,* III, 1950, pp. 199–203; Cailleux 1960, pp. 37–45; M. Laclotte, "Nouvelles Acquisitions des musées de province depuis 1960, peintures et dessins des primitifs au XVIIIe siècle," *Revue du Louvre,* IV–V, 1964, p. 161; Paris 1974–75, p. 151; E. Launay, *Les Frères Goncourt, collectionneurs de dessins,* Paris 1991, pp. 173 n. 605, 319–21, no. 128

This drawing, executed probably about 1767, is a rare example of Greuze's copying a French artist. Théophile Thoré was the first to note—in the Caroline Greuze sale catalogue—that the subject of this sheet derives from Jacob Van Loo's (1614–1670) *Le Coucher à l'italienne* (fig. 157).[1] This picture, executed in 1650, in turn was inspired by Jacob Jordaens's *Candaules Showing His Wife to Gyges* (fig. 158) executed only a few years earlier. In addition, there exists an engraving after Van Loo's picture by Greuze's colleague Carlo Antonio Porporati (1741–1816), but that print postdates the present drawing by about five years.[2]

The subject as treated by the three artists became increasingly abstract. Jordaens included in his composition the figures of Gyges and King Candaules observing Nyssia, the wife of the latter; Van Loo discarded Jordaens's dramatic subject for the simply

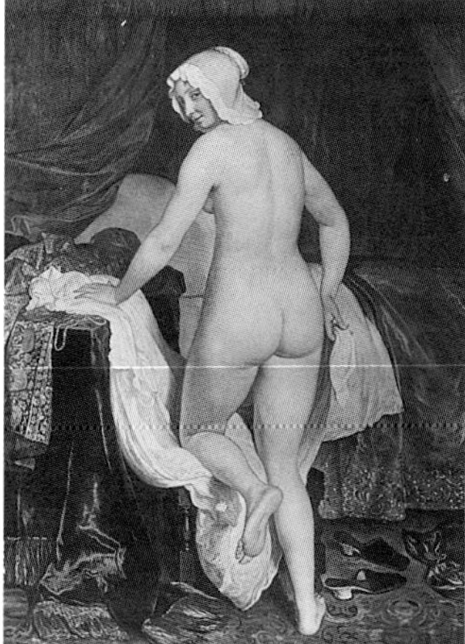

Fig. 157 J. Van Loo, *Le Coucher à l'italienne,* 1650, oil on canvas, Lyon, Musée des Beaux-Arts

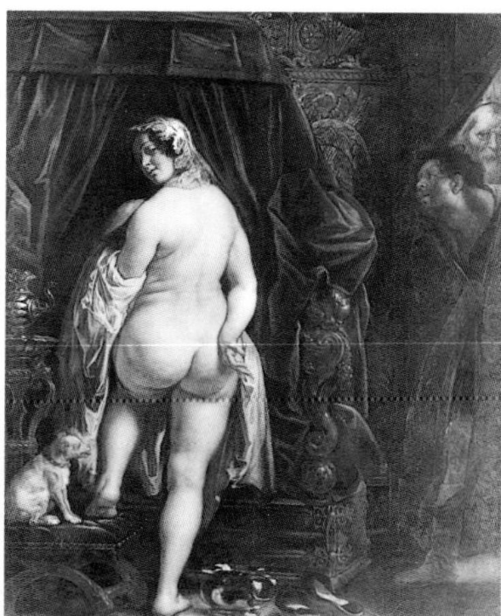

Fig. 158 J. Jordaens, *King Candaules Showing His Wife to Gyges,* 1646, oil on canvas, Stockholm, Nationalmuseum

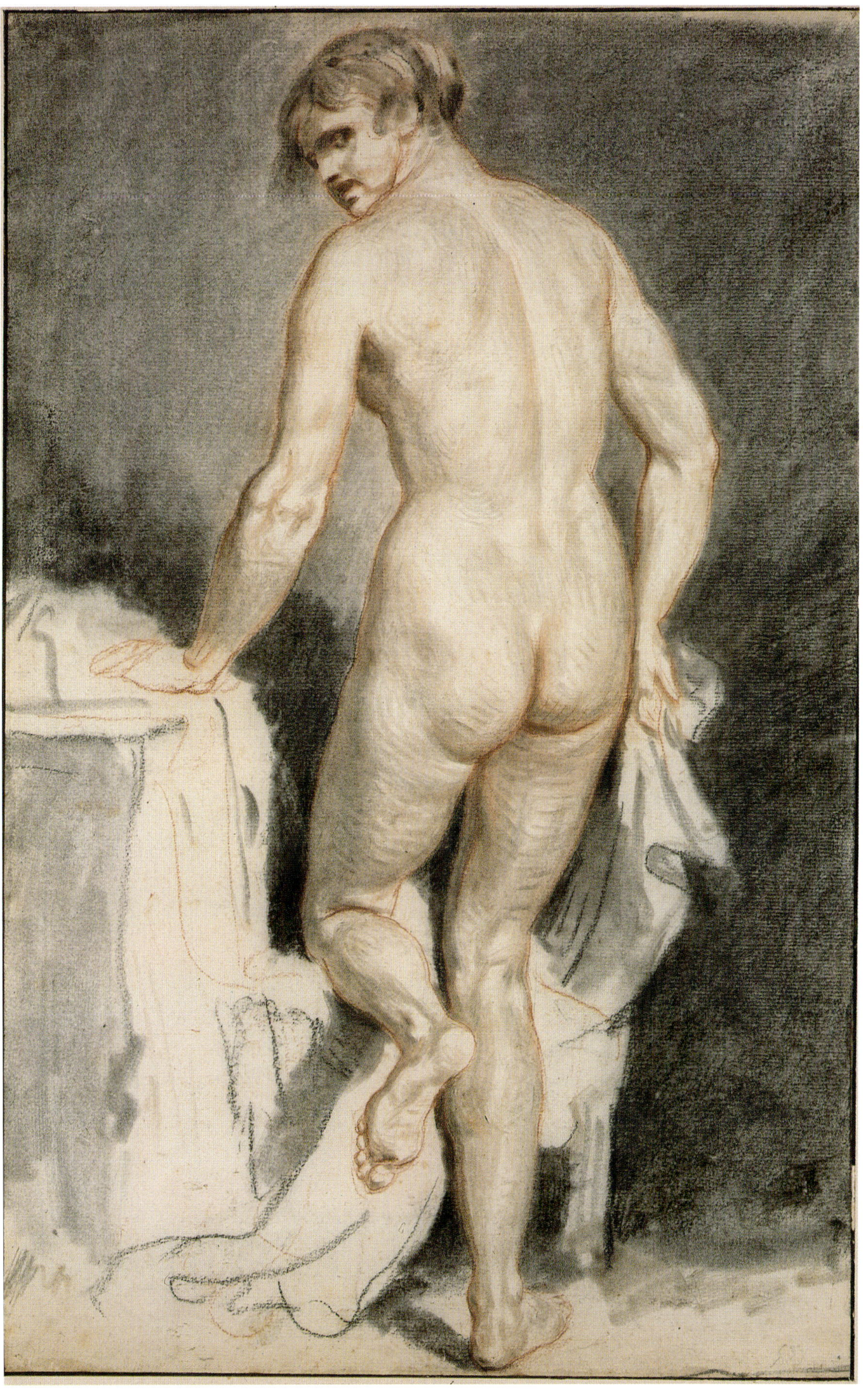

titillating one of a woman preparing to sleep in the nude *(à l'italienne),* rendering all the details of a bedroom setting; Greuze concentrated on the figure alone, yet seemingly was returning to the original subject. Far more than Jordaens, Greuze evoked its ominous mood in the harrowed expression of his androgynous figure, for Nyssia was to demand that the voyeur Gyges kill Candaules and replace him as her husband and as king in punishment for having exposed her nudity. At a time when Greuze was searching for an appropriate subject for his debut as a history painter, he may well have considered King Candaules as a possibility and executed this drawing as a preparation for it. Ultimately, he discarded the subject, probably because it would reveal him as recycling images by other artists.

Greuze executed another study of this same figure (fig. 159), which also appeared in the Caroline Greuze sale (lot 37).[3] In reference to it and the present drawing, it is worth quoting the opinion of a former owner of the latter—Edmond de Goncourt—as he contemplated it in the *petit salon* of his villa at Auteuil: "a drawing almost disagreeable because of the masculinity of the torso, but whose fine and highly colored modeling of the legs shows what a powerful artist Greuze was at certain times."[4]

Surprisingly enough, Edgar Degas (1834–1917) made two variations on the theme of a woman going to bed that recall the works of Greuze and his predecessors, with two monotypes of about 1880–83.[5]

1. "It is the figure in the painting by Vanloo, in the same pose, the left hand resting on a dressing table, the right one holding some drapery. There is no bonnet on the head as in the picture by Vanloo" *("C'est la figure du tableau de Vanloo, dans la même attitude, la main gauche posée sur la toilette, et la main droite laissant couler une draperie. La tête n'est pas coiffée comme dans le tableau de Vanloo").* T. Thoré, *Catalogue de tableaux et dessins de Greuze provenant de la succession de sa fille Mademoiselle Caroline Greuze,* Paris 1843, p. 6, lot 35.

2. See Cailleux 1960, pp. 294, 296–97; and Portalis and Béraldi 1880–82, III, pt. 1, pp. 341, 343.

3. Martin and Masson 1906, no. 1320. See Cailleux 1960, p. 292.

4. *"un dessin presque désagréable par la masculinité du torse, mais dont le fier et coloré modelage des jambes montre le puissant artiste qu'était Greuze à certaines heures."* Goncourt 1881, pp. 89–90.

5. E.P. Janis, *Degas Monotypes,* Greenwich CT 1968, nos. 129, 130.

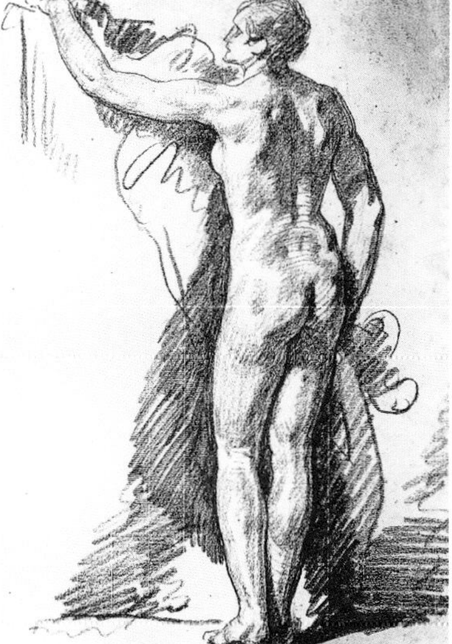

Fig. 159 Greuze, *Female Nude Seen from the Back,* 1767, red chalk on white paper, private collection

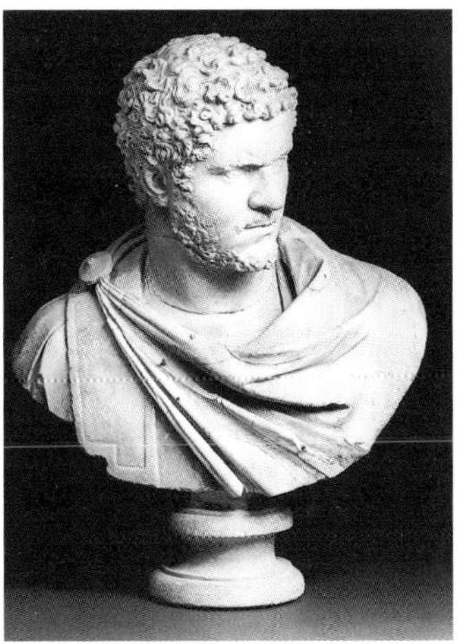

Fig. 160 Roman, *Caracalla,* third century AD, marble, Paris, Musée du Louvre

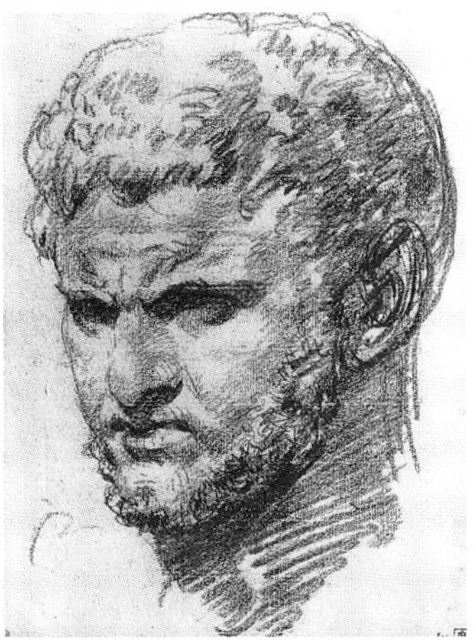

Fig. 161 Greuze, *Head of Caracalla,* 1767, red chalk on white paper, Bayonne, Musée Bonnat

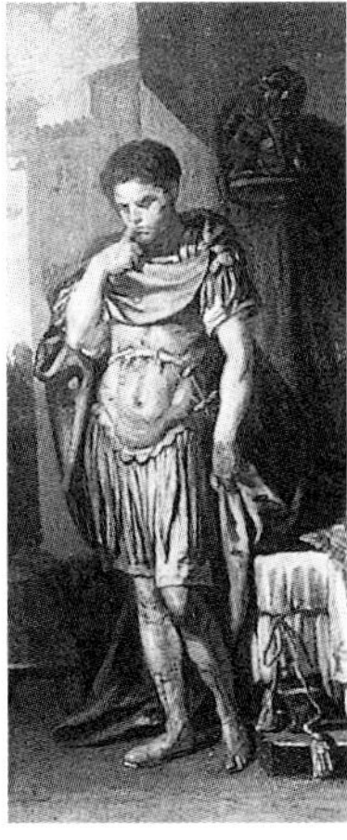

Fig. 162 Greuze, *Sketch for "Septimius Severus and Caracalla"* (detail), 1767, oil on canvas, whereabouts unknown

67 *Head of Caracalla*

Red chalk on cream paper, 388 × 303 mm (15 ¼ × 11 ¹⁵⁄₁₆ in.)
The Cleveland Museum of Art, Purchase from the J.H. Wade Fund

Provenance: M and Madame Jules Porgès, Paris; comtesse de Fitz-James, Paris; William H. Schab Gallery, New York; Julian Raskin, Scarsdale NY, acquired in 1956, and by descent through family; Spink-Leger Pictures, London; acquired by museum in 1999
Exhibition: Master Drawings from The Cleveland Museum of Art, Cleveland *et al.* 2000–2001, no. 43
Bibliography: Cailleux 1960, p. 294 n. 7; Hartford *et al.* 1976–77, p. 148; Paris 1984, p. 258; *Triumph und Tod des Helden,* exhib. cat., Cologne *et al.* 1988, p. 237; "A Selection of 1999 Museum Acquisitions," *Apollo,* December 1999, p. 33

Executed probably in 1767 as a preparatory study for the head of the young emperor Caracalla as depicted in Greuze's ill-fated *morceau de réception* of 1769, *Septimius Severus and Caracalla* (fig. 13),[1] the drawing is simultaneously an evocation of the appearance of the emperor as recorded in Roman sculpture (fig. 160) and an attempt to convey his emotions when challenged by his father whom he had attempted to assassinate.

An earlier study for the head of Caracalla (fig. 161) was executed probably after one of the innumerable versions or casts of the original ancient bust of Caracalla now in Naples, but which Greuze could have seen at the Palazzo Farnese during his Roman sojourn.[2] The present drawing eliminates the facial hair almost entirely, giving the man a more youthful appearance appropriate to historical fact.

In a preliminary oil sketch of *Septimius Severus and Caracalla,* Greuze depicted Caracalla precisely as he appears in the present drawing—his right index finger supporting his lower lip in a curiously childish way, his eyes directed to the left (fig. 162). In a study of the full figure (fig. 163), the right hand is shown lowered, the index finger now touching the upper chest, as in the final version of the painting (fig. 164).

When Diderot described to Falconet the oil sketch he had seen in Greuze's studio in August 1767, he described the appearance of Caracalla there (fig. 162) as follows: "Caracalla is standing, at the foot of the bed. He dares not confront the look of his father. He really has the air of a villain."[3] But two years later, he would describe Caracalla's appearance in Greuze's final version of his composition (fig. 164) thus: *Caracalla is even more ignoble than his father; he's a vile and contemptible rogue; the artist didn't have the art to fuse wickedness with nobility.... Greuze has abandoned his genre; a scrupulous student of nature, he didn't know how to elevate himself to the sort of exaggeration required by history painting. His Caracalla would be marvelous in a rustic and domestic scene; if need be, he could be the brother of that older boy standing listening to that* Old Man Reading to His Children [i.e., *The Family Bible Reading* of 1755; fig. 9].[4]

Quite correctly recognizing that Greuze adapted the hip-shot pose of Caracalla from the Belvedere Antinous (Rome, Musei Vaticani),[5] Diderot steadily insisted that the artist knew ancient sculpture only from plaster casts: "Conclude from what preceded that he who has seen beautiful antique statues only as plaster casts, no matter how perfect they be, has not seen them."[6]

Certain other critics who viewed *Septimius Severus and Caracalla* at the Salon of 1769 also spoke of Caracalla (fig. 164). Daudet de Jossan, for instance, wrote: "The heads are quite beautiful, modeled and drawn skillfully, and painted in that style that you recognize as his,"[7] while M.-B. Beaucousin, who thought the heads were copied from ancient medals, said they had "the hardness and coloring of copper," and added:

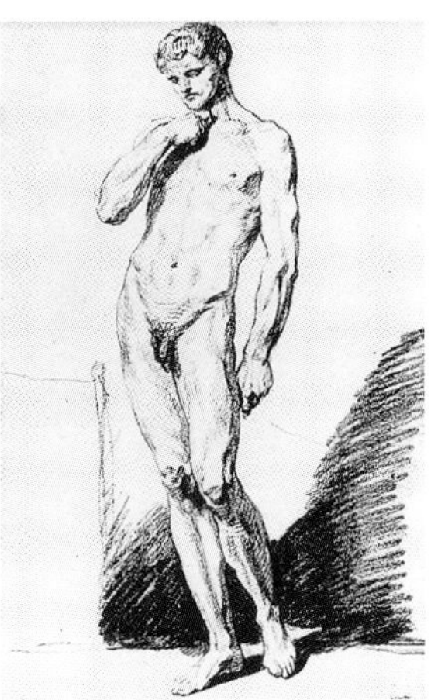

Fig. 163 Greuze, *Study for the Figure of Caracalla,* 1767, red chalk on white paper, Tournus, Musée Greuze

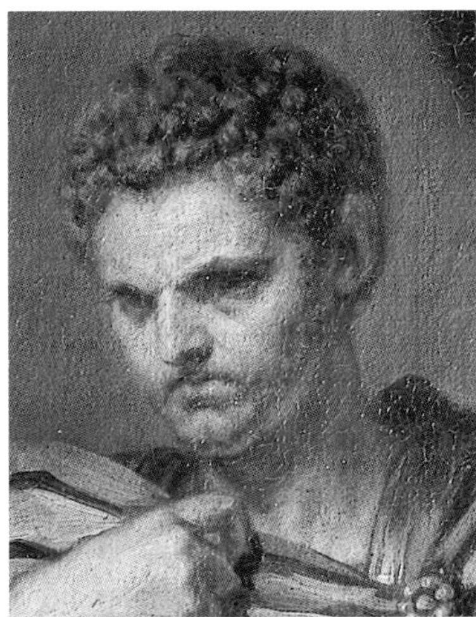

Fig. 164 Greuze, *Septimius Severus and Caracalla* (detail), 1769, oil on canvas, Paris, Musée du Louvre

"You wanted to give your characters somber looks, and all they have are deep-set eyes."[8] "Raphaël" noted: "The son is quite stupid, I say stupid because he is not troubled as an illustrious scoundrel would be, but more ashamed, like a simple workman."[9] Louis P. de Bachaumont remarked of this "second character in the drama": "[He] does not have a face wound up, so to say, to the highest degree of passion."[10]

Only the critic of *L'Avant-Coureur* hinted at the complex emotions Greuze had tried to convey with his Caracalla: "The face of Caracalla, whose head was drawn from antique sculpture, expresses the dark side of his character. One perceives that it is less the words of the emperor and the shame of his crime than the regret of having failed his attempt that has him confused."[11] In Greuze's celebrated response to the last critic's suggestion that he might have profited from a study of the example of Poussin, the artist wrote: "I beg you to believe that I have studied as well as you could have the works of that great man, and that in them I sought above all the art of giving my figures expression."[12] This *Head of Caracalla* is a convincing demonstration of that accomplishment.

A counterproof of the present drawing is in the collection of the Musée des Beaux-Arts, Besançon (inv. no. D936).[13]

1. For the history of this picture, see Seznec in Diderot *Salons,* IV, pp. 42–44; Hartford *et al.* 1976–77, no. 70; and Paris 1984, no. 69.

2. For the history of the bust, see Haskell and Penny 1981, pp. 172–73, no. 18; and K. de Kersanson, *Musée du Louvre, Département des antiquités grecques, étrusques et romaines, Catalogue des portraits romains,* Paris 1996, II, pp. 388–91.

3. *"Caracalla est debout, au pié de la couche. Il n'ose supporter le regard de son père. Il a bien l'air d'un scélérat."* Diderot *Correspondance,* VII, pp. 102–03.

4. *"Le Caracalla est plus ignoble encore que son père, c'est un vil et bas coquin; l'artiste n'a pas eu l'art d'allier la méchanceté avec la noblesse.... Greuze est sorti de son genre; imitateur scrupuleux de la nature, il n'a pas su s'élever à la sorte d'exagération qu'exige la peinture historique. Son Caracalla irait à merveille dans une scène champêtre et domestique; ce serait dans un besoin le frère de ce grand garçon qui écoute debout le* Vieillard qui fait la lecture à ses enfans." Diderot *Salons,* IV, p. 106.

5. Haskell and Penny 1981, p. 141, no. 4.

6. *"Concluez de ce qui précède que celui qui n'a vu les belles statues antiques que d'après des plâtres, quelque parfaits qu'ils fussent, ne les a pas vues."* Diderot *Salons,* IV, p. 106.

7. *"Les têtes en sont fort belles, modelées et dessinées sçavamment, et peintes de ce style que vous lui connoissez."* Daudet de Jossan, *Sentimens sur les tableaux exposés au Salon, 1769,* Paris 1769, p. 20.

8. *"la dureté et le ton du cuivre. Vous avez voulu donner à vos personnages des regards sombres, et ils n'ont que des yeux enfoncés."* M.-B. Beaucousin, *Lettres sur le Salon de peinture de 1769,* Paris 1769, p. 23.

9. *"Le fils est très sot; je dis sot, car il n'est pas confondu comme un illustre scélérat, mais honteux comme un fondeur de cloches." Lettre sur les peintures... exposées cette année au Louvre,* Paris 1769, p. 27.

10. *"le second personnage, n'a pas le visage monté, pour ainsi dire, au plus haut degré de passion."* Louis P. de Bachaumont, *Mémoires secrets pour servir à l'histoire de la république des lettres en France...,* London 1777–89, XIII, p. 58.

11. *"Caracalla, dont la tête est dessinée d'après l'antique, exprime sur son visage la noirceur de son caractère. On s'aperçoit que c'est moins la parole de l'Empereur et la honte de son crime que le chagrin d'avoir manqué son coup qui l'interdit."* "Exposition des peintures, sculptures, gravures de M.M. de l'Académie Royale," *L'Avant-Coureur,* 11 September 1769, p. iv.

12. *"Je vous supplie d'être persuadé que j'ai étudié aussi bien que vous l'avez pu faire, les ouvrages de ce grand homme, et que j'y ai surtout cherché l'art de mettre l'expression dans les figures."* J.-B. Greuze, "Lettre à l'auteur de *L'Avant-Coureur,*" *Nouvelles littéraires,* 25 September 1769, p. 407.

13. *Master Drawings from The Cleveland Museum of Art 2000–2001,* p. 114, fig. 1.

Facing page:
67 *Head of Caracalla*

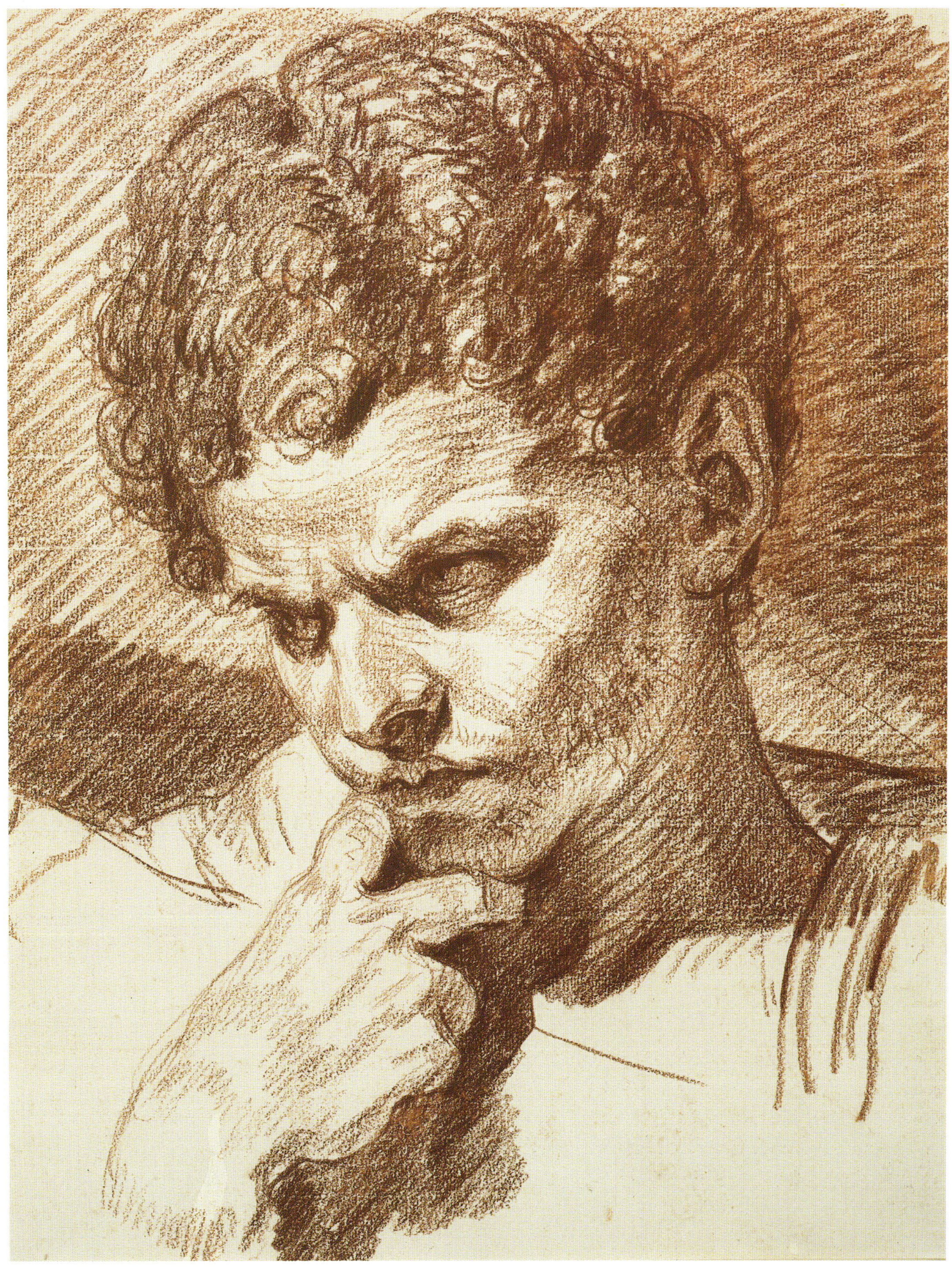

68 *Compositional Study for "Sophronie"*

Brush, brown and gray ink on tan paper, 247 × 246 mm (9 ¾ × 9 ¹¹⁄₁₆ in.)
Karlsruhe, Staatliche Kunsthalle, Kupferstichkabinett

Provenance: perhaps Camille Groult, Paris; Henri Baderou, Paris; anonymous sale, Paris, 9 December 1961, lot 6; Matthiesen Gallery, London; Z. Bruck, Buenos Aires, 1964; Faerber and Maison Ltd, London; acquired by the museum in 1970
Exhibitions: Hartford *et al.* 1976–77, no. 62; *Die französischen Zeichnungen, 1570–1930,* Karlsruhe, Staatliche Kunsthalle, 1983, no. 30
Bibliography: H. Cohen, *Guide de l'amateur de livres à vignettes du XVIIIe siècle,* Paris 1873, pp. 17–18; Portalis and Béraldi 1880–82, III, pt. 1, p. 169; Martin and Masson 1906, no. 408; Munhall 1961, pp. 237–42; *Jahrbuch der Staatlichen Kunstsammlungen in Baden-Württemberg,* VIII, 1971, p. 230, fig. 12; Laveissière 1980, p. 249

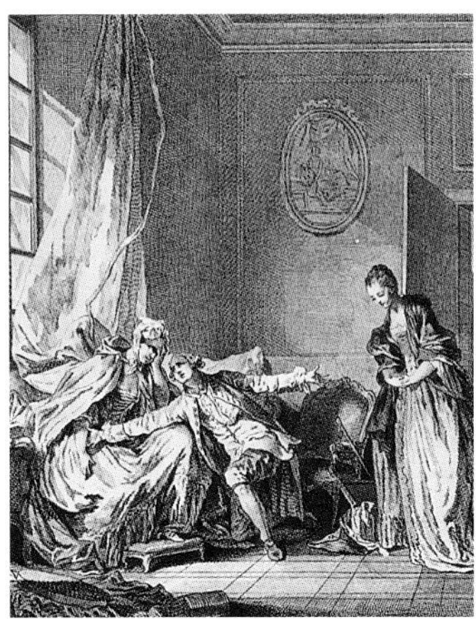

Fig. 165 J.-M. Moreau *le jeune, Frontispiece for "Sophronie,"* 1768, engraving, Paris, Bibliothèque nationale de France

The inscription below Jean-Michel Moreau *le jeune*'s engraving of this subject (fig. 165) indicates that Greuze created the engraver's model drawing in 1768, a work now lost. The present sheet—a Rembrandtesque explosion of ink—must have been an earlier, preliminary study for the composition, which was intended to serve as the frontispiece of Madame Benoist's novel *Sophronie, ou la leçon prétendue d'une mère à sa fille,* published in London in 1769.

The scene Greuze chose to illustrate is the book's climactic incident, in which Sophronie (at right), who had staged for her daughter Adelle's edification a mock seduction with Valzan, is surprised by Adelle's entrance into her boudoir. Valzan, surprised as well, implores the mother to grant him her daughter's hand. The relevant text reads: "He throws himself at her feet. You see her, cries he, darting a touching glance at her. Ah! Madame, let yourself be moved; deign to grant me her hand; you will fulfill all my wishes. Sophronie appears confused, shame lowers her brow, while a charming modesty shines on her daughter's face."[1]

Barred from exhibiting at the Salon of 1767 and still undecided about his intentions for that of 1769, Greuze decided to enter the field of literary illustration, then very profitable. His only other known illustrations are number 71 and one he made for Louis-Edme Billardon de Sauvigny's *La Rose, ou la fête de Salency,* known only from Moreau's engraving.[2]

Baron Grimm, a regular admirer of Greuze's work in the Salons and apparently a friend, noted this career change with regret:

he is rather annoyed that his friend Greuze wastes his time working like a Gravelot or a Charles Eisen instead of working like a Greuze... the habit of making such trifles... and the rage to put illustrations into books will ruin the arts in France, precisely because they enable

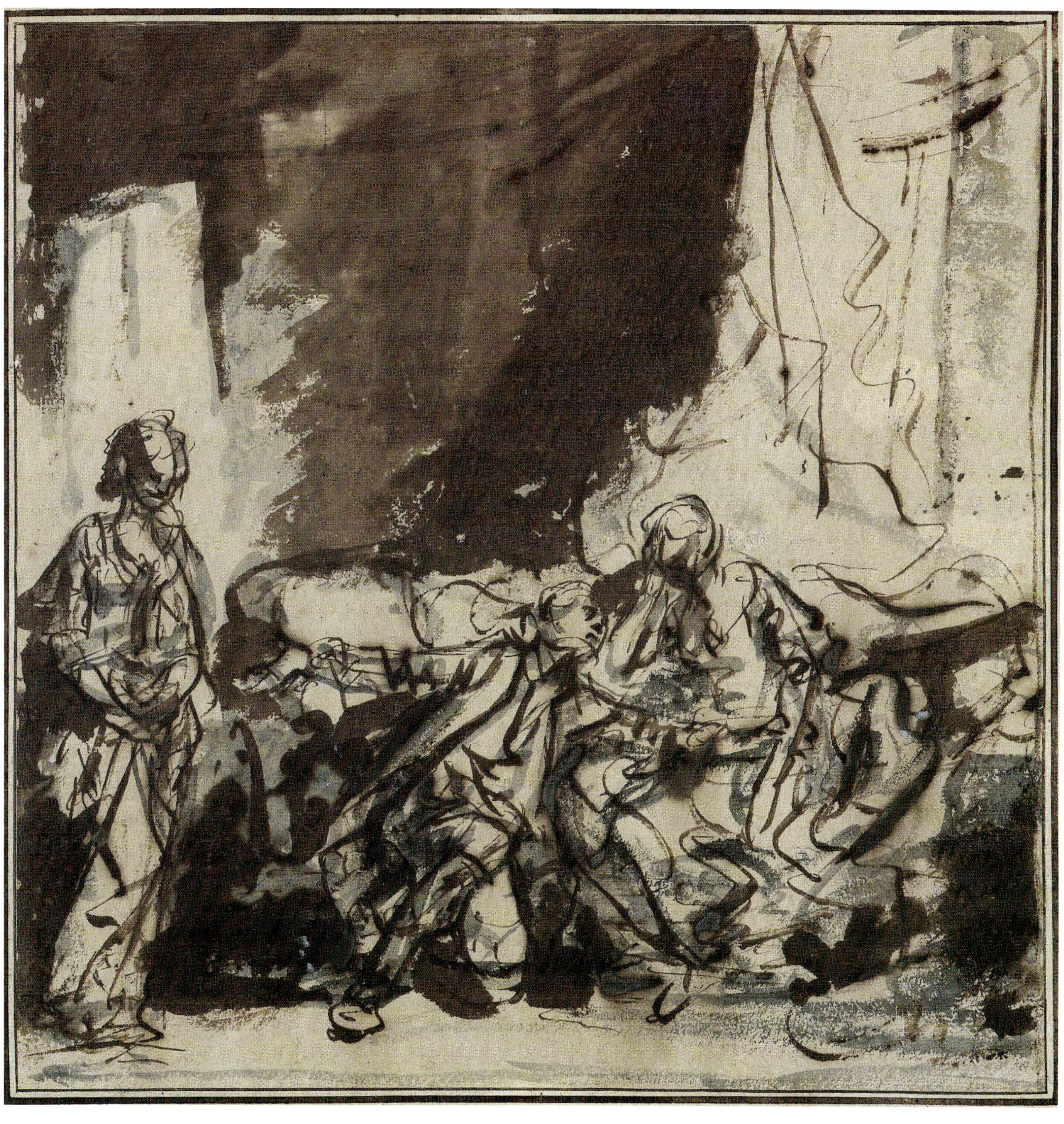

artists to earn a lot of money in a short time; finally, he wishes his friend Greuze would concern himself only with glory and scorn money, which, moreover, he does not lack.[3]

As an indication of the attention Greuze was devoting to this single literary illustration, two figural studies for it survive. One is a carefully detailed depiction of Valzan, his arms outstretched in supplication (fig. 166), his face expressive of a passion absent in Moreau's engraving (fig. 165).[4] The other is a study for Adelle, her head inclined with "charming modesty" (fig. 167).

1. *"Il se jette à ses pieds. Vous la voyez, s'écrie-t-il en jettant sur elle un regard touchant. Ah! Madame, laissez-vous fléchir; daignez m'accorder sa main, vous comblerés tous mes voeux. Sophronie paroit confondue; la honte abbaisse son front, tandis qu'une pudeur charmante brille sur le visage de sa fille."* Madame Benoist [F.-A. Puzin de la Martinière], *Sophronie,* London 1769, p. 40.

2. Cohen 1873, p. 21; Martin and Masson 1906, no. 407.

3. *"qu'il est assez fâché que son ami Greuze perde son temps à faire le Gravelot ou le Charles Eisen au lieu de faire le Greuze… l'habitude de faire de pareilles minuties… et la fureur de mettre des images dans les livres perdront les arts en France, précisément parce qu'elles font gagner aux artistes beaucoup d'argent en peu de temps; enfin qu'il voudrait que son ami Greuze ne fît cas que de la gloire et méprisât l'argent, qui, d'ailleurs, ne lui manque pas."* Baron Melchior von Grimm, *Correspondance littéraire, philosophique et critique,* ed. M. Tourneux, Paris 1879, VIII, pp. 356–57.

4. Hartford *et al.* 1976–77, no. 63.

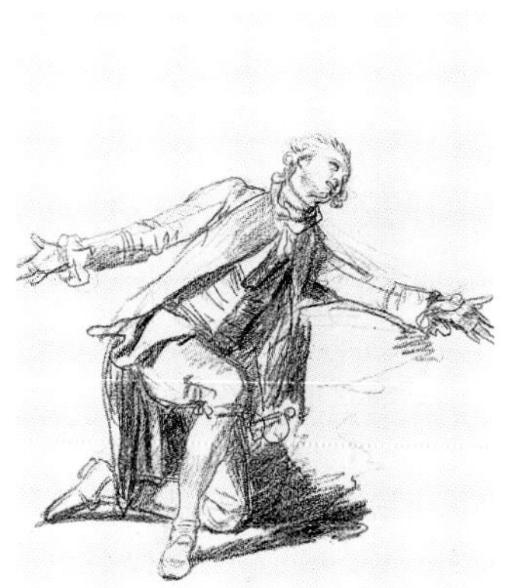

Fig. 166 Greuze, *Kneeling Youth with Arms Outstretched,* 1768, red chalk on white paper, Cambridge MA, Fogg Art Museum, Meta and Paul J. Sachs Collection

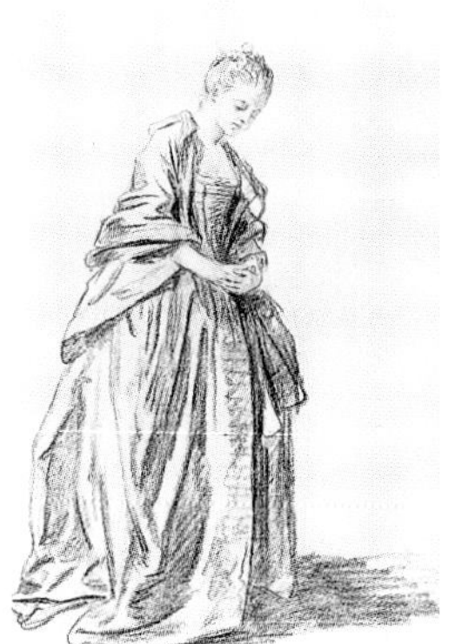

Fig. 167 Greuze, *Standing Young Woman,* 1768, red chalk on white paper, London, Victoria and Albert Museum

69 *The Death of a Cruel Father Abandoned by His Children*

Brush, black and brown ink wash over graphite on white paper, 468 × 640 mm (18 7/16 × 25 3/16 in.)
Signed in ink at lower right *Greuze*
Tournus, Musée Greuze

Provenance: perhaps Hippolyte Destailleurs, Paris;[1] acquired by the museum in 1898
Exhibitions: Salon of 1769, no. 161; Hartford *et al.* 1976–77, no. 52
Bibliography: Goncourt 1880, p. 341; Martin and Masson 1906, no. 190; Munhall 1965, pp. 28, 59; Seznec in Diderot *Salons,* IV, pp. 44–45; Brookner 1972, p. 111; Paris 1974–75, p. 151; Rosenblum 1977, p. 146; review of *Jean-Baptiste Greuze/1725–1805,* "Expositions," *La Revue du Louvre,* March 1977, p. 194; Schnapper 1977, p. 88; Fermigier 1977, p. 17; E.-M. Bukdahl, *Diderot critique d'art,* II, *Diderot, les salonniers et les esthéticiens de son temps,* Copenhagen 1982, p. 191; Rochette 2000, pp. 36, 74–75, no. 16; C. Rochette, "Avant première: Prochaine Inauguration du Musée Greuze à Tournus," *La Gazette de l'Hôtel Drouot,* 30 June 2000, p. 15; C. Guennec, "Jean-Baptiste Greuze (1725–1805) ou les deux cents ans de solitude du Maître de Tournus," *Valeurs de l'art,* March–April 2001, p. 28

The shock this drawing provokes is as astonishing today as it was when first exhibited at the Salon of 1769. For those who might not yet have seen it there, the composition was described vividly in the *Avant-Coureur:* "This last piece is frightening, the body of this wretched dying man is thrown half out of bed; someone is stealing his purse, and even the sheet that covers him; the candle placed at the foot of his bed breaks, and the flame will consume him in an instant."[2] The critic Daudet de Jossan then wrote: "While I am busy reproaching the bad choice of subjects, I must in the same breath express my discontent over a drawing by the same Author which he no doubt proposes to treat on a grand scale. *The Death of the Cruel Father Abandoned by His Children*... What a subject!... this scandalizes me; I am sorry that a Frenchman should have thought of it."[3] E.-C. Fréron felt the same way: "One would wish also that he prohibit himself such atrocious subjects... the sight of it is horrible... one sees nothing in it but a revolting and unprecedented barbarity toward a dying man."[4]

Bachaumont alone was able to categorize Greuze's achievement correctly. Noting that the drawing "tears apart the soul of him who views it and makes his hair stand on end," he described its subject in detail, concluding: "In a word, everything proclaims the despair of the dead man, the disorder of his abandonment, and the horror of his condition." In response to those who felt such scenes should not be depicted, he replied: "But you know, Sir, there is a sublime of terror, all the more beautiful in that few souls are strong enough to endure it. Should the weakness of the viewers be the measure of the merit of the creator? Oughtn't we to admire him all the more for having elevated himself above the sphere of the ordinary?"[5] As recently as 1977, one of our foremost and savvy historians was similarly stunned by this sheet: "The wash drawing... of *The Death of a Cruel Father Abandoned by His Children*... is a scene of such gruesome, hallucinatory horror... that, despite the humble setting and the moralizing pendant of the death of a good father, the mood is more of demonic, Fuselian fantasy than of a didactic genre scene."[6] Francisco de Goya's (1746–1828) name was evoked as well.

With his habit of exhibiting pairs of subjects, Greuze offered at the Salon of 1769 a contrast to the present drawing with *The Death of a Father Mourned by His Children* (fig. 168).[7] Daudet de Jossan contemplated it with relief, writing: "and to heal myself by the same fire that wounded me, I leave this nasty sketch to go see that of the death of the good Father; there is a worthy subject, interesting; I recognize in this drawing the touching and sublime author of the paralytic Father cared for by his Children (fig. 24)."[8] The conjunction of these two drawings must have appealed to Gabriel de Saint-Aubin, for he sketched them both in his Salon catalogue (fig. 169).[9]

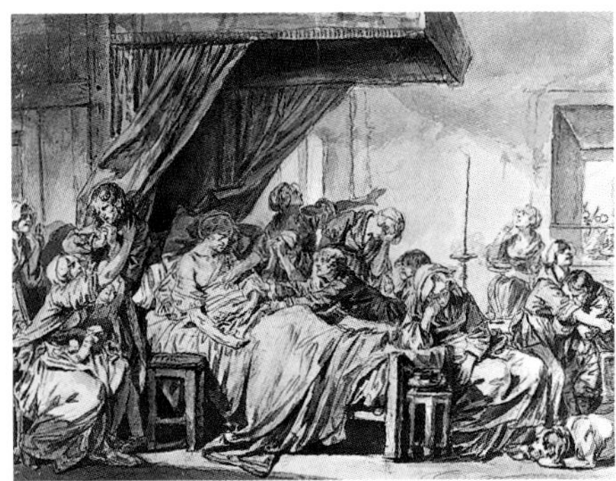

Fig. 168 Greuze, *The Death of a Father Mourned by His Children, c.* 1768, brush, black and brown ink over graphite on white paper, Paris, Musée du Louvre, Département des arts graphiques, on deposit at the Musée des Beaux-Arts, Strasbourg

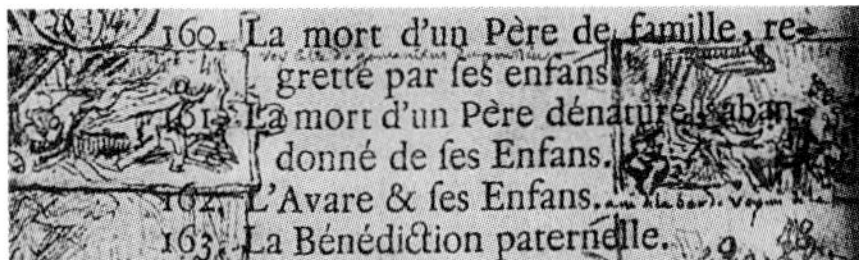

160. La mort d'un Père de famille, regretté par ses enfans.
161. La mort d'un Père dénaturé, abandonné de ses Enfans.
162. L'Avare & ses Enfans.
163. La Bénédiction paternelle.

Fig. 169 G. de Saint-Aubin, *Sketches in a Salon Catalogue of 1769,* 1769, pen and black ink, Paris, Bibliothèque nationale de France

1. Provenance given by Martin and Masson 1906.

2. *"Ce dernier morceau est effrayant, le corps de ce malheureux mourant est à moitié jetté hors du lit; on lui enlève la bourse, et jusqu'au drap qui le couvre; le cierge placé au pied de son lit se brise, et la flamme le dévore en un instant."* "Arts: Exposition des peintures, sculptures, gravures de M.M. de l'Académie Royale," *L'Avant-Coureur,* 11 September 1769, p. 396.

3. *"Pendant que je suis occupé à reprocher le mauvais choix des sujets, il faut que tout d'une haleine, j'exprime mon mécontentement d'un dessin du même Auteur qu'il propose sans doute de traiter en grand.* La Mort du père dénaturé abandonné de ses enfans... *Quel sujet!... ce sujet me scandalise; je suis fâché qu'un François l'ait imaginé."* Daudet de Jossan, *Lettre sur les peintures, gravures et sculptures qui ont été exposés cette année au Louvre,* Paris 1769, p. 29.

4. *"On voudroit aussi qu'il s'interdit les sujets atroces... le spectacle en est horrible... on n'y apperçoit qu'une barbarie révoltante et sans exemple contre un mourant."* E.-C. Fréron, "Lettre XIII: Exposition des peintures, sculptures et gravures de Messieurs de l'Académie Royale," *L'Année littéraire,* Paris 1769, pp. 310–11.

5. *"lui déchire l'ame et lui fait dresser les cheveux à la tête.... En un mot, tout annonce le désespoir du mort, le desordre de son abandon et l'horreur de son état.... Mais vous savez, Monsieur, qu'il y a un sublime de terreur d'autant plus beau, qu'il est peu d'ames en état de le soutenir. Faut-il que la foiblesse du Spectateur soit la mesure du mérite du compositeur? Et ne le doit-on pas admirer d'autant plus qu'il s'élève davantage au-dessus de la sphere ordinaire?"* Bachaumont, XIII, pp. 59–60.

6. Rosenblum 1977, p. 146.

7. Hartford *et al.* 1976–77, no. 51.

8. *"et pour me quérir par le même feu qui m'a blessé, je quitte ce vilain croquis pour aller voir celui de la mort du bon Père; voilà un sujet digne, intéressant; je reconnois à ce dessin l'auteur pathétique et sublime du Père paralytique servi par ses Enfans."* Daudet de Jossan 1769, pp. 28–29.

9. Dacier 1909–21, II, pp. 81–82.

Facing page:
69 *The Death of a Cruel Father Abandoned by His Children*

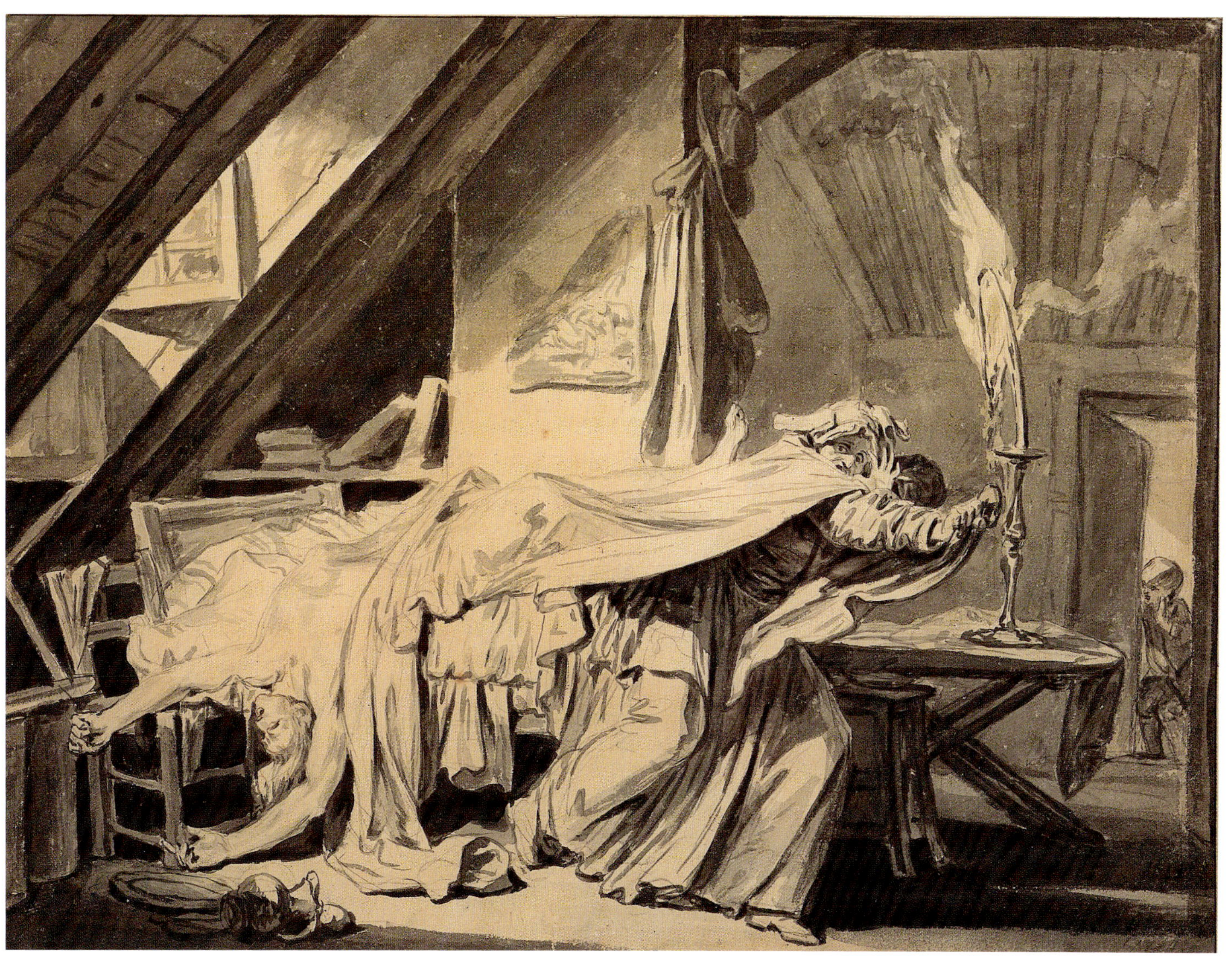

70 *The Beloved Mother*

Brush and gray ink wash over black chalk on white paper, 490 × 624 mm (19 5/16 × 24 5/8 in.)
Sydney, Art Gallery of New South Wales

Provenance: Jean-Baptiste Greuze, Paris, 1775; marquise de Boisgelin, Paris; Maurice Segoura, Paris, 1988; David Tunick, Inc., New York, 1988; James Fairfax, Sydney, 1992; given by him to the museum in 2000
Exhibitions: None known
Bibliography: Arquié-Bruley 1983, pp. 127, 134–35; A.F. Collins, "Drawn to the Master," *House and Garden,* April 1991, p. 90; A. Brandt, "The Prince of Prints and the Duke of Drawings—David Tunick," *Town and Country,* October 1993, p. 119

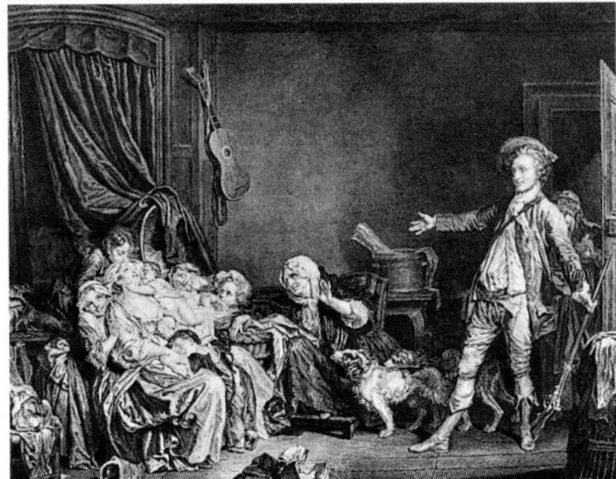

Fig. 170 J. Massard, after Greuze, *The Beloved Mother,* 1775, engraving, private collection

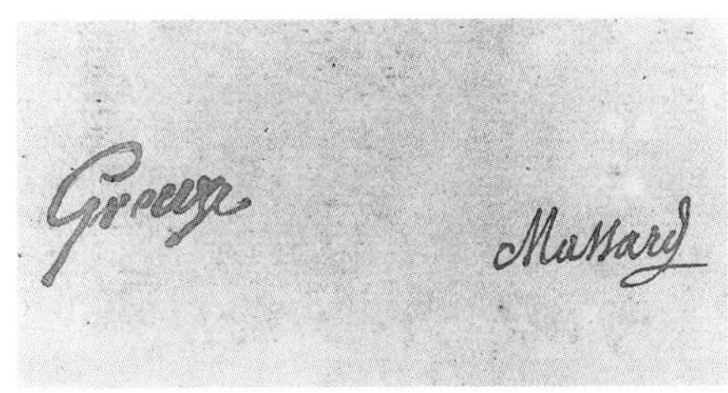

Fig. 171 J. Massard and J.-B. Greuze, signatures on verso of fig. 170, 1775, pen and brown ink, private collection

This must be the drawing Greuze executed after his painting *The Beloved Mother* (fig. 14) to serve as a model for the engraver Carlo Antonio Porporati. The latter had on 9 March 1771 signed a contract with Greuze and his wife whereby he agreed to execute an engraving "after the drawing by Monsieur Greuze of *The Beloved Mother*" and to participate in the sale of the prints he would produce, for a fee of 1500 livres.[1] Six weeks later, for unspecified reasons, Porporati withdrew from his contract, returning the 375 livres he had received as an advance. The following year, 1772, Jean Massard entered into a similar agreement with Greuze and his wife, but his engraving of *The Beloved Mother,* presumably based on this same drawing, was not published until 1775 (fig. 170).[2] The example reproduced here bears on the verso the signatures of Greuze and Massard required by the contract (Lugt 1103) (fig. 171).

According to the original contract, "after the plate has been engraved to perfection, the drawing of the said Greuze will be returned to him as his property, to do with as he wishes."[3] Greuze was very particular that the engraver not "interpret" his drawing, but copy it precisely and to size. This explains why the engraving of *The Beloved Mother* looks identical to the present drawing (though both are only roughly half the size of the painting), and why other such drawing-models, now lost, were routinely described in sale catalogues as "precious," "very finished," or "finely rendered."[4] In 1983 Françoise Arquié-Bruley lamented that no such drawings existed to compare to their related paintings and engravings.[5] Fortunately, the present sheet reappeared after her remark, and Greuze's drawing-models for *The Spoiled Child* (no. 33), *The Torn-up Will* (no. 77), and *The Father's Curse: The Ungrateful Son* (no. 82) were recognized by the present author as other examples.

The delay in Massard's execution of his reproductive print was normal at the time and explains why Greuze executed this drawing in the first place: the owner of a newly acquired painting was unlikely to be willing to give it up for two, three, or four years.

This was particularly true in the case of *The Beloved Mother* (fig. 14), for this apparent genre scene was in fact a group portrait of one of the richest families in France, commissioned by its principal male subject, the marquis Jean-Joseph de Laborde (1724–1794). Born in Spain, he became in 1746 the head of his family's bank and was naturalized as a French citizen in 1749. Over the next two decades, he experienced phenomenal financial success and was highly regarded by Louis XV, for whom in 1758 he procured a loan from King Ferdinand V of Spain of thirty million livres, a loan previously refused to the king. He lived sumptuously in Paris and in a series of

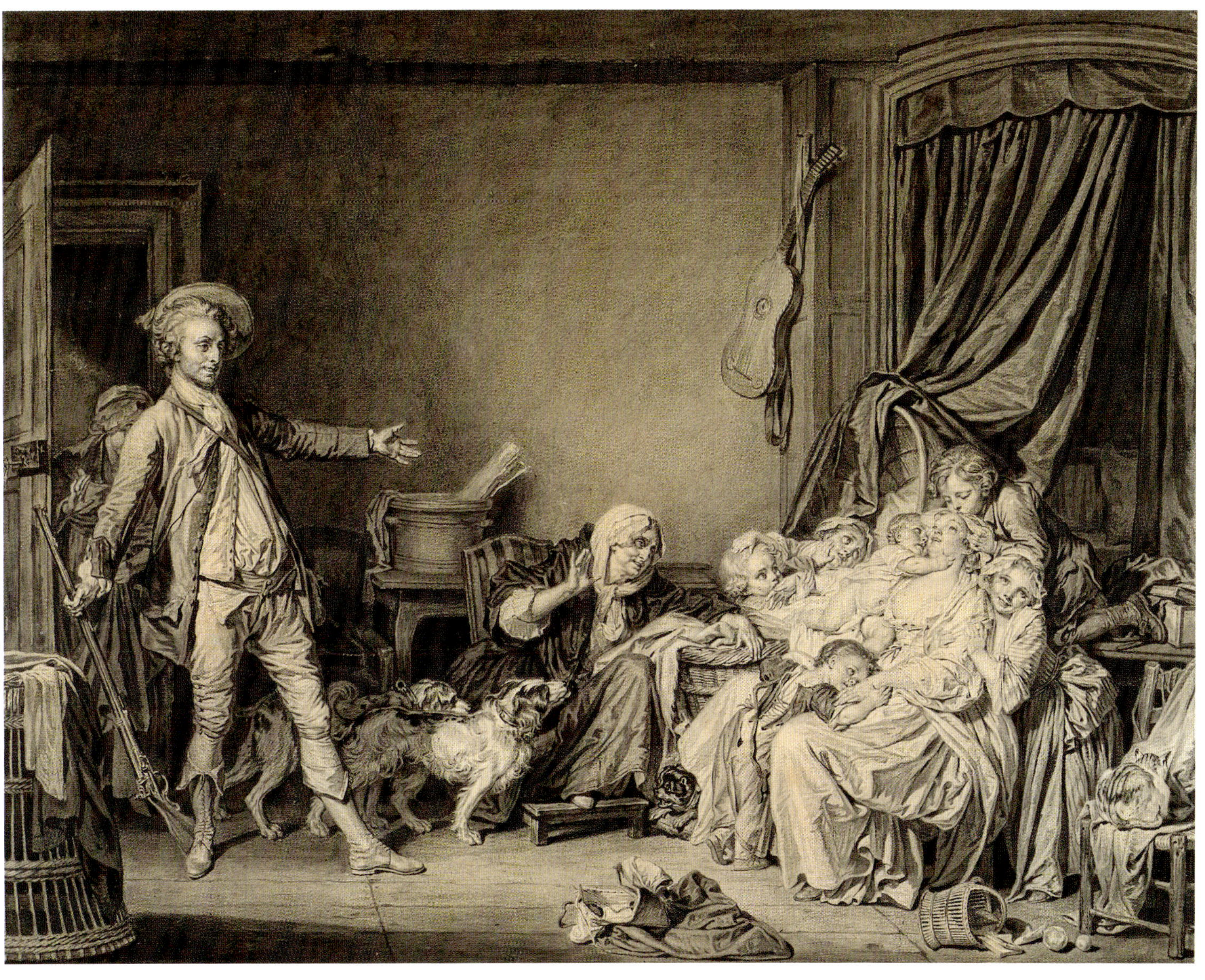

châteaux, and was a notable patron of the arts. In 1760 he married Rosalie-Claire-Josèphe Nettine (see no. 42), with whom he had two daughters and four sons. He was guillotined on 18 April 1794.

In 1765 Greuze exhibited at the Salon a sketch *("esquisse")* entitled *La Mère bien-aimée.* Diderot waxed enthusiastic about it: "This is excellent, both for talent and for morals. This preaches in favor of population, and paints in a very touching way the happiness and the inestimable value of domestic peace."[6] In his minute description of the composition, there are too many differences from the composition of the present sheet and from number 43 for either of them to have been number 123 in the Salon of 1765—such as his mention of "a fireplace with a mirror over it" behind the grandmother.[7] Nor did Diderot or any other critic mention the name Laborde or suggest that *The Beloved Mother* was a group portrait rather than a genre scene.

Mathon de La Cour described the composition with similar enthusiasm and added the detail that "M. Greuze has taken pleasure of placing in this beloved mother the portrait of Madame Greuze, and he has executed a sketch of her in pastel."[8] The latter would correspond to number 115 in the Salon, *A Head in Pastel* (no. 41). Again, no mention of the Laborde family.

However, when the painting *The Beloved Mother Caressed by Her Children* was announced in the catalogue of the Salon of 1769 as number 152, Gabriel de Saint-Aubin noted in his copy, "see M. de la Borde," providing the clue to the identification of the subject of that picture.[9] Though the critic Daudet de Jossan must have been early enough in his visits to the Salon to describe *The Beloved Mother,*[10] others complained that it never appeared, as well as other works belonging to the marquis de Laborde. Diderot, for instance, remarked: "Don't forget that we are lacking eight enormous compositions by Vernet of which that nasty M. de la Borde has deprived us."[11]

There remain the questions of how and when *The Beloved Mother* became a portrait of the Laborde family. Since the sketch of 1765 was not recognized as such, the mother being identified as Madame Greuze, and the painting of 1769 was so identified by all, the transformation occurred at some point in between. Diderot provides a clue in his text of 1765, wherein he wished he were rich enough to commission a painting after Greuze's sketch and went on to describe a type of charade in which people assume the poses of figures in a painting, a *tableau vivant:*

I have occasionally seen elegant society people, assembled out in the country, amuse themselves during autumn evenings by playing a totally interesting and amusing game. That is to imitate the compositions of well-known pictures with living figures.... Once the whole scene and the actors are arranged according to the composition of the painter, and the scene properly lighted, they invite the spectators in who give their opinion on the way in which the picture was executed.[12]

Might the Laborde family not have played such a game of charades at their château of La Ferté-Vidame, which the marquis acquired in 1764? Greuze might even have been there, for he contributed to the decoration of both that château and the marquis's previous one at Marolles-en-Beauce. In such circumstances, the marquis could well have acted as Diderot had wanted to and commissioned Greuze to execute a painting based on the sketch of 1765, transforming his generalized characters into Laborde portraits. Certainly the father's appearance—with his angular face and sharp nose—

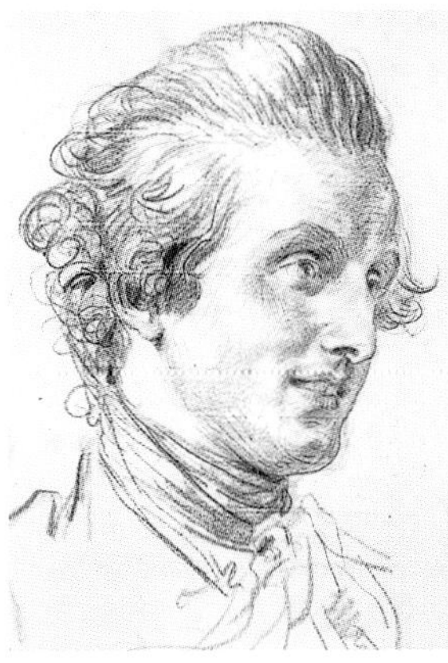

Fig. 172 Greuze, *Portrait of Jean-Joseph de Laborde, c.* 1768, red chalk on white paper, Madrid, collection comte de la Viñaza, marquis de Laborde

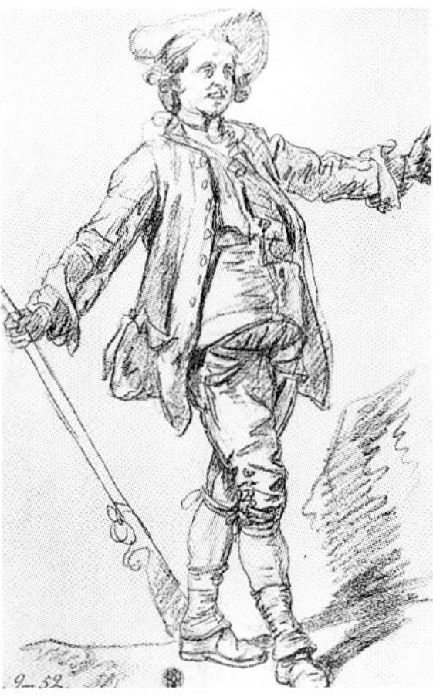

Fig. 173 Greuze, *Study for the Husband in "The Beloved Mother,"* 1765, red chalk on white paper, St Petersburg, The State Hermitage Museum

in the painting (fig. 14), in a study preserved in the Laborde family (fig. 172), and in the present drawing differs significantly from the same figure's appearance in pre-1765 studies (fig. 173).[13]

In the composition of *The Beloved Mother* there is no problem in identifying the husband and the grandmother with the marquis de Laborde and his mother-in-law (though the mother still looks like Madame Greuze), but what about the six children swarming around the mother? The Labordes, who married in 1760, did indeed have six children but three of them were born after 1769. However, as the head of a large family, the marquis de Laborde was likely to have had many of them around him at any time. As the family "Mémorial" recorded: "Jean-Joseph de Laborde, because of his great fortune, had become the center of his whole family, by providing dowries for them all, and housing them . . . nephews, nieces, cousins, etc."[14] In any case, the composition already included six children before it became a Laborde family portrait, as Diderot noted in 1765: "There are at least six of them."[15]

1. The contract, preserved in the Archives Nationales (Minutier Central XXIII, 713), was published in Wildenstein 1960, pp. 280–30, 232–34.

2. Portalis and Béraldi 1880–82, III, pt. 1, p. 47. In view of the general lack of appreciation of such reproductive engravings, it is worth quoting those authors' opinion of Massard's rendition of Greuze's drawing: "His work with the burin, very soft, corresponds well to that caressing painterly manner, consisting entirely of delicate planes and nuances" *("Son travail du burin, très doux, convenait bien à cette peinture caressée, faite toute de méplats et de nuances").* See also A. Griffiths, "Greuze et ses graveurs," *Nouvelles de l'estampe,* July–October 1980, pp. 9–11.

3. *"Après que la dite planche aura été mise à sa perfection, le dessein du dit Greuze lui sera rendu comme lui appartenant en particulier pour en disposer à son profit ainsi qu'il avisera."* Wildenstein 1960, p. 233.

4. *"Précieux," "très terminés," "les plus rendus du maître."* Quoted from the Vaudreuil sale catalogue of 26 November 1787 by Arquié-Bruley 1983, p. 127.

5. Arquié-Bruley 1983, p. 127.

6. *"Cela est excellent, et pour le talent, et pour les moeurs. Cela prêche la population, et peint très-pathétiquement le bonheur et le prix inestimable de la paix domestique."* Diderot *Salons,* II, p. 155.

7. *"une cheminée couverte d'une glace."* Diderot *Salons,* II, p. 155.

8. *"M. Greuze s'est plû à placer dans cette mere bien aimée le Portrait de Madame Greuze,et il en a fait l'esquisse en pastel."* Mathon de La Cour 1765, pp. 11–12.

9. *"Voy. M. de la Borde."* Dacier 1909–21, II, p. 81.

10. *Lettre sur les Peintures . . . par M. Raphaël . . . ,* p. 29.

11. *"N'oubliez pas qu'il nous manque huit énormes compositions de Vernet dont ce vilain M. de la Borde nous a privés."* Diderot *Salons,* IV, p. 89.

12. *"J'ai vu quelquefois des sociétés choisies, rassemblées à la campagne, s'amuser pendant les soirées d'automne à un jeu tout-à-fait intéressant et agréable. C'est d'imiter les compositions de tableaux connus avec des figures vivantes. . . . Lorsque toute la scène et tous les acteurs sont arrangés suivant l'ordonnance du peintre, et le lieu convenablement éclairé, on appelle les specta-teurs qui disent leur avis sur la manière dont le tableau est exécuté."* Diderot *Salons,* II, p. 155.

13. Monod and Hautecoeur 1922, no. 50.

14. *"Jean-Joseph de Laborde, par la haute situation de sa fortune, était devenu le centre de ses familles, en en dotant tous les membres, les hébergeant . . . neveux, nièces, cousins, cousines, etc."* "Mémorial des Laborde," p. 115. See also C. Duncan, "Happy Mothers and Other New Ideas in French Art," *The Art Bulletin,* December 1973, p. 572.

15. *"Il y en a six au moins."* Diderot *Salons,* II, p. 154.

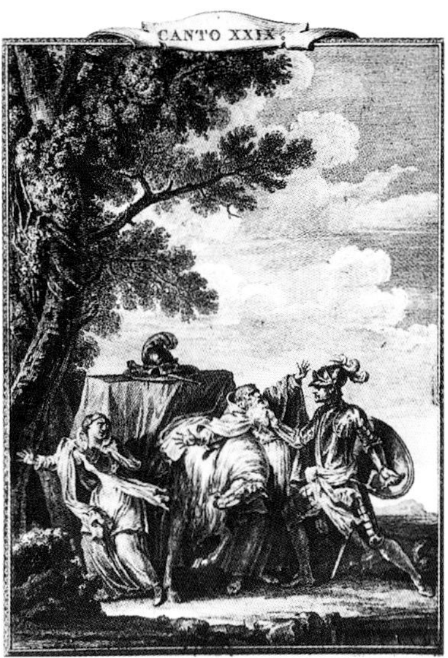

Fig. 174 J.-M. Moreau *le jeune,* after Greuze, *La Mano al mento... An Illustration for Ariosto's "Orlando furioso,"* 1771, engraving, Paris, Bibliothèque nationale de France

71 *An Illustration for "Orlando furioso"*

Brush and gray ink wash over graphite on white paper, 279 × 216 mm (11 × 8 ½ in.)
Frankfurt am Main, Städelsches Kunstinstitut

Provenance: Calonne Angelot, Paris; his sale, Paris, 11 May 1789, lot 261; Cornillon, Paris; Johann Friedrich Städel, Frankfurt; original collection of the museum
Exhibition: Französische Zeichnungen im Städelschen Kunstinstitut, Frankfurt am Main, Städelsches Kunstinstitut, 1986–87, no. 108
Bibliography: E. Bocher, *Jean-Michel Moreau le jeune, Catalogue raisonné des estampes, vignettes, eaux-fortes,* Paris 1882, p. 117, no. 288; Martin and Masson 1906, no. 409; G. Rouchès, "L'Interprétation du Roland furieux par la gravure," *L'Amateur d'estampes,* October 1925, pp. 145–53; Munhall 1961, pp. 240, 242 n. 7; Hartford *et al.* 1976–77, pp. 23, 25, fig. 13; R. Lee, *Names on Trees: Ariosto into Art,* Princeton NJ 1977, p. 107 n. 121

The third and last of Greuze's drawings intended as models for book illustrations (see no. 68), this one was prepared for the luxurious four-volume Italian edition of Ariosto's *Orlando furioso* printed by John Baskerville at Birmingham. Though Moreau's engraving of Greuze's model (fig. 174) is dated 1771, and the title page, 1773, the edition did not in fact appear until two years later. Other artists creating illustrations for the project included Giovanni Battista Cipriani (1727–1785), Charles-Nicolas Cochin *fils* (1715–1790), Charles-Dominique-Joseph Eisen (1720–1778), and Moreau *le jeune.* The production is regarded as the finest *Orlando furioso* of the eighteenth century.[1]

Greuze's drawing illustrates the last four lines of canto XXIX stanza 5:

Steps to him and with hand and toung ungracious
First bids him get him to his cell againe,
Then his long beard growne on his aged chin
All at one pull he pilleth from the skin.[2]

While Isabella flees to the left, looking like one of the daughters of Niobe,[3] Rodomont is depicted attacking the monk who had overcome her, traveling with her dead lover Zerbino's remains in a coffin mounted on his horse. The illustration appears in volume III, p. 207.

What is peculiar about this illustration and its engraving by Moreau *le jeune* is that the latter does not reverse the former, as is usually the case with such reproductions. One possibility is that Greuze executed the drawing after Moreau's print, his original model having been damaged or lost. Alternatively, while Moreau might have delicately traced the present drawing to flop its composition, the great difference in size between it and Moreau's print, which measures only 129 × 91 mm (5 1/16 × 3 9/16 in.), would seem to argue against that. A third possibility, proposed by Hubert Prouté,[4] is that an intermediary, Cochin for instance, might have executed after the present sheet a drawing reversed in composition but the size of the future print, which Moreau could then have used as his model.

1. See P. Hofer in *Fragonard Drawings for Ariosto,* New York 1954, p. 37.

2. *E che nuocer vi vede a viso aperto,*
E che seco non vuol triegua né pace:
La mano al mento con furor gli stese,
E tanto ne pelò, quanto ne prese.
Ludovico Ariosto, *Orlando furioso,* ed. N. Zingarelli, Milan 1949, p. 311; *Orlando furioso,* trans. Sir John Harrington (1591), ed. Robert McNulty, Oxford 1972, p. 325.

3. See Haskell and Penny 1981, figs. 144, 145.

4. Letter to the author dated 6 December 2000.

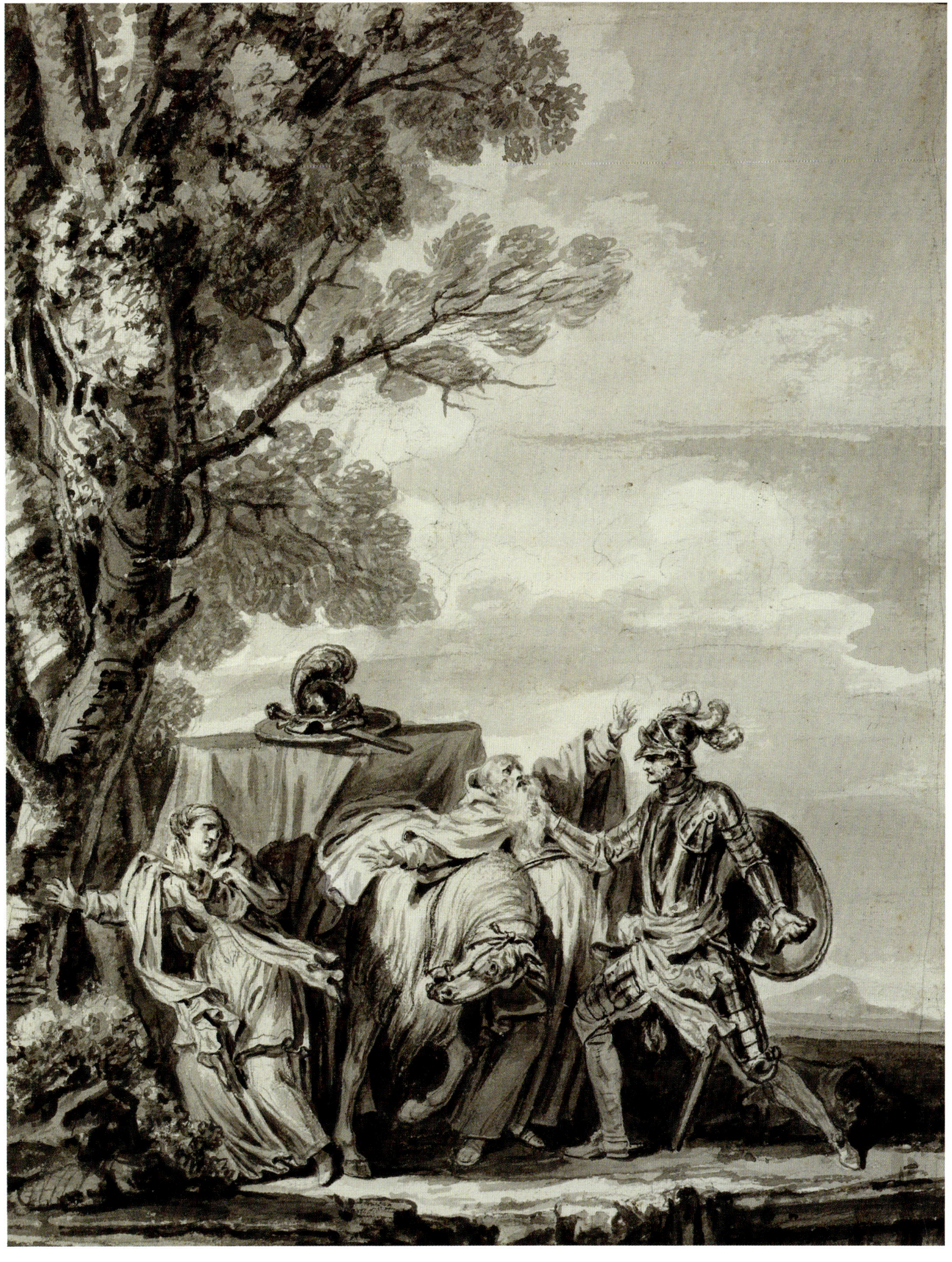

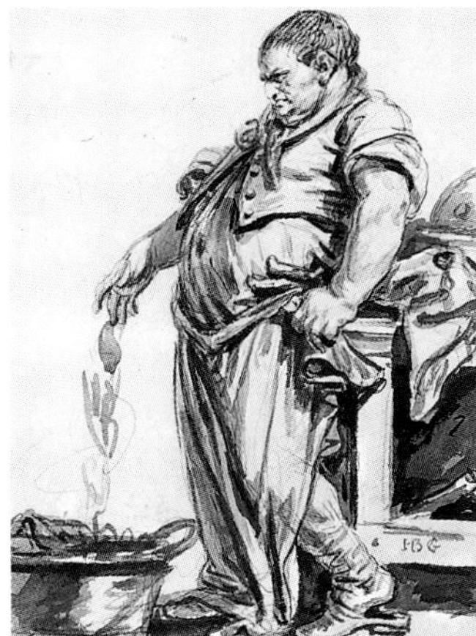

Fig. 175 Greuze, *The Pork Butcher, c.* 1775, brush and gray ink wash over graphite on white paper, Paris, École Nationale Supérieure des Beaux-Arts

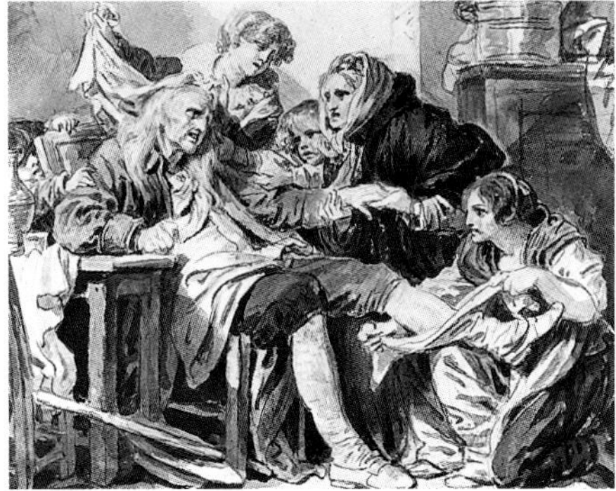

Fig. 176 Greuze, *Return of the Hunter, c.* 1775, brush with black, gray, and brown ink on white paper, Ottawa, National Gallery of Canada

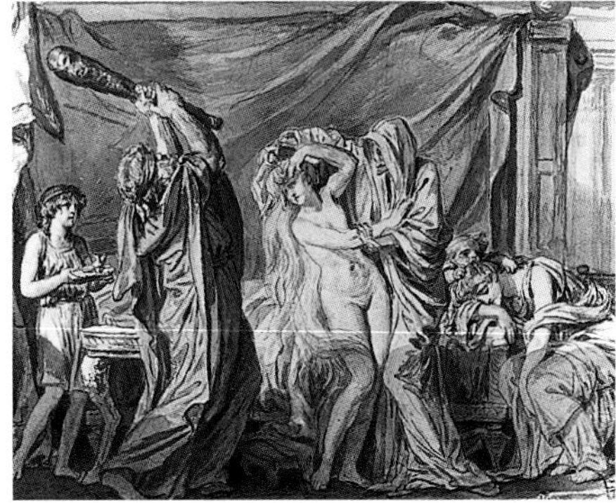

Fig. 177 Greuze, *Death and the Maiden, c.* 1790, brush with brown and gray ink wash over black chalk, Rouen, Musée des Beaux-Arts

72 *The Guilty and Repentant Daughter or Old Man Accused of Ruining a Young Girl*

Brush with black and gray ink wash over black chalk on cream paper, perimeter mounted on cream board, 498 × 643 mm (19 9/16 × 25 3/16 in.)
The Cleveland Museum of Art, Leonard C. Hanna Jr. Fund

Provenance: comte Magne, Marseille; his sale, Paris, 25 January 1907, lot 21; sale, London, 4 July 1984, lot 121; Kate de Rothschild-Didier Aaron & Cie, 1988; acquired by the museum in 1989
Exhibitions: Master Drawings: 1550–1850, New York and London, Kate de Rothschild-Didier Aaron & Cie., 1988, no. 41; *The Year in Review: Selections 1989,* The Cleveland Museum of Art, 1990; *French Drawings from the Collection,* The Cleveland Museum of Art, 1994–95; *Master Drawings from The Cleveland Museum of Art,* The Cleveland Museum of Art *et al.* 2000–2001, no. 44
Bibliography: E. Munhall in *Maîtres français 1550–1800. Dessins de la donation Mathias Polakovits à l'École des Beaux-Arts,* exhib. cat., Paris, École Nationale Supérieure des Beaux-Arts, 1989, p. 240, no. 99, fig. 1; *Maîtres français 1550–1800. Dessins de la donation Mathias Polakovits à l'École des Beaux-Arts,* exhib. cat., Tokyo, Museum of Western Art, 1992, p. 240, no. 90; D. Bull, "Exhibition Reviews: London Old Master Drawings," *The Burlington Magazine,* January 1989, p. 49; *The Bulletin of The Cleveland Museum of Art,* February 1990, pp. 47–48, 75, fig. 151; "Acquisitions at The Cleveland Museum of Art," *The Burlington Magazine,* January 1991, p. 65, no. 44; *The Cleveland Museum of Art Handbook,* Cleveland 1991, p. 116; *The Cleveland Museum of Art, Masterpieces from East and West,* Cleveland 1992, p. 132

There is little to add to Carter Foster's thorough analysis of this enigmatic drawing in the *Master Drawings from The Cleveland Museum of Art* exhibition catalogue, wherein he suggests—in the absence of any contemporary references to the work—that the central male figure is being accused by the mother of the embarrassed pregnant young woman at right for having ruined her. This image was neither engraved nor rendered as a painting.

The same robust male model with his short hair *à la Titus* posed for *The Pork Butcher* (fig. 175),[1] and the old woman behind the screen at left resembles the similarly hooded figure in the *Presentation of a Vestal Virgin* (no. 85). There is also a parallel between the central male figure shown here being cared for by two young men and the old man in Greuze's *Return of the Hunter* (fig. 176).[2] Finally, another drawing with an equally enigmatic subject—*Death and the Maiden* (fig. 177)—was similarly conceived on a grand scale by Greuze and has nearly identical dimensions: 490 × 631 mm (19 5/16 × 24 13/16 in.), a rich architectural setting, and a similar facture.

The diagonal lines rendered in graphite from lower right to upper left and upper right to lower left corners and from top to bottom in the center of the composition may have been aids in rendering the perspective of this elaborate architectural interior, one of the most complex and sumptuous Greuze ever attempted.

1. See Munhall 1989.

2. See *Master Drawings from The National Gallery of Canada,* exhib. cat., Washington D.C., National Gallery of Art, 1988, pp. 175–76, no. 55.

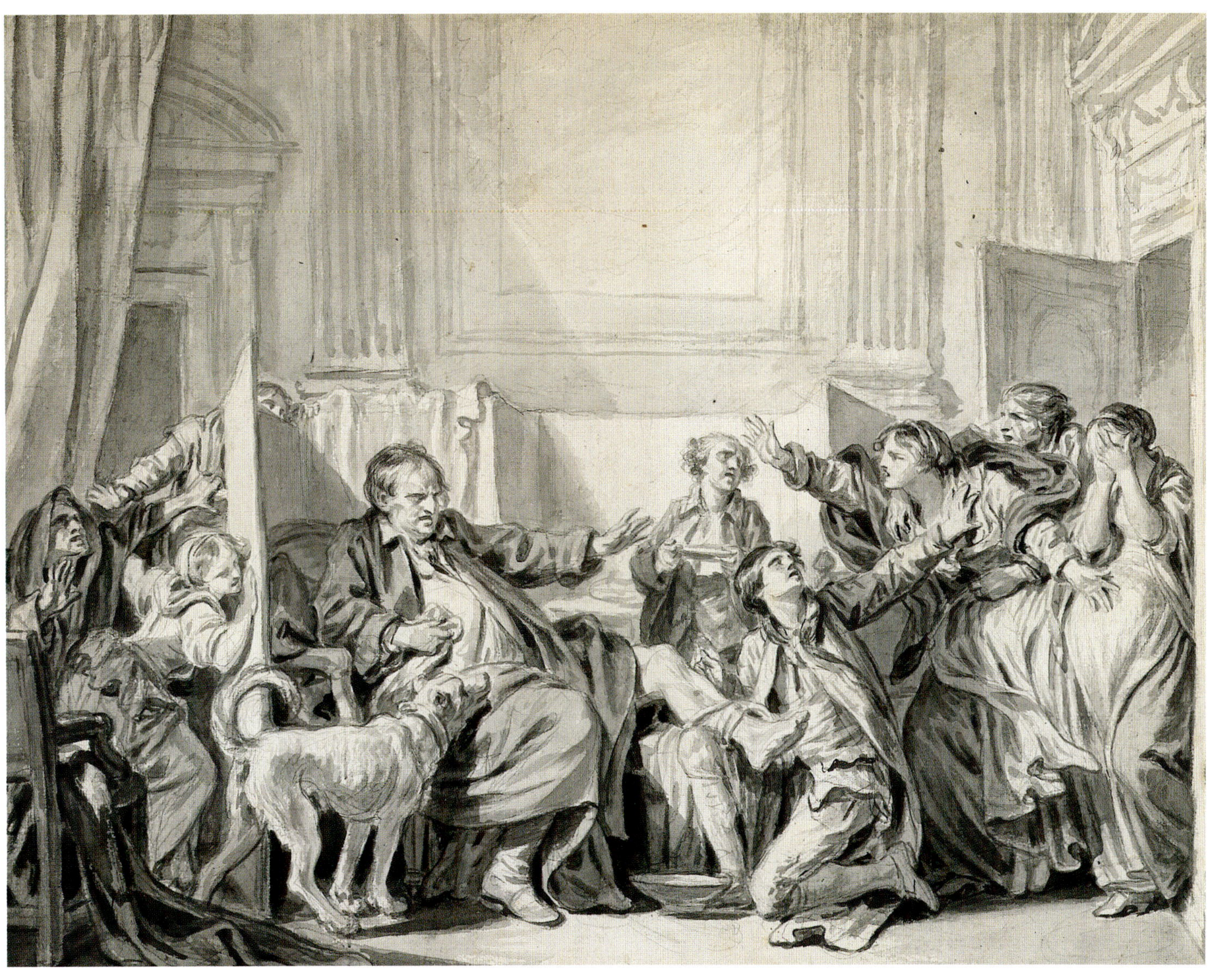

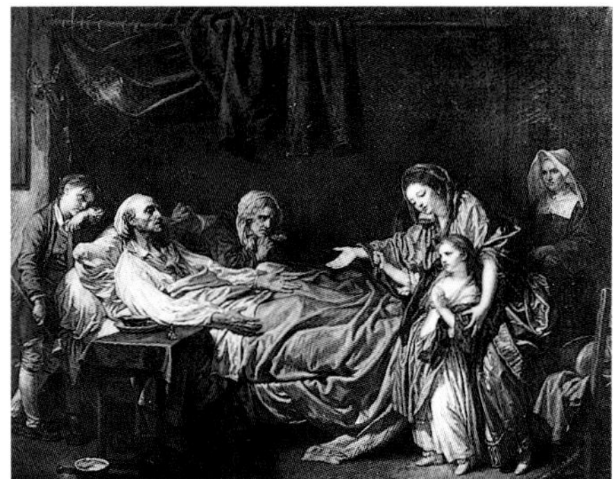

Fig. 178 Greuze, *The Woman of Good Deeds,* 1772–75, oil on canvas, Lyon, Musée des Beaux-Arts

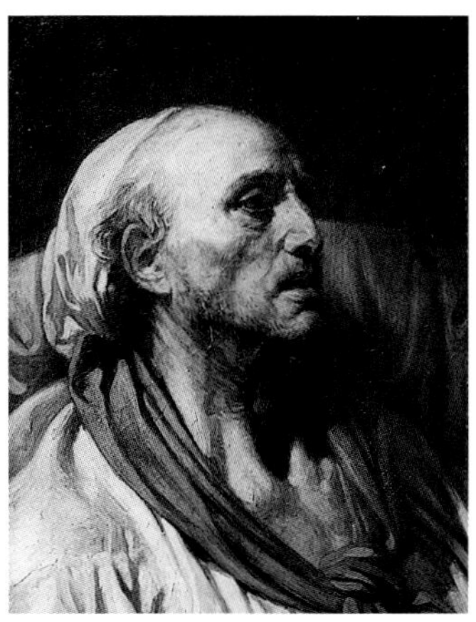

Fig. 179 Greuze, *Bust of a Dying Man,* *c.* 1773–74, oil on canvas, Montpellier, Musée Fabre

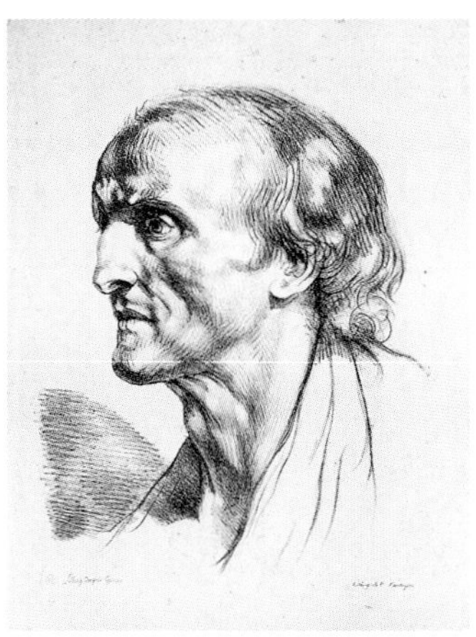

Fig. 180 C.-P. de Lasteyrie, after Greuze, *Bust of a Dying Man,* before 1849, lithograph, New York, The Metropolitan Museum of Art, Rogers Fund, 1922

73 *Head of a Man in Profile*

Red chalk on white paper, 409 × 201 mm (16 1/16 × 7 5/16 in.)
Inscribed in graphite at lower left *étude pour son paralytique*
Paris, Musée du Louvre, Département des arts graphiques

Provenance: original collection of the Cabinet des Dessins, Musée du Louvre
Exhibitions: None known
Bibliography: Reiset 1866–69, II, no. 768; Normand 1892, repr. facing p. 34; Martin and Masson 1906, no. 1685; Guiffrey and Marcel 1911, no. 4565; Hartford *et al.* 1976–77 (Dijon only), pp. 168, no. 76 *bis,* 171, no. 76 *ter;* T. Crow, *Painters and Public Life in Eighteenth-Century Paris,* New Haven 1985, fig. 61; E. Munhall in *Triumph und Tod des Helden,* exhib. cat., Cologne *et al.*, 1987–88, p. 224, no. 33

This haunting *tête d'expression* is a study for the figure of the dying man in *The Woman of Good Deeds* (fig. 178), for which Greuze executed, among many other drawings, a unique life-size study in oil based on this sheet (fig. 179). *The Woman of Good Deeds* was the first major picture undertaken by the artist after his *Septimius Severus and Caracalla* (fig. 13) of 1769. He had begun preparations for it by 1772 and exhibited it in his studio at the time of the biennial Salon in 1775.

Though he is sometimes referred to as a "paralyzed man," the catalogue of the Lebrun sale of 11 December 1780 (lot 168) correctly described the man as "dying" *("mourant").* The pathos of the emaciated subject is beyond that of the physical handicap of paralysis; it evokes the spiritual agony of a dying man, and specifically a nobleman (a quality Greuze suggested by including a sword hanging over his bed in the final painting). In his painted study based on this drawing, Greuze depicted his subject speaking, as though acknowledging the generous action of his benefactress.

In his remarks about *The Woman of Good Deeds* published in 1775, Bachaumont described the figure based on this study: "The unknown man visited by *The Charitable Woman* is an uncomplaining poor person, a worthy gentleman.... The nobility of his physiognomy confirms that first impression, no matter that his emaciation, his wrinkles, and the color of his muscular body add to the sympathy of the viewer, who rightly supposes that this is a sick man."[1] The author of the Lebrun sale catalogue mentioned above conveyed the power of this image: "Everyone knows the merit of the Heads of Monsieur Greuze, but this one especially has a character and nobility equal to the most beautiful creations of Italian art."[2]

Comte Charles-Philibert de Lasteyrie (1759–1849), a fervent promoter of lithography in France,[3] produced one of the rare lithographs of a Greuze *tête d'expression* based on the present drawing (fig. 180).

1. *"L'inconnu visité par la Dame de charité est un pauvre honteux, un bon gentilhomme.... La noblesse de sa physionomie en confirme cette première idée n'empêche pas que la maigreur, les rides et la couleur imprimés sur les muscles n'ajoutent encore à la sensibilité du spectateur, qui suppose avec raison que c'est un malade....* P. de Bachaumont, "Observations de Bachaumont sur la Dame de charité, tableau de M. Greuze," ms., 1775, Bibliothèque nationale de France, Cabinet des Estampes, Fonds Deloynes, pp. 1–2.

2. *"Tout le monde connaît le mérite des Têtes de M. Greuze mais celle-ci a surtout un caractère et une noblesse qui égalent les plus belles productions de l'Italie."* Lebrun sale catalogue, Paris, 11 December 1780, lot 168.

3. H. Béraldi, *Les Graveurs du XIXe siècle,* Paris 1889, VIII, pp. 54–55.

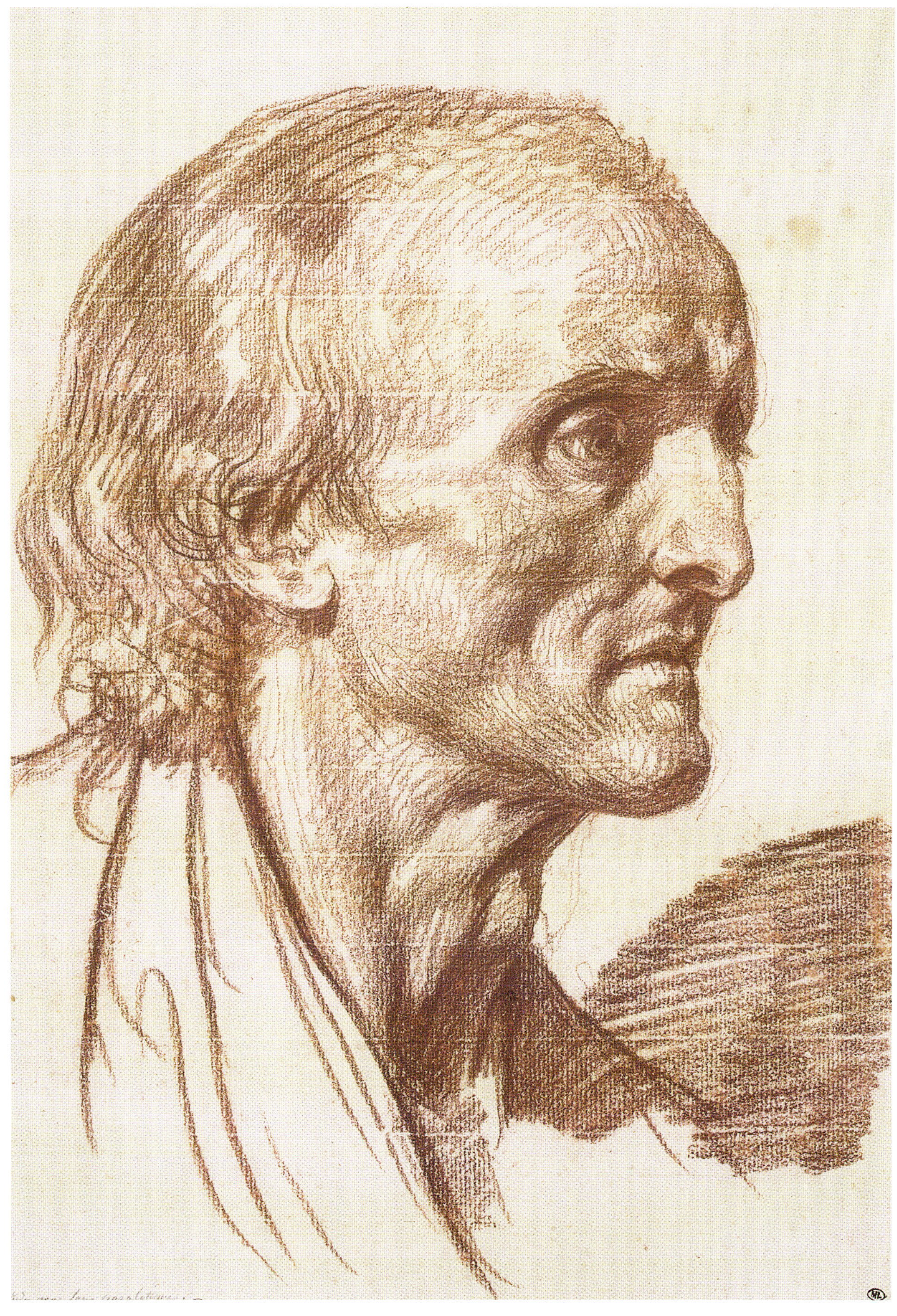

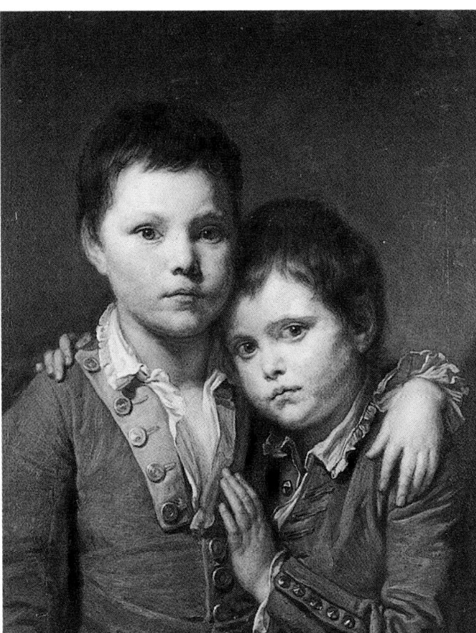

Fig. 181 Greuze, *Portrait of François and Alexandre de La Rochefoucauld, c.* 1775, oil on canvas, Houston, Mr William Carloss Morris III Collection

74 *Portrait of Two Boys*

Brush with dark brown oil on white paper (counterproof), 435 × 383 mm (17 1/8 × 15 1/16 in.)
Inscribed in graphite at lower left *Greuze*
Paris, Musée du Louvre, Département des arts graphiques

Provenance: original collection of the Cabinet des Dessins, Musée du Louvre (Saint-Morys collection)
Exhibitions: None known
Bibliography: Morel d'Arleux, no. 12647; Martin and Masson 1906, nos. 1771, 1206; Guiffrey and Marcel 1911, no. 4569; Munhall 1966, pp. 91, fig. 16, 92; Arquié-Bruley *et al.* 1987, II, p. 499

Executed in the same technique of oil on paper, counterproofed, as number 78, this poignant image of two boys is roughly contemporary with it.

Recognizing the features of the same boys in a Braun photograph of a rare double portrait by Greuze exhibited in Paris in 1897[1]—by the duc de La Roche-Guyon, according to Martin—the present author was able to propose identifying them as, at the left, François-Armand-Frédéric de La Rochefoucauld, duc de Liancourt (1765–1848) and, at the right, Alexandre-François, comte de La Rochefoucauld, duc d'Estissac (1767–1841), the two sons of Félicité-Sophie de Lannion and of François-Alexandre-Frédéric, duc de la Rochefoucauld de Roye, duc d'Estissac, and duc de Liancourt (1747–1827), one of the most extraordinary courtiers, politicians, and philanthropists of his time.[2] On 26 November 2000 this same portrait reappeared at an auction in Nice and was acquired by an American collector (fig. 181).[3]

Although not unique in Greuze's oeuvre as a double portrait (see no. 94), the present drawing and its resulting portrait are rare demonstrations of Greuze's empathy toward the more troubled sensibility of children, as opposed to his frequent recordings of their carefree and even giddy enthusiasms. The rendition of the eyes, with the full pupils revealed, confers a disquieting aura on such a rapidly executed study.

In the painting, the green coat with rose facing and set with silver buttons worn by François, on the left, was a uniform adapted from that of his father's regiment, the de La Rochefoucauld dragoons, which his son would join in 1780 as a *cadet-gentilhomme* under his father's command. It had been Louis XV's decision in 1762 that all the regiments of dragoons would wear green uniforms.[4]

After three years of military training, François then followed his father's example and spent four years in England with the agriculturist Arthur Young. The result of this experience was a publication, *Voyage particulier en Suffolk, et voyage particulier en Norfolk.* Back in France by 1787, he rejoined the military, but, again like his father, he emigrated in 1792 and joined the British Army. The following year he married Marie-Françoise de Tott. After returning definitively to France in 1800, he held various political and military posts under Louis XVIII, Charles X, and Louis-Philippe. In 1829 he purchased the château de La Roche-Guyon, which has remained in the family ever since. Dying at the age of eighty-three, he declared that his life had been "full of exhaustion, disappointments, and many errors of judgment."[5]

Alexandre-François de La Rochefoucauld, on the right, traveled widely as a child with his elder brother, in France, England, Switzerland, and Germany. He too joined the army and intended to serve under La Fayette, but because of his father's loyalty to Louis XVI, he was ill-regarded by the Revolutionary powers and, like his brother, emigrated. He settled in Santo Domingo, where his wife's family had business interests. The comtesse de La Rochefoucauld, née Adélaïde-Marie-Françoise Pyvart de Chastullé, was a first cousin of Joséphine de Beauharnais and became the empress's lady-in-waiting. Through her influence, Alexandre-François was named ambassador to Vienna in 1805. In his later years, he was elected to the Chambre des Députés as a constitutional royalist. This comte de La Rochefoucauld died seven years earlier than his brother.[6]

1. Munhall 1966, p. 91, fig. 17.

2. See *Dictionnaire des Parlementaires français,* Paris 1890, pp. 601–02; *Almanach de Gotha,* Gotha 1944, pp. 456, 459; G. Martin, *Histoire et Généalogie de la maison de La Rochefoucauld,* La Ricamarie 1975, pp. 56–87; *Les Préfets du 11 ventôse an VIII au 4 septembre 1870,* Paris 1981, p. 183; R. de Warren, *Les Pairs de France au XIXe siècle,* Paris 1959, II, no. 268. The author is grateful to the vicomte Jacques d'Arjuzon for providing these references, as well as those concerning uniforms.

3. Lot 109, *Portrait de François et d'Alexandre de La Rochefoucauld,* oil on canvas, 56.5 x 46 cm (22 1/4 × 18 1/8 in.), property of comtesse de La Rochefoucauld, château de La Roche-Guyon.

4. Martin 1975, p. 65; L. Rousselot, *L'Armée française,* Paris 1960, pl. 73.

5. *"remplie de fatigue, de revers et de beaucoup de mécomptes."* Martin 1975, p. 66.

6. This biographical summary is based on material published by Martin 1975, pp. 65–66, 85–87.

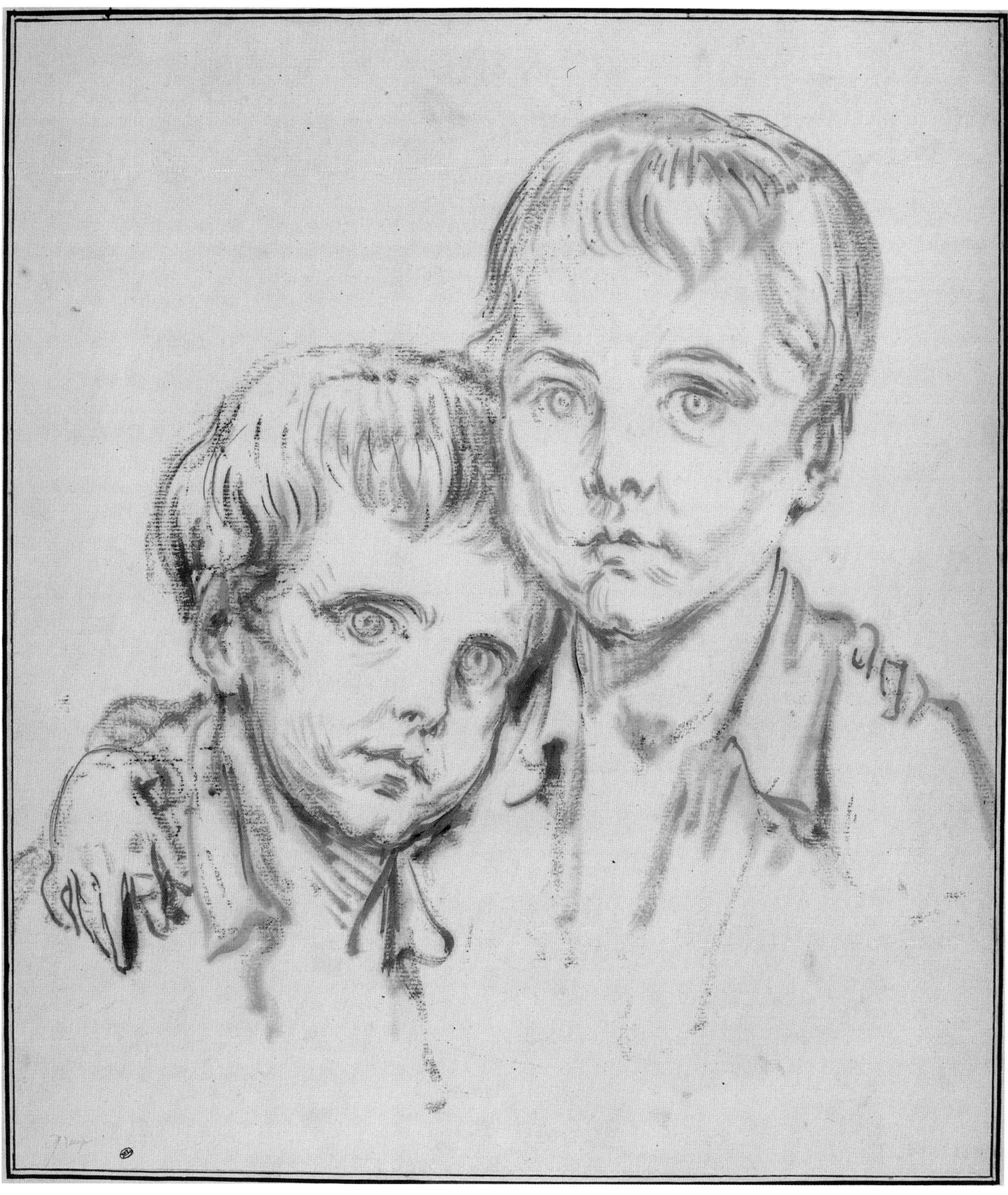

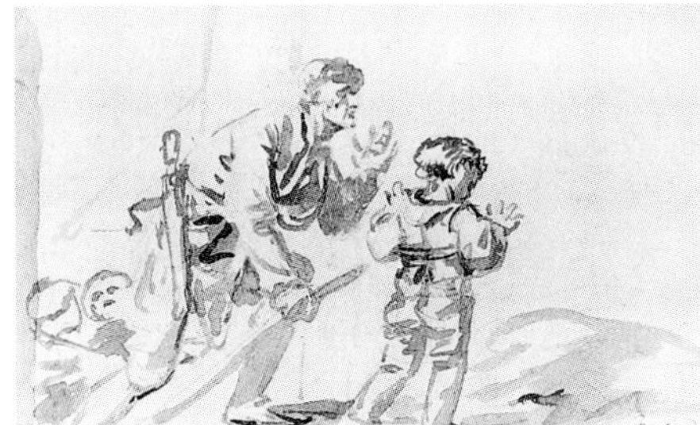

Fig. 182 Greuze, *A Child with a Man Holding a Gun, c.* 1775, brush with black ink over graphite on white paper, Compiègne, Musée Vivenel

75 *Figural Composition: Two Men Tying up a Dead Deer*

Brush, with brown and gray ink over graphite on white paper, 228 × 360 mm (8 15/16 × 14 3/16 in.)
Signed in brown ink at lower right *Greuze*
Frankfurt am Main, Städelsches Kunstinstitut

Provenance: chevalier de Damery, Paris (Lugt 2862); Johann Friedrich Städel, Frankfurt; original collection of the museum
Exhibition: Französiche Zeichnungen im Städelschen Kunstinstitut 1550 bis 1800, Frankfurt am Main, Städelsches Kunstinstitut, 1986–87, no. 106
Bibliography: Hartford *et al.* 1976–77, p. 196

This powerful drawing, which invites comparison to Goya, relates to two other hastily executed scenes of the hunt by Greuze. One—*A Child with a Man Holding a Gun* (fig. 182)—nearly identical in size to the present drawing, must have been sketched just shortly before it, considering the even greater roughness of its execution.[1] The bold brushstrokes at lower right would indicate the dead deer that the hunters in the present sheet are shown tying up. As Margret Stuffman states, this is not a scene intended to evoke the pleasures of the hunt, nor is it a tender Chardinesque elegy for a rabbit, but rather a scene of brutal confrontation with death on the part of some very young children.[2]

Dating from the same period in the mid-1770s are two renderings of a *Return from the Hunt,* one depicting a hunter with a wolf draped over his shoulders (fig. 183).[3] Here, the barely indicated figure at the right consisting of a ball of a head and some columnar indications of a body corresponds to the figure at the far right of the present sheet. Greuze's other treatment of the theme (fig. 184) places this same figure in a dramatic context.[4]

About a decade later, Greuze would produce a more elegant and anecdotal composition on the hunting theme with *The Recompense Refused* (fig. 185), but even here, a child raises his hands in horror before the grim cadaver at his feet.[5]

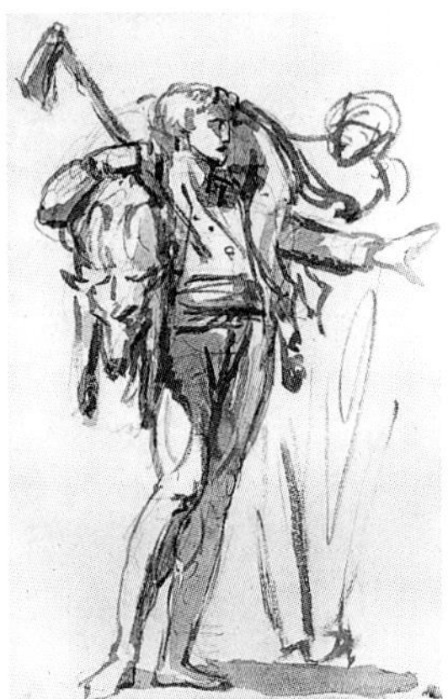

Fig. 183 Greuze, *Return from the Hunt, c.* 1775, brush with gray ink over black chalk on white paper, Besançon, Musée d'Art et d'Archéologie

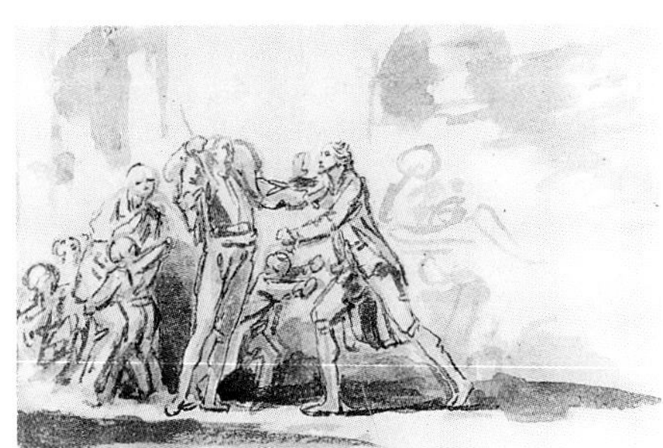

Fig. 184 Greuze, *Return from the Hunt, c.* 1775, brush and black ink wash over graphite on white paper, London, The Courtauld Institute of Art

1. P. Rosenberg, "Expositions. *Dessins connus et inconnus,* Compiègne, Musée Vivenel, 1969," *Revue de l'art,* no. 9, 1970, p. 95, fig. 4.

2. In Frankfurt am Main 1986–87.

3. *Old Master Drawings Presented by Adolphe Stein and Lorna Lowe,* London, H. Terry-Engell Gallery, 1972, no. 85; "La Chronique des arts. Principales Acquisitions des musées en 1992," *GBA,* March 1993, p. 11, no. 45; "Acquisitions," *La Revue du Louvre et des musées de France,* 1, 1994, p. 81, no. 22.

4. *French Drawings, XVI–XIX Centuries, Courtauld Institute Galleries,* exhib. cat., London, University of London, Courtauld Institute Galleries, 1991, no. 25; F. Borne, "French Drawings at the Courtauld Institute of Art," *Apollo,* September 1991, p. 194.

5. Hartford *et al.* 1976–77, no. 98.

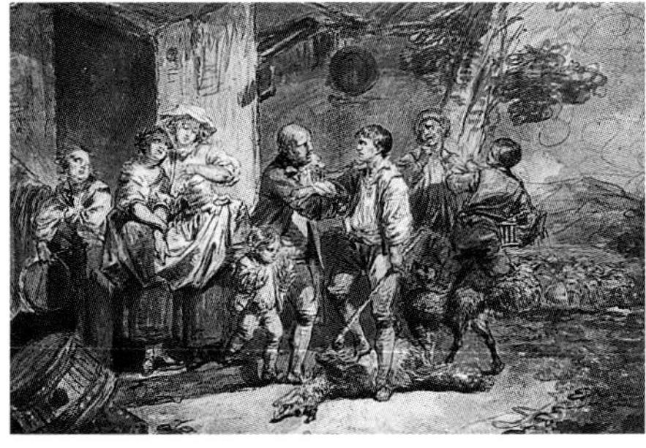

Fig. 185 Greuze, *The Recompense Refused, c.* 1785, brush with gray ink, heightened with white, on blue paper, London, British Museum

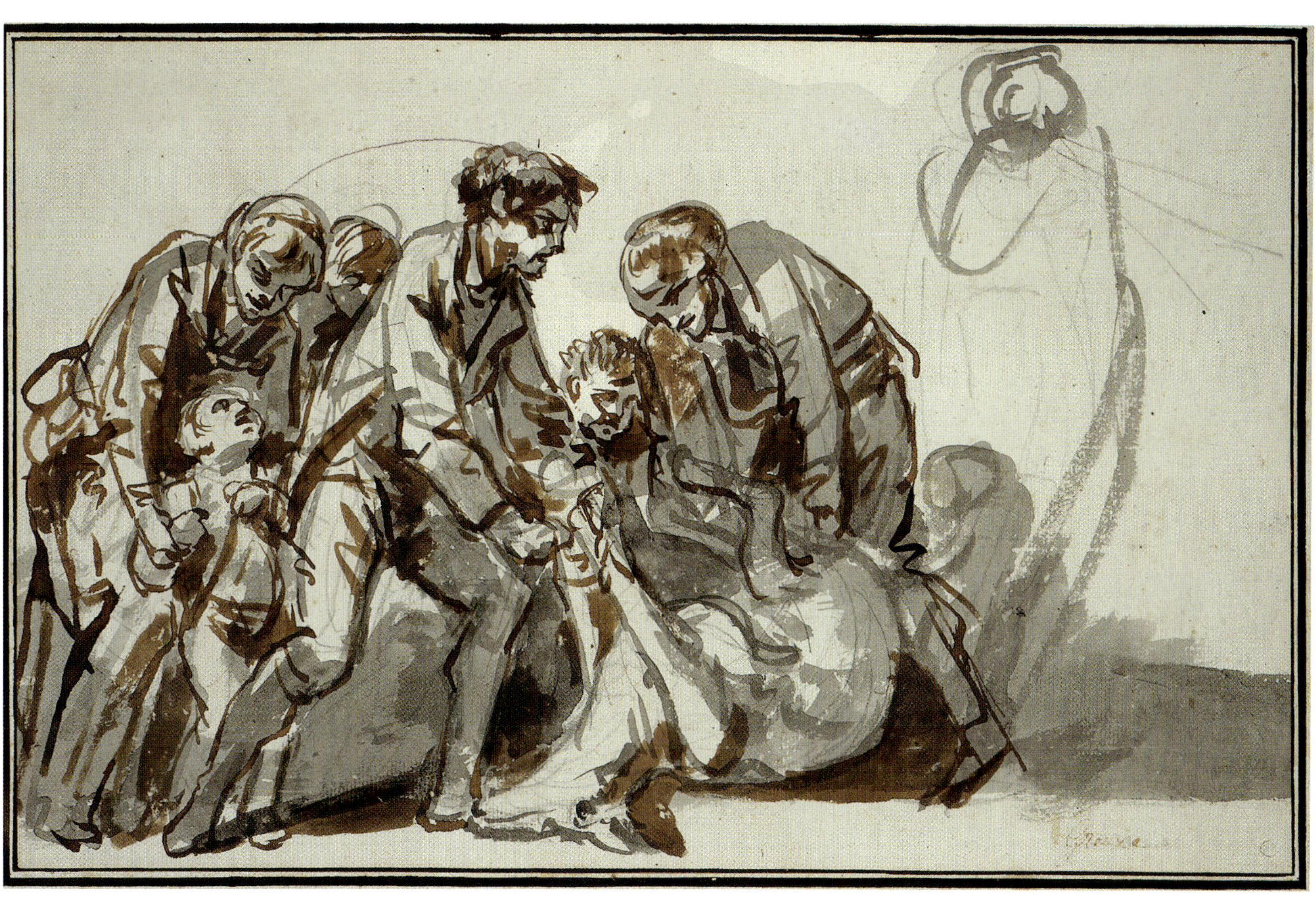

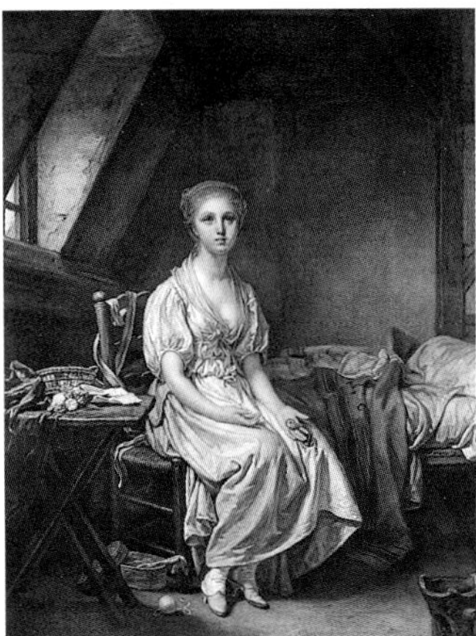

Fig. 186 Greuze, *Wavering Virtue, c.* 1774–75, oil on canvas, Munich, Alte Pinakothek

76 *Seated Young Woman, Study for "Wavering Virtue"*

Red and black chalks, stumped, brush with gray ink wash on white paper, 445 × 312 mm (17 1/2 × 12 5/16 in.)
Signed in graphite bottom left *Greuze*
Paris, Musée du Louvre, Département des arts graphiques

Provenance: original collection of the Cabinet des Dessins, Musée du Louvre (Saint-Morys collection)
Exhibitions: Chefs d'oeuvre de l'art français, Paris, Palais National des Arts, 1937, no. 551; Hartford *et al.* 1976–77, no. 77
Bibliography: Morel d'Arleux, no. 12646/21; Martin and Masson 1906, nos. 216, 1407; Guiffrey and Marcel 1911, VI, no. 4543; *Le Dessin français dans les collections hollandaises,* exhib. cat., Paris, Institut Néerlandais; Amsterdam, Rijksmuseum, 1964, p. 76, no. 93; Wakefield 1984, p. 128; Arquié-Bruley *et al.* 1987, II, p. 499

This is one of several studies by Greuze for *Wavering Virtue* (fig. 186), a painting engraved by Jean Massard in 1776.[1] The closest and most interesting study is a counterproof of the present sheet, reworked in brush and ink over the chalk transfer (fig. 187).[2] Probably earlier in date than these was the study in red chalk and ink wash (fig. 188), in which the head is a blank oval but a spot on the subject's left hand corresponds to the watch so crucial to the meaning of the painting. Finally, a study of the same figure seen from the side (fig. 189) would suggest that the artist was working up this subject, or at least the pose of the seated young woman, prior to 1767, when this sheet was acquired by Betskoy.[3]

The garret interior in the painting of *Wavering Virtue,* with its casement window and the chair placed alongside the bed, recalls the setting of *The Death of a Cruel Father Abandoned by His Children* (no. 69), exhibited in 1769. In this disheveled room, Greuze's pathetic heroine reflects on the ominous gift she has received, a gold watch that reads six o'clock (AM, judging from the pale light at the window). Élisabeth-Louise Vigée-Lebrun executed a painting with the subject Wavering Virtue at about the same time as Greuze; her picture depicts a partially dressed young woman sitting up in bed, wanly contemplating an open letter.[4]

1. *H. Bauer, Meisterwerke des 18. Jahrhunderts… in der Alten Pinakothek,* Munich 1966, pp. 30–31; S. Steingräber and C. Lenz, *Alte Pinakothek und Neue Pinakothek im München,* London and Bonn 1985, p. 106.

2. See *Le Dessin français dans les collections hollandaises* 1964, no. 93.

3. Monod and Hautecoeur 1922, no. 62; sale, Leipzig, 29 April 1931, lot 102; sale, New York, 26 January 2000, lot 88; sale, New York, 24 January 2001, lot 121.

4. Sale, New York, 23 May 2000, lot 140.

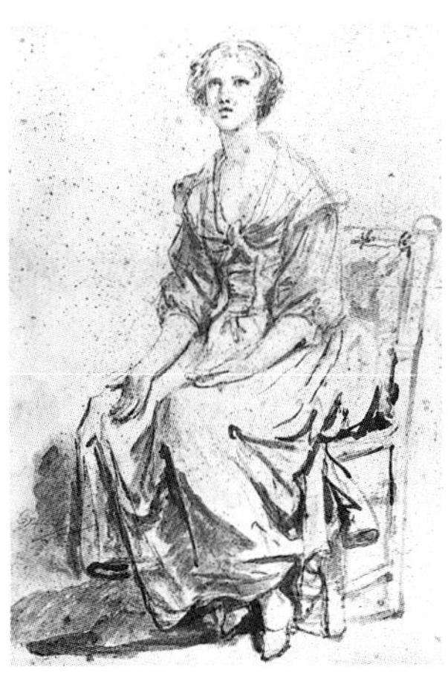

Fig. 187 Greuze, *Seated Young Woman, c.* 1769–74, red chalk and brush with gray ink on white paper, Rotterdam, Museum Boijmans-van Beuningen

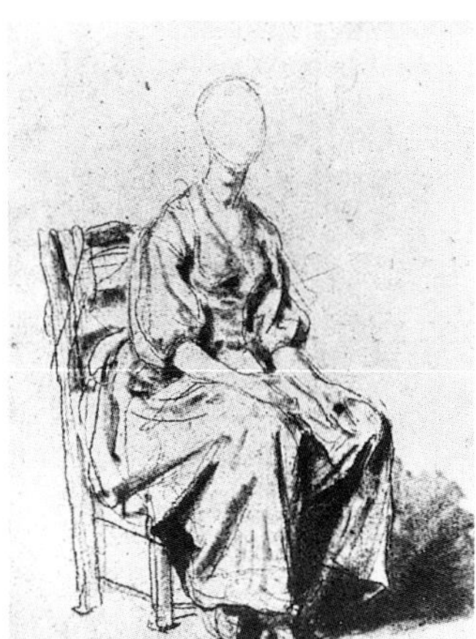

Fig. 188 Greuze, *Seated Young Woman, c.* 1769–74, red chalk and brush with gray ink on white paper, whereabouts unknown

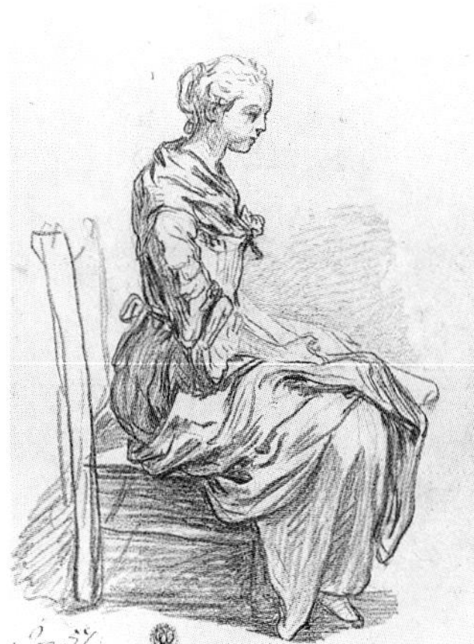

Fig. 189 Greuze, *Seated Young Woman, c.* 1767, red chalk on white paper, whereabouts unknown

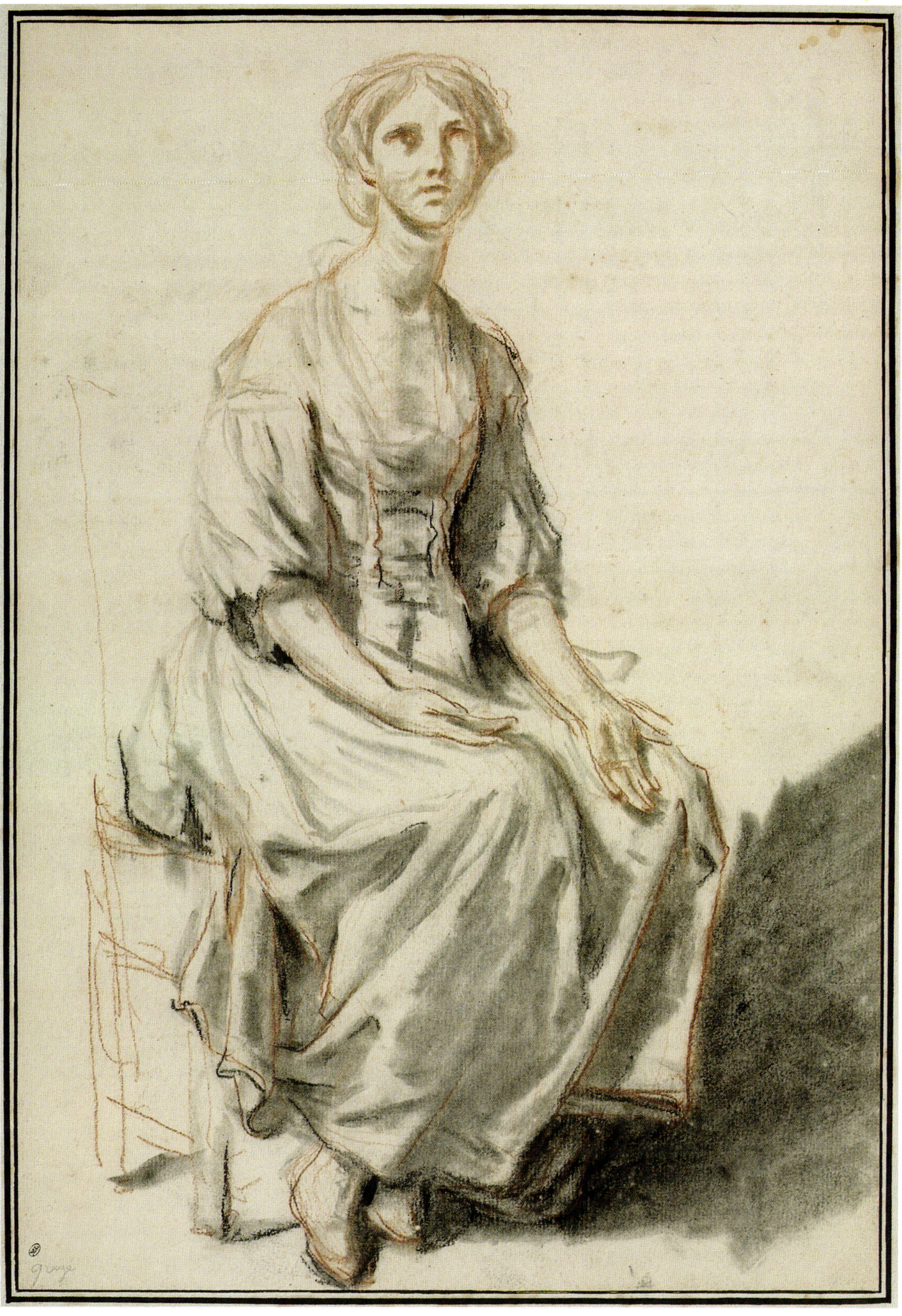

77 *The Torn-up Will*

Brush, with gray ink, heightened with white, over graphite on brown-gray paper (originally blue), 310 × 408 mm (12 3/16 × 16 1/16 in.)
Inscribed in ink on the original mount *J.B. Greuze 1775/ Arrete malheureux/ Le Testament déchiré/ Respecte les dernières volontés de ton père*[1]
Private collection

Provenance: T.C. Bruun-Neergaard, Paris;[2] his sale, Paris, 29 August–7 September 1814, lot 147; sale, Paris, 17–18 February 1834, lot 55; Destouches, Paris; his sale, Paris, 4–5 March 1847, no. 47; Hippolyte Walferdin, Paris; his sale, Paris, 18 May 1860, lot 77; Didier Aaron & Cie, Paris, 1996
Exhibitions: None known
Bibliography: Smith, no. 144; Portalis and Béraldi 1880–82, II, pt. 2, pp. 687, 688, 691; Martin and Masson 1906, nos. 214, 251; Barker 1994, p. 281

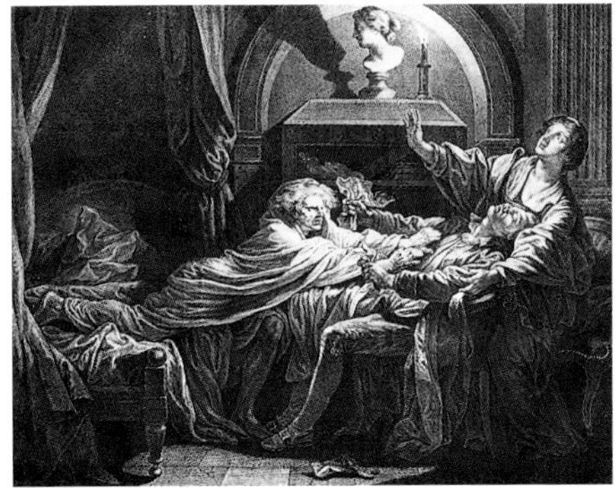

Fig. 190 J.-C. Le Vasseur, after Greuze, *The Torn-up Will*, after 1785, engraving, Paris, Bibliothèque nationale de France

Another highly finished drawing prepared as a model for an engraver, *The Torn-up Will* was delivered to Jean-Charles Le Vasseur on 30 April 1785 in an agreement signed with the notary Boulard in which Le Vasseur was promised 1500 livres for his work.[3] An earlier agreement had been established in 1780 among Greuze, his wife, and the engraver Jean-Jacques Flipart, but he died in 1782, before completing his work. Legal complications with his sister Marie-Cornélie ensued and were settled only in 1785, when Greuze turned to Le Vasseur to complete the job.[4] The final result (fig. 190) was dedicated to Greuze's notary and major patron Duclos-Dufresnoy.

Madame de Valori, Greuze's goddaughter, quoted the artist's description of *The Torn-up Will* in her "Notice sur Greuze." The text, as passionate as the one Greuze published at the time of *The Stepmother* (see no. 36), has an authentic tone:

A father of a family, with a considerable fortune, had two children, a son and a daughter-in-law. This father, having reached the age when all men lose their illusions, and consider the future with composure, made his will, which the blind confidence he had had in his son prevented him from taking to a notary.

A short time afterward, this father fell ill; the result of this sickness was a lethargy so profound, that his descendants took it for death itself. Their first concerns were to send away the servants and take advantage of the middle of the night to remove the last wishes of their father! Criminal avarice! *With a lighted candle in hand, pale of face and dry-eyed, accompanied by his wife, the son silently enters the bedroom of the respectable old man, opens the desk, and extends his trembling patricidal hand over the sacred deposit it contained. But, terrible moment! the father notices the light, and silently watches his guilty son. Wretched father! What a court of justice! Beneath this funeral veil, without knowing it, you are plunging your son into his tomb, where he believed you to be already descended.*

The daughter-in-law was then standing behind the chair of her husband, who, after reading the will, cries out, as he tears it up: "It exists no longer!" The old man, his eyes burning with rage and contempt, throws himself upon his son, and says to him: "Stop, wretched man! respect the last wishes of your father!" Stunned by this reproach, the guilty young man falls dead, the scraps of the will in his hands; and his wife, overwhelmed, holds him in her arms.[5]

In contrast to earlier scenes of children stealing jars of jam (Martin and Masson 1906, no. 289), Greuze by the mid-1770s was clearly heightening the level of crime

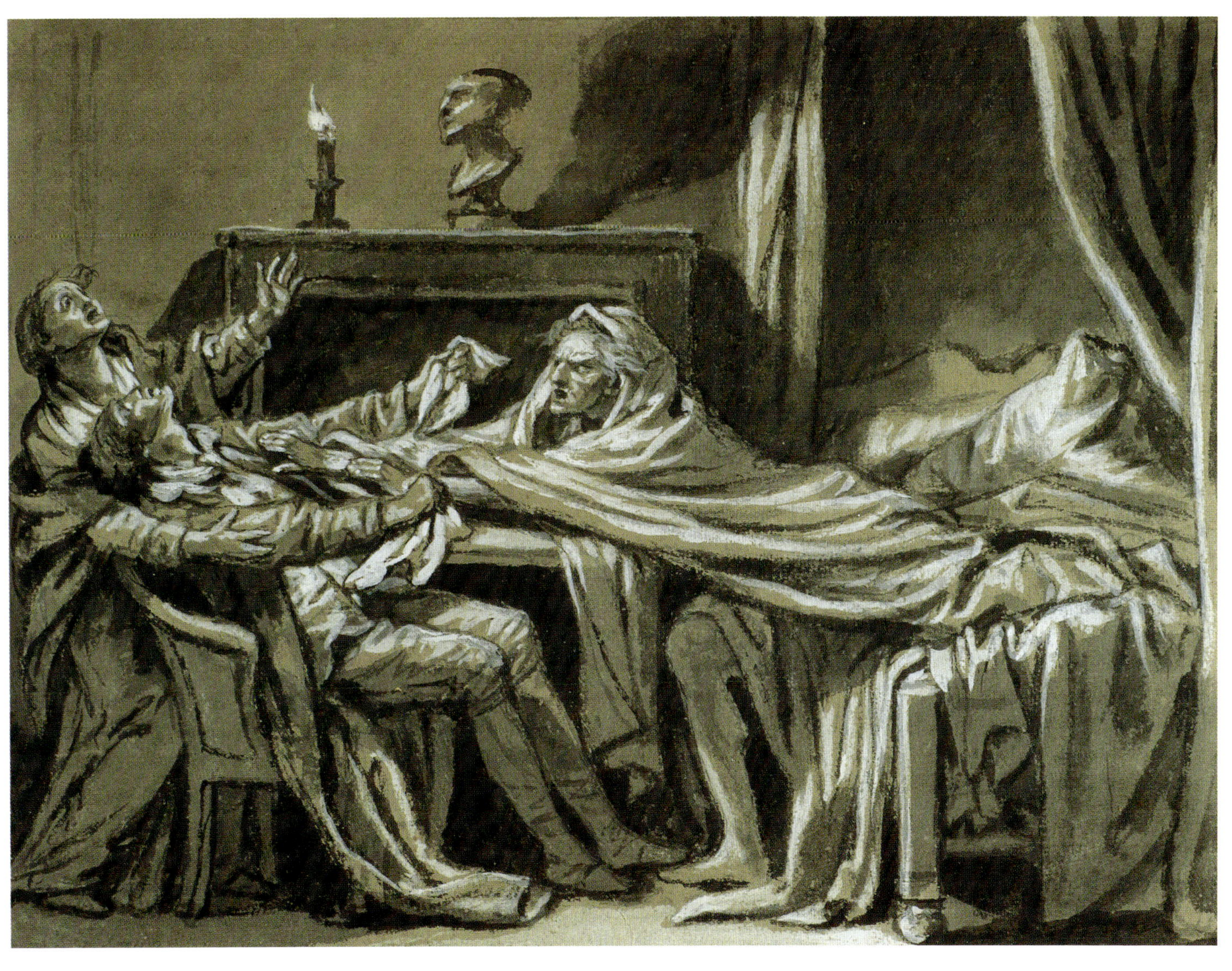

in which his protagonists were caught. It is worth recalling that when this drawing appeared in the Walferdin sale of 1860, it was described as "executed under the inspiration of Diderot, [and as] full of action as any drawing by Fragonard."[6]

As usual with Greuze, the subject of the present drawing may have autobiographical overtones. The artist's father, Jean-Louis Greuze, died in 1769, aged seventy-two. Of his nine children, his eldest son Jacques inherited the totality of his estate — two houses in Tournus, their furnishings, and 4000 livres. Knowing that the latter would leave the artist only thirty livres in 1792, it is not difficult to imagine the hypersensitive Greuze harboring dark thoughts about wills at the time he executed *The Torn-up Will*.[7]

Though Greuze's contracts with the engravers of *The Torn-up Will* refer to the present drawing as being after a painting, no such picture exists. However, a number of related drawings do. A full compositional study in red chalk appeared in the Caroline Greuze sale, 25–26 January 1843 (lot 50), described by Thoré as: "*The Avaricious Man.* A finished drawing for the painting of that name: figure of a naked man who throws himself out of his bed to protect his treasure. The movement is of great energy, and the physiognomy of a startling expression. In red chalk."[8] For the head of the son, Greuze may have recalled an earlier red chalk study of a dead man's head (fig. 191), which formed part of the collection of his drawings sold to Betskoy in 1767.[9] Another, of the father's head (fig. 192)—"his eyes burning with rage and contempt"—was given to the Fogg Art Museum in 1931 by Richard Owen. For a long time it was mistakenly described as a "head of an old woman."[10] A sketch for the latter (fig. 193), executed on the back of a playing card (Jack of Hearts), was sold in Paris, 20 November 2000, lot 77. *The Avaricious Man and His Children* that Greuze exhibited at the Salon of 1769 (no. 162) and that appeared in the Laborde sale, Paris, 16 May 1783, lot 42, was a different composition.

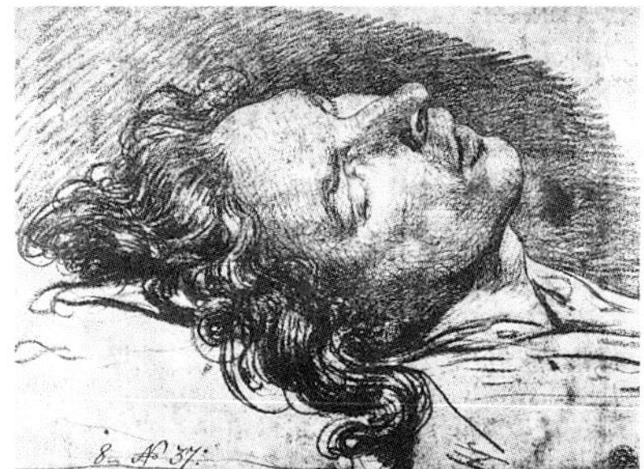

Fig. 191 Greuze, *Head of a Dead Man,* before 1767, red chalk on white paper, formerly St Petersburg, Imperial Academy of Fine Arts, whereabouts unknown

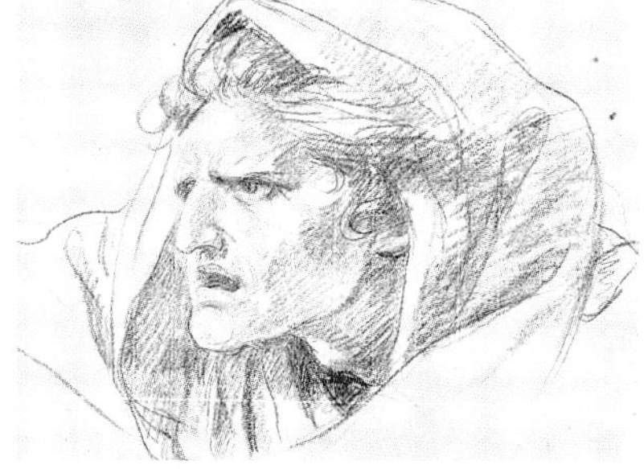

Fig. 192 Greuze, *Study for the Father in "The Torn-up Will," c.* 1775, red chalk on white paper, Cambridge MA, Fogg Art Museum, Gift of Richard Owen

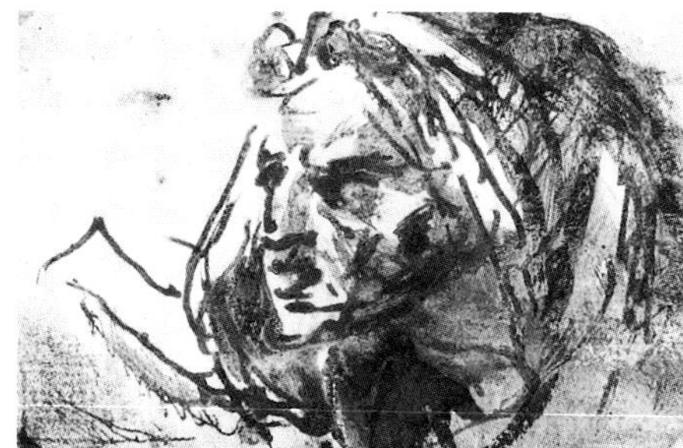

Fig. 193 Greuze, *Study for the Father in "The Torn-up Will," c.* 1775, pen and brush with brown ink on white board, whereabouts unknown

1. "J.B. Greuze 1775/ Stop, wretched man/ The torn-up Will/ Respect the last wishes of your father."

2. In the catalogue of his sale in 1814, Bruun-Neergaard was identified as a member of the court of the king of Denmark *("gentilhomme de la chambre du Roi de Danemark").* In 1801 he published in Paris a pamphlet, *Sur la Situation des Beaux-Arts en France ou Lettres d'un Danois à son ami,* in which he had this to say about Greuze: "*Greuze* is an old man who appeared after *Boucher.* His coloring is not true, and his drawing is not pure. David has so accustomed us to such purity that we expect to encounter it everywhere. However, the compositions of Greuze are simple, and one finds character in them" ("Greuze *est un vieillard qui a paru après* Boucher. *Son coloris n'est pas vrai, et son dessin n'est pas pur. David nous a tellement habitués à cette pureté, que nous prétendons la rencontrer par-tout. Au reste, les compositions de Greuze sont simples, et on y remarque du caractère"*). Bruun-Neergard 1801, p. 67. Nevertheless, his sale included thirteen drawings by Greuze, compared to one by David, twenty-five by Fragonard, and fifteen by Boucher.

3. Arquié-Bruley 1983, pp. 13, fig. 6, 134–35, 138–39.

4. See Arquié-Bruley 1983, pp. 128, 137–38; and H. Macqueron, *Procès d'artistes,* Abbeville 1911, pp. 6–8.

5. *"Un père de famille, possesseur d'une fortune considérable, avait deux enfants, son fils et sa bru. Ce père, parvenu à l'âge où les hommes perdent leurs illusions, et voient l'avenir avec sang-froid, fit son testament, que l'aveugle confiance qu'il avait eu en son fils l'emphêcha de porter chez un notaire. Peu de temps après, ce père tomba malade; l'issue de cette maladie fut une léthargie si profonde, que ses enfants la prirent pour la mort même. Leurs premiers soins furent d'écarter les domestiques et de profiter du milieu de la nuit pour soustraire les dernières volontés de leur père!* Criminelle avarice! *Le fils, un flambeau à la main, le visage pâle et l'oeil sec, accompagné de sa femme, entre sans bruit dans la chambre du respectable vieillard, ouvre le secrétaire, et porte en tremblant sa parricide main sur le dépôt sacré qu'il contenait. Mais, moment terrible! le père revoit la lumière, et observe dans le silence son coupable fils. Malheureux père! quel tribunal! Sous ce voile funèbre, sans le savoir tu vas précipiter ton fils dans le tombeau, où il te croyait déjà descendu. La bru se tenait alors debout derrière le fauteuil de son mari qui, après la lecture du testament, s'écrit, en le déchirant: 'Il n'existe plus!' Le vieillard, les yeux étincelants de colère et de mépris, s'élance aussitôt sur son fils, et lui dit: 'Arrête, malheureux! respecte les dernières volontés de ton père!' Foudroyé par ce reproche, le coupable jeune homme meurt, les débris du testament dans les mains; et sa femme, éperdue, le soutient dans ses bras."* Valori 1860, p. 360.

6. *"exécuté sous l'inspiration de Diderot… [et] aussi mouvementé qu'un dessin de Fragonard."* The influence of Diderot on Greuze at this late date seems unlikely.

7. For the Greuze family wills, see J. Tupinier, "Histoire d'un portrait," *Annales de l'Académie de Mâcon,* XXIX, 1934, pp. 364–66.

8. "L'Avare.—*C'est un dessin terminé pour le tableau qui porte ce nom: figure d'homme nu qui s'élance hors du lit pour défendre son trésor. Le mouvement est d'une grande énergie, et la physionomie d'une expression saisissante. Sanguine."* Caroline Greuze sale, Paris, 25–26 January 1843, lot 50.

9. Monod and Hautecoeur 1922, no. 83.

10. A. Mongan and P.J. Sachs, *Drawings in The Fogg Museum of Art,* Cambridge MA 1940, I, p. 332, no. 625 (inv. no. 1931.244); J.M. Wilson, *The Painting of the Passions in Theory, Practice and Criticism in Later Eighteenth-Century France,* New York 1981, pp. 175–76.

78 *Head of a Sorrowing Man*

Brush with dark brown oil (counterproof), reworked with brush and brown ink on white paper, 216 × 187 mm ($8\frac{1}{2} \times 7\frac{3}{8}$ in.)
Paris, Musée du Louvre, Département des arts graphiques

Provenance: original collection of the Cabinet des Dessins, Musée du Louvre (Saint-Morys collection)
Exhibitions: Le Théâtre et la danse en France au XVIIIe siècle, Paris, Musée du Louvre, Cabinet des Dessins, 1959, no. 66; Hartford *et al.* 1976–77, no. 87
Bibliography: Morel d'Arleux, no. 11400; Reiset 1866–69, II, p. 39, no. 775; Normand 1892, p. 37; Martin and Masson 1906, no. 1686; Guiffrey and Marcel 1911, VI, no. 4549; Hartford *et al.* 1976–77, p. 180; Arquié-Bruley *et al.* 1987, II, p. 497

Of the many drawings relating to the all-important figure of the sorrowing son in *The Father's Curse: The Punished Son* of 1778, this one, though reversed, comes closest in detail and feeling to his appearance in the painting (fig. 195). The hand is here depicted delicately supporting the brow rather than pounding it; that is the only essential difference from the same head in Greuze's drawing of 1765 (no. 49), which Diderot described thus: "The ungrateful son appears overwhelmed; his head falls forward, and he strikes his forehead with his fist."[1] More succinct and less contrived than most of Greuze's *têtes d'expression,* this final, working study still manages to convey a complex mixture of emotions—surprise, regret, guilt, with just a hint of narcissism. The important blurred shadow across the man's chest is repeated strongly in the final painting to emphasize the brilliantly lighted head.

Other related studies include three in the Musée du Louvre,[2] three among the ensemble acquired by Betskoy in 1767—executed therefore nearly a decade before Greuze painted *The Father's Curse: The Punished Son*[3]—and the one perhaps closest to the artist's final realization of the stricken young man in that picture, a drawing that may well have been executed after it (fig. 194).[4]

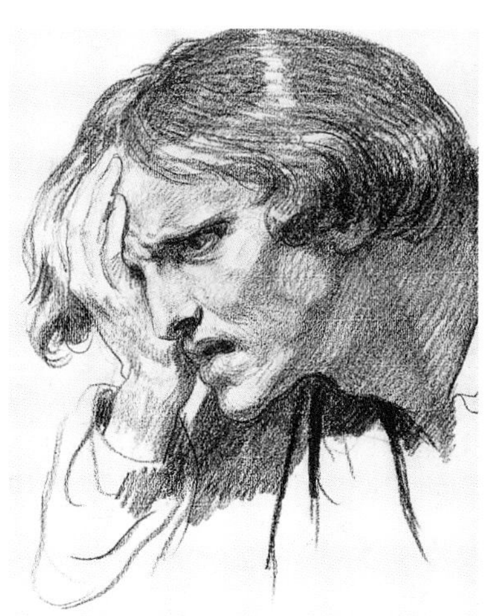

Fig. 194 Greuze, *Study of the Head of a Distraught Young Man,* 1777, red chalk on white paper, whereabouts unknown

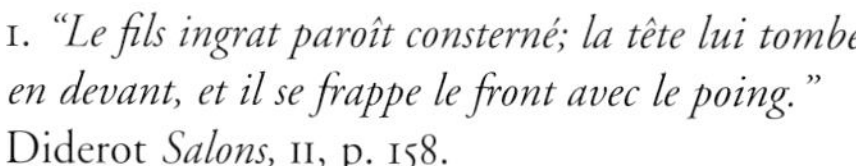

1. *"Le fils ingrat paroît consterné; la tête lui tombe en devant, et il se frappe le front avec le poing."* Diderot *Salons,* II, p. 158.

2. Inv. no. 26956 (Guiffrey and Marcel 1911, no. 4578); inv. no. 26975 (Guiffrey and Marcel 1911, no. 4548); inv. no. 26977 (Guiffrey and Marcel 1911, no. 4579).

3. Monod and Hautecoeur 1922, nos. 87, 89, 90.

4. Sale, London, 5 July 1993, lot 65.

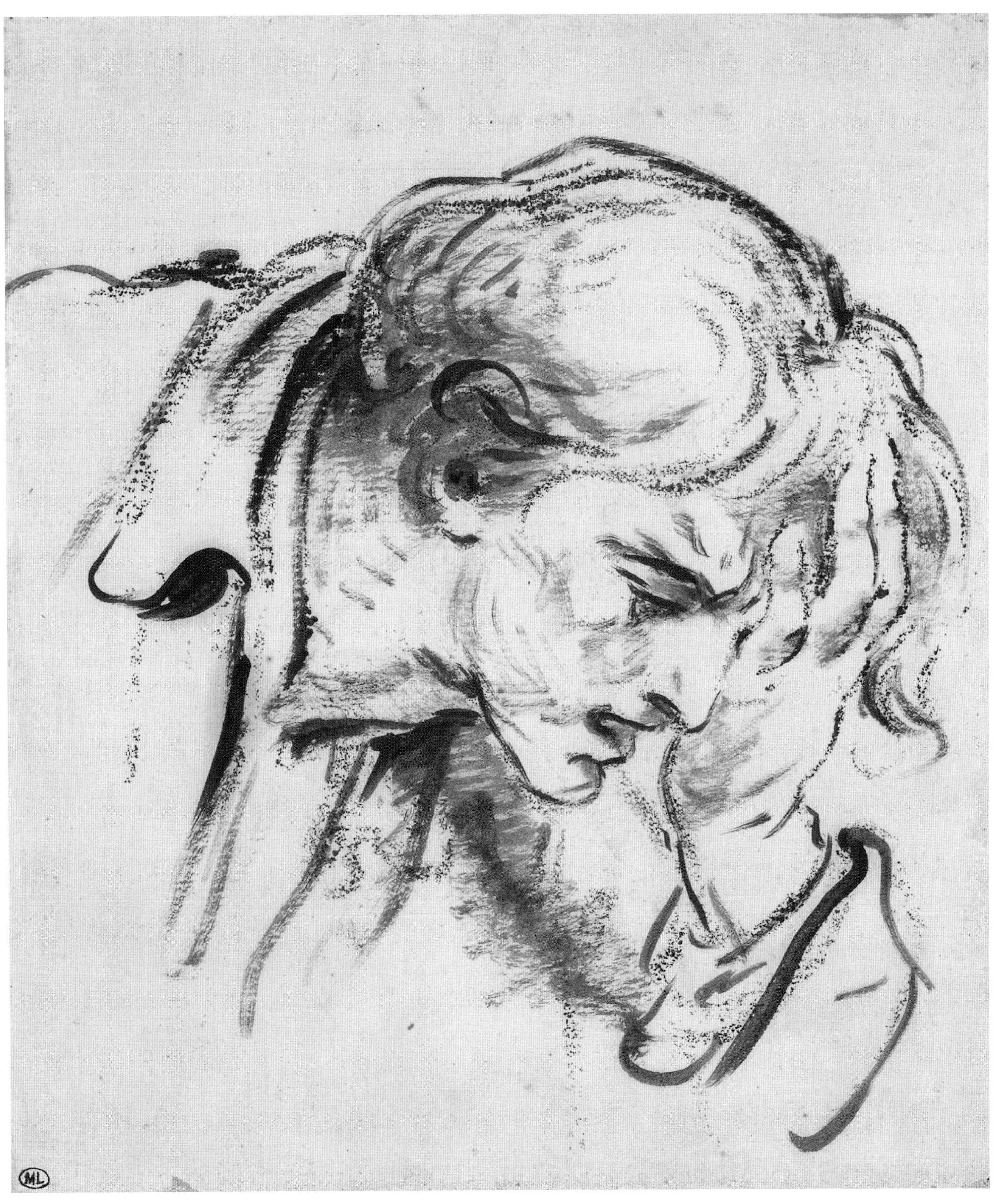

79 *Head of a Woman in Distress, Study for "The Father's Curse: The Punished Son"*

Red chalk on cream paper, 400 × 311 mm (15 ¾ × 12 ¼ in.)
Inscribed in graphite on verso *Aug. L. 28/ z–p/ no. 3/ Greuze/ RNSWC/ Coll. Baron L. A. de Schwiter (1805–1889)/ L.N. 1768 vente a Paris/ 20–21 Avril 1883*
Jeffrey E. Horvitz Collection

Provenance: baron Louis-Auguste de Schwiter, Paris (Lugt 1768); his sale, Paris, 20–21 April 1883, lot 59; Kurt Meissner, Zurich, 1969; Thomas Le Claire, Hamburg, 1989; acquired in 1990
Exhibitions: Old Master Drawings from the Collection of Kurt Meissner, Stanford CA, University Art Museum *et al.*, 1969–70, no. 14; *Ansichten menschlicher Köpfe,* Hamburg, Thomas Le Claire, 1989, no. 13
Bibliography: E. Haverkamp-Begeman, review of *Old Master Drawings from the Collection of Kurt Meissner, Old Master Drawings,* summer 1972, p. 165; Hartford *et al.* 1976–77, pp. 180, 181, fig. 25

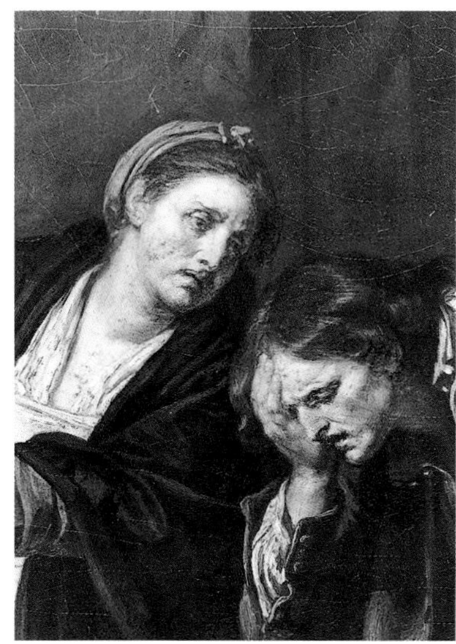

Fig. 195 Greuze, *The Father's Curse: The Punished Son* (detail), 1778, oil on canvas, Paris, Musée du Louvre

At first glance, this drawing seems to be only another of Greuze's *têtes d'expression,* easy to interpret and powerfully affective. But it is in fact the precise model for the head of the mother in *The Father's Curse: The Punished Son* (fig. 195), in which Greuze has depicted that pathetic, heavy-set, middle-aged woman in the climactic moment of her life—witnessing her husband's death, which she then must indicate to her wayward son, whose departure had been its cause. Her brow furrowed with anger and confusion, her mouth hanging open with shock, her eyes somehow conveying an undiminished love for her child—Greuze has transformed this study into a mask of tragedy. But in addition to being a model of facial expression, this drawing is also a careful preparation for the pattern of lighting Greuze would follow in his painting: the varying shadow along the right side of the head, and the strong accents below the jaw and along the left side of the breast.

Though many people viewed *The Father's Curse: The Punished Son* in Greuze's studio in the fall of 1778, few critical comments on it survive. Jean-François La Harpe could have been thinking of the figure of the mother when he observed: "M. Greuze, they say, does not rise up to the level of history painting, but isn't the history of the passions just as worthy as Greek and Roman history?"[1]

A full-length study for this figure in her gown *à l'antique* appeared in the Hippolyte Walferdin sale, Paris, 18 May 1860, lot 85, and another study for her head was sold in Leipzig, 27 June 1899, lot 241.

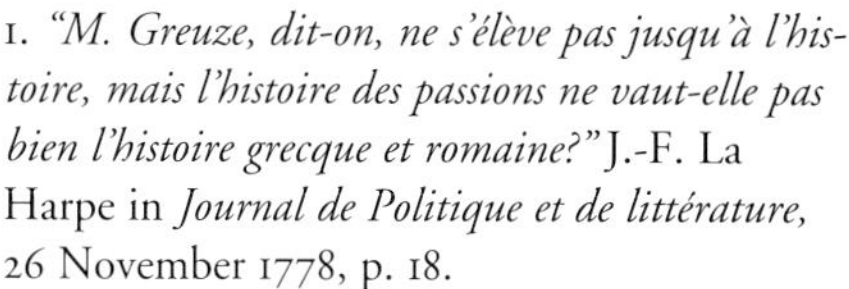

1. *"M. Greuze, dit-on, ne s'élève pas jusqu'à l'histoire, mais l'histoire des passions ne vaut-elle pas bien l'histoire grecque et romaine?"* J.-F. La Harpe in *Journal de Politique et de littérature,* 26 November 1778, p. 18.

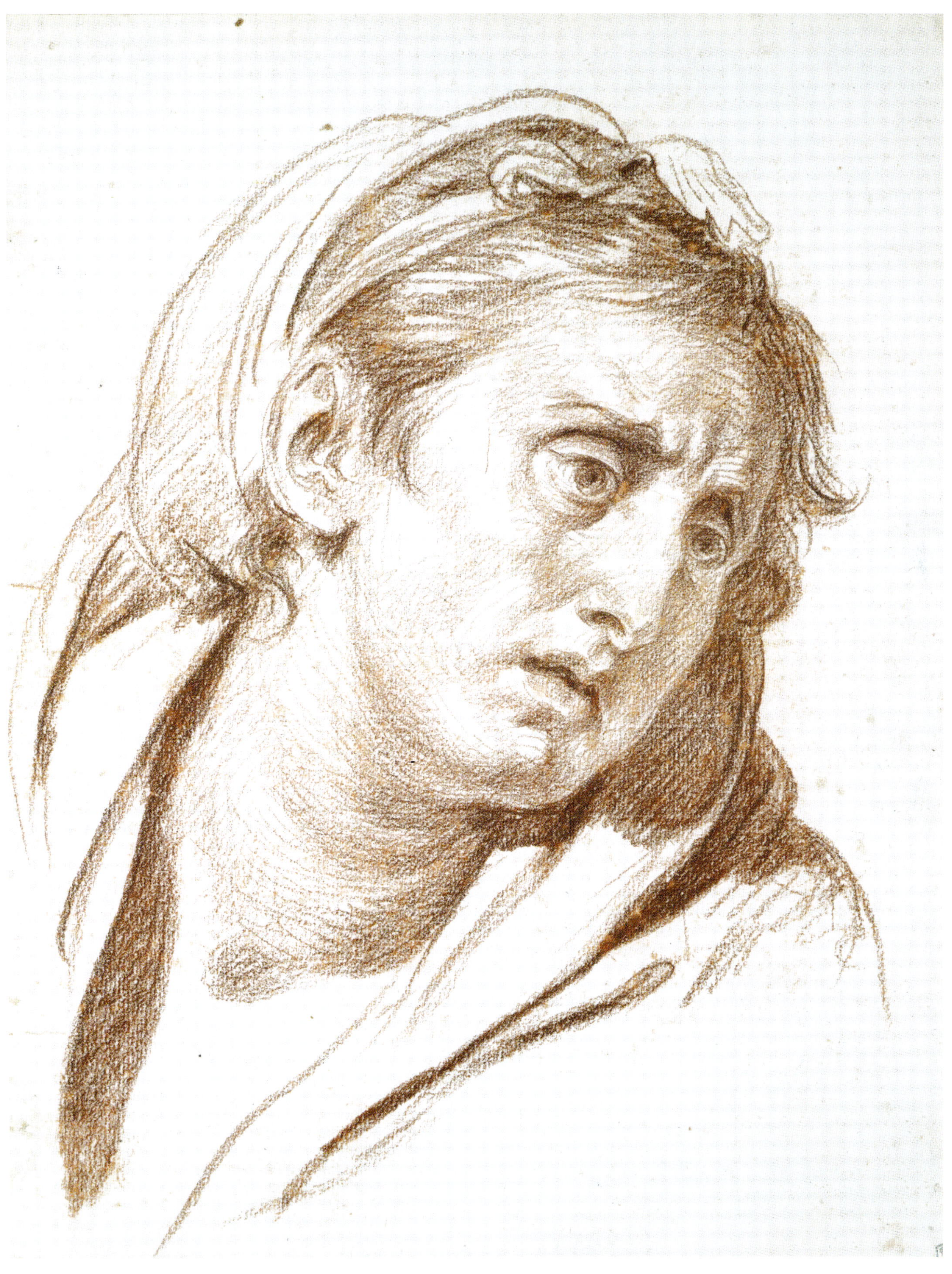

80 *Woman Embracing a Recumbent Old Man, Study for "The Father's Curse: The Punished Son"*

Pen and brush with brown ink on white paper, 120 × 202 mm (4 ¾ × 7 15/16 in.)
Signed in graphite at lower right *Greuze*
Paris, Collection Frits Lugt, Fondation Custodia, Institut Néerlandais

Provenance: Grosjean et Maupin, Paris; acquired in 1959
Exhibition: Hartford *et al.* 1976–77, no. 86
Bibliography: None known

In evolving the composition of his large painting *The Father's Curse: The Punished Son,* Greuze imbued this tiny study of a daughter embracing her expiring father with an emotional force far greater than that of his original version of this subject (no. 49) or even the painting of 1778 (fig. 17). In both of those, the young woman is depicted hovering over the bed rather than being in direct contact with the dying man. As Diderot so aptly phrased it, it is as if Greuze were trying to convey that she "cannot bring herself to believe she no longer has a father." [1]

In a drawing executed probably soon after this one (fig. 196), Greuze separated the two figures, giving greater emphasis to the woman's extended right arm, in a pose curiously anticipatory of that of the woman with the lamp in Picasso's *Guernica* (fig. 197).[2]

1. *"ne sauroit pas se persuader qu'elle n'a plus de père."* Diderot *Salons,* II, p. 157.

2. See Hartford *et al.* 1976–77, p. 180 n. 9.

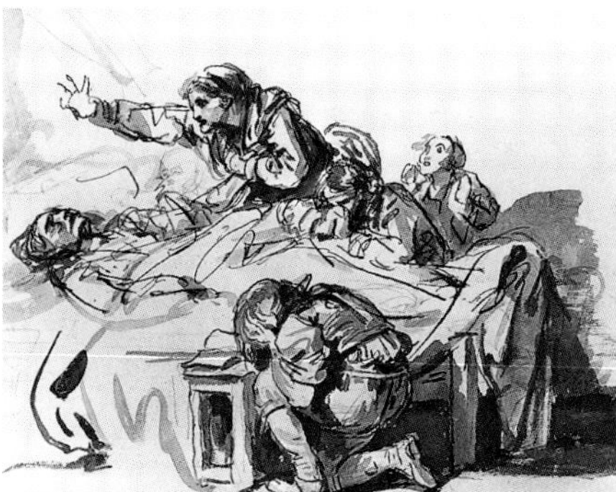

Fig. 196 Greuze, *Study for "The Father's Curse: The Punished Son,"* 1777, pen and brush with gray ink over graphite on white paper, Schmitz-Hille collection

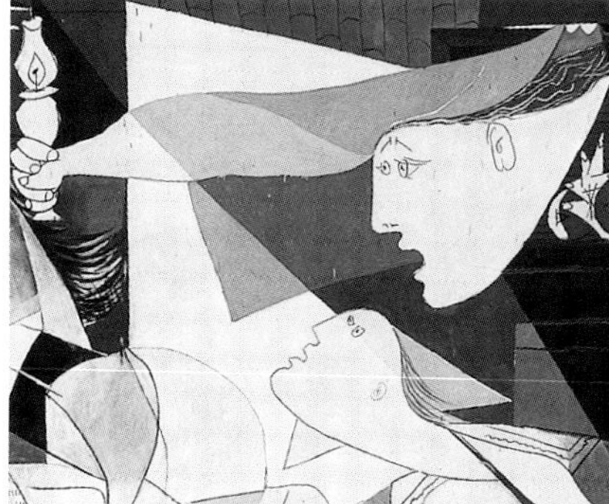

Fig. 197 P. Picasso, *Guernica* (detail), 1936, oil on canvas, Madrid, Reina Sofía Museum

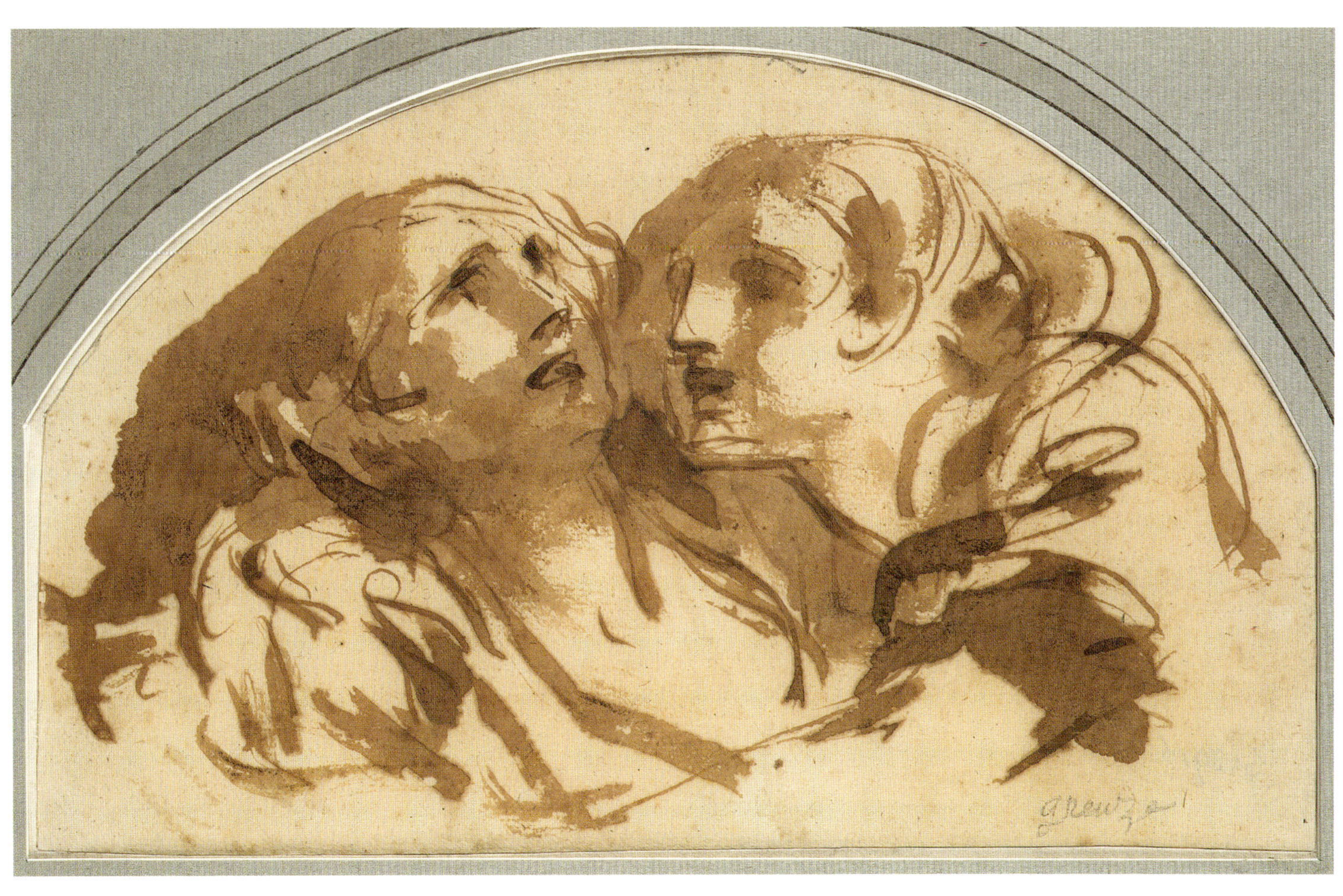

81 *The Father's Curse: The Ungrateful Son*

Brush with black ink, heightened with white, on blue paper, 319 × 432 mm (12 9/16 × 17 in.)
Vienna, Graphische Sammlung Albertina

Provenance: Duke Albert von Sachsen und Teschen, Vienna (Lugt 174)
Exhibition: L'Empire du temps, Paris, Musée du Louvre, 2000, no. 208
Bibliography: Hartford *et al.* 1976–77, pp. 112, 172; Raux 1995, pp. 103, fig. 26a, 104

Executed on the same scale as and with the loose painterly technique characteristic of the final compositional studies Greuze must have had before him as he worked on such canvases as *The Father's Curse: The Ungrateful Son* (fig. 16), this drawing nevertheless displays a few crucial differences from that painting. The most obvious change involves the helmeted recruiting officer at the right, whose pose in the drawing continues the diagonal sweep across the picture, halted only partially by the wide-eyed figure behind him. In the painting, that secondary figure is omitted and the officer has a less virile and more depraved air—complete with a plumed hat, a pencil-thin mustache, and a gesture of indifference (fig. 198). His slouching posture effectively brings everything to a halt. In the present drawing, Greuze has maintained the son's impertinent gesture from the earlier study (no. 48), but changed it in the painting to the open-fingered gesture so evocative of shock. Finally, the storage alcove in the wall at the left in the drawing is replaced by a large *armoire* in the painting.

But more than establishing such crucial details, the artist seemed concerned in this drawing, as in his *Compositional Study for "The Paralytic"* (no. 23), with setting the grand patterns of light that define the drama and create the visual excitement of his final composition—accentuating the lurching thrust of the father's arms, the enveloping draperies of the restraining mother, the monumental and tormented posture of the son.

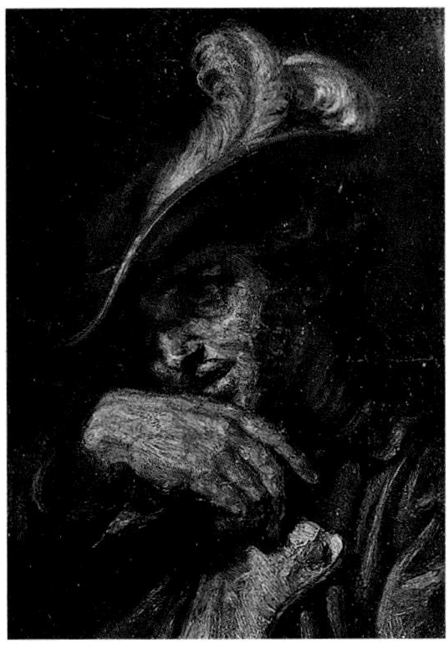

Fig. 198 Greuze, *The Father's Curse: The Ungrateful Son* (detail), 1777, oil on canvas, Paris, Musée du Louvre

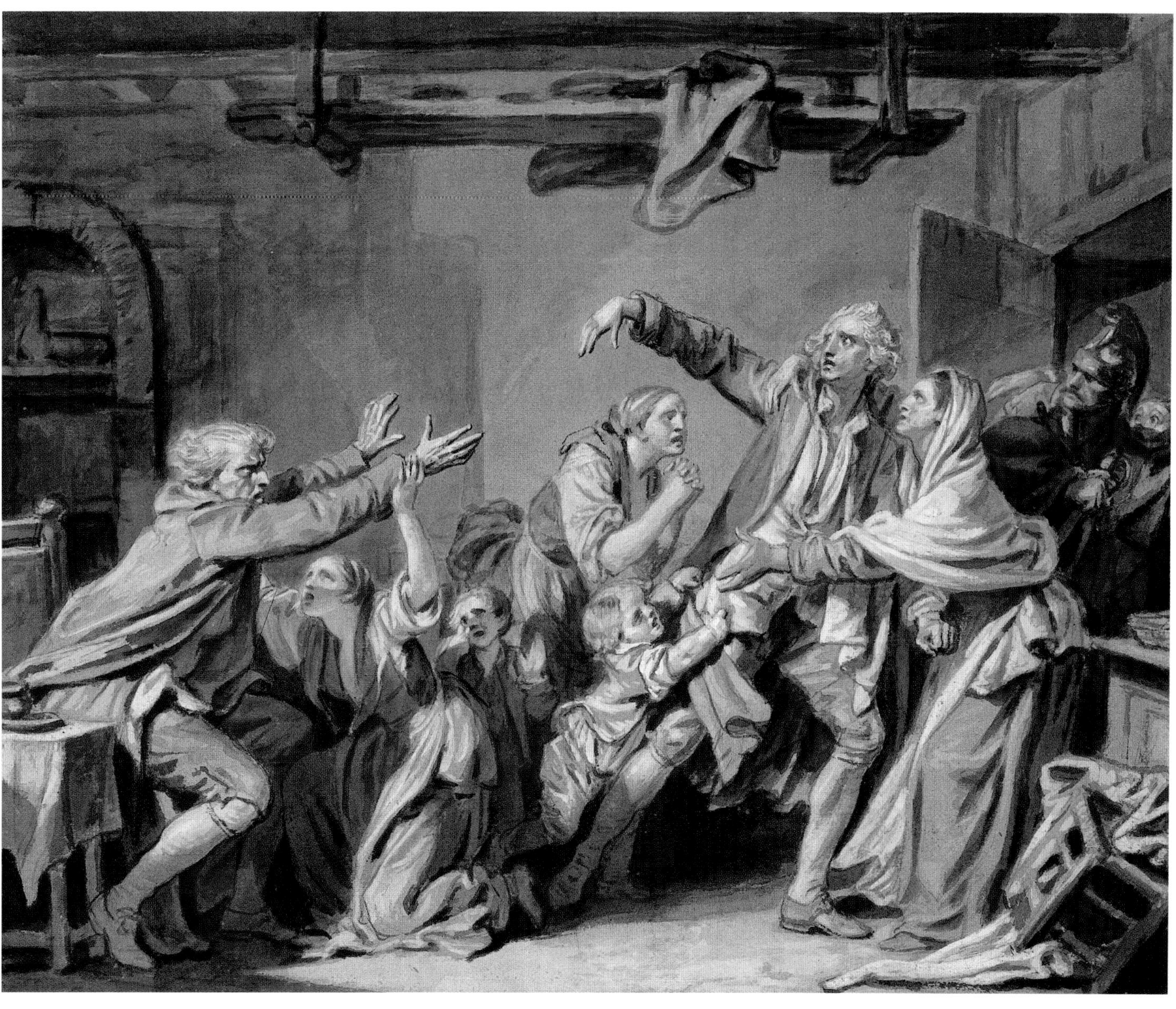

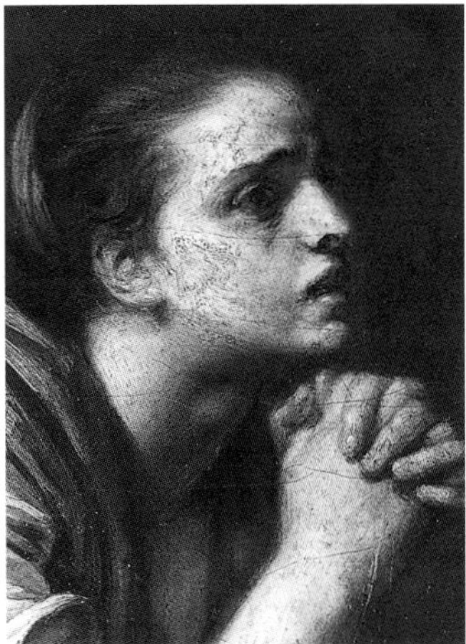

Fig. 199 Greuze, *The Father's Curse: The Ungrateful Son* (detail), 1777, oil on canvas, Paris, Musée du Louvre

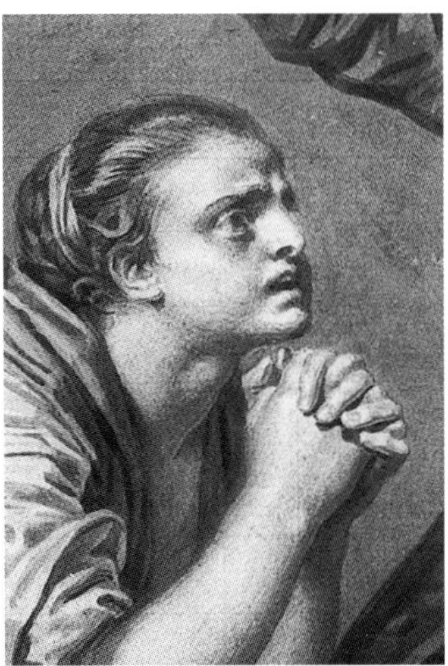

Fig. 200 Greuze, detail of no. 82

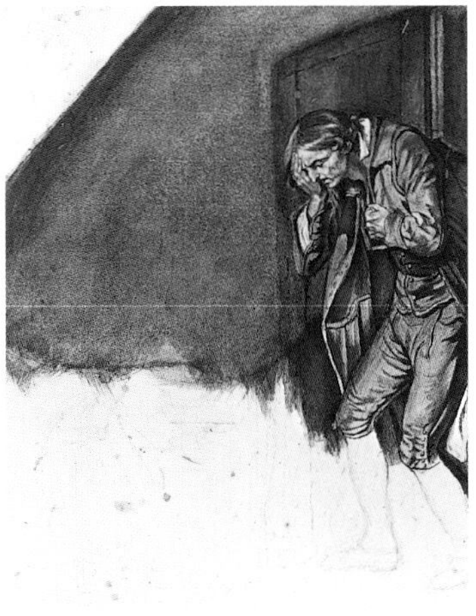

Fig. 201 Greuze, *A Young Man Entering a Room,* 1779, brush and gray ink over black chalk on white paper, whereabouts unknown

82 *The Father's Curse: The Ungrateful Son*

Brush and gray ink on white paper, squared in graphite, 489 × 625 mm (19 ¼ × 24 ⅝ in.)
Signed in brown ink at lower right *J. B. Greuze;* inscribed in black chalk on verso *No. 2726*
Los Angeles, The J. Paul Getty Museum

Provenance: perhaps comte Adolphe-Narcisse Thibaudeau, Paris;[1] baron Salomon de Rothschild (d. 1911), Paris; René Fribourg, New York, 1935; his sale, London, 16 October 1963, no. 548; Harry Spiro, New York; A.C.A. Heritage Gallery, New York; Mr and Mrs Lester Francis Avnet, New York, 1967; Christophe Janet, New York; acquired in 1983
Exhibitions: L'Art français au XVIIIe siècle, Copenhagen, Palais de Charlottenborg, 1935, no. 391; *Old Master Drawings from the Collection of Mr and Mrs Lester Francis Avnet,* West Palm Beach FL, Norton Gallery and School of Art *et al.*, 1969–70, no. 25; *Drawings from The J. Paul Getty Museum,* New York, The Metropolitan Museum of Art, 1993, no. 56; *Drawings from The J. Paul Getty Museum,* London, The Royal Academy of Arts, 1993–94, no. 108
Bibliography: Martin and Masson 1906, no. 167, p. 107; Hartford *et al.* 1976–77, p. 172; "Acquisitions/1983," *The J. Paul Getty Museum Journal,* XII, 1984, p. 272, no. 18; G. Goldner *et al.*, *European Drawings I, Catalogue of the Collections,* Malibu CA 1988, pp. 168–69, no. 74; Raux 1995, p. 104

Like numbers 33 and 70, this drawing was prepared by Greuze as a model for the engraver chosen to execute the reproductive print based on a painting of his, in this case, *The Father's Curse: The Ungrateful Son* of 1777 (fig. 16).[2] Roughly only a third the size of that picture, this sheet nevertheless reproduces it in complete detail. The engraver in question was Robert Gaillard (1719–1790),[3] who signed his contract with the artist on 6 June 1779 in the presence of Greuze's notary Duclos-Dufresnoy. This agreement was dissolved following the death of Gaillard on 11 April 1790, but the print—precisely the size of this drawing—had been completed by then.[4]

Comparison of components of the painting with comparable ones in this drawing (figs. 199, 200) reveals that Greuze, though working on a much reduced scale, added more detail to his copy than existed in the original painting. There, he had been working in a broad, painterly manner which, on a larger scale and at a distance, enabled him to convey the dramatic essence of his subject—mainly through the manipulation of effects of light and shade. With the engraving in mind, he had to accentuate details such as a furrowed brow, a staring eye, and the pressure of clasped fingers against the back of a hand to achieve the same effects. The squaring indicated in graphite on the drawing would have helped him reduce the composition in a balanced way.

Gaillard also produced the engraving after the pendant of this picture—*The Father's Curse: The Punished Son*[5]—but the comparable drawing-model by Greuze has not survived. However, a probable essay toward such a reproductive image exists in a fragmentary study after the figure of the returning son (fig. 201).[6]

1. Martin and Masson cited comte Thibaudeau's name in association with this drawing. However, in his posthumous sales, the only item that might correspond to this sheet was a *Réunion de famille* that appeared in Paris, 13–14 March 1857, lot 75.

2. See Hartford *et al.* 1976–77, no. 84.

3. Portalis and Béraldi 1880–82, II, pt. 1, pp. 222, 224, no. 18.

4. Arquié-Bruley 1983, pp. 129, 134–35.

5. See Hartford *et al.* 1976–77, no. 88.

6. Sale, London, 3 July 1975, lot 177.

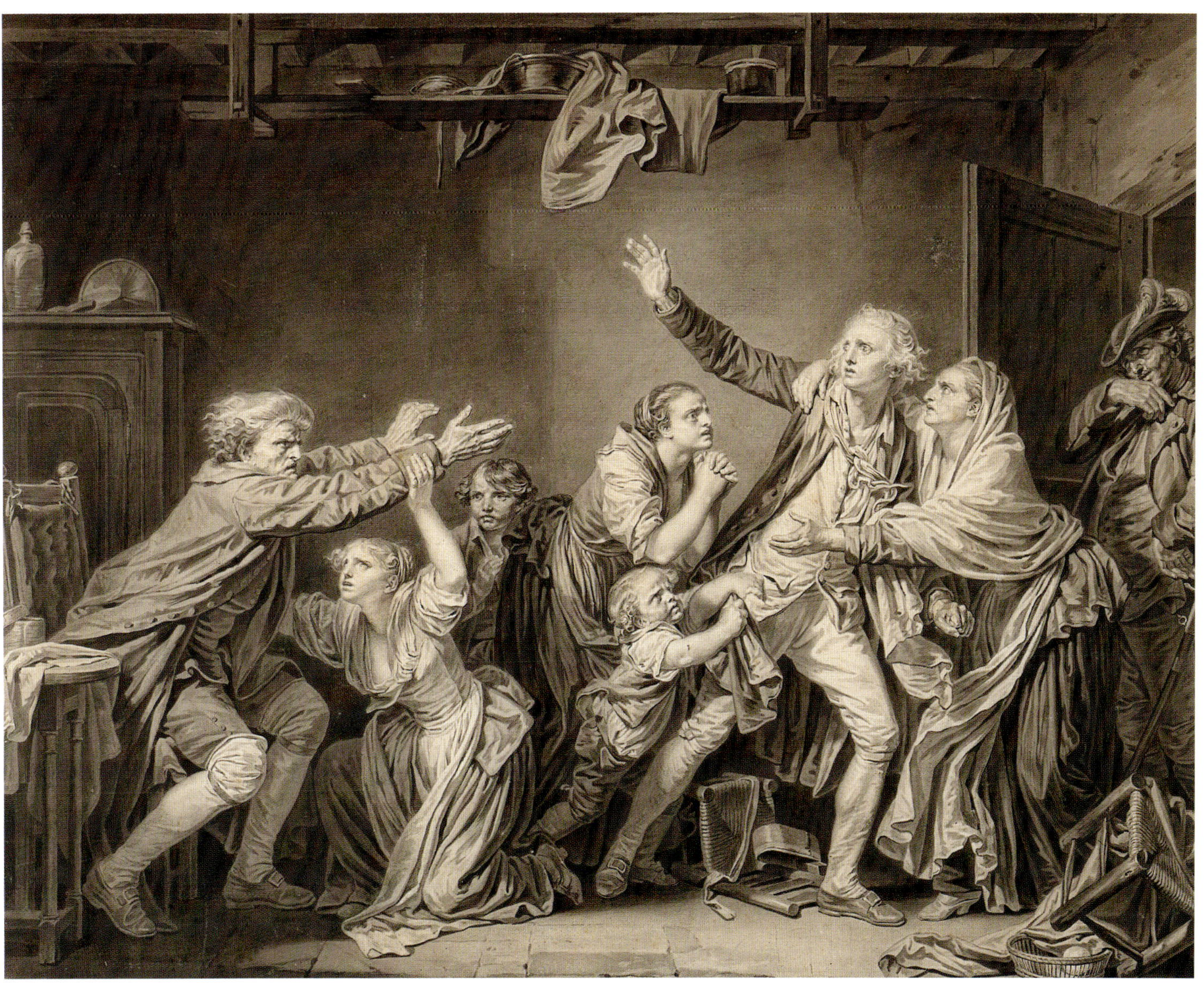

83 *Head of a Woman Facing Left*

Dark red chalk on white paper, 406 × 312 mm (16 × 12 5/16 in.)
Collection of the Art Gallery of Greater Victoria, Gift of baron Rudolf Gutmann

Provenance: perhaps Caroline Greuze (d. 1842), Paris; her sale, Paris, 25–26 January 1843, no. 73;[1] baron Rudolf, Ritter von Gutmann; given by him to the museum in 1958
Exhibitions: European Drawings from Canadian Collections, 1500–1900, Ottawa, National Gallery of Canada, 1976, no. 32; *European Old Master Drawings,* Victoria, Art Gallery of Greater Victoria, 1979, no. 14
Bibliography: Art Gallery of Greater Victoria, *Permanent Collection Catalogue,* Victoria 1964, no. 26

Rather than being a preparatory study for the grieving daughter in *The Father's Curse: The Punished Son* (fig. 17), the present drawing, like number 84 and figure 194, was more likely executed by Greuze after the painting, to serve independently as a *tête d'expression.* Indeed, this powerful image was engraved as such by Claude-François Letellier for his *IIIème Cahier des Têtes d'expression* (fig. 202).

The crucial highlight that Greuze added to the woman's left eye in the painting (fig. 203) was repeated here, by scratching out the red chalk, and again by Letellier in his print. This single point suffices to evoke the subject's horrified state.

1. Described by Théophile Thoré as "Astonishment—*Head of a Woman, Her Head Wrapped in a Kerchief.—Study for one of the pictures in the Louvre*" ("L'Étonnement—*Tête de femme, coiffée d'un mouchoir.—Étude pour un des tableaux du Louvre*").

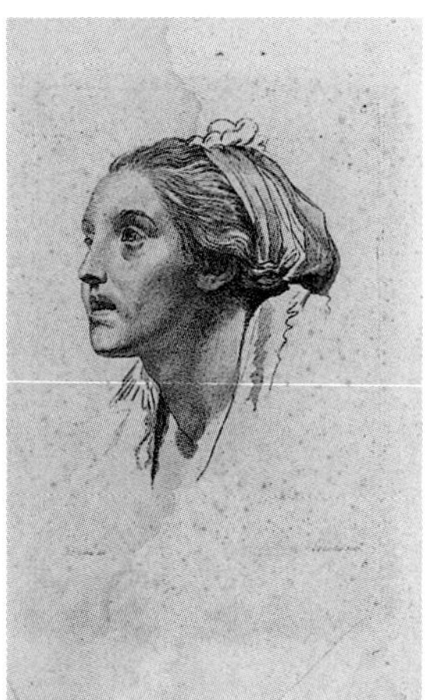

Fig. 202 C.-F. Letellier, *Head of a Woman Facing Left, c.* 1780, engraving, Tournus, Musée Greuze

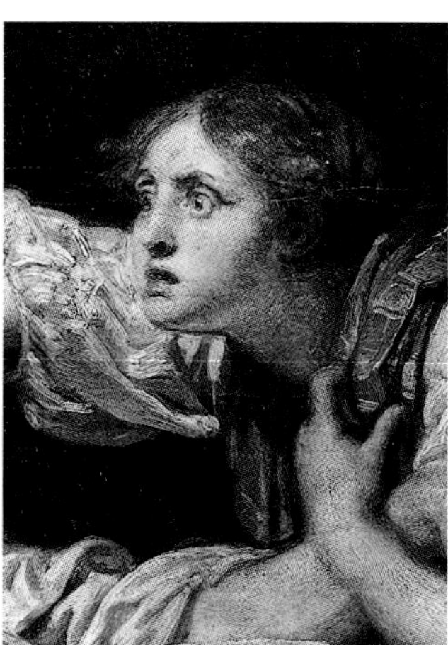

Fig. 203 Greuze, *The Father's Curse: The Punished Son* (detail), 1778, oil on canvas, Paris, Musée du Louvre

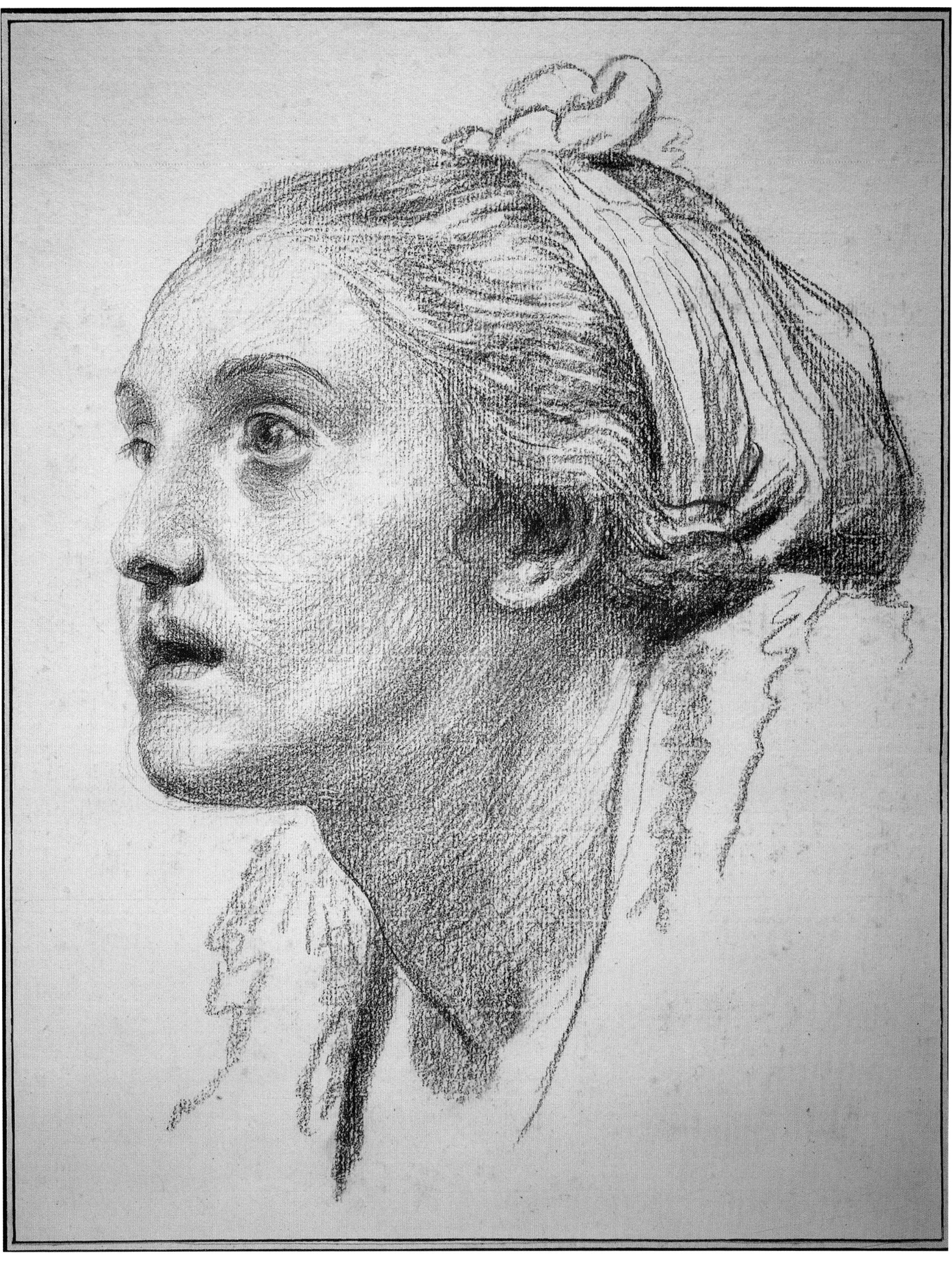

84 *The Ungrateful Son*

Red chalk on white paper, 419 × 324 mm (16½ × 12¾ in.)
Washington D.C., National Gallery of Art, Gift in Memory of Douglas Huntly Gordon and in Honor of the 50th Anniversary of the National Gallery of Art

Provenance: Prince W. Argoutinsky-Dolgoronkoff, Paris (Lugt 2602d); his sale, London, 4 July 1923, lot 41; Tancred Borenius, London; Mrs W.H. Hill, Boston; Mrs Smith, New York; Douglas Gordon, Baltimore, 1942; acquired by the National Gallery of Art in 1991, Gift in Memory of Douglas Huntly Gordon
Exhibitions: French Masters: Rococo to Romanticism, Los Angeles, University of California Art Council, 1961, no. 42; Hartford *et al.* 1976–77, no. 85; *Baltimore Collects: French and Italian Drawings, 1715–1814,* Baltimore Museum of Art, 1984; *Art for the Nation: Gifts in Honor of the 50th Anniversary of the National Gallery of Art,* Washington D.C., National Gallery of Art, 1991 (not in cat.; see "Supplement to *Art for the Nation*")
Bibliography: C.D. Denison in *French Master Drawings from The Pierpont Morgan Library,* exhib. cat., Paris, Musée du Louvre; New York, The Pierpont Morgan Library, 1993–94, pp. 150–51, no. 66

Though clearly related to *The Father's Curse: The Ungrateful Son,* this is not a preparatory study for the head of the departing son as he appears in either the drawing of 1765 (no. 48) or the painting of 1777 (fig. 16). Rather, this is another example—indeed, one of the greatest—of Greuze's *têtes d'expression.* Here, the emotional state depicted is so intense that it registers as physical pain: the complex mixture of shock, sorrow, and guilt that a son would feel as his father places a curse on him. To imagine the experience, hear the words Diderot had supplied for Greuze's pictorial drama in his *Père de famille* of 1758: "Get away from me, ungrateful and unnatural son. I curse you; go far away from me."[1]

This *Ungrateful Son* and a earlier, related one that Betskoy acquired from the artist in 1767 (fig. 204)[2] are evidence of Greuze's adapting Charles Lebrun's studies of expression, in this case, his representation of *douleur corporelle* (physical pain) in his *Conférence sur l'expression générale et particulière* (fig. 205), which in turn was based on the figure of the elder son in the Laocoön group.[3] It is worth noting that the inventory of Greuze's possessions after his death included "plaster casts of two heads of the

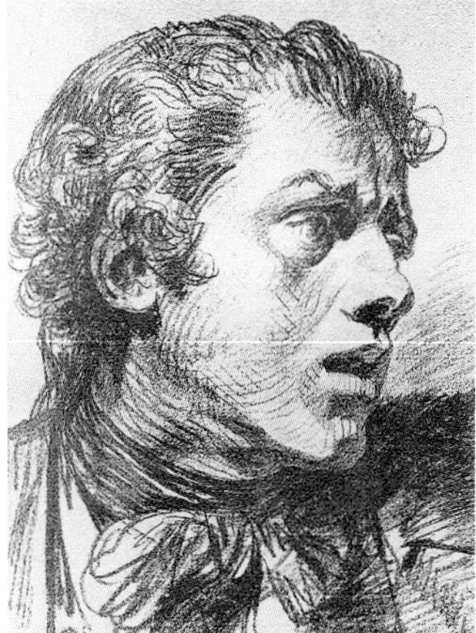

Fig. 204 Greuze, *Head of a Young Man,* *c.* 1767, red chalk on white paper, whereabouts unknown

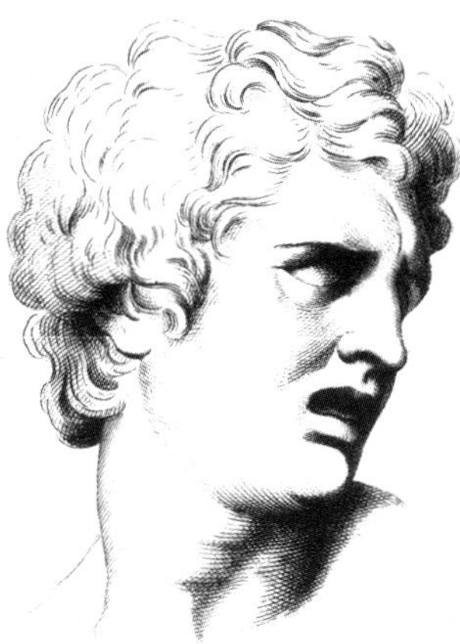

Fig. 205 After Charles Lebrun, *Physical Pain,* 1701, engraving from the *Conférence sur l'expression générale et particulière*

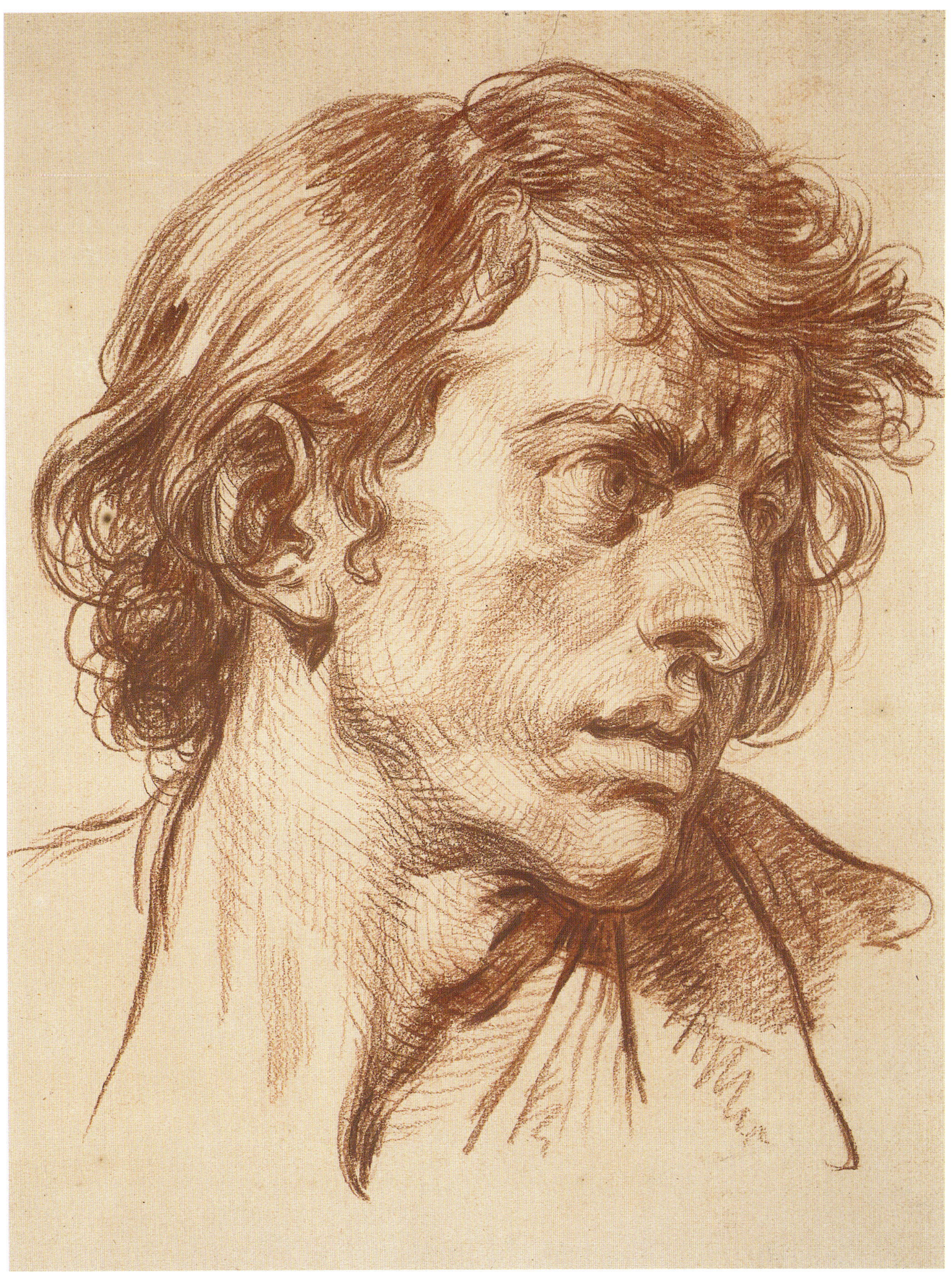

sons of Laocoön."[4] While bringing Lebrun's images up to date, Greuze nevertheless conformed closely to the seventeenth-century artist's description of the physical manifestations of pain:

But if the sorrow is caused by some physical pain, and if that pain is intense, all the movements of the face will appear intense, for the eyebrows, which are raised up, will be even more so than in the preceding passion [sadness], and will be drawn closer to one another, the pupil will be concealed beneath the eyebrow, the nostrils will also be raised in the same way and will form a crease in the cheeks, the mouth will be more open... and drawn back further, and will form a sort of square shape in that area. All parts of the face will appear more or less affected, and more or less agitated according to the violence of the pain.[5]

Only a few years after executing this *Ungrateful Son,* Greuze would be praised for his skill in depicting emotions in a naturalistic way: "Having often drawn from nature, he knows how to indicate by appropriate masses the principal characteristics of the passions peculiar to his subject."[6]

Though never engraved, this sheet was copied at least four times, in versions of varying quality preserved at the Pierpont Morgan Library, New York,[7] in the Musée du Louvre,[8] in the Musée des Beaux-Arts, Lyon,[9] and in a private collection, Paris.[10] A counterproof of yet another copy is in the Musée Greuze, Tournus.[11]

1. *"Éloignez-vous de moi, fils ingrat et dénaturé. Je vous donne ma malédiction; allez loin de moi."* Diderot, *Oeuvres complètes,* ed J. d'Assézat, Paris 1876, VIII, p. 227.

2. Monod and Hautecoeur 1922, no. 78.

3. Haskell and Penny 1981, pp. 243–47.

4. *"deux têtes des enfans de Laocoön... le tout en plâtre."* Arquié-Bruley 1983, p. 148.

5. *"Mais si la tristesse est causée par quelque douleur corporelle, et que cette douleur soit aiguë, tous les mouvemens du visage paroîtront aigus, car les sourcils qui s'élèvent en haut, le seront encore plus que dans la precedente passion, et s'approcheront plus près l'un et l'autre; la prunelle sera cachée sous le sourcil, les narines s'éleveront aussi de ce côté-là, et marqueront un plis aux jouës, la bouche sera plus ouverte que dans la precedente action, et plus retirée en arriere, et fera une espece de figure carrée en cet endroit-là. Toutes les parties du visage paroîtront plus ou moins marquées, et plus agitées selon que la douleur sera violente."* Montagu 1994, p. 121.

6. *"Ayant souvent copié la nature il sait indiquer par de justes masses, les principaux traits de caractère des passions propres à son sujet."* Anonymous, *Lettres d'un voyageur à Paris à son ami Charles Lovers... sur les nouvelles estampes de Mr Greuze,* Paris 1779, p. 5.

7. Denison 1993–94, pp. 150–51, no. 66.

8. Guiffrey and Marcel 1911, no. 4580.

9. Inv. no. 322.

10. Sale, Paris, 22 June 1965, lot 23.

11. Rochette 2000, pp. 94–95, no. 26.

85 *Presentation of a Vestal Virgin*

Brush with black ink wash over graphite on white paper, 420 × 355 mm (16 9/16 × 13 15/16 in.)
Private collection

Provenance: perhaps sale, Paris, 29 April 1863;[1] sale, Paris, 15 March 1973, lot A
Exhibitions: None known
Bibliography: Martin and Masson 1906, no. 36; "Conseils aux acheteurs: Aimez-vous Greuze?" *Connaissance des arts,* June 1973, p. 149; B. de Rochebouët, "L'âge d'or du dessin," *Le Figaro,* 23 March 2001, p. 17; "Dessins: l'envolée des prix," *Le Figaro Patrimoine,* 11 May 2001, p. 34

With this harrowing image of youth and old age, Greuze joined the company of his contemporaries fascinated with the lore of the Vestal Virgins—Jacques Gamelin (1738–1803), Lagrenée, François Lemoine (1688–1737), Jean-Marc Nattier (1685–1766), Jean Raoux (1677–1734), Pierre-Charles Trémolières (1703–1739), Anne Vallayer-Coster (1744–1818), Vien—but his image is imbued with a troubling, dark sexuality that has its closest parallels in Goya and Henry Fuseli (1741–1825).

Relying on correct archaeological precedents, as he had with *Septimius Severus and Caracalla* (fig. 13), Greuze has depicted here a Vestal Virgin in her pristine nudity being unveiled (or veiled) by what appears to be a hag but might be the *Pontifex Maximus.* This high priest supervised the lives and activities of the six Vestal Virgins, including sentencing those guilty of unchastity to living entombment. The sacred fire that the virgins tended, Ovid's *ignis inextinctus,* burns at the right in an elaborate neoclassical *guéridon* that could have been designed by Philippe Caffiéri (1714–1774). Since the Temple of Vesta—near the Forum, at the foot of the Palatine—could be entered solely by the Vestal Virgins and the *Pontifex Maximus,* the appearance of its interior could be only a matter of conjecture. Greuze properly represented it as a round structure, as Ovid described it in the *Fasti:* "That is brought about by its round shape. The form of the temple is similar; there is no projecting angle in it; a dome protects it from the showers of rain.... Long did I foolishly think that there were images of Vesta; afterwards I learned that there are none under her curved dome. An undying fire is hidden in that temple."[2] Greuze rendered the architectural setting here with considerable panache, as he did in a number of other late works.

In 1761 Greuze had exhibited at the Salon a *Portrait of Madame Greuze as a Vestal Virgin,* provoking Diderot's hilarity: "That one, a Vestal Virgin! Greuze, my dear friend, you are pulling our leg." In his description of that lost work, Diderot cited one detail that recurs in the present drawing: "the drapery brought over the head with long

Facing page:
85 *Presentation of a Vestal Virgin*

folds," just as he had two years earlier, in discussing Nattier's *Vestal Virgin:* "a drapery with great folds, brought over the head and exposing part of the brow."[3]

Closer in date and spirit to the present drawing is the enigmatic *Death and the Maiden* (fig. 177). Within a similarly elaborate interior, a young woman strongly resembling this Vestal Virgin is depicted about to meet her untimely and gruesome end, restrained by a hooded figure who is now Death itself.[4] Another frontal female nude enveloped in transparent draperies appears as Modesty in Greuze's *Psyche Crowning Cupid* (see fig. 20), also of about 1790. The ewer and basin in the foreground of that picture are the same as appear in *Death and the Maiden.*

1. Martin and Masson 1906 described this drawing as appearing at that auction, but the only sale on that date listed by Lugt did not include it. See F. Lugt, *Répertoire des Catalogues de ventes publiques,* The Hague, 1964, III, no. 27307.

2. Ovid, *Fasti,* trans. Sir James George Frazer, Cambridge MA and London 1951, p. 341.

3. *"Cela, une vestale! Greuze, mon cher, vous vous moquez de nous.... cette draperie ramenée à grands plis sur la tête."* Diderot *Salons,* I, p. 134. *"Une draperie à grands plis, ramenée sur la tête et dérobant une partie du front."* Diderot *Salons,* I, p. 65.

4. *La Jeune Fille et la mort,* brush with brown and gray ink wash over black chalk on white paper, 495 x 631 mm (19 9/16 × 24 13/16 in.), Rouen, Musée des Beaux-Arts (inv. no. 975.4.1307). See J. Vilain in *La Donation Suzanne et Henri Baderou au musée de Rouen, Peintures et dessins de l'École Française,* Paris 1980, pp. 113–14, fig. 7; F. Bergot, *Le Musée des Beaux-Arts de Rouen,* Rouen 1989, pp. 63, 67; *The Loves of the Gods: Mythological Painting from Watteau to David,* exhib. cat., Paris *et al.,* 1991–92, pp. 525–27, fig. 6.

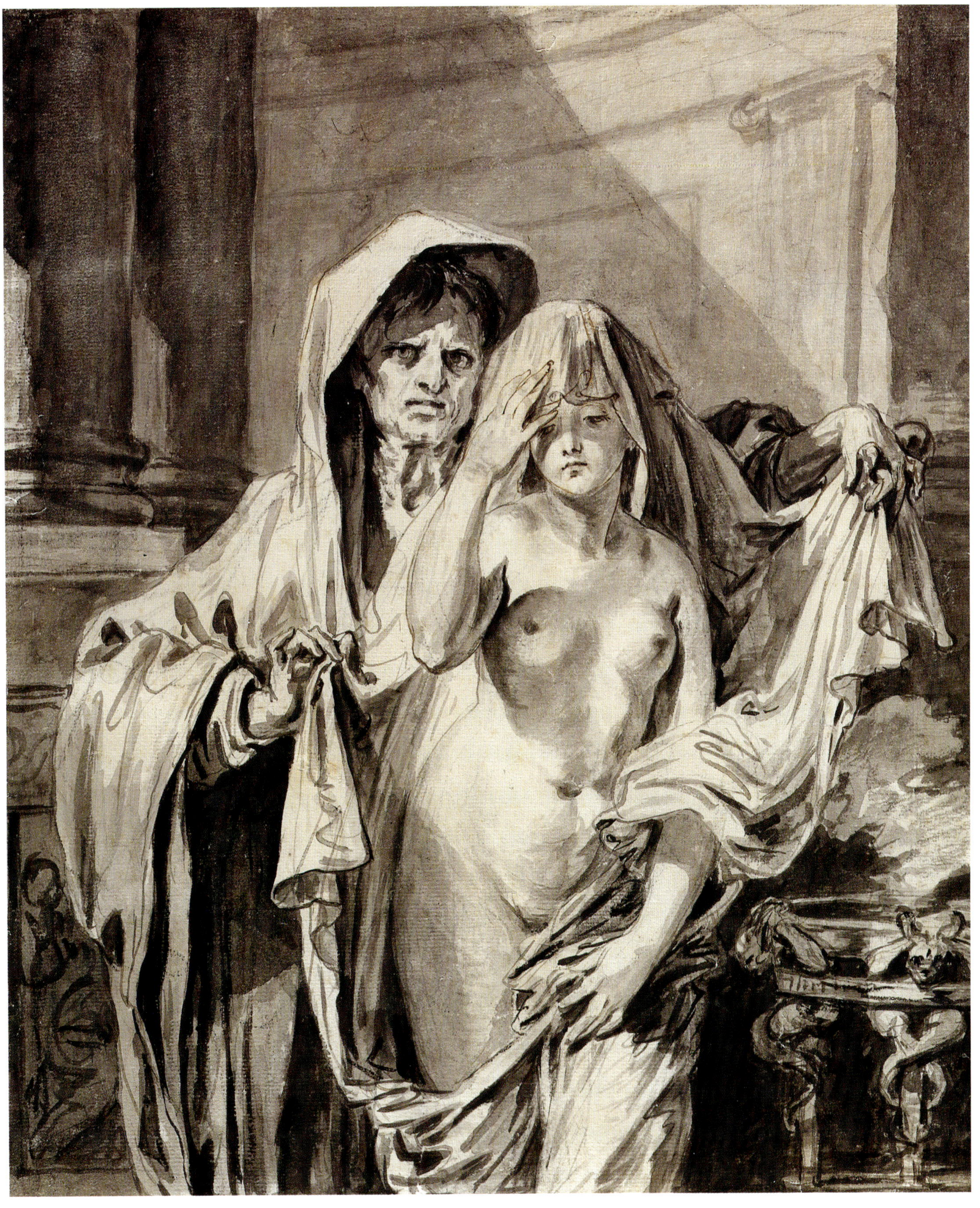

86 *Study of an Arm*

Red and black chalks, stumped, on buff paper, 425 × 283 mm ($16\frac{13}{16} \times 11\frac{1}{8}$ in.)
Signed in graphite on verso at lower left *Greuze*
Notre Dame IN, The Snite Museum of Art, University of Notre Dame
Gift of an Anonymous Benefactor

Provenance: probably Frédéric Villot sale, Paris, 16–18 May 1859, lot 130; Mr and Mrs Robert Meltzer, New York; Benjamin Sonnenberg, New York; his sale, New York, 5–9 June 1979, lot 49; Paul Weis, New York; private collection, USA; acquired by the museum in 1983
Exhibitions: None known
Bibliography: Martin and Masson 1906, no. 1428; *Selected Works from The Snite Museum of Art, University of Notre Dame,* Notre Dame 1987, p. 120

In addition to his numerous *académies* (see nos. 2, 3), Greuze drew many studies of body parts—feet, hands, arms, legs, skulls—but none so expressive as this study of the right arm of *The Milkmaid* (fig. 206).[1]

Since that work postdated Greuze's dissociation from the Académie, and since it was acquired apparently immediately by a resident of Montpellier—a Monsieur Daché, *conseiller d'honneur à la cour des aides de Montpellier*—it provoked no critical comment in Paris.

Its date of execution can be surmised from the fact that the engraving executed after the painting by Jean-Charles Le Vasseur, the engraver of *The Stepmother* (see no. 36) and *The Torn-up Will* (no. 77), was exhibited at the Salon of 1783.[2] Allowing Le Vasseur the time to produce such a large print, *The Milkmaid* must have been completed about 1781–82, and this preliminary study, shortly before.

With *The Broken Pitcher* (fig. 207), of which Jean Massard's engraving was also exhibited at the Salon of 1783, *The Milkmaid* is the last in a long series of images of young women in which Greuze cunningly mingled strains of innocence and sexuality, evoking as no other artist had the first stirrings of passion. Even this arm, excitingly bare, well-muscled, and elegant in proportion, contributes to that provocative allure, just like the slight swell of the breast emerging from the young woman's bodice in the

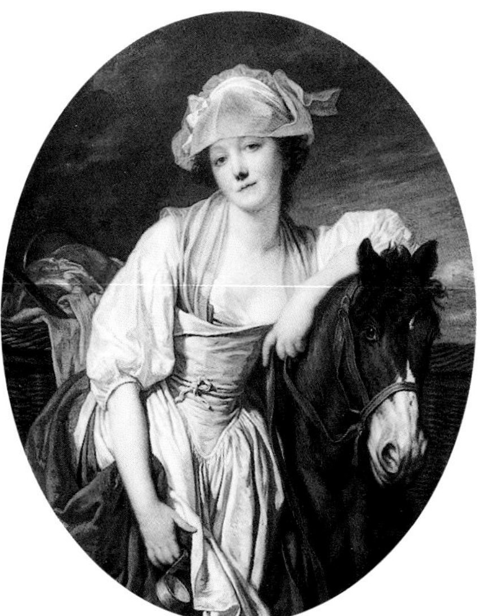

Fig. 206 Greuze, *The Milkmaid,* 1781–82, oil on canvas, Paris, Musée du Louvre

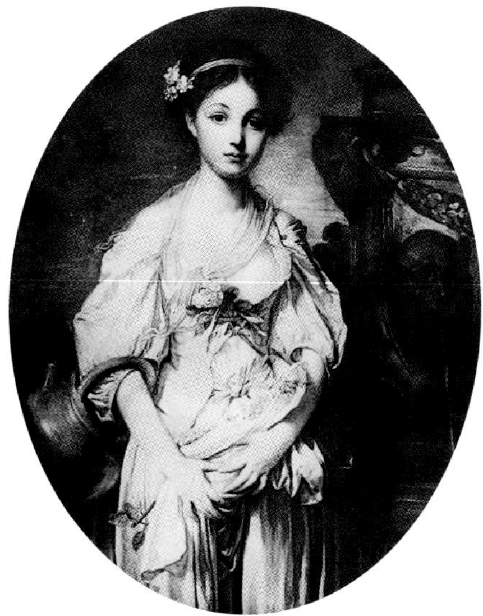

Fig. 207 Greuze, *The Broken Pitcher,* 1781–82, oil on canvas, Paris, Musée du Louvre

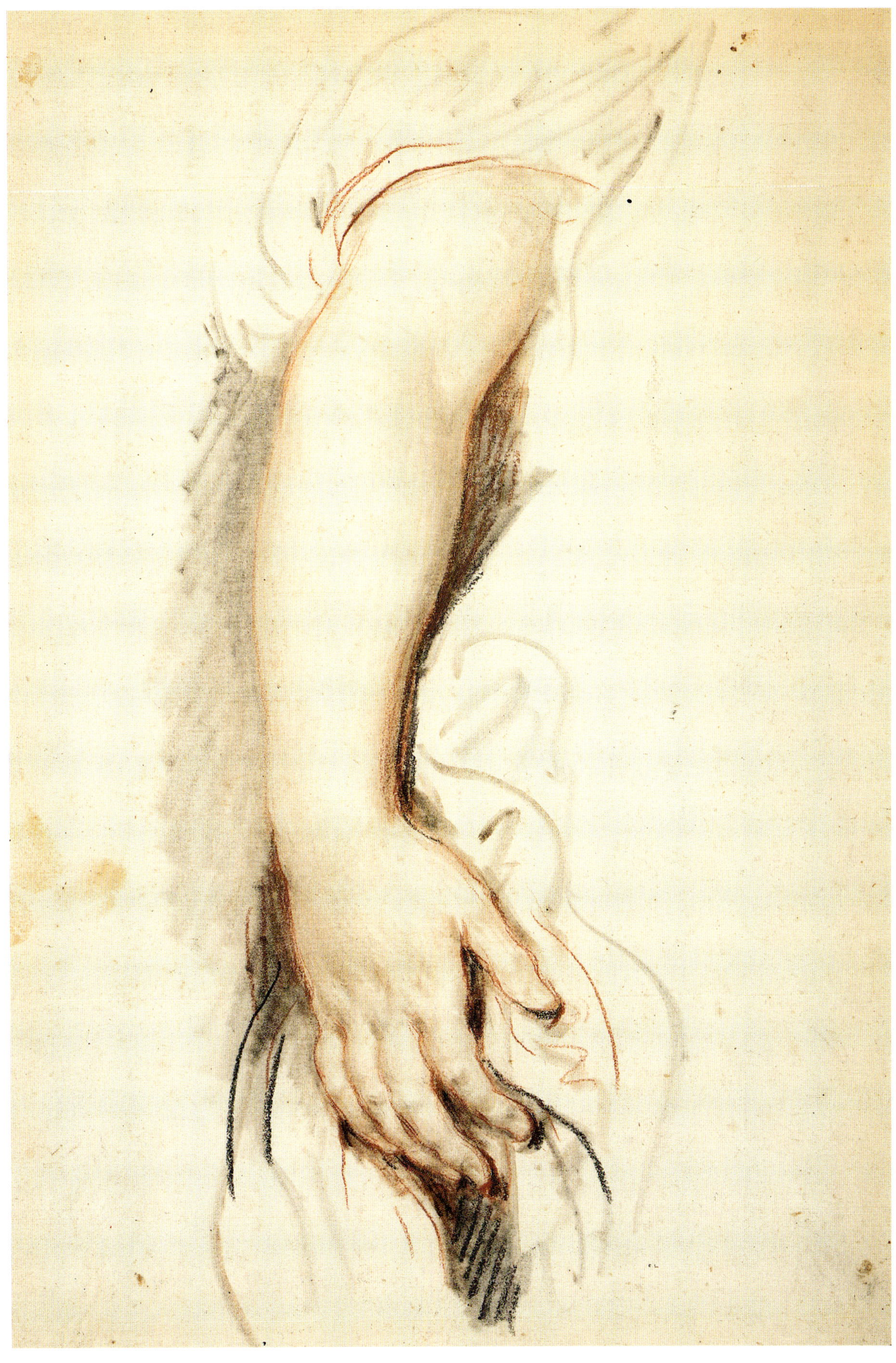

final painting. While, in the drawing, the fingers nestle amid some folds of drapery, in the painting they lightly hold the handle of the milkmaid's measuring cup.

If the art critics were silent about *The Milkmaid,* Louis-Sébastien Mercier, that tireless chronicler of daily life in Paris in the late eighteenth century, was not. Under the heading *Laitières* ("Milkmaids") in his *Tableau de Paris,* he had this to say:

These milkmaids with their red petticoats, swarthy and for the most part wrinkled faces, do not resemble those that Greuze had drawn. The creations of this painter are just as deceiving as the idylls of the poets, who copy Theocritus and Gessner, over there by the cabbages and carrots of the faubourg St-Marceau. We try in our rapid sketches to bring ourselves in touch with the truth, in depriving ours of those artificial improvements that disfigure the image of reality. Greuze has created fantastical portraits; but these voluptuous and seductive figures that he has taken pleasure in representing are not those who come to sell us milk, butter, and fruit.[3]

1. See Rosenberg, Reynaud, and Compin 1974, p. 274, no. 32; Compin and Roquebert 1986, p. 289.

2. Portalis and Béraldi 1880–82, II, pt. 2, p. 691; É. Dacier, *La Gravure de genres et de moeurs,* Paris 1925, pp. 29, 112–13, pl. LII.

3. *"Ces laitières en cotte rouge, basannées, et le plus souvent ridées, ne ressemblent pas à celles que Greuze a dessinées. Les tableaux de ce Peintre sont tout aussi menteurs que les idylles des Poëtes, qui copient Théocrite et Gessner, près des choux et carottes du fauxbourg Saint-Marceau. Nous tâchons dans nos esquisses rapides de nous rapprocher de la vérité, en les privant de ces embellissements factices qui défigurent le trait réel. Greuze a fait des portraits de fantaisie; mais ces figures voluptueuses et séduisantes qu'il s'est plu à représenter, ne sont pas celles qui viennent nous vendre du lait, du beurre et des fruits."* L.-S. Mercier, *Tableau de Paris,* Paris 1781, VII, p. 161.

87 *Anacreon in His Old Age Crowned by Love*

Pen with black and brown ink, brush with gray ink wash, heightened with white tempera, over graphite on brown paper, 314 × 407 mm (12 3/8 × 16 1/16 in.)
Signed in brown ink at lower right *Greuze;* original mount inscribed by Greuze in black ink: *Anacreon couronne par l'amour... dans sa vieillesse. Greuze*[1]
New York, The Pierpont Morgan Library, Bequest of Mrs Therese Kuhn Straus in Memory of Her Husband, Mr Herbert N. Straus

Provenance: perhaps Gil de Meestre; his sale, Paris, 1 April 1862;[2] Jacques Seligman and Co., New York, 1959; Mrs Herbert N. Straus, New York, 1976; bequeathed by Mrs Straus to The Pierpont Morgan Library in 1977
Exhibition: Hartford *et al.* 1976–77, no. 101
Bibliography: Martin and Masson 1906, no. 77; M. Levey, "Jean-Baptiste Greuze/1725–1805," review, *Master Drawings,* autumn 1977, p. 281; Paris 1984, p. 242; Roland Michel 1987, pp. 219, fig. 263, 220

This image of Love alighting on the bare knee of the startled Greek poet Anacreon and crowning him with a wreath of roses relates to that poet's Ode IV, in which the old man pleads with Love to grant him some pleasures before it is too late: "Instead, perfume me while I am still alive, place crowns of roses upon my head; have my mistress appear, and know, Love, that before I go off to the dance of death, I want to amuse myself here."[3]

As was the case with many of Greuze's historical or literary subjects, the present drawing has its autobiographical overtones. Not only did the artist, like Anacreon, have a lifelong affectionate regard for children, whom he drew over and over with unusual sympathy, but his own gallantry toward women led him to be compared specifically with the Greek poet of the sixth century BC. In one of the earliest articles published about Greuze after his death, Charles-Louis François Lecarpentier noted: "He had the delicacy of Anacreon, and like that agreeable poet of antiquity, he lightly stroked the roses of pleasure until the most advanced age."[4] Anacreon's poetry was much imitated among Greuze's contemporaries, including Pierre-Jean Béranger, Antoine Bertin, Claude-Joseph Dorat, Evariste-Désiré de Forge de Parny, and Voltaire (1694–1778).

The statuette represented on Anacreon's writing table is a reduction of the Venus de' Medici (Florence, Galleria degli Uffizi),[5] first sketched in roughly with the arms in their proper position and then rendered more completely with the placement of the arms reversed. Like many another eighteenth-century artist, Greuze was enamored of this Greek sculpture, which he had surely seen in Florence during his visit there in November 1755. A bronze-colored plaster replica of its torso appeared in the inventory of Greuze's possessions made after his divorce, and it figured again among his possessions inventoried after his death: "a torso of the Venus [Medici]... in plaster."[6] In 1763 Greuze had introduced another reduction of the Venus de' Medici into his *Portrait*

Facing page:
87 *Anacreon in His Old Age Crowned by Love*

of Claude-Henri Watelet (fig. 208), in which that *amateur* was represented studying the statuette just as Anacreon might have been doing prior to the unexpected arrival of Love in the present composition.[7]

A complete compositional study, reversed, for *Anacreon in His Old Age Crowned by Love,* along with a study of Love with his arm raised, suggests the importance Greuze attached to the subject (fig. 209). For the features of Anacreon himself, for instance, Greuze utilized a drawing he had made of a bust of Homer (fig. 210), probably from a cast in the royal collection after the original in the Capitoline Museum, Rome.[8]

1. "Anacreon crowned by Love... in his old age. Greuze."

2. Information given by Martin and Masson 1906, but no such sale is listed in Lugt *(Catalogues de ventes).* The present drawing does bear a mark (a large G in a vertical rectangle, with a line across the G), also not listed in Lugt *(Marques de collections),* which could be that of Gil de Meestre.

3. *"Parfume-moi plûtôt pendant que je suis en vie, mets des couronnes de roses sur ma tête; fai venir ma maîtresse, et sçache, Amour, qu'avant que d'aller aux danses des morts, je veux me divertir ici."* Anacreon, *Les Poésies d'Anacréon et de Sapho traduites en françois par Madame Dacier,* Amsterdam 1716. For the history of the theme of Anacreon and Love, see G.M. Ackerman, "Three Drawings by Gérôme in the Yale Collection," *Yale University Art Gallery Bulletin,* fall 1976, pp. 14–17. The author is grateful to Julianna Bark for her help in preparing this entry.

4. *"Il eut la délicatesse d'Anacréon, et comme cet agréable poëte de l'antiquité, il effleura les roses du plaisir jusque dans l'âge le plus avancé."* C.-L. F. Lecarpentier, *Notice sur Greuze lu dans la séance de la Société libre d'Émulation de Rouen,* [Rouen] 1805, pp. 6–7.

5. See Haskell and Penny 1981, pp. 325–28.

6. *"Un buste de Vénus Medicis, en plâtre bronzé"; "un torse de la Vénus... en plâtre."* Arquié-Bruley 1983, pp. 143, 148.

7. See *Nouvelles Acquisitions du Département des Peintures (1980–82),* exhib. cat., Paris, Musée du Louvre, 1983, pp. 6, 10, 50–52; Paris 1984, no. 64.

8. See S. Bocconi, *Collezioni Capitoline,* Rome 1950, pl. 30. The drawing reproduced here as fig. 209 was sold at Monaco, 5 December 1992, lot 104.

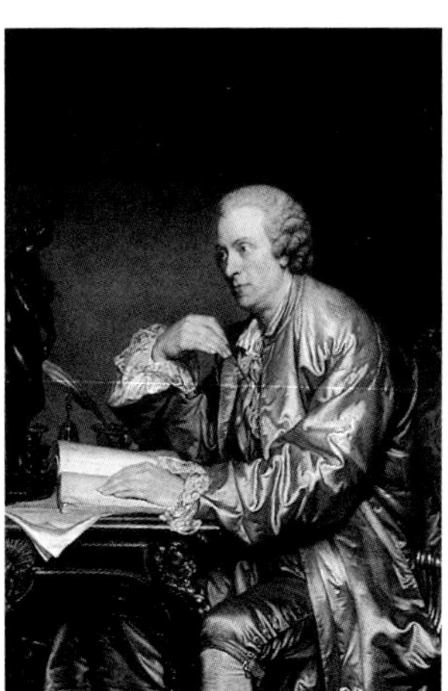

Fig. 208 Greuze, *Portrait of Claude-Henri Watelet,* 1763, oil on canvas, Paris, Musée du Louvre

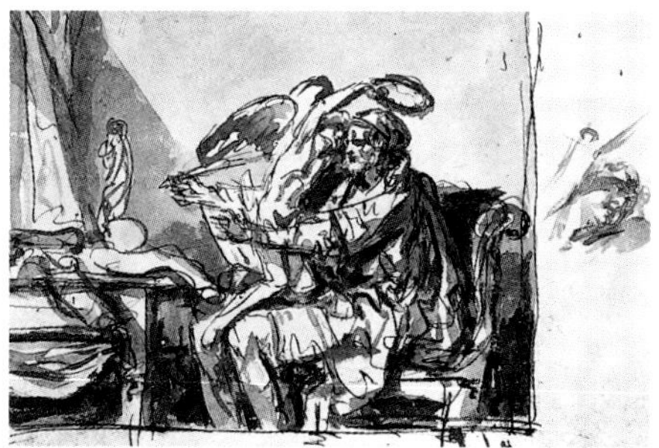

Fig. 209 Greuze, *Study for "Anacreon in His Old Age Crowned by Love," c.* 1788, pen and brush with brown and gray ink wash, Paris, private collection

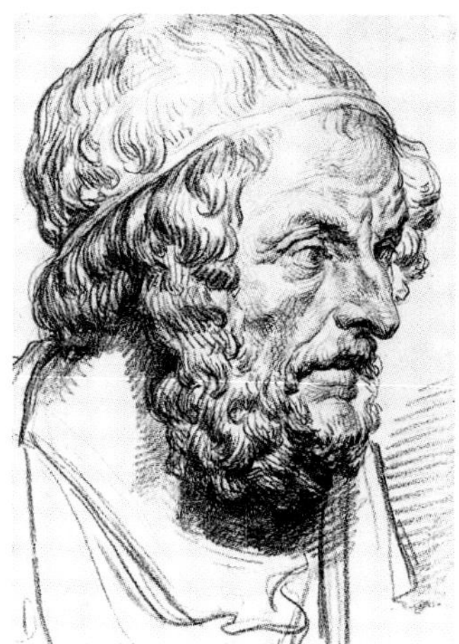

Fig. 210 Greuze, *A Bust of Homer, c.* 1768, red chalk on white paper, whereabouts unknown

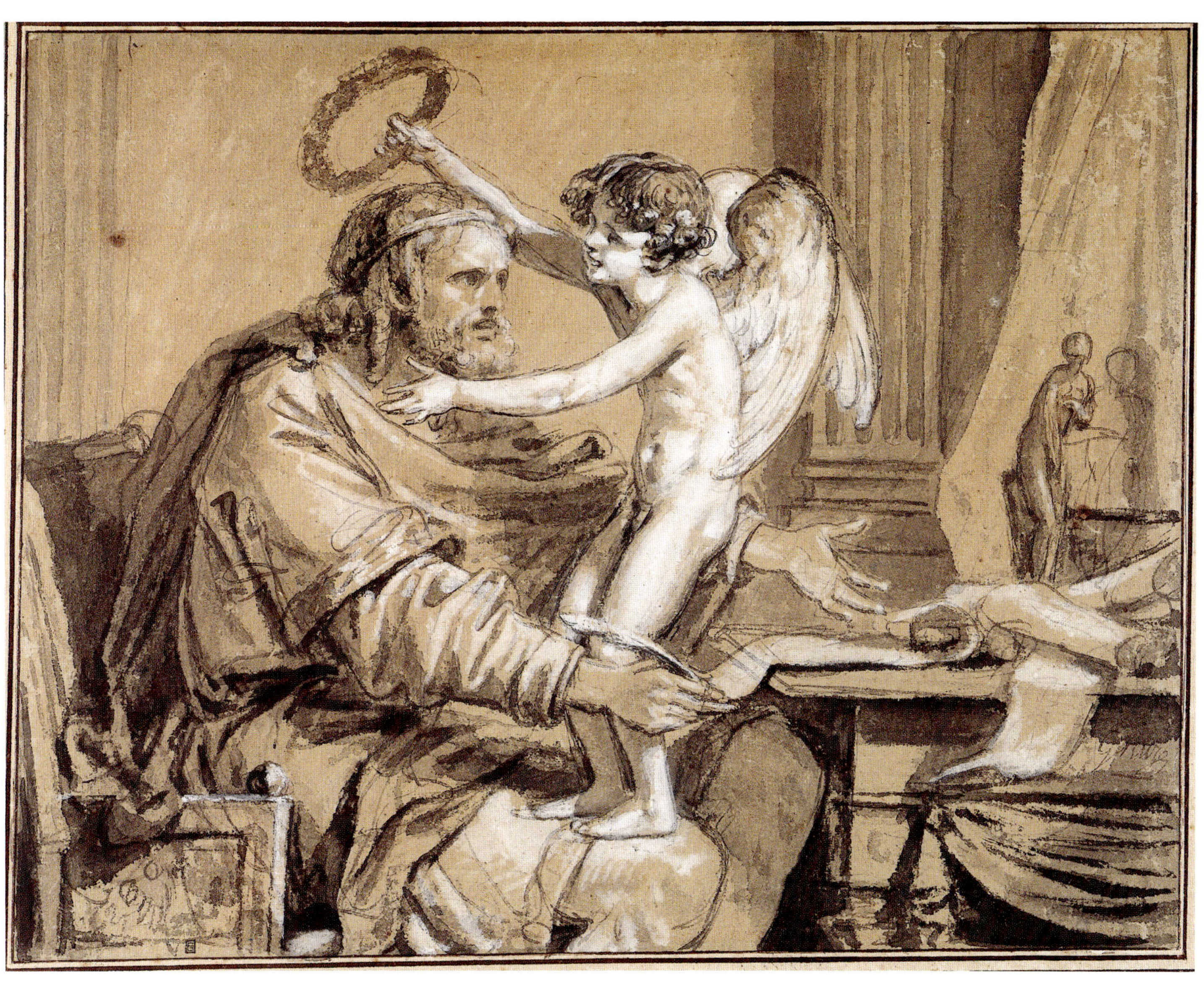

88 *Domestic Scene*

Pen and brown ink, brush with gray and brown ink wash over black chalk on white paper, 330 × 508 mm (13 × 20 in.)
New York, The Metropolitan Museum of Art, Harry Brisbane Dick Fund

Provenance: Caroline Greuze (d. 1842), Paris; her sale, Paris, 25–26 January 1843, lot 21; Mailand, Paris; his sale, Paris, 4–19 April 1881, lot 72; Franc-Lamy, Paris; his sale, Paris, 25–26 November 1912, lot 102; Jacques Petithory, Paris (his mark [JPH in a triangle] not in Lugt); purchased from him by the museum in 1972
Exhibitions: European Drawings Recently Acquired, 1972–1975, New York, The Metropolitan Museum of Art, 1976, no. 47; *Jean-Baptiste Greuze,* New York, The Metropolitan Museum of Art, 1990
Bibliography: Martin and Masson 1906, no. 312;[1] *The Metropolitan Museum of Art Annual Report,* 1972–73, p. 34; The Metropolitan Museum of Art, *Notable Acquisitions, 1965–1975,* New York 1975, p. 63; Hartford *et al.* 1976–77, p. 164; Bean and Tuŕcic 1986, p. 120, no. 126; Thompson 1989–90, p. 7, fig. 3, p. 36, fig. 31

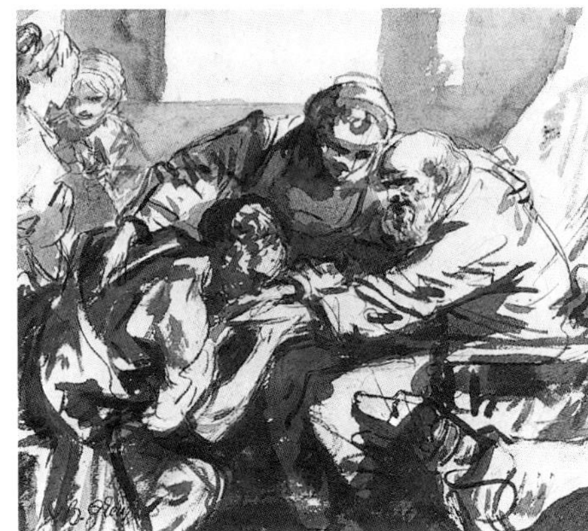

Fig. 211 Greuze, *Family Group,* 1793, pen and brown ink, brush with gray and brown ink, New York, private collection

Another turbulent, many-figured composition by Greuze whose meaning remains an enigma, this *Domestic Scene* transcribes directly a superanimated state of mind, which must have been Greuze's condition as he began to conceive a visual format for a new subject. The pen and ink lines seem to have been laid down almost automatically and the washes float over them without any specific connection. Even the dog at lower right morphoses over the lines of the table previously set down.

Inherited from the artist by his daughter Caroline, this drawing was described in the catalogue of her sale as "*A Family Scene.* An old man surrounded by his children" ("Intérieur de famille. *Un vieillard entouré de ses enfants*"). When it appeared in the Mailand sale seven years later, it was more accurately described as "An old man in an armchair and surrounded by all the members of his family" *("Un vieillard dans un fauteuil et entouré de tous les membres de sa famille").* Greuze never developed the subject in a painting.

A similarly aged man bending over in a gesture of benediction appears on a sheet depicting a family group (fig. 211) that Greuze inscribed *Donné à Lebrun par son ami Greuze le 6 7*[?]*bre 1793,* a likely date for the present drawing too. The same

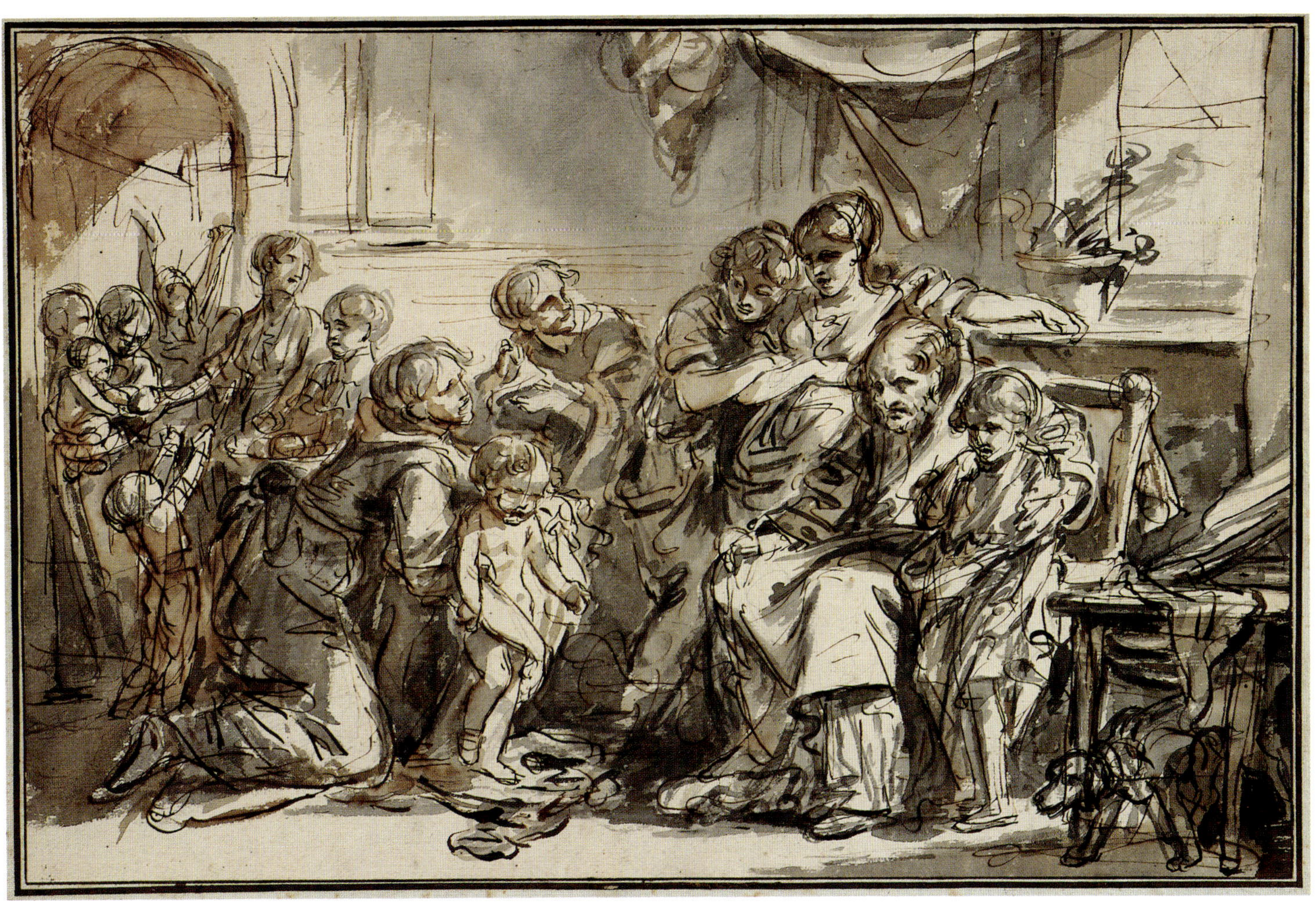

bearded man, crouched over in a togalike garment, is shown in a contemporary work implausibly entitled *The Return of the Prodigal Son* (fig. 212).

Even wilder in its graphic fervor is a contemporary *Scene of a Murder* (fig. 213).[2] Kate de Rothschild's description of the above-mentioned *Family Group* applies equally well to all these frantic exercises of Greuze: "Everything is understood without being literally defined.... The lack of detail also allows the artist to concentrate on expressing his emotions and results in some of the most powerful studies he ever produced."[3]

1. I am grateful to Perrin Stein for suggesting this reference.

2. Paris, Musée du Louvre, Département des arts graphiques, inv. no. 26988; Roland Michel 1987, p. 218, fig. 261.

3. In Brame & Lorenceau, Kate de Rothschild, Didier Aaron, *Master Drawings 1996,* no. 34.

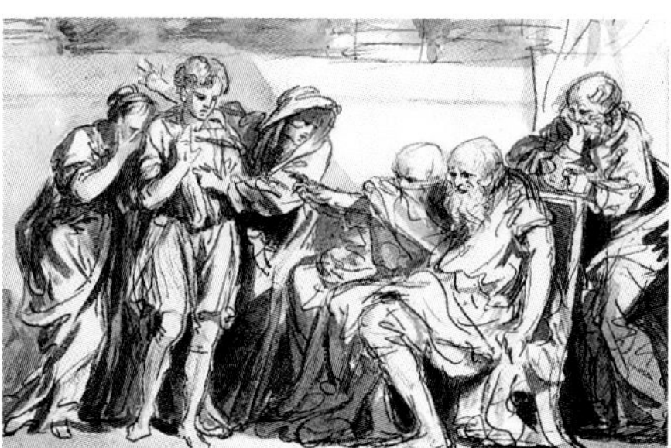

Fig. 212 Greuze, *The Return of the Prodigal Son, c.* 1790, pen and brush with gray ink wash, private collection

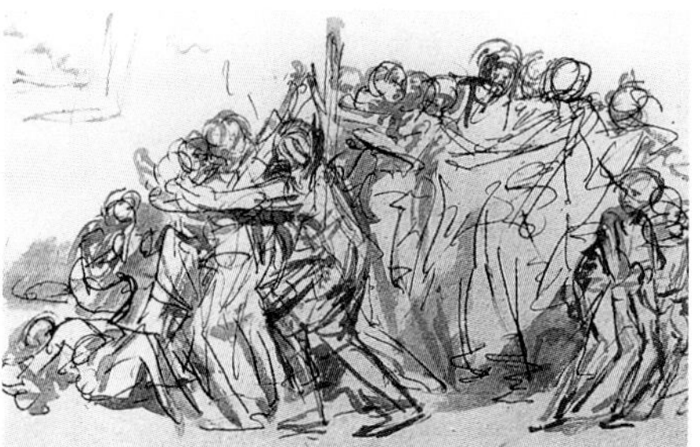

Fig. 213 Greuze, *Scene of a Murder, c.* 1790, pen and brown ink, brush with gray and brown ink, Paris, Musée du Louvre, Département des arts graphiques

89 *The Angry Wife*

Pen and black ink, brush with gray and black ink wash, heightened with white chalk, over graphite and black chalk on white paper, 521 × 640 mm (20½ × 25 3/16 in.)
Inscribed on the back of the original mat *dessin original de Greuze. Acheté dans son cabinet après sa mort par Monsieur Joseph Joubert, auteur des Pensées et Maximes*[1]
New York, The Metropolitan Museum of Art, Purchase, Joseph Pulitzer Bequest

Provenance: Joseph Joubert, Paris (d. 1824); Hesme, Paris; his sale, Paris, 3–4 March 1856, lot 89; sale, Paris, 9 March 1950, lot 16; Galerie Cailleux, Paris; purchased by the museum in 1961
Exhibitions: Paris 1951, no. 187; London 1968, no. 326; *French Drawings and Prints of the Eighteenth Century,* New York, The Metropolitan Museum of Art, 1972–73, no. 25; Hartford *et al.* 1976–77, no. 96; *Eighteenth-Century French Drawings in New York Collections,* New York, The Metropolitan Museum of Art, 1999, no. 84
Bibliography: Martin and Masson 1906, nos. 143, 1692; *The Metropolitan Museum of Art Annual Report,* 1960–61, p. 64; J. Bean, *One Hundred European Drawings in The Metropolitan Museum of Art,* New York 1964, no. 59; P. Hulton, "'France in the Eighteenth Century' at the Royal Academy," review, *Master Drawings,* autumn 1968, p. 167; M. Amaya, "The Moralist," *Art in America,* November–December 1976, p. 84; Preston 1977, p. 138; Fermigier 1977, p. 17; Rosenblum 1977, pp. 146, 148; Arquié-Bruley 1983, pp. 129, 133, nos. 57, 58, 134–35; Bean and Turcic 1986, p. 119, no. 125; Thompson 1989–90, pp. 38–39; Barker 1994, p. 282; Rand 1996, pp. 230–31; M. Simat, "The Drawing of 'The Fortune Teller' by Jean-Baptiste Greuze from the Mimara Museum," *Studije Muzeja Mimara,* no. 11, 1997, p. 14

With his usual willingness to share with one and all the most intimate details of his private life, Greuze has here introduced the viewer into his own household at a time when his already-unstable marriage was seriously coming apart, about 1785, when the artist and his wife had separated. In a legal deposition the artist dictated with the intent of obtaining a legal separation, at least two scenes are described reminiscent of that represented here: one, in which Madame Greuze responded to a request her husband had made to her by "slapping [him] with all her might," and another, in which "in the glow of a night light I saw Madame Greuze about to smash my head with her chamber pot."[2] Greuze recounted to a friend yet another humiliating scene, when he had to arm himself with a chair to fend off his wife brandishing fire tongs and her lover the fire dogs, adding with a remark particularly pertinent here: "Struck by the picture I had before my eyes I return trembling to my studio. I take some chalk and make a sketch of that scene of horror. It is one of the most beautiful drawings I have done. I invite you to come see it."[3] It was for such frankness in sharing his own woes that his contemporary Jean-Baptiste-Pierre Le Brun wrote of the artist: "To paint man in his private life is the great talent of M. Greuze," and another contemporary, Charles-Louis François Lecarpentier: "Greuze created a genre of painting unknown in France before him, that of private life.... [He] wanted, in painting different events of human life, to inspire a love of goodness, and a hatred of vice."[4]

As though it were not enough that his marital problems were already the talk of the town (Diderot compared the Greuze ménage to a Punch and Judy show), the artist then drew up before his notary Duclos-Dufresnoy on 16 December 1786 one of his customary contracts with the engraver Gaillard to produce and sell an engraving based on the present drawing. Although on 6 November 1788 the *Journal de Paris* announced the publication of the resulting print, entitled in curious French *La Femme colère,* and although the inventory of Gaillard's possessions after his death on 11 April 1790

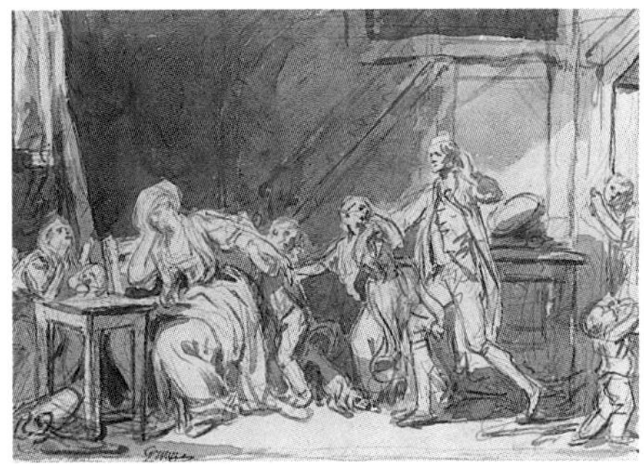

Fig. 214 Greuze, *Study for "The Reconciliation,"* *c.* 1785, brush with gray wash over graphite on white paper, Notre Dame IN, The Snite Museum of Art

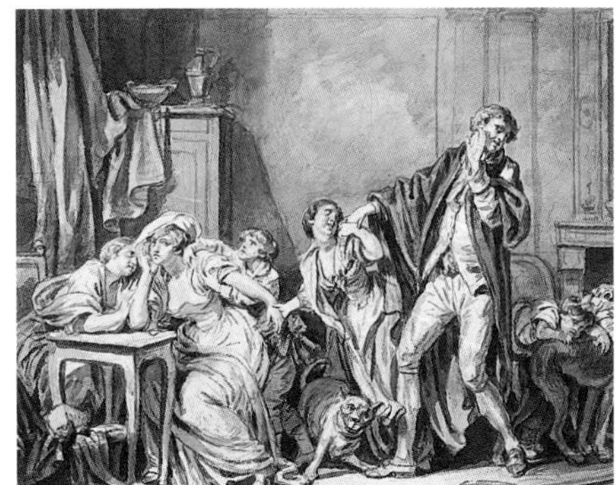

Fig. 215 Greuze, *The Reconciliation, c.* 1785, brush with black and gray wash over graphite on white paper, Phoenix Art Museum

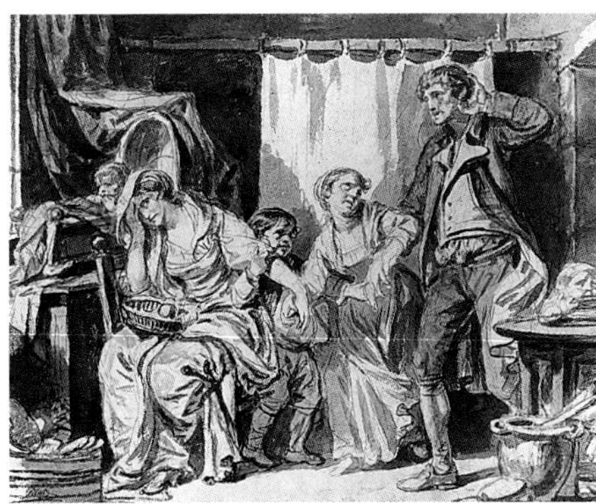

Fig. 216 Greuze, *The Reconciliation, c.* 1785, brush with gray and brown ink wash over graphite on white paper, Paris, Prat collection

mentions the copperplate and various states of this subject, not a single example of the print has survived.[5]

The elaborate and subtly rendered details of this drawing, including the use of a straightedge to lay out the architectural details, are consistent with other drawings Greuze produced as engravers' models (see nos. 33, 70, 82).

In his ingenious interpretation of *The Angry Wife,* Rand pointed out how atypically male the wife's appearance is, with her strident pose, clenched fist, and raised weapon, and how feminine is her husband's attitude, recoiling sinuously into his daughters' pliant arms. The verses appended to Gaillard's engraving make clear that such a reversal of the "natural" order of things can be disastrous: "Lise, restrain your anger/ You cease to be a woman and you are no longer a mother/ Everything speaks in favor of your husband/ Your daughters wiser than you/ Fulfill their duty, remain good daughters/ By repairing your wrongs and console their father."[6]

With his penchant for pairing dramatic subjects, it is not surprising that Greuze should have conceived a scene depicting a familial reconciliation that, ideally, should have followed such an altercation as depicted in this work. But the subject must have been so close to his heart that he executed no fewer than three variants on it (figs. 214, 215, 216).[7] However, the interiors of these waver between rustic and elegant, the cast of characters, both human and animal, is different from that in *The Angry Wife,* and none of the designs was ever brought to the perfection required of an engraver's model.

1. "original drawing by Greuze. Bought in his studio after his death by Monsieur Joseph Joubert, author of the Pensées and Maximes."

2. *"elle m'appliqua un soufflet à tour de bras"; "j'aperçu Madame Greuze à la lumière d'une lampe de nuit qui alloit m'écraser la tête avec son pot de chambre."* J. Boilly (ed.), "Mémoire de Greuze contre sa femme," *Archives de l'art français,* II, 1852–53, pp. 161, 170.

3. *"Frappé du tableau que j'avais sous les yeux je rentre en frémissant dans mon cabinet. Je prends un crayon et je fais un croquis de cette scène d'horreur. C'est un des plus beaux dessins que j'aye faits. Je vous invite à le venir voir."* M. Nitot [called C. Dufresne], "Cahiers," ms., Paris, Musée des Arts Décoratifs, Bibliothèque, VIII, p. 49.

4. *"Peindre l'homme dans sa vie privée, est le grand talent de M. Greuze."* J.-B.-P. Le Brun, *Almanach historique,* Paris 1776 (Minkoff reprint, 1972), p. 92. *"Greuze créa un genre en peinture inconnu en France avant lui, celui de la vie privée.... [Il] voulut, en peignant des différens événements de la vie humaine, inspirer l'amour du bien, et la haine du vice."* C.-L.F. Lecarpentier, *Notice sur Greuze lu dans la séance de la Société libre d'Émulation de Rouen,* [Rouen] 1805, pp. 2, 1.

5. Cabinet des Estampes de la Bibliothèque nationale, *Inventaire du fonds français,* "Gaillard," no. 193.

6. *"Lise, calmez votre courroux/ Vous cessez d'être Femme, et vous n'êtes plus Mère/ Tout parle ici pour votre Époux/ Vos filles plus sages que vous/ Remplissent leur devoir, gardent leur caractère/ En réparant vos torts, et consolent leur Père."* Quoted in Bean 1964, no. 59.

7. Hartford *et al.* 1976–77, no. 97; *The University of Notre Dame Friends and Alumni Collect,* exhib. cat., The Snite Museum of Art, University of Notre Dame, 1992, p. 43; S.S. Spiro in *Drawings from the Reilly Collection,* The Snite Museum of Art, University of Notre Dame, 1993, pp. 34–35, no. 36; P. Rosenberg, *Dessins français de la collection Prat,* exhib. cat., Paris, Musée du Louvre *et al.,* 1995, pp. 130–31, no. 48.

Facing page:
89 *The Angry Wife*

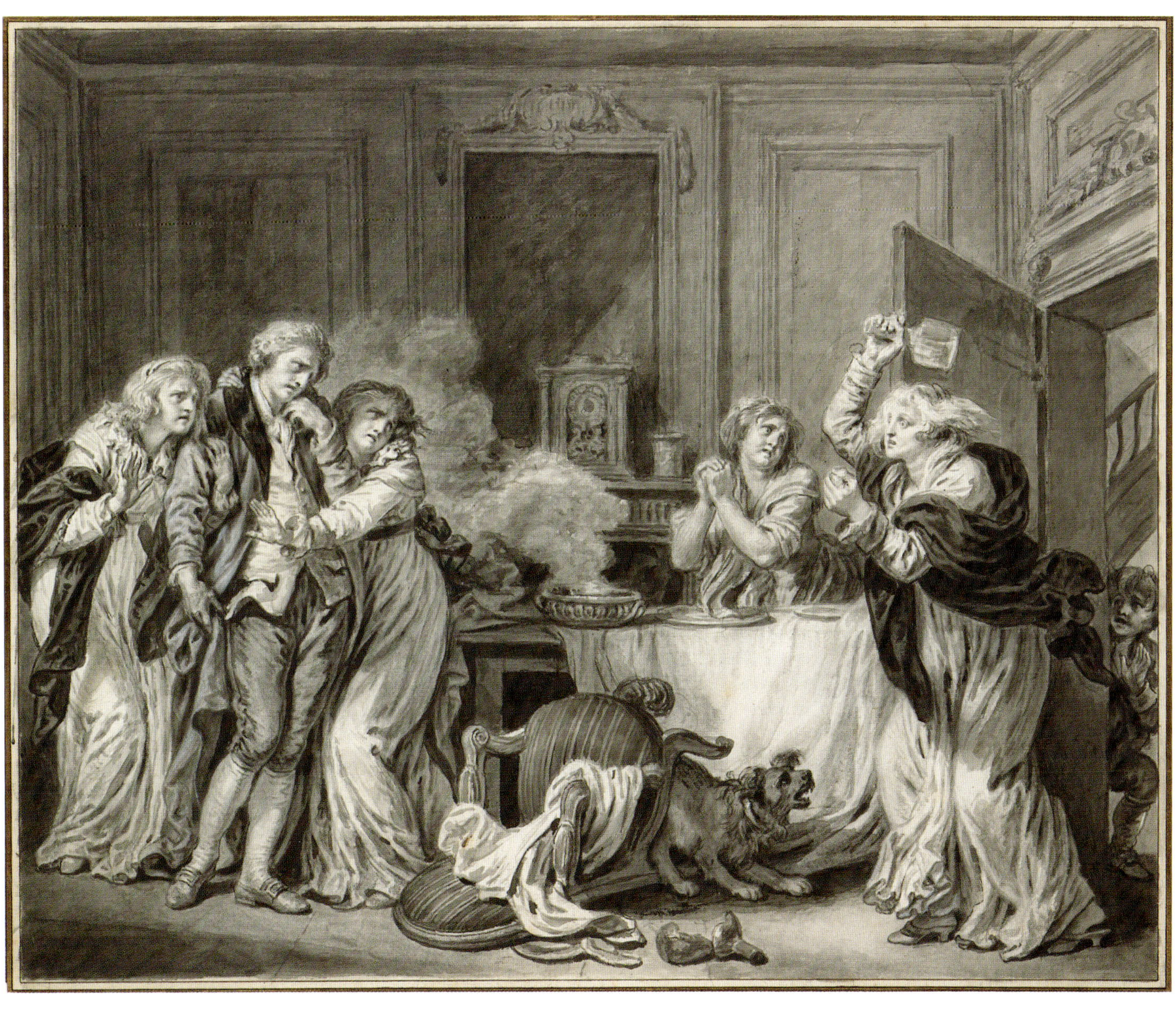

90 *Lamentation over the Dead Christ* (recto); *Studies of a Seated Woman* (verso)

Pen and brush with brown ink (recto) and black chalk (verso) on white paper,
362 × 257 mm (14 ¼ × 10 ⅛ in.)
Paris, private collection

Provenance: Charles Gasc, Paris, *c.* 1860 (Lugt 544); perhaps sale, Paris, 12 May 1863;[1] Sir Kenneth Clark, London, 1968; his sale, London, 5 July 1984, lot 175; acquired at that sale
Exhibition: London 1968, no. 324
Bibliography: Martin and Masson 1906, no. 10; P. Hulton, "'France in the Eighteenth Century' at the Royal Academy," *Master Drawings,* autumn 1968, p. 167; S. Sitwell, "The Pleasures of the Senses," *Apollo,* February 1968, p. 128, fig. 15; Brookner 1972, p. 129, pl. 83; O. Aaron, *Dessins insolites du XVIIIe siècle,* Paris 1985, pp. 58, 109, no. 48

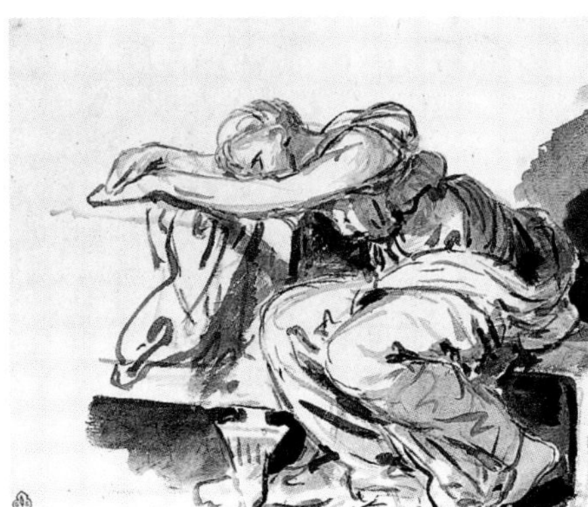

Fig. 217 Greuze, *Woman Weeping at a Tomb,* *c.* 1790, brush with gray and brown ink wash over black chalk, whereabouts unknown

This rare example of Greuze treating a traditional religious subject, the lamentation over the dead Christ, provoked an equally rare paean of praise from Brookner, who characterized it as "desperate, haggard, and impressive."[2] The dead Christ is represented only by his lower legs and feet, projecting beyond the edge of a bier at lower left. At the upper right, John comforts the Virgin, and in the center, Mary Magdalen with her cascading hair, Mary Cleophas, and another Holy Woman lament over the body of Christ.

The extraordinary freedom and boldness of both the linear elements of this drawing and the torrent of brown wash flowing down from the upper left give it an intensity far beyond its modest scale. Something of Romney's manner is apparent here, perhaps owing to the Englishman's visiting Greuze during his trip to Paris in the summer of 1790, the two artists' first encounter in twenty-five years.[3]

Probably related to this composition is a *Woman Weeping at a Tomb* (fig. 217), the foot of the tomb and the bench appearing much like the foot of the bier and the bench under Mary Magdalen in the present drawing.[4]

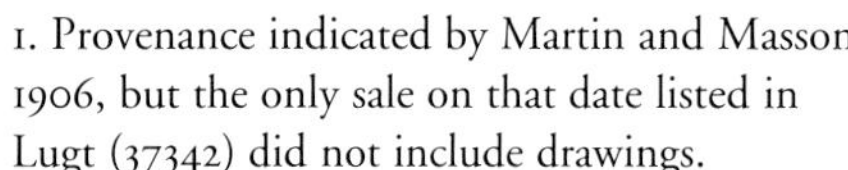

1. Provenance indicated by Martin and Masson 1906, but the only sale on that date listed in Lugt (37342) did not include drawings.

2. Brookner 1972, p. 129.

3. See W. Hayley, *The Life of Romney,* London 1809, p. 148; D.A. Cross, *A Striking Likeness, The Life of George Romney,* London 2000, p. 168.

4. Paris 1951, no. 64; sale, Paris, 15 March 1968, lot 26; Paris, Paul Prouté S.A., Catalogue "Gavarni," 1969, no. 28.

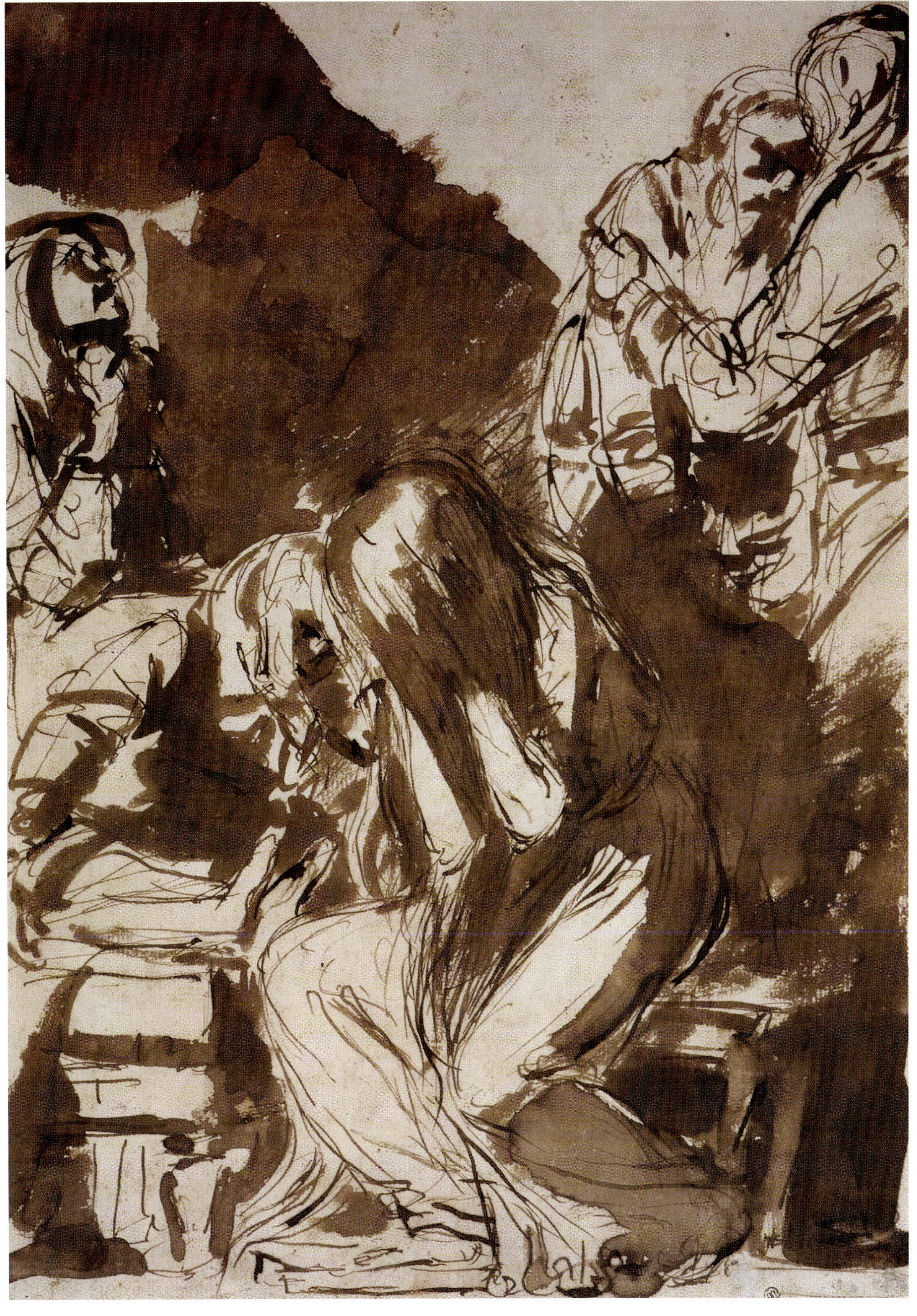

91 *Portrait of Baptiste* aîné

Pastel on cream paper, 419 × 337 mm (16 ½ × 13 ¼ in.), affixed at the time of execution to a larger sheet of blue paper, 451 × 375 mm (17 ¾ × 14 ¾ in.), mounted on canvas
New York, The Frick Collection

Provenance: L. Godard, Paris, 1860; Senator Antonio Santamarina, Buenos Aires, acquired *c.* 1950–52 in Paris, until 1974; bequeathed to his son Miguel M. Santamarina, Buenos Aires; acquired by The Frick Collection in 1996 with funds bequeathed in memory of Suzanne and Denise Falk
Exhibitions: Tableaux et dessins de l'école française principalement du XVIIIe siècle tirés de collections d'amateurs, Paris, Association des artistes, 26, boulevard des Italiens, 1860, no. 315; *Greuze, A Portraitist for the 90s,* New York, The Frick Collection, 1996; *Eighteenth-Century French Drawings in New York Collections,* New York, The Metropolitan Museum of Art, 1999, no. 100
Bibliography: G. Monval, *Les Collections de la Comédie-Française,* Paris 1897, p. 134; Martin and Masson 1906, no. 1067; P. Jeromack, "Two Greuzes for the Frick and a del Sarto for the Met," *The Art Newspaper,* March 1996, p. 17; S.G. Galassi, "Henry Clay Frick as a Collector of Drawings and Later Additions to The Frick Collection," *Master Drawings,* fall 2000, p. 289, repr. front cover

Nicolas-Pierre-Baptiste Anselme, called Baptiste *aîné* (for *fils aîné*), was born in Bordeaux on 18 June 1761, the son of Joseph-François Anselme, called Baptiste *l'ancien,* and Marie Bourdais. He died in the Batignolles quarter of Paris on 30 November 1835. Baptiste *aîné* was the most illustrious of several generations of a family of actors and actresses. After performing hither and yon with his parents, he established himself as an actor and singer in Rouen between 1783 and 1790. Prior to 1785, he had married there Anne-Françoise Gourville (see no. 92). By 1791 the entire Anselme family was performing in Paris at the Théâtre du Marais—Baptiste *aîné* and his wife, his parents, his younger brother, and his uncle. In 1792 Baptiste established his reputation with the principal role in Jean-Henri-Ferdinand La Martelière's *Robert, Chef des brigands.* The following year, he joined the company of the Théâtre de la République, in 1798, that of the Théâtre Feydeau, and the next year, the newly reorganized Comédie-Française, where he remained until his retirement on 1 April 1828. Between 1809 and 1828 he also taught acting at the Conservatoire. Two of Baptiste *aîné*'s children pursued careers in the theater, his son Joseph playing occasionally at the Comédie-Française and his daughter Françoise-Joséphine becoming a *sociétaire* of that company.

Among the more than one hundred roles Baptiste *aîné* performed at the Comédie-Française were parts in classics by Corneille, Molière, and Racine, as well as in many contemporary works by Beaumarchais, André Chénier, Fabre d'Églantine, Michel-Jean Sedaine, and Voltaire. During his stay at the Théâtre de la République, he was described by Jean-François La Harpe, writing to the grand duke of Russia, as "combining a deeply intelligent dramatic sense with a clear diction, sophisticated manners, and a realistic tone." Other contemporary accounts were more critical, such as this one: "His good qualities include a perfect intelligence, a relaxed manner, a precise diction, a pure voice, an attractive physiognomy, a passionate love of his art.... His faults are: a height too great for the theater, a way of performing that is mannered, a delivery that is precious and slow, the affectation of stressing every word, of underlining every detail; in short, an absence of feeling.... He enunciates everything, including periods and commas." Besides being renowned for his professional assiduity, Baptiste *aîné* also, as one colleague recalled, "made himself loved by everyone through his proverbial affability; never, over his long career, did he appear jealous of a comrade's

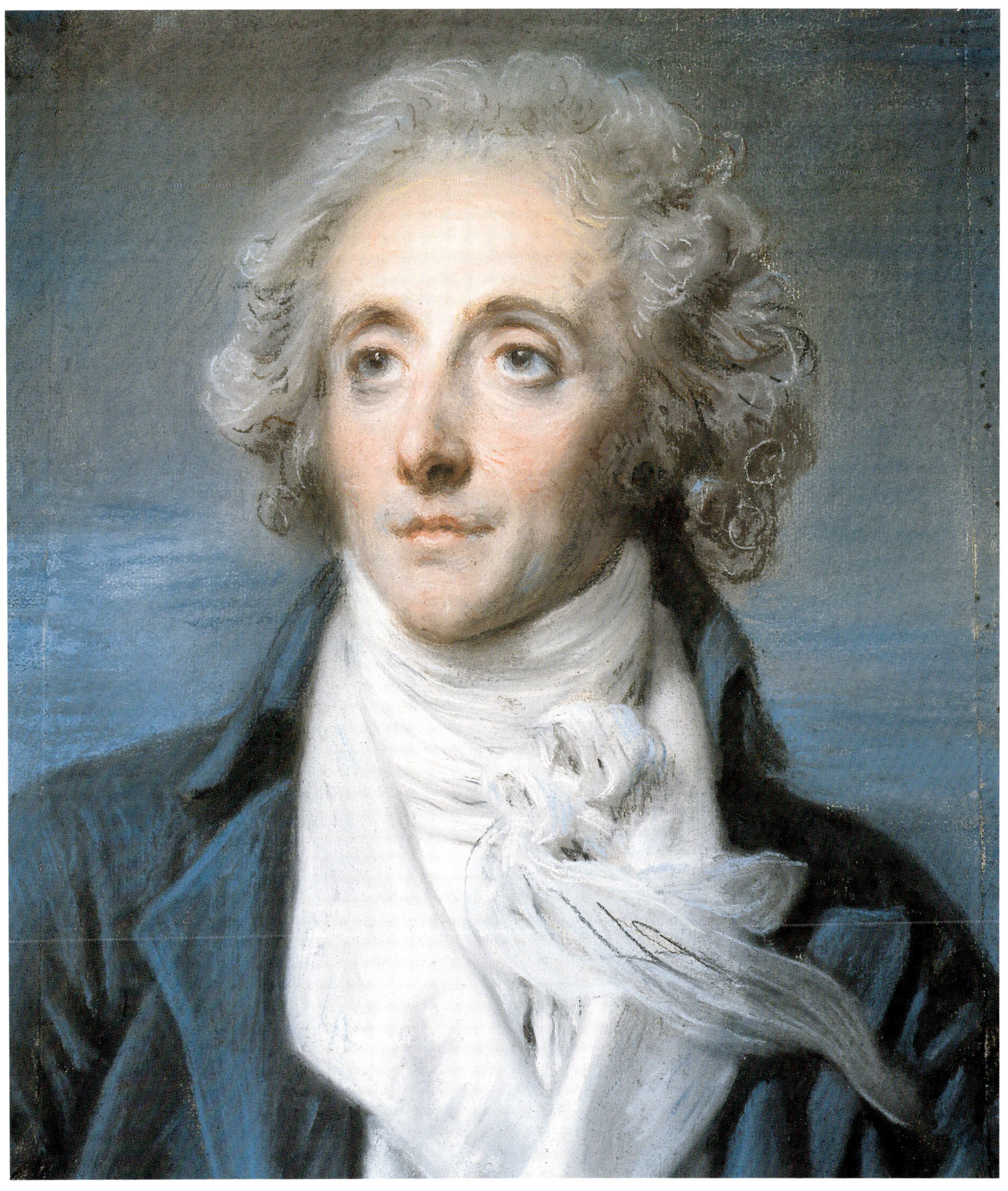

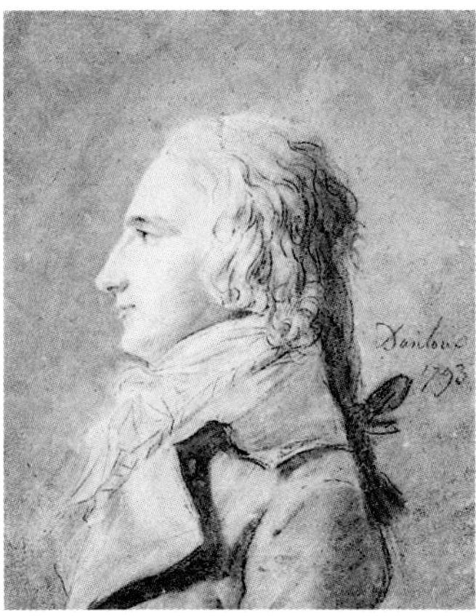

Fig. 218 H.-P. Danloux, *Portrait of a Gentleman (Baptiste* aîné), 1793, brush and gray ink wash, black and white chalks on white paper, whereabouts unknown

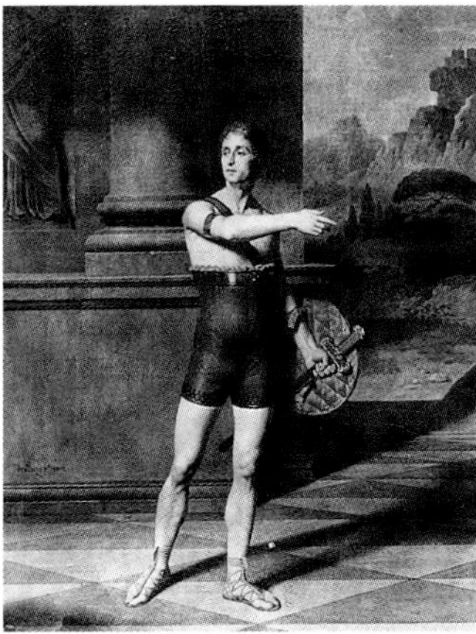

Fig. 219 M. Drolling, *Portrait of Baptiste* aîné *on Stage,* 1803, oil on canvas, Caen, Musée des Beaux-Arts

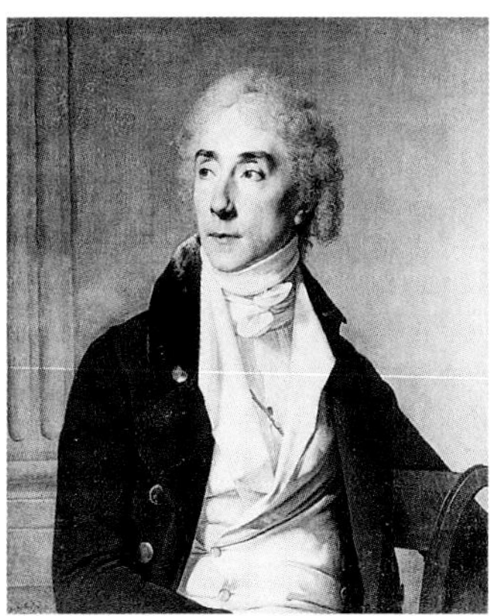

Fig. 220 M. Drolling, *Portrait of Baptiste* aîné, *c.* 1800, oil on canvas, Paris, Comédie-Française

success." Another added: "In his private life, Baptiste was most gentle and easy-going."

Commenting on the sparse turnout for the benefit performance that concluded the actor's career, one critic noted: "If one considers the so-called gratitude the public owes an actor, Baptiste *aîné* would certainly have had claim to it, his public and private conduct never having been anything but praiseworthy."[1]

Baptiste's fame, his unusual height—the source of his nickname *Le Télégraphe*—and his generally striking appearance inspired many artists to execute portraits of him. Besides Greuze, they include: Étienne Bouchardy (1797–1849) (Comédie-Française),[2] Henri-Pierre Danloux (fig. 218),[3] Martin Drolling (1752–1817) (figs. 219, 220),[4] Frédéric-Désiré Hillemacher (1811–1886),[5] Jean-Baptiste Isabey (1767–1855) (fig. 221),[6] and his pupil Muneret (Comédie-Française).[7] But it was Louis-Léopold Boilly (1761–1845) who seemed most fascinated with the actor. He first portrayed him, full-length, seated, and in profile right, at the center of his *Reunion of Artists in Isabey's Studio* (fig. 222), shown at the Salon of 1798.[8] The engraver Alexandre Clément reproduced from this group portrait a selection of heads that he published in 1804 as a *Réunion d'artistes,* in which Baptiste *aîné*'s profile appears at center left, identified in the accompanying key as *"Baptiste aîné du Théâtre Français."*[9]

Boilly then introduced Baptiste's unmistakable profile into the center of the crowd depicted in *The Public Viewing David's "Coronation of Napoleon and the Empress Josephine" in the Great Hall of the Louvre,* both in the preparatory study for that work, begun in 1808, and in the final painting (fig. 223).[10]

Unfortunately, there exists no documentation of the relations between Boilly and his distinctive model, but it is recorded that at the end of the eighteenth century such well-known theatrical personalities as Baptiste *aîné* were the object of an impassioned *théatromanie.* "Actors and actresses inspire passions; their private life is the object of an already insatiable curiosity; their playing inspires... a philosophy of the theater."[11]

Based on the evidence of Baptiste's clothing and hairstyling—and more specifically on that of Madame Baptiste in her pendant portrait (no. 92)—the costume historian Michele Majer suggested a date at the very end of the eighteenth century (1798–1800) for the two portraits by Greuze. Otherwise, there is no documentation concerning their execution that could suggest a more precise dating. However, Baptiste's joining the Comédie-Française in 1799 might have been the occasion for his commissioning the two portraits. Greuze's familiarity with the theatrical world is attested to by his slightly earlier pastel portrait of the former actor, playwright, and politician Fabre d'Églantine (Jeffrey E. Horvitz collection).[12]

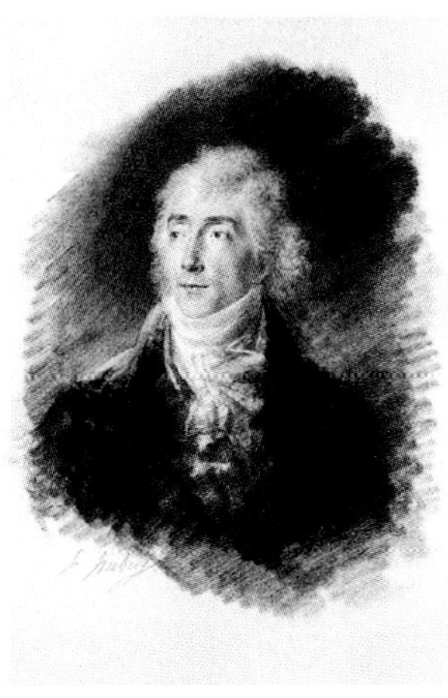

Fig. 221 J.-B. Isabey, *Portrait of Baptiste* aîné, *c.* 1800, black and white chalks on white paper, Paris, Comédie-Française

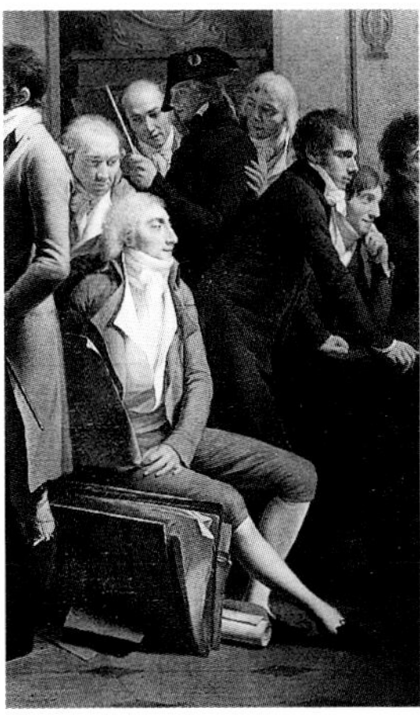

Fig. 222 L.-L. Boilly, *Reunion of Artists in Isabey's Studio* (detail), 1798, oil on canvas, Paris, Musée du Louvre

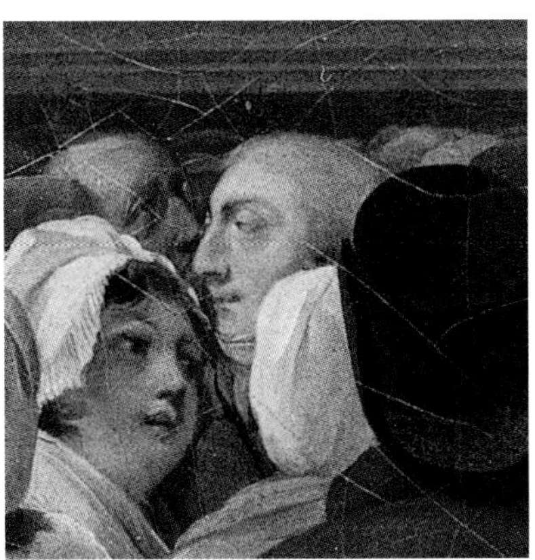

Fig. 223 L.-L. Boilly, *The Public Viewing David's "Coronation of Napoleon and the Empress Josephine" in the Great Hall of the Louvre* (detail), 1808, oil on canvas, Paris, Musée du Louvre

1. This summary biography and that of Madame Baptiste *aîné* (no. 92) are based primarily on archives preserved in the Collection Auguste Rondel at the Bibliothèque de l'Arsenal, Paris, as well as those held in the Bibliothèque de la Comédie-Française and in the Archives of the City of Paris. See also E. Laugier, *Documents historiques sur la Comédie Française pendant le règne de S.M. L'Empereur Napoléon Ier,* Paris 1853, pp. 94–168, *passim;* E.D. de Manne, *Galerie historique des comédiens de la troupe de Talma, Notices sur les principaux secrétaires de la Comédie Française depuis 1789 jusqu'aux trente premières années de ce siècle,* Lyon 1866, pp. 181–90; and H. Lyonnet, *Dictionnaire des comédiens français,* Geneva 1969, I, pp. 7–74.

2. Monval 1897, p. 90, no. 202.

3. Sale, New York, 30 January 1997, lot 163, as *Portrait of a Gentleman.*

4. Monval 1897, p. 83, no. 169; G. Monval, *La Comédie-Française,* Paris 1931, pp. 18–19, repr. p. 51; M. Guibert and J. Razgonikoff, *Le Journal de la Comédie-Française, 1787–1799,* Antony 1989, p. 30.

5. See Monval 1897, pp. 180–81.

6. See R. Delorme, *Le Musée de la Comédie-Française,* Paris 1878, no. 30; Monval 1897, p. 68, no. 146.

7. See Monval 1897, p. 76, no. 161.

8. C. Sterling and H. Adhémar, *Musée National du Louvre, Peintures, École Française, XIXe siècle,* Paris 1958, I, p. 7, pl. XXV, no. 85; Compin and Roquebert 1986, III, p. 66; S. Laveissière, "L'Atelier d'Isabey: Un Panthéon de l'Amitié," in *Boilly,* exhib. cat., Lille *et al.,* 1988–89, p. 57.

9. See Lille *et al.* 1988–89, p. 60, nos. 23–24.

10. See J.S. Hallam, *The Genre Works of Louis-Léopold Boilly,* Seattle 1979, p. 101. The author is indebted to Philippe Bordes for having pointed out the presence of Baptiste *aîné* in these works by and after Boilly.

11. G. Morel, *Histoire des spectacles, Le XVIIIe Siècle, Le Théâtre et la Société,* Paris 1965, p. 767.

12. See Cambridge *et al.* 1998–2000, no. 81.

92 *Madame Baptiste* aîné

Pastel on cream paper, 456 × 366 mm (18 × 14 7/16 in.)
New York, The Frick Collection

Provenance: same as no. 91
Exhibitions: Tableaux et dessins de l'école française principalement du XVIIIe siècle tirés de collections d'amateurs, Paris, Association des artistes, 26, boulevard des Italiens, 1860, no. 316; *Greuze, A Portraitist for the 90s,* New York, The Frick Collection, 1996
Bibliography: G. Monval, *Les Collections de la Comédie-Française,* Paris 1897, p. 134; Martin and Masson 1906, no. 1068; P. Jeromack, "Two Greuzes for the Frick and a del Sarto for the Met," *The Art Newspaper,* March 1996, p. 17; S.G. Galassi, "Henry Clay Frick as a Collector of Drawings and Later Additions to The Frick Collection," *Master Drawings,* fall 2000, p. 289

Far less is known about Madame Baptiste *aîné* than about her celebrated husband (no. 91). Née Anne-Françoise Gourville, she married Baptiste in Rouen at some point between 1783 and 1785. By 1791, known as *Madame Baptiste bru,* she was performing in Paris at her husband's side, the two described as *le jeune ménage.* By the time the couple were performing two years later at the Théâtre de la République, she was being assigned roles of increasingly lesser importance. Finally, *L'Opinion du parterre* of Germinal, An XI, recorded the end of her career in unflattering terms: "She had a terrible fault, which consisted of not allowing to be heard a single verse that she delivered. Never did she dare look at the audience; her eyes were fixed on the wings, to which she addressed her entire role. She has been offered her retirement."[1]

Extant correspondence suggests that a deep and mutual affection linked Baptiste *aîné* and his wife and family. A letter he addressed to her from Metz dated 18 Pluviôse An II attests to this:

Until we meet again, my good and dear friend... a thousand and thousand kisses for you, for our children, and for our respectable family—from your faithful husband... if you want to prove to me upon my return that you really love me, take great care of yourself, so that I find you in vigorous and good health. It takes only seven hours for me to go to Nancy, where I hope to find some letters from you; because I had none yesterday despite the great desire I had to receive some, and probably I shall not be any more happy today. Tell my little franc [a son's nickname] to behave himself well, and that Papa will bring him a trunk completely full, completely full of beautiful things.[2]

With his own marriage a tissue of bitter memories by the time he executed the portraits of Baptiste *aîné* and his wife, the aging Greuze must have envied their happy union. He seems to have conceived the portraits of Baptiste and his wife, not as individual studies, but rather as the parts of a diptych, in which two independent characters complement one another with great harmony: Baptiste, exuberant and dashing, set against a blue sky, turned slightly to the left; his wife, pensive and modest, drawn in a cool interior, and turned slightly to the right.

There are no other portraits known of Madame Baptiste *aîné.*

1. Quoted in H. Lyonnet, *Dictionnaire des comédiens français,* Geneva 1969, 1, p. 75.

2. *"Au revoir, ma bonne et chère amie... mille et mille baisers à toi, à nos enfants, et à notre respectable famille, Ton fidelle mari... Si tu veux me prouver à mon retour que tu m'aimes bien, soigne toi beaucoup, et que je te trouve en vigoureuse et bonne santé. Il ne me faut que sept heures pour aller à Nancy où j'espère trouver de tes lettres; car je n'en ai point eu hier malgré tout le désir que j'avois d'en recevoir; et probablement je ne serai pas plus heureux aujourdhuy. Recommande à mon petit franc d'être bien sage, et Papa lui apportera tout plein, tout plein de belles choses."* Collection of the Bibliothèque de la Comédie-Française, Paris.

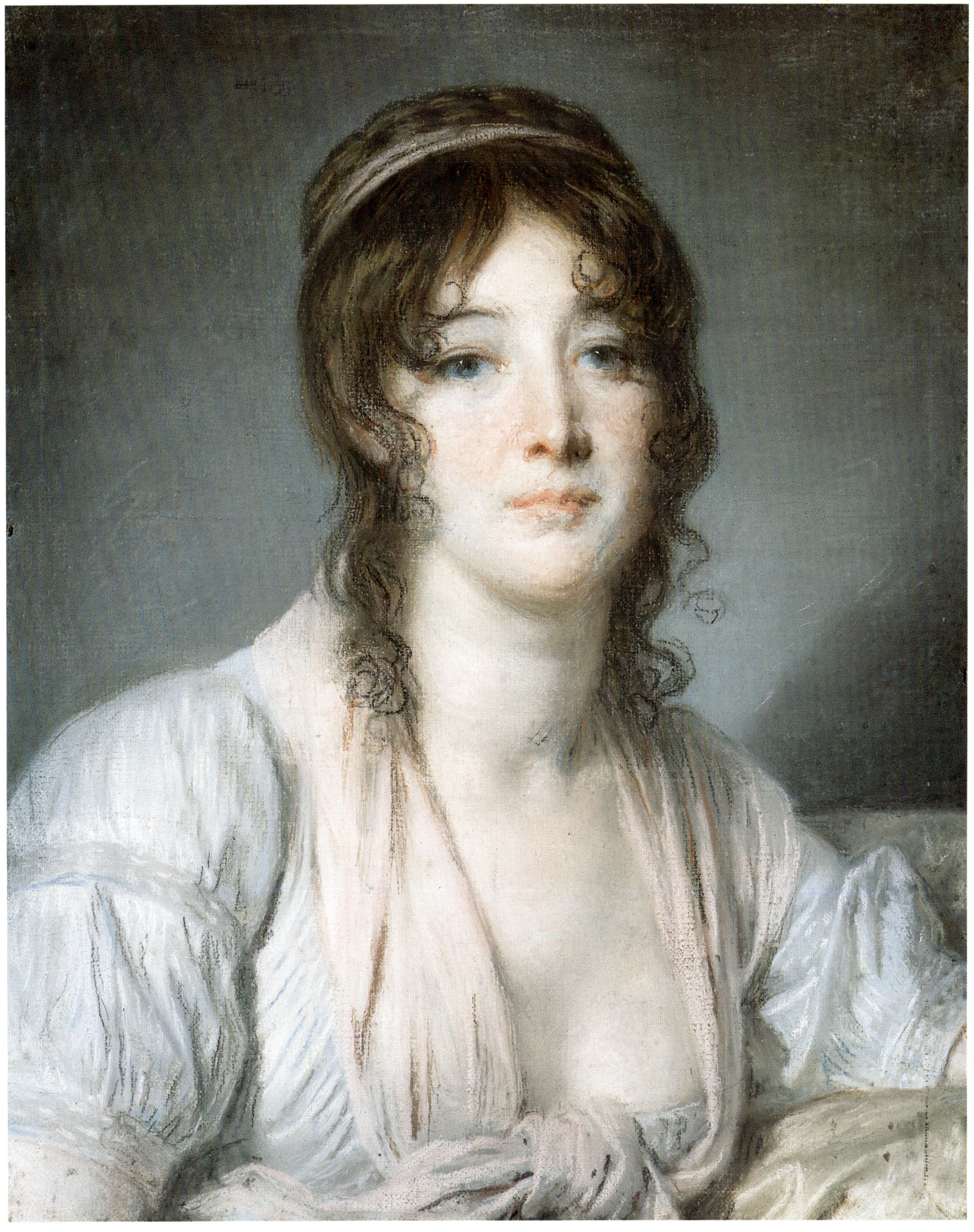

93 *Study of the Head of a Dog*

Black and red chalks, stumped, on white paper, 267 × 324 mm (10½ × 12¾ in.)
Richmond, Virginia Museum of Fine Arts, Gift of George Corbin Harwell and Kathleen Leigh Williams Harwell and The Fabergé Society of the Virginia Museum of Fine Arts

Provenance: sale, London, 3 July 1995, lot 132; private collection, Paris; Brame & Lorenceau, Kate de Rothschild, Didier Aaron, Inc., 1996; acquired by the museum in 1997
Exhibition: Master Drawings 1996, New York, Didier Aaron, Inc., 1996, no. 36
Bibliography: None known

This is a study for the dog depicted thrusting his head over the balustrade at the far right in *The Departure for the Hunt* (no. 94), eagerly straining to observe any possible sign of action on the part of his master. Described as a springer spaniel type, he appears to be smaller than the hunting hound standing next to him. In a compositional study for number 94 (fig. 224),[1] both dogs occupy a more prominent position than in the final drawing.

Greuze frequently included dogs in his work, beginning with *The Family Bible Reading* (fig. 225), first exhibited in 1755. Although their significance in his pictures may often be symbolic—images of fidelity, of nurturing care—independently of that, the artist clearly had a deep affection for them, understanding their character, and was knowledgeable about their anatomy, movements, and postures.

1. Sale, London, 3 July 1995, lot 201.

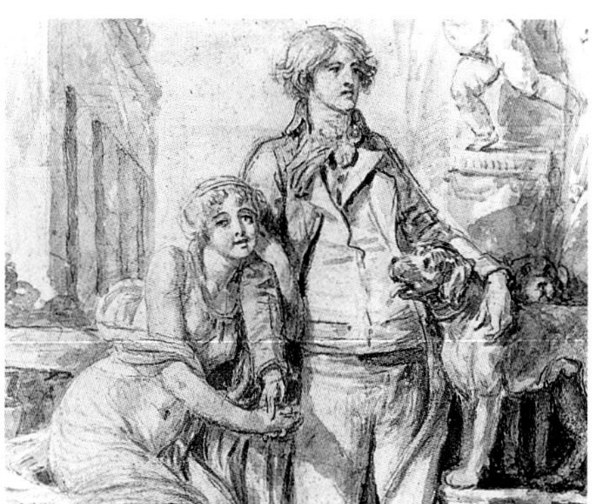

Fig. 224 Greuze, *Study for "The Departure for the Hunt,"* 1800, brush and gray wash over black chalk, private collection

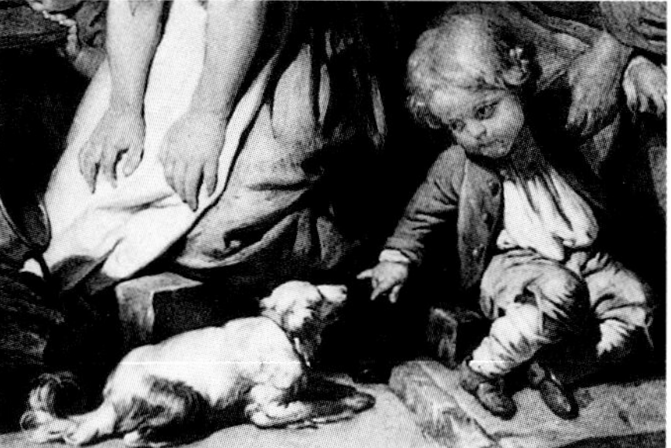

Fig. 225 Greuze, *The Family Bible Reading* (detail), 1755, oil on canvas, Paris, private collection

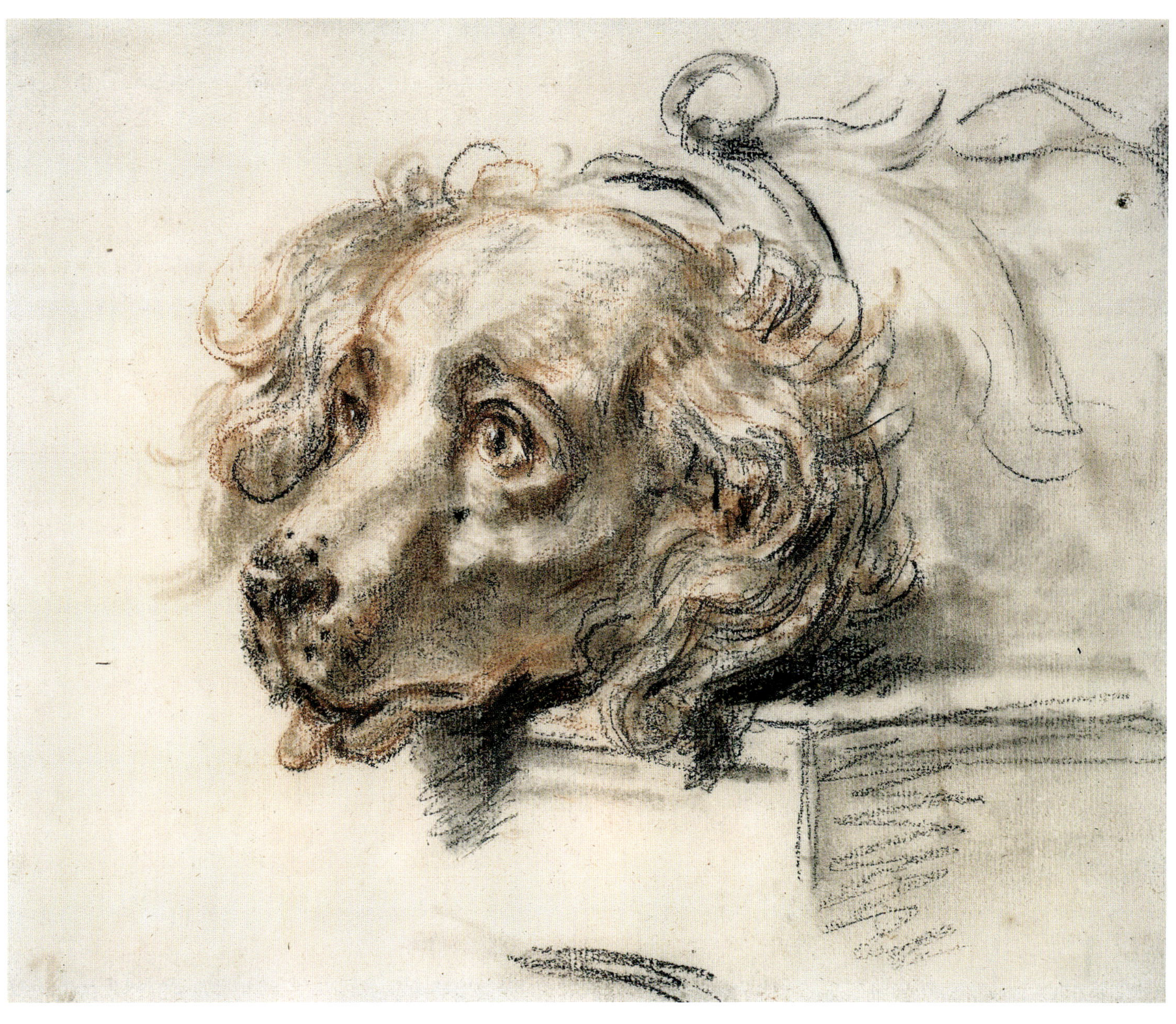

94 *The Departure for the Hunt*

Brush, gray ink wash, over graphite on tan paper, 380 × 350 mm ($14^{15}/_{16}$ × $13^{3}/_{4}$ in.)
Paris, Musée du Louvre, Département des arts graphiques

Provenance: Edmond and Jules de Goncourt, Paris, acquired after 25 April 1857 (Lugt 1089); Goncourt sale, Paris, 15–17 February 1897, lot 118, acquired by the museum (Lugt 1886a)
Exhibitions: perhaps Salon of 1800, no. 173; *Dessins de maîtres anciens,* Paris, École des Beaux-Arts, 1879, no. 564; *Les Goncourt,* Paris, Gazette des Beaux-Arts, 1933, no. 203; *La Révolution française,* Paris, Musée Carnavalet, 1939; *Les Goncourt,* Paris, Musée des Arts Décoratifs, 1946, no. 384; Hartford *et al.* 1976–77, no. 112
Bibliography: P. de Chennevières, "Les Dessins de maîtres anciens exposés à l'École des beaux-arts," *GBA,* 11, 1879, p. 203; E. de Goncourt, *La Maison d'un artiste,* Paris 1881, 1, p. 89; Mauclair 1906, repr. p. 128; Martin and Masson 1906, nos. 130, 308, 1287; Guiffrey and Marcel 1911, no. 4541; Hautecoeur 1913, p. 122, pl. XXIII; B.A. Waldram, *Greuze, 1725–1805,* New York 1923, p. 92; Bouchot-Saupique 1939, no. 14, pl. XIV; P. Lavallée, *Le Dessin français,* Paris 1948, p. 80; Brookner 1972, pp. 86, 132, pl. 94; P. Rosenberg in *Dessins français du 17e et du 18e siècles des collections américaines,* exhib. cat., Ottawa *et al.,* 1972–73, p. 164; R. Bacou, *Dessins et aquarelles des grands maîtres, Le XVIIIe siècle,* Paris 1976, p. 87, pl. XXXIV; D. Sutton, "The Ambiguities of Jean-Baptiste Greuze," *Financial Times,* 11 January 1977, p. 17; Preston 1977, p. 139, fig. 7; Tisserand 1984, p. 130; É. Launay, *Les Frères Goncourt Collectionneurs de dessins,* Paris 1991, pp. 145, fig. 65, 318, no. 125

In 1800, after a self-imposed absence of thirty-one years, Greuze decided to exhibit again at the Salon. By then, the organization that used to sponsor the exhibition, and to whose members it was restricted—the Académie Royale de Peinture et de Sculpture—had been dissolved, and the exhibition catalogue was now entitled *Explication des ouvrages... des artistes vivans, exposés au Muséum central des arts* ("Exhibition of the works of... living artists, exhibited at the Muséum Central des Arts"). It was open to all artists who wished to participate.

Greuze submitted eleven works, his list headed by number 173, *Le Départ pour la chasse, portrait du C.*** et de sa femme, dans un paysage (The Departure for the Hunt, Portrait of the C[ount]*** and His Wife, in a Landscape).* The author and others have long supposed that this number 173 at the Salon of 1800 was the present drawing. However, Martin and Masson, in one of the three catalogue entries they accorded this work (no. 308), had written: it "appears to be the first version *("pensée")* of *The Departure for the Hunt,* shown at the Salon of the year VIII." More recently, Élisabeth Launay also questioned whether this sheet was indeed number 173 at that Salon, citing the fact that Edmond de Goncourt, who once owned it and wrote about it at various times, had never made that association, describing it rather as "a study for the portrait of a young couple."[1] To support the argument that the work exhibited in 1800 might have been a painting rather than a drawing, there is the evidence of a horizontal line in graphite extending across the chest of the man to the right edge of the sheet and another one at lower left, lines that might have been part of a scheme of squaring the sheet for transfer to canvas.

In defense of the argument that the present sheet was the work exhibited in 1800—besides the fact that no painted version of the composition has ever been recorded—it should be remembered that Greuze frequently included drawings among

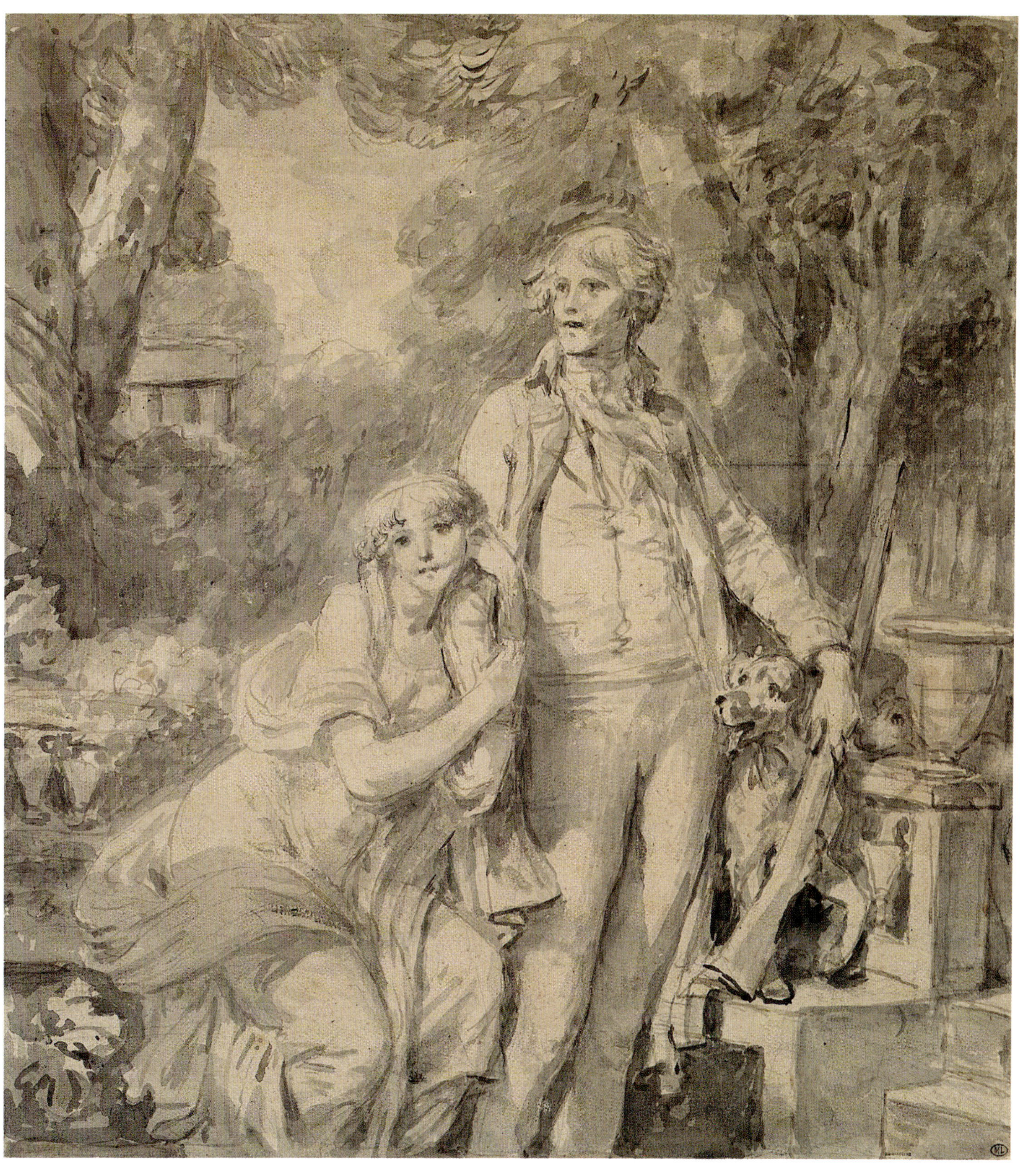

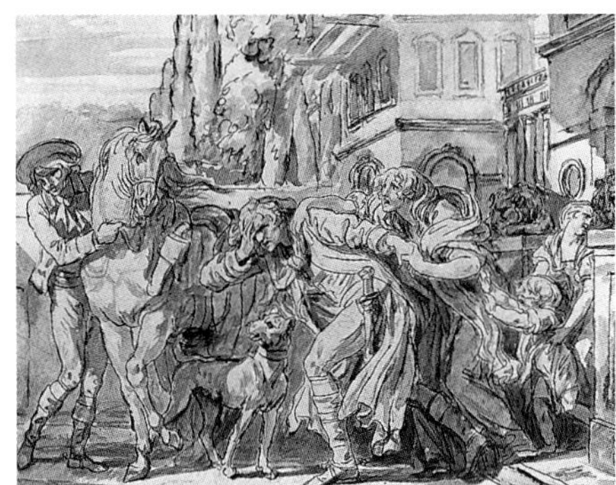

Fig. 226 Greuze, *The Departure of the Outlaw, c.* 1800, pen and brush, with gray and brown ink wash on white paper, Bayonne, Musée Bonnat, Donation Petithory

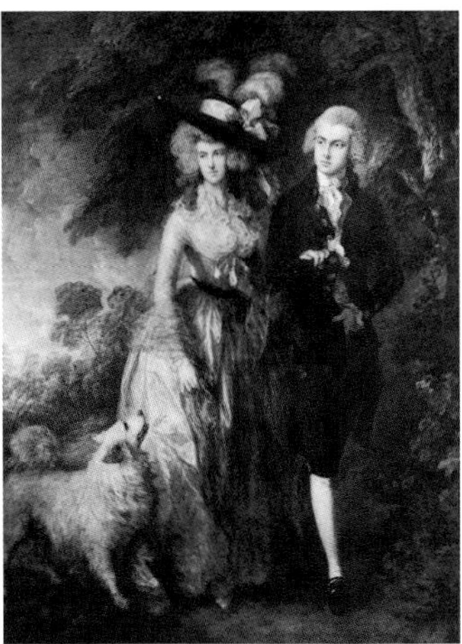

Fig. 227 T. Gainsborough, *The Morning Walk,* 1786, oil on canvas, London, The National Gallery

his Salon entries and that in 1800 he took the trouble to specify in the exhibition catalogue that the two items following number 173 were *"tableaux"* ("painted pictures"). While many critics commented on Greuze's work at the Salon of 1800, not one referred specifically to number 173.

What is more intriguing in Goncourt's remarks cited above is his suggestion that *The Departure for the Hunt,* already identified by Greuze as a "portrait," was intended to represent members of the Laborde family *("peut-être celui des de La Borde").*[2] Greuze's deep involvement with that family is discussed in relation to number 70. By 1800 the artist's patron Jean-Joseph de Laborde was dead, having been guillotined in 1794. Of his two sons, François-Louis-Jean-Joseph had fled to England the year of his father's death and would die in exile there in 1802. His brother Louis-Joseph-Alexandre (1772–1842) could therefore be the only de Laborde who might have been the subject of Greuze's portrait, having returned to France from Vienna in 1797 and leaving only in 1800, when he was posted to the French embassy in Madrid. This military man had a long political career and was a prolific author.[3] He was married to Marie-Anne-Thérèse de Sabatier de Cabre, daughter of the French *chargé d'affaires* in St Petersburg and widow of the marquis de Gillier.[4]

While the colonnade at upper left resembles a similar one in Greuze's *The Votive Offering to Cupid* of 1767 (London, The Wallace Collection),[5] there is evidence of a more contemporary interest on Greuze's part in such Neoclassical architectural details in his *The Departure of the Outlaw* (fig. 226), a composition that includes as well a hunting hound like the two depicted by the young man's side in *The Departure for the Hunt,* though less amiable. A similar façade appears in a study for *The Departure for the Hunt* (fig. 224).

Many have found an English character in this drawing—being a double portrait of husband and wife, depicted happily united in a luxuriant outdoor setting, accompanied by their pets—that recalls contemporary works by Romney, Sir Joshua Reynolds (1723–1792), and, especially, Thomas Gainsborough (1727–1788) (fig. 227). How this influence may have come about is difficult to explain, beyond the general Anglomania that affected Paris at the end of the eighteenth century. Brookner attributed it to Greuze's awareness of English mezzotints.[6]

An experienced hunter has pointed out that Greuze has depicted his subject holding his gun—probably a muzzle-loading musket, used for hunting deer or boar—in a careless, though elegant way, rather than gripping it firmly on the forestock, or cradling it in his arm.[7]

1. Launay 1991, p. 318; Goncourt 1881, p. 89.

2. See *Dictionnaire de biographie française,* Paris 1994, XVIII, pp. 1363, 1366–67, 1370–71.

3. Goncourt 1881, p. 89.

4. See *Dictionnaire de biographie française* 1994, VII, pp. 768, 769.

5. J. Ingamells, *The Wallace Collection. Catalogue of Pictures,* III, *French before 1815,* London 1989, p. 204.

6. Brookner 1972, p. 132.

7. Information kindly provided by John Rose.

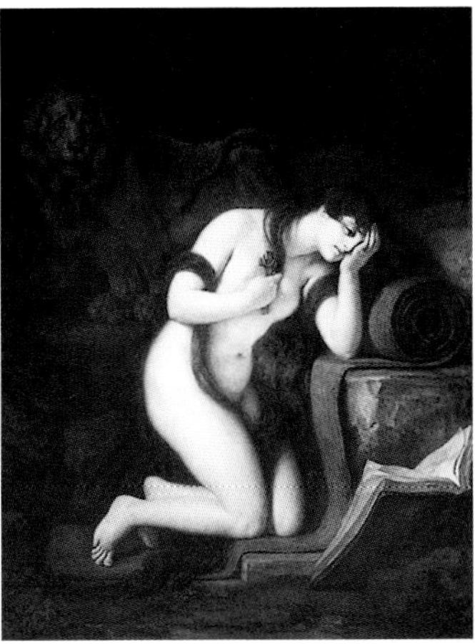

Fig. 228 Greuze, *The Repentance of St Mary of Egypt in the Desert*, *c.* 1800, oil on canvas, Norfolk VA, The Chrysler Museum of Art

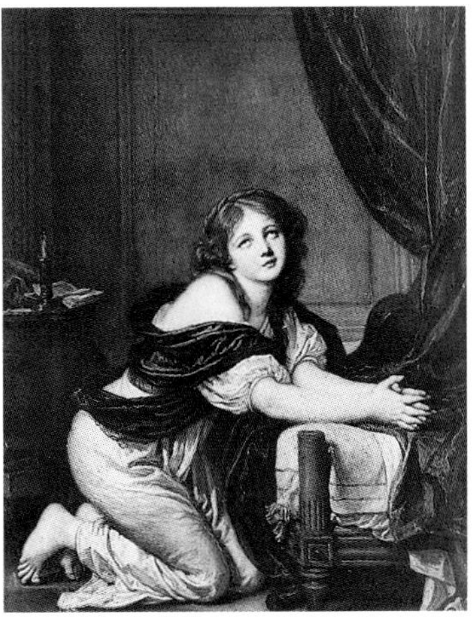

Fig. 229 Greuze, *Morning Prayer*, *c.* 1775, oil on canvas, Montpellier, Musée Fabre

95 *St Mary of Egypt with a Skull*

Brush with black ink wash, black chalk, heightened with white gouache, on tan paper, 305 × 408 mm (12 × 16 1/8 in.)
Inscribed on an old label attached to the mount *Voyez sur cette Sainte Marie Egyptienne par Greuze correspondant de l'Académie de Dijon, Galerie de Portraits du XVIIIè siècle par Arsène Houssaye, 1848, 2è série, p. 263*[1]
Dijon, Musée des Beaux-Arts

Provenance: given to the Académie des Sciences, Arts et Belles-Lettres de Dijon by Claude Hoin in 1802[2]
Exhibition: Hartford *et al.* 1976–77, no. 110
Bibliography: None known

As the inscription on the mount indicates, the subject of this somber and powerful drawing is St Mary of Egypt and not St Mary Magdalen, as one might think. It was entirely characteristic of Greuze to eschew the latter subject, treated by so many of his predecessors and contemporaries—Claude Mellan (1598–1668), Simon Vouet (1590–1649), Charles Lebrun, Eustache Le Sueur (1616–1655), Philippe de Champaigne (1602–1674), Annibale Carracci (1560–1609), Reni, Sir Antony van Dyck (1599–1641), Pierre Mignard (1612–1695), Nattier, Natoire, Piazzetta, Pompeo Batoni (1708–1787), Antonio Canova (1757–1822), Clodion (1738–1814), among others—in favor of one hardly ever represented at all, save by Jacques Callot (1592/3–1635) and Pier Francesco Mola (1612–1666).[3]

The fifth-century St Mary of Egypt, after a debauched career in Alexandria, was converted by a vision of the Virgin on the threshold of the Church of the Holy Sepulcher in Jerusalem. Retiring to the desert east of Palestine, she spent the rest of her life in isolation. After many years, an old hermit, Zosimus, found her corpse and was helped by a lion in digging her grave.[4] Greuze would include a lion in the major picture dealing with the subject that he exhibited at the Salon of 1801, *The Repentance of St Mary of Egypt in the Desert* (fig. 228).

It is that work Arsène Houssaye discussed in the text cited on the mount of the present drawing. Speaking of *A Marriage Contract* (fig. 10), of all things, he wrote:

It is more than a drama and an idyll, it is almost a page from the Bible: there is in this scene a religious gravity that recalls the earliest ages of the world. I should say as much of the "St Mary of Egypt"; this is more than a picture, it is St Mary herself in her physical splendor, in the divine and human beauty that enables us to imagine angels, Voltaire would say. The penitent, hidden away in the agrarian solitude of a cave, is clothed in her long hair, but especially in her modesty and in her repentance. Greuze could not help but endow her mouth and eyes with a hint of voluptuousness that recalls the world and its passions. This is a magical figure; one comes back to her again and again, as to a lover who weeps, as to a lover one has lost forever.[5]

As an earlier version of that work appeared in the Duclos-Dufresnoy sale of 1795, the present experiment with the subject must date from about 1790. Some fifteen years before that, Greuze produced *Morning Prayer* (fig. 229), an image depicting another

Facing page:
95 *St Mary of Egypt with a Skull*

woman at prayer, but in a totally different spirit. Here, the artist was still indulging in a salacious game, exploiting the subject of morning prayer as a means of presenting the physical charms of a young woman clad only in her nightgown and a shawl, apparently not overly beset by problems of the soul.

By the time of the many versions of *St Mary of Egypt,*[6] however, Greuze had moved into the realm of genuine, spiritual ardor, capable of conveying vividly the state of someone overcome by guilt and sorrow. Did these unusual religious subjects (see no. 90) and their troubled tone reflect the dark night of Greuze's own soul at this late point in his life, or was he fancifully transferring the torment to his estranged wife, imagining Anne-Gabrielle as a repentant sinner like St Mary of Egypt? Whoever's troubles they reflect, Greuze's meditations on the subject of St Mary of Egypt—in the words of one noted art historian—"inaugurate . . . a tradition of Romantic religious painting that will include in its succession Prud'hon's and Delacroix's almost autobiographical projections of personal anxieties into public Christian tragedies."[7]

1. "On this St Mary of Egypt by Greuze, corresponding member of the Académie of Dijon, see Galerie de Portraits du XVIIIe siècle by Arsène Houssaye, 1848, 2e série, p. 263."

2. P. Milsand, "Liste générale . . . des membres de l'Académie des Sciences, Arts et Belles-Lettres de Dijon, *Mémoires de l'Académie . . . de Dijon,* Dijon 1870, p. 323. The author is grateful to Sylvain Laveissière for providing this information.

3. See F. Bardon, "Le Thème de la Madeleine pénitente au XVIIe siècle en France," *Journal of the Warburg and Courtauld Institutes,* XXXI 1968, pp. 274–306; A. West, *From Pigalle to Préault: Neoclassicism and the Sublime in French Sculpture, 1760–1840,* London 1998, pp. 178–80, fig. 224; *Clodion,* exhib. cat., Paris, Musée du Louvre, 1992, pp. 115–21, nos. 11, 12; P.-P. Plan, *Jacques Callot, Maître Graveur,* Paris 1914, p. 92, no. 578 *(Les Images de tous les Saincts).* In contrast to all these artists' representations of St Mary Magdalen as a troubled beauty, Pier Francesco Mola chose to depict St Mary of Egypt as a hag (repr. *Apollo,* April 1992, p. 25).

4. See G. Ferguson, *Signs and Symbols in Christian Art,* New York 1954, pp. 21, 240–41; G. Duchet-Suchaux and M. Pastoureau, *The Bible and the Saints,* Paris and New York 1994, pp. 236–37.

5. *"C'est plus qu'un drame et une idylle, c'est presque une page de la Bible: il y a dans cette scène une gravité religieuse qui rappelle les premiers âges du monde. J'en dirai autant de la 'Sainte Marie Égyptienne'; c'est plus qu'un tableau, c'est sainte Marie elle-même dans la splendeur corporelle, dans la beauté divine et humaine qui a fait imaginer les anges, dirait Voltaire. La pénitente, réfugiée dans la solitude agreste d'un rocher, est vêtue de sa longue chevelure, mais surtout de sa pudeur et de son repentir. Greuze n'a pu s'empêcher de répandre sur la bouche et dans les yeux une teinte de volupté qui est le souvenir du monde et de ses passions. C'est une figure magique; on y revient sans cesse comme à une amante qui pleure, comme à une amante qu'on a perdue à jamais."* A. Houssaye, *Galerie de portraits du dix-huitième siècle,* Paris 1860, p. 318.

6. See Hartford *et al.* 1976–77, pp. 216, no. 110, 222, 224, no. 113.

7. Rosenblum 1977, p. 149.

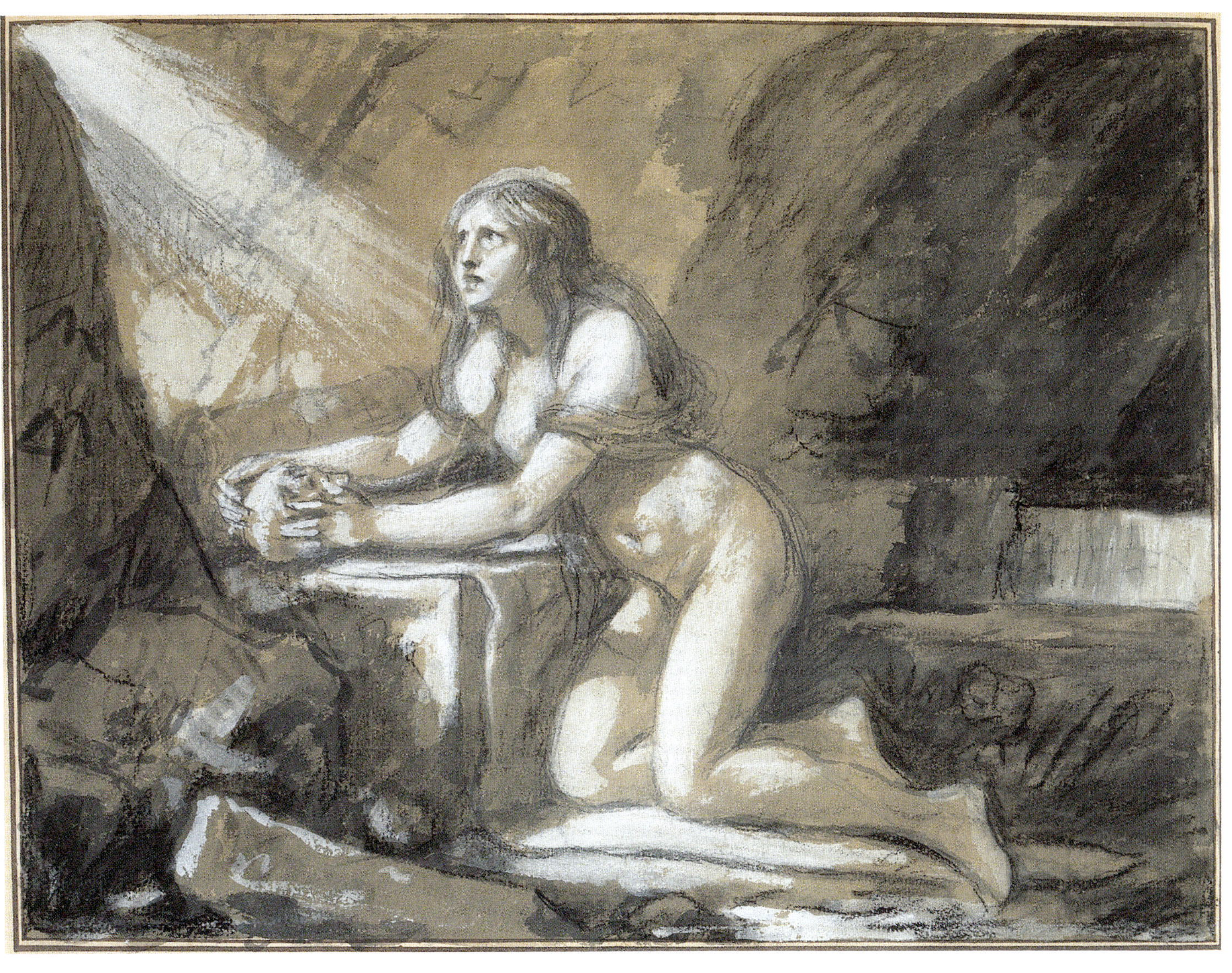

96 *Portrait of the Artist*

Oil on panel, 520 × 450 mm ($20\frac{1}{2}$ × $17\frac{11}{16}$ in.)
Marseille, Musée des Beaux-Arts

Provenance: marquis de Valori-Rustichelli, Paris; his sale, Paris, 16–18 April 1866, lot 87; Félix Abram, Marseille; bequeathed by his widow to the museum in 1925
Exhibitions: Salon of 1804, no. 211; *Exposition des Beaux-Arts, concours régional,* Marseille, 1861, no. 438; *L'Autoportrait du XVIIe siècle à nos jours,* Pau, Musée des Beaux-Arts, 1973, no. 31; Hartford *et al.* 1976–77, no. 114
Bibliography: Valori 1860, p. 374; Martin and Masson 1906, nos. 1139, 1143; B.A. Waldram, *Greuze, 1725–1805,* New York 1923, p. 76; Brookner 1956, p. 199; J. Vergnet-Ruiz and M. Laclotte, *Les Petits et Grands Musées de France,* Paris 1962, p. 238; G. Wildenstein, "Table alphabétique des portraits peints, sculptés, dessinés et gravés exposés à Paris au Salon entre 1800 et 1826," *GBA,* January 1963, p. 36; S. Collin and M. Latour, *Le Musée des Beaux-Arts de Marseille,* Marseille 1964, no. 75; Brookner 1972, pp. 87, 133, pl. 96; P. Rosenberg in *French Painting, 1774–1830: The Age of Revolution,* exhib. cat., The Detroit Institute of Arts; New York, The Metropolitan Museum of Art, 1974–75, no. 86; Rosenblum 1977, p. 149; Laveissière 1980, p. 249; A.-M. Lecoq in *La Peinture dans la peinture,* exhib. cat., Dijon, Musée des Beaux-Arts, 1982–83, p. 181, fig. 318; Tisserand 1984, pp. 26–27, 124, 128; A. Schnapper in *Au temps de Watteau, Fragonard et Chardin. Les Pays-bas et les peintres français du XVIIIe siècle,* exhib. cat., Lille, Musée des Beaux-Arts, 1985, p. 103; Novosselskaya 1987, p. 4; E. Munhall, "The Variety of Genres in the Work of Greuze, 1725–1805," *Porticus,* X–XI, 1987–88, pp. 28, fig. 6, 29; O. Michel, *Parcours, Catalogue guide du Musée des Beaux-Arts,* Marseille 1990, p. 85; Munhall 1994, p. 643; Rochette 2000, p. 51

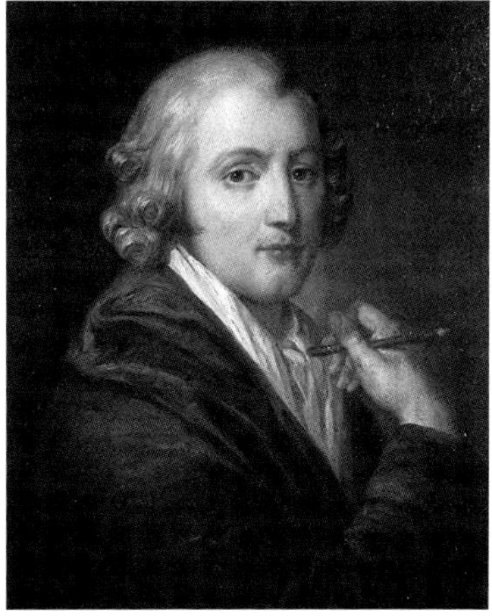

Fig. 230 Greuze, *Portrait of the Artist,* 1750, oil on canvas, Tournus, Musée Greuze

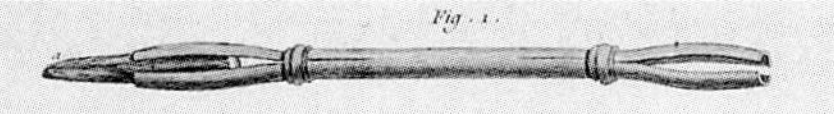

Fig. 231 Anonymous, *A Portecrayon,* 1762–77, engraving, from the *Encyclopédie,* "Dessein, Instrumens," pl. II

Eager as always to have the last word, Greuze startled the Parisian art world by presenting this self-portrait at the Salon of 1804, just a year before his death at the age of seventy-nine.

When Greuze had reappeared at the Salon of 1800 after an absence of thirty-one years (see no. 94), the critics had given him a sympathetic reception. Though everyone today recalls Bruun-Neergard's remark that year—"Greuze is an old man who appeared after Boucher"[1]—few are familiar with the same critic's reworking of that very phrase in his *Coup d'oeil sur le Salon de l'An VIII:* "he came after Boucher and left him far behind,"[2] or his generous conclusion: "May he rejoice in his old age with the consoling idea of having contributed to the restoration of taste, and may he applaud the progress of the art which established his glory and his happiness."[3] Another critic kindly remarked that "Greuze is still Greuze. The number of his productions [this year] cannot add anything to his reputation; but isn't he lucky at his age to be able to remind people this way of the existence of his talent?"[4] But all these gracious comments did not produce work for the "old man," and soon Greuze would be reduced to begging for an advance on a commission from Lucien Bonaparte, employing the memorable phrase: "I have lost everything but talent and courage."[5]

With the present portrait, Greuze proved those words to be true, by painting himself in the very same attitude—pointing emphatically to himself with his *portecrayon* ("This is me!")—that he had employed in another self-portrait painted over fifty years earlier (fig. 230). The pose, the garb, the coiffure, the simple drawing tool (fig. 231) are the same, and though the subject now appears shrunken, fragile, and even in pain, he possesses an air of lasting self-confidence.

Furthermore, the portrait was conceived and executed with all the subtlety and audacity the artist had mastered over a lifetime. Against a luminous, warm gray background, Greuze employed a strange and very personal palette, setting off his

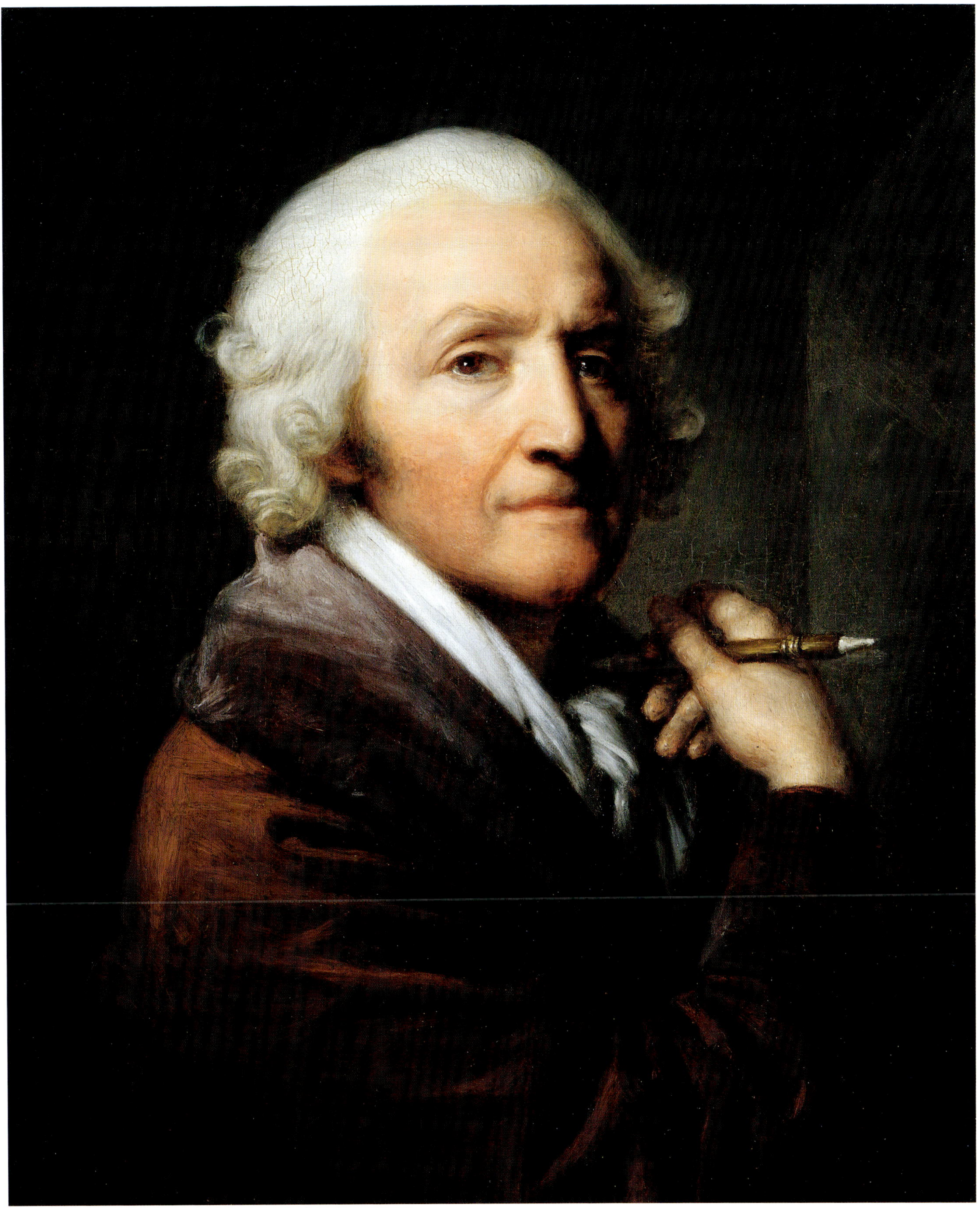

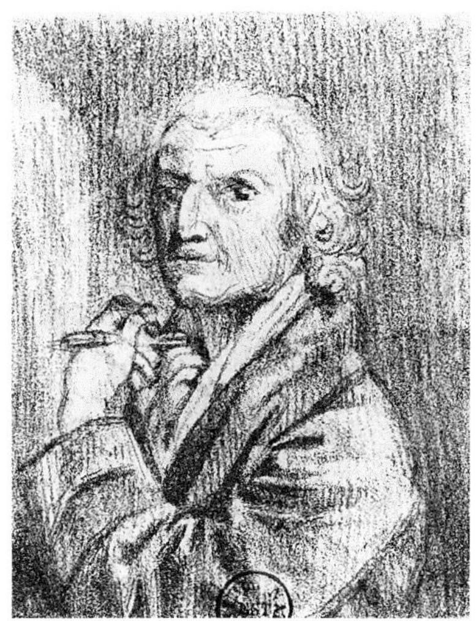

Fig. 232 A.-M. Monsaldy, after Greuze, *Portrait of the Artist,* 1804, black chalk on white paper, Paris, Bibliothèque nationale de France

bronze-colored dressing gown with a lavender-gray collar and band on the sleeve, with reflections from the white scarf accenting its inner edge. The flesh appears vibrant, almost tanned. Though moist, the brown eyes are highlighted in a challenging way. The cropping of the image is bold, drawing the viewer into an intimate confrontation with the subject. This eerie sense of a living presence is precisely what an unknown critic of 1800 characterized as Greuze's greatest achievement: "a tone so true that one can say without exaggerating that in their immobility, one has difficulty distinguishing them [Greuze's portraits] from the viewers who surround them. More than once we have had that experience and the paintings of Greuze are the only ones in the Salon to produce such a perfect illusion."[6]

With the canvas at the right still blank, and the hand still strong and muscular, one senses that the work of this artist will go on until death.

C.-L. F. Lecarpentier recorded that the portrait met with great success at the Salon of 1804: "They applauded especially the portrait he had just painted of himself."[7] That this was the *Portrait de l'auteur* from the Salon of 1804 is attested to by Antoine-Maxime Monsaldy's (1768–1816) sketch of it (fig. 232), made in reverse in anticipation of an engraving (never executed) intended to show panoramic views of the Salon's installation with visitors milling about, such as Monsaldy had made of the Salons of 1800 and 1803.[8]

Early copies of the portrait are in the collections of the State Hermitage Museum, St Petersburg,[9] and the Phoenix Art Museum.[10]

1. *"Greuze est un vieillard qui a paru après Boucher."* T.C. Bruun-Neergard, *Sur la situation des beaux-arts en France ou lettres d'un Danois à son ami,* Paris 1801, p. 67. Quoted in Normand 1892, p. 94; A.E. Macklin, *Greuze,* New York 1907, p. 67; Hautecoeur 1913, p. 143; Brookner 1972, p. 86.

2. *"il venoit après Boucher et le laissoit bien derrière lui." Coup d'oeil* etc., p. 44.

3. *"Qu'il jouisse dans sa vieillesse de l'idée consolante d'avoir contribué à la restauration du goût, et qu'il applaudisse au progrès de l'art qui fit sa gloire et son bonheur."* Bruun-Neergard 1801, p. 44.

4. *"Greuze est encore Greuze. Le nombre de ses productions ne peut rien ajouter à sa réputation; mais n'est-il pas heureux à son age de pouvoir ainsi rappeller l'existence de son talent?" Lettre de Monsieur Hennequin, peintre, aux auteurs du "Journal des arts,"* Paris 1800, p. 1.

5. *"J'ai tout perdu, or le talent et le courage."* Quoted in Goncourt 1880, p. 329.

6. *"un ton si vrai que l'on peut dire sans exagération, que sous leur immobilité on les distinguerait difficilement des spectateurs qui les entourent. Plus d'une fois nous en avons fait l'expérience et les tableaux de Greuze sont les seuls qui produisent au Salon une illusion parfaite."* "Exposition des ouvrages de peinture, sculpture, gravure, architecture, composés par les artistes vivans," *Journal du Bulletin universel des sciences, des lettres et des arts,* Paris 1800, p. 96.

7. *"On applaudit sur-tout à son portrait qu'il venoit de peindre lui-même."* C.-L. F. Lecarpentier, *Notice sur Greuze lu dans la séance de la Société libre d'émulation de Rouen,* [Rouen] 1805, p. 7.

8. H. Béraldi, *Les Graveurs du XIXe siècle,* Paris 1890, x, pp. 108–09. On Monsaldy's project, see G. Wildenstein, "Un tableau attribué à David et rendu à Mme Davin-Mirvault: 'Le Portrait du violiniste Bruni,'" *GBA,* February 1962, pp. 94–95.

9. I.S. Nemilova, *The Hermitage, Catalogue of Western European Painting, French Painting, Eighteenth Century,* Moscow and Florence 1986, p. 122, no. 67.

10. *French Paintings and Sculpture from the Phoenix Art Museum Collection,* Phoenix 1965, p. 6, no. 24; J. Harithas, *Paintings, Drawings, and Sculpture in The Phoenix Art Museum,* Phoenix 1965, p. 50.

Selected Bibliography

Abbreviations: *GBA*=*Gazette des Beaux Arts; BSHAF*=*Bulletin de la Société de l'histoire de l'art français*

Arquié-Bruley 1983
F. Arquié-Bruley, "Documents notariés sur Greuze," *BSHAF,* année 1981, 1983, pp. 125–54

Arquié-Bruley *et al.* 1987
F. Arquié-Bruley *et al., La Collection Saint-Morys au Cabinet des Dessins du Musée du Louvre,* 2 vols., Paris 1987

Bailey 2000
C.B. Bailey, *"Toute seule elle peut remplir et satisfaire l'attention.* The Early Appreciation and Marketing of Watteau's Drawings, with an Introduction to the Collecting of Modern French Drawings during the Reign of Louis XV," in New York and Ottawa 2000, pp. 68–92

Barker 1994
E. Barker, "Greuze and the Painting of Sentiment: The Family in French Art 1755–1785," diss., Courtauld Institute of Art, University of London, 1994

Barker 1997
E. Barker, "Painting and Reform in Eighteenth-Century France: Greuze's *L'Accordée de village," Oxford Art Journal,* xx, no. 2, 1997, pp. 42–52

Bean and Turčić 1986
J. Bean and L. Turčić, *15th–18th Century French Drawings in The Metropolitan Museum of Art,* New York 1986

Bouchot-Saupique 1939
J. Bouchot-Saupique, *J.-B. Greuze: Quatorze dessins,* Paris 1939

Brookner 1956
A. Brookner, "Jean-Baptiste Greuze—I," *The Burlington Magazine,* May 1956, pp. 157–62; "Jean-Baptiste Greuze—II," *The Burlington Magazine,* June 1956, pp. 192–99

Brookner 1972
A. Brookner, *Jean-Baptiste Greuze: The Rise and Fall of an Eighteenth-Century Phenomenon,* London and Greenwich CT 1972

Cailleux 1960
J. Cailleux, "Jacob van Loo, Greuze et Porporati, à propos d'un dessin du Musée des Beaux-Arts de Lyon," *Bulletin des musées et monuments Lyonnais,* III, no. 3, 1960, pp. 37–45

Compin and Roquebert 1986
I. Compin and A. Roquebert, *Catalogue sommaire illustré des peintures du Musée du Louvre et du Musée d'Orsay,* vols. 3–5, Paris 1986

Dacier 1909–21
E. Dacier, *Catalogues de ventes et livrets de Salons illustrés par Gabriel de Saint-Aubin,* 11 vols., Paris 1909–21

Diderot *Correspondance*
D. Diderot, *Correspondance, 1741–84,* ed. G. Roth, 16 vols., Paris, 1955–70

Diderot *Salons*
D. Diderot, *Salons (1759–81),* ed. J. Adhémar and J. Seznec, 4 vols., Oxford 1957–67; rev. 1983

Fermigier 1977
A. Fermigier, "Une Exposition Greuze à Dijon, La Dignité des pères et leur puissance terrible," *Le Monde des arts et spectacles,* 23 June 1977, p. 17

Fischer *et al.* 2000
C. Fischer, I. Novosselskaya, E.-M. Bukdahl, and T. Lederballe, *Greuze: Hjertets Dannelse,* Copenhagen 2000

Goncourt 1880
E. and J. de Goncourt, *L'Art du dix-huitième siècle,* Paris 1880, I, pp. 289–360

Gougenot
L. Gougenot, abbé de Chezal-Benoît, "Album de voyage en Italie," ms., I–III, Paris, private collection

Griffiths 1980
A. Griffiths, "Greuze et ses graveurs," *Nouvelles de l'estampe,* July–October 1980, pp. 9–11

Guicharnaud 1999
H. Guicharnaud, "Un Collectionneur Parisien, ami de Greuze et de Pigalle, l'abbé Louis Gougenot (1724–1767)," *GBA,* July–August 1999, pp. 1–74

Guiffrey and Marcel 1911
J. Guiffrey and P. Marcel, *Inventaire général des dessins du Musée du Louvre et du Musée de Versailles,* VI, Paris 1911

Haskell and Penny 1981
F. Haskell and N. Penny, *Taste and the Antique. The Lure of Classical Sculpture, 1500–1900,* New Haven CT and London 1981

Hautecoeur 1913
L. Hautecoeur, *Greuze,* Paris 1913

Jombert 1973
C.-A. Jombert, *Méthode pour apprendre le dessein,* Paris 1755; Minkoff reprint, Geneva 1973

Kamenskaya 1934
T. Kamenskaya, "Cherty realizma v risunkakh J.-B. Greuze" (Traits of realism in Jean-Baptiste Greuze's drawings), *Mir Iskusstvo,* v, 1934, pp. 79–93

Kamenskaya 1947
T. Kamenskaya, "Zhan-Batist Grez: Selskaia shkola (mest 'khudozhnika)" (Jean-Baptiste Greuze: *The Village School* [*The Artist's Revenge*]), Leningrad 1947

Laveissière 1980
S. Laveissière, *Dictionnaire des artistes et ouvriers d'art de Bourgogne,* I, Paris, 1980

Lugt
F. Lugt, *Les Marques de collections de dessins et d'estampes,* Amsterdam 1921

Lugt S.
F. Lugt, *Supplément,* The Hague 1956; facsimile reprint, San Francisco 1988

Mariette 1851–60
P.-J. Mariette, *Abécédario de P.-J. Mariette et autres notes inédites de cet amateur sur les arts et les artistes,* ed. P. de Chennevières and A. de Montaiglon, 6 vols., Paris 1851–60; reprinted, Paris 1966

Martin 1910
J. Martin, *Catalogue du Musée de Tournus (Musée Greuze),* Tournus 1910

Martin and Masson 1906
J. Martin and C. Masson, *Catalogue raisonné de l'oeuvre peint et dessiné de J.-B. Greuze,* in Mauclair 1906; published separately as *Oeuvre de J.-B. Greuze,* Paris 1908

Mathon de La Cour 1765
C.-J. Mathon de La Cour, *Troisième Lettre à M.*** sur les Peintures, les Sculptures, et les Gravures, exposées au Sallon du Louvre en 1765,* Paris 1765

Mauclair 1906
C. Mauclair, *Jean-Baptiste Greuze* (with catalogue raisonné by J. Martin and C. Masson), Paris 1906

McPherson 1985
H. McPherson, "Jean-Baptiste Greuze's Italian Sojourn, 1755–57," *Studies in Eighteenth-Century Culture,* XIV, 1985, pp. 93–107

"Mémorial des Laborde"
"Mémorial des Laborde," "Iconographie," IX, ms., private collection

Monod and Hautecoeur 1922
F. Monod and L. Hautecoeur, *Les Dessins de Greuze conservés à l'Académie des Beaux-Arts de Saint-Pétersbourg,* Paris 1922

Montagu 1994
J. Montagu, *The Expression of the Passions: The Origin and Influence of Charles Le Brun's "Conférence sur l'expression générale et particulière,"* New Haven CT and London 1994

Morel d'Arleux
L.M.J. Morel d'Arleux, "Inventaire des dessins du Louvre," [1797–1827], ms., Paris, Louvre, IX

Munhall 1961
E. Munhall, "Greuze's Frontispiece for *Sophronie,*" *GBA,* October 1961, pp. 237–42

Munhall 1964
E. Munhall, "Greuze and the Protestant Spirit," *Art Quarterly,* spring 1964, pp. 1–21

Munhall 1965
E. Munhall, "Les Dessins de Greuze pour 'Septime Sévère,'" *L'Oeil,* April 1965, pp. 22–29, 59

Munhall 1966
E. Munhall, "Quelques découvertes sur Greuze," *La Revue du Louvre et des musées de France,* II, 1966, pp. 85–92

Munhall 1968
E. Munhall, "Savoyards in French Eighteenth-Century Art," *Apollo,* February 1968, pp. 86–94

Munhall 1994
E. Munhall, "Greuze, Jean-Baptiste," *The Dictionary of Art,* London 1994, XIII, pp. 638–44

Normand 1892
C. Normand, *J.-B. Greuze,* Paris 1892

Novosselskaya 1975
I. Novosselskaya, "French Drawings from Watteau to Greuze," *Apollo,* June 1975, pp. 470–74

Novosselskaya 1985
I. Novosselskaya, "Rol'risunka v tvorchestve Zhana-Batista Greza" (The role of drawings in the work of Jean-Baptiste Greuze"), in *Zapadnoevropeiskaia grafika XV–XX vekov; sbornik statei* (Western European graphic art of the fifteenth–twentieth centuries: collected articles), Leningrad 1985, pp. 72–90

Novosselskaya 1987
I. Novosselskaya, *Masters of World Painting. Jean-Baptiste Greuze,* Leningrad 1987

Portalis and Béraldi 1880–82
R. Portalis and H. Béraldi, *Les Graveurs du dix-huitième siècle,* 3 vols. in 6, Paris 1880–82

Preston 1977
S. Preston, "The Revaluation of Greuze," *Apollo,* February 1977, pp. 136–39

Rand 1996
R. Rand, "Civil and Natural Contract in Greuze's 'L'Accordée de village,'" *GBA,* May–June 1996, pp. 221–34

Raux 1995
S. Raux, *Catalogue des dessins français du XVIIIe siècle de Claude Gillot à Hubert Robert, Palais des Beaux-Arts, Lille,* Lille 1995

Réau 1920
L. Réau, "Greuze et la Russie," *L'Art et les artistes,* July 1920, pp. 273–86

Reiset 1866–69
F. Reiset, *Notice des dessins, cartons, pastels, miniatures et émaux exposés... au Musée Impérial du Louvre,* 2 vols., Paris 1866–69

Rochette 2000
C. Rochette, *Jean-Baptiste Greuze (1725–1805) et les collections du musée Greuze de Tournus,* Tournus 2000

Roland Michel 1987
M. Roland Michel, *Le Dessin français au XVIIIe siècle,* Paris 1987

Rosenberg, Reynaud, and Compin 1974
P. Rosenberg, N. Reynaud, and I. Compin, *Musée du Louvre: Catalogue illustré des peintures: École française, XVIIe et XVIIIe siècles,* 2 vols., Paris 1974

Rosenblum 1977
R. Rosenblum, "The Greuze Exhibition at Hartford and Elsewhere," *The Burlington Magazine,* February 1977, pp. 145–49

Schnapper 1977
A. Schnapper, "Greuze un précurseur?" *Connaissance des arts,* June 1977, pp. 86–91

Schnapper 1978
A. Schnapper, "Edgar Munhall. *Jean-Baptiste Greuze, 1725–1805,*" review, *The Art Bulletin,* June 1978, pp. 374–75

Smith
J. Smith, *Catalogue raisonné of the Works of the Most Eminent Dutch, Flemish and French Painters,* VIII, London 1837; *Supplement,* London 1842

Thompson 1989–90
J. Thompson, "Jean-Baptiste Greuze," *The Metropolitan Museum of Art Bulletin,* winter 1989–90, pp. 4–52

Tisserand 1984
G. Tisserand (ed.), *Greuze et Diderot, Vie familiale et éducation dans la seconde moitié du XVIIIe siècle,* Clermont-Ferrand 1984

Valori 1860
C. de Valori, "Notice sur Greuze et sur ses ouvrages," in *Greuze, ou l'Accordée de village,* Paris 1813; reprinted by A. de Montaiglon (ed.), in *Revue universelle des arts,* XI, 1860, pp. 248–61, 362–77

Wakefield 1984
D. Wakefield, *French Eighteenth-Century Painting,* London 1984

Wildenstein 1960
G. Wildenstein, "Quelques documents sur Greuze," *GBA,* October 1960, pp. 227–34

Wille 1857
J.G. Wille, *Journal* (1759–93), ed. G. Duplessis as part of *Mémoires et journal,* 2 vols., Paris 1857

Exhibitions

Budapest 1970
Kiallitas a Leningradi Ermitazs legszebb rajzai-bol, Budapest, Szépmüvészeti Múzeum, 1970

Cambridge *et al.* 1998–2000
Mastery and Elegance. Two Centuries of French Drawings from the Collection of Jeffrey E. Horvitz, Cambridge MA, Harvard University Art Museums; Toronto, Art Gallery of Ontario; Paris, Musée Jacquemart-André; Edinburgh, National Gallery of Scotland; New York, National Academy Museum and School of Fine Arts; Los Angeles County Museum of Art, 1998–2000

Copenhagen 2000
Hjertets dannelse Greuze, Copenhagen, Statens Museum for Kunst, 2000

Florence 1982
Disegni dell'Europa occidentale dall'Ermitage di Leningrado, Florence, Gabineto Disegni et Stampi degli Uffizi, 1982

Hartford *et al.* 1976–77
Jean-Baptiste Greuze/1725–1805, Hartford CT, Wadsworth Atheneum; San Francisco, California Palace of the Legion of Honor, 1976–77; Dijon, Musée des Beaux-Arts, 1977

Karlsruhe 1996
Vom Glück des Lebens: französische Kunst des 18. Jahrhunderts aus der Staatlichen Eremitage St Petersburg, Karlslruhe, Städtische Galerie Karlsruhe im Landesgewerbeamt, 1996

Leningrad 1926
Dessins des maîtres anciens. Exposition de 1926, Leningrad, The State Hermitage Museum, 1926

Leningrad 1956
Vystavka frantsuzskogo iskusstva XII–XX vv. (Exhibition of French art of the twelfth–twentieth centuries), Leningrad, The State Hermitage Museum, 1956

Leningrad 1977
Jean-Baptiste Greuze, Drawings in the Collection of the Hermitage, Leningrad, The State Hermitage Museum, 1977

Leningrad 1983
French Eighteenth-Century Drawings in the Hermitage Collection, Leningrad, The State Hermitage Museum, 1983

Leningrad and Moscow 1969
Selected Drawings from The State Hermitage Museum: The C. Cobenzl Collection, Leningrad, The State Hermitage Museum; Moscow, The Pushkin State Museum of Fine Arts, 1969

Leningrad and Moscow 1987
Rossiia-Franttsiia: vek proveshcheniia, Russko-frantsuzskie kulturnye sviazi v 18 stoletii, Leningrad, The State Hermitage Museum; Moscow, The Pushkin State Museum of Fine Arts, 1987

London 1932
Exhibition of French Art, 1200–1900, London, The Royal Academy of Arts, 1932

London 1968
France in the Eighteenth Century, London, The Royal Academy of Arts, 1968

Moscow 1955
Vystavka frantsuzskogo iskusstva XV–XX vv. (Exhibition of fifteenth–twentieth-century French art), Moscow, The Pushkin State Museum of Fine Arts, 1955

New York 1990
Greuze in The Metropolitan Museum of Art, New York, The Metropolitan Museum of Art, 1990

New York 1998–99
Master Drawings from the Hermitage and Pushkin Museums, New York, The Pierpont Morgan Library, 1998–99

New York and Ottawa 2000
Watteau and His World: French Drawing from 1700 to 1750, New York, The Frick Collection; Ottawa, National Gallery of Canada, 2000

Paris 1951
Le Dessin français de Watteau à Prud'hon, Paris, Galerie Cailleux, 1951

Paris 1974–75
Le Néoclassicisme français. Dessins des musées de province, Paris, Galeries Nationales du Grand Palais, 1974–75

Paris 1984
Diderot et l'art de Boucher à David, Paris, Hôtel de la Monnaie, 1984

Paris 1986–87
La France et la Russie au Siècle des Lumières. Relations culturelles et artistiques de la France et de la Russie au XVIIIe siècle, Paris, Galeries nationales du Grand Palais, 1986–87

Prague 1972
Kresby evropskych mistru XV–XX stolelti ze sbirek statni Ermitaze v Leningrade, Prague, Narodni Galerie v Praze, 1972

St Petersburg 1903
Blanc et noir, "The World of Art," St Petersburg, Imperial Academy of Fine Arts, 1903

Stockholm 1963
Mastarteckningar fran Eremitaget, Leningrad, Stockholm, Nationalmuseum, 1963

Tokyo 1994
French Baroque and Rococo Art from the State Hermitage Museum, Tokyo, Mie Prefectural Art Museum, 1994

Illustration Credits

Aix-en-Provence, Jean Bernard Photographe: frontispiece, no. 96; fig. 20
Aix-en-Provence, Musée Granet: fig. 28 (Bernard Terlay)
Amsterdam, Amsterdams Historisch Museum: no. 56; fig. 136
Amsterdam, Rijksmuseum Foundation: no. 38
Austin TX, Jack S. Blanton Museum of Art: fig. 54 (The Suida-Manning Collection; © 2001 The University of Texas at Austin)
Basel, Peter Heman, Photograph: fig. 168
Bayonne, Musée Bonnat (Réunion des Musées Nationaux/Art Resource NY): figs. 3 (Bellot), 161, 226 (courtesy of Jacques Petithory)
Berlin, Kupferstichkabinett, Staatliche Museen zu Berlin–Preussischer Kulturbesitz: fig. 41 (Jörg P. Anders)
Besançon, Musée des Beaux-Arts et d'Archéologie: fig. 183 (Charles Choffet)
Boston, Jeffrey E. Horvitz Collection: no. 54 (inv. no. D-F-120); fig. 153 (inv. no. D-F-820)
Boston, Museum of Fine Arts: fig. 139 (Bequest of William A. Sargent, 1937; Courtesy, Museum of Fine Arts, Boston; © 2000. All rights reserved)
Caen, Musée des Beaux-Arts (Agence Photographique de la Réunion des Musées Nationaux): fig. 219 (© Photo RMN)
Cambridge MA, Harvard University Art Museums: nos. 64, 79 (© Harvard University; Collection of Jeffrey E. Horvitz [inv. no. D-F-124], Boston; photographer: Rick Stafford); figs. 166, 192
Chalon-sur-Saône, Musée Denon: no. 16
Chaumont, Musée Municipal: no. 61 (Christophe Jobard)
Chicago, The Art Institute of Chicago: no. 19 (photograph © 2001, The Art Institute of Chicago, All Rights Reserved)
The Cleveland Museum of Art: nos. 67, 72 (© The Cleveland Museum of Art)
Compiègne, Musée Vivenel: fig. 182
Copenhagen, Den Kongelige Kobberstiksamling, Statens Museum for Kunst: fig. 76
Dijon, Musée des Beaux-Arts: no. 95; fig. 34
Dijon, Musée Magnin: fig. 98
Dublin, National Gallery of Ireland: fig. 144
Düsseldorf, Kunstmuseum (Medienzentrum Rheinland): fig. 26
Edinburgh, National Galleries of Scotland: figs. 53 (Annan), 69 (Tom Scott)
Epinal, Musée départemental des Vosges: fig. 91
Florence, Gabinetto Disegni e Stampi degli Uffizi: fig. 148
Fort Worth TX, Kimbell Art Museum: fig. 113
Frankfurt am Main, Städelsches Kunstinstitut, Graphische Sammlung (© Ursula Edelmann): nos. 71, 75; fig. 18
Hartford CT, The Wadsworth Atheneum: fig. 112 (Courtesy Wadsworth Atheneum, Hartford)
Houston TX, William Carloss Morris III Collection: fig. 181
Kansas City MO, The Nelson-Atkins Museum of Art: figs. 88, 95
Karlsruhe, Staatliche Kunsthalle Karlsruhe: nos. 39, 68
Le Havre, Musée des Beaux-Arts: fig. 71
Lille, Musée des Beaux-Arts (Réunion des Musées Nationaux—P. Bernard): nos. 48, 49
London, British Museum: figs. 56, 185
London, Christie's: figs. 15 (A.C. Cooper), 90 (A.C. Cooper), 100, 130, 194, 210, 218
London, Mike Fear Photography: fig. 212
London, The National Gallery: fig. 227
London, The Royal Collection, Her Majesty Queen Elizabeth II: fig. 44
London, Victoria and Albert Museum: fig. 167
London, The Wallace Collection (By kind permission of the Trustees of the Wallace Collection; © The Wallace Collection): figs. 78, 83, 149
London, Witt Library, Courtauld Institute: figs. 25, 184
Los Angeles, The J. Paul Getty Museum: nos. 51 (Louis Meluso), 82; figs. 85, 154, 200
Lyon, Musée des Beaux-Arts: nos. 59, 66; figs. 157 (J. Camponogara), 178 (J. Camponogara)
Madison WI, Elvehjem Museum of Art, University of Wisconsin–Madison: no. 1
Madrid, Museo Nacional Centro de Arte Reina Sofía: fig. 197
Madrid, comte de la Viñaza, marquis de Laborde: figs. 13, 103, 172
Manchester NH, The Currier Gallery of Art: fig. 52
Montpellier, Musée Fabre: figs. 49 (© Musée Fabre, Montpellier; Frédéric Jaulnes), 179, 229
Moscow, The Pushkin State Museum of Fine Arts: figs. 79, 125
Munich, Alte Pinakothek, Bayerische Staatsgemäldesammlungen: fig. 186
Munich, BLV Verlagsgesellschaft: fig. 73 (photo Steimer)
New Haven CT, Yale University Art Gallery: figs. 63, 109
New York, Artists Rights Society: fig. 135 (© Estate of Pablo Picasso/Artists Rights Society [ARS], New York)

New York, W.M. Brady & Co., Inc.: figs. 123, 143
New York, The Frick Collection: nos. 91, 92 (© The Frick Collection; photographs: Richard di Liberto)
New York, Richard di Liberto: nos. 6, 17, 18; figs. 1, 8, 127, 170, 171
New York, The Metropolitan Museum of Art: nos. 36 (Photograph © 2001, All rights reserved), 52 (Schecter Lee; Photograph © 1987), 62 (Malcolm Varon; Photograph © 1989), 88 (Malcolm Varon; Photograph © 1989), 89 (Photograph © 1996); figs. 6, 7, 39, 57, 61, 70, 84, 99, 138, 141, 180, 223
New York, The Pierpont Morgan Library (Joseph Zahevi): nos. 55, 87
New York, Sotheby's: figs. 189, 201, 224
New York, Wildenstein & Co.: fig. 114
New York, The Woodner Family Collections: no. 26 (Jim Strong)
Norfolk VA, The Chrysler Museum of Art: fig. 228 (E. Irving Blomstrann)
Notre Dame IN, The Snite Museum of Art, University of Notre Dame: no. 86; fig. 214
Ottawa, National Gallery of Canada: fig. 176
Oxford, The Ashmolean Museum: no. 21
Paris, Didier Aaron & Cie: nos. 14, 77, 85; fig. 211
Paris, Arts graphiques de la Cité (Photographies Agraci): figs. 164, 198, 199
Paris, Bibliothèque nationale de France: no. 2; figs. 36, 38 (Studios Josse Lalance), 55, 68, 87, 89, 92, 117 (Studios Josse Lalance), 126 (Studios Josse Lalance), 128, 134, 137, 140, 165, 169, 174, 190, 232
Paris, Bonafous-Murat: fig. 67
Paris, Jean-Loup Charmet, Photographe: no. 90; fig. 151
Paris, Collection Prat: fig. 216
Paris, Comédie-Française: figs. 220, 221
Paris, Photographie Jean Dubout: fig. 209
Paris, École Nationale Supérieure des Beaux-Arts: figs. 116, 119, 175
Paris, Fondation Custodia, Collection Frits Lugt, Institut Néerlandais: no. 80
Paris, Galerie de Bayser: fig. 193
Paris, Galerie Cailleux: figs. 22, 94
Paris, Thomas Henoch Photographe: figs. 29, 30, 31, 32, 33
Paris, J. Michel Photographe: no. 47
Paris, Musée du Louvre (Réunion des Musées Nationaux/Art Resource, NY): nos. 20 (Bellot), 22, 23, 42 (Bellot), 63 (Bellot), 65 (Bellot), 73 (Bellot), 74 (Bellot), 76 (Bellot), 78, 94 (Bellot); figs. 10 (Berizzi), 14 (Ojeda), 16 (Ojeda), 17 (Lewandowski), 60, 62 (Agraci), 64, 66 (Berizzi), 82 (Arnaudet), 101, 105, 133, 145, 146, 150, 160 (Lewandowski), 195, 203, 206, 207, 213, 222
Paris, Musée du Petit Palais: no. 15 (© Photothèque des Musées de la Ville de Paris/negative: P. Pierrain)
Paris, Jacques Petithory: fig. 93
Paris, Paul Prouté S.A.: fig. 108
Paris, Philippe Sebert, Photographe: figs. 11, 12
Paris, Maurice Segoura: fig. 59
Phoenix AZ, Phoenix Art Museum: fig. 215
Portland OR, Portland Art Museum: fig. 19
Richmond, The Virginia Museum of Fine Arts: no. 93
Rotterdam, Museum Boijmans-Van Beuningen: figs. 81, 187
Rouen, Musée des Beaux-Arts: figs. 51, 177
St Petersburg, The State Hermitage Museum: nos. 3, 7, 8, 9, 10, 11, 12 13, 24, 25, 27, 28, 30, 34, 35, 37, 40, 44, 45, 46, 50, 53; figs. 21, 23, 24, 27, 42, 46, 72, 74, 77, 86, 110, 115, 124, 131, 132, 173, 191, 204
Stockholm, Nationalmuseum (© Foto Nationalmuseum): figs. 48, 97, 158
Stuttgart, Staatsgalerie Stuttgart, Graphische Sammlung: fig. 147
Sydney, Art Gallery of New South Wales: no. 70
Tournus, Hôtel-Dieu-Musée Greuze de Tournus (Pascal Tournier): no. 69; figs. 4, 50, 156, 163, 202, 230
Versailles, Photo Queste: fig. 45
Victoria BC, Art Gallery of Greater Victoria: no. 83
Vienna, Graphische Sammlung Albertina: nos. 5, 32, 33, 43, 57, 58, 81; figs. 80, 118, 120, 121
Warsaw, Print Room of the Warsaw University Library: fig. 152
Washington D.C., National Gallery of Art: nos. 29 (Ricardo Blanc), 41 (Ricardo Blanc), 84 (Dean Beasom); figs. 43, 106
Wijhe, The Netherlands, Stichting Hannema-de Stuers Fundatie: fig. 75
Worcester MA, Worcester Art Museum: fig. 40
Zurich, Collection Rau: fig. 96

The following numbers will not be seen at The Frick Collection: 8, 9, 11, 13, 20, 27, 30, 32, 33, 35, 37, 44, 46, 50, 57, 58, 63, 65, 67, 72, 74, 76, 80, 94, 95; at The J. Paul Getty Museum: 2, 3, 5, 7, 10, 12, 15, 19, 22, 23, 24, 25, 28, 34, 38, 40, 41, 42, 43, 45, 53, 54, 73, 78, 81.

Index

by Laura Hicks

Page numbers in *italics* refer to illustrations or captions to illustrations; those in **bold** refer to catalogue entries.

Designed by Nathan Garland,
New Haven CT
Composed in a modern version
of Garamond
Printed and bound in Italy

Greuze the Draftsman

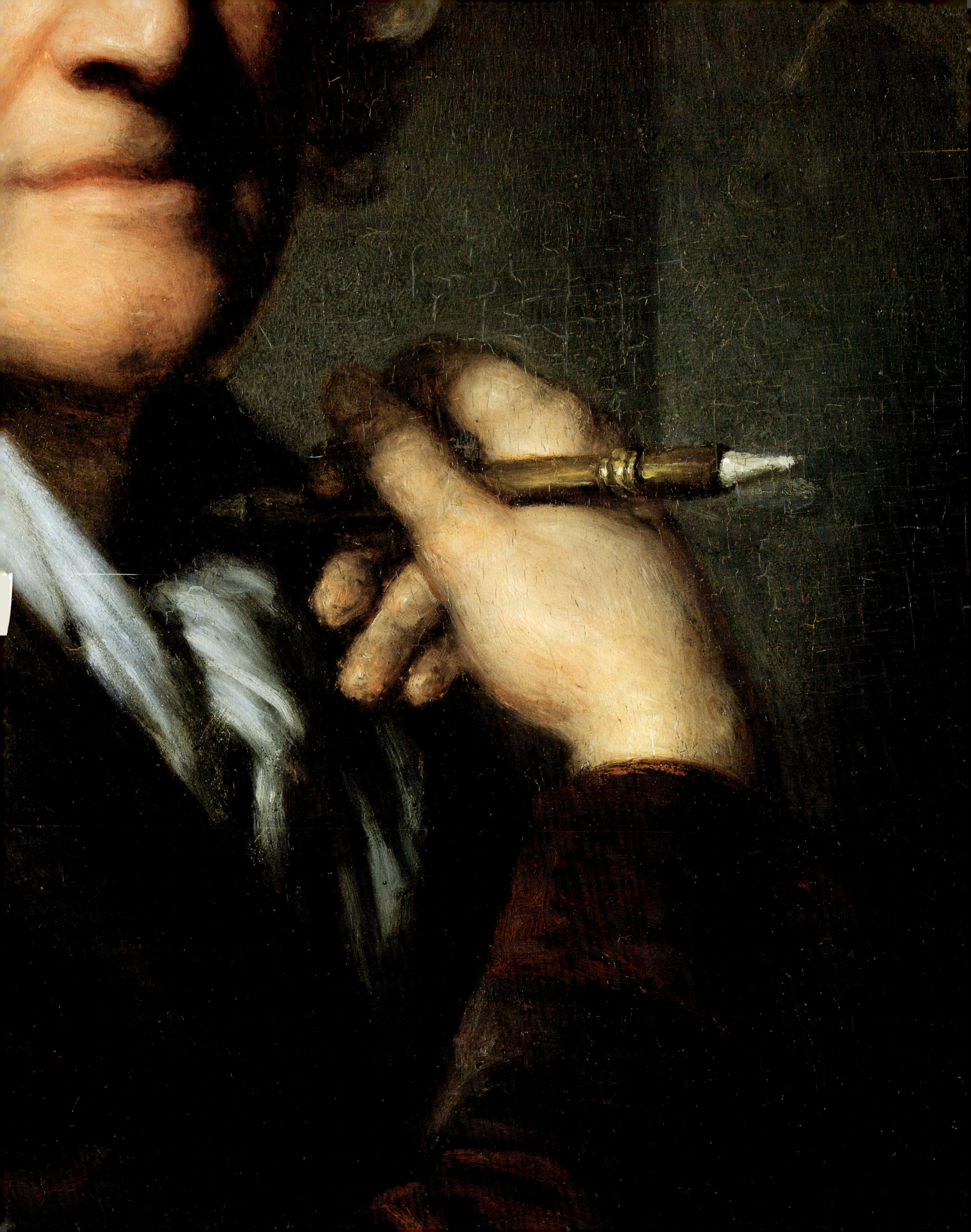

Greuze the Draftsman

Edgar Munhall

With an essay by Irina Novosselskaya

MERRELL in association with
The Frick Collection, New York

First published 2002 by
Merrell Publishers Limited
42 Southwark Street
London SE1 1UN

in association with
The Frick Collection
1 East 70th Street
New York, NY 10021

Published on the occasion
of the exhibition *Greuze the Draftsman*,
organized by Edgar Munhall

Exhibition itinerary:

The Frick Collection
New York
14 May – 4 August 2002

The J. Paul Getty Museum
Los Angeles
10 September – 1 December 2002

Front cover:
Greuze, *The Ungrateful Son*,
c. 1777 (no. 84)

Back cover:
Greuze, *Head of a Woman*,
c. 1765 (no. 47)

Frontispiece:
Greuze, *Portrait of the Artist* (detail),
1804 (no. 96)

Distributed in the USA by Rizzoli International
Publications, Inc. through St. Martin's Press,
175 Fifth Avenue, New York, NY 10010

A catalog record for this book is available from
the Library of Congress

British Library Cataloging-in-Publication Data:
Munhall, Edgar
Greuze the draftsman
1. Greuze, Jean-Baptiste, 1725–1805 – Criticism
and interpretation 2. Drawing – France
I. Title II. Frick Collection
741 ′.092

ISBN 1 85894 158 X (hardback)
ISBN 1 85894 159 8 (paperback)

Produced by Merrell Publishers Limited
Printed and bound in Italy

Designed by Nathan Garland
Edited by Fronia W. Simpson

Contents

Foreword

We are pleased to present at our respective institutions *Greuze the Draftsman,* the first exhibition devoted to the drawings of Jean-Baptiste Greuze. The selection of drawings comprises the finest and most representative sheets from international institutions and presents his graphic achievement in its fullest and most compelling scope.

While early photographs of Clayton, Henry Clay Frick's residence in Pittsburgh, show a Greuze-like *Head of a Girl* hanging in the Parlor, records indicate that the young collector returned it to Arthur Tooth & Sons less than a year after purchasing it in 1899 ("a wise decision," according to Edgar Munhall). Mr Frick never acquired another work by the artist, but in 1943 the Trustees of The Frick Collection purchased *The Wool Winder,* a major early painting that had formerly belonged to J. Pierpont Morgan. This picture will travel to Los Angeles to be part of an ancillary exhibition that The J. Paul Getty Museum is organizing to complement *Greuze the Draftsman.* In 1991, with funds recently bequeathed in memory of Suzanne and Denise Falk, The Frick Collection had the chance to acquire the extraordinary pair of pastel portraits by Greuze depicting the actor Baptiste *aîné* and his wife, which demonstrate in the present exhibition what the artist was capable of producing at the age of seventy-five (nos. 91, 92).

In 1983 The J. Paul Getty Museum had acquired Greuze's *The Laundress,* a work nearly contemporary with the Frick's *The Wool Winder.* By happy coincidence, the monograph devoted to it that the museum published in 2000 was written by Colin B. Bailey, who subsequently succeeded Edgar Munhall as the Chief Curator of The Frick Collection. In the same year *The Laundress* joined its collection, the Getty acquired its first Greuze drawing, *The Father's Curse: The Ungrateful Son* (no. 82)—a rare example of the sort of model Greuze prepared for engravers contracted to execute reproductive prints after his paintings—and a year later, in 1984, acquired the *Head of an Old Man* (no. 51). In 1999 the Getty made the daring acquisition of Greuze's painting *Cimon and Pero: Roman Charity* (fig. 154), which is based on a famous drawing in the collection of the Musée du Louvre (no. 65).

Greuze the Draftsman would have been inconceivable without the participation of its Guest Curator, Edgar Munhall. From the completion in 1959 of his PhD dissertation, "Jean-Baptiste Greuze: An Artist and His Critics," at Yale University, through his 1996 exhibition at The Frick Collection, *Greuze, a Portraitist for the 90s,* Mr Munhall has been the indefatigable keeper of the Greuze flame, which more than once has threatened to flicker out. Most notably, in 1976 he organized the first exhibition ever devoted to Greuze, *Jean-Baptiste Greuze/1725–1805,* which was seen at the Wadsworth Atheneum, the California Palace of the Legion of Honor, and the Musée des Beaux-Arts, Dijon.

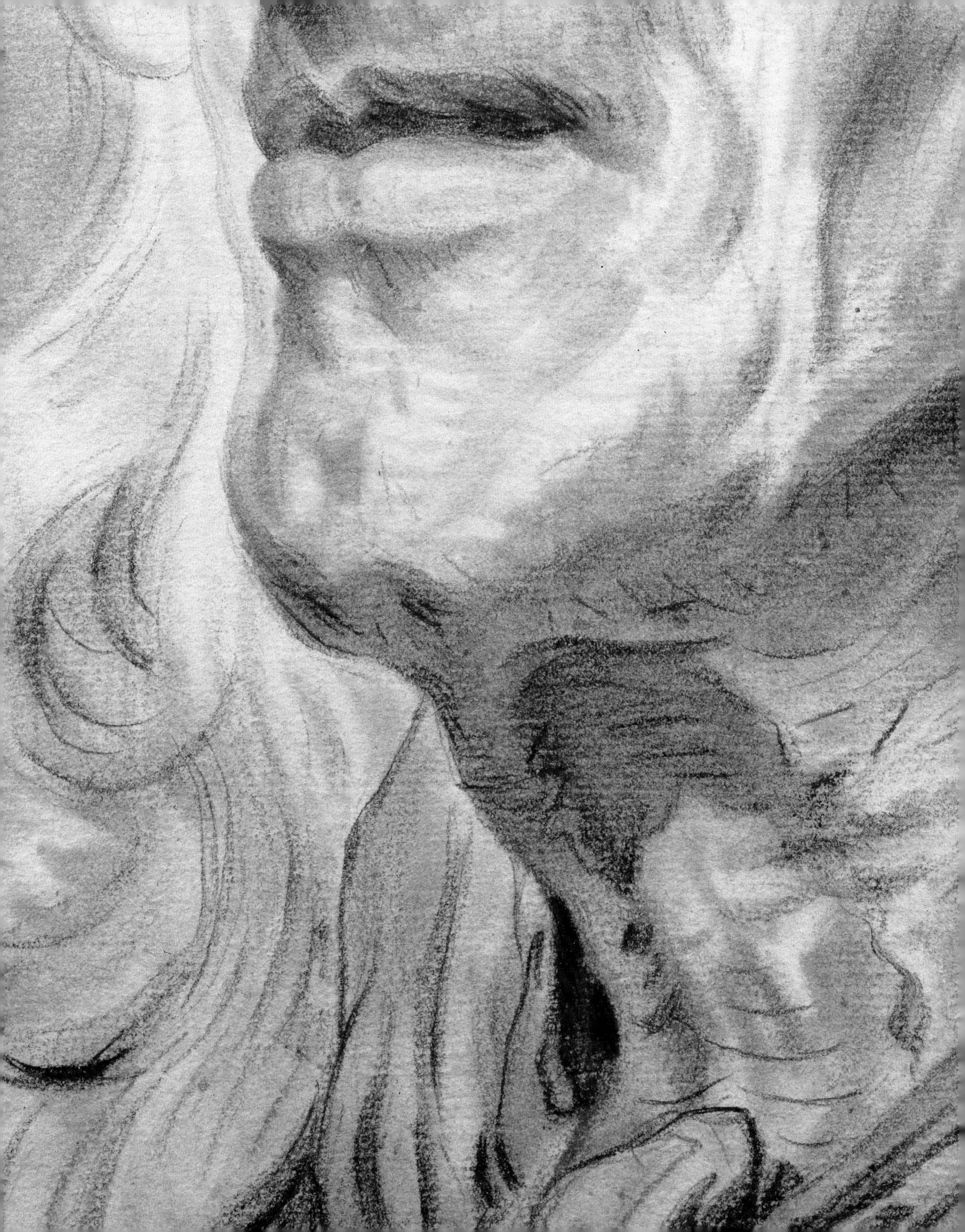

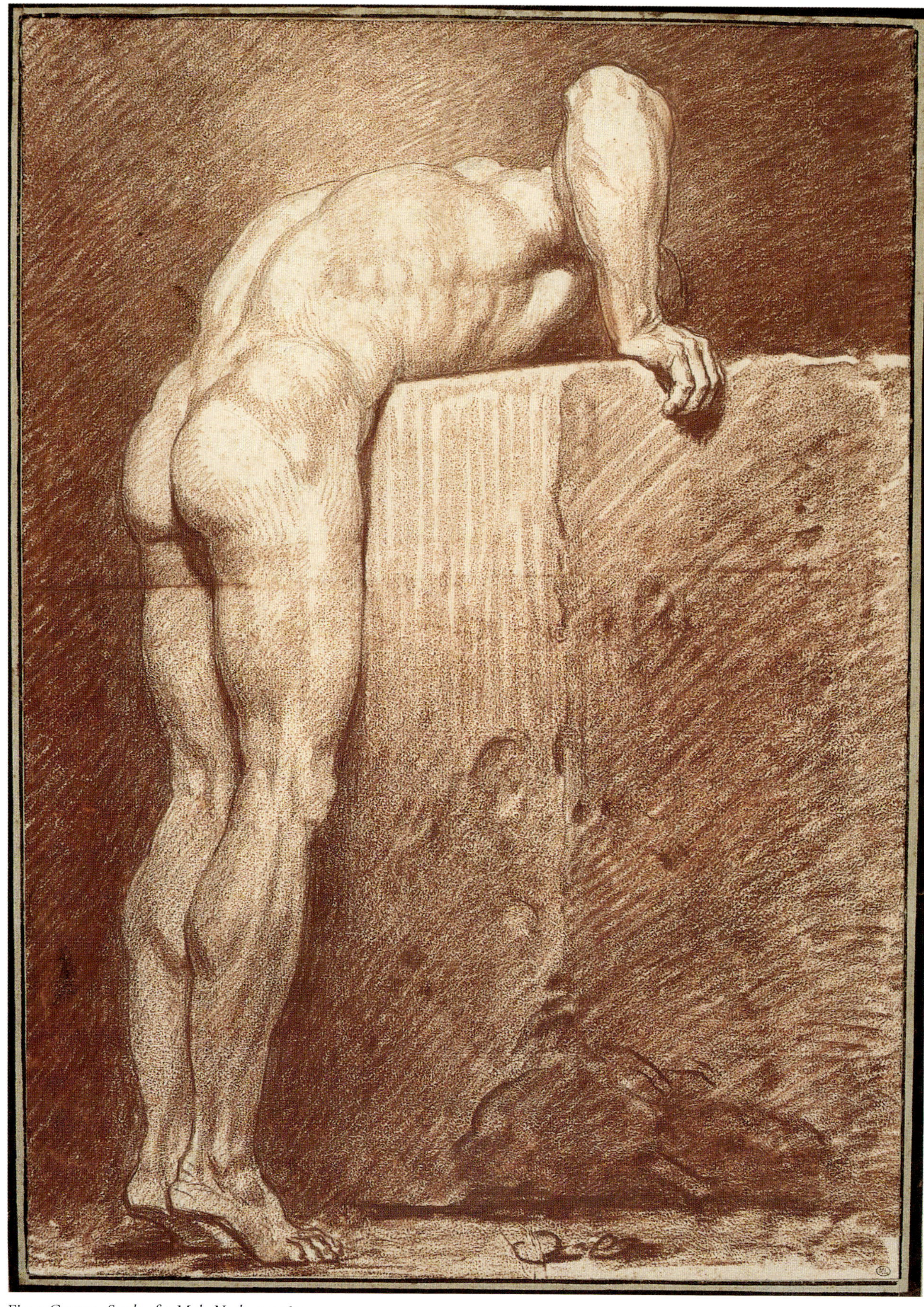

Fig. 3 Greuze, *Study of a Male Nude, c.* 1767, red chalk on cream paper, Bayonne, Musée Bonnat, Donation Petithory

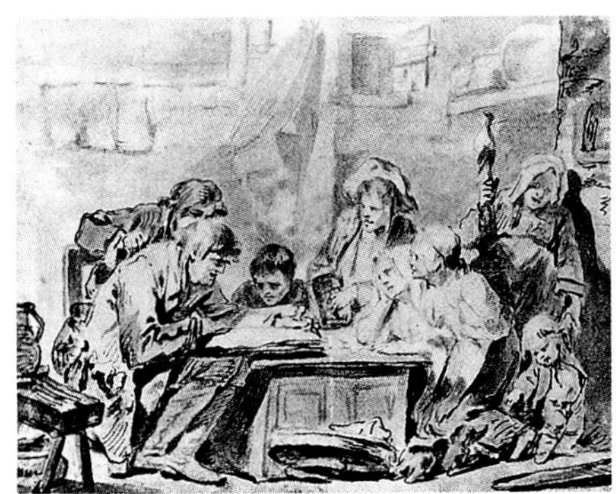

Fig. 2 Greuze, *Compositional Study for "The Family Bible Reading," c.* 1750–55, pen and brush with gray and brown ink wash on white paper, Paris, private collection

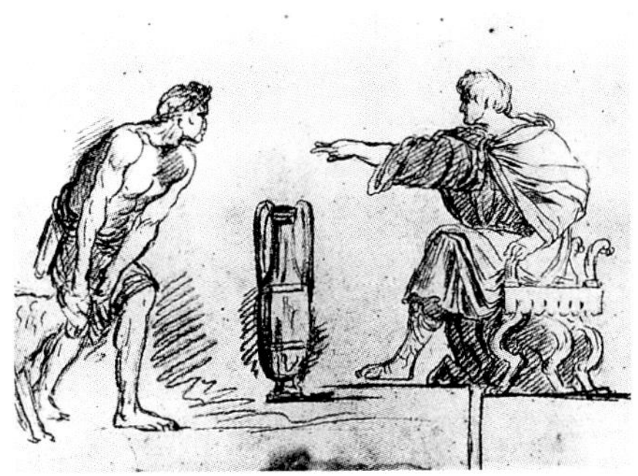

Fig. 4 Greuze, *Study after Domenichino's "Trial of Saint Cecilia,"* 1755–56, red chalk on cream paper, Tournus, Musée Greuze

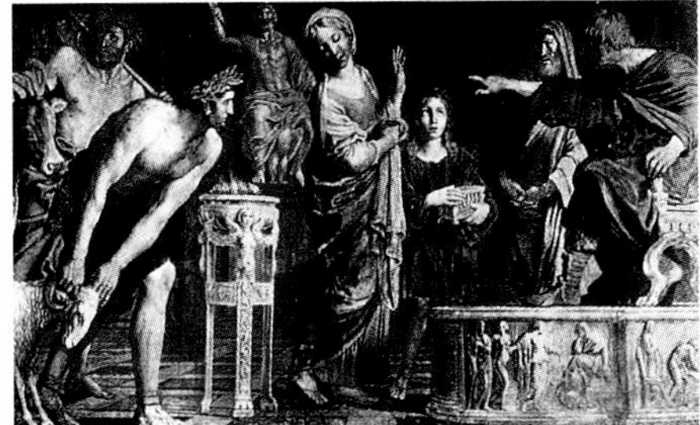

Fig. 5 Domenichino, *Trial of Saint Cecilia,* 1616–17, fresco, Rome, San Luigi dei Francesi

The two figural studies that this author earlier assigned to Greuze's period in Lyon exhibit a similar concentration on minute, even macabre details.[9] But this Grandonesque concern for precision was offset in them by a Rembrandtesque freedom with ink washes that characterizes even more Greuze's highly important compositional study for his first major work, *The Family Bible Reading* (figs. 2, 9). Apart from its stylistic significance, this drawing provides the first evidence of Greuze's unique ability to create a scene of many figures interacting with emotional intensity. Some perceptive amateur acquired this drawing early on, for Greuze's friend Johann Georg Wille (1715–1808) recalled purchasing it at a Paris auction in December 1759: "I bought at the sale that was held in M. Rémy's rooms... the first sketch that M. Greuze made for his picture *The Father of the Family Reading the Bible,* thirty-six livres.... The drawing has since passed into a German collection."[10] Perhaps it was the drawing's arresting drama that provoked Wille to describe its creator as "profound and solid."[11]

The next crucial phase in Greuze's development as a draftsman took place in Paris, where he must have arrived about 1750. Both Madame de Valori[12] and Louis Gougenot, abbé de Chezal-Benoît (see no. 4), recount the difficulties that Greuze, bereft of a protector, had in attending drawing classes at the Académie Royale de Peinture et de Sculpture. But the evidence of the large number of *académies*—studies of posed nude models—that Greuze would later sell General Ivan Ivanovitch Betskoy[13] and others (no. 2) suggest that the young artist spent many hours, presumably under the direction of Charles-Joseph Natoire (1700–1770) and Louis de Sylvestre (1675–1760), mastering his depiction of the human figure. Greuze's knowledge of anatomy, which he later claimed to disdain, is revealed in his lifelong ability to depict an ear, an eye, a finger—seen from any perspective—with perfect precision, something that connoisseurs keep in mind when faced with a copy or an imitation of an original drawing by Greuze. Also, his familiarity, perhaps even his boredom, with the genre of the *académie* led him to indulge in such highly original variations on it as number 66 and figure 3.

Greuze's year and a half in Italy (see no. 4) was highly productive, as reflected in what he brought back to exhibit at the Salon of 1757. In addition to the complex *Four Pictures in Italian Costume, The Neapolitan Sailor,* and the portrait of his patron the abbé Gougenot (fig. 34), the artist for the first time included a drawing in that exhibition: *A Sketch in Black Ink, Representing Some Italians Playing Morra* (Moscow, The Pushkin State Museum of Fine Arts). With Pierre Parrocel (1670–1739), Greuze was the only artist to exhibit a drawing in 1757—aside from the pastels of Maurice-Quentin de La Tour (1704–1788) and Jean-Baptiste Perronneau (1715?–1783).

By this time, according to Madame de Valori, Greuze felt he had developed his talents "so to say, to perfection."[14] Certainly the drawings that survive from the Italian sojourn (nos. 4–7) demonstrate a mastery of a broad range of types, as well as of media. The major change from this point on would be the artist's abandonment of the delicate, slightly Rococo style apparent in these Italian costume studies in pen and ink, the so-called *petite manière* that had been his speciality before leaving for Rome. While there, in addition to creating his own major works, he dutifully drew after ancient sculptures, Raphael (1483–1520), Michelangelo (1475–1564), Guido Reni (1575–1642), and Domenichino (1581–1641), but in a desultory manner, judging from a previously unidentified study after Domenichino's fresco *Trial of Saint Cecilia* in San Luigi dei Francesi (figs. 4, 5).[15]

Facing page:
Fig. 6 Greuze, *Head of a Girl* (no. 52), detail

From 1759 until his crisis-fraught Salon of 1769, Greuze regularly included drawings among his showings at the biennial exhibitions of the Académie: two in 1759, three in 1761 (see nos. 14, 23), none in 1763, four major works in 1765 (see nos. 41, 48, 49), none in 1767, when he was denied admission, and six in 1769 (see nos. 56, 69, Hartford *et al.* 1976–77, no. 51). On an average, only five or six other artists, including pastelists, would include drawings among their Salon entries—Jean-Baptiste Henri Deshays (1729–1765), Jean-Honoré Fragonard (1732–1806), Pierre-Antoine de Machy (1723–1807), André Portail (1695–1759), and Hubert Robert (1733–1808) among them. Greuze's decision to exhibit drawings at the Salon may reflect the influence of his patron Gougenot, who, as early as 1748, was urging artists to show their drawings this way: "One wishes that artists, instead of burying them [drawings] in the darkness of their portfolios, would make an effort to display them at the Salon more often than they have done to date.... By sharing their thoughts among themselves by such an exhibition, the masters could present at a glance the most serious aspect of their art."[16] In 1800, when Greuze reappeared at the Salon for the first time in thirty-one years, a drawing headed his list of entries: *The Departure for the Hunt* (no. 94).

From his Salon debut in 1755, when one critic characterized *The Family Bible Reading* (fig. 9) as "well drawn,"[17] to his surprise return appearance there in 1800, when his style of drawing was judged "too mannered,"[18] the ever-more-numerous critics focused on Greuze's drawings with considerable care. Concerning the three major drawings the artist showed in 1761, for instance, the abbé Philippe Bridard de la Garde wrote: "The several drawings by M. Greuze shown in the Salon do him as much honor by their execution as by the choice and genius of their invention. The subjects this young painter dreams up and renders so well could one day constitute a complete treatise on domestic morality."[19] They did, in fact, range from images of thieving children, to a family caring for a paralyzed father, to another family pathetically begging in unison.

That same year, 1761, Denis Diderot (1713–1784), the philosopher turned art critic, first spoke of Greuze's drawings in some detail, describing their subjects minutely and concluding with a vivid description of Greuze the draftsman that suggests he knew him well: "Greuze possesses a lot of spirit and taste. When he's working, he is completely wrapped up in what he's doing; he is profoundly moved: he expresses in the street the character of the subject he's dealing with in his studio, sad or gay, sprightly or serious, flirtatious or reserved, according to whatever engaged his brush and imagination in the morning."[20]

Two years later, when Diderot reached the apogee of his admiration for Greuze—exclaiming "That's really my man, that Greuze"[21]—he continued his description of him, specifically as a draftsman, in a highly personal and vivid way:

It's not surprising that this artist excels.... He is enthusiastic about his art; he makes endless studies; he spares neither care nor expenses in order to have the models that suit him. If he meets a head that strikes him, he would willingly fall on his knees before the bearer of that head to attract him to his studio. He is constantly on the lookout in the streets, in churches, in markets, at the theater, on promenades, in public gatherings. When he's thinking about a subject, he is obsessed with it, constantly preoccupied. Even his character is marked by it; he assumes that of his picture: he is brusque, sweet, insinuating, caustic, flirtatious, sad, gay, warm, serious, or mad, according to whatever he's working on.[22]

Diderot's final word on Greuze the draftsman was included in his lengthy review of the Salon of 1769, when he referred to the six drawings the artist was exhibiting:

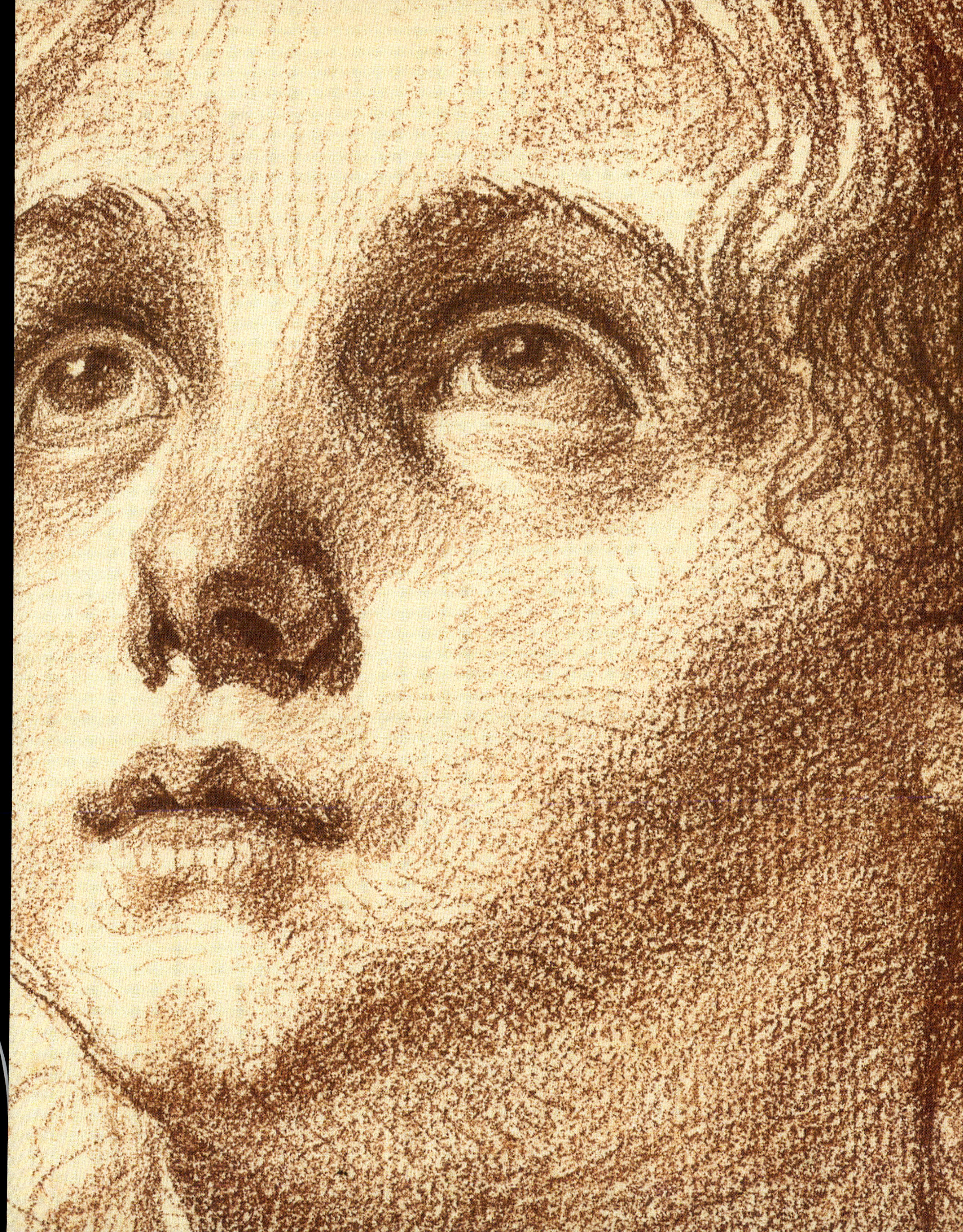

Facing page:
Fig. 7 Greuze, *Domestic Scene* (no. 88), detail

"And what about those *drawings*? Because that's where Greuze truly shows himself to be a man of genius. The one of *The Death of a Father Mourned by His Children* [fig. 168] is especially beautiful in composition, expression, and effect. He who understands art can imagine it painted."[23]

In 1767, when relations between Greuze and Diderot were souring, the latter sought to prevent the artist's being invited by Catherine II to Russia by writing in a letter to Étienne-Maurice Falconet (1716–1791) (that he knew the empress would probably see): "Say, my friend, all things considered, I think we shall never be sending Greuze to Russia. He's an excellent artist, but a very disagreeable character. One should have his drawings and his paintings, and leave the man at that."[24] Catherine II took the hint, as Dr Novosselskaya's essay here recounts in detail, writing to Falconet: "I renounce, not the works of Greuze, but indeed the man himself. . . ."[25]

With the eighteenth-century vogue not only for collecting contemporary drawings but for displaying them in frames,[26] Greuze had an enthusiastic and rich market for his work. Fellow artists and dealers possessed his drawings—Pierre-François Basan (1723–1797), Aignan-Thomas Desfriches (1715–1800), Claude Hoin (1750–1817), Jean-Baptiste-Pierre Le Brun (1748–1813), Joseph-Marie Vien (1716–1809), Johann Georg Wille—as well as collectors, such as Jean-Baptiste-Laurent Boyer de Fonscolombe, the chevalier de Damery, Louis-Antoine Vassal de Saint-Hubert, Vialart de Saint-Morys; aristocrats, such as the baron de Besenval, the marquis Jean-Joseph de Laborde, the comte de Vaudreuil; writers, such as Diderot, T.C. Bruun-Neergard; and distinguished foreigners, such as General Betskoy (with Catherine II behind him), count Karl Cobenzl, the baron d'Holbach, Duke Albert von Sachsen und Teschen, and Johann Friedrich Städel. Down to the present day, the greatest connoisseurs have savored their Greuze drawings—from Pierre-Jean Mariette in the eighteenth century (no. 57), to Edmond and Jules de Goncourt in the nineteenth (nos. 66, 94), to Frits Lugt in the twentieth (no. 80), and Pierre Rosenberg in the twenty-first.